SEVENTH EDITION

Criminal Procedure for the Criminal Justice Professional

John N. Ferdico, J. D.

Member of the Maine Bar
Former Assistant Attorney General and
Director of Law Enforcement Education for the State of Maine

West/Wadsworth
I⊤P® An International Thomson Publishing Company

Belmont, CA • Albany, NY • Boston • Cincinnati • Johannesburg
London • Madrid • Melbourne • Mexico City • New York
Pacific Grove, CA • Scottsdale, AZ • Singapore • Tokyo • Toronto

Criminal Justice Editor: Sabra Horne
Development Editor: Dan Alpert
Project Development Editor: Claire Masson
Editorial Assistant: Cherie Hackelberg
Marketing Manager: Christine Henry
Project Manager: Debby Kramer
Print Buyer: Karen Hunt

Permissions Manager: Bob Kauser
Production: Hal Lockwood
Text and Cover Designer: Carolyn Deacy
Copy Editor: Laura Larson
Compositor: R&S Book Composition
Printer: R.R. Donnelley & Sons Co., Crawfordsville

For more information, contact Wadsworth Publishing Company, 10 Davis Drive, Belmont, CA 94002,
or electronically at http://www.wadsworth.com

International Thomson Publishing Europe
Berkshire House 168-173
High Holborn
London, WC1V 7AA, England

Thomas Nelson Australia
102 Dodds Street
South Melbourne 3205
Victoria, Australia

Nelson Canada
1120 Birchmount Road
Scarborough, Ontario
Canada M1K 5G4

International Thomson Editores
Seneca, 53
Colonia Polanco
11560 México D.F. México

International Thomson Publishing Asia
60 Albert Street #15-01
Albert Complex
Singapore 189969

International Thomson Publishing Japan
Hirakawa-cho Kyowa Building, 3F
2-2-1 Hirakawa-cho, Chiyoda-ku
Tokyo 102, Japan

International Thomson Publishing
  Southern Africa
Building 18, Constantia Park
138 Sixteenth Road, P.O. Box 2459
Halfway House, 1685 South Africa

Library of Congress Cataloging-in-Publication Data

Ferdico, John N.
    Criminal procedure for the criminal justice professional / John N.
Ferdico.—7th ed.
        p.   cm.
    Includes index.
    ISBN 0-534-54693-5
    1. Criminal procedure—United States.   I. Title.
KF9619.F47   1998
345.73′05—dc21   98-389985

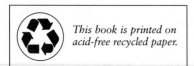

*This book is printed on
acid-free recycled paper.*

Brief Contents

Contents

Admissions and Confessions and Pretrial Identification   431

Preface

Criminal Procedure for the Criminal Justice Professional was originally published in 1975 as *Criminal Procedure for the Law Enforcement Officer* and was written with the primary emphasis on providing practical guidelines for law enforcement officers with respect to the legal aspects of their daily duties. Over the years, in response to suggestions and comments from professors and students who have used the book, many changes have been made to enhance the book's suitability for use as a classroom text. Chapters dealing with individual rights under the Constitution and basic underlying concepts have been added, and chapters dealing with evidence, testifying in court, and investigation of crime have been eliminated. Review and discussion questions were added to stimulate discussion and to expand understanding beyond the principles and examples used in the text. In 1993 the Fifth Edition of this book featured two pedagogical devices added to assist the student's comprehension of basic concepts:

- *Key Points*—concise, clear statements of the essential principles of criminal procedure. These appear at the end of major sections of chapters and serve as mini-summaries of those sections. Their purpose is to aid the student in "separating the wheat from the chaff" and to expedite review by boiling down the complexities into understandable statements of fundamentals.

- *Key Holdings from Major Cases*—essential principles from U.S. Supreme Court cases, usually presented in the form of quotations. These appear at the end of chapters. Their purpose is to familiarize the student with judicial language and to give a sense of the historical development of particular aspects of criminal procedure in the words of the Supreme Court. These holdings also serve as summaries of important principles.

The purpose of the various improvements to the book has been to provide the student with a broad and sophisticated understanding of the law of criminal procedure while maintaining a practical, real-life orientation.

The Seventh Edition of *Criminal Procedure for the Criminal Justice Professional* retains all these features and expands and revises them where necessary. New pedagogical features in this edition are:

- Chapter *Objectives* and *Outline*—statements of student learning goals followed by a profile of the chapter's major contents. These appear at the beginning of each chapter and are designed to provide purpose, structure, and context.

- *Real-Life Fact Situations*—verbatim statements of fact situations from actual reported court cases. These appear at the end of chapters and are designed to supplement the sometimes theoretical Review and Discussion Questions by challenging students to apply their knowledge to practical, everyday situations.

- *Glossary*—definitions of major terms used in criminal procedure law taken from Ferdico's *Criminal Law and Justice Dictionary.*

In addition, every chapter has been thoroughly reviewed, revised, and updated to reflect modern developments in the law. The revisions include discussions of all relevant U.S. Supreme Court cases decided since the publication of the Sixth Edition and all amendments to relevant legislation and court rules. Also, all forms and exhibits have been reviewed and updated where necessary.

The Seventh Edition adds discussions of over 100 new cases decided by the U.S. Supreme Court and other federal and state courts. Many of these new cases replace old and archaic cases with modern examples illustrating important legal principles. Some of these new cases establish new principles of criminal procedure law or provide instructive examples of the operation of existing law. In addition to these general changes, the following notable changes have been made to individual chapters.

Chapter 1: Individual Rights Under the United States Constitution. This chapter adds *Hudson v. United States,* clarifying that the Double Jeopardy Clause protects against multiple *criminal* punishments for the same offense. Also included is an expanded discussion of the Sixth Amendment right to a public trial and clarification of the Sixth Amendment right to effective assistance of counsel.

Chapter 2: An Overview of the Criminal Court System. This chapter adds the following:

- Definition of trial de novo
- Clarification of the test for determining a defendant's competency to stand trial
- Additional information on court discretion in determining sentence
- Discussion of the Antiterrorism and Effective Penalty Act's limitations on habeas corpus relief

Chapter 3: Basic Underlying Concepts. This chapter adds a new section on alternatives to the exclusionary rule and expands the discussion of "adequate and independent state grounds."

Chapter 4: Arrest. This chapter adds an expanded discussion of the *Payton* requirement of an arrest warrant before entering a suspect's home to arrest him or her. Other new material is a discussion of exceptions to the requirement of a search warrant to enter a third person's home to arrest a suspect and a clarification that exigent circumstances allowing a warrantless entry of premises must not be created by police.

Chapter 5: Search Warrants. This chapter adds the following new material:

- Discussion of the interests to be balanced in determining whether a search requiring surgery is constitutional
- Enhanced discussion of circumstances justifying the securing of a dwelling while a warrant is being sought
- Discussion of *Richards v. Wisconsin,* which refused to allow a blanket exception to the knock-and-announce requirement in felony drug cases
- Discussion of the exception to the knock-and-announce requirement for entries achieved by ruse or deception
- Expanded discussion of the reduced probable cause standard for administrative search warrants

- Discussion of *Vernonia School District 47J v. Acton,* which held that a public school's interest in deterring drug use by students constituted a special need justifying suspicionless random testing of student athletes

- Discussion of *Chandler v. Miller,* which held unconstitutional a Georgia statute requiring candidates for designated state offices to certify that they have passed a drug test within 30 days prior to nomination or election

Chapter 6: Probable Cause.   This chapter is essentially unchanged except for updating and refining.

Chapter 7: Stop and Frisk.   This chapter adds a discussion of two new U.S. Supreme Court cases: *Ohio v. Robinette,* holding that once a driver has been ordered out of a lawfully stopped vehicle, the officer may request consent to search the car, whether or not the officer has a subjective intention to arrest or issue a traffic ticket; and *Maryland v. Wilson,* holding that an officer making a traffic stop may order passengers to get out of the car pending completion of the stop. Also added is the following new material:

- Discussion of what constitutes reasonable investigative procedure pursuant to a traffic stop

- Enhanced discussion of the amount of force allowed to be used in connection with an investigative stop

- Enhanced discussion of how reasonable suspicion may be developed from a series of lawful acts

- Enhanced discussion of criteria justifying traffic stops

- Discussion of detention and search of carry-on luggage at airline security checkpoints

Chapter 8: Search Incident to Arrest.   This chapter adds a discussion of the U.S. Supreme Court case of *Whren v. United States,* holding that, if police conduct is justified by probable cause, subjective intent or pretext is irrelevant for Fourth Amendment purposes. Also added is an enhanced discussion of protective sweeps.

Chapter 9: Consent Searches.   This chapter adds a discussion of a different aspect of *Ohio v. Robinette,* holding that police are not required to always inform detainees that they are free to go before a consent to search may be deemed voluntary. Also added is an enhanced explanation of *Illinois v. Rodriguez*'s holding that a consent search may be valid if the searching officer reasonably believed that the consenting person had authority over the premises.

Chapter 10: The Plain View Doctrine.   This chapter is essentially unchanged except for updating and refining.

Chapter 11: Search and Seizure of Vehicles and Containers.   This chapter adds the U.S. Supreme Court case of *Pennsylvania v. Labron,* reasserting that, if a car is readily mobile and probable cause exists to believe it contains contraband, the Fourth Amendment permits police to search the vehicle without additional justification. Also added is the following new material:

- An enhanced discussion of the scope of a *Carroll* Doctrine search

- A new discussion of reasons justifying police impoundment of a vehicle

- A brief discussion of the rule in some states that requires officers to consider reasonable alternatives to impoundment of vehicles in certain circumstances
- A new discussion of the need to *complete* a vehicle inventory in order to validate it

Chapter 12: Open Fields and Abandoned Property.   This chapter adds a discussion of the U.S. Supreme Court case of *Dow Chemical Co. v. United States,* dealing with aerial photography of an outdoor industrial complex. Also added is an expanded discussion of the rule prohibiting, in the absence of exigent circumstances, the warrantless entry of premises and seizure of incriminating evidence even though the officer had probable cause.

Chapter 13: Admissions and Confessions.   This chapter adds the following:

- Expanded and updated discussion of the test for voluntariness of a statement
- Expanded discussion of the *McNabb-Mallory* rule
- Expanded discussion of the location of the interrogation as a factor determining "custody" for *Miranda* purposes
- Expanded discussion of the meaning of "interrogation" for *Miranda* purposes
- Cautionary advice on the application of the "public safety" exception to *Miranda*
- New discussion of what constitutes an invocation of the right to silence
- New discussion of the effect of the passage of time on the integrity of *Miranda* warnings

Chapter 14: Pretrial Identification Procedures.   This chapter adds expanded discussions of *United States v. Wade, Gilbert v. California, Kirby v. Illinois,* and on-the-scene showups.

Acknowledgments

I am grateful to the following criminal justice instructors for their time and effort in reviewing the Seventh Edition and providing helpful comments and suggestions for the book's improvement: Charles Dreveskracht, Northeastern State University; G. G. Hunt, Wharton County Junior College; James Hague, Virginia Commonwealth University; Susan Jacobs, University of Nebraska at Omaha; Richard Janikowski, University of Memphis; and Elizabeth Lewis, Waycross College. I also want to thank again the following professors for their reviews of previous editions of the book: Jack E. Call, Joseph Robert Caton, Charles Dreveskracht, Jack Elrod, David V. Guccione, James Hague, G. G. Hunt, Susan Jacobs, Joseph G. Sandoval, Susette M. Talarico, and Alvin J. T. Zumbrun. My appreciation also to the staff at Wadsworth Publishing Company and those who worked with them at all stages of the production of this Seventh Edition. Finally, and most importantly, I express my deepest appreciation to my wife, Barbara Duff, and my son, Rocky, for their loving support and understanding through my absences and engrossment in the preparation of the Seventh Edition. When the task sometimes seemed overwhelming, their presence gave me the solace and encouragement to carry on.

JOHN N. FERDICO

Introduction

A *crime* is an act committed or omitted in violation of a law specifically prohibiting or commanding it. Crimes differ from other prohibited behavior in that, upon conviction, an adult may be penalized by fine, incarceration, or both; a corporation may be penalized by fine or forfeiture; and a juvenile may be adjudged delinquent or transferred to criminal court for prosecution. Generally, a crime consists of conduct that violates the duties a person owes to the community or society, as distinguished from a private wrong committed against one or more persons or organizations. *Criminal law* is the body of law that defines what acts or omissions constitute crimes and provides for the punishment of that behavior. *Criminal procedure* can be defined as the body of laws and rules governing the process of detecting and investigating crime and gathering evidence against, apprehending, prosecuting, trying, adjudicating, sentencing, and punishing persons accused of crimes.

Criminal Procedure—Complex and Dynamic

The law of criminal procedure is not only complex, but constantly changing. The criminal justice professional, and especially the law enforcement officer, is expected to understand these complexities and keep abreast of the changes. More importantly, criminal procedure law must be applied to a variety of situations that do not always neatly conform to the established principles. To compound the problem, criminal procedure law is derived primarily from judicial opinions that are often written in a rambling, legalistic style that even lawyers and judges have trouble understanding. The result is a gap of communication and understanding between those who make the rules (judges) and those who must enforce and apply them (law enforcement officers and other criminal justice professionals). Violations of rights of citizens by criminal justice personnel who are not aware or not heedful of court-imposed limitations on their activities is a main cause of the failure of many prosecutions and the reversal of many convictions.

This book is an attempt to bridge the gap of communication and understanding between judges and criminal justice professionals. All who operate within the criminal justice system need understandable guidelines for performing their particular functions within the system. For example, law enforcement officers need understandable rules and procedures for conducting arrests, searches and seizures, interrogations, and lineups. Also, all criminal justice personnel should be familiar with the language and reasoning of the courts defining rights and obligations in the criminal justice area. Nonlawyers, however, should not be expected to read through long, involved opinions of every state and federal case that affects them and to extract principles of law to guide them in the execution of their duties. They already carry a heavy enough burden. Therefore, this book attempts to reduce the complexity of the law of criminal procedure into simple, straightforward advice, illustrated with examples of actual cases. Quotations from cases are used if they are written in clear, understandable language.

Criminal Procedure—The Constitution and the Courts

Most of the principles governing criminal procedure are derived from the United States Constitution, constitutions of individual states, and court decisions interpreting those constitutions. This book begins with a discussion of individual rights under the U.S. Constitution and an overview of the criminal court system. The remainder and greater portion of the book is a discussion of various specific areas of criminal procedure, presented primarily through appellate court decisions. An *appellate court* is a court that hears appeals from lower courts, usually trial courts. An *appeal* in a criminal case is a request to an appellate court by either the defendant or the prosecution to review alleged errors by the trial court or alleged official misconduct or violation of rights by one of the participants in the criminal justice process. Most appeals are by convicted defendants attempting to overturn their convictions. After the appellate court reviews the allegations presented, it issues a written opinion explaining its decision.

Most of the principles in this book are illustrated by decisions of the U.S. Supreme Court. The Supreme Court has a significant role in the development of the law of criminal procedure, because criminal procedure is prominently featured in the Constitution and because the Supreme Court has the ultimate responsibility for interpreting the Constitution. Of the twenty-three separate rights set out in the first eight amendments to the Constitution, more than half concern criminal procedure. Although the Court has had little to say about some constitutional rights, the Court has, since the early 1960s especially, developed complex and comprehensive bodies of law around other constitutional rights. Lower federal courts and state appellate courts have responded to this development with increased activity of their own in the criminal procedure area in recent years. Decisions of these lower courts are used in this book primarily to give examples of important principles and to clarify the law in areas where the U.S. Supreme Court has not spoken, or has spoken only superficially or sketchily. In rare situations, a lower court case may be used to set out a principle or doctrine not addressed by the U.S. Supreme Court or to illustrate a state court's disagreement with and departure from guidelines established by the Supreme Court. The reader is apprised of these uses of lower court decisions.

Because most criminal procedure principles and doctrines derive from U.S. Supreme Court decisions interpreting the Constitution, the reader should know how to recognize these cases. An example of a U.S. Supreme Court case citation follows: *Miranda v. Arizona,* 384 U.S. 436, 86 S.Ct. 1602, 16 L.Ed.2d 694 (1966). The title of the case appears in italics. The designation "384 U.S. 436" means that the *Miranda* case appears in volume 384 of the *United States Reports,* beginning at page 436. The *United States Reports* is the official published collection of U.S. Supreme

Court decisions. "S.Ct." refers to the *Supreme Court Reporter,* a compilation of U.S. Supreme Court decisions published by West Publishing Company, Eagan, Minnesota. "L.Ed.2d" refers to the *U.S. Supreme Court Reports Lawyer's Edition,* Second Series, published by Lawyers Cooperative Publishing, Rochester, New York. These published collections of Supreme Court decisions can be found in law libraries. All U.S. Supreme Court decisions in this book are cited according to this format.

This book uses the West Publishing Company Reporter system for all citations for lower federal and state court decisions. For example, *United States v. Guyon,* 717 F.2d 1536 (6th Cir. 1983), means that the *Guyon* case appears in volume 717 of West's *Federal Reporter,* Second Series, beginning at page 1536. "6th Cir." means that the case was decided by the U.S. Court of Appeals for the Sixth Circuit. All decisions of U.S. Courts of Appeals appear in West's *Federal Reporter.* Decisions of the U.S. District Courts appear in West's *Federal Supplement.* A typical citation to that reporter follows: *United States v. Gallego-Zapata,* 630 F.Supp. 655 (D.Mass 1986). "D.Mass." indicates that the case was decided by the U.S. District Court for the District of Massachusetts. A typical state court citation follows: *People v. Eddington,* 198 N.W.2d 297 (Mich. 1972). "N.W.2d" means that the case appears in West's *Northwestern Reporter,* Second Series. West Publishing Company publishes state court decisions in reporters covering different regions of the United States. The designation "Mich." means that the case was decided by the Michigan Supreme Court. A more detailed discussion of citations and the reporter systems is beyond the scope of this book.

PART ONE

A Framework for the Study of Criminal Procedure

CHAPTER ONE

Individual Rights Under the United States Constitution

OBJECTIVES

1. Understand the historical context out of which came the concern for the individual rights that are embodied in the United States Constitution.

2. Be able to explain how the legislative, judicial, and executive branches of government are involved in the protection of the constitutional rights of citizens.

3. Understand the individual rights protected by the original Constitution of 1788, and be familiar with the terms *habeas corpus, bill of attainder, ex post facto law,* and *treason.*

4. Be able to explain the general nature and limits of the rights embodied in the Bill of Rights, especially the First Amendment freedoms of

religion, speech, press, assembly, and petition; the Fourth Amendment prohibition against unreasonable searches and seizures; the Fifth Amendment protection against double jeopardy and self-incrimination and the right to due process of law; the Sixth Amendment rights to a speedy and public trial, notice of charges, confrontation with adverse witnesses, compulsory process for favorable witnesses, and assistance of counsel; and the Eighth Amendment rights against excessive bail and fines and against cruel and unusual punishment.

5. Have a general understanding of the concepts of due process and equal protection as guaranteed by the Fourteenth Amendment.

OUTLINE

The law of criminal procedure can be described as rules designed to balance the conflicting governmental functions of maintaining law and order and protecting the rights of citizens. These functions, common to every government that is not totally authoritarian or anarchistic, are necessarily conflicting because an increased emphasis on maintaining law and order will necessarily involve increased intrusions on individual rights. And, conversely, an increased emphasis on protecting individual rights will necessarily hamper the efficient maintenance of law and order. For example, an overprotective policy toward preserving individual rights is likely to result in an atmosphere conducive to increased violation of and disrespect for the law. Potential criminals will perceive that restrictions on police authority to arrest, detain, search, and question will decrease the likelihood of their getting caught and that complex and technical procedural safeguards designed to ensure the fairness of court proceedings will enable them to avoid punishment if they do get caught. The ultimate result, it is argued, is a society in which people do not feel secure in their homes or communities and in which illegal activity abounds in government, business, and other aspects of daily life, to the detriment of everyone.

On the other hand, enforcement of the criminal laws would be much easier if persons suspected of crime were presumed guilty; if they had no privilege against self-incrimination; if their bodies, vehicles, and homes could be searched at will; and if they could be detained for long periods of time without a hearing. Life in many totalitarian countries today is characterized by such governmental abuses, and the citizenry of these countries lives in daily fear of official intrusion into the home, the disappearance of a loved one, or tighter restrictions on movement, speech, or association.

Because the United States was founded as a direct response to British abuses against the early colonists—although those abuses were certainly not as severe as the abuses under present-day dictatorships—our form of government has, from the beginning, reflected a strong commitment to the protection of individual rights from governmental abuse. This commitment was embodied in the original Constitution of 1788 and in the Bill of Rights, which was adopted shortly thereafter. This discussion of individual rights begins with a brief history of events leading to the adoption of the Constitution. ■

History

On September 17, 1787, a convention of delegates from all the original thirteen states except Rhode Island proposed a new Constitution to the Continental Congress and the states for ratification. The rights expressed and protected by this Constitution, and by the amendments adopted four years later, were not new. Some had roots in the societies of ancient Rome and Greece, and all were nurtured during almost six hundred years of English history since the signing of the Magna Carta.

As colonists under English rule, Americans before the Revolution were familiar with the ideas that government should be limited in power and that the law was superior to any government, even the king. As the Declaration of Independence shows, the colonists rebelled because the English king and Parliament refused to allow them their historic rights as free English citizens. In September 1774, delegates from twelve colonies met in the First Continental Congress to petition England for their rights "to life, liberty, and property" and to trial by jury; "for a right peaceably to assemble, consideration of their grievances, and petition the King"; and for other rights that they had been denied. The petition was ignored, and soon afterward fighting broke out at Lexington and Concord. Meanwhile, citizens in Mecklenburg County, North Carolina, declared the laws of Parliament to be null and void and instituted their own form of local government with the adoption of the Mecklenburg Resolves in May 1775. In June 1776, a resolution was introduced in the Continental Congress, and a month later, on July 4, 1776, the Thirteen United Colonies declared themselves free and independent. Their announcement was truly revolutionary. They listed a large number of abuses they had suffered, and justified their independence in the historic words "We hold these truths to be self-evident, that all men are created equal, that they are endowed by their Creator with certain Inalienable Rights, that among these are Life, Liberty and the pursuit of Happiness."

Two years later, in July 1778, the newly independent states joined in a united government under the Articles of Confederation, which was our nation's first Constitution. But it soon became clear that the Articles of Confederation did not adequately provide for a working, efficient government. Among their other weaknesses, the articles gave Congress no authority to levy taxes or to regulate foreign or interstate commerce. In May 1787, a convention of delegates, meeting in Philadelphia with Congress's approval, began to consider amendments to the articles. But the delegates realized that a new system of government was necessary. After much debate, and several heated arguments, a compromise Constitution was negotiated.

Although we now honor the wisdom of the delegates, they themselves had a different opinion of their work. Many were dissatisfied, and a few even thought a new Constitution should be written. No delegate from Rhode Island attended the convention or signed the document on September 17, 1787, when the proposed Constitution was announced. Delaware was the first state to accept this Constitution, ratifying it on December 7, 1787, by a unanimous vote. Not all states were as pleased, and in some states the vote was extremely close. For a while it was not certain that a sufficient number of states would ratify. A major argument against ratification was the absence of a Bill of Rights. Only after it became generally agreed that the first order of business of the new government would be to propose amendments for a Bill of Rights was acceptance of the Constitution obtained by a sufficient number of states. On June 21, 1788, New Hampshire became the ninth state to sign on, and ratification of the new Constitution was completed. By the end of July 1788, the important states of Virginia and New York had joined New Hampshire.

On September 25, 1789, Congress proposed the first ten amendments to the new Constitution—the Bill of Rights. With the proposal of these guarantees, the states of North Carolina and Rhode Island, the last of the thirteen original colonies, ratified the Constitution. Ratification of the Bill of Rights was completed on December 15, 1791. Since that date, the Bill of Rights has served as our nation's testimony to its belief in the basic and inalienable rights of the people and in the limitations on the power of government. Together with provisions of the original Constitution, it protects that great body of liberties that belongs to every citizen.

For ease of discussion, the remainder of this chapter treats the original Constitution separately from the Bill of Rights and later amendments.

The Original Constitution

The Constitution of 1789 has served as the fundamental instrument of our government for almost all of our country's history as an independent nation. Drawn at a time when there were only thirteen original states, dotted with small towns, small farms, and small industry, the Constitution has provided a durable and viable instrument of government despite enormous changes in the political, social, and economic environment.

From serving a weak country on the Atlantic seaboard to serving a continental nation of fifty states with over 260 million people producing goods and services at a rate thousands of times faster than in 1789, the framework for democratic government set out in the Constitution has remained workable and progressive. Similarly, the individual rights listed in the Constitution and its twenty-seven amendments have also retained an extraordinary vitality despite their being applied to problems and situations that could not have been envisioned by the Founding Fathers. Freedom of the press, for example, could have been understood only in the context of the small, still primitive printing presses of the late eighteenth century. Yet today that freedom applies not only to modern presses but to radio, television, and motion pictures—all products of the twentieth century.

The purpose of this chapter is to explain how these basic rights have been applied and to develop a sensitivity to them as a prelude to the study of criminal procedure, in which these rights will confront the countervailing demands of society for the enforcement of the law and the detection and prevention of crime.

Each branch of the government—legislative, judicial, and executive—is charged by the Constitution with the protection of individual liberties. Within this framework, the judicial branch has assumed perhaps the largest role. Chief Justice John Marshall, speaking for the Supreme Court in the early case of *Marbury v. Madison*, 5 U.S. (1 Cranch) 137, 2 L.Ed. 60 (1803), declared that it was the duty of the judiciary to say what the law is, adding that this duty included expounding and interpreting the law. Marshall stated that the law contained in the Constitution was paramount and that other laws that were repugnant to its provisions must fall. It was the province of the courts, he concluded, to decide when other laws were in violation of the basic law of the Constitution and, where this was found to occur, to declare those laws null and void. This is the doctrine known as **judicial review**, which became the basis for the application of constitutional guarantees by courts in cases brought before them.

> Judicial review is the exercise by courts of their responsibility to determine whether acts of the other two branches are illegal and void because those acts violate the constitution. The doctrine authorizes courts to determine whether a law is constitutional, not whether it is necessary or useful. In other words, judicial review is the power to say what the constitution means and not whether such a law reflects a wise policy. Adherence to the doctrine of judicial review is essential to achieving balance in our government. . . . Judicial review, coupled with the specified constitutional provisions which keep the judicial branch separate and independent of the other branches of government and with those articles of the constitution that protect the impartiality of the judiciary from public and political pressure, enables the courts to ensure that the constitutional rights of each citizen will not be encroached upon by either the legislative or the executive branch of the government. *State v. LaFrance*, 471 A.2d 340, 343–44 (N.H. 1983).

The Congress has played an important role in the protection of constitutional rights by enacting legislation designed to guarantee and apply those rights in specific contexts. Laws that guarantee the rights of Native Americans, afford due process to military service personnel, and give effective right to counsel to poor defendants are examples of the legislative role.

Finally, the executive branch, which is charged with implementing the laws enacted by Congress, contributes to the protection of individual rights by devising its own regulations and procedures for administering the law without intruding on constitutional guarantees.

To properly understand the scope of constitutional rights, one must realize that, because of our federal system, an American lives under two governments rather than one: the federal government and the government of the state in which that person lives. The authority of the federal government is limited by the Constitution to the powers specified in the Constitution; the remainder of governmental powers is reserved to the states. The federal government is authorized, for example, to settle disputes between states, conduct relations with foreign governments, and act in certain matters of common national concern. States, on the other hand, retain the remainder of governmental power to be exercised within their respective boundaries.

The Bill of Rights

Only a few individual rights were specified in the Constitution when it was adopted in 1788. Shortly after its adoption, however, ten amendments—called the Bill of Rights—were added to the Constitution to guarantee basic individual liberties. These liberties include freedom of speech, freedom of the press, freedom of religion, and freedom to assemble and petition the government.

The guarantees of the Bill of Rights originally applied only to actions of the federal government and did not prevent state and local governments from taking action that might threaten civil liberty. As a practical matter, states had their own constitutions, some containing their own bills of rights that guaranteed the same rights as (or similar rights to) those guaranteed by the Bill of Rights against federal intrusion. These rights, however, were not guaranteed by all the states; if they did exist, they were subject to varying interpretations. In short, citizens were protected only to the extent that the states themselves recognized their basic rights.

In 1868, the Fourteenth Amendment was added to the Constitution. In part it provides that no state shall "deprive any person of life, liberty, or property without due process of law." Not until 1925, in the case of *Gitlow v. New York,* 268 U.S. 652, 45 S.Ct. 625, 69 L.Ed. 1138, did the Supreme Court interpret the phrase "due process of law" to mean, in effect, "without abridgement of certain of the rights guaranteed by the Bill of Rights." Since that decision, the Supreme Court has ruled that a denial by a state of certain of the rights contained in the Bill of Rights represents a denial of due process of law. The members of the Court, however, have had a long-standing controversy as to which of the provisions of the Bill of Rights were applicable to the states and to what extent they are applicable. Essentially three major positions, with many variations, have evolved over the years:

1. The "total incorporation" approach held that the due process clause of the Fourteenth Amendment made the entire federal Bill of Rights applicable to the states. This view never commanded a majority of the court and was rejected repeatedly in *Twining v. New Jersey,* 211 U.S. 78, 29 S.Ct. 14, 53 L.Ed. 97 (1908); *Palko v. Connecticut,* 302 U.S. 319, 58 S.Ct. 149, 82 L.Ed. 288 (1937); and *Adamson v. California,* 332 U.S. 46, 67 S.Ct. 1672, 91 L.Ed. 1903 (1947). The Court in *Twining* noted, however, that "it is possible that some of the personal rights safeguarded by the first eight Amendments against National action may also be safeguarded against state

action, because a denial of them would be a denial of due process of law. . . . If this is so, it is not because those rights are enumerated in the first eight amendments, but because they are of such a nature that they are included in the conception of due process of law." 211 U.S. at 99, 29 S.Ct. at 19–20, 53 L.Ed. at 106.

2. The possibility mentioned in the *Twining* quote became known as the "fundamental rights" or "ordered liberty" approach to due process, which was adopted by the Court in *Palko, Adamson,* and other cases and held sway until the early 1960s. Under this approach, the Court found no necessary relationship between the due process clause of the Fourteenth Amendment and the Bill of Rights. The due process clause was said to have an "independent potency" existing apart from the Bill of Rights. Due process was viewed as prohibiting state action that violated those rights that are "implicit in the concept of ordered liberty," that are "so rooted in the traditions and conscience of our people as to be ranked fundamental," that represent "fundamental fairness essential to the very concept of justice," or some like phrase suggesting fundamental rights. Under the fundamental rights–ordered liberty approach, the Court looked to the "totality of the circumstances" of the particular case to determine what right, or what aspect or phase of a right, is "fundamental."

3. The "selective incorporation" approach combines aspects of the other two approaches and has prevailed since the early 1960s. This approach accepts the basic tenet of the fundamental rights–ordered liberty approach (that is, that Fourteenth Amendment due process protects only rights that are "fundamental"). Also, under selective incorporation, every right in the Bill of Rights was not necessarily considered fundamental, and some rights outside the Bill of Rights might be considered fundamental. But the selective incorporation approach rejected the examination of the "totality of the circumstances" to determine whether particular aspects or phases of rights in the Bill of Rights were or were not fundamental. Instead, if a right was determined to be fundamental, it was incorporated into the Fourteenth Amendment and applicable to the states *to the same extent* as to the federal government. As the Court said in *Duncan v. Louisiana,* "Because we believe that trial by jury in criminal cases is fundamental to the American scheme of justice, we hold that the Fourteenth Amendment guarantees a right of jury trial in all criminal cases which—*were they to be tried in a federal court*—would come within the Sixth Amendment's guarantee" (emphasis added). 391 U.S. 145, 149, 88 S.Ct. 1444, 1447, 20 L.Ed.2d 491, 496 (1968). The reference in this quotation to the *American* scheme of justice is not without significance, as is pointed out in footnote 14 of the *Duncan* opinion:

> In one sense recent cases applying provisions of the first eight amendments to the States represent a new approach to the "incorporation" debate. Earlier the Court can be seen as having asked, when inquiring into whether some particular procedural safeguard was required of a State, if a civilized system could be imagined that would not accord the particular protection. . . . The recent cases, on the other hand, have proceeded upon the valid assumption that state criminal processes are not imaginary and theoretical schemes but actual systems bearing virtually every characteristic of the common-law system that has been developing contemporaneously in England and in this country. The question thus is whether given this kind of system a particular procedure is fundamental— whether, that is, a procedure is necessary to an Anglo-American regime of ordered liberty. . . . Of immediate relevance for this case are the Court's holdings that the States must comply with certain provisions of the Sixth Amendment,

specifically that the States may not refuse a speedy trial, confrontation of witnesses, and the assistance, at state expense if necessary, of counsel. . . . Of each of these determinations that a constitutional provision originally written to bind the Federal Government should bind the States as well it might be said that the limitation in question is not necessarily fundamental to fairness in every criminal system that might be imagined but is fundamental in the context of the criminal processes maintained by the American States. 391 U.S. at 149 n.14, 88 S.Ct. at 1447 n.14, 20 L.Ed.2d at 496 n.14.

At present, the following guarantees of the Bill of Rights have been applied to the states under the terms of the Fourteenth Amendment: Amendments I, IV, and VI; the self-incrimination, double jeopardy, and just compensation clauses of Amendment V; and the guarantee against cruel and unusual punishment of Amendment VIII. The only guarantees specifically concerning criminal procedure that have not been applied to the states are the right to indictment by grand jury in Amendment V and the prohibition against excessive bail or fines in Amendment VIII.

To place these rights in a broader perspective, one should realize that they make up only the core of what are considered to be **civil rights**—the privileges and freedoms that are accorded all Americans by virtue of their citizenship. Many other civil rights are not specifically mentioned in the Constitution but nonetheless have been recognized by the courts, have often been guaranteed by statute, and are embedded in our democratic traditions. The right to buy, sell, own, and bequeath property; the right to enter into contracts; the right to marry and have children; the right to live and work where one desires; and the right to participate in the political, social, and cultural processes of the society in which one lives are a few of the rights that must be considered as fundamental to a democratic society as those specified by the Constitution.

Despite the inherent nature of the rights of American citizenship, the rights guaranteed by the Constitution or otherwise are not absolute rights in the sense that they entitle citizens to act in any way they please. Rather, to be protected by the law, people must exercise their rights in such a way that the rights of others are not denied. Thus, as Justice Oliver Wendell Holmes pointed out, "Protection of free speech would not protect a man falsely shouting 'Fire' in a theater and causing a panic." Nor does freedom of speech and press sanction the publication of libel and obscenity. Similarly, the rights of free speech and free assembly do not permit one to engage knowingly in conspiracies to overthrow by force the government of the United States. Civil liberties thus carry with them an obligation on the part of all Americans to exercise their rights within a framework of law and mutual respect for the rights of their fellow citizens.

This obligation implies not only a restraint on the part of those exercising these rights but a tolerance on the part of those who are affected. Thus, citizens may on occasion be subjected to annoying political tirades, or disagreeable entertainment, or noisy demonstrations of protest. They may feel annoyed when a defendant refuses to testify or when they see a seemingly guilty defendant go free because certain evidence was not admissible in court. But these annoyances or inconveniences are a small price to pay for the freedom American citizens enjoy. If the rights of one are suppressed, it is, in the final analysis, the freedom of all that is jeopardized. Ultimately, a free society is a dynamic society, where thoughts and ideas are forever challenging and being challenged. Such a society is not without the risk that the wrong voice will be listened to or the wrong plan pursued. But a free society is one that learns by its mistakes and can freely pursue the happiness of its citizens.

Individual Rights in the Original Constitution

ARTICLE I, SECTION 9, CLAUSE 2

The Privilege of the Writ of Habeas Corpus shall not be suspended, unless when in Cases of Rebellion or Invasion the public Safety may require it. ■

This guarantee enables a person whose freedom has been restrained in some way to petition a federal court for a writ of habeas corpus, to test whether the restraint was imposed in violation of the Constitution or laws of the United States. This right under the Constitution applies to all cases in which a person is confined by governmental authority. It can be suspended only when the president, pursuant to congressional authorization, declares that a national emergency requires its suspension and probably only when the courts are physically unable to function because of war, invasion, or rebellion. Habeas corpus is an important safeguard to prevent unlawful imprisonment and is discussed in further detail in Chapter 2.

ARTICLE I, SECTION 9, CLAUSE 3

No Bill of Attainder . . . shall be passed [by the federal government]. ■

ARTICLE I, SECTION 10, CLAUSE 1

No State shall . . . pass any Bill of Attainder. . . . ■

Historically, a **bill of attainder** is a special act of a legislature that declares that a person or group of persons has committed a crime and that imposes punishment without a trial by court. Under our system of separation of powers, only courts may try a person for a crime or impose punishment for violation of the law. Section 9 restrains Congress from passing bills of attainder, and Section 10 restrains the states.

ARTICLE I, SECTION 9, CLAUSE 3

No . . . ex post facto Law shall be passed [by the federal government]. ■

ARTICLE I, SECTION 10, CLAUSE 1

No state shall . . . pass any . . . ex post facto Law. . . . ■

These two clauses prohibit the states and the federal government from enacting any **ex post facto law**. "[A]ny statute which punishes as a crime an act previously committed, which was innocent when done; which makes more burdensome the punishment for a crime, after its commission, or which deprives one charged with crime of any defense available according to law at the time when the act was committed, is prohibited as ex post facto." *Beazell v. Ohio*, 269 U.S. 167, 169–70, 46 S.Ct. 68, 68–69, 70 L.Ed. 216, 217 (1925). However, laws that retroactively determine how a person is to be tried for a crime may be changed so long as the substantial rights of the accused are not curtailed. Laws are not ex post facto if they make punishment less severe than it was when the crime was committed.

ARTICLE III, SECTIONS 1 AND 2

(Article III, Sections 1 and 2, of the Constitution deal with the judicial system of the United States and for purposes of this book are too long to be reproduced.) ■

Article III, Section 1, of the Constitution outlines the structure and power of our federal court system and establishes a federal judiciary that helps maintain the rights of American citizens. Article III, Section 2, also contains a guarantee that the trial of all federal crimes, except that of impeachment, shall be by jury. The Supreme Court has interpreted this guarantee as containing exceptions for "trials of petty offenses," cases rightfully tried before a court martial or other military tribunal, and some cases in which the defendant has voluntarily relinquished the right to jury. The right to a jury trial is discussed further in Chapter 2.

Section 2 also requires that a federal criminal trial be held in a federal court sitting in the state where the crime was committed. Thus, a person is given protection against being tried without his or her consent in some part of the United States far distant from the place where the alleged violation of federal laws occurred.

ARTICLE III, SECTION 3

Treason against the United States, shall consist only in levying War against them, or in adhering to their Enemies, giving them Aid and Comfort. No Person shall be convicted of Treason unless on the Testimony of two Witnesses to the same overt Act, or on Confession in open Court.

The Congress shall have power to declare the Punishment of Treason, but no Attainder of Treason shall work Corruption of Blood, or Forfeiture except during the Life of the Person attainted. ■

Treason is the only crime defined by the Constitution. The precise description of this offense reflects an awareness by our forebears of the danger that unpopular views might be branded as traitorous. Recent experience in other countries with prosecutions for conduct loosely labeled treason confirms the wisdom of the authors of the Constitution in expressly stating what constitutes this crime and how it shall be proved.

ARTICLE VI, CLAUSE 3

[N]o religious Test shall ever be required as a Qualification to any Office or public Trust under the United States. ■

Together with the First Amendment, this guarantee expresses the principle that church and government are to remain separate and that religious beliefs are no indication of patriotism, ability, or the right to serve this country. Thus, a citizen need not fear that religious affiliations or convictions may legally bar him or her from holding office in the United States.

Individual Rights in the Bill of Rights

AMENDMENT I

Congress shall make no law respecting an establishment of religion, or prohibiting the free exercise thereof; or abridging the freedom of speech, or of the press; or the right of the people peaceably to assemble, and to petition the Government for a redress of grievances.

Freedom of Religion

Two express guarantees are given to the individual citizen with respect to religious freedom. First, neither Congress nor a state legislature because of the Fourteenth Amendment may "make any law respecting an establishment of religion." This means no law may be passed that establishes an official church that all Americans must accept and support or to whose tenets all must subscribe or that favors one church over another. Second, no law is constitutional if it "prohibits the free exercise" of religion. Citizens are guaranteed the freedom to worship in the way they choose.

The Supreme Court described the establishment clause as providing a "wall of separation between church and state." *Everson v. Board of Education,* 330 U.S. 1, 16, 67 S.Ct. 504, 512, 91 L.Ed. 711, 723 (1947):

> The "establishment of religion" clause of the First Amendment means at least this: Neither a state nor the Federal Government can set up a church. Neither can pass laws which aid one religion, aid all religions, or prefer one religion over another. Neither can force nor influence a person to go to or remain away from church against his will or force him to profess a belief or disbelief in any religion. No person can be punished for entertaining or professing religious beliefs or disbeliefs, for church attendance or non-attendance. No tax in any amount, large or small, can be levied to support any religious activities or institutions, whatever they may be called, or whatever form they may adopt to teach or practice religion. Neither a state nor the Federal Government can, openly or secretly, participate in the affairs of any religious organizations or groups and *vice versa.* 330 U.S. at 15–16, 67 S.Ct. at 511–12, 91 L.Ed. at 723.

In *Lemon v. Kurtzman,* 403 U.S. 602, 612–13, 91 S.Ct. 2105, 2111, 29 L.Ed.2d 745, 755 (1971), the Court sought to refine these principles by focusing on three tests for determining whether a statute or government practice is permissible under the establishment clause: (1) it must have a secular purpose, (2) its principal or primary purpose must be one that neither advances nor inhibits religion, and (3) it must not foster an excessive government entanglement with religion. Thus, Court decisions have held that a state may not require prayer in the public schools, nor may it supplement or reimburse parochial schools for teachers' salaries and textbooks. To permit or authorize such activities would constitute governmental support of the religious organization affected. On the other hand, the Court held that it is permissible for public schools to release students, at the students' own request, from an hour of class work so that those students may attend their own churches for religious instruction; or for a state to provide free bus transportation to children attending church or parochial schools if transportation is also furnished to children in the public schools. Furthermore, the Court upheld the tax-exempt status of church property used exclusively for worship purposes, and it has sanctioned federal aid programs for new construction at church-related universities. It also held that the establishment clause does not prevent a state from designating Sunday as a day of rest.

Freedom to worship, as interpreted by the Supreme Court, must not conflict with otherwise valid government enactments. For example, a man may not have two wives and escape conviction for bigamy by attributing his conduct to his religious beliefs. Nor could a person commit an indecent act or engage in immoral conduct and then validly justify the actions on grounds of religious freedom. The Supreme Court also declared that it is an unconstitutional invasion of religious freedom to exclude from public schools children who, because of their religious beliefs, refuse to salute the American flag. The Court further ruled that requiring children of the Amish religious sect to attend public schools beyond the eighth grade was an impairment of the free exercise clause, since such attendance prevented education in the traditional Amish framework.

Freedom of Speech

As a general rule, citizens may freely speak out on any subject they choose. In addition, they may join organizations, wear buttons, buy books, and carry signs that represent their views. And they may take their cases to court when they feel they have been wronged.

The Supreme Court ruled, however, that the protections afforded by the First Amendment do not extend to all forms of expression. Highly inflammatory remarks that are spoken to a crowd and that advocate violence and clearly threaten the peace and safety of the community, or present a "clear and present danger" to the continued existence of the government, are not protected. Obscenity, too, has been judged unprotected by the First Amendment, although the Court has held that the mere possession of obscene materials in the home may not be punished.

Courts have also recognized that "symbolic speech," which involves more tangible forms of expression, falls within the protection of the First Amendment. Wearing buttons or clothing with political slogans, displaying a sign or a flag, or burning a flag as a mode of expression are examples of symbolic speech. The wearing of black armbands by secondary school students in protest against the Vietnam War has been ruled protected by the First Amendment, so long as the activity was not disruptive or injurious to the rights of other students. The display of a black flag in protest to organized government has also been protected. On the other hand, burning draft cards in protest against the Vietnam War has not been protected, since it could be shown to disrupt or undermine the operation of the Selective Service System. Courts have also been reluctant to overturn hair and dress codes of public schools when the schools could show that the codes were designed to prevent disruption or distraction of classes.

Finally, the courts have frequently condemned censorship imposed by requiring official approval or a license in advance for speaking. Nevertheless, although a citizen is free to make speeches on the public streets, he or she may be prevented from doing so when using a loud and raucous amplifier in a hospital zone or when the location chosen is such that the address is likely to interfere with the movement of traffic.

Freedom of the Press

Freedom of the press is a further guarantee of the right to express oneself, in this case by writing or publishing one's views on a particular subject. The Founding Fathers recognized the importance of a free interplay of ideas in a democratic society and sought to guarantee the right of all citizens to speak or publish their views, even if those views were contrary to the views of the government or the society as a whole.

Accordingly, the First Amendment generally forbids censorship or other restraint on speech or the printed word. Thus, a school board's dismissal of a teacher who had protested school board activities in a letter to the editor of the local newspaper was held to infringe on the teacher's First Amendment rights. And a state court order, issued in anticipation of the trial of an accused mass murderer, restraining the press and broadcasting media from reporting any confessions or incriminating statements made by the defendant or from reporting other facts "strongly implicative" of the defendant was similarly struck down.

As with speech, however, freedom to write or publish is not an absolute right of expression. The sale of obscene materials is not protected, nor are printed materials that are libelous. The Supreme Court ruled, however, that public figures cannot sue for defamation unless the alleged libelous remarks were printed with knowledge of their falsity or with a reckless disregard for the truth.

The Court also ruled that the publication of a secret study into the origins of the United States' involvement in the Vietnam War could not be prevented owing to the First Amendment guarantee. The Court indicated, however, that freedom of the press may not extend to other similar matters that could be shown to have a more direct and substantial bearing on national security.

Finally, broadcasting, including radio, television, and motion pictures, receives the protections of the free press guarantee and is also subject to its limitations.

The Right to Assembly and Petition

American citizens, whether they are meeting for political activity, religious services, or other purposes, have the right to assemble peaceably. Public authorities cannot impose unreasonable restrictions on such assemblies, but they can impose limitations reasonably designed to prevent fire, hazard to health, or a traffic obstruction. The Supreme Court emphasized that freedom of assembly is just as fundamental as freedom of speech and press. Thus, although no law may legitimately prohibit demonstrations, laws or other governmental actions may legitimately restrict demonstrations to certain areas or prohibit the obstruction and occupation of public buildings.

Picketing is also protected under the free speech guarantee. It may, however, be reasonably regulated to prevent pickets from obstructing movement onto and from the property involved. Picketing on private property has been upheld, but only where the property is open to the public and the picketing relates to the business being conducted on the property. Thus, the distribution of antiwar handbills on the premises of a privately owned shopping center has been held to be unprotected.

The right of petition is designed to enable citizens to communicate with their government without obstruction. When citizens exercise their First Amendment freedom to write or speak to their senator or member of Congress, they partake of "the healthy essence of the democratic process."

AMENDMENT II

A well regulated Militia, being necessary to the security of a free State, the right of the people to keep and bear Arms, shall not be infringed. ■

The Second Amendment provides for the freedom of citizens to protect themselves against both disorder in the community and attack from foreign enemies. This right to bear arms has become much less important in recent decades as well-trained military and police forces have been developed to protect the citizenry. No longer do people usually need to place reliance on having their own weapons available. Furthermore, the Supreme Court held that the state and federal governments may pass laws prohibiting the carrying of concealed weapons, requiring the registration of firearms, and limiting the sale of firearms for other than military uses.

AMENDMENT III

No Soldier shall, in time of peace be quartered in any house, without the consent of the Owner, nor in time of war, but in a manner to be prescribed by law. ■

Before the Revolution, American colonists had, against their will, frequently been required to provide lodging and food for British soldiers. The Third Amendment prohibited the continuation of this practice.

AMENDMENT IV

The right of the people to be secure in their persons, houses, papers, and effects, against unreasonable searches and seizures, shall not be violated, and no Warrants shall issue, but upon probable cause, supported by Oath or affirmation, and particularly describing the place to be searched, and the persons or things to be seized. ■

In some countries, even today, police officers may invade a citizen's home, seize the citizen's property, or arrest the citizen whenever they see fit. In the United States, on the other hand, the Fourth Amendment protects the person and his or her property from unreasonable search and seizure by governmental officers. In general, although there are many exceptions to the rule, a police officer may not search the home of a private citizen, seize any of the citizen's property, or arrest the citizen without first obtaining a court order, called a **warrant.** Before the warrant will be issued, the police officer must convince a magistrate that there is **probable cause**—fair probability—either that the person involved has committed a crime or that evidence of a crime is in a particularly described place.

Because the major portion of this book deals with the topics of arrest, search and seizure, and probable cause, further discussion of the Fourth Amendment appears in the chapters dealing with those topics.

AMENDMENT V

No person shall be held to answer for a capital, or otherwise infamous crime, unless on a presentment or indictment of a Grand Jury, except in cases arising in the land or naval forces, or in the Militia, when in actual service in time of War or public danger; nor shall any person be subject for the same offense to be twice put in jeopardy of life or limb; nor shall be compelled in any criminal case to be a witness against himself, nor be deprived of life, liberty, or property, without due process of law; nor shall private property be taken for public use, without just compensation. ■

Indictment by Grand Jury

The Fifth Amendment requires that before a person is tried in *federal* court for an infamous crime, he or she must first be indicted by a grand jury. The grand jury's duty is to make sure that there is probable cause to believe that the accused person is guilty. This provision prevents a person from being subjected to a trial when there is not enough proof that he or she has committed a crime.

An infamous crime, generally, is a felony (a crime for which a sentence of more than one year's imprisonment can be given) or a lesser offense that can be punished by confinement in a penitentiary or at hard labor. An indictment is not required for a trial by court martial or by other military tribunal. Furthermore, the constitutional requirement of grand jury indictment does not apply to trials in state courts. *Hurtado v. California,* 110 U.S. 516, 4 S.Ct. 111, 28 L.Ed. 232 (1884). However, where states do use grand juries in their criminal proceedings, the Supreme Court has ruled that the grand juries must be free of racial bias. The grand jury is discussed in further detail in Chapter 2.

Freedom from Double Jeopardy

The clause "nor shall any person be subject for the same offense to be twice put in jeopardy of life or limb" is often referred to as the **double jeopardy** clause. The U.S. Supreme Court has recognized three separate guarantees embodied in the double jeopardy clause: "It protects against a second prosecution for the same offense after acquittal, against a second prosecution for the same offense after conviction, and against multiple punishments for the same offense." *Justices of Boston Municipal Court v. Lydon,* 466 U.S. 294, 306–07, 104 S.Ct. 1805, 1812, 80 L.Ed.2d 311, 323 (1984). Note that the double jeopardy clause "protects only against the imposition of multiple *criminal* punishments for the same offense." *Hudson v. United States,* ___ U.S. ___, ___, 118 S.Ct. 488, 493, 139 L.Ed.2d 450, 458 (1997). It does not protect against criminal prosecution of a person after the person has been penalized in a civil proceeding. The double jeopardy protections were explained in *Ohio v. Johnson,* 467 U.S. 493, 498–99, 104 S.Ct. 2536, 2540–41, 81 L.Ed.2d 425, 433 (1984):

> [T]he bar to retrial following acquittal or conviction ensures that the State does not make repeated attempts to convict an individual, thereby exposing him to continued embarrassment, anxiety, and expense, while increasing the risk of an erroneous conviction or an impermissibly enhanced sentence. . . . [P]rotection against cumulative punishments is designed to ensure that the sentencing discretion of courts is confined to the limits established by the legislature.

Jeopardy attaches in a jury trial when the jury is impaneled and sworn and in a nonjury trial when the judge begins to hear evidence. Jeopardy attaches to all criminal proceedings, whether felony or misdemeanor, and to juvenile adjudicatory proceedings, even though they are civil in nature.

There are many exceptions to the general rules protecting a person from double jeopardy. Some of the important exceptions are mentioned here. First, a second trial for the same offense may occur when the first trial results in a mistrial (for example, deadlocked jury), if there is a "manifest necessity" for the mistrial declaration or "the ends of public justice would otherwise be defeated." *Richardson v. United States,* 468 U.S. 317, 324, 104 S.Ct. 3081, 3085, 82 L.Ed.2d 242, 250 (1984). Generally, the double jeopardy clause does not bar reprosecution of a defendant whose conviction is overturned on appeal.

While different theories have been advanced to support the permissibility of re-trial, of greater importance than the conceptual abstractions employed to explain the . . . principle are the implications of that principle for the sound administration of justice. Corresponding to the right of an accused to be given a fair trial is the societal interest in punishing one whose guilt is clear after he has obtained such a trial. It would be a high price indeed for society to pay were every accused granted immunity from punishment because of any defect sufficient to constitute reversible error in the proceedings leading to conviction. *United States v. Tateo,* 377 U.S. 463, 466, 84 S.Ct. 1587, 1589, 12 L.Ed.2d 448, 451 (1964).

Reprosecution after a conviction is reversed on appeal is prohibited, however, if the reason for the reversal was insufficiency of the evidence to support the conviction. *Burks v. United States,* 437 U.S. 1, 98 S.Ct. 2141, 57 L.Ed.2d 1 (1978). Double jeopardy does not arise when a single act violates both federal and state laws and the defendant is exposed to prosecution in both federal and state courts. This is called the **dual sovereignty** doctrine, and it also applies to prosecutions by two different states. In *Heath v. Alabama,* 472 U.S. 82, 106 S.Ct. 433, 88 L.Ed.2d 387 (1985), the U.S. Supreme Court held that the key question under this doctrine was whether the two entities seeking to prosecute the defendant for the same criminal act are separate sovereigns that derive their power to prosecute from independent sources. Because local governments are not sovereigns for double jeopardy purposes, the double jeopardy clause prohibits successive prosecutions by a state and a municipality in that state or by two municipalities in the same state. A criminal prosecution in either a state court or a federal court does not exempt the defendant from being sued for damages by anyone who is harmed by his or her criminal act. Finally, a defendant may be prosecuted more than once for the same conduct if that conduct involves the commission of more than one crime. For instance, a person who kills three victims at the same time and place can be tried separately for each killing.

The double jeopardy clause also embodies the **collateral estoppel** doctrine. The U.S. Supreme Court explained that collateral estoppel "means simply that when an issue of ultimate fact has once been determined by a valid and final judgment, that issue cannot again be litigated between the same parties in any future lawsuit." *Ashe v. Swenson,* 97 U.S. 436, 443, 90 S.Ct. 1189, 1194, 25 L.Ed.2d 469, 475 (1970).

Privilege Against Self-Incrimination

The Fifth Amendment protects a person against being incriminated by his or her own compelled **testimonial communications.** This protection is applicable to the states through the Fourteenth Amendment. *Malloy v. Hogan,* 378 U.S. 1, 84 S.Ct. 1489, 12 L.Ed.2d 653 (1964). To be testimonial, a "communication must itself, explicitly or implicitly, relate a factual assertion or disclose information" that is "the expression of the contents of an individual's mind." *Doe v. United States,* 487 U.S. 201, 210 n.9, 108 S.Ct. 2341, 2347 n.9, 101 L.Ed.2d 184, 197 n.9 (1988). Therefore, the privilege against self-incrimination is not violated by compelling a person to appear in a lineup, produce voice exemplars, furnish handwriting samples, be fingerprinted, shave a beard or mustache, or take a blood-alcohol or breathalyzer test. With respect to the requirement that the communication be incriminating, the U.S. Supreme Court said:

> The privilege afforded not only extends to answers that would in themselves support a conviction under a . . . criminal statute but likewise embraces those which would furnish a link in the chain of evidence needed to prosecute the claimant for a . . . crime. . . . But this protection must be confined to instances

where the witness has reasonable cause to apprehend danger from a direct answer. . . . To sustain the privilege, it need only be evident from the implications of the question, in the setting in which it is asked, that a responsive answer to the question or an explanation of why it cannot be answered might be dangerous because injurious disclosure could result. The trial judge in appraising the claim must be governed as much by his personal perception of the peculiarities of the case as by the facts actually in evidence. *Hoffman v. United States,* 341 U.S. 479, 486–87, 71 S.Ct. 814, 818, 95 L.Ed. 1118, 1124 (1951).

The protection against self-incrimination enables a person to refuse to testify against him- or herself at a criminal trial in which the person is a defendant and also "privileges him not to answer official questions put to him in any other proceeding, civil or criminal, formal or informal, where the answers might incriminate him in future criminal proceedings." *Minnesota v. Murphy,* 465 U.S. 420, 426, 104 S.Ct. 1136, 1141, 79 L.Ed.2d 409, 418 (1984). The privilege also applies to the compelled preparation of incriminating documents. *United States v. Doe,* 465 U.S. 605, 104 S.Ct. 1237, 79 L.Ed.2d 552 (1984). When a defendant chooses not to testify at trial, neither the prosecutor nor the trial judge may make any adverse comment about the defendant's failure to testify. *Griffin v. California,* 380 U.S. 609, 85 S.Ct. 1229, 14 L.Ed.2d 106 (1965). Moreover, the defendant is entitled to a jury instruction that no inference of guilt may be drawn from the failure to testify. The *Miranda* safeguards to secure the privilege against self-incrimination when a defendant is subjected to custodial interrogation are discussed in detail in Chapter 13.

Under the Fifth Amendment privilege, a *witness* at a civil or criminal proceeding is protected from answering questions when the answers might be incriminating in some future criminal prosecution. If authorized by statute, however, the prosecution may compel the witness to testify by granting **immunity** from prosecution. The type of immunity usually granted is **use immunity,** which prevents the prosecution from using the compelled testimony and any evidence derived from it in a subsequent prosecution. If a witness has been granted immunity and still refuses to testify, he or she can be held in contempt of court for the refusal.

The Right to Due Process

The words **due process of law** express the fundamental ideas of American justice. A due process clause is found in both the Fifth and Fourteenth Amendments as a restraint on both the federal and state governments. "The Due Process Clause of the Constitution prohibits deprivations of life, liberty, or property without 'fundamental fairness' through governmental conduct that offends the community's sense of justice, decency and fair play." *Roberts v. Maine,* 48 F.3d 1287, 1291 (1st Cir. 1995). Notice of a hearing or trial that is timely and adequately informs the accused of the charges against him or her is a basic concept included in due process. The opportunities to present evidence in one's own behalf before an impartial judge or jury, be presumed innocent until proven guilty by legally obtained evidence, and have the verdict supported by the evidence presented are other rights repeatedly recognized within the protection of the due process clause.

The due process clauses of the Fifth and Fourteenth Amendments also provide other basic protections whereby the state and federal governments are prevented from adopting arbitrary and unreasonable legislation or other measures that would violate individual rights. Thus, constitutional limitations are imposed on governmental interference with important individual liberties—such as the freedom to enter into contracts, engage in a lawful occupation, marry, and move without unnecessary restraints. To be valid, governmental restrictions placed on one's liberties must be reasonable and consistent with due process. (See the discussion of incorporation in this chapter under "Bill of Rights.")

The Right to Just Compensation

The power of the government to acquire private property is called *eminent domain.* The Fifth Amendment requires that whenever the government takes a person's property, the property acquired must be taken for public use and its full value must be paid to the owner. Thus, property cannot be taken by the federal government from one person simply to be given to another. But the Supreme Court has held that it is permissible to take private property for such purposes as urban renewal, even though ultimately the property taken will be returned to private ownership, since the taking is for the benefit of the community as a whole. To qualify for just compensation, property does not have to be physically taken from the owner. If governmental action leads to a lower value of private property, that action may constitute a "taking" and therefore require payment of compensation. Thus, the Supreme Court held that the disturbance of the egg-laying habits of chickens on a man's poultry farm, caused by the noise of low-level flights by military aircraft from a nearby air base, lessened the value of that farm and that, accordingly, the landowner was entitled to receive compensation equal to his loss.

AMENDMENT VI

In all criminal prosecutions, the accused shall enjoy the right to a speedy and public trial, by an impartial jury of the State and district wherein the crime shall have been committed, which district shall have been previously ascertained by law, and to be informed of the nature and cause of the accusation; to be confronted with the witnesses against him; to have compulsory process for obtaining witnesses in his favor, and to have the Assistance of Counsel for his defence. ■

The Right to a Speedy and Public Trial

The right to a speedy and public trial requires that, after arrest or indictment, the accused be brought to trial without unnecessary delay and that the trial be open to the public. Intentional or negligent delay by the prosecution that prejudices the defendant's right to defend him- or herself has been held to be grounds for dismissal of the charges. *Barker v. Wingo,* 407 U.S. 514, 92 S.Ct. 2182, 33 L.Ed.2d 101 (1972). In the *Barker* case, the Court identified four factors that courts should assess in determining whether a particular defendant has been deprived of the right to a speedy trial: "Length of delay, the reason for the delay, the defendant's assertion of his right, and prejudice to the defendant." 407 U.S. at 530, 92 S.Ct. at 2192, 33 L.Ed.2d at 117. The Court said that the length of the delay was to some extent a "triggering mechanism." If there is no presumptively prejudicial delay, inquiry into the other factors that go into the balance is not necessary. The Court also said that prejudice should be assessed in the light of the interests of defendants that the speedy trial right was designed to protect: (1) to prevent oppressive pretrial incarceration; (2) to minimize anxiety and concern of the accused; and, most important, (3) to limit the possibility that the defense will be impaired.

While the Sixth Amendment guarantees a criminal defendant the right to a *public* trial, the First Amendment implicitly provides the press and the general public the right to attend criminal trials. Therefore, the "right to an open public trial is a shared right of the accused and the public, the common concern being the assurance of fairness." *Press-Enterprise Co. v. Superior Court,* 478 U.S. 1, 7, 106 S.Ct. 2735, 2739, 92 L.Ed.2d 1, 9 (1986). In addition to ensuring fairness, the constitutional commitment to public trials helps maintain confidence in the criminal justice system, promote informed discussion of governmental affairs, ensure that judges and prosecutors perform their duties responsibly, encourage witnesses to come forward, and discourage perjury. *Waller v. Georgia,* 467 U.S. 39, 104 S.Ct. 2210, 81 L.Ed.2d 31 (1984). Although a defendant may waive the Sixth Amendment right to a public trial and request a closed proceeding, such a request must be balanced against the press's and public's First Amendment right to access.

Trial by an Impartial Jury

The guarantee of trial by an impartial jury supplements the earlier jury trial guarantee contained in Article III of the Constitution. Jury trials are discussed further in Chapter 2.

The Right to Notice of Charges

The Sixth Amendment requirement that a person "be informed of the nature and cause of the accusation" means that an accused person must be given notice in what respects it is claimed he or she has broken the law, to provide the person with an opportunity to prepare a defense. This means that an indictment or information must be sufficiently specific in setting forth the charges to enable the defendant to plead and prepare a defense. (The indictment and information are discussed in detail in Chapter 2.) This also means that the crime must be established by statute beforehand so that all persons are aware of what is illegal before they act. The statute must not be so vague or unclear that it does not inform people of the exact nature of the crime.

The Right to Confrontation with Witnesses

The **confrontation** clause guarantees the accused a right to confront **hostile witnesses** at his or her criminal trial. This right is designed to promote the truth-finding function of a trial by "ensur[ing] the reliability of the evidence against a criminal defendant by subjecting it to rigorous testing in the context of an adversary proceeding before the trier of fact." *Maryland v. Craig,* 497 U.S. 836, 845, 110 S.Ct. 3157, 3163, 111 L.Ed.2d 666, 678 (1990). This rigorous testing is accomplished both through the defendant's face-to-face confrontation during the witness's testimony and through the opportunity for cross-examination. Therefore, the defendant is entitled to be present at all important stages of the criminal trial, unless the right to be present is waived (1) by voluntarily being absent from the courtroom, *Taylor v. United States,* 414 U.S. 17, 94 S.Ct. 194, 38 L.Ed.2d 174 (1973), or (2) by continually disrupting the proceedings after being warned by the court. *Illinois v. Allen,* 397 U.S. 337, 90 S.Ct. 1057, 25 L.Ed.2d 353 (1970).

> It is essential to the proper administration of criminal justice that dignity, order, and decorum be the hallmarks of all court proceedings in our country. The flagrant disregard in the courtroom of elementary standards of proper conduct

should not and cannot be tolerated. We believe trial judges confronted with disruptive, contumacious, stubbornly defiant defendants must be given sufficient discretion to meet the circumstances of each case. No one formula for maintaining the appropriate courtroom atmosphere will be best in all situations. We think there are at least three constitutionally permissible ways for a trial judge to handle an obstreperous defendant like Allen: (1) bind and gag him, thereby keeping him present; (2) cite him for contempt; (3) take him out of the courtroom until he promises to conduct himself properly. 397 U.S. at 343–44, 90 S.Ct. at 1061, 25 L.Ed.2d at 359.

The defendant's right to the opportunity for cross-examination permits the defendant to test both the witness's credibility and the witness's knowledge of relevant facts of the case.

> The opportunity for cross-examination . . . is critical for ensuring the integrity of the fact finding process. Cross-examination is "the principal means by which the believability of a witness and the truth of his testimony are tested." Indeed the Court has recognized that cross-examination is the "'greatest legal engine ever invented for the discovery of the truth.'" *Kentucky v. Stincer,* 482 U.S. 730, 736, 107 S.Ct. 2658, 2662, 96 L.Ed.2d 631, 641 (1987).

Cross-examination is discussed further in Chapter 2.

In general, the admission of **hearsay evidence** is prohibited by the confrontation clause, because the defendant cannot confront the absent declarant. Hearsay evidence is defined by Rule 801(c) of the *Federal Rules of Evidence* as "a statement, other than one made by the declarant while testifying at the trial or hearing, offered in evidence to prove the truth of the matter asserted." The U.S. Supreme Court held that the confrontation clause does not prohibit the admission of hearsay evidence if the prosecution establishes (1) that it is unable to procure the witness's attendance at trial, despite good-faith efforts, and (2) that the evidence introduced bears sufficient "indicia of reliability." *Ohio v. Roberts,* 448 U.S. 56, 100 S.Ct. 2531, 65 L.Ed.2d 597 (1980). A statement is reliable if it falls within one of the established exceptions to the hearsay rule or if the prosecution shows that it is "trustworthy" in the totality of the circumstances.

Guarantee of Compulsory Process

The **compulsory process** clause guarantees the defendant's right to compel the attendance of *favorable* witnesses at trial, usually by means of a court-issued subpoena. To obtain compulsory process, the defendant must show that the witness's testimony would be relevant, material, favorable to the defendant, and not cumulative. *United States v. Valenzuela-Bernal,* 458 U.S. 858, 102 S.Ct. 3440, 73 L.Ed.2d 1193 (1982).

The Right to Representation by Counsel

Finally, the Sixth Amendment provides a right to be represented by counsel in all criminal prosecutions that result in imprisonment. "[A]bsent a knowing and intelligent waiver, no person may be imprisoned for any offense, whether classified as petty, misdemeanor, or felony unless he was represented by counsel at his trial." *Argersinger v. Hamlin,* 407 U.S. 25, 37, 92 S.Ct. 2006, 2012, 32 L.Ed.2d 530, 538 (1972). As the quotation implies, by knowingly and intelligently waiving the right to counsel, a defendant has the right to conduct his or her own defense in a criminal case. "[I]t is one thing to hold that every defendant, rich or poor, has the right to the assistance of counsel, and quite another to say that a state may compel a defendant to accept a lawyer he does not *want*." *Faretta v. California,* 422 U.S. 806, 832–33, 95 S.Ct. 2525, 2540, 45 L.Ed.2d 562, 580 (1975).

The right to counsel attaches at the initiation of adversary judicial criminal proceedings "whether by way of formal charge, preliminary hearing, indictment, information or arraignment." *Kirby v. Illinois,* 406 U.S. 682, 689, 92 S.Ct. 1877, 1882, 32 L.Ed.2d 411, 417 (1972). A person is entitled to the assistance of counsel, however, *only* at a "critical stage" of the prosecution "where substantial rights of a criminal accused may be affected." *Mempa v. Rhay,* 399 U.S. 128, 134, 88 S.Ct. 254, 257, 19 L.Ed.2d 336, 340 (1967). Thus, courts have accorded this right at

- Preindictment preliminary hearing—*Coleman v. Alabama,* 399 U.S. 1, 90 S.Ct. 1999, 26 L.Ed.2d 387 (1970)

- Postindictment pretrial lineup—*United States v. Wade,* 388 U.S. 218, 87 S.Ct. 1926, 18 L.Ed.2d 1178 (1967)

- Postindictment interrogation—*Massiah v. United States,* 377 U.S. 201, 84 S.Ct. 1199, 12 L.Ed.2d 246 (1964)

- Arraignment—*Hamilton v. Alabama,* 368 U.S. 52, 82 S.Ct. 157, 7 L.Ed.2d 114 (1961)

- Interrogation after arraignment—*Brewer v. Williams,* 430 U.S. 387, 97 S.Ct. 1232, 51 L.Ed.2d 424 (1977)

- First appeal as a matter of right—*Douglas v. California,* 372 U.S. 353, 83 S.Ct. 814, 9 L.Ed.2d 811 (1963)

The right to counsel is also assured at all stages of the trial process. In addition, prior to the initiation of adversary judicial criminal proceedings, a person has a *Fifth* Amendment right to counsel during custodial interrogation (see Chapter 13).

For many years, the guarantee of representation by counsel was interpreted to mean only that defendants had a right to be represented by a lawyer if they could afford one. In the 1930s, however, the U.S. Supreme Court began to vastly expand the class of persons entitled to the right to counsel in preparing and presenting a defense. In *Powell v. Alabama,* 287 U.S. 45, 53 S.Ct. 55, 77 L.Ed. 158 (1932), the Court held that the right to counsel was so fundamental that the due process clause of the Fourteenth Amendment required the *states* to provide all defendants charged with *capital* crimes with the effective aid of counsel. Six years later, *Johnson v. Zerbst,* 304 U.S. 458, 58 S.Ct. 1019, 82 L.Ed. 1461 (1938), held that the Sixth Amendment required *all federal* defendants to be provided legal counsel for their defense, unless the right to counsel was properly waived. That decision raised the question of whether the constraint on the federal courts expressed a rule so fundamental and essential to a fair trial, and thus to due process of law, that it was made obligatory on the states by the Fourteenth Amendment. The Supreme Court said no in *Betts v. Brady,* 316 U.S. 455, 62 S.Ct. 1252, 86 L.Ed. 1595 (1942). The Court held that

> the Fourteenth Amendment prohibits the conviction and incarceration of one whose trial is offensive to the common and fundamental ideas of fairness and right, and while want of counsel in a particular case may result in a conviction lacking in such fundamental fairness, we cannot say that the amendment embodies an inexorable command that no trial for any offense, or in any court, can be fairly conducted and justice accorded a defendant who is not represented by counsel. 316 U.S. at 473, 62 S.Ct. at 1262, 86 L.Ed.2d at 1607.

Twenty-one years later, the Court changed its mind and finally recognized that "lawyers in criminal courts are necessities, not luxuries." In *Gideon v. Wainwright,* 372 U.S. 335, 83 S.Ct. 792, 9 L.Ed.2d 799 (1963), the Supreme Court overruled *Betts v. Brady,* holding that the Sixth Amendment imposed an affirmative obligation on the part of the federal and state governments to provide at public expense legal counsel for those who could not afford it, in order that their cases could be adequately presented to the court. In addition, indigents were given the right to a free copy of their trial transcript for purposes of appealing their conviction.

The Sixth Amendment right to counsel is a right to the *effective* assistance of counsel. "The very premise of our adversary system of criminal justice is that partisan advocacy on both sides of a case will promote the ultimate objective that the guilty be convicted and the innocent go free." *Herring v. New York,* 422 U.S. 853, 862, 95 S.Ct. 2550, 2555, 45 L.Ed.2d 593, 600 (1975). The absence of effective counsel undermines faith in the proper functioning of the adversarial process. In *Strickland v. Washington,* 466 U.S. 668, 104 S.Ct. 2052, 80 L.Ed.2d 674 (1984), the Court held that to establish a claim of ineffective assistance of counsel, a defendant must show (1) that counsel's representation fell below an objective standard of reasonableness and (2) that there is a reasonable probability that, but for counsel's unprofessional errors, the result of the proceeding would have been different. A reasonable probability is a probability sufficient to undermine confidence in the outcome. In *Lockhart v. Fretwell,* 506 U.S. 364, 113 S.Ct. 838, 122 L.Ed.2d 180 (1993), the Court refined the *Strickland* test to require that not only would a different trial result be probable because of attorney performance but that the actual trial result was fundamentally unfair or unreliable.

AMENDMENT VII

In suits at common law, where the value in controversy shall exceed twenty dollars, the right of trial by jury shall be preserved, and no fact tried by a jury, shall be otherwise re-examined in any Court of the United States, than according to the rules of the common law. ■

The Seventh Amendment applies only to federal civil trials and not to civil suits in state courts. Except as provided by local federal court rules, if a case is brought in a federal court and a money judgment is sought that exceeds twenty dollars, the party bringing the suit and the defendant are entitled to have the controversy decided by the unanimous verdict of a jury of twelve people.

AMENDMENT VIII

Excessive bail shall not be required, nor excessive fines imposed, nor cruel and unusual punishments inflicted. ■

The Right to Bail

Bail has traditionally meant the money or property pledged to the court or actually deposited for the release from custody of an arrested or imprisoned person as a guarantee of the person's appearance in court at a specified date and time. Accused persons who are released from custody and subsequently fail to appear for trial forfeit their bail to the court.

The Eighth Amendment does not specifically provide that all citizens have a *right* to bail but only that bail will not be excessive. A right to bail has, however, been recognized in common law and in statute since 1789. Excessive bail was defined in *Stack v. Boyle,* 342 U.S. 1, 4–5, 72 S.Ct. 1, 3, 96 L.Ed. 3, 6 (1951):

> From the passage of the Judiciary Act of 1789 . . . to the present . . . federal law has unequivocally provided that a person arrested for a non-capital offense *shall* be admitted to bail. This traditional right to freedom before conviction permits the unhampered preparation of a defense, and serves to prevent the infliction of punishment prior to conviction. . . . Unless this right to bail before trial is preserved, the presumption of innocence, secured only after centuries of struggle, would lose its meaning.
>
> The right to release before trial is conditioned upon the accused's giving adequate assurance that he will stand trial and submit to sentence if found guilty. . . . Like the ancient practice of securing the oaths of responsible persons to stand as sureties for the accused, the modern practice of requiring a bail bond or the deposit of a sum of money subject to forfeiture serves as additional assurance of the presence of an accused. *Bail set at a figure higher than an amount reasonably calculated to fulfill this purpose is "excessive" under the Eighth Amendment.* (Emphasis supplied.)

The excessive bail clause "has been assumed" to be applicable to the states through the Fourteenth Amendment. *Schilb v. Kuebel,* 404 U.S. 357, 92 S.Ct. 479, 30 L.Ed.2d 502 (1971). Under many state constitutions, when a capital offense such as murder is charged, bail may be denied altogether if "the proof is evident or the presumption great."

In 1966, Congress enacted the Bail Reform Act to provide for pretrial release of persons accused of noncapital federal crimes. Congress sought to end pretrial imprisonment of indigent defendants who could not afford to post money bail and who were, in effect, confined only because of their poverty. The act also discouraged the traditional use of money bail by requiring the judge to seek other means as likely to ensure that the defendant would appear when the trial was held.

The Bail Reform Act of 1984 substantially changed the 1966 act to allow an authorized judicial officer to impose conditions of release to ensure community safety. This change marked a significant departure from the basic philosophy of the 1966 act, which was that the *only* purpose of bail laws was to ensure the defendant's appearance at judicial proceedings. The 1984 act also expanded appellate review and eliminated the presumption in favor of bail pending appeal. Most significantly, however, the 1984 act allowed an authorized judicial officer to detain an arrested person pending trial if the government demonstrates by clear and convincing evidence after an adversary hearing that no release conditions "will reasonably assure . . . the safety of any other person and the community." In *United States v. Salerno,* 481 U.S. 739, 107 S.Ct. 2095, 95 L.Ed.2d 697 (1987), the U.S. Supreme Court held that pretrial detention under the act, based solely on risk of danger to the community, did not violate due process or the Eighth Amendment.

Freedom from Cruel and Unusual Punishment

The prohibition against the infliction of cruel and unusual punishment is concerned with punishments imposed after a formal adjudication of guilt. The prohibition is applicable to the states through the Fourteenth Amendment. *Robinson v. California,* 370 U.S. 660, 82 S.Ct. 1417, 81 L.Ed.2d 758 (1962). The cruel and unusual punishment clause of the Eighth Amendment limits the punishment that may be imposed on conviction of a crime in three ways. First, the clause "imposes substantive limits on what can be made criminal and punished as such." *Ingraham v. Wright,* 430 U.S. 651, 667, 97 S.Ct. 1401, 1410, 51 L.Ed.2d 711, 728 (1977). The U.S. Supreme Court held that a statute making the status of narcotics addiction a crime was unconstitutional because it imposed punishment for personal characteristics rather than illegal acts. *Robinson, supra.* Also, a person may not be punished in retaliation for exercising a constitutional right. *United States v. Heubel,* 864 F.2d 1104 (3d Cir. 1988). Second, the cruel and unusual punishment clause proscribes certain kinds of punishment such as torture and divestiture of citizenship. Third, the clause prohibits punishment that is excessive in relation to the crime committed. In *Coker v. Georgia,* a case holding that the state may not impose a death sentence on a rapist who does not take human life, the Court said that a "punishment is 'excessive' and unconstitutional if it (1) makes no measurable contribution to acceptable goals of punishment and hence is nothing more than the purposeless and needless imposition of pain and suffering; or (2) is grossly out of proportion to the severity of the crime." 433 U.S. 584, 592, 97 S.Ct. 2861, 2866, 53 L.Ed.2d 982, 989 (1977). In *Solem v. Helm,* 463 U.S. 277, 103 S.Ct. 3001, 77 L.Ed.2d 637 (1983), the U.S. Supreme Court set forth three criteria for analyzing the proportionality of sentences:

> [A] court's proportionality analysis under the Eighth Amendment should be guided by objective criteria, including (i) the gravity of the offense and the harshness of the penalty; (ii) the sentences imposed on other criminals in the same jurisdiction; and (iii) the sentences imposed for the commission of the same crime in other jurisdictions. 463 U.S. at 292, 103 S.Ct. at 3011, 77 L.Ed.2d at 650.

The cruel and unusual punishment clause does not prohibit capital punishment. *Gregg v. Georgia,* 428 U.S. 153, 96 S.Ct. 2909, 49 L.Ed.2d 859 (1976). Mandatory death statutes leaving the jury or trial judge no discretion to consider the individual defendant and his or her crime are cruel and unusual, however. The Court also held that standards and procedures may be established for imposing death that would remove or mitigate the arbitrariness and irrationality characteristic of many death penalty laws. Further discussion of the many Supreme Court cases decided in recent years dealing with capital punishment is beyond the scope of this chapter.

AMENDMENT IX

The enumeration in the Constitution, of certain rights, shall not be construed to deny or disparage others retained by the people. ■

The Ninth Amendment emphasizes the Founding Fathers' view that powers of government are limited by the rights of the people and that it was not intended, by expressly guaranteeing in the Constitution certain rights of the people, to grant the government unlimited power to invade other rights of the people.

The Supreme Court has on at least one occasion suggested that this amendment is a justification for recognizing certain rights not specifically mentioned in the Constitution or for broadly interpreting those that are. The case involving the Ninth Amendment was *Griswold v. Connecticut,* 381 U.S. 479, 85 S.Ct. 1678, 14 L.Ed.2d 510 (1965), in which a statute prohibiting the use of contraceptives was voided as an infringement of the right of marital privacy. At issue was whether the right to privacy was a constitutional right and, if so, whether the right was one reserved to the people under the Ninth Amendment or only derived from other rights specifically mentioned in the Constitution.

Courts have long recognized particular rights to privacy that are part of the First and Fourth Amendments. As the Court in *Griswold* said, the "specific guarantees in the Bill of Rights have penumbras, formed by emanations from those guarantees that help give them life and substance." 381 U.S. at 484, 85 S.Ct. at 1681, 14 L.Ed.2d at 514. Thus, freedom of expression guarantees freedom of association and the related right to be silent and free from official inquiry into such associations. It also includes the right not to be intimidated by government for the expression of one's views. The Fourth Amendment's guarantee against unreasonable search and seizure confers a right to privacy because its safeguards prohibit unauthorized entry onto one's property and tampering with one's person, property, or possessions.

The court in *Griswold* ruled that the Third and Fifth Amendments, in addition to the First and Fourth, created "zones of privacy" safe from governmental intrusion and, without resting its decision on any one of these or on the Ninth Amendment itself, simply held that the right of privacy was guaranteed by the Constitution.

AMENDMENT X

The powers not delegated to the United States by the Constitution, nor prohibited by it to the States, are reserved to the States respectively, or to the people. ■

The Tenth Amendment embodies the principle of federalism, which reserves for the states the residue of powers not granted to the federal government or withheld from the states.

Later Amendments Dealing with Individual Rights

AMENDMENT XIII

Section 1. Neither slavery nor involuntary servitude, except as a punishment for crime whereof the party shall have been duly convicted, shall exist within the United States, or any place subject to their jurisdiction.

Section 2. Congress shall have power to enforce this article by appropriate legislation. ■

The Thirteenth Amendment prohibits slavery in the United States. It has been held that certain state laws were in violation of this amendment because they had the effect of jailing a debtor who did not perform his or her financial obligations. The Supreme Court has ruled that selective service laws, which authorize the draft for military duty, are not prohibited by this amendment.

The courts have also justified certain civil rights legislation that condemned purely private acts of discrimination but that did not constitute "state action," on the basis of the authority granted in Section 2 of this amendment and Section 5 of the Fourteenth Amendment, which is similar. An example is the civil rights legislation of 1866 and 1964 designed to end discrimination in the sale or rental of real or personal property. These discriminatory practices were seen as "badges of servitude," which the Thirteenth Amendment was intended to abolish.

AMENDMENT XIV

Section 1. All persons born or naturalized in the United States, and subject to the jurisdiction thereof, are citizens of the United States and of the State wherein they reside. No State shall make or enforce any law which shall abridge the privileges or immunities of citizens of the United States; nor shall any State deprive any person of life, liberty, or property, without due process of law; nor deny to any person within its jurisdiction the equal protection of the laws. . . .

Section 5. The Congress shall have power to enforce, by appropriate legislation, the provisions of this article. ■

The Right to Due Process

The Fourteenth Amendment limits the states from infringing on the rights of individuals. The Bill of Rights—the first ten amendments—does not specifically refer to actions by the states but applies only to actions by the federal government. Through judicial interpretation of the phrase "due process of law" in the Fourteenth Amendment, many of the Bill of Rights guarantees have been made applicable to actions by state governments and their subdivisions, such as counties, municipalities, and cities. Under this principle, certain rights and freedoms are deemed so basic to the people in a free and democratic society that state governments may not violate them, even though states are not specifically barred from doing so by the Constitution. (See the discussion of incorporation of guarantees in the Bill of Rights into the Fourteenth Amendment, in this chapter under "The Bill of Rights.") In determining whether state action violates the due process clause, a court considers

[f]irst, the private interest that will be affected by the official action; second, the risk of an erroneous deprivation of such interest through the procedures used, and the probable value, if any, of additional or substitute procedural safeguards; and finally, the Government's interest, including the function involved and the fiscal and administrative burdens that the additional or substitute procedural requirement would entail. *Mathews v. Eldridge,* 424 U.S. 319, 335, 96 S.Ct. 893, 903, 47 L.Ed.2d 18, 33 (1976).

The Fifth Amendment, discussed earlier, also contains a due process clause that applies to actions of the federal government.

The Right to Equal Protection of the Laws

In addition to containing the due process clause, the Fourteenth Amendment also prohibits denial of the **equal protection of the laws.** This requirement prevents the state from making unreasonable, arbitrary distinctions between different persons as to their rights and privileges. Therefore, because "all people are created equal," no law could deny red-haired men the right to drive an automobile. The state does, however, remain free to make reasonable classifications. Therefore, the law can deny minors the right to drive.

Some classifications, such as those based on race, religion, and national origin, have been held to be patently unreasonable. Thus, racial segregation in public schools and other public places, laws that prohibit the sale or use of property to certain races or minority groups, and laws that prohibit interracial marriage have been struck down. Furthermore, the Supreme Court held that purely private acts of discrimination can be in violation of the equal protection clause if they are customarily enforced throughout the state, whether or not there is a specific law or other explicit manifestation of action by the state.

The equal protection clause has been interpreted to mean that a citizen may not arbitrarily be deprived of the right to vote and that every citizen's vote must be given equal weight to the extent possible. Thus, the Supreme Court held that state legislatures and local governments must be apportioned strictly in terms of their populations in such a way as to accord one person one vote.

Section 5 of this amendment provided the authority for much of the civil rights legislation passed by Congress in the 1960s.

AMENDMENT XV

Section 1. The right of citizens of the United States to vote shall not be denied or abridged by the United States or by any State on account of race, color, or previous condition of servitude.

Section 2. The Congress shall have power to enforce this article by appropriate legislation. ■

AMENDMENT XIX

Section 1. The right of citizens of the United States to vote shall not be denied or abridged by the United States or by any State on account of sex.

Section 2. Congress shall have power to enforce this article by appropriate legislation. ■

AMENDMENT XXVI

Section 1. The right of citizens of the United States, who are eighteen years or older, to vote shall not be denied or abridged by the United States or any State on account of age.

Section 2. The Congress shall have power to enforce this article by appropriate legislation. ■

The intent and purpose of these three amendments are clear. The right to vote, which is the keystone of our democratic society, may not be denied any citizen over the age of eighteen because of race, color, previous condition of servitude, or sex. The Twenty-Sixth Amendment, which lowered the voting age for all elections from twenty-one to eighteen years of age, became law on July 1, 1971. These amendments, together with the Fifth and Fourteenth, prohibit any arbitrary attempt to disenfranchise any American citizen.

AMENDMENT XXIV

Section 1. The right of citizens of the United States to vote in any primary or other election for President or Vice President, for electors for President or Vice President, or for Senator or Representative in Congress, shall not be denied or abridged by the United States or any State by reason of failure to pay any poll tax or other tax.

*Section 2. The Congress shall have power to enforce this article by appropri-
ate legislation.* ◼

The Twenty-Fourth Amendment prohibits denial of the right to vote for federal officials because a person has not paid a tax. This amendment was designed to abolish
the requirement of a poll tax, which, at the time of its ratification, five states imposed
as a condition to voting. The Supreme Court subsequently held that poll taxes were
unconstitutional under the equal protection clause of the Fourteenth Amendment on
the basis that the right to vote should not be conditioned on one's ability to pay a tax.
Accordingly, poll taxes in any election, state or federal, have been prohibited.

Conclusion

In addition to the specific constitutional rights outlined in
this chapter, certain safeguards for the individual are inherent in the structure of American government. The separation
of powers among legislative, executive, and judicial branches
of government is the basis for a system of checks and balances—which prevents excessive concentration of power,
with the inevitable threat to individual liberties that accompanies such concentration. With respect to the legislative
power itself, the existence of two houses of Congress—each
chosen by a different process—is itself a protection against
ill-advised laws that might threaten constitutional rights.
Similarly, our federal system, which divides authority between the national government and the governments of the
various states, has provided a fertile soil for the nourishment
of constitutional rights.

No matter how well a constitution may be written, the
rights it guarantees have little meaning unless there is popu-
lar support for those rights and that constitution. Fortu-
nately, that support has existed in the United States. Indeed,
in this country the most fundamental protection of personal
liberty rests in the well-established American traditions of
constitutional government, obedience to the rule of law,
and respect for the individual. These traditions provide the
groundwork for the entire body of law dealing with criminal
procedure and should be foremost in the minds of students
of and participants in our criminal justice system. The remainder of this book shows how the criminal justice system
operates to achieve a balance between the protection of individual rights guaranteed by the Constitution and the maintenance of the rule of law and public order in our society.

Review and Discussion Questions

1. How has the Constitution been able to remain a durable
   and viable instrument of government despite the enormous changes that have occurred in our society since its
   adoption? Discuss this issue in terms of specific changes.

2. Discuss generally the most important roles and functions
   under the Constitution of each of the following: the
   three branches of the federal government, the state governments, the average citizen, and the law enforcement
   officer. Explain some of the interrelationships among
   those roles and functions.

3. The Constitution speaks predominantly in terms of the
   protection of individual rights from governmental abuse
   or abridgment. What corresponding obligations and burdens must each citizen undertake or bear to ensure that
   everyone remains free to exercise these rights to their full
   extent?

4. Name three constitutional sources for the protection of
   the right to privacy, and explain how they differ.

5. If a state legislature passed a law requiring all book-
   stores that have, in the last six months, sold or adver-
   tised for sale pictures of the pope to be immediately
   closed down and their owners immediately arrested and
   jailed, what provisions of the Constitution might be
   violated?

6. If a terminally ill cancer patient wishes to refuse medical
   treatment and die a "natural" death because of religious
   beliefs, can that person be required under state law to
   undergo treatment? What if the wish to die is not based
   on a religious belief, but the person is a minor or mentally incompetent? What if the cancer was caused by exposure to radiation and the person wishes the death to
   be a political statement on the dangers of nuclear power
   and nuclear war?

7. Discuss the constitutional issues involved in compelling a newsperson to reveal a confidential source of information when the source would be useful to the government in a criminal investigation or helpful to a criminal defendant at trial. Should the government be able to obtain a search warrant to look into files, audit tapes, or view films in the possession of the news media to find evidence of crime?

8. Should members of the news media have greater access than that of members of the general public to court proceedings and court records? What about greater access to prisons to interview prisoners? What about greater access to police investigative files?

9. Would the Fifth Amendment privilege against self-incrimination prohibit the government from any of the following: requiring all participants in a lineup to speak certain words; requiring a person to produce income tax records; threatening a person with a reduction in pay in his government job if he does not make incriminating testimonial admissions about a non-job-related matter?

10. What does the term *checks and balances* mean? What aspects of the Constitution other than separation of powers help fulfill the purposes of checks and balances?

CHAPTER TWO

An Overview of the Criminal Court System

OBJECTIVES

1. Be able to explain the structure of the court system of the United States and of the student's state.

2. Be able to trace the progress of a criminal case through its various stages from initial complaint through appeal and postconviction remedies.

3. Understand the meanings of the following terms: acquittal; affidavit; appeal; appellate jurisdiction; arraignment; arrest warrant; bench trial; beyond a reasonable doubt; burden of proof; challenge for cause; complaint; court of general jurisdiction; court of limited jurisdiction; cross-examination; deposition; direct examination; discovery; grand jury; habeas corpus; indictment; information; instruction; judgment; jury nullification; motion; nolo contendere; original jurisdiction; peremptory challenge; plea; preliminary examination; probation; rebuttal; rule of four; sentence; subpoena; summons; transactional immunity; trial de novo; true bill; use immunity; venue; verdict; voir dire; writ of certiorari.

OUTLINE

Most of the law enforcement officer's daily law-related duties involve enforcing the laws, keeping the public peace, and investigating and preventing crime. To perform these duties properly, officers must be sensitive to the constitutional rights of all persons, as discussed in Chapter 1; must be familiar with the criminal laws of their jurisdictions; and must understand the law dealing with arrest, search and seizure, confessions, and pretrial identifications, with which most of the remainder of this book is concerned.

Most law enforcement officers are not as familiar with the rules and procedures that govern the course of a prosecution beyond the investigatory stage. Law enforcement officers play an important role in this process, often as chief witnesses for the prosecution in their cases. Nevertheless, outside their roles as witnesses, officers are often ignored as their cases move through pleadings, motions, jury selection, trial, and appeal. To many officers, the entire process may look like a complex legal jumble involving the prosecuting attorney, the defense attorney, and the judge. Because law enforcement officers are an integral part of the criminal justice system, and because their actions early on in a case vitally affect its outcome at nearly all stages of the prosecution, they should have a basic understanding of what happens to their case when it reaches the prosecutor and the courts, and why. Other criminal justice professionals, who are usually less involved in a criminal case than are law enforcement officers, can function more effectively within the criminal justice system if they have a general knowledge of that system's structure and operation.

Criminal court procedure in most states is governed by court rules and statutes designed for use by judges and attorneys to ensure the just and efficient processing of criminal offenders. Many of the rules and statutes are quite complex and do not directly concern law enforcement officers or other criminal justice professionals. Therefore, this chapter highlights pertinent court procedures and legal terms to provide a comprehensive view of how the system works, without dwelling too heavily on details that are of little direct concern to the criminal justice professional.

So far as possible, this chapter presents the different stages of criminal court procedure in chronological order, following a criminal case from beginning to end. The discussion is limited to court procedures for serious offenses and does not cover procedures for traffic offenses and other petty misdemeanors. Wherever certain aspects of criminal court procedure are covered in another chapter, reference is made to that chapter. Because the information in this chapter is general, and because criminal court procedure differs by state, do not take the information presented here as a final authority; be sure to consult your own state's pertinent statutes or rules. ■

Structure of the Court System

Before discussing the preliminary proceedings in a criminal case, this chapter first outlines the basic structure of the federal court system and a typical state court system and then briefly describes the criminal trial jurisdiction of the different courts. As used here, the term **jurisdiction** simply means the authority of a court to deal with a particular type of case.

The federal court system is larger and more complex than any state court system, but the basic structures of the two court systems are similar. Both the federal and the state system consist of courts that have original jurisdiction over criminal matters and courts that have appellate jurisdiction. **Original jurisdiction** means the authority to deal with a case from the beginning, try the case, and pass judgment on the facts and the law. **Appellate jurisdiction** means the authority to deal with a case, not in its initial stages but only after it has been finally decided by an inferior court, and then only to revise or correct the proceedings in the inferior court.

Courts are further classified as courts of limited jurisdiction and courts of general jurisdiction. A **court of limited jurisdiction** is a court whose trial jurisdiction either includes no felonies or is limited to less than all felonies and that may or may not hear appeals. A court of limited jurisdiction is limited to a particular class or classes of cases. It often has jurisdiction over misdemeanor or traffic cases, over the initial setting of bail and preliminary hearings in felony cases, and occasionally over felony trials in which the penalty prescribed for the offense is below a statutorily specified limit. A **court of general jurisdiction** is a court that has trial jurisdiction over all criminal offenses, including all felonies, and that may or may not hear appeals. A court of general jurisdiction has original jurisdiction over all felonies and frequently has appellate jurisdiction over the decisions of a court of limited jurisdiction. The decisions of a court of general jurisdiction may be reviewed by an appellate court.

Federal Courts

The U.S. district courts are the trial courts of *general* federal jurisdiction. Each state has at least one district court, while some of the larger states have as many as four. There are ninety-four district courts in the fifty states, the District of Columbia, the Commonwealth of Puerto Rico, and the territories of Guam, the U.S. Virgin Islands, and the Northern Mariana Islands. Some district courts have divisions (for example, Eastern and Western Divisions of North Dakota), usually in districts covering a large geographic area, and may have several places where the court hears cases. With the exception of the territorial courts, all district court judges are appointed for life by the president with the advice and consent of the Senate. Congress authorizes judgeships for each district based in large part on the caseload. At this writing, there are 649 district court judges. Usually only one judge is required to hear and decide a case in a district court. The district courts have original jurisdiction over criminal cases, and the great majority of federal criminal cases begin in the district courts. Cases from the district courts are reviewable on appeal by the applicable court of appeals. Each district court has one or more bankruptcy judges, a clerk, a U.S. attorney, a U.S. marshal, probation officers, court reporters, and their staffs.

Each district court also has one or more U.S. magistrate judges. Magistrate judges are appointed for eight-year terms by district court judges and are required to be members of the bar. A magistrate judge, at the designation of the district court judge, may issue search warrants, hear and determine certain kinds of pretrial matters, conduct preliminary examinations and other hearings, and submit for the court's approval proposed findings and recommendations on motions. Perhaps the most important power magistrate judges possess is the authority to conduct misdemeanor trials with the defendant's consent and to conduct trials in civil cases with the consent of the parties involved. Since the enactment of the Federal Magistrates Act in 1968, Congress has expanded the services allowed to be performed by magistrate judges. As a result, magistrate judges are playing an increasingly significant role in the administration of the justice in the federal system.

The U.S. courts of appeals (often referred to as circuit courts) are intermediate appellate courts created by act of Congress to relieve the U.S. Supreme Court of considering all appeals in cases originally decided by the federal trial courts. The courts of appeal are empowered to review all final decisions and certain interlocutory decisions of district courts. They also have the power to review and enforce orders of many federal administrative bodies. The decisions of the courts of appeals are final, except that they are subject to discretionary review or appeal in the U.S. Supreme Court. The United States is divided geographically into twelve judicial circuits, including the District of Columbia. Each circuit has a court of appeals. Each of the fifty states is assigned to one of the circuits, and the territories are assigned variously to the first, third, and ninth circuits. A thirteenth federal circuit court, the U.S. Court of Appeals for the Federal Circuit, was created by act of Congress in 1982 with nationwide jurisdiction to hear appeals in patent and contract cases and various other matters. Appeals court judges are appointed for life by the president with the advice and consent of the Senate. Each court of appeals has from six to twenty-eight permanent circuit judgeships, depending on the amount of judicial work in the circuit. At this writing, there are 167 judges in the twelve judicial circuits. One of the justices of the U.S. Supreme Court is assigned as a circuit justice for each of the thirteen judicial circuits. Each court of appeals normally hears cases in panels consisting of three judges but may sit *en banc* with all judges present.

The U.S. Supreme Court is composed of the chief justice of the United States and such number of associate justices as may be fixed by Congress. By act of Congress in 1948, the number of associate justices is eight. Power to nominate the justices is vested in the president of the United States, and appointments are made with the advice and consent of the Senate. Article III, section 1, of the Constitution further provides that "[t]he Judges, both of the supreme and inferior Courts, shall hold their Offices during good Behaviour, and shall, at stated Times, receive for their Services, a Compensation, which shall not be diminished during their Continuance in Office."

The U.S. Supreme Court is the appellate court of last resort, meaning that it is a court from which no appeal is possible. The Court has original jurisdiction in certain limited areas, but its greatest work load is to review the decisions of the lower federal courts and the highest state courts. The Supreme Court exercises its appellate jurisdiction through the granting of a **writ of certiorari,** which means that the Court, upon petition of a party, agrees to review a case decided by one of the circuit courts of appeals or the highest court of a state. A vote of four Supreme Court justices is required to grant certiorari to review a case (sometimes referred to as the rule of four). Certiorari is granted at the Court's discretion when a case presents questions whose resolution will have some general "importance beyond the facts and parties involved." *Boag v. MacDougall,* 454 U.S. 364, 368, 102 S.Ct. 700, 702, 70 L.Ed.2d 551, 555 (1982). (REHNQUIST, J., dissenting). For example, the Court may grant certiorari in cases involving important and unsettled questions of federal law or in situations involving confusion among the state and federal courts. Note that failure to grant certiorari is not affirmance of the lower court's decision in disguise. It simply means that the petitioner failed to persuade four of the nine justices to hear the appeal. Legislation effective in 1988 essentially eliminated the Supreme Court's former so-called mandatory or obligatory appeal jurisdiction. With very minor exceptions, petitioning for a writ of certiorari is now the only path to Supreme Court review of federal and state court decisions. Exhibit 2.1 depicts U.S. courts with criminal jurisdiction.

Besides the courts mentioned, the federal court system also includes a number of specialized courts that have been established to hear particular classes of cases. Examples are the U.S. Court of International Trade, the U.S. Court of Military Appeals, and the U.S. Tax Court. In addition, there are quasi-judicial boards or commissions, which have special and limited jurisdiction under specific federal statutes.

```
┌─────────────────────────────────────────────┐
│        UNITED STATES SUPREME COURT            │
│   Discretionary appellate jurisdiction over   │
│   decisions of U.S. courts of appeals.        │
│   Discretionary appellate jurisdiction over   │
│   decisions of the highest court of a state if│
│   a constitutional question or federal law    │
│   involved.                                    │
└─────────────────────────────────────────────┘
            │
┌─────────────────────────────────────────────┐
│      UNITED STATES COURTS OF APPEALS          │
│   Appellate jurisdiction over decisions of    │
│   U.S. district courts.                        │
└─────────────────────────────────────────────┘
            │
┌─────────────────────────────────────────────┐
│      UNITED STATES DISTRICT COURTS            │
│   Original jurisdiction over federal criminal │
│   cases.                                       │
└─────────────────────────────────────────────┘
            │
┌─────────────────────────────────────────────┐
│      UNITED STATES MAGISTRATE JUDGES          │
│   If designated by the district court judge,  │
│   jurisdiction over misdemeanor trials (with  │
│   the defendant's consent) and over trials in │
│   civil cases (with the consent of the parties│
│   involved).                                   │
└─────────────────────────────────────────────┘
```

EXHIBIT 2.1   United States Courts with Criminal Jurisdiction

State Courts

A typical state court system has the same basic structure as the federal system. Courts of original jurisdiction are usually divided into (1) courts of limited jurisdiction whose trial jurisdiction either includes no felonies or is limited to less than all felonies and (2) higher courts of general jurisdiction with trial jurisdiction over all criminal offenses, including *all* felonies. The courts of limited jurisdiction are usually established on a local level and may be called municipal courts, police courts, magistrate courts, district courts, or something similar. These courts have jurisdiction over misdemeanor cases, traffic cases, initial setting of bail and preliminary hearings in felony cases, and occasionally over felony trials in which the penalty prescribed for the offense is below a statutorily specified limit. The courts of general jurisdiction have original jurisdiction over all criminal offenses and are usually established on a county or regional level. They may be called circuit courts, district courts, superior courts, or something similar. Generally, the more serious criminal cases are tried in these courts. In some states, these courts may also exercise a limited appellate jurisdiction over certain cases appealed from the courts of limited jurisdiction. Such appeals result in a **trial de novo** in the court of general jurisdiction. A trial de novo is a new trial or retrial in which the whole case is examined again as if no trial whatever had been held in the court of limited jurisdiction. In a trial de novo, matters of fact as well as law may be considered,

```
┌─────────────────────────────────────┐
│  NEBRASKA SUPREME COURT              │
│  Highest appellate court. May        │
│  exercise original jurisdiction in   │
│  certain cases. Hears discretionary  │
│  appeals from the court of appeals.  │
└─────────────────────────────────────┘
                  │
┌─────────────────────────────────────┐
│  NEBRASKA COURT OF APPEALS           │
│  Intermediate appellate court. Hears │
│  appeals from district courts except │
│  for cases involving the death       │
│  penalty or life imprisonment or     │
│  cases raising constitutional        │
│  questions.                          │
└─────────────────────────────────────┘
                  │
┌─────────────────────────────────────┐
│  NEBRASKA DISTRICT COURTS            │
│  Trial courts of general             │
│  jurisdiction. Try all felony cases. │
│  Hear and determine appeals from     │
│  county courts and juvenile courts.  │
└─────────────────────────────────────┘
```

NEBRASKA COUNTY COURTS
Trial courts of limited jurisdiction. Try misdemeanors, including traffic and municipal ordinance violations. Conduct preliminary hearings in felony cases. Function as juvenile courts, except in Douglas, Lancaster, and Sarpy Counties.

SEPARATE JUVENILE COURTS
Established in Douglas, Lancaster, and Sarpy Counties. Same juvenile jurisdiction as county courts.

EXHIBIT 2.2   Nebraska Courts with Criminal Jurisdiction

witnesses may be heard, and new evidence may be presented, regardless of what happened at the first trial. Some states have lower-level specialized courts, such as juvenile courts, traffic courts, or family courts, which may have criminal jurisdiction or partial criminal jurisdiction.

From the court of general jurisdiction, a case may proceed through an intermediate appellate court until it reaches the highest court (or the court of last resort) of the state, usually called the state supreme court. If a case involves important constitutional issues or questions of federal law, it may finally reach the U.S. Supreme Court for review. Generally the state supreme court also has the power to prescribe rules of pleading, practice, and procedure before itself and the other lower courts of the state. Exhibit 2.2 depicts the courts with criminal jurisdiction in Nebraska.

Preliminary Proceedings

This chapter focuses on the progress of a felony case through the criminal court system. A brief note about misdemeanor cases is useful at the outset to emphasize the differences between the two types of cases. Generally, misdemeanors are crimes for which the maximum possible sentence is less than one year imprisonment. Misdemeanors are tried in courts of limited jurisdiction. Although misdemeanor proceedings are similar to felony proceedings, they are usually less formal and more abbreviated. For example, jury trials are available but unusual in misdemeanor cases, and six-person juries are common. Also, in some jurisdictions, if the defendant pleads guilty, misdemeanor charges may be disposed of at the initial appearance before the magistrate. Because misdemeanor proceedings differ greatly from jurisdiction to jurisdiction, and because they are similar in many ways to felony proceedings, the remainder of this chapter focuses primarily on felony proceedings. Exhibit 2.3 gives a general view of the progress of a case through the criminal justice system, and the reader may wish to refer to it as an aid to understanding the following material.

The Complaint

A criminal process against a defendant formally begins with a **complaint.** The word *formally* is used here because a person can be arrested for an offense before a complaint is filed or a warrant is issued. Such an arrest would be considered the beginning of the criminal process. However, because an arrest without a warrant is considered an exception to the basic warrant requirement, the complaint is still considered the formal beginning of proceedings. Also, a person may be arrested based on a report of, or a law enforcement officer's observation of, the commission of a crime, but for various reasons the prosecutor decides not to charge the defendant. The most common reason for releasing without prosecution is insufficient evidence, but other reasons may be the minimal harm caused by the offense, the victim's disinclination to press charges, and adequate alternative remedies. Once the decision to charge is made, however, the next step is the filing of the complaint.

The complaint can serve a dual purpose in a criminal proceeding. If the defendant has been arrested without a warrant, the complaint is prepared, signed, and filed at the defendant's initial appearance before the magistrate. The complaint serves as the charging document on which the preliminary examination will be held. If the defendant has not been arrested and is not before the court, the complaint serves as the basis for determining whether there is probable cause (fair probability) to justify issuing a warrant for his or her arrest.

The complaint must be made on oath or affirmation, must state the essential facts of the offense being charged, must be in writing, and must be made before a judicial officer authorized to issue process in criminal cases. This officer is usually called a **magistrate.** The information in the complaint does not have to be derived from personal observation or experience, but it may be based on information from others or circumstantial evidence. Nevertheless, the evidence put forth in the complaint must be strong enough to convince the magistrate that there is probable cause to believe that an offense has been committed and that the defendant committed it. (Probable cause is discussed in Chapters 3 and 6.)

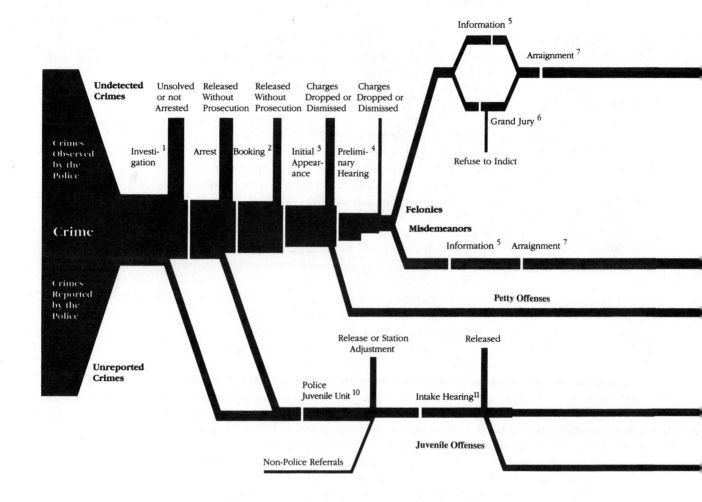

Police   **Prosecution**   **Courts**

1. May continue until trial.
2. Administrative record of arrest. First step at which temporary release on bail may be available.
3. Before magistrate, commissioner, or justice of peace. Formal notice of charge, advice of rights. Bail set. Summary trials for petty offenses usually conducted here without further processing.
4. Preliminary testing of evidence against defendant. Charge may be reduced. No separate preliminary hearing for misdemeanors in some systems.

5. Charge filed by prosecutor on basis of information submitted by police or citizens. Alternative to grand jury indictment; often used in felonies, almost always in misdemeanors.
6. Reviews whether government evidence sufficient to justify trial. Some states have no grand jury system; others seldom use it.

Report by the President's Commission on Law Enforcement and Administration of Justice: The Challenge of Crime in a Free Society 8, 9 (1967).

EXHIBIT 2.3   A General View of the Criminal Justice System

Corrections

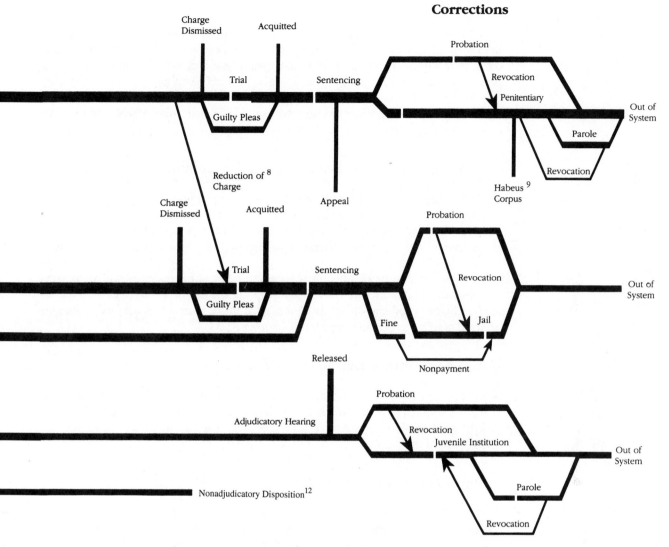

7. Appearance for plea; defendant elects trial by judge or jury (if available); counsel for indigent usually appointed here in felonies. Often not at all in other cases.

8. Charge may be reduced at any time prior to trial in return for plea of guilty or for other reasons.

9. Challenge on constitutional grounds to legality of detention. May be sought at any point in process.

10. Police often hold informal hearings, dismiss or adjust many cases without further processing.

11. Probation officer decides desirability of further court action.

12. Welfare agency, social services, counseling, medical care, etc., for cases where adjudicatory handling not needed.

Affidavits

Information that is not contained in the complaint or that comes from witnesses other than the complainant may be brought to the court's attention in the form of an affidavit. An **affidavit** is a sworn written statement of the facts relied on in seeking the issuance of a warrant. An affidavit need not be prepared with any particular formality. It is filed with the complaint, and together these documents can provide a sufficient written record for a reviewing court to examine in determining whether probable cause existed for the issuance of a warrant.

Warrant or Summons Issued on the Complaint

Once the magistrate has determined from the complaint and accompanying affidavits that there is probable cause to believe that an offense has been committed and that the defendant committed it, the magistrate issues either a summons or a warrant for the defendant's arrest. If the defendant is already before the court, no summons or warrant is necessary.

Once the summons or warrant is issued, the law enforcement officer must serve the summons or execute the warrant by arresting the defendant and bringing the defendant before a judicial officer as commanded in the warrant. A detailed discussion of arrest warrant procedure appears in Chapter 4.

Initial Appearance Before the Magistrate

Once a person has been arrested, either with or without a warrant, he or she is required by statute to be brought before a magistrate "without unnecessary delay," or "forthwith," or some similar statutory language. The details of this procedure are also discussed in Chapter 4.

Preliminary Examination

At the **preliminary examination** (also called the preliminary hearing), the magistrate must determine whether there is probable cause to believe that an offense was committed and that the defendant committed it. The purpose of the preliminary examination is to provide another judicial determination of the existence of probable cause and to protect the defendant from a totally baseless prosecution. Rule 5(c) of the *Federal Rules of Criminal Procedure* provides that the preliminary examination must occur "within a reasonable time but in any event not later than 10 days following the initial appearance if the defendant is in custody and no later than 20 days if the defendant is not in custody. . . ." The rule also provides that "the preliminary examination shall not be held if the defendant is indicted or if an information against the defendant is filed in district court before the date set for the preliminary examination."

The preliminary examination is a formal adversarial proceeding conducted in open court with a transcript made of the proceedings. The U.S. Supreme Court held that the preliminary examination is a critical stage of a criminal prosecution, and, as such, the defendant is entitled to have an attorney present at the hearing. *Coleman v. Alabama,* 399 U.S. 1, 90 S.Ct. 1999, 26 L.Ed.2d 387 (1970). Indigent defendants who cannot afford an attorney must be provided one at the government's cost. The preliminary examination consists mainly of the presentation of evidence against the defendant by the prosecuting attorney. The defense attorney's function was described by the Court in *Coleman v. Alabama*:

> First, the lawyer's skilled examination and cross-examination of witnesses may expose fatal weaknesses in the State's case that may lead the magistrate to refuse to bind the accused over. Second, in any event, the skilled interrogation of witnesses by an experienced lawyer can fashion a vital impeachment tool for use in cross-examination of the State's witnesses at the trial, or preserve testimony favorable to the accused of a witness who does not appear at the trial. Third, retained counsel can more effectively discover the case the State has against his client and make possible the preparation of a proper defense to meet that case at the trial. Fourth, counsel can also be influential at the preliminary hearing in making effective arguments for the accused on such matters as the necessity for early psychiatric examination or bail. 399 U.S. at 9, 90 S.Ct. at 2003, 26 L.Ed.2d at 397.

If probable cause to believe that the defendant committed the offense is found, the defendant is bound over either to the grand jury or, in jurisdictions that allow prosecution by information, to the trial court for adjudication. The magistrate may admit the defendant to bail at the preliminary examination or may continue, increase, or decrease the original bail. (Bail is discussed in further detail in Chapter 1.) If no probable cause is found, the magistrate dismisses the complaint and discharges the defendant. A dismissal does not prevent the prosecution from recharging the defendant and submitting new evidence at a later preliminary examination. Nor does a dismissal prevent the prosecution from going to the grand jury and obtaining an indictment in states that have both grand jury and preliminary hearing procedures.

Exhibit 2.4 compares the preliminary examination with grand jury proceedings.

Indictment and Information

In felony cases, the **indictment** or the **information** replaces the complaint as the document that charges the defendant with an offense and on which the defendant is brought to trial. The indictment and the information are very similar in nature and content. Each is a "plain, concise and definite written statement of the essential facts constituting the offense charged." *Fed. R.Crim.P.* 7(c)(1). The main difference between the indictment and the information is that the indictment is returned by a grand jury and signed by the foreperson of the grand jury and the prosecuting attorney. The information is signed and sworn to *only* by the prosecuting attorney, without the approval or intervention of the grand jury. Laws governing when the indictment or the information is used vary in different jurisdictions. An example of a typical indictment appears in Exhibit 2.5. Note the language "a true bill" in the example. This means that the grand jury found probable cause to justify the prosecution of the defendant. If the grand jury had rejected the prosecutor's accusations and found no ground for prosecution (which is rare), it would have endorsed on the indictment form "no true bill," "not a true bill," "no bill," or some similar language.

A variety of technical statutes and rules deal with drafting, amending, and dismissing indictments and informations. These provisions are of direct concern only to judges and attorneys and so are not discussed here.

GRAND JURY PROCEEDINGS	PRELIMINARY EXAMINATION
Primary function is to determine whether there is probable cause to believe that the defendant committed the crime or crimes charged.	Primary function is to determine whether there is probable cause to believe that the defendant committed the crime or crimes charged.
If probable cause is found, indictment against the defendant is returned.	If probable cause is found, the defendant is bound over to the grand jury or to the trial court for adjudication.
Held in the grand jury room in closed session.	Held in open court.
Held in secret.	Open to the public.
Informal proceeding.	Formal judicial proceeding.
Nonadversarial proceeding in which grand jury hears only evidence presented by the prosecution.	Adversarial proceeding in which both the prosecution and defense may present evidence.
No judge or magistrate presides.	Judge or magistrate presides.
Defendant has no right to be present or to offer evidence.	Defendant has the right to be present and to offer evidence.
Defendant has no right to counsel.	Defendant has the right to counsel.
Power to investigate crime on grand jury's own initiative.	No power to investigate crime.
Power to subpoena witnesses and evidence.	No subpoena power.
Power to grant immunity.	No power to grant immunity.

EXHIBIT 2.4 A Comparison of Grand Jury Proceedings with the Preliminary Examination

Sufficiency of Indictment

An indictment is sufficient if it adequately informs the accused of the facts and elements of the charge so that the accused is able to prepare an adequate defense or enter a plea of double jeopardy in a subsequent prosecution for the same offense. In determining the sufficiency of an indictment, courts construe the indictment in a commonsense manner and generally ignore technical errors or omissions. An indictment that tracks statutory language is usually held to be sufficient. *Hamling v. United States,* 418 U.S. 87, 94 S.Ct. 2887, 41 L.Ed.2d 590 (1974). A defendant can obtain more specific details about the crime charged by requesting the court to require the government to provide a *bill of particulars*. The grant or denial of this request is within the discretion of the trial court.

Joinder and Severance

Statutes and court rules permit the joinder of offenses or defendants in the same indictment or information. Rules 8 and 14 of the *Federal Rules of Criminal Procedure* are illustrative and are reproduced here:

RULE 8. JOINDER OF OFFENSES AND OF DEFENDANTS

(a) *Joinder of Offenses. Two or more offenses may be charged in the same indictment or information in a separate count for each offense if the offenses charged, whether felonies or misdemeanors or both, are of the same or similar character or are based on the same act or transaction or on two or more acts or transactions connected together or constituting parts of a common scheme or plan.*

(b) *Joinder of Defendants. Two or more defendants may be charged in the same indictment or information if they are alleged to have participated in the same act or transaction or in the same series of acts or transactions constituting an offense or offenses. Such defendants may be charged in one or more counts together or separately and all of the defendants need not be charged in each count.* ∎

RULE 14. RELIEF FROM PREJUDICIAL JOINDER

If it appears that a defendant or the government is prejudiced by a joinder of offenses or of defendants in an indictment or information or by such joinder for trial together, the court may order an election or separate trials of counts, grant a severance of defendants or provide whatever other relief justice requires. In ruling on a motion by a defendant for severance the court may order the attorney for the government to deliver to the court for inspection in camera *any statements or confessions made by the defendants which the government intends to introduce in evidence at the trial.* ∎

A detailed discussion of joinder and severance is beyond the scope of this chapter.

Duplicity and Multiplicity

A **duplicitous indictment** or information is one that unites two or more separate and distinct offenses in the same count. By obscuring the exact charge, duplicitous indictments or informations may violate the defendant's constitutional right to notice of charges and may impair the defendant's ability to plead double jeopardy in a subsequent prosecution. A **multiplicitous indictment** or information is one that charges the commission of a single offense in several counts. The evil of a multiplicitous indictment or information is that it may lead to multiple sentences for the same offense, or it may have some psychological effect on a jury by suggesting that the defendant has committed more than one crime. If a duplicitous or multiplicitous indictment or

UNITED STATES DISTRICT COURT
DISTRICT OF MAINE

UNITED STATES OF AMERICA	)	
	)	Criminal Number
VS.	)	(21 U.S.C. §§841(a)(1), 841(b)(1)(B),
	)	853(a); 18 U.S.C. §2)
ROY L. PAINE	)	

INDICTMENT

The Grand Jury Charges:

Count One

On or about February 15, 1996, in the District of Maine,

ROY L. PAINE

defendant herein, did unlawfully, knowingly and intentionally manufacture and aid and abet the manufacture of in excess of one hundred (100) marijuana plants, a Schedule I controlled substance listed in Title 21, United States Code, Section 812, in violation of Title 21, United States Code, Sections 841(a)(1) and 841(b)(1)(B) and Title 18, United States Code, Section 2.

Count Two

On or about February 15, 1996, in the District of Maine,

ROY L. PAINE

defendant herein, did unlawfully, knowingly and intentionally possess with intent to distribute and aid and abet the possession with intent to distribute in excess of one hundred (100) marijuana plants, a Schedule I controlled substance listed in Title 21, United States Code, Section 812, in violation of Title 21, United States Code, Sections 841(a)(1) and 841(b)(1)(B) and Title 18, United States Code, Section 2.

EXHIBIT 2.5   A Typical Indictment

information is prejudicial to the defendant and the prejudice is not corrected, the indictment may be dismissed.

Prosecutorial Discretion

In our criminal justice system, the Government retains "broad discretion" as to whom to prosecute.... "[S]o long as the prosecutor has probable cause to be-

<u>Count Three</u>

In committing violations of Title 21, United States Code, Section 841(a)(1) which are punishable by imprisonment for more than one year, to wit: the offenses charged by Counts One and Two of this indictment,

ROY L. PAINE

defendant herein, used and intended to use real property located off the John Tarr Road in the Town of Bowdoin, County of Sagadahoc and State of Maine which is better described in a deed from Guy Dwyer to the said ROY L. PAINE, defendant herein, dated November 9, 1985 and recorded in the Sagadahoc County Registry of Deeds at Book 733 and Page 231, including any buildings and structures located thereon, to commit and facilitate the commission of said offenses, and by virtue of the commission of said felony offenses, ROY L. PAINE, defendant herein, is forfeit of any and all interest in the said real property and such interest is vested in the United States of America and is forfeitable thereto pursuant to Title 21, United States Code, Section 853.

A TRUE BILL.

_____
Foreperson

_____
Assistant U.S. Attorney   A TRUE COPY
Dated: ATTEST: William S. Brownell, Clerk

By _____
                     Deputy Clerk

EXHIBIT 2.5   *(continued)*

lieve that the accused committed an offense defined by statute, the decision whether or not to prosecute, and what charge to file or bring before a grand jury, generally rests entirely in his discretion." *Wayte v. United States,* 470 U.S. 598, 607, 105 S.Ct. 1524, 1530, 84 L.Ed.2d 547, 555–56 (1985).

A prosecutor also has broad discretion in determining when to bring charges, whether to investigate, and whether to grant immunity or to plea-bargain. The prosecutor may dismiss charges against a person without giving reasons. Prosecutorial discretion is not absolute, however, but is subject to judicial review in cases of selective prosecution or vindictive prosecution.

Selective prosecution is a violation of the equal protection clause of the Constitution. To establish selective prosecution, a defendant bears a heavy burden to show that others similarly situated were not prosecuted *and* that the defendant's prosecution was "deliberately based upon an unjustifiable standard such as race, religion, or other arbitrary classification." *Bordenkircher v. Hayes,* 434 U.S. 357, 364, 98 S.Ct. 663, 668–69, 54 L.Ed.2d 604, 611 (1978).

Vindictive prosecution violates due process. Vindictive prosecution occurs when a prosecutor increases the number or severity of charges to penalize a defendant who exercises constitutional or statutory rights. In *Blackledge v. Perry,* 417 U.S. 21, 94 S.Ct. 2098, 40 L.Ed.2d 628 (1974), a case involving a felony charge brought against a defendant who exercised a statutory right to appeal from a misdemeanor conviction for the same offense, the Court said the real basis of the vindictiveness rule is that "the fear of such vindictiveness may unconstitutionally deter a defendant's exercise of the right to appeal or collaterally attack his first conviction. . . ." 417 U.S. at 28, 94 S.Ct. at 2102, 40 L.Ed.2d at 634. In *United States v. Goodwin,* 457 U.S. 368, 381, 102 S.Ct. 2485, 2492–93, 73 L.Ed.2d 74, 85 (1982), the Court recognized a distinction between alleged vindictiveness before trial and alleged vindictiveness during or after trial:

> There is good reason to be cautious before adopting an inflexible presumption of prosecutorial vindictiveness in a pretrial setting. In the course of preparing a case for trial, the prosecutor may uncover additional information that suggests a basis for further prosecution or he simply may come to realize that information possessed by the State has a broader significance. At this stage of the proceedings, the prosecutor's assessment of the proper extent of prosecution may not have crystallized. In contrast, once a trial begins—and certainly by the time a conviction has been obtained—it is much more likely that the State has discovered and assessed all of the information against an accused and has made a determination, on the basis of that information, of the extent to which he should be prosecuted. Thus, a change in the charging decision made after an initial trial is completed is much more likely to be improperly motivated than is a pretrial decision.

Grand Jury

The Fifth Amendment provides that "[n]o person shall be held to answer for a capital, or otherwise infamous crime, unless on a presentment or indictment of a Grand Jury." As explained in Chapter 1, this Fifth Amendment requirement applies only to the federal government, although the states have on their own developed varying laws and rules regarding the use of the grand jury. The primary duty of the grand jury is to receive complaints in criminal cases, hear the evidence put forth by the state, and return an indictment when the jury is satisfied that there is probable cause that the defendant has committed an offense. The concurrence of a specified number of grand jurors is required to return an indictment.

The grand jury is unique in that

> the whole theory of its function is that it belongs to no branch of the institutional Government, serving as a kind of buffer or referee between the Government and the people. . . . Although the grand jury normally operates, of course, in the courthouse and under judicial auspices, its institutional relationship with the Judicial Branch has traditionally been, so to speak, at arm's length. Judges' direct involvement in the functioning of the grand jury has generally been confined to the constitutive one of calling the grand jurors together and administering their oaths of office. *United States v. Williams,* 504 U.S. 36, 47, 112 S.Ct. 1735, 1742, 118 L.Ed.2d 352, 365 (1992).

The grand jury usually consists of sixteen to twenty-three jurors, selected from their communities according to law to serve during the criminal term of the appropriate court. The composition of a grand jury can be challenged by either the prosecution or the defendant on the grounds of improper selection or legal disqualification. Bias in grand jury selection results in dismissal of the indictment. In *Rose v. Mitchell,* the U.S. Supreme Court said:

> Selection of members of a grand jury because they are of one race and not another destroys the appearance of justice and thereby casts doubt on the integrity of the judicial process. The exclusion from grand jury service of Negroes, or any group otherwise qualified to serve, impairs the confidence of the public in the administration of justice. As this Court repeatedly has emphasized, such discrimination "not only violates our Constitution and the laws enacted under it but is at war with our basic concepts of a democratic society and a representative government." 443 U.S. 545, 555–56, 99 S.Ct. 2993, 3000, 61 L.Ed.2d 739, 749 (1979).

Grand jury proceedings are nonadversarial and traditionally conducted in secrecy. During deliberations or voting, no one other than the jurors is allowed to be present. When the grand jury is taking evidence, however, the attorneys for the state, the witnesses under examination, and, when ordered by the court, an interpreter and an official court reporter may be present. Matters occurring before the grand jury, other than the deliberations or the votes of any juror, may be disclosed to the prosecuting attorney for use in performing his or her duties. Otherwise, these matters are to be kept secret, unless the court orders that they be disclosed.

The reasons for keeping grand jury proceedings secret were summarized by the U.S. Supreme Court in *United States v. Procter & Gamble Co.,* 356 U.S. 677, 681 n.6, 78 S.Ct. 983, 986 n.6, 2 L.Ed.2d 1077, 1081 n.6 (1958):

> (1) to prevent the escape of those whose indictment may be contemplated; (2) to insure the utmost freedom to the grand jury in its deliberations, and to prevent persons subject to indictment or their friends from importuning the grand jurors; (3) to prevent subornation of perjury or tampering with the witnesses who may testify before grand jury and later appear at the trial of those indicted by it; (4) to encourage free and untrammeled disclosures by persons who have information with respect to the commission of crimes; (5) to protect innocent accused who is exonerated from disclosure of the fact that he has been under investigation, and from the expense of standing trial where there was no probability of guilt.

The grand jury also has broad investigative powers:

> Traditionally the grand jury has been accorded wide latitude to inquire into violations of criminal law. No judge presides to monitor its proceedings. It deliberates in secret and may alone determine the course of its inquiry. The grand jury may compel the production of evidence or the testimony of witnesses as it considers appropriate, and its operation generally is unrestrained by the technical procedural and evidentiary rules governing the conduct of criminal trials. *United States v. Calandra,* 414 U.S. 338, 343, 94 S.Ct. 613, 617, 38 L.Ed.2d 561, 568–69 (1974).

The grand jury can use its broad subpoena power to compel witnesses to testify or provide physical evidence. The Fourth Amendment prohibits unreasonably vague or overbroad subpoenas for documents, and some courts hold that the evidence sought must be relevant to the investigation. Failure to obey a subpoena is punishable as contempt of court. A grand jury can also grant immunity to compel testimony from witnesses who exercise their Fifth Amendment privilege against self-incrimination and refuse to testify. So-called **use immunity** protects a witness from use of his or her testimony and any evidence derived from the testimony in future prosecutions. **Transactional immunity,** on the other hand, protects a witness only from prosecution for crimes to which his or her compelled testimony relates. Exhibit 2.4 compares grand jury proceedings with the preliminary examination.

Waiver of Indictment

In some jurisdictions, a defendant who does not wish to be prosecuted by indictment may waive the indictment and be prosecuted by information. The waiver of an indictment procedure is of great advantage to a defendant who wishes to plead guilty or **nolo contendere.** (These pleas are discussed in further detail later in this chapter.) In effect, the waiver of indictment procedure enables a defendant to begin serving a sentence sooner instead of having to wait for a grand jury, which sits only during the criminal term of court. The defendant can thereby secure release from custody at an earlier date than by going through the indictment procedure.

Warrant or Summons Issued on the Indictment

An indictment may sometimes be found against a defendant before the defendant has been taken into custody and brought before the court. In these cases, on the request of the prosecuting attorney or by direction of the court, the clerk shall issue a summons or a warrant for the arrest of each defendant named in the indictment. This process indicates no change of procedure for law enforcement officers, who are required to execute the warrant or serve the summons in the same way as they would any other warrant or summons. Procedures for executing an arrest warrant or serving a summons appear in Chapter 4.

Arraignment and Preparation for Trial

The next step in the criminal proceeding, after the indictment or information, is the **arraignment.** The meaning of the term *arraignment* is often confused with the initial appearance before a magistrate by a defendant who has been arrested. Part of the reason for the confusion is that, in misdemeanor proceedings in courts of limited jurisdiction, the two procedures are combined. The essence of the arraignment is that the defendant is called on to plead to the charge after the magistrate reads the substance of the charge. In misdemeanor proceedings, if there is no requirement of prosecution by indictment or information, the complaint is read to the defendant, and the **plea** is made to the complaint. However, in courts in which prosecution must be by indictment or information, the indictment or information is read to the defendant, and the plea is made to the indictment or information. Therefore, in courts that require prosecution by indictment or information, the arraignment proceeding must be separate from the initial appearance before the magistrate.

Pleas

In general, the pleas available to the defendant vary in different jurisdictions. Three of the most common pleas are as follows:

- Not guilty
- Guilty
- Nolo contendere (no contest)

A plea of not guilty puts in issue all the material facts alleged in the indictment, information, or complaint. A defendant has a right to refuse to plead at all, in which case the court must enter a plea of not guilty. Refusing to plead is sometimes called *standing mute,* and it may occur for various reasons, such as obstinacy, dumbness, insanity, mental illness or retardation, or ignorance of the language used in the proceedings.

To plead guilty or nolo contendere, the defendant must obtain the court's consent. Both these pleas simply mean that the defendant does not wish to contest the charge but will submit to the judgment of the court. A guilty plea may constitute an admission of guilt by the defendant and may be used against him or her in a civil action based on the same facts. A plea of nolo contendere, however, is not an admission of guilt and cannot be used against the defendant in a civil action.

By pleading guilty, a defendant waives many constitutional rights. Therefore, the court may not accept a plea of guilty or nolo contendere in a felony proceeding unless the court is satisfied, after inquiry, that the defendant committed the crime charged and that the plea is made knowingly and voluntarily with the advice of competent counsel. Rule 11 of the *Federal Rules of Criminal Procedure* and similar state provisions establish guidelines for courts in making these and other determinations. Relevant portions of Rule 11 follow:

RULE 11. PLEAS

(a) *Alternatives.*
    (1) *In General. A defendant may plead not guilty, guilty, or nolo contendere. If a defendant refuses to plead or if a defendant corporation fails to appear, the court shall enter a plea of not guilty.*
    (2) *Conditional Pleas. With the approval of the court and the consent of the government, a defendant may enter a conditional plea of guilty or nolo contendere, reserving in writing the right, on appeal from the judgment, to review of the adverse determination of any specified pretrial motion. A defendant who prevails on appeal shall be allowed to withdraw the plea.*
(b) *Nolo Contendere. A defendant may plead nolo contendere only with the consent of the court. Such a plea shall be accepted by the court only after due consideration of the views of the parties and the interest of the public in the effective administration of justice.*
(c) *Advice to Defendant. Before accepting a plea of guilty or nolo contendere, the court must address the defendant personally in open court and inform the defendant of, and determine that the defendant understands, the following:*
    (1) *the nature of the charge to which the plea is offered, the mandatory minimum penalty provided by law, if any, and the maximum possible*

*penalty provided by law, including the effect of any special parole or su-
pervised release term, the fact that the court is required to consider any
applicable sentencing guidelines but may depart from those guidelines
under some circumstances, and, when applicable, that the court may also
order the defendant to make restitution to any victim of the offense; and*

*(2) if the defendant is not represented by an attorney, that the defendant has
the right to be represented by an attorney at every stage of the proceeding and, if necessary, one will be appointed to represent the defendant;
and*

*(3) that the defendant has the right to plead not guilty or to persist in that
plea if it has already been made, the right to be tried by a jury and at
that trial the right to the assistance of counsel, the right to confront and
cross-examine adverse witnesses, and the right against compelled self-
incrimination; and*

*(4) that if a plea of guilty or nolo contendere is accepted by the court there
will not be a further trial of any kind, so that by pleading guilty or nolo
contendere the defendant waives the right to a trial; and*

*(5) if the court intends to question the defendant under oath, on the record,
and in the presence of counsel about the offense to which the defendant
has pleaded, that the defendant's answers may later be used against the
defendant in a prosecution for perjury or false statement.*

*(d) **Insuring that the Plea is Voluntary.** The court shall not accept a plea of
guilty or nolo contendere without first, by addressing the defendant personally in open court, determining that the plea is voluntary and not the result
of force or threats or of promises apart from a plea agreement. The court
shall also inquire as to whether the defendant's willingness to plead guilty
or nolo contendere results from prior discussions between the attorney for
the government and the defendant or the defendant's attorney.*

*(e) **Plea Agreement Procedure.** [Paragraph (e) is reproduced in the next section,
"Plea Bargaining."]*

*(f) **Determining Accuracy of Plea.** Notwithstanding the acceptance of a plea of
guilty, the court should not enter a judgment upon such plea without making such inquiry as shall satisfy it that there is a factual basis for the plea.*

*(g) **Record of Proceedings.** A verbatim record of the proceedings at which the
defendant enters a plea shall be made and, if there is a plea of guilty or nolo
contendere, the record shall include, without limitation, the court's advice to
the defendant, the inquiry into the voluntariness of the plea including any
plea agreement, and the inquiry into the accuracy of a guilty plea.*

*(h) **Harmless Error.** Any variance from the procedures required by this rule
which does not affect substantial rights shall be disregarded.* ■

The court must also ensure the defendant's competency to plead guilty. This determination involves the same considerations as the determination of competency to
stand trial, discussed later in this chapter.

A defendant may withdraw a guilty plea with the court's permission. Rule 32(e)
of the *Federal Rules of Criminal Procedure* and similar state provisions govern this
procedure:

*(e) **Plea Withdrawal.** If a motion to withdraw a plea of guilty or nolo contendere is made before sentence is imposed, the court may permit the plea to
be withdrawn if the defendant shows any fair and just reason. At any later*

*time, a plea may be set aside only on direct appeal or by motion under 28
U.S.C.A. § 2255.*

In some jurisdictions, a plea of not guilty by reason of insanity may be entered. This plea is required if the defendant intends to raise the defense of insanity. A defendant may plead not guilty and not guilty by reason of insanity to the same charge. When a plea of not guilty by reason of insanity is entered, the court may, on petition, order the defendant committed to an appropriate institution for the mentally ill for examination. The insanity plea is rarely raised in a misdemeanor proceeding.

Plea Bargaining

The disposition of criminal charges by agreement between the prosecutor and the accused, sometimes loosely called "plea bargaining," is an essential component of the administration of justice. Properly administered, it is to be encouraged. If every criminal charge were subjected to a full-scale trial, the States and the Federal Government would need to multiply by many times the number of judges and court facilities.

Disposition of charges after plea discussions is not only an essential part of the process but a highly desirable part for many reasons. It leads to prompt and largely final disposition of most criminal cases; it avoids much of the corrosive impact of enforced idleness during pretrial confinement for those who are denied release pending trial; it protects the public from those accused persons who are prone to continue criminal conduct even while on pretrial release; and, by shortening the time between charge and disposition, it enhances whatever may be the rehabilitative prospects of the guilty when they are ultimately imprisoned. . . .

This phase of the process of criminal justice, and the adjudicative element inherent in accepting a plea of guilty, must be attended by safeguards to insure the defendant what is reasonably due in the circumstances. Those circumstances will vary, but a constant factor is that when a plea rests in any significant degree on a promise or agreement of the prosecutor, so that it can be said to be part of the inducement or consideration, such promise must be fulfilled. *Santobello v. New York*, 404 U.S. 257, 260–62, 92 S.Ct. 495, 498–99, 30 L.Ed.2d 427, 432–33 (1971).

The federal government and most states have developed statutes or rules governing the plea bargaining process. Many states model their provisions after Rule 11(e) of the *Federal Rules of Criminal Procedure*:

*(e) **Plea Agreement Procedure.***
    *(1) **In General.** The attorney for the government and the attorney for the
    defendant or the defendant when acting pro se may engage in discus-
    sions with a view toward reaching an agreement that, upon the entering
    of a plea of guilty or nolo contendere to a charged offense or to a lesser
    or related offense, the attorney for the government will do any of the
    following:*
        (A) move for dismissal of other charges; or
        *(B) make a recommendation, or agree not to oppose the defendant's re-
        quest, for a particular sentence, with the understanding that such
        recommendation or request shall not be binding upon the court; or*

(C)   *agree that a specific sentence is the appropriate disposition of
the case.*

The court shall not participate in any such discussions.

(2) **Notice of Such Agreement.** *If a plea agreement has been reached by the
parties, the court shall, on the record, require the disclosure of the
agreement in open court or, on a showing of good cause, in camera, at
the time the plea is offered. If the agreement is of the type specified in
subdivision (e)(1)(A) or (C), the court may accept or reject the agreement, or may defer its decision as to the acceptance or rejection until
there has been an opportunity to consider the presentence report. If the
agreement is of the type specified in subdivision (e)(1)(B), the court
shall advise the defendant that if the court does not accept the recommendation or request the defendant nevertheless has no right to withdraw the plea.*

(3) **Acceptance of a Plea Agreement.** *If the court accepts the plea agreement, the court shall inform the defendant that it will embody in the
judgment and sentence the disposition provided for in the plea
agreement.*

(4) **Rejection of a Plea Agreement.** *If the court rejects the plea agreement,
the court shall, on the record, inform the parties of this fact, advise the
defendant personally in open court or, on a showing of good cause, in
camera, that the court is not bound by the plea agreement, afford the
defendant the opportunity to then withdraw the plea, and advise the defendant that if the defendant persists in a guilty plea or plea of nolo
contendere the disposition of the case may be less favorable to the defendant than that contemplated by the plea agreement.*

(5) **Time of Plea Agreement Procedure.** *Except for good cause shown, notification to the court of the existence of a plea agreement shall be given
at the arraignment or at such other time, prior to trial, as may be fixed
by the court.*

(6) **Inadmissibility of Pleas, Plea Discussions, and Related Statements.** *Except as otherwise provided in this paragraph, evidence of the following
is not, in any civil or criminal proceeding, admissible against the defendant who made the plea or was a participant in the plea discussions:*

(A)   *a plea of guilty which was later withdrawn;*

(B)   *a plea of nolo contendere;*

(C)   *any statement made in the course of any proceedings under this rule
regarding either of the foregoing pleas; or*

(D)   *any statement made in the course of plea discussions with an attorney for the government which do not result in a plea of guilty or
which result in a plea of guilty later withdrawn.*

*However, such a statement is admissible (i) in any proceeding wherein an-
other statement made in the course of the same plea or plea discussions has
been introduced and the statement ought in fairness be considered contemporaneously with it, or (ii) in a criminal proceeding for perjury or false
statement if the statement was made by the defendant under oath, on the
record, and in the presence of counsel.*

In general, plea agreements are treated as contracts. If the defendant breaches the
agreement, the prosecution may not only reprosecute the defendant but also bring

more serious charges. For example, in *Bordenkircher v. Hayes,* 434 U.S. 357, 98 S.Ct. 663, 54 L.Ed.2d 604 (1978), the U.S. Supreme Court found no due process violation where the prosecutor carried out a threat made during plea negotiations to reindict the defendant on more serious charges if the defendant did not plead guilty to the original charge. If the defendant alleges that the prosecution breached a plea agreement and the allegations are not "palpably incredible" or "patently frivolous or false," the defendant is entitled to an evidentiary hearing. *Blackledge v. Allison,* 431 U.S. 63, 97 S.Ct. 1621, 52 L.Ed.2d 136 (1977). If the defendant establishes such a breach, the court may allow the defendant to withdraw the plea, may alter the sentence, or may require the prosecution to honor the agreement.

Motions

A **motion** is an oral or written request asking a court to make a specified finding, decision, or order. Many standard motions are available, but an attorney may also fashion unique motions to respond to particular circumstances requiring court action. Some of the more common standard pretrial motions are as follows: motion to be admitted to bail, motion to quash a grand jury indictment, motion to inspect grand jury minutes, motion to challenge the sufficiency of the indictment, motion for a competency hearing, motion for discovery, motion for a continuance, motion for change of venue, motion to dismiss an indictment, motion for joinder or severance of codefendants, and motion to withdraw a guilty plea. Most of these motions either are discussed elsewhere in this chapter or are primarily of concern to judges and attorneys and therefore beyond the scope of this book.

Two pretrial motions, however, are central to criminal procedure law: (1) the motion to suppress evidence and (2) the motion to suppress a confession. These motions are made by defendants who believe they are aggrieved by either an unlawful search and seizure or an unlawfully obtained admission or confession. Some jurisdictions do not allow one or both of these motions to be made before trial. The purpose of a motion to suppress is twofold:

- To enable the defendant to invoke the exclusionary rule and prevent the use of illegally obtained evidence at trial
- To enable the court to resolve the issue of the legality of a search and seizure or confession without interrupting the trial

The hearing on the motion to suppress is often the point in the proceedings at which the court carefully scrutinizes a law enforcement officer's performance in a case. If the defendant is able to prove that an officer illegally obtained evidence, and if the evidence is essential to the prosecution's case, suppression of the evidence is likely to result in a dismissal of charges or the granting of a motion for judgment of acquittal. Therefore, law enforcement officers must know the law not only at the time they conduct a search and seizure or obtain a confession but also when they may be called on to justify their actions at a hearing on a motion to suppress.

Depositions

When a witness is unable to attend a criminal trial and it is shown that his or her testimony is material to a just determination of the case, the court may order that a **deposition** of the witness be taken at any time after the filing of an indictment or information. Obtaining a deposition involves taking the testimony of a witness out of court and preserving that testimony in writing for later use in court. A deposition is used only in exceptional circumstances and not for the mere convenience of a witness or party. It may be requested by either the prosecution or the defendant, and the opposing party may attend the taking of the deposition.

A deposition, or a part of a deposition, may be used at a trial or hearing if it appears that any of the following circumstances exist:

- The witness who gave the deposition is dead.
- The witness is out of the jurisdiction (unless the party offering the deposition caused the witness's absence).
- The witness is unable to attend or testify because of sickness or infirmity.
- The party offering the deposition is unable to procure the attendance of the witness by subpoena.

Furthermore, depositions may be used even if the witness does testify at the trial, but only for the purposes of contradicting or impeaching the witness's testimony.

Discovery

Discovery, also called pretrial discovery, is a procedure, largely governed by statute or court rule, whereby the defendant or the prosecution is enabled to inspect, examine, copy, or photograph items in the possession of the other party. Discovery in federal cases is governed by Rules 12.1, 16, and 26.2 of the *Federal Rules of Criminal Procedure*. Among the items subject to discovery are tangible objects, tape recordings, books, papers (including written or recorded statements made by the defendants or witnesses), and the results or reports of physical examinations and scientific tests, experiments, and comparisons. The general purpose of discovery is to make the criminal trial "less a game of blindman's bluff and more a fair contest with the basic issues and facts disclosed to the fullest practical extent." *United States v. Procter & Gamble Co.*, 356 U.S. 677, 682, 78 S.Ct. 983, 986–87, 2 L.Ed.2d 1077, 1082 (1958).

Ordinarily, to obtain the right to discovery, a party must make a timely motion before the court and must show that the specific items sought may be material to the preparation of its case and that its request is reasonable. Nevertheless, jurisdictions differ considerably with respect to both the conditions under which discovery is allowed and the items that are subject to discovery. Some jurisdictions do not allow discovery at all. Others allow discovery only for the defendant, in an effort to correct the imbalance between the investigative resources of the prosecution and the defendant, thereby enabling the defendant more adequately to prepare a defense. A recent development is automatic informal discovery for certain types of evidence, without the necessity for motions and court orders. The state of the law governing discovery is constantly changing, but the trend appears to be in favor of broadening the right of discovery for both the defense and the prosecution.

"There is no general constitutional right to discovery in a criminal case. . . ." *Weatherford v. Bursey*, 429 U.S. 545, 559, 97 S.Ct. 837, 846, 51 L.Ed.2d 30, 42 (1977). Nevertheless, to protect defendants' due process rights, courts have created constitutional rules requiring disclosure of evidence in certain situations. In *Brady v. Maryland*, 373 U.S. 83, 87, 83 S.Ct. 1194, 1196–97, 10 L.Ed.2d 215, 218 (1963), the U.S. Supreme Court held that "the suppression by the prosecution of evidence favorable to an accused upon request violates due process where the evidence is material either to guilt or punishment, irrespective of the good faith or bad faith of the prosecution." In *United States v. Bagley,* 473 U.S. 667, 682, 105 S.Ct. 3375, 3383, 87 L.Ed.2d 481, 494 (1985), the Court held:

> The evidence is material only if there is a reasonable probability that, had the evidence been disclosed to the defense, the result of the proceeding would have been different. A "reasonable probability" is a probability sufficient to undermine confidence in the outcome.

As the Court explained in *Kyles v. Whitley,* 514 U.S. 419, 434, 115 S.Ct. 1555, 1566, 131 L.Ed.2d 490, 506 (1995), "[t]he question is not whether the defendant would more likely than not have received a different verdict with the evidence, but whether in its absence he received a fair trial, understood as a trial resulting in a verdict worthy of confidence." The *Brady* rule does not require the prosecution to make its files available to the defendant for an open-ended "fishing expedition" or to disclose inculpatory, neutral, or speculative evidence or evidence that is available to the defendant from other sources through the defendant's own efforts.

Subpoena

The term **subpoena** describes the process used to secure the attendance of witnesses or the production of books, papers, documents, or other objects at a criminal proceeding. It is the primary vehicle by which the defendant exercises the Sixth Amendment right to "compulsory process for obtaining witnesses in his favor" (see Chapter 1). The subpoena is usually issued by a judicial officer, and it commands the person to whom it is directed to attend a trial, hearing, or deposition for the purpose of testifying at the proceeding or bringing a named document or object. As discussed earlier, the grand jury also has broad subpoena powers. A subpoena can be served by a law enforcement officer or any other adult person who is not a party to the proceedings. A typical form for a subpoena in a criminal case appears in Exhibit 2.6.

Competency to Stand Trial

The test for determining competency to stand trial is whether the defendant "has sufficient present ability to consult with his lawyer with a reasonable degree of rational understanding—and whether he has a rational as well as factual understanding of the proceedings against him." *Dusky v. United States,* 362 U.S. 402, 402, 80 S.Ct. 788, 789, 4 L.Ed.2d 824, 825 (1960). Due process requires a court to hold a competency hearing if there is sufficient doubt regarding a defendant's competency. "[E]vidence of a defendant's irrational behavior, his demeanor at trial, and any prior medical opinion on competence to stand trial are all relevant in determining whether further inquiry is required. . . ." *Drope v. Missouri,* 420 U.S. 162, 180, 95 S.Ct. 896, 908, 43 L.Ed.2d 103, 118 (1975).

When a court finds that a defendant is incompetent to stand trial, criminal proceedings against the defendant are suspended until such time as the defendant may be found competent. If future competency is highly probable, the defendant may be committed to a mental institution for a reasonable period of time to determine future competency. During this period, the court may order periodic examination of the defendant to determine whether competency has been regained. After such a reasonable time, the government must either institute civil commitment proceedings or release the defendant. *Jackson v. Indiana,* 406 U.S. 715, 92 S.Ct. 1845, 32 L.Ed.2d 435 (1972).

AO 89 (Rev. 11/91) Subpoena in a Criminal Case

United States District Court

_____ DISTRICT OF _____

**SUBPOENA IN A
CRIMINAL CASE**

V.

CASE NUMBER:

TO:

☐ YOU ARE COMMANDED to appear in the United States District Court at the place, date, and time specified below to testify in the above case.

PLACE	COURTROOM
	DATE AND TIME

☐ YOU ARE ALSO COMMANDED to bring with you the following document(s) or object(s):

U.S. MAGISTRATE JUDGE OR CLERK OF COURT	DATE
(By) Deputy Clerk	

ATTORNEY'S NAME, ADDRESS AND PHONE NUMBER:

EXHIBIT 2.6   A Typical Subpoena Form

A claim that a defendant is incompetent to stand trial must be distinguished from the claim that a defendant is not guilty by reason of insanity. The former concerns only the defendant's mental fitness at the *time of trial* and is unrelated to any determination of guilt. The latter is a defense to prosecution on the grounds that the defendant was mentally incompetent at the *time that an alleged crime was committed.*

AO 89 (Rev. 11/91) Subpoena in a Criminal Case

PROOF OF SERVICE

	DATE	PLACE
RECEIVED BY SERVER		
SERVED	DATE	PLACE

SERVED ON (PRINT NAME)	FEES AND MILEAGE TENDERED TO WITNESS
	☐ YES ☐ NO AMOUNT $_____

SERVED BY (PRINT NAME)	TITLE

DECLARATION OF SERVER

I declare under penalty of perjury under the laws of the United States of America that the foregoing information contained in the Proof of Service is true and correct.

Executed on _____ _____
　　　　　　　　　Date　　　　　*Signature of Server*

　　　　　　　　　　　　　　_____
　　　　　　　　　　　　　　Address of Server

ADDITIONAL INFORMATION

EXHIBIT 2.6 *(continued)*

Venue

One final pretrial matter to be considered is venue. Venue is often confused with jurisdiction. **Jurisdiction** refers to the authority of the court to deal with a particular type of case. For instance, a municipal court may have jurisdiction over misdemeanor offenses. **Venue,** on the other hand, merely refers to the place at which the authority of the court should be exercised. For example, Article III, section 2, paragraph 3, of the U.S. Constitution states that "[t]he Trial of all Crimes ... shall be held *in the State where the said Crimes shall have been committed, ...*" and the Sixth Amendment requires that "[i]n all criminal prosecutions, the accused shall enjoy the right to a speedy and public trial, by an impartial jury *of the State and district wherein the crime shall have been committed,* which district shall have been previously ascertained by law. . . ." (emphasis supplied). A typical state statute or rule requires that the trial of certain types of cases be held in the geographic division of the court in which the offense was committed. Most jurisdictions also have special rules relating to the proper venue for an offense that is committed on a boundary of two counties or for an offense partly committed in one county and partly in another. These technicalities are not discussed here.

Sometimes, because of heavy publicity or intense community feeling, a defendant may wish to have his or her case tried in a different place than the one authorized by statute. To accomplish this, a defendant may make a motion for a change of venue. The motion usually must be made before the jury is impaneled or, in cases in which there is no jury, before any evidence is received. The defendant must give adequate reasons in support of the motion. Typical grounds for granting a motion for change of venue are as follows:

- Such prejudice prevails in the county where the case is to be tried that the defendant cannot obtain a fair and impartial trial there.

- Another location is much more convenient for the parties and witnesses than the intended place of trial, and the interests of justice require a transfer of location.

The Trial

The Sixth Amendment to the U.S. Constitution guarantees a defendant in a criminal prosecution a speedy, public, and impartial trial *by jury.* The right to a jury trial was made applicable to the states in *Duncan v. Louisiana:*

> Because we believe that trial by jury in criminal cases is fundamental to the American scheme of justice, we hold that the Fourteenth Amendment guarantees a right of jury trial in all criminal cases which—were they to be tried in federal court—would come within the Sixth Amendment guarantee. 391 U.S. 145, 149, 88 S.Ct. 1444, 1447, 20 L.Ed.2d 491, 496 (1968).

This guarantee means that a defendant must be provided a jury trial in all criminal prosecutions except those for petty offenses. In *Baldwin v. New York,* the U.S. Supreme Court held that "no offense can be deemed 'petty' for purposes of the right to trial by jury where imprisonment for more than six months is authorized." 399 U.S 66, 69, 90 S.Ct. 1886, 1888, 26 L.Ed.2d 437, 440 (1970). A defendant who is prosecuted in a single proceeding for multiple counts of a petty offense, however, does not have a constitutional right to a jury trial, even if the aggregate of sentences authorized for the offense exceeds six months. *Lewis v. United States,* 518 U.S. 322, 116 S.Ct. 2163, 135 L.Ed.2d 590 (1996). For an offense punishable by a sentence of six months or less, a defendant has a constitutional right to a jury trial only if the additional statutory penalties "are so severe that they clearly reflect a legislative determination that the offense in question is a 'serious' one." *Blanton v. City of North Las Vegas,* 489 U.S. 538, 543, 109 S.Ct. 1289, 1293, 103 L.Ed.2d 550, 556 (1989). There is no right to jury trial in juvenile court proceedings. *McKeiver v. Pennsylvania,* 403 U.S. 528, 91 S.Ct. 1976, 29 L.Ed.2d 647 (1971). Defendants who do not wish to be tried by a jury may, with the approval of the court, waive in writing their right to a jury trial. The waiver must be voluntary, knowing, and intelligent. A defendant has no absolute constitutional right to a trial without a jury.

Trial Without a Jury

A trial without a jury is also called a **bench trial** or a **nonjury trial.** When a case is tried without a jury, the judge must perform the jury's functions of weighing the evidence, determining the credibility of witnesses, and finding the facts, in addition to performing his or her regular duties as judge. The judge must also make a finding as to the guilt or innocence of the defendant based on the evidence presented. Outside the performance of these jury functions in a nonjury trial, the judge's other regular duties are essentially the same in either a jury or a nonjury trial. Therefore, the remainder of this chapter is concerned primarily with jury trials.

Selection of Jurors

Once it has been determined that the trial will be by jury, the next step in the criminal proceeding is the selection of the jurors. The jurors will perform the crucial tasks of finding the facts, determining the credibility of witnesses, weighing the evidence, and ultimately issuing a verdict of guilty or not guilty. Because of the importance of the jury's function, detailed rules governing the selection of jurors have been devised. These rules are designed to protect the prosecution or the defendant from having a person who is prejudiced against its cause sitting as a member of the jury during the trial of the case.

The jury is selected by the court through an examination of prospective jurors on the jury panel (also called venire). The **jury panel** is a list of members of the community considered eligible for jury service. Most states have minimum qualifications for juror eligibility based on factors such as age, residence, normal intelligence, and literacy in English. The list is compiled by local officials, often according to statute. It must be indiscriminately drawn and must not systematically exclude any class of persons. The U.S. Supreme Court held that "the selection of a petit jury from a representative cross section of the community is an essential component of the Sixth Amendment right to a jury trial." *Taylor v. Louisiana,* 419 U.S. 522, 528, 95 S.Ct. 692, 697, 42 L.Ed.2d 690, 697 (1975). Federal law, and the law of most states, requires that no citizen be excluded from service as a juror on account of race, color, religion, sex, national origin, or economic status.

The examination of prospective jurors on the panel is commonly referred to as **voir dire.** The usual method of examination is to question the prospective jurors with regard to their feelings and views on various matters. The trial judge generally has broad discretion in conducting the voir dire. The judge may allow the parties or their attorneys to conduct the examination, or the judge may elect to conduct the examination.

The purpose of the examination or voir dire is to determine whether any prospective juror is prejudiced about the case in any way. Typical questions relate to whether prospective jurors know the defendant, the attorneys, or any of the witnesses; whether they have read about the case in the newspapers; whether they have racial, nationality, or gender biases; and whether they have formed any opinions on the case. If either attorney wishes to have a prospective juror dismissed on the basis of these questions or for any other reason, the attorney may issue a challenge to that juror. Two types of challenges are available. One is a **challenge for cause** and is directed toward the qualifications of a juror. Most jurisdictions have statutes or rules setting out the permissible grounds for a challenge for cause. Typical grounds are as follows:

- The juror is related to one of the parties.
- The juror has given or formed an opinion in the case.
- The juror has a bias, prejudice, or particular interest in the case.

Each party has available an unlimited number of challenges for cause, assuming that the grounds for such a challenge can be established to the judge's satisfaction.

The other form of challenge is known as the **peremptory challenge.** Peremptory challenges are available to each party as a means for dismissing prospective jurors who may be qualified but for some other reason are felt to be undesirable by one party's attorney. No reason need be given for a peremptory challenge. Peremptory challenges have to be exercised with great care. It is often difficult to determine from a few questions whether a prospective juror will be receptive or antagonistic to a party's position. Furthermore, the number of peremptory challenges available to each side is limited in number. The prosecutor's use of peremptory challenges to deliberately produce racially unbalanced juries is unconstitutional.

> [T]he State's privilege to strike individual jurors through peremptory challenges, is subject to the command of the Equal Protection Clause. Although a prosecutor ordinarily is entitled to exercise peremptory challenges "for any reason at all, as long as that reason is related to his view concerning the outcome" of the case to be tried . . . the Equal Protection Clause forbids the prosecutor to challenge potential jurors solely on account of their race or on the assumption that black jurors as a group will be unable impartially to consider the State's case against a black defendant. *Batson v. Kentucky,* 476 U.S. 79, 89, 106 S.Ct. 1712, 1719, 90 L.Ed.2d 69, 82–83 (1986).

In *J.E.B. v. Alabama ex rel. T.B.,* 511 U.S. 127, 114 S.Ct. 1419, 128 L.Ed.2d 89 (1994), the U.S. Supreme Court held that the equal protection clause forbids intentional discrimination on the basis of gender, just as it prohibits discrimination on the basis of race. Therefore, the use of peremptory challenges to strike potential jurors solely on the basis of gender is unconstitutional.

> Discrimination in jury selection, whether based on race or on gender, causes harm to the litigants, the community, and the individual jurors who are wrongfully excluded from participation in the judicial process. The litigants are harmed by the risk that the prejudice which motivated the discriminatory selection of the jury will infect the entire proceedings. . . . The community is harmed by the State's participation in the perpetuation of invidious group stereotypes and the inevitable loss of confidence in our judicial system that state-sanctioned discrimination in the courtroom engenders. 511 U.S. at 140, 114 S.Ct. at 1427, 128 L.Ed.2d at 104.

Once all the challenges available to both the prosecution and the defense are exercised, a jury is chosen and sworn in by the judge. In some cases, additional jurors are selected as alternates; they hear the evidence just as the other jurors do but do not enter deliberations unless one of the regular twelve jurors becomes ill, dies, or is unable to serve for some other reason. After administering an oath to the jurors, the judge admonishes the jurors to discuss the case with no one until the jury goes into deliberations to decide the case after hearing all the evidence.

Jury Composition

Historically, juries have been composed of twelve members. In *Williams v. Florida*, however, the U.S. Supreme Court held that a six-member jury satisfied the Sixth Amendment:

> The purpose of the jury trial . . . is to prevent oppression by the Government. . . . Given this purpose, the essential feature of a jury obviously lies in the interposition between the accused and his accuser of the common-sense judgment of a group of laymen, and in the community participation and shared responsibility which results from this group's determination of guilt or innocence. The performance of this role is not a function of the particular number of the body which makes up the jury. To be sure, the number should probably be large enough to promote group deliberation, free from outside attempts at intimidation, and to provide a fair possibility for obtaining a representative cross-section of the community. But we find little reason to think that these goals are in any meaningful sense less likely to be achieved when the jury numbers six, than when it numbers 12—particularly if the requirement of unanimity is retained. And, certainly the reliability of the jury as a fact-finder hardly seems likely to be a function of its size. . . .
>
> Similarly, while in theory the number of viewpoints represented on a randomly selected jury ought to increase as the size of the jury increases, in practice the difference between the 12-man and the six-man jury in terms of the cross-section of the community represented seems likely to be negligible. 399 U.S. 78, 100–02, 90 S.Ct. 1893, 1905–7, 26 L.Ed.2d 446, 460–61 (1970).

In *Ballew v. Georgia*, 435 U.S. 223, 98 S.Ct. 1029, 55 L.Ed.2d 234 (1978), the Court held that a five-person jury violated the Sixth Amendment.

Presentation of Evidence

Once the jury has been impaneled, the presentation of evidence begins with the opening statement of the prosecuting attorney. The prosecuting attorney gives an outline of what the government intends to prove by the evidence to be presented. Usually, the defense counsel then makes an opening statement to the jury outlining what the defense intends to prove. Sometimes, however, the defense counsel will wait until the prosecutor has presented the government's evidence before giving an opening statement, thereby concealing the course of the defense until the government has disclosed its proof.

After the opening statement or statements are given, the prosecutor begins the introduction of the government's proof. The prosecution is entitled to present its evidence first in a criminal case because it is the plaintiff and therefore has the burden of proof. The **burden of proof** means the duty to establish the truth of facts alleged in support of every element of the offense charged against the defendant. The burden of proof is upon the prosecution from the beginning to the end of the trial because of the presumption that the accused is innocent. Furthermore, the due process clause requires the prosecution to prove all the elements included in the definition of the crime with which the defendant is charged beyond a reasonable doubt. If the prosecution fails to do so on any element, the defendant must be acquitted. *In re Winship*, 397 U.S. 358, 90 S.Ct. 1068, 25 L.Ed.2d 368 (1970).

Reasonable doubt is a term requiring little interpretation, although various courts have attempted to formulate somewhat involved definitions that add little beyond its plain meaning. Suffice it to say that proof beyond a reasonable doubt requires that the guilt of the defendant be established to a reasonable, but not absolute or mathematical, certainty. Probability of guilt is not sufficient. In other words, to satisfy the "beyond a reasonable doubt" standard, the jury must be satisfied that the charges against the defendant are almost certainly true.

Rules of Evidence

The rules of evidence govern which evidence will be admissible in court and which will be excluded. These rules deal with matters such as relevancy, privileges, presumptions, witnesses, expert testimony, hearsay, authentication, and judicial notice. A discussion of the rules of evidence is beyond the scope of this chapter.

Order of Presentation of Evidence

The order of presentation of evidence begins with the **direct examination** or examination in chief of the prosecution's first witness. This witness will be someone the prosecution has called and will be expected to give evidence favorable to the government's position. The examination of the witness is designed to produce evidence that will prove the prosecution's case against the defendant. A law enforcement officer is usually involved as a witness for the prosecution, sometimes as its only witness.

When the prosecutor is through questioning the prosecution's witness, the defense counsel has a right to question the same witness. This is known as **cross-examination**. Its purpose is either to discredit information given by the witness or to impeach the person's credibility as a witness. This is done by showing inadequacy of observation, confusion, inconsistency, bias, contradiction, and the like. In some jurisdictions, the defense attorney on cross-examination is limited to questioning the witness on matters raised by the prosecutor during direct examination. In other jurisdictions, the defense attorney is not so limited, and the witness may be cross-examined concerning any matter that is relevant and material to an issue in question. The judge determines what is relevant and material and may also limit cross-examination if questions are prejudicial, cumulative, confusing, or lacking a sufficient factual base. (See Chapter 1 for additional material on cross-examination.)

After cross-examination, the prosecutor may wish to reexamine the prosecution's witness in order to rehabilitate him or her in the eyes of the jury. This is called redirect examination. Unlike cross-examination, the scope of redirect examination is limited to the matters brought out in the previous examination by the adverse party. This same rule applies if the defense counsel wishes to conduct a recross-examination. This order of presenting evidence by direct examination, cross-examination, redirect, and recross is followed for all the prosecution's witnesses until all the government's evidence has been presented.

Motion for Acquittal

After the prosecutor has presented the government's evidence, the defense counsel may move for a judgment of acquittal. A judgment of acquittal will be granted in cases in which the evidence is insufficient to sustain a conviction on the offense or offenses charged. This usually means the judge has decided that reasonable persons could not conclude that guilt has been proven beyond a reasonable doubt. If the motion is not granted at the close of the prosecution's evidence, the defense may then offer its evidence. The motion for acquittal may be renewed at the close of all the evidence; or, at the judge's discretion, it may be renewed after the jury returns a verdict or is discharged without having returned a verdict.

The Defendant's Evidence

Assuming that the court does not grant a motion for judgment of acquittal at the close of the prosecution's evidence, the defense counsel then has an opportunity to present evidence. The defense may put forth one or more of several possible defenses to refute the proof offered by the prosecution. Among the defenses available to the defendant are alibi, insanity, duress, self-defense, and entrapment. In presenting any of these defenses, the defense counsel may call witnesses on direct examination. The prosecutor has a right to cross-examine each of the defense witnesses, just as the defense counsel had a right to cross-examine the prosecution's witnesses.

Defendants may choose to testify in their own behalf or to exercise their constitutional privilege against self-incrimination and not testify. Defendants who do testify are treated much like any other witness. If a defendant chooses not to testify, the prosecuting attorney is not permitted to comment to the jury upon the failure to testify. *Griffin v. California,* 380 U.S. 609, 85 S.Ct. 1229, 14 L.Ed.2d 106 (1965).

Rebuttal by the Prosecution

Assuming that a motion for judgment of acquittal is not granted at the close of defendant's evidence, the prosecution is entitled to present rebuttal proof at this time. Rebuttal proof is designed to controvert evidence presented by the defense and to rebut any special defenses raised. Rebuttal proof is limited to new matter brought out in the defendant's presentation of evidence. Law enforcement officers may be called as witnesses again at this stage of the prosecution to correct any errors or misleading impressions that might be left after the defendant's presentation of evidence. After rebuttal, the defense may present additional evidence.

Closing Arguments

After all the evidence has been presented, both the prosecutor and the defense attorney are allotted certain amounts of time, usually specified by statute or rule, for final argument. In the final argument, attorneys for each side attempt to convince the jury (or in nonjury cases, the judge) of the correctness of their positions. The prosecutor presents the government's argument first and is followed by the attorney for the defense. The prosecutor is then allowed to present a short rebuttal. Much leeway is given for the attorneys for both sides to use their wit and imagination to win the jury over to their respective positions. However, the attorneys are required to confine themselves to a discussion of the evidence presented and reasonable inferences to be derived from that evidence.

Instructions to the Jury

After the final arguments and before the jury retires for deliberations, the judge must give **instructions** to the jury regarding the law of the case. Attorneys for both sides are given an opportunity to submit written requests to the judge for particular instructions that they wish to be given. In a typical case, the instructions cover such matters as the respective responsibilities of the court and the jury, the presumption of innocence and the burden of proof, various evidentiary problems, a definition of the offense or offenses charged, additional clarification of the critical elements of those offenses, any defenses that are available in the case, and the procedures to be followed in the jury room. The exact content of the instructions is a matter for the judge's discretion, but the attorneys are given an opportunity to object to any portion of the charge or any omission from it.

The judge may summarize the evidence for the jury, help them recall details, and attempt to resolve the complicated evidence into its simplest elements. However, the judge may not express any opinion on any issue of fact in the case or favor either side in summarizing the evidence. Furthermore, when a jury has no sentencing function, it should be instructed to "reach its verdict without regard to what sentence might be imposed." *Rogers v. United States,* 422 U.S. 35, 40, 95 S.Ct. 2091, 2095, 45 L.Ed.2d 1, 7 (1975).

> The principle that juries are not to consider the consequences of their verdicts is a reflection of the basic division of labor in our legal system between judge and jury. The jury's function is to find the facts and to decide whether, on those facts, the defendant is guilty of the crime charged. The judge, by contrast, imposes sentence on the defendant after the jury has arrived at a guilty verdict. Information regarding the consequences of a verdict is therefore irrelevant to the jury's task. Moreover, providing jurors sentencing information invites them to ponder matters that are not within their province, distracts them from their factfinding responsibilities, and creates a strong possibility of confusion. *Shannon v. United States,* 512 U.S. 573, 579, 114 S.Ct. 2419, 2424, 129 L.Ed.2d 459, 466–67 (1994).

Verdict

After receiving instructions, the jury retires to the jury room to begin deliberations on a verdict. The **verdict** is the decision of the jury as to the defendant's guilt or innocence. In federal cases, court decisions and Rule 31(a) of the *Federal Rules of Criminal Procedure* require a unanimous verdict for conviction. In state jury trials, however, a verdict of fewer than twelve members of a twelve-member jury satisfies the Sixth Amendment. *Apodaca v. Oregon,* 406 U.S. 404, 92 S.Ct. 1628, 32 L.Ed.2d 184 (1972), held that conviction by ten votes of a twelve-member jury in a state court did not violate the Sixth Amendment right to a jury trial. And *Johnson v. Louisiana,* 406 U.S. 356, 92 S.Ct. 1620, 32 L.Ed.2d 152 (1972), held that conviction by nine votes of a twelve-member jury in a state court did not violate the due process guarantee of the Fourteenth Amendment. If, however, the state uses six-member juries, the verdict must be unanimous. *Burch v. Louisiana,* 441 U.S. 130, 99 S.Ct. 1623, 60 L.Ed.2d 96 (1979). If the jurors are so irreconcilably divided in opinion that they are unable to agree on a verdict, a hung jury results. The jurors are then dismissed, and the case must be either retried or dismissed. If, however, an agreement is reached, the jurors return to the courtroom, and the verdict is read in open court by the jury foreperson. Any party, or the court itself, may then request a poll of the jury. This simply involves asking each juror whether he or she concurs in the verdict. The purpose of polling the jury is to make sure that the verdict was not reached as a result of the coercion or domination of one juror by others or as a result of sheer mental or physical exhaustion of a juror. If, during the poll, it is found that any juror did not concur in the verdict, the whole jury may be directed to retire for further deliberations or may be discharged by the judge.

Jury nullification is the power of a jury to acquit regardless of the strength of the evidence against a defendant. An acquittal is, of course, final and cannot be appealed by the prosecution. Nor can the prosecution bring charges based on the same offense against the defendant again. Nullification usually occurs when the defendant is particularly sympathetic or when the defendant is prosecuted for violating an unpopular law. In a decision that rejected the appellants' request to have the jury informed of its power of nullification, the court said:

> The way the jury operates may be radically altered if there is alteration in the way it is told to operate. The jury knows well enough that its prerogative is not limited to the choices articulated in the formal instructions of the court. The jury gets its understanding as to the arrangements in the legal system from more than one voice. There is the formal communication from the judge. There is the informal communication from the total culture—literature (novel, drama, film, and television); current comment (newspapers, magazines and television); conversation; and, of course, history and tradition. The totality of input generally convey adequately enough the idea of prerogative, of freedom in an occasional case to depart from what the judge says. *United States v. Dougherty*, 473 F.2d 1113, 1135 (D.C.Cir. 1972).

Some states require their courts to instruct juries on the power of nullification, and the issue continues to be debated.

Sentence and Judgment

After the defendant's guilt or innocence has been determined, either by verdict of the jury or by a judge without a jury, the judge must enter a judgment in the case. The **judgment** is merely the written evidence of the final disposition of the case, signed by the judge. A judgment of conviction sets forth the plea, the verdict or findings, and the adjudication and **sentence.** If the defendant is found not guilty or for some other reason is entitled to be discharged, the judgment is entered accordingly, and the defendant is guaranteed by the double jeopardy clause of the Constitution to be free forever from any further prosecution for the crime for which he or she was tried. (See Chapter 1 for a discussion of double jeopardy.) If the defendant is found guilty, the judge must pass sentence on the defendant before entering judgment.

The determination of the sentence is perhaps the most sensitive and difficult decision the judge has to make, because of the effect it will have on the defendant's life. For this reason, most jurisdictions have laws directing and guiding the judge in this determination. In general, sentencing courts have broad discretion to consider various kinds of information. 18 U.S.C.A. § 3661 states that "[n]o limitation shall be placed on the information concerning the background, character, and conduct of a person convicted of an offense which a court of the United States may receive and consider for the purpose of imposing an appropriate sentence." A sentencing court may even consider conduct of which a defendant has been acquitted, so long as that conduct has been proved by a preponderance of the evidence. *United States v. Watts*, ___ U.S. ___, 117 S.Ct. 633, 136 L.Ed.2d 554 (1997). Rule 32(a)(1) of the *Federal Rules of Criminal Procedure* and similar state provisions require judges to impose sentence without unnecessary delay. This protects the defendant from a prolonged period of uncertainty about the future. In addition, Rule 32(c)(3) provides that, before imposing sentence, the judge must "(B) afford defendant's counsel an opportunity to speak on behalf of the defendant;" and "(C) address the defendant personally and determine whether the defendant wishes to make a statement and to present any information in mitigation of the sentence." The purpose of these provisions is to enable the defendant and defense counsel to present any information that may assist the court in determining punishment. The prosecution is also given an equivalent opportunity to speak to the court. In addition, in most jurisdictions, the victim of the crime is provided an opportunity to participate at sentencing either by an oral statement in open court or by written statement to the court. The court, in its discretion, may allow others, such as family and friends of the victim and members of the victim's community, to participate at sentencing. After imposing sentence, the court is required to notify the defendant of the defendant's right to appeal, including any right to appeal the sentence.

Another typical provision designed to assist the court in fixing sentence either allows or mandates the court to consider the report of a presentence investigation before the imposition of sentence. This report is prepared by a probation and parole board or similar agency and contains the prior criminal record of the defendant and such other information on personal history and characteristics, financial condition, and the circumstances affecting the defendant's behavior that may be helpful to the court in imposing sentence. The presentence investigation report may also include specific sentence recommendations, information on the effects of the offense on the victims, and available alternatives to imprisonment.

The Constitution also restricts the information that the judge may properly consider in determining sentence; for example:

- Due process prohibits a judge from relying on materially untrue assumptions. *Townsend v. Burke,* 334 U.S. 736, 68 S.Ct. 1252, 92 L.Ed. 1690 (1948).

- Due process prohibits a judge from vindictively imposing a harsher punishment on a defendant for exercising constitutional rights. *North Carolina v. Pearce,* 395 U.S. 711, 89 S.Ct. 2072, 23 L.Ed.2d 656 (1969).

- The First Amendment prohibits a judge from considering the defendant's religious or political beliefs. *United States v. Lemon,* 723 F.2d 922 (D.C.Cir. 1983). In *Wisconsin v. Mitchell,* 508 U.S. 476, 113 S.Ct. 2194, 124 L.Ed.2d 436 (1993), however, the U.S. Supreme Court held that, although the First Amendment protects the defendant's "abstract beliefs" from being considered at sentencing, a sentence may be enhanced because the defendant intentionally selected the victim on account of the victim's race. The court explained that the "Constitution does not erect a per se barrier to the admission of evidence concerning one's beliefs and associations at sentencing simply because those beliefs and associations are protected by the First Amendment." 508 U.S. at 486, 113 S.Ct. at 2200, 124 L.Ed.2d at 445.

- The Eighth Amendment prohibits the imposition of excessive fines and the infliction of cruel and unusual punishments on persons convicted of a crime. (See Chapter 1 for a discussion of the Eighth Amendment.)

The court has a number of alternatives open to it with respect to sentencing, depending largely on individual criminal statutes. Some criminal statutes have mandatory sentences, some have fixed maximum sentences, some have fixed minimum sentences, and others leave the matter of sentencing to the judge. Therefore, depending on the offense for which the defendant has been convicted, the court may have very broad discretion in fixing sentence or no discretion whatsoever. In a few jurisdictions, the jury has the power to fix the sentence as well as to determine guilt or innocence.

In federal courts, sentencing is determined through the use of guidelines promulgated by the U.S. Sentencing Commission under the Sentencing Reform Act of 1984. The guidelines (18 U.S.C.A. Appx. Chapters 1–7) consist of a grid of forty-three offense levels and six criminal history categories. They became effective on November 1, 1987, and apply to offenses committed on or after that date. The Sentencing Reform Act abolished indeterminate sentencing and parole and created a sentencing structure that attempts to establish similar sentences for similarly situated defendants and varies the sentence imposed to reflect differences in the severity of the criminal conduct. The act also creates a sentencing method in which the sentence imposed by the judge generally determines the actual time that the convicted person will serve in prison. Restitution is a mandatory sentence for conviction of certain crimes. Judges are allowed to depart from the sentencing guidelines when a defendant has provided substantial assistance in the investigation or prosecution of another person and to correct perceived unjust effects of the guidelines in extraordinary cases. A detailed discussion of the Sentencing Reform Act is beyond the scope of this chapter.

The court also has the power to place a defendant on **probation** for certain offenses. Probation is usually controlled by statute. It is a procedure by which a person found guilty of an offense is released by the court, subject to conditions imposed by the court, without being committed to a penal or correctional institution. Probation of a defendant is usually effected in one of two ways. The court may sentence the defendant, suspend the execution of the sentence, and place the defendant on probation; or the court may continue the matter for sentencing for no more than two years and during that period place the defendant on probation. A defendant placed on probation is usually under the control and supervision of a probation and parole board or similar agency, although still under the jurisdiction of the court.

In some jurisdictions, a different type of probation may be imposed by the court for cases that involve the violation of certain statutes concerning controlled or illegal drugs or narcotics. In these cases, the court may impose sentence, place the defendant on probation, and require as a condition of probation that the defendant participate in programs at an approved drug treatment facility.

In federal cases, probation is governed by the Sentencing Reform Act of 1984, which treats probation as a sentence in its own right and not as a suspension of sentence. The act specifically limits the offenses for which probation may be granted and imposes mandatory conditions that the person on probation not commit another crime and not possess illegal controlled substances. If the conviction is for a felony, the act requires that one or more of the following be imposed as conditions of probation: a fine, an order of restitution, or community service.

The U.S. Sentencing Commission *Guidelines Manual* recommends that the following conditions be imposed on all probationers: restricted travel without prior permission, regular reporting to a probation officer, answering all inquiries of the probation officer, supporting all dependents and meeting other family responsibilities, working at a regular occupation, notifying the probation officer of change in residence or employment, refraining from possession of drugs and drug paraphernalia and excessive use of alcohol, not frequenting places where illegal drugs are sold, not associating with those known to engage in criminal activity, permitting a probation officer to visit at any time, notifying the probation officer of any arrest, not becoming a government informant without court permission, and notifying any applicable third party of the probationer's criminal record. The *Guidelines Manual* suggests that the following special conditions be imposed if appropriate: prohibition on ownership of weapons, restitution, fines, credit limitations, financial disclosure, community confinement, home detention, community service, occupational restrictions, participation in a mental health or substance abuse program, intermittent confinement, and curfew.

Probation revocation and modification are governed by the Sentencing Reform Act of 1984 and Rule 32.1 of the *Federal Rules of Criminal Procedure*. In general, probation can be revoked at any time before the end of the probationary period for any violation of probation conditions that occurs during the probation period.

Posttrial Motions

After judgment has been entered, several motions are still available to the defendant to challenge the court's decision. One of these is the motion for judgment of acquittal, sometimes called a motion for "judgment notwithstanding the verdict." The statutes or rules in some jurisdictions provide that this motion can be made after the jury has been discharged so long as it is made within a specified time after the discharge. Courts do not usually grant such a motion unless

- the prosecution's evidence was insufficient or nonexistent on a vital element of the offense charged or
- the indictment or information did not state a criminal offense under the law of the jurisdiction.

Another motion open to the defendant is the motion for a new trial. This motion may be made in addition to a motion for acquittal. When it is made alone, it is sometimes deemed to include a motion for acquittal. In the latter case, if the defendant moves for a new trial, the court in granting it may either enter a final judgment of acquittal or grant a new trial. A new trial may be granted by the court if it is required in the interest of justice. The usual ground for granting a new trial is the insufficiency of the evidence to support the verdict. Some courts have also considered errors of law and improper conduct of trial participants during the trial under the motion.

Another ground for granting a motion for a new trial is the discovery of new evidence, which carries with it the procedural difference of an extended time period during which the motion may be made. The time period varies in different jurisdictions but is usually longer than the period for a motion based on any other ground. This longer period allows a reasonable amount of time for the discovery of new evidence. To justify the granting of a motion for a new trial on the ground of newly discovered evidence, it must be shown that the new evidence was discovered after the trial, that it will probably change the result of the trial, that it could not have been discovered before the trial by the exercise of due diligence, that it is material to the issues involved, and that it is not merely cumulative or impeaching.

In some jurisdictions, by motion of either the defendant or the court, the defendant may obtain a revision or correction of sentence. The power to revise a sentence is granted to enable the trial court to change a sentence that is inappropriate in a particular case, even though the sentence may be legal and was imposed in a legal manner. This power to revise a sentence includes a limited power to increase as well as reduce the sentence.

In contrast to the power to revise, the power to correct a sentence is granted to enable the court to change a sentence because the sentence was either illegal or imposed in an illegal manner. An example of an illegal sentence is one that was in excess of the statutory maximum. An example of an illegally imposed sentence is one in which the defendant was not personally addressed by the judge and given an opportunity to be heard before sentencing, where such a procedure is required by statute. The court must exercise both its power to revise and its power to correct a sentence within specific time periods, or the powers are lost. A federal court's power to correct a sentence is limited by the Sentencing Reform Act of 1984.

Remedies After Conviction

There are two major forms of relief for a defendant after being convicted of a crime: **appeal** and **habeas corpus.** Each is discussed separately here.

Appeal

A defendant has a right to appeal after being convicted of a crime and after the trial judge has decided all posttrial motions. The appeal procedure varies in different jurisdictions and is not detailed here. It involves, among other things, the filing of a notice of appeal, the designation of the parts of the trial record to be considered on appeal, the filing of a statement of points on appeal, the filing of briefs, and the arguing of the briefs before the appellate court. If a defendant is unable to afford a lawyer to handle the appeal, provision is made by statute or court rule for a lawyer to be appointed by the court free of charge.

In some jurisdictions, by statute, the prosecution is also given a right to appeal adverse decisions of the trial court. The prosecution's right to appeal, however, is usually much more limited than the defendant's right. Typical statutes allow appeal by the prosecution of adverse rulings made before the jury hears the case or in cases in which the defendant has appealed. The procedure for appeal by the prosecution is essentially the same as it is for appeal by the defendant.

The appeal procedure is *not* a retrial of the case, nor is it ordinarily a reexamination of factual issues. The determination of factual issues is the function of the jury or, in a nonjury case, the lower court judge. The appellate court's function in an appeal is primarily to review the *legal* issues involved in the case. The following example illustrates this point:

> Suppose a law enforcement officer obtained a confession from a defendant but forgot to give the *Miranda* warnings before a custodial interrogation. During the case's trial, the trial judge erroneously permitted the officer who obtained the confession to read it to the jury over the objection of the defense. The jury convicted the defendant. On appeal, the defendant argues that the trial judge committed an error of law in allowing the jury to hear the confession.
>
> The appellate court would very likely reverse the conviction on the basis of the error of law made by the trial judge. Along with reversal, the usual procedure is to remand the case (send it back to the trial court for a new trial) with instructions to exclude the confession from the jury in the new trial. A different jury would then hear the evidence in the case, without the illegally obtained confession, and render another verdict. Therefore, even though a conviction is reversed on appeal, it does not necessarily mean that the defendant is acquitted and can go free. It usually means simply that the defendant has won the right to be tried again.

Generally, to obtain appellate court review of an issue, the appealing party (appellant) must preserve its claim by making a specific timely objection at or before trial. This is called the contemporaneous objection rule. If the appellant failed to make a timely objection, the appellate court will consider the claim only if it constitutes "plain error." Plain errors are defects seriously affecting substantial rights that are so prejudicial to a jury's deliberations "as to undermine the fundamental fairness of the trial and bring about a miscarriage of justice." *United States v. Polowichak,* 783 F.2d 410, 416 (4th Cir. 1986).

On the other hand, even though the appellant preserved its claim by timely objection and the appellate court found that an error occurred in the trial court, the appellate court may still affirm the conviction if it finds that the error was "harmless." This so-called harmless error rule avoids "setting aside of convictions for small errors or defects that have little, if any, likelihood of having changed the result of the trial." *Chapman v. California,* 386 U.S. 18, 22, 87 S.Ct. 824, 827, 17 L.Ed.2d 705, 709 (1967). If the error was of constitutional dimensions, the appellate court must determine "beyond a reasonable doubt that the error complained of did not contribute to the verdict obtained." 386 U.S. at 23, 87 S.Ct. at 828, 17 L.Ed.2d at 710. If the error was not of constitutional dimensions, the appellate court must determine with "fair assurance after pondering all that happened without stripping the erroneous action from the whole that the judgment was not substantially swayed by the error. . . ." *Kotteakos v. United States,* 328 U.S. 750, 765, 66 S.Ct. 1239, 1248, 90 L.Ed. 1557, 1566–67 (1946).

Most types of error are subject to harmless error analysis, including classic trial errors involving the erroneous admission of evidence. *Arizona v. Fulminante,* 499 U.S. 279, 111 S.Ct. 1246, 113 L.Ed.2d 302 (1991). Some types of error, however, involve rights so basic to a fair trial that they can never be considered harmless. Examples of these types of errors are as follows:

- Conflict of interest in representation throughout the entire proceeding. *Holloway v. Arkansas,* 435 U.S. 475, 98 S.Ct. 1173, 55 L.Ed.2d 426 (1978).

- Denial of the right to an impartial judge. *Chapman v. California,* 386 U.S. 18, 87 S.Ct. 824, 17 L.Ed.2d 705 (1967).

- Racial discrimination in grand jury selection. *Vasquez v. Hillery,* 474 U.S. 254, 106 S.Ct. 617, 88 L.Ed.2d 598 (1986).

- Failure to inquire whether a defendant's guilty plea is voluntary. *United States v. Gonzalez,* 820 F.2d 575 (2d Cir. 1987).

If the appellate court finds that the trial court committed no errors of law or only harmless errors, it will affirm the defendant's conviction. The defendant may, however, still have a chance for further appeal. If the appeal was heard in an intermediate appellate court, an additional appeal to the highest appellate court in the jurisdiction is possible. If the defendant's appeal was heard in the highest appellate court in a *state,* an appeal may be made to the U.S. Supreme Court. Note that the U.S. Supreme Court and the highest appellate courts of some states have discretionary jurisdiction and may select the cases they will hear. Defendants have no right to insist on having their appeal heard by such a court.

Appeals may be taken only from cases that have come to a final judgment. This means that an appellate court will not decide any legal issues, nor will it review the denial of any motions until the case has been finally disposed of by the trial court. The reason for this rule is to prevent unnecessary delays in the conduct of trials that would result if the parties could appeal issues during the course of a trial. There are some minor exceptions to the final judgment rule, but they are not discussed here.

When an appellate court decides a case, it delivers a written opinion to explain and justify its decision. In this way the higher court explains the trial judge's errors and also informs the party losing the appeal that it has lost and why. The decisions of the appellate courts are compiled and published in books of reported court decisions, which can be found in law libraries. Attorneys and judges use these reported decisions as authorities for arguing and deciding future cases that raise issues similar to those already decided.

Habeas Corpus

FEDERAL HABEAS CORPUS FOR STATE PRISONERS. State prisoners who challenge the *fact* or *duration* of their confinement on constitutional grounds and seek immediate or speedier release may petition for a writ of habeas corpus (also known as the Great Writ) in federal district court. The federal statute governing the habeas corpus remedy is 28 U.S.C.A. § 2254. (A state prisoner who challenges the *conditions* of confinement or attempts to obtain *damages* should seek relief by means of a civil action under 42 U.S.C.A. § 1983.)

Since the Judiciary Act of February 5, 1867, habeas corpus has been available to state prisoners "in all cases where any person may be restrained of his or her liberty in violation of the constitution or of any treaty or law of the United States." Initially, the constitutional grounds for which habeas corpus relief could be granted were limited to those relating to the jurisdiction of the state court, but the U.S. Supreme Court extended the scope of the writ to all constitutional challenges by its decision in *Fay v. Noia,* 372 U.S. 391, 83 S.Ct. 822, 9 L.Ed.2d 837 (1963).

> Although in form the Great Writ is simply a mode of procedure, its history is inextricably intertwined with the growth of fundamental rights of personal liberty. For its function has been to provide a prompt and efficacious remedy for whatever society deems to be intolerable restraints. Its root principle is that in a civilized society, government must always be accountable to the judiciary for a man's imprisonment: if the imprisonment cannot be shown to conform with the fundamental requirements of law, the individual is entitled to his immediate release. Thus there is nothing novel in the fact that today habeas corpus in the federal courts provides a mode for the redress of denials of due process of law. Vindication of due process is precisely its historic office. 372 U.S. at 401–02, 83 S.Ct. at 828–29, 9 L.Ed.2d at 846–47.

In *Brecht v. Abrahamson,* 507 U.S. 619, 623, 113 S.Ct. 1710, 1714, 123 L.Ed.2d 353, 363 (1993), the Court held that the standard for determining whether habeas corpus relief must be granted for constitutional trial errors is whether the error "had substantial and injurious effect or influence in determining the jury's verdict."

In 1976, the U.S. Supreme Court limited federal habeas corpus review of state prisoners' claims of violations of federal constitutional rights, holding that "where the State has provided an opportunity for full and fair litigation of a Fourth Amendment claim, a state prisoner may not be granted federal habeas corpus relief on the ground that evidence obtained in an unconstitutional search or seizure was introduced at his trial." *Stone v. Powell,* 428 U.S. 465, 494, 96 S.Ct. 3037, 3052, 49 L.Ed.2d 1067, 1088 (1976). With that limitation, however, other constitutional claims of state prisoners may be heard in a federal habeas corpus proceeding even though a state court has fully adjudicated the claims. *Townsend v. Sain,* 372 U.S. 293, 83 S.Ct. 745, 9 L.Ed.2d 770 (1963). Furthermore, "*Stone*'s restriction on the exercise of federal habeas jurisdiction does not extend to a state prisoner's claim that his conviction rests on statements obtained in violation of the safeguards mandated by *Miranda v. Arizona.* . . ." *Withrow v. Williams,* 507 U.S. 680, 681, 113 S.Ct. 1745, 1748, 123 L.Ed.2d 407, 413 (1993).

Prisoners must exhaust available state remedies before a federal court will consider their constitutional claim on habeas corpus. This rule means that, if an appeal or other procedure to hear a claim is still available by right in the state court system, the prisoner must pursue that procedure before a federal habeas corpus application will be considered. Federal habeas corpus review may likewise be barred if a defendant is unable to show cause for noncompliance with a state procedural rule and to show some actual prejudice resulting from the alleged constitutional violation. *Wainwright v. Sykes,* 433 U.S. 72, 97 S.Ct. 2497, 53 L.Ed.2d 594 (1977).

In 1996, Congress, in response to the bombing of the federal building in Oklahoma City, passed the Antiterrorism and Effective Penalty Act. The habeas corpus provisions of that act establish a one-year limitation on filing habeas corpus petitions and provide new procedures governing the disposition of second or successive petitions. Before the district court will hear a second or successive petition, the petitioner is required to obtain an authorization order from a three-judge panel in the appropriate court of appeals. The grant or denial of an authorization order is not appealable to the U.S. Supreme Court and is not subject to rehearing. In *Felker v. Turpin,* 518 U.S. ___, 116 S.Ct. 2333, 135 L.Ed.2d 827 (1997), the Court found the "gatekeeping" requirements constitutional but found nothing in the law to limit or remove its authority to hear *original* petitions for habeas corpus, thereby preserving its own power to review.

The remedies available to courts deciding habeas corpus petitions include reclassifying a petitioner's conviction or ordering the state to retry or resentence a petitioner. Release of the prisoner is granted only if the state fails to comply with the court's order of relief. *Burkett v. Cunningham,* 826 F.2d 1208 (3rd Cir. 1987).

HABEAS CORPUS RELIEF FOR FEDERAL PRISONERS. In 1948, Congress enacted a statute (28 U.S.C.A. § 2255) that was designed to serve as a substitute for habeas corpus for federal prisoners. The primary purpose of the statute was to shift the jurisdictions of the courts hearing habeas corpus applications. The basic scope of the remedy that had been available to federal prisoners by habeas corpus was not changed by the statute. Section 2255 provides, in part, as follows:

> A prisoner in custody under sentence of a court established by Act of Congress claiming the right to be released upon the ground that the sentence was imposed in violation of the Constitution or laws of the United States, or that the court was without jurisdiction to impose such sentence, or that the sentence was in excess of the maximum authorized by law, or is otherwise subject to collateral attack, may move the court which imposed the sentence to vacate, set aside or correct the sentence. . . .
>
> An application for a writ of habeas corpus in behalf of a prisoner who is authorized to apply for relief by motion pursuant to this section, shall not be entertained if it appears that the applicant has failed to apply for relief, by motion, to the court which sentenced him, or that such court has denied him relief, unless it also appears that the remedy by motion is inadequate or ineffective to test the legality of his detention.

In *Hill v. United States,* 386 U.S. 424, 428, 82 S.Ct. 468, 471, 7 L.Ed.2d 417, 421 (1962), the U.S. Supreme Court held that a petitioner is not entitled to habeas corpus relief under section 2255 unless the violation of federal law was a "fundamental defect which inherently results in a complete miscarriage of justice [or] an omission inconsistent with the rudimentary demands of fair procedure." The section 2255 remedy is similar to the habeas corpus remedy for state prisoners, discussed earlier. Although there are some significant distinctions between the two remedies, they are beyond the scope of this book and not discussed here.

STATE POSTCONVICTION RELIEF. Almost all states have postconviction procedures permitting prisoners to challenge constitutional violations. These procedures may derive from statutes, court rules, or the common law. Many of these state remedies are as extensive in scope as federal habeas corpus for state prisoners. Other states provide much narrower remedies. The differences in postconviction remedies among the states are also beyond the scope of this book and not discussed here.

Summary

The purpose of this chapter is to provide law enforcement officers and other criminal justice professionals with a better understanding of some of the legal terms and procedures involved in a criminal case from the initial report of a crime through an appeal to the U.S. Supreme Court. Although much of the information is not immediately useful for the carrying out of daily duties, it can help enhance the criminal justice professional's perception of his or her role in the entire criminal justice system and the importance of properly performing that role to the effective and just operation of the system.

Review and Discussion Questions

1. Draw a diagram of the hierarchy of federal and state courts with criminal jurisdiction in your state. Indicate whether each court has original or appellate criminal jurisdiction, and explain any peculiarities in the jurisdiction of each court (for example, whether it handles only misdemeanors, or whether it has a limited appellate jurisdiction).

2. Draw a diagram of the progress of a felony case in your state from warrantless arrest through appeal to the U.S. Supreme Court. Assume that, at each stage of the proceedings, the decision is adverse to the defendant, who then seeks relief at the next highest tribunal.

3. Discuss the differences and similarities among a complaint, an affidavit, an indictment, and an information.

4. Why is the arraignment sometimes confused with the initial appearance before the magistrate?

5. What is the grand jury, and what is its function? Discuss the similarities and differences between grand jury proceedings and a preliminary examination.

6. What pleas are available to a person charged with a crime, and what is the effect of each?

7. What is the difference between jurisdiction and venue, and between a challenge for cause and a peremptory challenge?

8. Why is a motion to suppress important to a law enforcement officer?

9. Explain the meaning of burden of proof in a criminal case, discussing the standard of proof in a criminal case.

10. Name and briefly describe three ways in which a defendant can obtain relief from the courts after a verdict of guilty.

CHAPTER THREE

Basic Underlying Concepts

OBJECTIVES

1. Understand the history of and reasons for the exclusionary rule and its exceptions and the significance of the exclusionary rule in the law of criminal procedure.

2. Understand generally the nature of the right of privacy in the law of criminal procedure and how it has affected court resolutions of Fourth Amendment issues.

3. Be able to define probable cause and reasonableness and understand generally their importance in the law of criminal procedure, especially with respect to arrests, searches, and seizures.

OUTLINE

1. Exclusionary rule
   a. Alternatives to the exclusionary rule
   b. Federal-state conflict
   c. Criticism of the exclusionary rule
   d. Fruit of the poisonous tree doctrine
      (1) Independent source
      (2) Attenuation
      (3) Inevitable discovery
   e. Good-faith exception
   f. Standing
2. Privacy
3. Probable cause
4. Reasonableness

Before discussing in detail the law of arrest, search and seizure, admissions and confessions, and pretrial identification, it is helpful to lay some further groundwork by presenting four basic concepts that underlie much of what is to follow. The concepts discussed here are the exclusionary rule, privacy, probable cause, and reasonableness. Later in this book these concepts are developed in greater detail and clarified by examples. Because these concepts are so pervasive and so essential to an understanding of criminal procedure, treating them at the outset should make the later chapters more meaningful. ■

Exclusionary Rule

The exclusionary rule requires that any evidence obtained by police using methods that violate a person's constitutional rights be excluded from being used in a criminal prosecution against that person. This rule is of rather recent vintage in the development of our legal system. Under the common law, the seizure of evidence by illegal means did not affect its admissibility in court. Any evidence, however obtained, was allowed as long as it satisfied other criteria for admissibility, such as relevance and trustworthiness. The exclusionary rule was first developed in 1914 in the case of *Weeks v. United States*, 232 U.S. 383, 34 S.Ct. 341, 58 L.Ed. 652, and was limited to a prohibition on the use of evidence illegally obtained by federal law enforcement officers. Not until 1949, in the case of *Wolf v. Colorado*, 338 U.S. 25, 27–28, 69 S.Ct. 1359, 1361, 93 L.Ed. 1782, 1785, did the U.S. Supreme Court rule that the Fourth Amendment was applicable to the states through the due process clause of the Fourteenth Amendment:

> The security of one's privacy against arbitrary intrusion by the police—which is at the core of the Fourth Amendment—is basic to a free society. It is therefore implicit in the "concept of ordered liberty" and as such enforceable against the States through the Due Process Clause.

The Court, however, left enforcement of Fourth Amendment rights to the discretion of the states and did not require application of the exclusionary rule. That mandate did not come until 1961, in the landmark decision of *Mapp v. Ohio*, 367 U.S. 643, 655, 81 S.Ct. 1684, 1691, 6 L.Ed.2d 1081, 1090, in which the Court said:

> Since the Fourth Amendment's right of privacy has been declared enforceable against the States through the Due Process Clause of the Fourteenth, it is enforceable against them by the same sanction of exclusion as is used against the Federal Government. Were it otherwise, then just as without the Weeks rule the assurance against unreasonable federal searches and seizures would be "a form of words," valueless and undeserving of mention in a perpetual charter of inestimable human liberties, so too, without that rule the freedom from state invasions of privacy would be so ephemeral and so neatly severed from its conceptual nexus with the freedom from all brutish means of coercing evidence as not to merit this Court's high regard as a freedom "implicit in the 'concept of ordered liberty.'"

As discussed in Chapter 1, the Supreme Court has made other constitutional guarantees in the Bill of Rights applicable to the states through the due process clause of the Fourteenth Amendment. For example, the Fifth Amendment privilege against self-incrimination was made applicable to the states in *Malloy v. Hogan*, 378 U.S. 1,

84 S.Ct. 1489, 12 L.Ed.2d 653 (1964), and the Sixth Amendment right to counsel was made applicable to the states in *Gideon v. Wainwright,* 372 U.S. 335, 83 S.Ct. 792, 9 L.Ed.2d 799 (1963). The manner in which the exclusionary rule is used to enforce the rights guaranteed in these amendments and others is discussed in detail in later chapters.

The U.S. Supreme Court has also invoked the exclusionary rule to protect certain "due process of law" rights that are not specifically contained in the Constitution or its amendments. For example, a confession that has been coerced and is therefore involuntary will be excluded from evidence, not because of the privilege against self-incrimination but because a coerced confession is a violation of due process of law. Similarly, pretrial identification procedures that are not fairly administered may be violations of due process of law.

The exclusionary rule was historically designed to deter police misconduct. It follows that evidence illegally obtained by persons other than the police will not be rendered inadmissible in court—that is, such evidence is admissible. In *Burdeau v. Mc-Dowell,* 256 U.S. 465, 41 S.Ct. 574, 65 L.Ed. 1048 (1921), a private citizen illegally seized certain papers from another private citizen and turned them over to the government. The Court said:

> The papers having come into the possession of the government without a violation of petitioner's right by governmental authority, we see no reason why the fact that individuals, unconnected with the government, may have wrongfully taken them, should prevent them from being held for use in prosecuting an offense where the documents are of an incriminatory character. 256 U.S. at 476, 41 S.Ct. at 576, 65 L.Ed. at 1051.

If, however, police instigate, encourage, or participate in an illegal search or other constitutional violation, and if the private citizen acts with the intent of assisting the police, he or she will be considered an agent of the government and subject to the exclusionary rule in the same way as a governmental official. *United States v. Lambert,* 771 F.2d 83, 89 (6th Cir. 1985).

Alternatives to the Exclusionary Rule

Theoretically, there are several alternatives to the exclusionary rule. An illegal search and seizure may be criminally actionable, and an officer performing an illegal search or seizure may be subject to prosecution. However, examples of officers being criminally prosecuted for overzealous law enforcement are extremely rare. An officer who makes an illegal search and seizure is subject to internal departmental discipline, which may be backed up in the few jurisdictions that have adopted them by the oversight of and participation of police review boards. Again, however, the examples of disciplinary actions are exceedingly rare.

Persons who have been illegally arrested or have had their privacy invaded will usually have a tort action available under state statute or common law. Moreover, law enforcement officers acting under color of state law who violate a person's Fourth Amendment rights are subject to a suit for damages and other remedies in federal courts under a federal civil rights statute (42 U.S.C. § 1983). While federal officers and others acting under color of federal law are not subject jurisdictionally to this statute, the Supreme Court has held that a right to damages for violation of Fourth Amendment rights arises by implication out of the guarantees secured and that this right is enforceable in federal courts. *Bivens v. Six Unknown Named Agents of the Federal Bureau of Narcotics,* 403 U.S. 388, 91 S.Ct. 1999, 29 L.Ed.2d 619 (1971).

Although a damage remedy might be made more effectual, a number of legal and practical problems stand in the way. Law enforcement officers have available to them the usual common-law defenses, the most important of which is the claim of good faith. Federal officers are entitled to qualified immunity based on an objectively reasonable belief that a warrantless search later determined to violate the Fourth Amendment was supported by probable cause or exigent circumstances. *Anderson v. Creighton,* 483 U.S. 635, 107 S.Ct. 3034, 97 L.Ed.2d 523 (1987). And on the practical side, persons subjected to illegal arrests and searches and seizures are often disreputable persons toward whom juries are unsympathetic, or they are indigent and unable to bring suit. The U.S. Supreme Court, therefore, has emphasized exclusion of unconstitutionally seized evidence in subsequent criminal trials as the only effective enforcement method.

Federal-State Conflict

Mapp v. Ohio did not require the states to follow all interpretations of federal courts in the area of criminal procedure but only interpretations dealing with constitutional guarantees. Some of the rulings handed down by the U.S. Supreme Court are based on the Court's statutory authority to promulgate rules for the supervision of federal law enforcement. These rulings apply only in federal courts. In *Ker v. California,* 374 U.S. 23, 83 S.Ct. 1623, 10 L.Ed.2d 726 (1963), the Court explicitly stated that *Mapp* established no assumption by the Supreme Court of supervisory authority over state courts, and it therefore implied no total obliteration of state laws relating to arrests and searches in favor of federal law. The Court went on to say:

> The States are not thereby precluded from developing workable rules governing arrests, searches and seizures to meet "the practical demands of effective criminal investigation and law enforcement" in the States, provided that those rules do not violate the constitutional proscription of unreasonable searches and seizures and the concomitant command that evidence so seized is inadmissible against one who has standing to complain. 374 U.S. at 34, 83 S.Ct. at 1630, 10 L.Ed.2d at 738.

The practice of state courts affording the accused greater protection under state law than that required by the U.S. Constitution is sometimes called the **new federalism.** It is derived from the well-established rule that state court decisions based on "adequate and independent state grounds" are immune to federal review. *Murdock v. Memphis,* 87 U.S. (20 Wall.) 590, 22 L.Ed. 429 (1875). Under this rule, state courts are free, as a matter of state constitutional, statutory, or case law, to expand individual rights by imposing greater restrictions on police than those imposed under federal constitutional law. State courts may not, however, decrease individual rights below the level established by the U.S. Constitution. Nor may state courts impose greater restrictions on police activity as a matter of federal constitutional law when the U.S. Supreme Court specifically refrains from imposing such restrictions. *Oregon v. Hass,* 420 U.S. 714, 95 S.Ct. 1215, 43 L.Ed.2d 570 (1975).

A state court has several options in responding to a U.S. Supreme Court decision raising issues of federal law:

- Apply the ruling as it thinks the Supreme Court would. This might include adopting the ruling as a matter of state law.

- Factually distinguish the case before it from the Supreme Court case, whereupon the decision would be subject to reversal by the Supreme Court.

- Reject the Supreme Court ruling on adequate and independent state grounds by interpreting the state constitution or state statutes to provide rights unavailable under the U.S. Constitution as interpreted by the Supreme Court. This approach clearly expresses disapproval of the Supreme Court ruling and insulates the state court decision from Supreme Court review. When the state court opinion is ambiguous as to whether it is based on an adequate and independent ground, the Supreme Court applies the so-called plain statement rule:

> [W]hen . . . a state court decision fairly appears to rest primarily on federal law, or to be interwoven with the federal law, and when the adequacy and independence of any possible state law ground is not clear from the face of the opinion, we will accept as the most reasonable explanation that the state court decided the case the way it did because it believed that federal law required it to do so. If a state court chooses merely to rely on federal precedents as it would on the precedents of all other jurisdictions, then it need only make clear by a plain statement in its judgment or opinion that the federal cases are being used only for the purpose of guidance, and do not themselves compel the result that the court has reached. In this way, both justice and judicial administration will be greatly improved. If the state court decision indicates clearly and expressly that it is alternatively based on bona fide separate, adequate, and independent grounds, we, of course, will not undertake to review the decision. *Michigan v. Long,* 463 U.S. 1032, 1040–41, 103 S.Ct. 3469, 3476, 77 L.Ed.2d 1201, 1214 (1983).

In recent years, many state courts, reacting against the Burger and Rehnquist Courts' reluctant and sparing approach to protecting the rights of the accused, have resorted to this option to keep alive the Warren Court's active commitment to the protection and expansion of individual rights.

One example of this trend is the case of *South Dakota v. Opperman,* 428 U.S. 364, 96 S.Ct. 3092, 49 L.Ed.2d 1000 (1976). In that case, the South Dakota Supreme Court ruled that an automobile inventory conducted by South Dakota law enforcement officers violated the Fourth Amendment, but the U.S. Supreme Court reversed the decision, holding that the police conduct was reasonable. On remand, the South Dakota Supreme Court, in *State v. Opperman,* 247 N.W.2d 673 (S.D. 1976), decided that the police inventory procedure violated the South Dakota Constitution and held that the evidence seized was inadmissible. This South Dakota court's decision is noteworthy because the search and seizure provision of the South Dakota Constitution is essentially similar to the Fourth Amendment of the U.S. Constitution and because neither the prosecution nor the defense in the case had raised the issue of the state constitution. Other examples of the new federalism are presented in later chapters dealing with particular areas of conflict.

Criticism of the Exclusionary Rule

The exclusionary rule has, throughout its existence, been the object of criticism and attempted reform. In recent years, no less a public authority than the chief justice of the U.S. Supreme Court has complained of the ineffectiveness of the exclusionary rule to achieve its purpose: the deterrence of police misconduct. In his dissent in the case of *Bivens v. Six Unknown Named Agents of the Federal Bureau of Narcotics,* 403 U.S. 388, 416–18, 91 S.Ct. 1999, 2015, 29 L.Ed.2d 619, 638–39 (1971), Chief Justice Warren E. Burger said:

> The rule does not apply any direct sanction to the individual official whose illegal conduct results in the exclusion of evidence in a criminal trial. With rare

exceptions law enforcement agencies do not impose direct sanctions on the individual officer responsible for a particular judicial application of the suppression doctrine. . . . Thus there is virtually nothing done to bring about a change in his practices. The immediate sanction triggered by application of the rule is visited upon the prosecutor whose case against a criminal is either weakened or destroyed. The doctrine deprives the police in no real sense; except that apprehending wrongdoers is their business, police have no more stake in successful prosecutions than prosecutors or the public.

The suppression doctrine vaguely assumes that law enforcement is a monolithic governmental enterprise. . . . But the prosecutor who loses his case because of police misconduct is not an official in the police department; he can rarely set in motion any corrective action or administrative penalties. Moreover, he does not have control or direction over police procedures or police actions that lead to the exclusion of evidence. It is the rare exception when a prosecutor takes part in arrests, searches, or seizures so that he can guide police action.

Whatever educational effect the rule conceivably might have in theory is greatly diminished in fact by the realities of law enforcement work. Policemen do not have the time, inclination, or training to read and grasp the nuances of the appellate opinions that ultimately define the standards of conduct they are to follow. The issues that these decisions resolve often admit of neither easy nor obvious answers, as sharply divided courts on what is or is not "reasonable" demonstrate. Nor can judges, in all candor, forget that opinions sometimes lack helpful clarity.

The presumed educational effect of judicial opinions is also reduced by the long time lapse—often several years—between the original police action and its final judicial evaluation. Given a policeman's pressing responsibilities, it would be surprising if he ever becomes aware of the final result after such a delay. Finally, the exclusionary rule's deterrent impact is diluted by the fact that there are large areas of police activity that do not result in criminal prosecutions—hence the rule has virtually no applicability and no effect in such situations.

The criticism and attempts at reform of the exclusionary rule have resulted in limitations on the application of the rule and refusals to further extend the application of the rule beyond the criminal trial context. For example, in *United States v. Calandra,* 414 U.S. 338, 94 S.Ct. 613, 38 L.Ed.2d 561 (1974), the Supreme Court held that the Fourth Amendment did not prevent the use of illegally obtained evidence by a grand jury. In *United States v. Janis,* 428 U.S. 433, 96 S.Ct. 3021, 49 L.Ed.2d 1046 (1976), the Court held that illegally obtained evidence need not be suppressed at trial in a civil case brought by the United States. In *Harris v. New York,* 401 U.S. 222, 91 S.Ct. 643, 28 L.Ed.2d 1 (1971), the Court allowed the use of illegally obtained evidence to impeach the defendant's testimony at trial. In *Pennsylvania Board of Probation v. Scott,* the Court held that "the federal exclusionary rule does not bar the introduction at parole revocation hearings of evidence seized in violation of parolees' Fourth Amendment rights." __ U.S. __, __, 118 S.Ct. 2014, 2020, __ L.Ed.2d __, __ (1998). And in *Stone v. Powell,* 428 U.S. 465, 494, 96 S.Ct. 3037, 3052, 49 L.Ed.2d 1067, 1088 (1976), the Court held that "where the State has provided an opportunity for full and fair litigation of a Fourth Amendment claim, a state prisoner may not be granted federal habeas corpus relief on the ground that evidence obtained in an unconstitutional search or seizure was introduced at his trial." The *Stone v. Powell* decision is noteworthy not only because it limited the application of the exclusionary rule but also because it strengthened the authority of state courts in interpreting the Fourth Amendment.

Despite the Supreme Court's cutting back on certain applications of the exclusionary rule in recent years, the basic holding of *Mapp v. Ohio* remains good law, and the basic tenets of the exclusionary rule remain valid legal doctrine. Any further limitations or changes in the exclusionary rule will depend largely on the makeup of the Supreme Court and the opportunities presented to the Court in the cases brought before it.

Fruit of the Poisonous Tree Doctrine

The exclusionary rule is not limited to evidence that is the direct product of illegal police behavior, such as a coerced confession or the items seized as a result of an illegal search. The rule also requires exclusion of evidence that is obtained *indirectly* as a result of a violation of one's constitutional rights. This type of evidence is sometimes called **derivative evidence** or **secondary evidence.** In *Silverthorne Lumber Co. v. United States,* 251 U.S. 385, 392, 40 S.Ct. 182, 183, 64 L.Ed. 319, 321 (1920), the U.S. Supreme Court invalidated a subpoena that had been issued on the basis of information obtained through an illegal search:

> The essence of a provision forbidding the acquisition of evidence in a certain way is that not merely evidence so acquired shall not be used before the Court but that it shall not be used at all. Of course this does not mean that the facts thus obtained become sacred and inaccessible. If knowledge of them is gained from an independent source they may be proved like any others, but the knowledge gained by the Government's own wrong cannot be used by it in the way proposed.

Thus, the prosecution may not use in court evidence obtained directly *or indirectly* from an unconstitutional search. The prohibition against using this derivative or secondary evidence is often called the rule against admission of "fruit of the poisonous tree," the tree being the illegal search and the fruit being the evidence obtained as an indirect result of that search. The fruit, or the evidence indirectly obtained, is sometimes referred to as tainted evidence. Although the rule against the admission of fruit of the poisonous tree was originally developed in applying the exclusionary rule to unconstitutional searches, it has been applied equally to evidence obtained as the indirect result of other constitutional violations. Thus, evidence may be inadmissible if it is acquired indirectly as a result of an illegal arrest, an illegal identification procedure, or an involuntary confession.

The fruit of the poisonous tree doctrine applies only when a person's constitutional rights have been violated and not when a violation of rights is not of constitutional dimensions, such as when *Miranda* procedures are violated. As stated by the Supreme Court, "If errors are made by law enforcement officers in administering the prophylactic *Miranda* procedures, they should not breed the same irremediable consequences as police infringement of the Fifth Amendment itself." *Oregon v. Elstad,* 470 U.S. 298, 309, 105 S.Ct. 1285, 1293, 84 L.Ed.2d 222, 232 (1985).

INDEPENDENT SOURCE. Several exceptions to the fruit of the poisonous tree doctrine are recognized, allowing the admission of tainted evidence under certain conditions. One exception already referred to in the *Silverthorne* case is the **independent source doctrine.** This exception allows the admission of tainted evidence if that evidence was also obtained through a source wholly independent of the primary constitutional violation. The independent source exception is compatible with the underlying rationale of the exclusionary rule: the deterrence of police misconduct. As stated by the U.S. Supreme Court:

> The independent source doctrine teaches us that the interest of society in deterring unlawful police conduct and the public interest in having juries receive all probative evidence of a crime are properly balanced by putting the police in the

same, not a *worse,* position than they would have been in if no police error or misconduct had occurred. *Nix v. Williams,* 467 U.S. 431, 443, 104 S.Ct. 2501, 2509, 81 L.Ed.2d 377, 387 (1984).

In a case applying the independent source doctrine, law enforcement officers illegally entered an apartment, secured it, and then remained there for about nineteen hours until a search warrant arrived. Despite the illegal entry, the U.S. Supreme Court admitted the evidence found during the execution of the warrant. The Court found an independent source for the tainted evidence because the information on which the warrant was based came from sources entirely separate from the illegal entry and was known to the officers well before that entry. The Court held that "[w]hether the initial entry was legal or not is irrelevant to the admissibility of the challenged evidence because there was an independent source for the warrant under which that evidence was seized." *Segura v. United States,* 468 U.S. 796, 813–14, 104 S.Ct. 3380, 3390, 82 L.Ed.2d 599, 614 (1984). In *Murray v. United States,* 487 U.S. 533, 108 S.Ct. 2529, 101 L.Ed.2d 472 (1988), federal agents made an unlawful search of a warehouse. They then obtained a warrant to search the warehouse without revealing the unlawful search to the issuing magistrate. The Supreme Court upheld the trial court's denial of motions to suppress evidence found in the warehouse.

> Knowledge that the marijuana was in the warehouse was assuredly acquired at the time of the unlawful entry. But it was also acquired at the time of entry pursuant to the warrant, and if that later acquisition was not the result of the earlier entry there is no reason why the independent source doctrine should not apply. Invoking the exclusionary rule would put the police (and society) not in the *same* position they would have occupied if no violation occurred, but in a *worse* one. 487 U.S. at 541, 108 S.Ct. at 2535, 101 L.Ed.2d at 483.

ATTENUATION. Another exception to the fruit of the poisonous tree doctrine was first established in *Nardone v. United States,* 308 U.S. 338, 60 S.Ct. 266, 84 L.Ed. 307 (1939), and is referred to as the **attenuation doctrine.** This doctrine states that, even where the tainted evidence would not have been discovered except through the constitutional violation, there being no independent source, the evidence may still be admissible if the means of obtaining the evidence were sufficiently remote from and distinguishable from the primary illegality. The key question, as posed in *Wong Sun v. United States,* 371 U.S. 471, 488, 83 S.Ct. 407, 417, 9 L.Ed.2d 441, 455 (1963), is "whether granting establishment of the primary illegality, the evidence to which instant objection is made has been come at by exploitation of that illegality or instead by means sufficiently distinguishable to be purged of the primary taint." If the tainted evidence is obtained by means sufficiently distinguishable from the primary illegality, the causal connection between the primary illegality and the evidence indirectly derived from it is said to be attenuated, and the evidence is admissible even though tainted. The rationale behind this exception is that the deterrent purpose of the exclusionary rule is not served where an officer could not have been aware of the possible benefit to be derived from his or her illegal actions at the time of taking those actions.

In the *Wong Sun* case, narcotics agents illegally broke into Toy's laundry and followed Toy into his living quarters, where they arrested and handcuffed him. Almost immediately thereafter, Toy told the agents that Yee had been selling narcotics. The agents subsequently seized heroin from Yee, who told them that it had been brought to him by Toy and Wong Sun. Wong Sun was illegally arrested, arraigned, and released on his own recognizance. Several days later, Wong Sun returned voluntarily and made an oral confession to a narcotics agent.

Toy argued that his statement and the heroin later seized from Yee were fruit of the illegal entry into his dwelling and his illegal arrest. The Court agreed and held both inadmissible. Wong Sun claimed that his statement was the fruit of his illegal arrest. The Court disagreed:

> We have no occasion to disagree with the finding of the Court of Appeals that his arrest, also, was without probable cause or reasonable grounds. At all events no evidentiary consequences turn upon that question. For Wong Sun's unsigned confession was not the fruit of that arrest, and was therefore properly admitted at trial. On the evidence that Wong Sun had been released on his own recognizance after a lawful arraignment, and had returned voluntarily several days later to make the statement, we hold that the connection between the arrest and the statement has "become so attenuated as to dissipate the taint." 371 U.S. at 491, 83 S.Ct. at 419, 9 L.Ed.2d at 457.

The U.S. Supreme Court has set out three factors for courts to consider in determining whether the connection between the primary illegality and the resulting evidence has been sufficiently attenuated: (1) the time elapsed between the illegality and the acquisition of the evidence, (2) the presence of intervening circumstances, and (3) the purpose and flagrancy of the official misconduct. *Brown v. Illinois,* 422 U.S. 590, 95 S.Ct. 2254, 45 L.Ed.2d 416 (1975). (See the discussion of the *Brown* case in Chapter 4 under "Effect of Illegal Arrest.")

Courts applying the attenuation doctrine make a distinction between physical and verbal evidence. In *United States v. Ceccolini,* 435 U.S. 268, 98 S.Ct. 1054, 55 L.Ed.2d 268 (1978), the Supreme Court held that because of the cost to the truth-finding process of disqualifying knowledgeable witnesses, the exclusionary rule should be invoked with much greater reluctance when the fruit of the poisonous tree is the testimony of a live witness rather than an inanimate object. Therefore, a court will not exclude the testimony of a witness discovered as the result of a constitutional violation, unless the court finds a more direct link between the discovery and the violation than is required to exclude physical evidence. Furthermore, the court must find that the constitutional violation is the kind that will be deterred by application of the exclusionary rule. In a case illustrating the kind of constitutional violation that should be deterred, police obtained an involuntary statement from the defendant for the very purpose of discovering the defendant's crimes and witnesses to testify to those crimes. The court held that legitimate concerns for the deterrence of police misconduct compelled the application of the exclusionary rule to the testimony of sexually abused children who were revealed through the defendant's coerced statement. *Commonwealth v. Lahti,* 501 N.E.2d 511 (Mass. 1986).

INEVITABLE DISCOVERY. Another exception to the fruit of the poisonous tree doctrine is the **inevitable discovery doctrine.** This doctrine is "in reality an extrapolation from the independent source doctrine. . . ." *Murray v. United States,* 487 U.S. 533, 539, 108 S.Ct. 2529, 2534, 101 L.Ed.2d 472, 481 (1988). Whereas the independent source doctrine allows the admission of tainted evidence if the tainted evidence was also obtained from an independent source, the inevitable discovery doctrine allows admission of the evidence if it would inevitably have been discovered in the normal course of events. Under this exception, the prosecution must establish by a preponderance of the evidence that, even though the evidence was actually discovered as the indirect result of a constitutional violation, the evidence would ultimately or inevitably have been discovered by lawful means—for example, as the result of the predictable and routine behavior of a law enforcement agency, some other agency, or a private person.

The U.S. Supreme Court specifically adopted the inevitable discovery doctrine in *Nix v. Williams,* 467 U.S. 431, 104 S.Ct. 2501, 81 L.Ed.2d 377 (1984). In that case, police initiated a search for a ten-year-old girl who had disappeared. While the search was going on, the defendant was arrested and, in response to illegal questioning, led police to the girl's body. The search was called off, but the girl's body was found in a place that was essentially within the area to be searched. Although the defendant's illegally obtained statements, leading to the discovery of the body, rendered evidence relating to the body inadmissible, the Court allowed the admission of the evidence under the inevitable discovery doctrine. The Court found that the volunteer search parties were approaching the actual location of the body, that they would have resumed the search had the defendant not earlier led the police to the body, and that the body would inevitably have been found.

The Court justified its adoption of the inevitable discovery doctrine using the rationale underlying the independent source exception:

> [I]f the government can prove that the evidence would have been obtained inevitably and, therefore, would have been admitted regardless of any overreaching by the police, there is no rational basis to keep that evidence from the jury in order to ensure the fairness of the trial proceedings. In that situation, the State has gained no advantage at trial and the defendant has suffered no prejudice. Indeed, suppression of the evidence would operate to undermine the adversary system by putting the State in a *worse* position than it would have occupied without any police misconduct. 467 U.S. at 447, 104 S.Ct. at 2511, 81 L.Ed.2d at 389–90.

Furthermore, in response to the defendant's contention that the prosecution must prove the absence of bad faith on the part of the police, the Court said that such a requirement

> would place courts in the position of withholding from juries relevant and undoubted truth that would have been available to police absent any unlawful police activity. Of course, that view would put the police in a worse position than they would have been in if no unlawful conduct had transpired. And, of equal importance, it wholly fails to take into account the enormous societal cost of excluding truth in the search for truth in the administration of justice. 467 U.S. at 445, 104 S.Ct. at 2509–10, 81 L.Ed.2d at 388.

Finally, the Court dismissed arguments that the inevitable discovery doctrine will promote police misconduct. A police officer who is faced with an opportunity to obtain evidence illegally will rarely, if ever, be in a position to calculate whether the evidence sought would inevitably be discovered. Even when an officer is aware that evidence will inevitably be discovered, there will be little to gain from taking dubious shortcuts to obtain the evidence. Other significant disincentives to obtaining evidence illegally include the possibility of departmental discipline and civil liability.

Lower courts have been careful to scrutinize claims of inevitable discovery. For example, in *United States v. Satterfield,* 743 F.2d 827, 846 (11th Cir. 1984), the court stated:

> To qualify for admissibility, there must be a reasonable probability that the evidence in question would have been discovered by lawful means, and the prosecution must demonstrate that the lawful means which made discovery inevitable were possessed by the police and were being actively pursued *prior* to the occurrence of the illegal conduct.

In the *Satterfield* case, despite the claim by police that they would have undoubtedly found a shotgun during a search of the defendant's home, no warrant was sought until several hours after an illegal search that uncovered the weapon. Therefore, the police did not possess *before* the illegal action the legal means that would have led to the discovery of the shotgun. The shotgun was ruled inadmissible.

Occasionally, courts will find inevitable discovery based on the behavior not of law enforcement officers but ordinary civilians. In *State v. Miller,* 680 P.2d 676 (Or. 1984), after obtaining, in violation of *Miranda,* the defendant's statement that he had "hurt someone" in his hotel room, a law enforcement officer conducted a warrantless search of the hotel room and discovered a dead body. The court held that evidence of the discovery of the body was admissible despite the *Miranda* violation, because the maid would inevitably have discovered the body and would normally be expected to come forward and cooperate with police authorities.

Good-Faith Exception

In *United States v. Leon,* 468 U.S. 897, 104 S.Ct. 3405, 82 L.Ed.2d 677 (1984), the U.S. Supreme Court adopted another exception to the exclusionary rule: the **good-faith exception** for searches conducted pursuant to a warrant. Under this exception, whenever a law enforcement officer acting with objective good faith has obtained a search warrant from a detached and neutral judge or magistrate and has acted within its scope, evidence seized pursuant to the warrant will not be excluded, even though the warrant is later determined to be invalid. The Court reasoned that excluding such evidence would not further the purposes of the exclusionary rule—deterrence of police misconduct—since the officer is acting as a reasonable officer would and should act under the circumstances. In determining what is good faith on the part of an officer, the Court said:

> [O]ur good-faith inquiry is confined to the objectively ascertainable question whether a reasonably well-trained officer would have known that the search was illegal despite the magistrate's authorization. In making this determination, all of the circumstances—including whether the warrant application has previously been rejected by a different magistrate—may be considered. 468 U.S. at 922–23 n.23, 104 S.Ct. at 3421 n.23, 82 L.Ed.2d at 698 n.23.

The Court described several circumstances under which an officer would *not* have reasonable grounds for believing that a warrant was properly issued:

- In issuing the warrant, the magistrate or judge was misled by information in an affidavit that the affiant knew was false or would have known was false except for a reckless disregard of the truth (see Chapter 5).

- The issuing magistrate wholly abandoned a neutral and detached judicial role and acted either as a "rubber stamp" or as an arm of the prosecution (see Chapter 5).

- The warrant was based on an affidavit so lacking in indicia of probable cause as to render official belief in its existence entirely unreasonable (see Chapter 6).

- The warrant was so facially deficient—in failing to particularize the place to be searched or the things to be seized—that the executing officers could not reasonably presume it to be valid (see Chapter 5).

Under such circumstances, not only would the warrant be declared invalid, but any evidence seized pursuant to the warrant would be ruled inadmissible.

The U.S. Supreme Court cited an example of good-faith behavior in *Massachusetts v. Sheppard,* the companion case to *United States v. Leon:*

> The officers in this case took every step that could reasonably be expected of them. Detective O'Malley prepared an affidavit which was reviewed and approved by the District Attorney. He presented that affidavit to a neutral judge. The judge concluded that the affidavit established probable cause to search Sheppard's residence . . . and informed O'Malley that he would authorize the search as requested. O'Malley then produced the warrant form and informed the judge that it might need to be changed. He was told by the judge that the necessary changes would be made. He then observed the judge make some changes and received the warrant and the affidavit. At this point, a reasonable police officer would have concluded, as O'Malley did, that the warrant authorized a search for the materials outlined in the affidavit. 468 U.S. 981, 989, 104 S.Ct. 3424, 3428, 82 L.Ed.2d 737, 744 (1984).

In *Arizona v. Evans,* 514 U.S. 1, 115 S.Ct. 1185, 131 L.Ed.2d 34 (1995), the Court found that the officer acted in good faith in arresting under authority of a warrant, even though the warrant had been quashed (annulled) several weeks before. In that case, when the defendant was stopped for a minor traffic violation, he told the officer that his license had been suspended. The officer checked his cruiser's computer data terminal, which revealed an outstanding misdemeanor warrant for the defendant's arrest. The officer arrested the defendant, searched his car, and found marijuana. Later, police were informed that the arrest warrant had been quashed seventeen days before and that the police had not been properly notified by court personnel. Since there was no indication that the arresting officer was not acting objectively reasonably when he relied on the computer record, the Court applied the good-faith exception and refused to exclude the evidence, despite the clerical error by court personnel. The Court said that the exclusion of evidence at trial would not sufficiently deter future errors so as to warrant such a severe sanction.

> First . . . the exclusionary rule was historically designed as a means of deterring police misconduct, not mistakes by court employees. . . . Second, respondent offers no evidence that court employees are inclined to ignore or subvert the Fourth Amendment or that lawlessness among these actors requires application of the extreme sanction of exclusion. . . . Finally, and most important, there is no basis for believing that application of the exclusionary rule in these circumstances will have a significant effect on court employees responsible for informing the police that a warrant has been quashed. Because court clerks are not adjuncts to the law enforcement team engaged in the often competitive enterprise of ferreting out crime, . . . they have no stake in the outcome of particular criminal prosecutions. 514 U.S. at 14–15, 115 S.Ct. at 1193, 131 L.Ed.2d 46–47.

Some courts, when reviewing suppression rulings, now proceed directly to the good-faith issue and bypass the issue of whether probable cause supported the warrant. For example, in *United States v. McLaughlin,* 851 F.2d 283, 284–85 (9th Cir. 1988), the court said:

> We need not decide whether the warrant was based on probable cause, because we find that even if the warrant lacked probable cause, the evidence was properly admitted under the exception to the exclusionary rule announced in *United States v. Leon* . . . . The officers in this case relied on the determination of a neutral magistrate that they had probable cause to search. . . . We cannot say that

their reliance was objectively unreasonable. There is no evidence that the affidavit upon which the warrant was based contained any knowing or reckless falsehood, or that the magistrate abandoned his judicial role. The warrant, even if not based on probable cause, was not so deficient that no officer could reasonably have believed it to be valid, and the affidavit did not lack all indicia of probable cause.

In *Illinois v. Krull,* 480 U.S. 340, 107 S.Ct. 1160, 94 L.Ed.2d 364 (1987), the U.S. Supreme Court extended the good-faith exception to the exclusionary rule, holding that the exclusionary rule does not apply to evidence obtained by police who acted in objectively reasonable reliance on a statute that authorized warrantless administrative searches but that was subsequently found to violate the Fourth Amendment. Following the approach used in the *Leon* case, the Court said that applying the exclusionary rule in this situation would have as little deterrent effect on an officer's actions as would excluding evidence when an officer acts in objectively reasonable reliance on a warrant.

Unless a statute is clearly unconstitutional, an officer cannot be expected to question the judgment of the legislature that passed the law. If the statute is subsequently declared unconstitutional, excluding evidence obtained pursuant to it prior to such judicial declaration will not deter future Fourth Amendment violations by an officer who has simply fulfilled his responsibility to enforce the statute as written. 480 U.S. at 349–50, 107 S.Ct. at 1167, 94 L.Ed.2d at 375.

Note that several states have opted not to embrace the good-faith exception. For example, the Georgia Supreme Court said:

[W]e declined to adopt the "good faith" exception to the exclusionary rule . . . holding that because the Georgia legislature has statutorily protected the right to be free from unreasonable search and seizure . . . "the State of Georgia has chosen to impose greater requirements upon its law enforcement officers than that required by the U.S. Supreme Court." *Davis v. State,* 422 S.E.2d 546, 549 n.1 (Ga. 1992).

The discussion of the exceptions to the exclusionary rule serves to highlight an important feature of the rule: The exclusionary rule does not necessarily bar or stop a prosecution. At most, it will cause the suppression of evidence obtained as the direct or indirect result of a constitutional violation. If that evidence is essential to the prosecution's case against a defendant, the prosecution may decide that it is futile to go on with the prosecution. If, however, the prosecution has sufficient other evidence, either legally obtained or falling within one of the exceptions to the exclusionary rule, the prosecution may go forward despite the illegal police conduct.

Standing

To invoke the exclusionary rule to challenge the admissibility of evidence, a defendant must have **standing.** A defendant has standing when his or her own constitutional rights have been violated. In *Rakas v. Illinois,* a police search of a car yielded a box of rifle shells found in the glove compartment and a sawed-off rifle found under the passenger seat. The U.S. Supreme Court held that the petitioners, who were passengers in the car and had no ownership interest in the rifle shells or sawed-off rifle, and no legitimate expectation of privacy in the area searched, had suffered no invasion of their Fourth Amendment rights.

"Fourth Amendment rights are personal rights which, like some other constitutional rights, may not be vicariously asserted." . . . A person who is aggrieved by an illegal search and seizure only through the introduction of damaging evidence secured by a search of a third person's premises or property has not had any of his Fourth Amendment rights infringed. . . . And since the exclusionary rule is an attempt to effectuate the guarantees of the Fourth Amendment, . . . it is proper to permit only defendants whose Fourth Amendment rights have been violated to benefit from the rule's protections. *Rakas v. Illinois,* 439 U.S. 128, 133–34, 99 S.Ct. 421, 425, 58 L.Ed.2d 387, 394–95 (1978).

In *Rakas,* the U.S. Supreme Court went on to say that "capacity to claim the protection of the Fourth Amendment depends not upon a property right in the invaded place but upon whether the person who claims the protection of the Amendment has a legitimate expectation of privacy in the invaded place." 439 U.S. at 143, 99 S.Ct. at 430, 58 L.Ed.2d at 401. A subjective expectation of privacy is legitimate if it is "one that society is prepared to recognize as 'reasonable.'" *Katz v. United States,* 389 U.S. 347, 361, 88 S.Ct. 507, 516, 19 L.Ed.2d 576, 588 (1976). For example, the Supreme Court held that a person's status as an overnight guest is alone enough to show that the person had an expectation of privacy in the home that society is prepared to recognize as reasonable. The Court said:

> To hold that an overnight guest has a legitimate expectation of privacy in his host's home merely recognizes the everyday expectations of privacy that we all share. Staying overnight in another's home is a longstanding social custom that serves functions recognized as valuable by society. We stay in others' homes when we travel to a strange city for business or pleasure, when we visit our parents, children, or more distant relatives out of town, when we are in between jobs or homes, or when we house-sit for a friend. We will all be hosts and we will all be guests many times in our lives. From either perspective, we think that society recognizes that a houseguest has a legitimate expectation of privacy in his host's home. *Minnesota v. Olson,* 495 U.S. 91, 98, 110 S.Ct. 1684, 1689, 109 L.Ed.2d 85, 94 (1990).

The U.S. Supreme Court held, however, that even a coconspirator or codefendant in a crime has no standing to object to a search, unless that person has a reasonable expectation of privacy in the place to be searched. *United States v. Padilla,* 508 U.S. 77, 113 S.Ct. 1936, 123 L.Ed.2d 635 (1993).

The topic of privacy is discussed further in the following section.

Privacy

In a criminal case, for the Fourth Amendment to be applicable to a particular fact situation, there must be a seizure or a search and seizure accompanied by an attempt by the prosecution to introduce what was seized as evidence in court. Whether there was a search or seizure within the meaning of the Fourth Amendment and, if so, whether the search or seizure violated someone's constitutional rights depend on the nature of the interest that the Fourth Amendment protects. Under the common law, it was clear that the security of one's property was a sacred right and that protection of that right was a primary purpose of government. In an early English case, the court said:

The great end for which men entered into society was to secure their property. That right is preserved sacred and incommunicable in all instances where it has not been taken away or abridged by some public law for the good of the whole. . . . By the laws of England, every invasion of private property, be it ever so minute, is a trespass. No man can set foot upon my ground without my license but he is liable to an action though the damage be nothing. . . . *Entick v. Carrington,* 19 Howell's State Trials 1029, 1035, 95 Eng.Rep. 807, 817–18 (1765).

The protection of property interests as the basis of the Fourth Amendment was adopted by the U.S. Supreme Court, and until relatively recently, analysis of Fourth Amendment issues centered around whether an intrusion into a "constitutionally protected area" had occurred. Three cases involving electronic surveillance illustrate this approach. In *Olmstead v. United States,* 277 U.S. 438, 48 S.Ct. 564, 72 L.Ed. 944 (1928), one reason for the Court's holding that wiretapping was not covered by the Fourth Amendment was that there had been no physical invasion of the defendant's premises. The Court said:

The evidence was secured by the use of the sense of hearing and that only. There was no entry of the houses or offices of the defendants. . . . The intervening wires are not part of his house or office, any more than are the highways along which they are stretched. 277 U.S. at 464–65, 48 S.Ct. at 568, 72 L.Ed. at 950.

In *Silverman v. United States,* 365 U.S. 505, 81 S.Ct. 679, 5 L.Ed.2d 734 (1961), however, a spike mike was pushed through a party wall until it hit a heating duct, and the Court held that the electronic surveillance was an illegal search and seizure. And in *Clinton v. Virginia,* 377 U.S. 158, 84 S.Ct. 1186, 12 L.Ed.2d 213 (1964), the Court ruled as inadmissible evidence obtained by means of a mechanical listening device stuck into the wall of an apartment adjoining the defendant's. The rationale for the *Silverman* and *Clinton* cases was that the listening devices had actually physically invaded the target premises, even though the invasion was slight.

This emphasis on property concepts in interpreting the Fourth Amendment began to lose favor in the 1960s. Justice William O. Douglas, concurring in the *Silverman* case, said that "our sole concern should be with whether the privacy of the home was invaded." 365 U.S. at 513, 81 S.Ct. at 683, 5 L.Ed.2d at 740. In a later case, the Court said:

The premise that property interests control the right of the Government to search and seize has been discredited. . . . We have recognized that the principal object of the Fourth Amendment is the protection of privacy rather than property, and have increasingly discarded fictional and procedural barriers rested on property concepts. *Warden v. Hayden,* 387 U.S. 294, 304, 87 S.Ct. 1642, 1648, 18 L.Ed.2d 782, 790 (1967).

Finally, in *Katz v. United States,* 389 U.S. 347, 88 S.Ct. 507, 19 L.Ed.2d 576 (1967), another electronic surveillance case, the Court dispensed with the requirement of an actual physical trespass in applying the Fourth Amendment. The issue was the admissibility of telephone conversations overhead by FBI agents who had attached an electronic listening and recording device to the *outside* of a public telephone booth. The Court said:

[T]his effort to decide whether or not a given "area," viewed in the abstract, is "constitutionally protected" deflects attention from the problem presented by this case. For the Fourth Amendment protects people, not places. What a person knowingly exposes to the public, even in his own home or office, is not a subject of Fourth Amendment protection. . . . But what he seeks to preserve as private, even in an area accessible to the public may be constitutionally protected. 389 U.S. at 351–52, 88 S.Ct. at 511, 19 L.Ed.2d at 582.

The Court held that the government's activities in electronically listening to and recording the defendant's words violated the privacy on which the defendant justifiably relied while using the telephone booth and thus constituted a search and seizure within the meaning of the Fourth Amendment. The Court added, "The fact that the electronic device employed to achieve that end did not happen to penetrate the wall of the booth can have no constitutional significance." 389 U.S. at 353, 88 S.Ct. at 512, 19 L.Ed.2d at 583.

The *Katz* case signaled a major shift in the interpretation of the Fourth Amendment away from a property approach toward a privacy approach. Court decisions since the *Katz* case no longer focus on whether there has been an intrusion into a constitutionally protected area. Now the formula for analysis of Fourth Amendment problems is that "wherever an individual may harbor a reasonable 'expectation of privacy,' . . . he is entitled to be free from unreasonable governmental intrusion." *Terry v. Ohio,* 392 U.S. 1, 9, 88 S.Ct. 1868, 1873, 20 L.Ed.2d 889, 899 (1968). It would seem that such a sweeping change in the interpretation of the Fourth Amendment would result in a large-scale overturning of earlier decisions. Yet, as Justice John Marshall Harlan noted in his concurring opinion in the *Katz* case, the determination of what protection the Fourth Amendment affords to people requires reference to a "place." Therefore, many of the pre-*Katz* decisions are not necessarily changed or overruled by the *Katz* decision. These cases should, however, be evaluated in terms of not only the reasoning employed in them but also the new standard announced in *Katz.* In later chapters considering the Fourth Amendment, both pre- and post-*Katz* cases are discussed, to help the reader gain as complete an understanding as possible of this continually developing area of the law.

In analyzing Fourth Amendment issues, most courts take the approach suggested by Justice Harlan in his concurring opinion in the *Katz* case. Justice Harlan said that "there is a twofold requirement, first that a person have exhibited an actual (subjective) expectation of privacy and, second, that the expectation be one that society is prepared to recognize as 'reasonable.'" 389 U.S. at 361, 88 S.Ct. at 516, 19 L.Ed.2d at 588. If these requirements are satisfied, any governmental intrusion on the expectation of privacy is a search for purposes of the Fourth Amendment. Reflecting Justice Harlan's approach, the U.S. Supreme Court defined the terms **search** and **seizure** as follows:

A "search" occurs when an expectation of privacy that society is prepared to consider reasonable is infringed. A "seizure" of property occurs when there is some meaningful interference with an individual's possessory interests in that property. *United States v. Jacobsen,* 466 U.S. 109, 113, 104 S.Ct. 1652, 1656, 80 L.Ed.2d 85, 94 (1984).

The case of *Maryland v. Macon,* 472 U.S. 463, 105 S.Ct. 2778, 86 L.Ed.2d 370 (1985), illustrates the application of these definitions. A county police detective, who was not in uniform, entered an adult bookstore. After browsing for several minutes, the detective purchased two magazines from a salesclerk, paying for them with a marked fifty-dollar bill. The detective then left the store and showed the magazines to his fellow officers, who were waiting nearby. The officers concluded that the magazines were obscene, reentered the store, and arrested the salesclerk. They also retrieved the marked fifty-dollar bill from the cash register but neglected to return the change received at the time of the purchase. In determining whether there had been a search, the Court said:

> [R]espondent did not have any reasonable expectation of privacy in areas of the store where the public was invited to enter and to transact business. . . . The mere expectation that the possibly illegal nature of a product will not come to the attention of the authorities, whether because a customer will not complain or because undercover officers will not transact business with the store, is not one that society is prepared to recognize as reasonable. The officer's action in entering the bookstore and examining the wares that were intentionally exposed to all who frequent the place of business did not infringe a legitimate expectation of privacy and hence did not constitute a search within the meaning of the Fourth Amendment. 472 U.S. at 469, 105 S.Ct. at 2782, 86 L.Ed.2d at 376–77.

In determining whether there had been a seizure, the Court said:

> [R]espondent voluntarily transferred any possessory interest he may have had in the magazines to the purchaser upon the receipt of the funds. . . . Thereafter, whatever possessory interest the seller had was in the funds, not the magazines. At the time of the sale the officer did not "interfere" with any interest of the seller; he took only that which was intended as a necessary part of the exchange. 472 U.S. at 469, 105 S.Ct. at 2782, 86 L.Ed.2d at 377.

Therefore, no seizure occurred for the purposes of the Fourth Amendment.

In *Warden v. Hayden,* 387 U.S. 294, 304, 87 S.Ct. 1642, 1649, 18 L.Ed.2d 782, 790 (1967), the U.S. Supreme Court observed that the "principal" object of the [Fourth] Amendment is the protection of privacy rather than property and that "this shift in emphasis from property to privacy has come about through a subtle interplay of substantive and procedural reform." Nevertheless, the Court did not suggest that this shift in emphasis had eliminated the previously recognized protection for property under the Fourth Amendment. In *Soldal v. Cook County, Ill.,* 506 U.S. 56, 113 S.Ct. 538, 121 L.Ed.2d 450 (1992), the Court ruled that the Fourth Amendment protects against unreasonable seizures of property, even though neither privacy nor liberty is also implicated and even though no search within the meaning of the amendment has taken place. The *Soldal* case involved the forcible repossession of a mobile home by deputy sheriffs and the owner of a mobile home park. The Court said:

> [T]he reason why an officer might enter a house or effectuate a seizure is wholly irrelevant to the threshold question of whether the [Fourth] Amendment applies. What matters is the intrusion on the people's security from governmental interference. Therefore, the right against unreasonable seizures would be no less transgressed if the seizure of the house was undertaken to collect evidence, verify compliance with a housing regulation, effect an eviction by the police, or on a whim, for no reason at all. . . . [I]t would be "anomalous to say that the individual and his private property are fully protected by the Fourth Amendment only when the individual is suspected of criminal behavior." 506 U.S. at 69, 113 S.Ct. at 548, 121 L.Ed.2d at 463–64.

In this book, the primary concern is with governmental actions that are sufficiently intrusive as to be considered searches and seizures, and with the legality of those actions. Generally, to be legal, a search or seizure must be reasonable. For most searches or seizures, this reasonableness requirement means that they must be conducted under the authority of a valid warrant, or they must fall within a recognized exception to the warrant requirement. Parts 2 and 3 of this book deal with the warrant requirement and its exceptions.

Note that privacy, as one of the basic rights guaranteed to individuals in our society, encompasses much more than the protections offered by the Fourth Amendment, even as interpreted under the *Katz* formula. This point is perhaps best stated in the *Katz* decision itself:

> [T]he Fourth Amendment cannot be translated into a general constitutional "right to privacy." That Amendment protects individual privacy against certain kinds of governmental intrusion, but its protections go further, and often have nothing to do with privacy at all. Other provisions of the Constitution protect personal privacy from other forms of governmental invasion. But the protection of a person's general right to privacy—his right to be let alone by other people—is, like the protection of his property and of his very life, left largely to the law of individual States. 389 U.S. at 350–51, 88 S.Ct. at 510–11, 19 L.Ed.2d at 581.

Probable Cause

The Fourth Amendment to the U.S. Constitution introduces the concept of **probable cause:**

> The right of the people to be secure in their persons, houses, papers, and effects, against unreasonable searches and seizures, shall not be violated, and no Warrants shall issue, but upon *probable cause,* supported by Oath or affirmation, and particularly describing the place to be searched, and the persons or things to be seized.

From this language, it is apparent that probable cause is necessary for the issuance of an arrest or search warrant. It is not so apparent that the other clause of the Fourth Amendment declaring the right of the people to be secure against "unreasonable searches and seizures" is also founded on probable cause. In general, that clause governs the various situations in which police are permitted to make warrantless arrests, searches, and seizures. These warrantless police actions are usually held to be unreasonable, if not based on probable cause. As the U.S. Supreme Court explained, if the requirements for warrantless arrests, searches, and seizures were less stringent than those for warrants, "a principal incentive now existing for the procurement of . . . warrants would be destroyed." *Wong Sun v. United States,* 371 U.S. 471, 479–80, 83 S.Ct. 407, 413, 9 L.Ed.2d 441, 450 (1963).

To explain what probable cause means, it is helpful to start with the Supreme Court's often-cited definition of probable cause to *arrest* set forth in *Brinegar v. United States:*

> Probable cause exists where "the facts and circumstances within their [the arresting officers'] knowledge and of which they had reasonably trustworthy information [are] sufficient in themselves to warrant a man of reasonable caution in the belief that" an offense has been or is being committed [by the person to be arrested]. 338 U.S. 160, 175–76, 69 S.Ct. 1302, 1310–11, 93 L.Ed. 1879, 1890 (1949).

The Court noted that probable cause has come to mean more than bare suspicion. In a more recent case, the Court defined probable cause to *search* as "a fair probability that contraband or evidence of a crime will be found in a particular place." *Illinois v.*

Gates, 462 U.S. 213, 238, 103 S.Ct. 2317, 2332, 76 L.Ed.2d 527, 548 (1983). The Court also said:

> Perhaps the central teaching of our decisions bearing on the probable cause standard is that it is a "practical, nontechnical conception." . . . "In dealing with probable cause, . . . as the very name implies, we deal with probabilities. These are not technical; they are the factual and practical considerations of everyday life on which reasonable and prudent men, not legal technicians, act." 462 U.S. at 231, 103 S.Ct. at 2328, 76 L.Ed.2d at 544 (1983).

Note that although these definitions seem to make a distinction between arrests and searches, the same *quantum* of evidence is required to establish probable cause to search and probable cause to arrest. The distinction only applies to the type of information needed. Probable cause to search requires a belief that certain items are contraband or fruits, instrumentalities, or evidence of crime and are in a particular place or on a particular person. Probable cause to arrest requires a belief that a particular person has committed or is committing a crime.

As discussed in detail in later chapters, many arrests and searches are conducted without a warrant. The quantum of evidence required to establish probable cause for a warrantless arrest or search is somewhat greater than that required under authority of a warrant. The reason that a greater degree of probable cause may be required in the warrantless situation is that the Supreme Court has expressed a strong preference for arrest warrants (*Beck v. Ohio,* 379 U.S. 89, 85 S.Ct. 223, 13 L.Ed.2d 142 [1964]) and for search warrants (*United States v. Ventresca,* 380 U.S. 102, 85 S.Ct. 741, 13 L.Ed.2d 684 [1965]). This preference is so strong that less persuasive evidence will justify the issuance of a warrant than would justify a warrantless search or warrantless arrest. In *Aguilar v. Texas,* the Supreme Court said that

> when a search is based upon a magistrate's, rather than a police officer's, determination of probable cause, the reviewing courts will accept evidence of a less "judicially competent or persuasive character than would have justified an officer in acting on his own without a warrant," . . . and will sustain the judicial determination so long as "there was a substantial basis for [the magistrate] to conclude that [seizable evidence was] probably present. . . ." 378 U.S. 108, 111, 84 S.Ct. 1509, 1512, 12 L.Ed.2d 723, 726 (1964).

The warrant procedure is preferred because it places responsibility for deciding the delicate question of probable cause with a neutral and detached judicial officer. Thereby, law enforcement is served, because law enforcement officers are enabled to search certain places and seize certain persons or things when the officers can show reasonable grounds that those persons, places, or things are significantly connected with criminal activity. The Fourth Amendment rights of citizens are also served by the warrant procedure, because the decision to allow a search and seizure is removed from the sometimes hurried and overzealous judgment of law enforcement officers engaged in the competitive enterprise of investigating crime.

Whether law enforcement officers are applying for a warrant or are determining their authority to arrest or search without a warrant, they must have sufficient information to establish probable cause. Probable cause may arise through facts or information that an officer has personally observed or gathered. It may also be based on apparently reliable information from third parties such as the victim, other police agencies, witnesses, reporters, and informants, or even on information from the defendant. Chapter 6 contains a detailed discussion of what information may and may not be considered in arriving at probable cause in addition to procedures to assist the law enforcement officer in establishing probable cause, both when the information comes from informants and when it does not.

Probable cause is evaluated by examining the collective information in the police's possession at the time of the arrest or search, not merely the personal knowledge of the arresting or searching officer. Therefore, if the police's knowledge is in its totality sufficient to establish probable cause, a law enforcement officer's actions in making a warrantless arrest or search upon orders to do so will be justified, even though that officer does not personally have all the information on which probable cause is based. *United States v. Thevis,* 469 F.Supp. 490 (D.Conn. 1979).

> [L]aw enforcement officers in diverse jurisdictions must be allowed to rely on information relayed from officers and/or law enforcement agencies in different localities in order that they might coordinate their investigations, pool information, and apprehend fleeing suspects in today's mobile society. In an era when criminal suspects are increasingly mobile and increasingly likely to flee across jurisdictional boundaries, this rule is a matter of common sense: it minimizes the volume of information concerning suspects that must be transmitted to other jurisdictions and enables police in one jurisdiction to act promptly in reliance on information from another jurisdiction. *United States v. Nafziger,* 974 F.2d 906, 910–11 (7th Cir. 1992).

Even if the collective knowledge of the police is not sufficient to establish probable cause, the officer arresting upon orders will be protected from civil and criminal liability.

Reasonableness

The final basic underlying concept to be discussed is **reasonableness.** The Fourth Amendment does not proscribe all searches and seizures, only those that are unreasonable. Reasonableness has therefore been called the touchstone of the Fourth Amendment. Other Fourth Amendment requirements, such as warrants, probable cause, exigency, and good faith, can all be thought of as subcriteria of the ultimate criteria of reasonableness. The U.S. Supreme Court has pointed out that reasonableness does not necessarily mean correctness.

> It is apparent that in order to satisfy the "reasonableness" requirement of the Fourth Amendment, what is generally demanded of the many factual determinations that must regularly be made by agents of the government—whether the magistrate issuing a warrant, the police officer executing a warrant, or the police officer conducting a search or seizure under one of the exceptions to the warrant requirement—is not that they always be correct, but that they always be reasonable. *Illinois v. Rodriguez,* 497 U.S. 177, 185–86, 110 S.Ct. 2793, 2800, 111 L.Ed.2d 148, 159 (1990).

Also, the Court has said that "[t]here is no formula for the determination of reasonableness. Each case is to be decided on its own facts and circumstances." *Go-Bart Importing Co. v. United States,* 282 U.S. 344, 357, 51 S.Ct. 153, 158, 75 L.Ed.2d 374, 382 (1931).

In evaluating the facts and circumstances of cases involving searches and seizures, the Supreme Court has used a balancing test to weigh the needs and demands of effective law enforcement against the privacy rights of individual citizens. The results have varied with the particularities of the cases and the philosophies of individual Supreme Court justices. Examples of the reasonableness approach can be found in the discussion of administrative searches in Chapter 5, the discussion of stop and frisk in Chapter 7, and elsewhere in this book. Essential to an understanding of the concept of reasonableness is an appreciation that it is a flexible standard to be liberally construed for the protection of individual freedom.

> Implicit in the Fourth Amendment's protection from unreasonable searches and seizures is its recognition of individual freedom. That safeguard has been declared to be "as of the very essence of constitutional liberty" the guaranty of which "is as important and as imperative as are the guaranties of the other fundamental rights of the individual citizen * * *." [Citations omitted.] While the language of the Amendment is "general," it "forbids every search that is unreasonable; it protects all, those suspected or known as to be offenders as well as the innocent, and unquestionably extends to the premises where the search was made * * *." *Go-Bart Importing Co. v. United States,* 282 U.S. 344, 357, 51 S.Ct. 153, 158, 75 L.Ed. 374 (1931). Mr. Justice Butler there stated for the Court that "(t)he Amendment is to be liberally construed and all owe the duty of vigilance for its effective enforcement lest there shall be impairment of the rights for the protection of which it was adopted." *Ibid.* He also recognized that "(t)here is no formula for the determination of reasonableness. Each case is to be decided on its own facts and circumstances." *Ibid.* [Citations omitted.]
>
> This Court's long-established recognition that standards of reasonableness under the Fourth Amendment are not susceptible of Procrustean application is carried forward when that Amendment's proscriptions are enforced against the States through the Fourteenth Amendment. And, although the standard of reasonableness is the same under the Fourth and Fourteenth Amendments, the demands of our federal system compel us to distinguish between evidence held inadmissible because of our supervisory powers over federal courts and that held inadmissible because prohibited by the United States Constitution. We reiterate that the reasonableness of a search is in the first instance a substantive determination to be made by the trial court from the facts and circumstances of the case and in the light of the "fundamental criteria" laid down by the Fourth Amendment and in opinions of this Court applying that Amendment. Findings of reasonableness, of course, are respected only insofar as consistent with federal constitutional guarantees. As we have stated above and in other cases involving federal constitutional rights, findings of state courts are by no means insulated against examination here. [Citations omitted.] While this Court does not sit as in nisi prius to appraise contradictory factual questions, it will, where necessary to the determination of constitutional rights, make an independent examination of the facts, the findings, and the record so that it can determine for itself whether in the decision as to reasonableness the fundamental—i.e., constitutional—criteria established by this Court have been respected. The States are not thereby precluded from developing workable rules governing arrests, searches and seizures to meet "the practical demands of effective criminal investigation and law enforcement" in the States, provided that those rules do not violate the constitutional proscription of unreasonable searches and seizures and the concomitant command that evidence so seized is inadmissible against one who has standing to complain. . . . Such a standard implies no derogation of uniformity in applying federal constitutional guarantees but is only a recognition that conditions

and circumstances vary just as do investigative and enforcement techniques. *Ker v. California*, 374 U.S. 23, 32–34, 83 S.Ct. 1623, 1629–30, 10 L.Ed.2d 726, 737–38 (1963).

It is fitting to conclude this chapter with a quotation from Justice Brennan that succinctly summarizes the essence of the Fourth Amendment and neatly ties together the concepts of privacy, probable cause, and reasonableness:

> The Fourth Amendment was designed not merely to protect against official intrusions whose social utility was less as measured by some "balancing test" than its intrusion on individual privacy; it was designed in addition to grant the individual a zone of privacy whose protections could be breached only where the "reasonableness" requirements of the probable cause standard were met. Moved by whatever momentary evil has aroused their fears, officials—perhaps even supported by a majority of citizens—may be tempted to conduct searches that sacrifice the liberty of each citizen to assuage the perceived evil. But the Fourth Amendment rests on the principle that a true balance between the individual and society depends on the recognition of "the right to be let alone—the most comprehensive of rights and the right most valued by civilized men." *New Jersey v. T.L.O.*, 469 U.S. 325, 361–62, 105 S.Ct. 733, 753, 83 L.Ed.2d 720, 747–48 (1985).

Summary

This chapter is designed to round out the reader's preparation for the detailed study of the law of criminal procedure. Chapter 1 introduced the Constitution, the wellspring from which flow all the rules and principles to follow. Emphasis was placed on the constitutional sources of individual rights, and the necessary conflict between the protection of individual rights and the maintenance of law and order was pointed out. Future chapters deal with specific instances of this conflict and show how the delicate balance between these competing interests is maintained.

Chapter 2 presented an overview of the criminal court system, the arena in which the balancing takes place and in which the reasonableness, appropriateness, and thoroughness of the law enforcement officer's activities are ultimately tested. Chapter 2 was designed to give an overall picture of the criminal justice system as a backdrop for a more integrated understanding of the law of criminal procedure.

Finally, this chapter introduces the basic concepts of the exclusionary rule, privacy, probable cause, and reasonableness, which wind through the following chapters of this book. The law enforcement officer or other criminal justice professional who knows the potentially devastating effects of the exclusionary rule, who is sensitive to the constitutional rights of all citizens, especially to their reasonable expectation of privacy, who understands the meaning and importance of probable cause, and who embraces the concept of reasonableness as a guide is well on the way to appreciating the constitutional restraints that characterize the operation of our criminal justice system. The remainder of this book provides the details of criminal procedure, the knowledge of which can enable a person to function effectively within that system.

Key Holdings from Major Cases

Wolf v. Colorado (1949). "The security of one's privacy against arbitrary intrusion by the police—which is at the core of the Fourth Amendment—is basic to a free society. It is therefore implicit in the 'concept of ordered liberty' and as such enforceable against the States through the Due Process Clause." 338 U.S. 25, 27–28, 69 S.Ct. 1359, 1361, 93 L.Ed. 1782, 1785.

Mapp v. Ohio (1961). "Since the Fourth Amendment's right of privacy has been declared enforceable against the States through the Due Process Clause of the Fourteenth, it is enforceable against them by the same sanction of exclusion as is used against the Federal Government. Were it otherwise, then just as without the Weeks rule the assurance against unreasonable federal searches and seizures would be 'a form of words,' valueless and undeserving of mention in a perpetual charter of inestimable human liberties, so too, without that rule the freedom from state invasions of privacy would be so ephemeral and so neatly severed from its conceptual nexus with the freedom from all brutish means of coercing evidence as not to merit this Court's high regard as a freedom 'implicit in the "concept of ordered liberty."'" 367 U.S. 643, 655, 81 S.Ct. 1684, 1691, 6 L.Ed.2d 1081, 1090.

"[A]s to the Federal Government, the Fourth and Fifth Amendments and, as to the States, the freedom from unconscionable invasions of privacy and the freedom from convictions based upon coerced confessions do enjoy an 'intimate relation' in their perpetuation of 'principles of humanity and civil liberty [secured] only after years of struggle.' . . . They express 'supplementing phases of the same constitutional purpose—to maintain inviolate large areas of personal privacy.' . . . The philosophy of each Amendment and of each freedom is complementary to, although not dependent upon, that of the other in its sphere of influence—the very least that together they assure in either sphere is that no man is to be convicted on unconstitutional evidence." 367 U.S. at 657, 81 S.Ct. at 1692, 6 L.Ed.2d at 1091.

"Having once recognized that the right to privacy embodied in the Fourth Amendment is enforceable against the States, and that the right to be secure against rude invasions of privacy by state officers is, therefore, constitutional in origin, we can no longer permit that right to remain an empty promise. Because it is enforceable in the same manner and to like effect as other basic rights secured by the Due Process Clause, we can no longer permit it to be revocable at the whim of any police officer who, in the name of law enforcement itself, chooses to suspend its enjoyment. Our decision, founded on reason and truth, gives to the individual no more than that which the Constitution guarantees him, to the police officer no less than that to which honest law enforcement is entitled, and, to the courts, that judicial integrity so necessary in the true administration of justice." 367 U.S. at 660, 81 S.Ct. at 1694, 6 L.Ed.2d at 1093.

Malloy v. Hogan (1964). The protection of the Fifth Amendment's privilege against self-incrimination is "to be enforced against the States under the Fourteenth Amendment according to the same standards that protect those personal rights against federal encroachment." 378 U.S. 1, 10, 84 S.Ct. 1489, 1495, 12 L.Ed.2d 653.

Gideon v. Wainwright (1963). "[I]n our adversary system of criminal justice, any person haled into court, who is too poor to hire a lawyer, cannot be assured a fair trial unless counsel is provided for him. . . . [L]awyers in criminal courts are necessities, not luxuries. The right of one charged with crime to counsel may not be deemed fundamental and essential to fair trials in some countries, but it is in ours. From the very beginning, our state and national constitutions and laws have laid great emphasis on procedural and substantive safeguards designed to assure fair trials before impartial tribunals in which every defendant stands equal before the law. This noble ideal cannot be realized if the poor man charged with crime has to face his accusers without a lawyer to assist him." 372 U.S. 335, 344, 83 S.Ct. 792, 796–97, 9 L.Ed.2d 799, 805.

Murdock v. Memphis (1874). The U.S. Supreme Court will not review state court judgments that rest on "adequate and independent state grounds" even if there are also federal grounds. 87 U.S. (20 Wall.) 590, 22 L.Ed. 429.

Silverthorne Lumber Co. v. United States (1920). "The essence of a provision forbidding the acquisition of evidence in a certain way is that not merely evidence so acquired shall not be used before the Court but that it shall not be used at all. Of course this does not mean that the facts thus obtained become sacred and inaccessible. If knowledge of them is gained from an independent source they may be proved like any others, but the knowledge gained by the Government's own wrong cannot be used by it in the way proposed." 251 U.S. 385, 392, 40 S.Ct. 182, 183, 64 L.Ed. 319, 321.

Wong Sun v. United States (1963). Not "all evidence is 'fruit of the poisonous tree' simply because it would not have come to light but for the illegal actions of the police. Rather, the more apt question in such a case is 'whether granting establishment of the primary illegality, the evidence to which instant objection is made has been come at by exploitation of that illegality or instead by means sufficiently distinguishable to be purged of the primary taint.'" 371 U.S. 471, 488, 83 S.Ct. 407, 417, 9 L.Ed.2d 441, 455.

Nix v. Williams (1984). "The independent source doctrine teaches us that the interest of society in deterring unlawful police conduct and the public interest in having juries receive all probative evidence of a crime are properly balanced by putting the police in the same, not a *worse*, position than they would have been in if no police error or misconduct had occurred." 467 U.S. 431, 443, 104 S.Ct. 2501, 2509, 81 L.Ed.2d 377, 387.

"[I]f the government can prove that the evidence would have been obtained inevitably and, therefore, would have been admitted regardless of any overreaching by the police, there is no rational basis to keep that evidence from the jury in order to ensure the fairness of the trial proceedings. In that situation, the State has gained no advantage at trial and the defendant has suffered no prejudice. Indeed, suppression of the evidence would operate to undermine the adversary system by putting the State in a *worse* position than it would have occupied without any police misconduct." 467 U.S. at 447, 104 S.Ct. at 2511, 81 L.Ed.2d at 389–90.

United States v. Leon (1984). The Fourth Amendment exclusionary rule does not "bar the use in the prosecution's case-in-chief of evidence obtained by officers acting in reasonable reliance on a search warrant issued by a detached and neutral magistrate but ultimately found to be unsupported by probable cause." 468 U.S. 897, 900, 104 S.Ct. 3405, 3409, 82 L.Ed.2d 677, 684.

Arizona v. Evans (1993). "[T]he exclusionary rule was historically designed as a means of deterring police misconduct. . . ." 514 U.S. at 14, 115 S.Ct. at 1193, 131 L.Ed.2d 46–47.

Illinois v. Krull (1987). "The application of the exclusionary rule to suppress evidence obtained by an officer acting in objectively reasonable reliance on a statute would have as little deterrent effect on the officer's actions as would the exclusion of evidence when an officer acts in objectively reasonable reliance on a warrant. Unless a statute is clearly unconstitutional, an officer cannot be expected to question the judgment of the legislature that passed the law. If the statute is subsequently declared unconstitutional, excluding evidence obtained pursuant to it prior to such judicial declaration will not deter future Fourth Amendment violations by an officer who has simply fulfilled his responsibility to enforce the statute as written." 480 U.S. 340, 349–50, 107 S.Ct. 1160, 1167, 94 L.Ed.2d 364, 375.

Rakas v. Illinois (1978). "'Fourth Amendment rights are personal rights which, like some other constitutional rights, may not be vicariously asserted.' . . . A person who is aggrieved by an illegal search and seizure only through the introduction of damaging evidence secured by a search of a third person's premises or property has not had any of his Fourth Amendment rights infringed. . . . And since the exclusionary rule is an attempt to effectuate the guarantees of the Fourth Amendment, . . . it is proper to permit only defendants whose Fourth Amendment rights have been violated to benefit from the rule's protections." 439 U.S. 128, 133–34, 99 S.Ct. 421, 425, 58 L.Ed.2d 387, 394–95.

Minnesota v. Olson (1990). A person's "status as an overnight guest is alone enough to show that he had an expectation of privacy in the home that society is prepared to recognize as reasonable." 495 U.S. 91, 96–97, 110 S.Ct. 1684, 1688, 109 L.Ed.2d 85, 93.

United States v. Padilla (1993). Even a coconspirator or codefendant in a crime has no standing to object to a search, unless that person has a reasonable expectation of privacy in the place to be searched. 508 U.S. 77, 113 S.Ct. 1936, 123 L.Ed.2d 635.

Katz v. United States (1967). "[T]he Fourth Amendment protects people, not places. What a person knowingly exposes to the public, even in his own home or office, is not a subject of Fourth Amendment protection. . . . But what he seeks to preserve as private, even in an area accessible to the public may be constitutionally protected." 389 U.S. 347, 351–52, 88 S.Ct. 507, 511, 19 L.Ed.2d 576, 582.

United States v. Jacobsen (1984). "A 'search' occurs when an expectation of privacy that society is prepared to consider reasonable is infringed. A 'seizure' of property occurs when there is some meaningful interference with an individual's possessory interests in that property." 466 U.S. 109, 113, 104 S.Ct. 1652, 1656, 80 L.Ed.2d 85, 94.

Soldal v. Cook County, Illinois (1992). "[T]he reason why an officer might enter a house or effectuate a seizure is wholly irrelevant to the threshold question of whether the [Fourth] Amendment applies. What matters is the intrusion on the people's security from governmental interference. . . . [I]t would be 'anomalous to say that the individual and his private property are fully protected by the Fourth Amendment only when the individual is suspected of criminal behavior.'" 506 U.S. 56, 69, 113 S.Ct. 538, 548, 121 L.Ed.2d 450, 463–64.

Brinegar v. United States (1949). "Probable cause exists where the facts and circumstances within their [the arresting officers'] knowledge and of which they had reasonably trustworthy information [are] sufficient in themselves to warrant a man of reasonable caution in the belief that an offense has been or is being committed [by the person to be arrested]." 338 U.S. 160, 175–76, 69 S.Ct. 1302, 1310–11, 93 L.Ed. 1879, 1890.

Illinois v. Gates (1983). Probable cause to search is "a fair probability that contraband or evidence of a crime will be found in a particular place." 462 U.S. 213, 238, 103 S.Ct. 2317, 2332, 76 L.Ed.2d 527, 548.

"Perhaps the central teaching of our decisions bearing on the probable cause standard is that it is a 'practical, nontechnical conception.' . . . 'In dealing with probable cause, . . . as the very name implies, we deal with probabilities. These are not technical; they are the factual and practical considerations of everyday life on which reasonable and prudent men, not legal technicians, act.'" 462 U.S. at 231, 103 S.Ct. at 2328, 76 L.Ed.2d at 544.

Aguilar v. Texas (1964). "[W]hen a search is based upon a magistrate's, rather than a police officer's, determination of probable cause, the reviewing courts will accept evidence of a less 'judicially competent or persuasive character than would have justified an officer in acting on his own without a warrant,' . . . and will sustain the judicial determination so long as 'there was a substantial basis for [the magistrate] to conclude that [seizable evidence was] probably present. . . .'" 378 U.S. 108, 111, 84 S.Ct. 1509, 1512, 12 L.Ed.2d 723, 726.

Illinois v. Rodriguez (1990). "It is apparent that in order to satisfy the 'reasonableness' requirement of the Fourth Amendment, what is generally demanded of the many factual determinations that must regularly be made by agents of the government—whether the magistrate issuing a warrant, the police officer executing a warrant, or the police officer conducting a search or seizure under one of the exceptions to the warrant requirement—is not that they always be correct, but that they always be reasonable." 497 U.S. 177, 185–86, 110 S.Ct. 2793, 2800, 111 L.Ed.2d 148, 159.

Review and Discussion Questions

1. Explain why the application of the exclusionary rule does not necessarily mean that the prosecution is ended and the defendant goes free.

2. Discuss the probable effectiveness in deterring illegal police conduct of the following suggested alternatives to the exclusionary rule: criminal prosecution of law enforcement officers; administrative disciplining of officers; bringing of civil actions for damages against officers.

3. Explain why a state court may refuse to follow certain holdings of the U.S. Supreme Court.

4. Give three reasons in support of the exclusionary rule and three reasons in support of its abolishment.

5. Discuss three theories under which evidence may be admissible in court even though it is fruit of the poisonous tree.

6. What did Justice Harlan mean when he said, in his concurring opinion in *Katz v. United States,* that the answer to the question of what protection the Fourth Amendment affords to people requires reference to a place?

7. Should a person in a telephone booth be given the same degree of Fourth Amendment protection as a person in his or her bedroom? As a person in his or her garage? As a person in his or her automobile?

8. Although *Katz v. United States* dispensed with the requirement of an actual physical trespass to trigger the Fourth Amendment, is a physical trespass always an intrusion on a person's reasonable expectation of privacy?

9. Compare the standard of probable cause against the following statements of degree of certainty: absolutely positive; pretty sure; good possibility; beyond a reasonable doubt; reasonable suspicion; preponderance of the evidence; reasonable probability; strong belief; convinced.

10. Why do reviewing courts accept evidence of a "less judicially competent or persuasive character" to justify the issuance of a warrant than they would to justify officers acting on their own without a warrant?

Arrest, Search Warrants, and Probable Cause

CHAPTER FOUR

Arrest

OBJECTIVES

1. Be able to define formal arrest.

2. Understand the distinctions between the terms seizure, stop, and seizure tantamount to arrest.

3. Know what an arrest warrant and a summons are and why arrests made pursuant to a warrant are preferred.

4. Know the difference between the warrantless arrest authority for misdemeanors and for felonies.

5. Know the procedures for effecting a formal arrest.

6. Know the law relating to citizen's arrest and fresh pursuit.

7. Know the limitations on the use of force in making arrests, self-defense, and entry of dwellings.

8. Know the legal requirements and procedures for dealing with an arrested person after the arrest is made.

9. Know the consequences of an illegal arrest.

OUTLINE

The power of arrest is the most important power that a law enforcement officer possesses. It enables the officer to deprive a person of the freedom to carry out daily personal and business affairs, and it initiates against a person the processes of criminal justice, which may ultimately result in that person being fined or imprisoned. Because an arrest potentially has a great detrimental effect on a person's life, liberty, and privacy, the law governing arrest provides many protections to ensure that a person will be arrested only when reasonable and necessary. These protections take the form of severe limitations and restrictions on the law enforcement officer's exercise of the power of arrest. The law governing arrest is based on guarantees in the Fourth Amendment to the U.S. Constitution, which provides as follows:

> The right of the people to be secure in their *persons,* houses, papers and effects, against unreasonable searches and *seizures,* shall not be violated and no Warrants shall issue, but upon probable cause, supported by Oath or affirmation, and particularly describing the place to be searched and the *persons* or things *to be seized.* (Emphasis supplied.) U.S. Const., Amend. 4

There is a common misunderstanding that the Fourth Amendment applies only to searches and seizures of material things and not to people. The word *persons* has been emphasized in the preceding passage to indicate clearly that this amendment is not so restricted but that it also protects individuals from illegal seizures of their persons. (Note that although the Fourth Amendment does not specifically mention arrest, an arrest is a type of seizure and is clearly governed by the Fourth Amendment.) With the Fourth Amendment as a backdrop, the discussion now turns to defining arrest and exploring the law enforcement officer's powers and duties with respect to arrest. ■

Definition of Formal Arrest

Arrest is a difficult term to define, because it is used in different senses. In its narrow sense, sometimes called a formal or technical arrest, **arrest** can be defined as "the taking of a person into custody for the commission of an offense as the prelude to prosecuting him for it." *State v. Murphy,* 465 P.2d 900, 902 (Or.App. 1970). In its broader sense, sometimes called a **seizure tantamount to arrest** or an arrest for constitutional purposes, *arrest* refers to any seizure of a person significant enough to resemble a formal arrest in important respects. This chapter refers to the narrow sense as a formal arrest and to the broad sense as a seizure tantamount to arrest, or simply an arrest. Seizures tantamount to arrest are discussed in the next section. The discussion of formal arrest begins with a listing of the basic elements necessary for a formal arrest:

- A purpose or intention of a law enforcement officer to take a person into the custody of the law

- Exercise of real or pretended authority

- Detention or restraint of the person to be arrested, whether by physical force or by submission to assertion of authority

- An understanding by the person to be arrested that it is the intention of the arresting officer then and there to arrest and detain him or her

Each of these elements is discussed separately.

Intention to Arrest

To satisfy the first requirement of formal arrest, a law enforcement officer must intend to take a person into the custody of the law. This intention is the basic element that distinguishes a formal arrest from lesser forms of detention. Examples of lesser forms of detention follow:

- Restraining a person who is behaving in a manner that is dangerous either to self or others
- Briefly stopping a person to seek information or to render assistance
- Serving a subpoena or other process such as a summons or notice to appear in court
- Asking a suspect or witness to appear at the station house for questioning
- Briefly stopping a vehicle to inspect license, equipment, or load

Although this is not a complete list, it illustrates the type of situation in which the law enforcement officer does *not* intend to take the person into the custody of the law and in which there is no formal arrest. Ways in which lesser forms of detention can develop into the constitutional equivalent of a formal arrest are discussed in the next section on seizures tantamount to arrest.

One further detention situation deserving mention is that in which a police officer detains a person under suspicious circumstances and conducts a brief, general on-the-scene investigation about possible criminal conduct. This type of encounter is commonly referred to as a **stop.** Because a separate body of law has developed to govern such encounters, the stop is discussed separately in Chapter 7. For purposes of this chapter, the ordinary stop does not involve an intention to arrest and therefore does not constitute a formal arrest.

Real or Pretended Authority

A law enforcement officer's taking a person into custody must be under real or pretended authority. Real authority is simply the legal right to make a formal arrest either with or without a warrant. That right may derive from the warrant itself or from the officer's observing the commission of a crime or having probable cause to believe that a particular person committed, or was in the process of committing, a particular crime. An example of pretended authority is an officer making a formal arrest without the legal right to do so but erroneously assuming that right. The arrest is still technically a formal arrest despite the officer's error. This authority requirement distinguishes arrest from the situation in which a person is seized and detained without any type of authority being apparent or claimed. An example is a kidnapping, in which a person is seized but no one claims any kind of authority to arrest.

Detention or Restraint

"An arrest requires *either* physical force . . . or, where that is absent, *submission* to the assertion of authority." *California v. Hodari D.,* 499 U.S. 621, 626, 111 S.Ct. 1547, 1551, 113 L.Ed.2d 690, 697 (1990).

PHYSICAL FORCE. To constitute an arrest, the mere grasping or application of physical force with lawful authority, whether or not it succeeds in subduing the arrestee, is sufficient. The following was quoted with approval by the U.S. Supreme Court in the *Hodari D.* case:

> There can be constructive detention, which will constitute an arrest, although the party is never actually brought within the physical control of the party making an arrest. This is accomplished by merely touching, however slightly, the body of the accused, by the party making the arrest and for that purpose, although he does not succeed in stopping or holding him even for an instant. . . . A. Cornelius, Search and Seizure 163–64 (2d ed. 1930) 499 U.S. at 625, 111 S.Ct. at 1550, 113 L.Ed.2d at 696.

To say that an arrest is effected by the slightest application of physical force, despite the arrestee's escape, is not to say that, for Fourth Amendment purposes, there is a *continuing* arrest during the period the person is not in custody. A seizure is a single act and not a continuous fact.

SHOW OF AUTHORITY. An arrest may be accomplished without any physical touching if the officer makes a show of authority *and* the person to be arrested submits. The following was also quoted with approval in the *Hodari D.* case:

> Mere words will not constitute an arrest, while, on the other hand, no actual, physical touching is essential. The apparent inconsistency in the two parts of this statement is explained by the fact that an assertion of authority and purpose to arrest followed by submission of the arrestee constitutes an arrest. There can be no arrest without either touching or submission. Perkins, The Law of Arrest, 25 Iowa L.Rev. 201, 206 (1940) 499 U.S. at 626–27, 111 S.Ct. at 1551, 113 L.Ed.2d at 697.

Understanding by the Arrestee

The final element of formal arrest is that the law enforcement officer's actions in making an arrest must result in the arrested person's understanding that an arrest is being made. This understanding is ordinarily conveyed by the officer's notifying the person of the arrest. Surrounding circumstances, however, such as handcuffing or other physical restraint or confinement, may make the fact of arrest obvious to the arrested person. The officer may never say a word, but the circumstances convey the idea anyhow. If the arrested person is unconscious, under the influence of drugs or alcohol, or mentally impaired, the requirement of understanding may be delayed or dispensed with.

The arrestee's understanding has been the subject of several court decisions in recent years. Problems concerning this issue arise when an encounter between the police and a person does not quite fit the description of a formal arrest, but the intrusion on the person's freedom of action is significantly greater than with an ordinary, brief investigative detention or other minimal street encounter. The next section discusses such seizures, which, although not formal arrests, may be tantamount to arrests for the purposes of Fourth Amendment protection.

KEY POINTS

1. The requirements for a formal arrest are a law enforcement officer's intention to take a person into the custody of the law to answer for an alleged crime, under real or pretended authority, accompanied by detention or restraint of the person and an understanding by the person that an arrest is being made.

2. The "detention or restraint" requirement of a formal arrest may be satisfied either by actually touching the person to be arrested or by the person's submitting to the officer's show of authority.

Seizures of the Person Tantamount to an Arrest

A law enforcement officer investigating crime or otherwise enforcing the laws or keeping the public peace will have contact with members of the public in degrees of intensity varying from the briefest observation or questioning to a full-fledged formal arrest with the use of force. With respect to the most minimal of these police contacts, the U.S. Supreme Court stated:

> [L]aw enforcement officers do not violate the Fourth Amendment by merely approaching an individual on the street or in another public place, by asking him if he is willing to answer some questions, by putting questions to him if the person is willing to listen, or by offering in evidence in a criminal prosecution his voluntary answers to such questions. . . . Nor would the fact that the officer identifies himself as a police officer, without more, convert the encounter into a seizure requiring some level of objective justifications. . . . The person approached, however, need not answer any question put to him; indeed, he may decline to listen to the questions at all and may go on his way. . . . He may not be detained even momentarily without reasonable, objective grounds for doing so; and his refusal to listen or answer does not, without more, furnish those grounds. . . . If there is no detention—no seizure within the meaning of the Fourth Amendment—then no constitutional rights have been infringed. *Florida v. Royer,* 460 U.S. 491, 497–98, 103 S.Ct. 1319, 1324, 75 L.Ed.2d 229, 236 (1983).

Some encounters with members of the public, however, are more intrusive than those described in the previous paragraph and involve a greater encroachment on a person's freedom of movement and privacy. An example is a so-called *Terry*-type investigative stop, which is a brief detention of a person for investigative purposes, sometimes accompanied by a limited search for weapons called a **frisk.** Officers may stop a person only if they have a reasonable and articulable suspicion that criminal activity is afoot. Officers may frisk a person they have stopped only if they have a reasonable and articulable suspicion that the person is armed and dangerous. Both the stop and the frisk must be reasonable under the circumstances. (Stop and frisk are discussed in Chapter 7.)

At a still higher level of intrusiveness are police contacts with members of the public involving a detention or temporary seizure of a person that restrains his or her freedom of action more than a brief investigatory stop but does not satisfy the four elements of a formal arrest (discussed earlier). The missing element is usually the officer's intention to arrest. In these instances, courts often hold that despite the lack of a formal arrest, the seizure is so similar to a formal arrest in important respects that it should be allowed only if supported by probable cause to believe a crime has been or is being committed. The leading case on this subject is the U.S. Supreme Court case of *Dunaway v. New York,* 442 U.S. 200, 99 S.Ct. 2248, 60 L.Ed.2d 824 (1979).

In the *Dunaway* case, the defendant was picked up at his neighbor's home by the police and taken to the police station for questioning about an attempted robbery and homicide. Although the defendant was not told that he was under arrest, he would have been physically restrained had he attempted to leave. The police did not have probable cause to arrest the defendant. He was given *Miranda* warnings, and he waived his right to counsel. He was questioned, and he eventually made statements and drew sketches incriminating himself. His motions at trial to suppress the statements and sketches were denied, and he was convicted.

On appeal, the Court examined the seizure of the defendant and held that the police violated his Fourth Amendment and Fourteenth Amendment rights. The seizure was much more intrusive than a traditional stop and frisk (see Chapter 7) and could not be justified on the mere grounds of "reasonable suspicion" of criminal activity. Whether or not technically characterized as a formal arrest, the seizure was in important respects indistinguishable from a formal arrest. Instead of being questioned briefly where he was found, the defendant was taken from a neighbor's home to a police car, transported to a police station, and placed in an interrogation room. He was never informed that he was free to go and would have been physically restrained had he refused to accompany the officers or tried to escape their custody. That the defendant was not formally placed under arrest, was not booked, and would not have had an arrest record if the interrogation had proven fruitless did not make his seizure something less than an arrest for purposes of Fourth Amendment protections. Because it was unsupported by probable cause, Dunaway's seizure was illegal.

Therefore, even though an officer does not intend to formally arrest a person, a court may find that the officer's actions are tantamount to an arrest if they are indistinguishable from an arrest in important respects. If an officer seizes or detains a person significantly, beyond a mere stop or other minor investigatory detention, the seizure or detention may be considered an arrest for purposes of the Fourth Amendment, even if the officer does not comply with all the requirements of a formal arrest. As such, the seizure or detention will be ruled illegal unless it is supported by probable cause.

In a case similar to *Dunaway,* in which police took a burglary-rape suspect against his will from his home to the police station for fingerprinting, the U.S. Supreme Court reiterated its principles regarding seizures tantamount to arrests:

> [W]hen the police, without probable cause or a warrant, forcibly remove a person from his home or other place in which he is entitled to be and transport him to the police station, where he is detained, although briefly, for investigative purposes . . . such seizures, at least where not under judicial supervision, are sufficiently like arrests to invoke the traditional rule that arrests may constitutionally be made only on probable cause. *Hayes v. Florida,* 470 U.S. 811, 816, 105 S.Ct. 1643, 1647, 84 L.Ed.2d 705, 710 (1985).

The Court did not rule out, however, the possibility that an investigative seizure on less than probable cause might be permissible if judicially authorized.

> [U]nder circumscribed procedures, the Fourth Amendment might permit the judiciary to authorize the seizure of a person on less than probable cause and his removal to the police station for the purpose of fingerprinting. . . . [S]ome States . . . have enacted procedures for judicially authorized seizures for the purpose of fingerprinting. The state courts are not in accord on the validity of these efforts to insulate investigative seizures from Fourth Amendment invalidation. 470 U.S. at 817, 105 S.Ct. at 1647, 84 L.Ed.2d at 711.

Many issues involving seizures tantamount to arrest arise as a result of investigative detentions of suspected drug law violators on the public concourses of airports. In one such case, *Florida v. Royer,* 460 U.S. 491, 103 S.Ct. 1319, 75 L.Ed.2d 229 (1983), the U.S. Supreme Court concluded that the detention of the defendant was tantamount to an arrest. In that case, narcotics agents had adequate grounds to suspect the defendant of carrying drugs, based on his traveling under an assumed name and his appearance and conduct fitting the "drug courier profile." The agents therefore had the right to temporarily detain the defendant, within the limits of the *Terry* case, in order to confirm or dispel their reasonable suspicions. The agents, however, not only asked the defendant for his identification and to accompany them to another room. They told him they were narcotics agents and had reason to believe he was carrying illegal drugs, they kept his identification and airline ticket, they took him to a small room where he found himself alone with two police officers, they retrieved his checked luggage from the airlines without his consent, they never informed him he was free to board his plane if he so chose, and they would not have allowed him to leave the interrogation room even if he had asked to do so. Under these circumstances, the Court held that the officers' conduct was more intrusive than necessary to effectuate an investigative detention authorized by the *Terry* case. The detention was therefore a seizure tantamount to an arrest, and since the officers did not have probable cause to arrest, it was an illegal seizure. The defendant's consent to a search of his luggage in the interrogation room was tainted by the illegal seizure, and therefore the search of the luggage was also illegal.

When a suspect is in a motor vehicle, police may have more leeway in stopping the suspect for investigation before the stop rises to the level of an arrest. In *United States v. Jones,* 759 F.2d 633 (8th Cir. 1985), the court found no seizure tantamount to arrest where two officers, acting on reasonable suspicion that a fleeing man was involved in a burglary, blocked the suspect's car with theirs, drew their guns, forcefully ordered the suspect out of his vehicle, and repeatedly demanded identification. Noting the danger inherent in the situation, the court said, "Blocking generally will be reasonable when the suspect is in a vehicle because of the chance that the suspect may flee upon the approach of police with resulting danger to the public as well as to the officers involved." 759 F.2d at 638.

KEY POINTS

3. A seizure of a person that is in important respects indistinguishable from a traditional formal arrest is illegal unless it is supported by probable cause to believe that the person has committed or is committing a crime.

Arrest Authority Under a Warrant

Even though the authority of law enforcement officers to arrest without a warrant in proper circumstances has been recognized for a long time, arrests made under the authority of a warrant have always been preferred. The warrant procedure is favored because it places the sometimes delicate decision of determining whether there is probable cause to justify an arrest in the hands of an impartial judicial authority. The U.S. Supreme Court said that "the informed and deliberate determinations of magistrates empowered to issue warrants . . . are to be preferred over the hurried action of officers . . . who may happen to make arrests." *Aguilar v. Texas,* 378 U.S. 108, 110–11, 84 S.Ct. 1509, 1512, 12 L.Ed.2d 723, 726 (1964). This preference for warrants attempts to avoid placing the responsibility for determining probable cause on law enforcement officers who, in their eagerness to enforce the law and investigate crime, might be tempted to violate constitutional rights.

Although warrants are often considered a hindrance by law enforcement officers, they protect officers in an important way. If a warrant is proper on its face and the officer does not abuse authority in executing the arrest, the officer is protected against civil liability for false arrest or false imprisonment, even though it is later determined that the issuance of the warrant was illegal. The officer is not so protected when making warrantless arrests.

A law enforcement officer has authority to arrest under a warrant whether or not the officer has possession of the warrant. If the warrant is outstanding, any officer may arrest under its authority.

Arrest Warrant

The **arrest warrant** is (1) a written order, (2) issued by a proper judicial authority, (3) in the name of the government, (4) upon probable cause, (5) directing the arrest of a particular person or persons. Typical forms for an arrest warrant appear in Exhibits 4.1 and 4.2. Note that Exhibit 4.2 is a combination form that can be used as a complaint, a summons, an arrest warrant, or an order of detention. The person issuing the arrest warrant could be a judge, a magistrate, a complaint justice, a justice of the peace, or a clerk of the court. Every jurisdiction authorizes different judicial officers to issue warrants. (For the remainder of this chapter, the term **magistrate** is used to designate the judicial officer authorized to issue arrest warrants.) The warrant is issued on the basis of a sworn complaint, charging that a particularly described suspect has committed a crime. The person swearing out the complaint is usually the victim of the crime or a law enforcement officer.

Complaint

The **complaint** must state the essential facts constituting the offense charged, including the time and place of the offense's commission and the name of the suspect or a reasonably definite description of the suspect if the name is not known. The complaint must be sworn to and signed by the person charging the offense (the complainant). A warrant issued on an unsworn complaint is void, and any arrest made under such a warrant is illegal. Typical complaint forms appear in Exhibits 4.2 and 4.3.

Besides serving as an application for an arrest warrant, in some jurisdictions the complaint is the charging instrument for misdemeanor cases or for the initial appearance or preliminary examination. In felony cases, the complaint is replaced as the charging instrument by the indictment or information. (The complaint is discussed in further detail in Chapter 2.)

Probable Cause

Before an arrest warrant can be issued, the magistrate must be satisfied from the complaint that there is **probable cause** to believe that the offense charged in the complaint was committed by the accused. (Probable cause is discussed briefly in Chapter 3 and in detail in Chapter 6.) If the complaint form has insufficient space, a separate **affidavit** or affidavits detailing the facts and circumstances on which probable cause is based must be filed with the complaint. An affidavit need not be prepared with any particular formality and may be merely a sworn statement of the facts on which the complainant relies in seeking the issuance of a warrant. The magistrate may require

AO 442 (Rev. 5/93) Warrant for Arrest

United States District Court

---- **DISTRICT OF** ----

UNITED STATES OF AMERICA

WARRANT FOR ARREST

V.

CASE NUMBER: _____

To: The United States Marshal
    and any Authorized United States Officer

YOU ARE HEREBY COMMANDED to arrest _____
                                                              Name
and bring him or her forthwith to the nearest magistrate judge to answer a(n)

☐ Indictment ☐ Information ☐ Complaint ☐ Order of Court ☐ Violation Notice ☐ Probation Violation Petition

charging him or her with (brief description of offense)

TQT

in violation of Title _____ United States Code, Section(s) _____

_____   _____
Name of Issuing Officer   Title of Issuing Officer

_____   _____
Signature of Issuing Officer   Date and Location

Bail fixed at $ _____ by _____
                                                          Name of Judicial Officer

RETURN
This warrant was received and executed with the arrest of the above-named defendant at _____

DATE RECEIVED	NAME AND TITLE OF ARRESTING OFFICER	SIGNATURE OF ARRESTING OFFICER
DATE OF ARREST		

EXHIBIT 4.1 Typical Arrest Warrant Form

additional affidavits of other persons having pertinent and reliable information bearing on probable cause. All the information on which probable cause is based must appear in the original complaint and the affidavits submitted in support of it. The reason for this requirement is to maintain a record of the evidence produced before the magistrate issuing the warrant, if the validity of the warrant is later questioned.

AO 442 (Rev. 5/93) Warrant for Arrest

THE FOLLOWING IS FURNISHED FOR INFORMATION ONLY:

DEFENDANT'S NAME: _____

ALIAS: _____

LAST KNOWN RESIDENCE: _____

LAST KNOWN EMPLOYMENT: _____

PLACE OF BIRTH: _____

DATE OF BIRTH: _____

SOCIAL SECURITY NUMBER: _____

HEIGHT: _____ WEIGHT: _____

SEX: _____ RACE: _____

HAIR: _____ EYES: _____

SCARS, TATTOOS, OTHER DISTINGUISHING MARKS: _____

_____

_____

FBI NUMBER: _____

COMPLETE DESCRIPTION OF AUTO: _____

_____

INVESTIGATIVE AGENCY AND ADDRESS: _____

_____

_____

EXHIBIT 4.1 *(continued)*

Requirements of Arrest Warrant

The arrest warrant must conform to certain requirements, which vary in different jurisdictions. The following list is representative of what an arrest warrant must contain:

- The caption of the court or division of the court from which the warrant issues
- The name of the person to be arrested, if known; if not known, any name or description by which the person can be identified with reasonable certainty. The warrant must show on its face that it is directed toward a particular, identifiable person to satisfy the Fourth Amendment requirement that a warrant particularly describe the person to be seized.
- A description of the offense charged in the complaint. This description should be in the language of the appropriate statute or ordinance. The important consideration, however, is that the description be in words definite enough for the defendant to readily understand the charge. Stating that the defendant is charged

State of Minnesota   County of   Court

| CCT | SECTION/Subdivision | U.O.C. | GOC | CTY. ATTY. FILE NO. | CONTROLLING AGENCY | CONTROL NO. |

COURT CASE NO.   DATE FILED

Complaint   SUMMONS
                     WARRANT
√ if more than 6 counts (see attached)   ORDER OF DETENTION

State of Minnesota   FELONY
                              GROSS MISDEMEANOR
        VS.   PLAINTIFF,

NAME: first, middle, last   Date of Birth   SJIS COMPLAINT NUMBER

DEFENDANT.
`COMPLAINT`

The Complainant, being duly sworn, makes complaint to the above-named Court and states that there is probable cause to believe that the Defendant committed the following offense (s). The complainant states that the following facts establish PROBABLE CAUSE:

THEREFORE, Complainant requests that said Defendant, subject to bail or conditions of release be:
    (1) arrested or that other lawful steps be taken to obtain defendant's appearance in court; or
    (2) detained, if already in custody, pending further proceedings,
and that said Defendant otherwise be dealt with according to law.
COMPLAINANT'S NAME: COMPLAINANT'S SIGNATURE:

Being duly authorized to prosecute the offense (s) charged, I hereby approve this Complaint.
DATE: PROSECUTING ATTORNEY'S SIGNATURE:

PROSECUTING ATTORNEY:
NAME/TITLE: ADDRESS/TELEPHONE:

FORM B.1

EXHIBIT 4.2A   Combination Form, Page 1

merely with a "felony" or a "misdemeanor," for example, is insufficient and will invalidate the warrant.

- The date of issuance
- The officer or officers to whom the warrant is directed, together with a command that the defendant be brought before the proper judicial official

Court Case #:   **PAGE**   *of*

FINDING OF PROBABLE CAUSE

From the above sworn facts, and any supporting affidavits or supplemental sworn testimony, I, the Issuing Officer, have determined that probable cause exists to support, subject to bail or conditions of release where applicable, Defendant(s) arrest or other lawful steps be taken to obtain Defendant(s) appearance in Court, or his detention, if already in custody, pending further proceedings. The Defendant(s) is/are thereof charged with the above-stated offense.

SUMMONS

THEREFORE You, THE ABOVE-NAMED DEFENDANT(S, ARE HEREBY SUMMONED to appear on the
day of   , 19   at   AM/PM before the above-named court at
                                    to answer this complaint.
IF YOU FAIL TO APPEAR in response to this SUMMONS, a WARRANT FOR YOUR ARREST shall be issued.

WARRANT

EXECUTE IN MINNESOTA ONLY
To the sheriff of the above-named county; or other person authorized to execute this WARRANT; I hereby order, in the name of the State of Minnesota, that the above-named Defendant(s) be apprehended and arrested without delay and brought promptly before the above-named Court (if in session, and if not, before a Judge or Judicial Officer of such Court without unnecessary delay, and in any event not later than 36 hours after the arrest or as soon thereafter as such Judge or Judicial Officer is available) to be dealt with according to law.

ORDER OF DETENTION

Since the above-named Defendant(s) is/are already in custody;
I hereby order; subject to bail or conditions of release, that the above-named Defendant(s) continue to be detained pending further proceedings.

Bail:

Conditions of Release:

This COMPLAINT – SUMMONS, WARRANT, ORDER OF DETENTION was sworn to subscribed before, and issued by the undersigned authorized Issuing Judicial Officer this   day of   , 19
JUDICIAL OFFICER:

Name: *Signature:*
Title:
       Sworn testimony has been given before the Judicial Officer by the following witnesses:

STATE OF MINNESOTA   COUNTY of   Clerk's Signature or File Stamp:

State of Minnesota
                    Plaintiff,

             vs.   *RETURN OF SERVICE*
                                          *I hereby Certify and Return that I have served
                                          a copy of this COMPLAINT - SUMMONS, WAR-
                                          RANT, ORDER OF DETENTION upon the Defen-
                                          dant(s) herein-named.*
                                          Signature of Authorized Service Agent:

                    Defendant(s)

FORM J-1

EXHIBIT 4.2B Combination Form, Page 2

- The signature of the issuing magistrate, together with a statement of the magistrate's official title

An officer to whom a warrant is directed should read the warrant carefully. If the warrant satisfies the requirements listed here, the officer may execute the warrant without fear of civil liability arising from a challenge to the validity of the warrant.

United States District Court

────────── **DISTRICT OF** ──────────

UNITED STATES OF AMERICA
V.

CRIMINAL COMPLAINT

CASE NUMBER: _____

(Name and Address of Defendant)

I, the undersigned complainant being duly sworn state the following is true and correct to the best of my

knowledge and belief. On or about _____ in _____ county, in the

_____ District of _____ defendant(s) did, (Track Statutory Language of Offense)

in violation of Title _____ United States Code, Section(s) _____.

I further state that I am a(n) _____ and that this complaint is based on the following
                                     Official Title
facts:

Continued on the attached sheet and made a part hereof: ☐ Yes   ☐ No

                                                          _____
                                                          Signature of Complainant

Sworn to before me and subscribed in my presence,

_____ at _____
Date   City and State

_____   _____
Name & Title of Judicial Officer   Signature of Judicial Officer

EXHIBIT 4.3   A Typical Criminal Complaint Form

Summons

A magistrate may issue a **summons** instead of an arrest warrant in certain situations. The requirements for a summons are generally the same as those for a warrant, except that a summons directs the defendant to appear before a court at a stated time and place rather than ordering the defendant's arrest. Court rules and statutes usually

AO 83 (Rev. 12/85) Summons in a Criminal Case

United States District Court

_____ DISTRICT OF _____

UNITED STATES OF AMERICA
V.

SUMMONS IN A CRIMINAL CASE

CASE NUMBER:

(Name and Address of Defendant)

YOU ARE HEREBY SUMMONED to appear before the United States District Court at the place, date and time set forth below.

Place	Room
	Date and Time

Before:

To answer a(n)
☐ Indictment ☐ Information ☐ Complaint ☐ Violation Notice ☐ Probation Violation Petition

Charging you with a violation of Title _____ United States Code, Section(s) _____

Brief description of offense:

Signature of Issuing Officer   Date

Name and Title of Issuing Officer

EXHIBIT 4.4A   A Typical Summons Form, Page 1

provide that, if a defendant fails to appear in response to a summons, a warrant will be issued for his or her arrest. Typical summons forms appear in Exhibits 4.2 and 4.4.

The summons is usually used when the offense charged in a complaint is a misdemeanor, a violation of a municipal ordinance, or some other petty offense. If the offender is a citizen with "roots firmly established in the soil of the community" and thus can be easily found for serving a warrant if the summons is ignored, the summons procedure is a much easier and better way of inducing the defendant to appear in court than arrest.

The term *summons* may be confusing because it is often used to describe a citation, ticket, or notice to appear issued by a law enforcement officer, especially in traffic cases. Such a notice is *not* a summons in the legal sense, because it is not issued by a magistrate on the basis of a complaint. A citation, ticket, or notice to appear merely

AO 83 (Rev. 12/85) Summons in a Criminal Case

RETURN OF SERVICE

Service was made by me on: ___ Date ___

Check one box below to indicate appropriate method of service

☐ Served personally upon the defendant at: _____

☐ Left summons at the defendant's dwelling house or usual place of abode with a person of suitable age and discretion then residing therein and mailed a copy of the summons to the defendant's last known address. Name of person with whom the summons was left: _____

☐ Returned unexecuted: _____

I declare under penalty of perjury under the laws of the United States of America that the foregoing information contained in the Return of Service is true and correct.

Returned on ___ Date ___   Name of United States Marshal

(by) Deputy United States Marshal

Remarks:

1) As to who may serve a summons see Rule 4 of the Federal Rules of Criminal Procedure.

EXHIBIT 4.4B   A Typical Summons Form, Page 2

gives notice to offenders that they may be arrested if they do not voluntarily appear in court to answer the charges against them.

KEY POINTS

4. An arrest warrant is a written order to arrest a person, issued by a proper judicial authority on the basis of a sworn complaint charging the commission of a crime, supported by a statement of facts and circumstances establishing probable cause.

5. A summons is similar to an arrest warrant, except that it directs a person to appear in court rather than ordering the person's arrest.

Arrest Authority Without a Warrant

Law enforcement officers are often faced with the decision of whether to apply for an arrest warrant or to arrest without a warrant. Since officers often have to make an immediate decision in this respect, they must have a clear working knowledge of the law governing arrest without a warrant.

Authority to arrest without a warrant depends on the difference between a **felony** and a **misdemeanor.** In most jurisdictions, a felony is defined as any crime that is or may be punished by death or imprisonment in a state prison. Since most jurisdictions do not provide for imprisonment in the state prison unless the term of the sentence is one year or more, a crime is probably not a felony unless the penalty is at least one year's incarceration. Note that it is the punishment that *may* be imposed under the statute defining the crime that determines whether a crime is a felony or misdemeanor, not the penalty that finally *is* imposed. *Therefore, a felony can be defined as any crime for which the punishment could possibly be imprisonment for a term of one year or more. All crimes that do not amount to a felony are classified as misdemeanors.*

Jurisdictions differ greatly as to which specific crimes are classified as felonies and which are misdemeanors. Law enforcement officers must familiarize themselves with the classifications of crimes as felonies or misdemeanors in their jurisdictions.

Misdemeanors

In most jurisdictions, unless otherwise provided by statute, a law enforcement officer may arrest without a warrant for a misdemeanor only when the misdemeanor is "committed in the officer's presence." Ordinarily, this means that the officer must personally observe the misdemeanor being committed before making an arrest. However, sight is not the only means of perceiving the commission of a crime. Therefore, courts have generally held that a misdemeanor is committed in an officer's presence if the officer is able to perceive it through any of the five senses: sight, hearing, touch, taste, or smell. For example, an officer had authority to make a warrantless misdemeanor arrest when he heard, through a door, a person dial a telephone and accept a bet on a horse race. *People v. Goldberg,* 280 N.Y.S.2d 646, 227 N.E.2d 575 (N.Y. 1967). In another case, an officer's smelling of alcohol on a driver's breath justified a conclusion that a misdemeanor was being committed in the officer's presence. *State v. Hines,* 504 P.2d 946 (Ariz.App. 1973). And an officer's sense of touch justified a warrantless misdemeanor arrest of a citizen who hit the officer in the face during an investigation of a domestic quarrel in the citizen's home. *Hoover v. Garfield Heights Municipal Court,* 802 F.2d 168 (6th Cir. 1986). Furthermore, an officer investigating crime may enhance his or her senses in various ways.

> Permissible techniques of surveillance include more than just the five senses of officers and their unaided physical abilities. Binoculars, dogs that track and sniff out contraband, search-lights, fluorescent powders, automobiles and airplanes, burglar alarms, radar devices, and bait money contribute to surveillance without violation of the Fourth Amendment in the usual case. *United States v. Dubrofsky,* 581 F.2d 208, 211 (9th Cir. 1978).

The "presence" requirement may even be satisfied by the defendant's admission of guilt. *People v. Ward*, 252 N.W.2d 514 (Mich.App. 1977). But information from other witnesses may not be used to satisfy the presence requirement:

> When the basis of the officer's belief that the defendant has committed a misdemeanor is information imparted to him by, say, victims, witnesses or informers, he must present the evidence to a magistrate and seek an arrest warrant. He may not act on his own appraisal of the reasonableness of the information. *People v. Dixon*, 222 N.W.2d 749, 751 (Mich. 1974).

An officer must perceive the commission of a misdemeanor *before* arresting the offender. If the officer arrests on mere suspicion or chance that a misdemeanor is being committed, the arrest is illegal, even if later developments show that a crime did take place. *In re Alonzo C.*, 151 Cal.Rptr. 192 (Cal.App. 1978).

An officer also has no authority to arrest without a warrant for a past or completed misdemeanor, even if the offender is still at the crime scene. If the misdemeanor was completed before the officer arrived, it could not have been committed in the officer's presence. In this situation, the officer may either

- issue a summons to the suspected offender or
- identify the offender and apply for an arrest warrant.

The rule allowing warrantless arrests only for misdemeanors committed in the officer's presence is based on the common law and is not required by the Fourth Amendment. (Note: The **common law** is a body of unwritten law developed in England and based on court decisions. It receives its binding force from traditional usage, custom, and universal acceptance.) "The United States Constitution does not require a warrant for misdemeanors not occurring in the presence of the arresting officer." *Fields v. City of Houston, Tex.*, 922 F.2d 1183, 1189 (5th Cir. 1991). Therefore, as discussed in the next section, states may enlarge the authority to arrest for misdemeanors without a warrant through statute or constitutional amendment.

MISDEMEANOR ARRESTS ON PROBABLE CAUSE. In recent years, some state legislatures have enacted laws making exceptions to the general rule that an arrest without a warrant for a misdemeanor is authorized only for offenses committed in an officer's presence. These laws authorize arrests on probable cause for certain types of misdemeanors, such as shoplifting, driving while intoxicated, fish and game violations, and liquor violations. Because the laws of each state are different, each law enforcement officer must determine for what misdemeanors, if any, state law allows warrantless arrests on probable cause.

PROMPTNESS OF ARREST. An arrest without a warrant for a misdemeanor committed in an officer's presence must be made promptly and without unnecessary delay. The officer must set out to make the arrest at the time the offense is perceived and must continue that effort until the arrest is accomplished or abandoned.

> The arrest for misdemeanors committed or attempted in the presence of officers must be made as quickly after commission of the offense as the circumstances will permit. After an officer has witnessed a misdemeanor, it is his duty to then and there arrest the offender. Under some circumstances, there may be justification for delay, as for instance, when the interval between the commission of the offense and the actual arrest is spent by the officer in pursuing the offender, or

in summoning assistance where such may reasonably appear to be necessary. . . . If, however, the officer witnesses the commission of an offense and does not arrest the offender, but departs on other business, or for other purposes, and afterwards returns, he cannot then arrest the offender without a warrant; for then the reasons for allowing the arrest to be made without a warrant have disappeared. *Smith v. State*, 87 So.2d 917, 919 (Miss. 1956).

Reasonable delay in making a warrantless misdemeanor arrest that is closely connected with the offense itself or with an attempted flight by the offender will usually not invalidate the arrest. Examples of reasonable delays are delays to summon assistance in making the arrest, plan strategy to overcome resistance to arrest, pursue a fleeing offender, or take safety precautions. If an officer delays a warrantless misdemeanor arrest for reasons unconnected with the process of arrest, however, the arrest will be unlawful. These types of delay require the officer to obtain a warrant and to arrest in accordance with the warrant.

Felonies

A law enforcement officer may make a warrantless public arrest for a felony if, at the time of arrest, the officer has probable cause to believe that a felony has been committed and that the person to be arrested is committing or has committed the felony. The U.S. Supreme Court said:

Law enforcement officers may find it wise to seek arrest warrants where practicable to do so, and their judgments about probable cause may be more readily accepted where backed by a warrant issued by a magistrate. . . . But we decline to transform this judicial preference into a constitutional rule when the judgment of the Nation and Congress has for so long been to authorize warrantless public arrests on probable cause rather than to encumber criminal prosecutions with endless litigation with respect to the existence of exigent circumstances, whether it was practicable to get a warrant, whether the suspect was about to flee, and the like. *United States v. Watson*, 423 U.S. 411, 423–24, 96 S.Ct. 820, 827–28, 46 L.Ed.2d 598, 608–09 (1976).

Some states, however, either by statute or by court interpretation of the state constitution, place greater restrictions on the arrest authority of law enforcement officers. In *People v. Hoinville*, 553 P.2d 777 (Colo. 1976), the court held that a state statute providing that "[a]n arrest warrant should be obtained when practicable" required police officers to obtain a warrant whenever possible.

FELONY ARRESTS ON PROBABLE CAUSE. Assuming that most states allow warrantless felony arrests on probable cause, the key terms law enforcement officers must know to determine their authority are *felony* and *probable cause*. Felony was defined earlier in this chapter as any offense for which the punishment could possibly be imprisonment for a term of one year or more. Probable cause was defined in Chapter 3 and is discussed in detail in Chapter 6. For purposes of this discussion, probable cause to arrest is a *fair probability* that the person to be arrested is committing or has committed a crime. Note that before making a warrantless arrest, a law enforcement officer must have specific facts or circumstances connecting the person to be arrested with a particular felony. If the officer is unable to later justify the arrest by articulating the facts and circumstances supporting probable cause, the arrest is likely to be declared illegal.

If an officer making an arrest has probable cause to believe that a felony has been committed and that the defendant committed it, it makes no difference whether the officer turns out to be right or wrong in making the arrest or whether the defendant is later acquitted of the crime for which the arrest is made. The officer is still justified in making the arrest, and it is a legal arrest. On the other hand, if the officer, on mere suspicion or chance, makes a warrantless arrest without probable cause, the arrest is illegal whether the defendant is guilty or not. Therefore, probable cause is the main consideration in determining the validity of an arrest.

PROMPTNESS OF ARREST. Unlike a warrantless arrest for a misdemeanor, which must be made immediately, a warrantless arrest for a felony may be delayed, whether or not the felony was committed in the officer's presence. *United States v. Drake*, 655 F.2d 1025 (10th Cir. 1981). Delay may be justified for a variety of reasons, so long as the delay is not designed to prejudice an offender's constitutional rights. Reasons justifying delay include an inability to locate the defendant, the need to complete additional undercover investigation, a desire to avoid alerting other potential offenders, and the need to protect the identity of undercover agents or informants.

> The police are not required to guess at their peril the precise moment at which they have probable cause to arrest a suspect, risking a violation of the Fourth Amendment if they act too soon, and a violation of the Sixth Amendment if they wait too long. Law enforcement officers are under no constitutional duty to call a halt to a criminal investigation the moment they have the minimum evidence to establish probable cause, a quantum of evidence which may fall far short of the amount necessary to support a criminal prosecution. *Hoffa v. United States*, 385 U.S. 293, 310, 87 S.Ct. 408, 417, 17 L.Ed.2d 374, 386 (1966).

Some courts hold that a person has no constitutional right to be arrested, suggesting that a warrantless felony arrest may be delayed indefinitely. *United States v. Hudgens*, 798 F.2d 1234 (9th Cir. 1986). The safer procedure for the law enforcement officer, however, is to arrest soon after a crime is committed unless there are good reasons for delay.

> [A] point can be reached where the delay is so great that the prejudice to the defendant caused by it—due to faded memories of parties and witnesses, loss of contact with witnesses, and loss of documents—becomes so great that due process and fundamental fairness require that the charges be dismissed. *People v. Hall*, 729 P.2d 373, 375 (Colo. 1986).

KEY POINTS

6. A law enforcement officer may make a warrantless public arrest for a felony if, at the time of arrest, the officer has probable cause to believe that a felony has been committed and that the person to be arrested is committing or has committed the felony. An officer may arrest without a warrant for a misdemeanor only when the misdemeanor is committed in the officer's presence, unless otherwise provided by statute or state constitution.

7. An arrest without a warrant for a misdemeanor committed in an officer's presence must be made as quickly after commission of the offense as the circumstances will permit. An arrest without a warrant for a felony on probable cause, however, may be delayed for various reasons, so long as the delay is not designed to prejudice the offender's constitutional rights.

Effecting a Formal Arrest

To effect a formal arrest, a law enforcement officer must satisfy the basic requirements of a formal arrest (discussed earlier in this chapter). Other aspects of effecting an arrest include notice, time of day, warrant requirements, service of a summons, assistance, and the use of discretion.

Notice

The notice required to be given by a law enforcement officer when making an arrest is usually governed by statute and differs from state to state. The following is a list of typical information to be included in that notice:

- Notice that the person is under arrest. "The obvious purpose of informing the suspect he is under arrest is not to make the arrest legal but to indicate to the person being arrested that his detention is legal, so that he will not resist." *Pullins v. State,* 256 N.E.2d 553, 556 (Ind. 1970).

- Notice of the officer's authority to arrest. This can be accomplished by the officer's announcing his or her identity as a law enforcement officer. This announcement is not necessary, however, if the officer's authority is already known to the defendant or is obvious from the display of a badge, uniform, or other indicia of authority. *State v. Erdman,* 292 N.W.2d 97 (S.D. 1980).

- Notice of the cause of the arrest. An otherwise lawful arrest is not rendered unlawful, however, if the arresting officer states the offense inaccurately or imprecisely, particularly where the officer acts in good faith and the defendant is not prejudiced by the error. *State Department of Public Safety v. Rice,* 323 N.W.2d 74 (Minn. 1982).

An officer may dispense with giving any notice before making an arrest when one or more of the following are true:

- It would endanger the officer to do so. *United States v. Manfredi,* 722 F.2d 519 (9th Cir. 1983).

- It would adversely affect the making of the arrest. *People v. Bigham,* 122 Cal.Rptr. 252, 49 Cal.App.3d 73 (Cal.App. 1975).

- The offense is being committed in the officer's presence. *Dillard v. State,* 543 S.W.2d 925 (Ark. 1976).

- The person to be arrested is reasonably likely to escape. *United States v. Nolan,* 718 F.2d 589 (3rd Cir. 1983).

- It would result in the destruction or concealment of evidence. *State v. Mueller,* 552 P.2d 1089 (Wash.App. 1976).

Time of Day

An arrest, with or without a warrant, may be made on any day of the week and at any time of the day or night, unless otherwise provided in the warrant or by statute. *State v. Perez,* 277 So.2d 778 (Fla. 1973). Unlike the execution of a search warrant, generally no specific provision in an arrest warrant is required to authorize a nighttime arrest. (See Chapter 5.) Note, however, that some states limit the time during which a *misdemeanor* warrant may be served, unless another time period is specifically authorized in the warrant.

Executing an Arrest Warrant

Several additional considerations are involved in effecting an arrest when the arrest is carried out under authority of a warrant. First, when officers are directed to serve a warrant of arrest, their belief in the guilt of the defendant or their personal knowledge of facts pertaining to the offense is immaterial. There is no requirement that the offense be committed in their presence or that they have probable cause to believe that the defendant committed the offense. Officers are simply required to carry out the command as stated in the warrant, and the only questions of concern are (1) whether the person to be arrested is the person identified in the warrant and (2) whether the warrant is valid on its face.

When the accused is identified in the warrant by name or description, a law enforcement officer is required to exercise reasonable diligence to make sure that no one else but the person designated in the warrant is arrested. If the person being arrested claims not to be the person identified in the warrant and there is a reasonably simple and direct means of checking that claim, the officer who arrests without checking may be civilly liable for false arrest or false imprisonment. The officer must be reasonably careful in determining whether the person arrested is the person identified in the warrant.

A warrant that is invalid on its face gives the law enforcement officer executing it no protection and no authority to arrest. The officer is bound to examine the warrant if it is available and acts at his or her peril in executing it if it is obviously invalid on its face. An arrest warrant is invalid on its face if one or more of the following are true:

- The court issuing the warrant clearly has no jurisdiction.
- The warrant fails to adequately indicate the crime charged.
- The warrant fails to name or describe any identifiable person.
- The warrant is not signed by the issuing magistrate.
- The warrant is not directed to the officer who is about to execute it. (If the warrant is directed to all law enforcement officers in the jurisdiction, any sworn officer may execute it. If, however, the warrant is directed only to the sheriff of a particular county, only that sheriff or a deputy sheriff may execute it.)

Once an officer determines that a warrant is valid on its face, the officer must carry out the warrant's commands and arrest the person identified in the warrant. The officer no longer has any personal discretion and is merely carrying out an order of the court:

> When the warrant purports to be for a matter within the jurisdiction of the justice (magistrate), the ministerial officer is obliged to execute it, and of course must be justified by it. He cannot inquire upon what evidence the judicial officer proceeded, or whether he committed an error or irregularity in his decision . . . the constable has nothing to look to but the warrant as his guide. . . . *Alexander v. Lindsey,* 55 S.E.2d 470, 473–74 (N.C. 1949).

Most states allow arrest warrants for violations of state law to be executed at any place within the boundaries of the state. However, a law enforcement officer of one state may not go into another state to arrest under a warrant except in fresh pursuit, which is discussed later.

Officers arresting with a warrant should give the same notice, discussed earlier, that they would ordinarily give in making any arrest. In addition, officers should have the warrant in their possession at the time of arrest and should show the warrant to the person arrested. In some states, however, officers may make a legal arrest pursuant to a warrant even though they do not possess the warrant. They must, however, inform the defendant of the offense charged and the existence of the warrant. If the defendant requests, officers must produce the warrant as soon as possible.

Like a warrantless felony arrest, an arrest made under a warrant (for a felony or misdemeanor) need not be made immediately. Officers have considerable discretion as to the time of making an arrest under a warrant. They may have lawful strategic reasons for delay, or they may wish to select a time when the arrest can be accomplished with the least difficulty. "[T]he general rule is that, while execution should not be unreasonably delayed, law enforcement officers have a reasonable time in which to execute a warrant and need not arrest at the first opportunity." *United States v. Drake,* 655 F.2d 1025, 1027 (10th Cir. 1981).

An officer executing an arrest warrant must make a return of the warrant. The return is made by entering on the warrant the date of the arrest, signing the warrant, and filing the warrant with the court. (See the arrest warrant forms in Exhibits 4.1 and 4.2.) Failure to return an arrest warrant may invalidate the arrest and subject the officer to civil liability for false arrest or false imprisonment.

Service of a Summons

As discussed earlier, a magistrate may, under certain circumstances, issue a summons instead of an arrest warrant. A summons is served by personally delivering a copy to the defendant or by leaving it at the defendant's home or usual place of abode with some person of suitable age and discretion who resides there. It may also be served by mailing it to the defendant's last known address. As with an arrest warrant, most states provide that a summons for a violation of state law may be served at any place within the state. In addition, a summons must be returned by the officer serving it to the proper magistrate before the return date appearing on the summons. (See the summons forms in Exhibits 4.2 and 4.4.)

Assistance

Law enforcement officers may request private citizens to aid them in making an arrest. The laws of some jurisdictions require that any person called on by a law enforcement officer to assist the officer in executing his or her official duties, including the arrest of another person, is legally obligated to obey the officer. Refusal to aid an officer may be punishable under state law.

When private citizens act in aid of a known law enforcement officer, they have the same rights and privileges as the officer. While so acting, they have the status of a temporary law enforcement officer, including the right to use force and to enter property. If the person called on acts in good faith, he or she is protected from liability even if the officer was acting illegally. "It would be manifestly unfair to impose civil liability upon a private person for doing that which the law declares it a misdemeanor for him to refuse to do." *Peterson v. Robison,* 277 P.2d 19, 24 (Cal. 1954).

Discretion

Even though a law enforcement officer clearly has the ability and authority to arrest, good police practice may call for the arrest to be delayed or not to be made at all. It is beyond the scope of this chapter to give detailed guidelines in this area, but a brief discussion is necessary to set out general principles.

A law enforcement officer's primary duty is to protect the public at large. Therefore, when an arrest may cause greater risk of harm to the public or will only cause embarrassment to a person who poses no real threat to the community, proper police practice may call for delay or restraint in exercising the power of arrest. For example, when a crowd is present, it is often unwise to arrest a person or persons who are creating a minor disturbance. An arrest may aggravate the disturbance and possibly precipitate a riot or civil disorder. Less drastic ways to handle the matter should be explored, even though legal grounds for an arrest may exist. The same considerations apply to minor domestic disputes and disturbances by intoxicated persons who are creating no danger and may need no more than an assist in getting home. *An arrest is a significant restraint on a person's freedom and should always be justified by circumstances.*

Some law enforcement agencies have policies covering discretion to arrest. Where no policies exist, officers must use their common sense and good judgment. *Authority to arrest does not always mean duty to arrest.*

KEY POINTS

8. Unless there are extenuating circumstances, an officer arresting a person should give notice that the person is under arrest as well as notice of the officer's authority and the cause of arrest.

9. If an arrest warrant is valid on its face, a law enforcement officer must execute the warrant within a reasonable time according to its terms, and the officer has no personal discretion in this matter.

10. Warrantless arrests are discretionary and should always be justified by the circumstances.

Place of Arrest

In most states, law enforcement officers acting under authority of a warrant may make an arrest at any place within the state where the defendant may be found. Similarly, officers may serve a summons at any place within the state.

However, with respect to warrantless arrests, "[a]s a general rule, a police officer acting outside his or her jurisdiction does not act in his or her official capacity and does not have any official power to arrest." *State v. Slawek,* 338 N.W.2d 120, 121 (Wis.App. 1983). Thus, sheriffs may not arrest without a warrant beyond the counties in which they have been elected, nor may municipal police officers arrest without a warrant beyond the limits of the cities in which they have been appointed. On the other hand, the authority of state law enforcement officers is statewide, and their power to arrest without a warrant runs throughout the state. However, a law enforcement officer of one state has no authority to arrest in another state. Two exceptions to the rule that an officer may not arrest without a warrant outside his or her jurisdiction should be noted:

- Arrests made as a private citizen
- Arrests made in fresh pursuit

Citizen's Arrest Authority

Law enforcement officers have the same authority as private citizens to arrest without a warrant. Under the common-law rule in force in most states, a private citizen may arrest a person if the citizen has probable cause to believe that the person has committed a felony. In *State v. Slawek*, 338 N.W.2d 120 (Wis.App. 1983), Chicago (Illinois) police officers in unmarked cars followed the defendants' van into Wisconsin on information that the defendants were involved in residential burglaries. The officers observed the defendants commit a burglary in Wisconsin and arrested them. There were no Wisconsin precedents on the issue of the citizen's arrest authority of police officers. Nevertheless, the court found the arrests legal based on an extensive line of cases from other states. Those cases upheld the validity of an extraterritorial arrest made by a police officer who lacked the official authority to arrest when the place of arrest authorizes a private person to make a citizen's arrest under the same circumstances. The court noted that "the reasoning which permits an officer to make a citizen's arrest in an adjoining jurisdiction within the same state also allows an officer from a different state to make a citizen's arrest in a neighboring state under those circumstances when the state allows private persons to make arrests." 338 N.W.2d at 122 n.1.

A private citizen may use the same degree of force as a law enforcement officer in making an arrest. (See the discussion of use of force, later in this chapter.) If, however, the private citizen is mistaken and no felony was *actually committed,* the citizen is subject to civil liability for false arrest or false imprisonment. In contrast, a law enforcement officer who arrests for a felony based on probable cause is protected from civil liability, even if the officer is mistaken.

Under the common law, private citizens have a *duty* to arrest for felonies *committed in their presence.* Also, a private citizen *may* arrest for "breach of the peace" misdemeanors *committed in their presence.* A breach of the peace misdemeanor can be defined generally as a misdemeanor that causes or threatens direct physical harm to the public.

Therefore, in a state where the common-law rule on citizen's arrest is followed, a law enforcement officer may arrest as a private citizen without a warrant in the previously described circumstances anywhere in the state. Furthermore, unless neighboring states have modified the common-law rule by statute, a law enforcement officer may also arrest outside the borders of his or her state as a private citizen. However, the officer making a felony arrest on probable cause as a private citizen risks civil liability if the officer cannot prove that a felony was actually committed.

Fresh Pursuit

Under the common law and most statutes, law enforcement officers may make a lawful arrest without a warrant beyond the borders of their jurisdiction in cases of fresh pursuit. **Fresh pursuit** means an officer's immediate pursuit of a criminal suspect into another jurisdiction after the officer has attempted to arrest the suspect in the officer's jurisdiction. The common law allowed a warrantless arrest in fresh pursuit only in felony cases, but today most state statutes allow warrantless arrests for both felonies and misdemeanors. For a warrantless arrest in fresh pursuit to be legal, all of the following conditions must be met:

- The officer must have authority to arrest for the crime in the first place.
- The pursuit must be of a fleeing criminal attempting to avoid immediate capture.
- The pursuit must begin promptly and be maintained continuously.

The main requirement is that the pursuit be fresh. The pursuit must flow out of the act of attempting to make an arrest and must be a part of the continuous process of apprehension. The pursuit need not be instantaneous, but it must be made without unreasonable delay or interruption. There should be no side trips or diversions, even for other police business. However, the continuity of pursuit is not legally broken by unavoidable interruptions connected with the act of apprehension, such as eating, sleeping, summoning assistance, or obtaining further information.

Fresh pursuit may lead a law enforcement officer outside the boundaries of his or her state. Ordinarily, an officer has no authority beyond that of a private citizen to make arrests in another state. However, many states have adopted the Uniform Act on Fresh Pursuit or similar legislation, which permits law enforcement officers from other states, entering in fresh pursuit, to make an arrest. The Uniform Fresh Pursuit Law of Iowa is typical:

> Any member of a duly organized state, county, or municipal law enforcing unit of another state of the United States who enters this state in fresh pursuit, and continues within this state in such fresh pursuit, of a person in order to arrest the person on the ground that the person is believed to have committed a felony in such other state, shall have the same authority to arrest and hold such person in custody, as has any member of any duly organized state, county, or municipal law enforcing unit of this state, to arrest and hold in custody a person on the ground that the person is believed to have committed a felony in this state. Iowa Code Ann. § 806.1.

Because some states extend the privilege to make an arrest in fresh pursuit to out-of-state officers only on a reciprocal basis, a law enforcement officer must be familiar with not only the statutes in his or her state but also the fresh pursuit statutes of all neighboring states.

A law enforcement officer who makes an arrest in fresh pursuit under such a statute in a neighboring state must take the arrested person before an appropriate judicial officer in that state without unreasonable delay. Some states allow an arresting officer from another state to take a person arrested in fresh pursuit back to the officer's home state after the arrested person is brought before an appropriate judicial officer. Other states allow this only upon extradition or waiver of extradition. **Extradition** is a procedure whereby authorities in one state (the demanding state) demand from another state (the asylum state) that a fugitive from justice in the demanding state, who is present in the asylum state, be delivered to the demanding state. Most states have adopted the Uniform Criminal Extradition Act, which provides uniform extradition procedures among the states.

KEY POINTS

11. In general, a law enforcement officer has no authority to make warrantless arrests outside the geographic limits of the jurisdiction for which he or she has been elected or appointed.

12. As a private citizen, a law enforcement officer may arrest outside his or her jurisdiction for felonies on probable cause and for felonies and "breach of the peace" misdemeanors if committed in the officer's presence.

13. A law enforcement officer may arrest outside his or her jurisdiction in "fresh pursuit." Fresh pursuit means an officer's immediate and continuously maintained pursuit of a criminal suspect into another jurisdiction after the officer has attempted to arrest the person in the officer's own jurisdiction.

Use of Force

A law enforcement officer's right to use force to make an arrest depends on the degree of force used and the context in which it is used. This section examines various aspects of arrest and discusses the degree of force appropriate in each situation.

Felony Arrests

Under the common-law rule, a law enforcement officer could use any reasonably necessary *nondeadly* force to arrest for a felony. Most jurisdictions retain this rule today, by either statute or court decision: "[T]he use of any significant force . . . not reasonably necessary to effect an arrest—as where the suspect neither resists nor flees or where the force is used after a suspect's resistance has been overcome or his flight thwarted—would be constitutionally unreasonable." *Kidd v. O'Neil*, 774 F.2d 1252, 1256–57 (4th Cir. 1985).

The common-law rule also allowed officers to use *deadly* force to arrest any fleeing felony suspect. Under the rule, an officer was not required to retreat from effecting an arrest to avoid extreme measures but was required to press on and use all necessary force to bring the offender into custody. The use of deadly force was therefore permitted as a last resort if the only alternative was to abandon the attempt to arrest.

An examination of the history of the common-law rule reveals that it originated in an era when all felonies were punishable by death, all felons were considered dangerous, defendants had meager rights, and few of those arrested and tried for felonies escaped conviction and death. Consequently, the use of deadly force to apprehend fleeing felons was viewed merely as a more timely and less costly implementation of the eventual penalty for their offenses.

In addition, police as such did not exist at that time; the responsibility for apprehending fleeing felons fell upon the unarmed and untrained citizens who responded to the hue and cry. Weapons were primitive, and the use of force often meant hand-to-hand combat, which was seldom deadly, although it posed significant danger to the arresting person.

Today, most felonies are not punishable by death; fewer felons are convicted or executed; and police are organized, trained, equipped with sophisticated weapons, and capable of killing accurately at a distance and under circumstances posing little danger to officers or others, especially if the felon is unarmed. Operation of the common-law rule under these changed circumstances would allow police to kill persons merely suspected of offenses that, upon conviction, would very likely result in only brief imprisonment or even probation.

Although it is generally agreed that the police should be able to use as much force as necessary to protect themselves and the public against violent offenders, the common-law rule on deadly force has been much criticized as overly broad to fulfill these legitimate functions. As a result, the U.S. Supreme Court in 1985 declared unconstitutional Tennessee's statute that codified the common-law rule. The Court reasoned that, in authorizing police to use deadly force to apprehend *any* fleeing felony suspect, under *any* circumstances, the statute violated the Fourth Amendment's guarantee against unreasonable seizures. Killing a suspect, the Court noted, is the ultimate seizure.

The use of deadly force to prevent the escape of all felony suspects, whatever the circumstances, is constitutionally unreasonable. It is not better that all felony suspects die than that they escape. Where the suspect poses no immediate threat to the officer and no threat to others, the harm resulting from failing to apprehend him does not justify the use of deadly force to do so. It is no doubt unfortunate when a suspect who is in sight escapes, but the fact that the police arrive a little late or are a little slower afoot does not always justify killing a suspect. A police officer may not seize an unarmed, nondangerous suspect by shooting him dead. . . . Where the officer has probable cause to believe that the suspect poses a threat of serious physical harm, either to the officer or to others, it is not constitutionally unreasonable to prevent escape by using deadly force. Thus, if the suspect threatens the officer with a weapon or there is probable cause to believe that he has committed a crime involving the infliction or threatened infliction of serious physical harm, deadly force may be used if necessary to prevent escape, and if, where feasible, some warning has been given. *Tennessee v. Garner,* 471 U.S. 1, 11–12, 105 S.Ct. 1694, 1701, 85 L.Ed.2d 1, 9–10 (1985).

Even before the Supreme Court decision in the *Garner* case, criticism of the common-law rule on deadly force in felony cases resulted in abolition of the rule in many jurisdictions and in changes such as Section 3.07(2)(b) of the Model Penal Code, which reads as follows:

> The use of deadly force is not justifiable under this Section unless:
>   (i) the arrest is for a felony; and
>   (ii) the person effecting the arrest is authorized to act as a peace officer or is assisting a person whom he believes to be authorized to act as a peace officer; and
>   (iii) the actor believes that the force employed creates no substantial risk of injury to innocent persons; and
>   (iv) the actor believes that:
>   (A) the crime for which the arrest is made involved conduct including the use or threatened use of deadly force; or
>   (B) there is substantial risk that the person to be arrested will cause death or serious bodily injury if his apprehension is delayed.

Some states have adopted this section of the Model Penal Code or variations of it. Other states have unclear policies on the use of deadly force.

Officers should make every effort to clearly ascertain the law on deadly force in their state and the policy in their department, but at a minimum, officers must comply with the standards of the Supreme Court as set out in the *Garner* case. Very serious consequences can result from the unwarranted use of deadly force, such as death or injury to the officer or other persons or liability of the officer both civilly and criminally.

Misdemeanor Arrests

As with felonies, most states retain the common-law rule allowing law enforcement officers to use any reasonably necessary nondeadly force to arrest for a misdemeanor. However, an officer is *never* justified in using deadly force to arrest for a misdemeanor. *State v. Wall,* 286 S.E.2d 68 (N.C. 1982). *The rule is that it is better that a misdemeanant escape rather than a human life be taken.* The use of deadly force on a misdemeanant is excessive force constituting an assault. An officer who kills the suspect may be guilty of murder or manslaughter.

Self-Defense

Whether an offense is a felony or misdemeanor, a law enforcement officer making a lawful arrest may use any force reasonably necessary under the circumstances, including deadly force, if the officer reasonably believes that the person to be arrested is about to commit an assault and that the officer is in danger of death or serious bodily injury. The law enforcement officer's duty is to be the aggressor and to press forward to bring the person under restraint. This cannot be accomplished by purely defensive action on an officer's part. Therefore, if an officer has lawful authority to arrest, the officer is not required to back down in the face of physical resistance to the arrest. *State v. Williams,* 148 A.2d 22 (N.J. 1959). An officer faced with the choice of abandoning an arrest or using deadly force in *self-defense* has the right to use deadly force if necessary for self-protection.

Resisting Arrest

Resisting arrest is a crime involving a person's opposition by direct, forcible means against a law enforcement officer to prevent the officer from taking the person into custody. Under statutes defining the crime, indirect interference or hindrance of an officer will usually not support a conviction. Resistance requires active opposition such as shooting, striking, pushing, or otherwise struggling with the officer. Mere flight, concealment, or other avoidance or evasion of arrest will not constitute resistance.

> The fact that the accused sought to escape the officer by merely running away was not such an obstruction as the law contemplates. While it is the duty of every citizen to submit to a lawful arrest, yet flight is not such an offense as will make a person amenable to the charge of resisting or obstructing an officer who is attempting to make an arrest, as there is a broad distinction between avoidance and resistance or obstruction. *Jones v. Commonwealth,* 126 S.E. 74, 76–77 (Va. 1925).

Nor will verbal objections, protests, or threats unaccompanied by force constitute resisting arrest. However, a serious threat that is accompanied by the apparent ability and present intention to execute it, and that prevents an officer from acting because of reasonable fear of serious bodily injury, may constitute resistance to arrest.

Under the common-law rule, the crime of resisting arrest requires that the arrest be lawful. If an arrest is unlawful, the person being arrested has the *right* to resist. A person being arrested also has a right to resist if the person making the arrest is not an officer of the law or if the officer does not proceed in a lawful manner in making the arrest. Therefore, it is very important for law enforcement officers making an arrest to

- establish their identity, if not already known or obvious; and
- explain their purpose and authority.

Under the common-law rule, a person threatened with an illegal arrest may not only resist the arrest but may use any force reasonably necessary for self-defense and prevention of impending injury. *State v. McGowan,* 90 S.E.2d 703 (N.C. 1956). Since the impending injury resulting from an arrest is ordinarily only a brief unlawful detention, the degree of force a person may use is strictly limited. A person who uses more force than is reasonably necessary for the purpose may be guilty of an assault and battery on the officer. Deadly force is rarely justified to resist an unlawful arrest, except when a person has reasonable grounds to fear death or serious bodily injury at the hands of an officer.

The law on resisting arrest and other interferences with law enforcement officers varies in different jurisdictions. For example, some jurisdictions prohibit a private citizen from using force to resist an arrest made by one whom the citizen knows or has good reason to believe is an authorized police officer engaged in the performance of official duties, whether or not the arrest is illegal. If, however, the officer uses excessive and unnecessary force in effecting the arrest, the citizen may respond or counter with reasonable force for self-protection.

> Despite his duty to submit quietly without physical resistance to an arrest made by an officer acting in the course of his duty, even though the arrest is illegal, his right to freedom from unreasonable seizure and confinement can be protected, restored and vindicated through legal processes. However, the rule permitting reasonable resistance to excessive force of the officer, whether the arrest is lawful or unlawful, is designed to protect a person's bodily integrity and health and so permits resort to self-defense. Simply stated, the law recognizes that liberty can be restored through legal processes but life or limb cannot be repaired in a courtroom. And so it holds that the reason for outlawing resistance to an unlawful arrest and requiring disputes over its legality to be resolved in the courts has no controlling application on the right to resist an officer's excessive force. . . .
>
> Two qualifications on the citizen's right to defend against and to repel an officer's excessive force must be noticed. He cannot use greater force in protecting himself against the officer's unlawful force than reasonably appears to be necessary. If he employs such greater force, then he becomes the aggressor and forfeits the right to claim self-defense to a charge of assault and battery on the officer. . . . Furthermore, if he knows that if he desists from his physically defensive measures and submits to arrest the officer's unlawfully excessive force would cease, the arrestee must desist or lose his privilege of self-defense. *State v. Mulvihill,* 270 A.2d 277, 280 (N.J. 1970).

As illustrated by the *Mulvihill* case, the modern trend is away from the common-law rule allowing resistance to any illegal arrest, because of the dangers inherent in the rule and because the consequences of an illegal arrest are at most a brief period of detention during which arrested persons can resort to nonviolent legal remedies for regaining their liberty.

Entry of Dwellings

Under the common law, the right of a law enforcement officer to enter a dwelling to arrest depended on whether the officer had legal authority to arrest. Legal authority to arrest, with or without a warrant, carried with it the authority to forcibly enter any dwelling and search for the suspect who the officer had probable cause to believe was in that dwelling.

> An agent must have probable cause to believe that the person he is attempting to arrest, with or without a warrant, is in a particular building at the time in question before that agent can legitimately enter the building by ruse or any other means. To hold otherwise is to grant the agent a license to go from house to house employing ruse entries in violation of the right of privacy of the respective occupants. *United States v. Phillips,* 497 F.2d 1131, 1136 (9th Cir. 1974).

This authority to enter a dwelling house to arrest applied even to misdemeanor arrests.

The common-law rule is no longer valid. In recent years the U.S. Supreme Court has decided cases dealing with the entry of dwellings to arrest. The general rule now is that a law enforcement officer may not enter a dwelling to arrest a person without a warrant, unless there is consent or **exigent circumstances.** Whether an arrest warrant or search warrant is required for entry depends on whether the dwelling to be entered is the suspect's home or someone else's home.

Entry of a Suspect's Home

In *Payton v. New York,* 445 U.S. 573, 100 S.Ct. 1371, 63 L.Ed.2d 639 (1980), the U.S. Supreme Court held that, absent exigent circumstances or consent, a law enforcement officer may not make a warrantless entry into a suspect's home to make a routine felony arrest. The Court said that the physical entry of the home is the chief evil against which the wording of the Fourth Amendment is directed and that the warrant procedure minimizes the danger of needless intrusions of that sort. The Court went on to say that an arrest warrant requirement, although providing less protection than a search warrant requirement, was sufficient to interpose the magistrate's determination of probable cause between a zealous officer and a citizen. The Court concluded that "an arrest warrant founded on probable cause implicitly carries with it the limited authority to enter a dwelling in which the suspect lives when there is reason to believe the suspect is within." 445 U.S. at 603, 100 S.Ct. at 1388, 63 L.Ed.2d at 661. Therefore, absent consent or exigent circumstances, a law enforcement officer must have at least an arrest warrant to lawfully enter a suspect's home to arrest the suspect.

With respect to the *Payton* requirement that an officer executing an arrest warrant at the suspect's home have "reason to believe the suspect is within," the following quotation from the 11th Circuit Court of Appeals is informative:

> [I]n order for law enforcement officials to enter a residence to execute an arrest warrant for a resident of the premises, the facts and circumstances within the knowledge of the law enforcement agents, when viewed in the totality, must warrant a reasonable belief that [1] the location to be searched is the suspect's dwelling, and that [2] the suspect is within the residence at the time of entry. . . . In evaluating this on the spot determination, as to the second *Payton* prong, courts must be sensitive to common sense factors indicating a resident's presence. For example, officers may take into consideration the possibility that the resident may be aware that police are attempting to ascertain whether or not the resident is at home, and officers may presume that a person is at home at certain times of the day—a presumption which can be rebutted by contrary evidence regarding the suspect's known schedule. *United States v. Magluta,* 44 F.3d 1530, 1535 (11th Cir. 1995).

In *United States v. Beck,* 729 F.2d 1329 (11th Cir. 1984), the court held that FBI officers and local police had reason to believe that Beck was in his apartment when the officers entered it to execute an arrest warrant. There were no outward signs of life in the apartment the evening before the search or the next morning, and as the agents had not monitored Beck's apartment, they were not aware of his comings and goings. Despite these evidentiary shortcomings, the court observed that Beck's car was parked near the home and that it was reasonable to believe that a person would be home sleeping at 7:30 A.M., which would account for the lack of outward signs of life. Finally, the court noted that the lack of response to the officer's knock and an-nouncement did not indicate that no one was at home "since it was reasonable to ex-pect a fugitive to hide or flee if possible." 729 F.2d at 1332. In *United States v. De Parias,* 805 F.2d 1447 (11th Cir. 1986), the court held that agents reasonably believed that the suspects were at home, where the apartment manager informed agents that the De Pariases were at home if a certain car was parked in front of the apartment.

In *United States v. Holland,* 755 F.2d 253 (2d Cir. 1985), the court held that the *Payton* rule did not apply to vestibules and common areas of multiple-tenant build-ings, because there can be no expectation of privacy in those areas and because police protection is needed in those areas. In that case, the court upheld a nonconsensual, nonemergency arrest of a defendant who answered the doorbell in the vestibule of his two-apartment building. The arresting officer had probable cause to believe that the defendant was involved in illegal drug sales.

Entry of a Third Person's Home

In *Steagald v. United States,* 451 U.S. 204, 101 S.Ct. 1642, 68 L.Ed.2d 38 (1981), the U.S. Supreme Court held that an arrest warrant does not authorize law enforcement officers to enter the home of a third person to search for the person to be arrested, in the absence of consent or exigent circumstances. To protect the Fourth Amendment privacy interests of persons not named in an arrest warrant, a search warrant must be obtained to justify the entry into the home of any person other than the person to be arrested. The Court said:

> In the absence of exigent circumstances, we have consistently held that [law en-forcement officers' determinations of probable cause] are not reliable enough to justify an entry into a person's home to arrest him without a warrant, or a search of a home for objects in the absence of a search warrant. We see no rea-son to depart from this settled course when the search of a home is for a person rather than an object.
>
> A contrary conclusion—that the police, acting alone and in the absence of exigent circumstances, may decide when there is sufficient justification for searching the home of a third party for the subject of an arrest warrant—would create a significant potential for abuse. Armed solely with an arrest warrant for a single person, the police could search all the homes of that individual's friends and acquaintances. . . . Moreover, an arrest warrant may serve as the pretext for entering a home in which the police have suspicion, but not probable cause to believe, that illegal activity is taking place. 451 U.S. at 215, 101 S.Ct. at 1649, 68 L.Ed.2d at 46–47.

This requirement places a heavy practical burden on law enforcement officers, causing them to seek both an arrest warrant and a search warrant in many situations. An alternative, suggested by the Supreme Court, is that in most instances the police may avoid altogether the need to obtain a search warrant simply by waiting for a sus-pect to leave the third person's home before attempting to arrest the suspect. When the suspect leaves either the home of a third person or the suspect's own home and is in a public place, officers may arrest on probable cause alone. Neither an arrest war-rant nor a search warrant is required to support an arrest made in a public place.

Some courts have allowed exceptions to the requirement of a search warrant to enter a third person's home to arrest a suspect. *United States v. Donaldson,* 793 F.2d 498 (2d Cir. 1986), held that a search warrant was not required where the third-party homeowner knowingly allowed a fleeing felon to enter his home. And *United States v. Riis,* 83 F.3d 212 (8th Cir. 1996), held that a search warrant was not required to arrest a suspect at the home of a third party where police reasonably believed that the suspect was the third party's girlfriend and that she possessed common authority over the home.

Exigent Circumstances

In neither *Payton* nor *Steagald* did the Supreme Court specify the nature of the exigent circumstances that would justify a warrantless entry of a home to make an arrest. In *Welsh v. Wisconsin,* 466 U.S. 740, 753, 104 S.Ct. 2091, 2099, 80 L.Ed.2d 732, 745 (1984), however, the Court held:

> [A]n important factor to be considered when determining whether any exigency exists is the gravity of the underlying offense for which the arrest is being made. Moreover, although no exigency is created simply because there is probable cause to believe that a serious crime has been committed . . . application of the exigent-circumstances exception in the context of a home entry should rarely be sanctioned when there is probable cause to believe that only a minor offense . . . has been committed.

In the *Welsh* case, the warrantless arrest of the defendant in his home for a noncriminal traffic offense (operating a motor vehicle while under the influence of an intoxicant) was held illegal. The need to obtain a blood sample quickly for blood-alcohol testing was not considered a sufficient exigency.

In *Minnesota v. Olson,* 495 U.S. 91, 110 S.Ct. 1684, 109 L.Ed.2d 85 (1990), the U.S. Supreme Court approved the Minnesota Supreme Court's standard for determining whether exigent circumstances exist. The Minnesota court observed that "a warrantless intrusion may be justified by hot pursuit of a fleeing felon, or imminent destruction of evidence . . . or the need to prevent a suspect's escape, or the risk of danger to the police or to other persons inside or outside the dwelling." 436 N.W.2d at 97. Furthermore, "in the absence of hot pursuit there must be at least probable cause to believe that one or more of the other factors justifying the entry were present and that in assessing the risk of danger, the gravity of the crime and likelihood that the suspect is armed should be considered." 495 U.S. at 100, 110 S.Ct. at 1690, 109 L.Ed.2d at 95–96. Applying this standard, exigent circumstances justifying the warrantless entry into a home were determined *not* to exist in the Olson case in which

- although a grave crime was involved, the defendant was known not to be the murderer;
- the police had already recovered the murder weapon;
- there was no suggestion of danger to the two women with whom the defendant was staying;
- several police squads surrounded the house;
- the time was 3 P.M. Sunday;
- it was evident the suspect was going nowhere; and
- if he came out of the house, he would have been promptly apprehended.

A case in which the U.S. Supreme Court found that **hot pursuit** of the perpetrator of a serious crime was exigent circumstances is *Warden v. Hayden,* 387 U.S. 294, 87 S.Ct. 1642, 18 L.Ed.2d 782 (1967). In that case, police officers had reliable information that an armed robbery had taken place and that the perpetrator had entered a certain house five minutes earlier. The Court held that the officers acted reasonably when they entered the house and began to search for a man of the description they had been given and for weapons which he had used in the robbery or might use against them. The Fourth Amendment does not require police officers to delay in the course of an investigation if to do so would gravely endanger their lives or the lives of others. Speed here was essential, and only a thorough search of the house for persons and weapons could have insured that Hayden was the only man present and that the police had control of all weapons which could be used against them or to effect an escape. 387 U.S. at 298–99, 87 S.Ct. at 1646, 18 L.Ed.2d at 787.

When the arrest of a suspect is set in motion in a public place, but the suspect retreats into his or her home, the right of officers to enter the home in hot pursuit is governed by the case of *United States v. Santana,* 427 U.S. 38, 96 S.Ct. 2406, 49 L.Ed.2d 300 (1976). In that case, police officers drove to the defendant's house after receiving information that she had in her possession marked money used to make a heroin buy arranged by an undercover agent. The defendant was standing in the doorway of her house holding a paper bag as the police pulled up within fifteen feet of her. The officers got out of the car, shouting "Police," and the defendant retreated into the vestibule of her house where she was apprehended. When the defendant tried to pull away, envelopes containing heroin fell to the floor from the paper bag. Some of the marked money was found on her person.

The Court held that, while standing in the doorway of her house, the defendant was in a "public place" for purposes of the Fourth Amendment. Since she was not in an area where she had any expectation of privacy and she was exposed to public view, speech, hearing, and touch, it was the same as if she had been standing completely outside her house. When police sought to arrest her, they merely intended to make a warrantless arrest in a public place upon probable cause. Under *United States v. Watson,* 423 U.S. 411, 96 S.Ct. 820, 46 L.Ed.2d 598 (1976), such an arrest would not violate the Fourth Amendment. By retreating into a private place, the defendant could not defeat an otherwise proper arrest that had been set in motion in a public place. Since the officers needed to act quickly to prevent the destruction of evidence, a true hot pursuit took place, even though it entailed only a very short chase. Thus, the warrantless entry to make the arrest was justified, as was the search incident to that arrest.

A case in which the court found that the risk of danger to persons inside a dwelling constituted exigent circumstances is *State v. York,* 464 N.W.2d 36 (Wis.App. 1990). In that case police, acting on a missing persons report, went to the home of the missing persons and detected an odor of a decomposing body emanating from an open window. Warrantless entry of the home was justified because the officers had reason to believe there might be another living victim in the area in need of assistance. The court pointed out that "the criterion is the reasonableness of the belief of the police as to the existence of an emergency, not the existence of an emergency in fact." 464 N.W.2d at 40. See pages 356 through 358 for a discussion of limitations on searches of murder scenes and for a broader discussion of emergency entries of dwellings and observations of evidence under the plain view doctrine.

Officers, of course, cannot deliberately create exigent circumstances to subvert the warrant requirements of the Fourth Amendment. In considering claims of manufactured exigency, courts "distinguish between cases where exigent circumstances arise naturally during a delay in obtaining a warrant and those where officers have deliberately created the exigent circumstances." *United States v. Webster,* 750 F.2d 307, 327 (5th Cir. 1984). In *United States v. Hultgren,* 713 F.2d 79 (5th Cir. 1983), the court held that exigent circumstances arose naturally when the transmitter worn by a confidential informant participating in a drug buy suddenly failed. Concern for the confidential informant's safety justified the warrantless entry. On the other hand, a warrantless entry was held to be illegal because of manufactured exigency in *United States v. Scheffer*, 463 F.2d 567 (5th Cir. 1972), in which codefendants who had already been arrested were helping agents catch other members of a drug conspiracy. Agents sent the cooperating defendants into a residence to consummate a drug deal and then made a warrantless entry to arrest the residents. The court refused to accept the government's argument that the agents lacked the time to obtain a warrant, because the agents controlled the timing of the drug buy.

Forced Entry

Assuming police officers have legal authority to enter a dwelling, they should first knock on the door, announce their authority and purpose, and then demand admittance before they force their way into the dwelling to arrest someone inside. This principle is an element of the reasonableness inquiry under the Fourth Amendment.

> Given the longstanding common-law endorsement of the practice of announcement, we have little doubt that the Framers of the Fourth Amendment thought that the method of an officer's entry into a dwelling was among the factors to be considered in assessing the reasonableness of a search or seizure. . . . [W]e hold that in some circumstances an officer's unannounced entry into a home might be unreasonable under the Fourth Amendment. *Wilson v. Arkansas,* 514 U.S. 927, 934, 115 S.Ct. 1914, 1918, 131 L.Ed.2d 976, 982 (1995).

If their demand to enter is refused or met with silence, officers may enter forcibly after waiting a reasonable time under the circumstances.

> The requirement of prior notice of authority and purpose before forcing entry into a home is deeply rooted in our heritage, and should not be given grudging application. . . . Every householder, the good and the bad, the guilty and the innocent, is entitled to the protection designed to secure the common interest against unlawful invasion of the house. The petitioner could not be lawfully arrested in his home by officers breaking in without first giving him notice of their authority and purpose. Because the petitioner did not receive that notice before the officers broke the door to invade his home, the arrest was unlawful, and the evidence seized should have been suppressed. *Miller v. United States,* 357 U.S. 301, 313–14, 78 S.Ct. 1190, 1198, 2 L.Ed.2d 1332, 1340–41 (1958).

> In this context, forcible entry of a dwelling does not necessarily mean only the violent breaking down of a door or the smashing of a window. The U.S. Supreme Court stated that "[a]n unannounced intrusion into a dwelling . . . is no less an unannounced intrusion whether officers break down a door, force open a chain lock on a partially open door, open a locked door by use of a passkey, or . . . open a closed but unlocked door." *Sabbath v. United States,* 391 U.S. 585, 590, 88 S.Ct. 1755, 1758, 20 L.Ed.2d 828, 834 (1968). Also, refusal of admittance is not restricted to an affirmative refusal but is determined from the totality of the circumstances. As stated in *United States v. James,* 528 F.2d 999, 1017 (5th Cir. 1976), "Failure to respond within a reasonable time [is] tantamount to a refusal. A reasonable time is ordinarily very brief." Furthermore, officers' knowledge that the occupants are drug dealers justifies a shorter wait before entry.

> Those within might reasonably be thought to be unusually attuned to a law-enforcement knock at the door, and ready to respond promptly in one form or another. As common sense, and bitter experience, would suggest, the law has

"uniformly . . . recognized that substantial dealers in narcotics possess firearms and that such weapons are as much tools of the trade as more commonly recognized drug paraphernalia." *United States v. Payne*, 805 F.2d 1062, 1065 (D.C. Cir. 1986). . . . Once police officers seeking to enter a drug traffickers' enclave have announced their identity and authority, they stand before the door blind and vulnerable. In such a danger-fraught situation, the officers may quite reasonably infer refusal more readily than under other circumstances. *United States v. Bonner*, 874 F.2d 822, 824 (D.C.Cir. 1989).

The U.S. Supreme Court held that although an officer's unannounced entry into a home might, in some circumstances, be unreasonable under the Fourth Amendment, not *every* entry must be preceded by an announcement.

> The Fourth Amendment's flexible requirement of reasonableness should not be read to mandate a rigid rule of announcement that ignores countervailing law enforcement interests. . . . [T]he common-law principle of announcement was never stated as an inflexible rule requiring announcement under all circumstances. *Wilson v. Arkansas*, 514 U.S. 927, 934, 115 S.Ct. 1914, 1918, 131 L.Ed.2d 976, 982 (1995).

Therefore, the failure to knock, announce, and demand admittance before forcibly entering may be excused in the following situations:

- When the officer's purpose is already known to the offender or other person upon whom demand for entry is made. As the Supreme Court stated in the *Miller* case:

  > It may be that, without an express announcement of purpose, the facts known to officers would justify them in being virtually certain that the petitioner already knows their purpose so that an announcement would be a useless gesture. 375 U.S. at 310, 78 S.Ct. at 1196, 2 L.Ed.2d at 1338.

- When the personal safety of the officer or other persons might be imperiled. "[T]he presumption in favor of announcement would yield under circumstances presenting a threat of physical violence." *Wilson v. Arkansas*, 514 U.S. 927, 936, 115 S.Ct. 1914, 1918–19, 131 L.Ed.2d 976, 983 (1995).

- When the delay to knock and announce might defeat the arrest by allowing the offender to escape. *State v. Fair*, 211 A.2d 359 (N.J. 1965).

- When a prisoner escapes from an officer and retreats into the prisoner's dwelling. "Proof of 'demand and refusal' was deemed unnecessary in such cases because it would be a 'senseless ceremony' to require an officer in pursuit of a recently escaped arrestee to make an announcement prior to breaking the door to retake him." *Wilson v. Arkansas*, 514 U.S. 927, 936, 115 S.Ct. 1914, 1919, 131 L.Ed.2d 976, 983 (1995).

- When knocking and announcing might allow persons inside to destroy evidence. In *Ker v. California*, 374 U.S. 23, 83 S.Ct. 1623, 10 L.Ed.2d 726 (1963), the U.S. Supreme Court held that an unannounced entry into the defendant's apartment was proper when evidence of narcotics activity would otherwise have been destroyed. However, officers must be able to justify an unannounced entry by the particular facts of a case. In the *Ker* case, not only did the officers reasonably believe that the defendant was in possession of narcotics, but the defendant's furtive conduct in eluding officers shortly before the arrest gave the officers grounds to believe that he might have been expecting the police. In *United States v. Stewart*, 867 F.2d 581 (10th Cir. 1989), the officers' justification for their unannounced entry consisted only of generalities about drug dealers that bore no relation to the particular premises or the particular circumstances. Finding the unannounced entry illegal, the court stated:

None of these facts specifically pertained to the defendant or the defendant's house. No officer had any information to the effect that the house had been barricaded or fortified or if the occupants were monitoring activity in the surrounding area. Most importantly, no effort was made to determine who was in the house at the time the entry was made. 867 F.2d at 585.

See the discussion on page 182 of *Richards v. Wisconsin*, holding that there is no automatic exception to the "knock and announce" requirement in drug cases.

KEY POINTS

14. In general, a law enforcement officer may not use deadly force to arrest or prevent the escape of a felon, unless the felon poses a threat of serious physical harm, to either the officer or others.

15. A law enforcement officer may use any reasonably necessary *nondeadly* force but may never use *deadly* force to arrest for a misdemeanor. It is better that a misdemeanant escape rather than a human life be taken.

16. A law enforcement officer making a lawful arrest (for either a misdemeanor or a felony) may use any force reasonably necessary under the circumstances in self-defense, including deadly force, if the officer reasonably believes that the person to be arrested is about to commit an assault and that the officer is in danger of death or serious bodily injury.

17. Resisting arrest is a crime involving a person's opposition by direct, forcible means against a law enforcement officer to prevent being taken into custody.

18. Absent exigent circumstances or consent, a law enforcement officer may not make a warrantless entry into a suspect's home to make a routine felony arrest.

19. Absent exigent circumstances or consent, an *arrest* warrant does not authorize a law enforcement officer to enter the home of a third person to search for the person to be arrested. A *search* warrant must be obtained to justify the entry into the home of any person other than the person to be arrested.

20. Exigent circumstances that would justify a warrantless entry of a dwelling to arrest are hot pursuit of a fleeing felon, imminent destruction of evidence, the need to prevent a suspect's escape, and the risk of danger to the police or to other persons. In assessing the risk of danger, the gravity of the crime and the likelihood that the suspect is armed should be considered.

21. If an arrest is begun in a public place, officers may enter a dwelling without a warrant in hot pursuit, to complete the arrest.

22. Absent extenuating circumstances, before law enforcement officers may lawfully force their way into a dwelling to arrest someone inside, they should first knock on the door, announce their authority and purpose, and then demand admittance and be refused admittance.

Disposition of an Arrested Person

The arrest of a person initiates a series of administrative and judicial processes dealing with the person and his or her property. These processes vary among jurisdictions and are necessary for the protection of the person and property of the arrestee, notification and opportunity to exercise certain rights, safety and security of law enforcement officials and places of confinement, identification, further investigation, record keeping, and avoidance of civil liability. Our discussion begins with booking, usually the first of these processes to take place after arrest.

Booking

Booking is a police administrative procedure officially recording an arrest in a police register. Booking involves, at the minimum, recording the name of the person arrested; the name of the officer making the arrest; and the time of, place of, circumstances of, and reason for the arrest. The meaning of booking, however, is sometimes expanded to include other procedures that take place in the station house after an arrest. For more serious offenses, booking may include a search of the arrested person, including in some cases a search of body cavities, fingerprinting, photographing, a lineup, or other identification procedures. The arrested person may be temporarily detained in a jail or lockup until release on bail can be arranged. For less serious offenses, the arrested person may be released on recognizance, under which the person agrees to appear in court when required but is not required to pay or promise to pay any money or property as security.

Booking is usually completed before the arrested person is taken for his or her initial appearance before the magistrate. It may, however, take place after the initial appearance, or parts of the booking procedures may take place both before and after the initial appearance. Booking procedures vary in different jurisdictions and different law enforcement agencies within a particular jurisdiction.

Initial Appearance Before the Magistrate

After arresting a person, with or without a warrant, and after the complaint has been filed, a law enforcement officer must take the person before a magistrate or deliver the person according to the mandate of the warrant. Statutes in different jurisdictions require that this be done promptly, using terms such as "immediately," "without unnecessary delay," "forthwith," or other similar language. These statutes confer a substantial right on the defendant and create a corresponding duty on law enforcement officers.

The reasons behind the rule requiring arrested persons to be brought before a magistrate without unnecessary delay are as follows:

- To verify that the person arrested is the person named in the complaint
- To advise the arrested person of the charges, so that the person may prepare a defense
- To advise the arrested person of his or her rights, such as the right to a preliminary hearing, the right to counsel, and the right to remain silent
- To protect arrested persons from being abandoned in jail and forgotten by, or otherwise cut off from contact with, people who can help them
- To prevent secret and extended interrogation of arrested persons by law enforcement officers
- To give the arrested person an early opportunity to secure release on bail while awaiting the final outcome of the proceedings. If the person has been bailed earlier, the magistrate will simply review that bail. Release on personal recognizance upon the defendant's promise to appear, without any pledge or deposit of money or property, may also be granted at the initial appearance.
- To give the arrested person an opportunity to speedily conclude proceedings on charges of minor offenses by pleading guilty to the charges, paying fines, and carrying on with his or her life

- To obtain a prompt, neutral "judicial determination of probable cause as a prerequisite to extended restraint of liberty following arrest." *Gerstein v. Pugh,* 420 U.S. 103, 114, 95 S.Ct. 854, 863, 43 L.Ed.2d 54, 65 (1975). Not all states provide for a judicial determination of probable cause at the initial appearance before a magistrate.

There is no single preferred pretrial procedure, and the nature of the probable cause determination usually will be shaped to accord with a State's pretrial procedure viewed as a whole. . . . It may be found desirable, for example, to make the probable cause determination at the suspect's first appearance before a judicial officer, . . . or the determination may be incorporated into the procedure for setting bail or fixing other conditions of pretrial release. In some States, existing procedures may satisfy the requirement of the Fourth Amendment. Others may require only minor adjustment, such as acceleration of existing preliminary hearings. Current proposals for criminal procedure reform suggest other ways of testing probable cause for detention. Whatever procedure a State may adopt, it must provide a fair and reliable determination of probable cause as a condition for any significant pretrial restraint of liberty, and this determination must be made by a judicial officer either before or promptly after arrest. 420 U.S. at 123–25, 95 S.Ct. at 868–69, 43 L.Ed.2d at 71–72.

In *County of Riverside v. McLaughlin,* 500 U.S. 44, 111 S.Ct. 1661, 114 L.Ed.2d 49 (1991), the U.S. Supreme Court held that, to satisfy the "promptness" requirement of *Gerstein,* a jurisdiction that chooses to combine probable cause determinations with other pretrial proceedings must do so as soon as is reasonably feasible, but in no event later than forty-eight hours after arrest. This is not to say that the probable cause determination in a particular case passes constitutional muster simply because it is provided within forty-eight hours. As the Court said:

Such a hearing may nonetheless violate *Gerstein* if the arrested individual can prove that his or her probable cause determination was delayed unreasonably. Examples of unreasonable delay are delays for the purpose of gathering additional evidence to justify the arrest, a delay motivated by ill will against the arrested individual, or delay for delay's sake. In evaluating whether the delay in a particular case is unreasonable, however, courts must allow a substantial degree of flexibility. Courts cannot ignore the often unavoidable delays in transporting arrested persons from one facility to another, handling late-night bookings where no magistrate is readily available, obtaining the presence of an arresting officer who may be busy processing other suspects or securing the premises of an arrest, and other practical realities. 500 U.S. at 56–57, 111 S.Ct. at 1670, 114 L.Ed.2d at 63.

The Court went on to say that, where an arrested person does not receive a probable cause determination within forty-eight hours, the burden shifts to the government to demonstrate the existence of a bona fide emergency or other extraordinary circumstance. The Court specifically stated that neither intervening weekends nor the fact that in a particular case it may take longer than forty-eight hours to consolidate pretrial proceedings qualifies as an extraordinary circumstance.

Safety Considerations

In *Washington v. Chrisman,* 455 U.S. 1, 102 S.Ct. 812, 70 L.Ed.2d 778 (1982), the U.S. Supreme Court held:

[I]t is not "unreasonable" under the Fourth Amendment for a police officer, as a matter of course, to monitor the movements of an arrested person, as his judgement dictates, following the arrest. The officer's need to ensure his own safety— as well as the integrity of the arrest—is compelling. Such surveillance is not an impermissible invasion of the privacy or personal liberty of an individual who has been arrested. 455 U.S. at 7, 102 S.Ct. at 817, 70 L.Ed.2d at 785.

In the *Chrisman* case, the officer arrested a college student for possession of alcoholic beverages by a person under twenty-one, and the student asked permission to go to his room to get his identification. The officer accompanied the student to his room, and while in the room, the officer observed marijuana in plain view. The Court held that the officer had a right to remain literally at the student's elbow at all times and that no showing of "exigent circumstances" was necessary to authorize the officer to accompany the student into the room. The Court said:

> Every arrest must be presumed to present a risk of danger to the arresting officer. . . . There is no way for an officer to predict reliably how a particular subject will react to arrest or the degree of potential danger. Moreover, the possibility that an arrested person will attempt to escape if not properly supervised is obvious. 455 U.S. at 7, 102 S.Ct. at 817, 70 L.Ed.2d at 785.

Protection and Welfare of an Arrested Person

When delay in taking an arrested person before a magistrate is unavoidable, the officer must keep the arrested person safely in custody for the period of the delay. The officer may reasonably restrain the person to prevent escape and may even confine the person in a jail or other suitable place. Handcuffs may be used at the officer's discretion, depending on the person's reputation or record for violence, the time of day, the number of other persons in custody, and the duration of the detention.

The officer is responsible for the health and safety of the arrested person, including the provision of adequate medical assistance, if necessary. Any unnecessary use of force or negligent failure to prevent the use of force by others against the arrested person may subject the officer to civil liability.

Station-House Search

When a person is arrested and taken into custody, police may, as part of the routine administrative procedure incident to booking and jailing the person, search the person and any container or article in his or her possession. In *Illinois v. Lafayette*, 462 U.S. 640, 103 S.Ct. 2605, 77 L.Ed.2d 65 (1983), the U.S. Supreme Court held that station-house inventory searches were an incidental step following arrest and preceding incarceration. The justification for these searches does not rest on probable cause; thus, the absence of a warrant is immaterial to the reasonableness of the searches. The Court said that the governmental interests justifying a station-house inventory search are different from, and may in some circumstances be even greater than, those supporting a search incident to arrest (see Chapter 8). Among those interests are prevention of theft of the arrested person's property; deterrence of false claims regarding that property; prevention of injury from belts, drugs, or dangerous instruments such as razor blades, knives, or bombs; and determination or verification of the person's identity. Furthermore, it does not matter that less intrusive means of satisfying those governmental interests might be possible. The Court said:

It is evident that a stationhouse search of every item carried on or by a person who has lawfully been taken into custody by the police will amply serve the important and legitimate governmental interests involved.

Even if less intrusive means existed of protecting some particular types of property, it would be unreasonable to expect police officers in the everyday course of business to make fine and subtle distinctions in deciding which containers or items may be searched and which must be sealed as a unit. 462 U.S. at 648, 103 S.Ct. at 2610, 77 L.Ed.2d at 72.

A station-house inventory search need not be conducted immediately upon the arrested person's arrival at the station house. The U.S. Supreme Court held that a seizure of a prisoner's clothing in the morning, several hours after his arrest and incarceration the previous evening, was reasonable. No substitute clothing had been available at the time of arrest and, therefore, the normal processes incident to arrest and custody had not been completed.

[O]nce the accused is lawfully arrested and is in custody, the effects in his possession at the place of detention that were subject to search at the time and place of his arrest may lawfully be searched and seized without a warrant even though a substantial period of time has elapsed between the arrest and subsequent administrative processing, on the one hand, and the taking of the property for use as evidence, on the other. *United States v. Edwards,* 415 U.S. 800, 807, 94 S.Ct. 1234, 1239, 39 L.Ed.2d 771, 778 (1974).

Sometimes, especially when a vehicle is involved, officers must take positive action to protect the defendant's property or become civilly liable for damages for failure to do so. To protect against liability of this nature, many law enforcement agencies have adopted standard procedures for impounding arrested persons' vehicles and making an inventory of their contents. (For a further discussion of impoundment and inventory of vehicles, see Chapter 11.)

Identification and Examination of an Arrested Person

Pretrial procedures for identifying and examining an arrested person take many different forms. One form is confrontation of the arrested person with victims or witnesses of the crime, sometimes accomplished through the use of a police lineup or showup. The arrested person has no right to object to being viewed by witnesses for identification purposes and also has no right to demand to be placed in a lineup. (For a discussion of pretrial identification techniques and the right to counsel, see Chapter 14.)

Law enforcement officers may take fingerprints, footprints, or photographs of the arrested person for purposes of identification or evidence. Officers may also obtain voice exemplars or have a dentist examine a defendant's mouth for a missing tooth for identification purposes.

[T]he Fourth Amendment does not protect "what a person knowingly exposes to the public even in his home or office. . . . Like a man's facial characteristics, or handwriting, his voice is repeatedly produced for others to hear. No person can have a reasonable expectation that others will not know the sound of his voice, any more than he can reasonably expect that his face will be a mystery to the world." This doctrine is applicable as well to a missing tooth. *United States v. Holland,* 378 F.Supp. 144, 155 (E.D.Pa. 1974).

Law enforcement officers may physically examine arrested persons for measurements, scars, bruises, tattoos, and so on, and may require persons to disrobe against their will.

> Such procedures and practices and tests may result in freeing an innocent man accused of crime, or may be part of a chain of facts and circumstances which help identify a person accused of a crime or connect a suspect or an accused with the crime of which he has been suspected or has been accused. The law is well settled that such actions, practices, and procedures do not violate any constitutional right. *Commonwealth v. Aljoe*, 216 A.2d 50, 52–53 (Pa. 1966).

These various forms of identifying and examining arrested persons may be accomplished by force, if necessary, but the methods used may not be such as to "shock the conscience," offend a "sense of justice," or run counter to the "decencies of civilized conduct." *Rochin v. California*, 342 U.S. 165, 72 S.Ct. 205, 96 L.Ed. 183 (1952).

The U.S. Supreme Court held that there is no denial of due process of law in taking a blood sample with proper medical supervision from a person who is unconscious and unable to give consent. *Breithaupt v. Abram*, 352 U.S. 432, 77 S.Ct. 408, 1 L.Ed.2d 448 (1957). Also, in *Schmerber v. California*, the Court held that there is no violation of the Fifth Amendment privilege against self-incrimination or the Fourth Amendment protection against unreasonable searches and seizures when a blood sample is taken without consent from an arrested person in lawful custody. The Court said that the privilege against self-incrimination "protects an accused only from being compelled to testify against himself, or otherwise provide the State with evidence of a testimonial or communicative nature, and that the withdrawal of blood and use of the analysis in question in this case did not involve compulsion to these ends." 384 U.S. 757, 761, 86 S.Ct. 1826, 1830–31, 16 L.Ed.2d 908, 914 (1966). The Court found that the Fourth Amendment standard of reasonableness was satisfied where (1) "there was plainly probable cause for the officer to arrest petitioner and charge him with driving an automobile under the influence of intoxicating liquor," and (2) the facts "suggested the required relevance and likely success of a test of petitioner's blood for alcohol. . . ." The blood sample was taken in a hospital by a physician following accepted medical procedures. Also, the officer "might reasonably have believed that he was confronted with an emergency" and that there was a need for immediate action because the sample was needed to measure the blood's alcoholic content, which would quickly dissipate. The Court said:

> [W]e reach this judgment only on the facts in the present record. The integrity of an individual's person is a cherished value of our society. That we today hold that the Constitution does not forbid the State's minor intrusions into an individual's body under stringently limited conditions in no way indicates that it permits more substantial intrusions or intrusions under other conditions. 384 U.S. at 772, 86 S.Ct. at 1836, 16 L.Ed.2d at 920.

In a case involving a more substantial intrusion, the Supreme Court refused, on Fourth Amendment grounds, to allow the prosecution to compel an armed robbery suspect to undergo a surgical procedure under a general anesthetic for removal of a bullet lodged in his chest. *Winston v. Lee*, 470 U.S. 753, 105 S.Ct. 1611, 84 L.Ed.2d 662 (1985). The Court applied the same balancing test used in *Schmerber* and found that the potential threat to the suspect's health and safety, combined with the extensive intrusion on the suspect's personal privacy and bodily integrity, were not counterbalanced by a compelling need for evidence. Of particular importance was the

Court's finding that the prosecution had substantial additional evidence that the suspect was the person who committed the robbery. The Court said:

> The Fourth Amendment is a vital safeguard of the right of the citizen to be free from unreasonable governmental intrusions into any area in which he has a reasonable expectation of privacy. Where the Court has found a lesser expectation of privacy . . . or where the search involves a minimal intrusion on privacy interests . . . the Court has held that the Fourth Amendment protections are correspondingly less stringent. Conversely, however, the Fourth Amendment's command that searches be "reasonable" requires that when the State seeks to intrude upon an area in which our society recognizes a significantly heightened privacy interest, a more substantial justification is required to make the search "reasonable." Applying these principles, we hold that the proposed search in this case would be "unreasonable" under the Fourth Amendment. 470 U.S. at 767, 105 S.Ct. at 1620, 84 L.Ed.2d at 673.

KEY POINTS

23. A state must provide a fair and reliable judicial determination of probable cause as a condition for any significant pretrial restraint on liberty either before arrest or as soon as is reasonably feasible after arrest, but in no event later than forty-eight hours after arrest.

24. A law enforcement officer may monitor the movements of an arrested person, as his or her judgment dictates, to ensure the officer's safety and the arrest's integrity.

25. Once a person is lawfully arrested and in custody, police may, as part of the routine administrative procedure incident to booking and jailing the person, search the person and any containers or articles in his or her possession.

26. An arrested person may be subjected to various identification and examination procedures, including the obtaining of a blood sample, so long as the reasonableness requirement of the Fourth Amendment is satisfied. Reasonable force may be used for these purposes if the methods do not "shock the conscience," offend a "sense of justice," or run counter to the "decencies of civilized conduct."

Effect of Illegal Arrest

Jurisdiction to try a person for a crime is not affected by an illegal arrest.

> [T]he power of a court to try a person for crime is not impaired by the fact that he had been brought within the court's jurisdiction by reason of a "forcible abduction." . . . [D]ue process of law is satisfied when one present in court is convicted of crime after having been fairly apprised of the charges against him and after a fair trial in accordance with constitutional procedural safeguards. There is nothing in the Constitution that requires a court to permit a guilty person rightfully convicted to escape justice because he was brought to trial against his will. *Frisbie v. Collins*, 342 U.S. 519, 522, 72 S.Ct. 509, 511–12, 96 L.Ed. 541, 545–46 (1952).

However, although an illegal arrest does not affect jurisdiction to try an offender, the exclusionary rule may affect the trial adversely. The exclusionary rule, as it relates to arrest, states that any evidence obtained by exploitation of an unlawful arrest will be inadmissible in court in a prosecution against the person arrested. Therefore, if the only evidence that the state has against an armed robbery suspect is a gun, a mask, and a roll of bills taken during a search incident to an unlawful arrest, the offender will very likely go free because these items will be inadmissible in court. (The exclusionary rule is discussed in detail in Chapter 3.)

A confession obtained by exploitation of an illegal arrest will also be inadmissible in court. In *Brown v. Illinois,* the defendant was illegally arrested in a manner calculated to cause surprise, fright, and confusion and taken to a police station. He was given *Miranda* warnings, and he waived his rights and made incriminating statements, all within two hours of the illegal arrest. The Court held that officers could not avoid the effect of the illegal arrest by simply giving the arrested person the *Miranda* warnings. *Miranda* warnings do not alone sufficiently deter a Fourth Amendment violation. The Court said:

> The *Miranda* warnings are an important factor, to be sure, in determining whether the confession is obtained by exploitation of illegal arrest. But they are not the only factor to be considered. The temporal proximity of the arrest and the confession, the presence of intervening circumstances, . . . and, particularly, the purpose and flagrancy of the official misconduct are all relevant. . . . And the burden of showing admissibility rests, of course, on the prosecution. *Brown v. Illinois,* 422 U.S. 590, 603–04, 95 S.Ct. 2254, 2261–62, 45 L.Ed.2d 416, 427 (1975).

The prosecution has a difficult burden in curing the effect of an illegal arrest on a subsequent confession. In *Taylor v. Alabama,* 457 U.S. 687, 102 S.Ct. 2664, 73 L.Ed.2d 314 (1982), police made an investigatory arrest without probable cause, based on an uncorroborated informant's tip, and transported the defendant against his will to the station for interrogation in the hope that something would turn up. The defendant was in police custody the entire time, and the police repeatedly questioned him, took his fingerprints, and subjected him to a lineup without counsel present. The Court held that there was no meaningful intervening event to break the causal connection between the arrest and the confession, even though (1) six hours elapsed between the arrest and the confession and (2) the confession may have been voluntary for purposes of the Fifth Amendment in the sense that *Miranda* warnings were given and understood, the defendant was permitted a short visit with his girlfriend, and the police did not physically abuse the defendant.

Many factors must be considered to determine whether a confession is obtained by exploitation of an illegal arrest; thus, it is difficult to predict how a particular court will rule. For example, despite only a two-hour lapse between an illegal arrest and a confession, in *People v. Vance,* 185 Cal.Rptr. 549 (Cal.App. 1982), the court held the defendant's confession admissible because of the following circumstances:

- Proper *Miranda* warnings were given,
- the defendant was confronted with information that tied him to the crimes,
- the defendant was allowed to speak privately with his common-law wife, and
- there was no purposeful or flagrant police activity.

Because circumstances in the police's control often determine the admissibility of a confession following an illegal arrest, officers should do everything possible to ensure that a confession is a product of the suspect's free will.

But if the evidence is not the *product* of the illegal arrest, the exclusionary rule does not apply. The indirect fruits of an illegal arrest should be suppressed only when they bear a sufficiently close relationship to the underlying illegality. In *New York v. Harris,* 495 U.S. 14, 110 S.Ct. 1640, 109 L.Ed.2d 13 (1990), police officers, who had probable cause to believe that the defendant committed murder, entered his home without first obtaining an arrest warrant in violation of *Payton v. New York* (see page 132). The officers read him his *Miranda* rights and obtained an admission of guilt. After the defendant was arrested, taken to the police station, and again given his *Miranda* warnings, he signed a written inculpatory statement. The first statement was inadmissible because it was obtained in the defendant's home by exploitation of the *Payton* violation. The statement taken at the police station, however, was admissible. That statement was *not* the product of being in unlawful custody; neither was it the fruit of having been arrested in the home rather than someplace else. The police had a justification to question the defendant prior to his arrest. Therefore, his subsequent statement was not an *exploitation* of the illegal entry into his home. Moreover, suppressing a station-house statement obtained after a *Payton* violation would have minimal deterrent value, since it is doubtful that the desire to secure a statement from a suspect whom the police have probable cause to arrest would motivate them to violate *Payton.* The Court therefore held that "where the police have probable cause to arrest a suspect, the exclusionary rule does not bar the State's use of a statement made by the defendant outside of his home, even though the statement is taken after an arrest made in the home in violation of *Payton.*" 495 U.S. at 21, 110 S.Ct. at 1644–45, 109 L.Ed.2d at 22.

Finally, a law enforcement officer may be subject to civil liability for false arrest or false imprisonment if an arrest is illegal or is made with excessive or unreasonable force. Civil liability may also be imposed if an officer's application for an arrest warrant is so lacking in indicia of probable cause as to render official belief in its existence unreasonable. *Malley v. Briggs,* 475 U.S. 335, 106 S.Ct. 1092, 89 L.Ed.2d 271 (1986).

KEY POINTS

27. Jurisdiction to try a person for a crime is not affected by an illegal arrest.

28. In general, evidence that is obtained by exploitation of an illegal arrest and is a *product* of that arrest will be inadmissible in court in a prosecution against the person arrested.

Summary

A formal arrest can be defined as the taking of a person into custody for the commission of an offense as the prelude to prosecuting him or her for it. The basic elements constituting a formal arrest are (1) an intention to take a person into the custody of the law, (2) exercise of real or pretended authority, (3) detention or restraint of the person to be arrested, and (4) an understanding of the officer's intention by the person to be arrested. Even though these basic elements are not all present, courts may find that an encounter between a law enforcement officer and a person entails such a significant intrusion on the person's freedom of action that it is in important respects indistinguishable from a formal arrest. Such an encounter, sometimes called a seizure tantamount to arrest, must be supported by probable cause or it is illegal. The test to determine whether a seizure is tantamount to arrest is whether, in view of all the circumstances surrounding the encounter, a reasonable person would have believed that he or she was not free to leave.

Although warrantless arrests on probable cause are permitted, courts always prefer arrests made under the authority of an arrest warrant. An arrest warrant is a written judicial order directing a law enforcement officer to arrest a particular person. The warrant is issued by a magistrate on the basis of a complaint stating the essential facts constituting the offense charged, if the magistrate is satisfied that the offense was committed and that the person to be arrested committed it. The magistrate may also issue a summons that merely directs the defendant to appear rather than ordering an arrest.

Law enforcement officers may make a warrantless public arrest for a felony if they have probable cause to believe that a felony has been or is being committed and that the person to be arrested has committed or is committing the felony. Officers may make a warrantless public arrest for a misdemeanor, however, only if (1) the misdemeanor was committed in their presence or (2) a state statute or constitution allows warrantless arrests on probable cause for certain misdemeanors. A warrantless misdemeanor arrest for offenses committed in the officer's presence must be made immediately, but a warrantless felony arrest may be delayed for various reasons, so long as the defendant's rights are not prejudiced by the delay.

When law enforcement officers make an arrest, they should notify the person arrested that he or she is under arrest and notify that person of the officers' authority and the cause of the arrest. If the arrest is made under authority of a warrant, officers should examine the warrant to make sure it is valid on its face before carrying out its commands. When the arrest warrant is executed, officers should return the warrant as directed and explain what they have done in carrying out its commands.

Officers have no official authority to arrest without a warrant outside their jurisdiction—the geographic area for which they were elected or appointed. Nevertheless, even though outside their jurisdiction, they have the authority of any private citizen to arrest for breach of the peace misdemeanors committed in their presence and for felonies on probable cause. They may also arrest outside their jurisdiction in fresh pursuit of a criminal who has fled their jurisdiction, if the pursuit is begun promptly inside the jurisdiction and maintained continuously.

Officers may use only the amount of force reasonably necessary under the circumstances to effect an arrest. Deadly force may be used only as a last resort and then only in specifically limited circumstances. Deadly force may never be used to accomplish an arrest for a misdemeanor. But officers may use deadly force in self-defense to protect themselves from death or serious bodily injury, and officers need not abandon an attempt to arrest in the face of physical resistance to the arrest.

Officers may not enter a dwelling to arrest a person without a warrant unless there is consent or exigent circumstances. An arrest warrant is required to enter a suspect's home to arrest the suspect. A search warrant is required to enter the home of a third person to arrest a suspect. Exigent circumstances that would justify a warrantless entry of a dwelling to arrest are hot pursuit of a fleeing felon, imminent destruction of evidence, the need to prevent a suspect's escape, and the risk of danger to the police or other persons. In assessing the risk of danger, the gravity of the crime and the likelihood that the suspect is armed should be considered. If an arrest is begun in a public place, officers may enter a dwelling without a warrant in hot pursuit, to complete the arrest. Before officers may lawfully enter a dwelling *forcibly* to arrest a person, they must be refused admittance after knocking, announcing their authority and purpose, and demanding admittance. Failure to knock and announce is excused if an officer's purpose is already known or if knocking and announcing would cause danger to the officer, cause the escape of the suspect, or result in the loss or destruction of evidence.

Duties of the officer after an arrest is effected include the following: booking; bringing the arrested person before a magistrate without unnecessary delay; ensuring the health and safety of the prisoner while in the officer's custody; conducting a station-house inventory search of the prisoner, which may include searching and seizing any container or object in the prisoner's possession; and conducting identification procedures, including fingerprinting, photographing, physical examinations, and lineups.

Although an illegal arrest will not affect the jurisdiction of the court to try a person, any evidence obtained as the product of the exploitation of an illegal arrest will be inadmissible in a criminal proceeding against the defendant. In addition, the law enforcement officer may be liable both civilly and criminally for making an illegal arrest or using excessive force.

Key Holdings from Major Cases

California v. Hodari D. (1990). "An arrest requires *either* physical force . . . *or*, where that is absent, *submission* to the assertion of authority." 499 U.S. 621, 626, 111 S.Ct. 1547, 1551, 113 L.Ed.2d 690, 697.

Hayes v. Florida (1985). "[W]hen the police, without probable cause or a warrant, forcibly remove a person from his home or other place in which he is entitled to be and transport him to the police station, where he is detained, although briefly, for investigative purposes . . . such seizures, at least where not under judicial supervision, are sufficiently like arrests to invoke the traditional rule that arrests may constitutionally be made only on probable cause." 470 U.S. 811, 816, 105 S.Ct. 1643, 1647, 84 L.Ed.2d 705, 710.

Aguilar v. Texas (1964). "[T]he informed and deliberate determinations of magistrates empowered to issue warrants . . . are to be preferred over the hurried action of officers . . . who may happen to make arrests." 378 U.S. 108, 110–11, 84 S.Ct. 1509, 1512, 12 L.Ed.2d 723, 726.

United States v. Watson (1976). "Law enforcement officers may find it wise to seek arrest warrants where practicable to do so, and their judgments about probable cause may be more readily accepted where backed by a warrant issued by a magistrate. . . . But we decline to transform this judicial preference into a constitutional rule when the judgment of the Nation and Congress has for so long been to authorize warrantless public arrests on probable cause rather than to encumber criminal prosecutions with endless litigation with respect to the existence of exigent circumstances, whether it was practicable to get a warrant, whether the suspect was about to flee, and the like." 423 U.S. 411, 423–24, 96 S.Ct. 820, 827–28, 46 L.Ed.2d 598, 608–09.

Hoffa v. United States (1966). "The police are not required to guess at their peril the precise moment at which they have probable cause to arrest a suspect, risking a violation of the Fourth Amendment if they act too soon, and a violation of the Sixth Amendment if they wait too long. Law enforcement officers are under no constitutional duty to call a halt to a criminal investigation the moment they have the minimum evidence to establish probable cause, a quantum of evidence which may fall far short of the amount necessary to support a criminal prosecution." 385 U.S. 293, 310, 87 S.Ct. 408, 417, 17 L.Ed.2d 374, 386.

Tennessee v. Garner (1985). "The use of deadly force to prevent the escape of all felony suspects, whatever the circumstances, is constitutionally unreasonable. It is not better that all felony suspects die than that they escape. Where the suspect poses no immediate threat to the officer and no threat to others, the harm resulting from failing to apprehend him does not justify the use of deadly force to do so. . . . Where the officer has probable cause to believe that the suspect poses a threat of serious physical harm, either to the officer or to others, it is not constitutionally unreasonable to prevent escape by using deadly force. Thus, if the suspect threatens the officer with a weapon or there is probable cause to believe that he has committed a crime involving the infliction or threatened infliction of serious physical harm, deadly force may be used if necessary to prevent escape, and if, where feasible, some warning has been given." 471 U.S. 1, 11–12, 105 S.Ct. 1694, 1701, 85 L.Ed.2d 1, 9–10.

Payton v. New York (1980). "[A]n arrest warrant founded on probable cause implicitly carries with it the limited authority to enter a dwelling in which the suspect lives when there is reason to believe the suspect is within." 445 U.S. 573, 603, 100 S.Ct. 1371, 1388, 63 L.Ed.2d 639, 661.

Steagald v. United States (1981). "In the absence of exigent circumstances, we have consistently held that [law enforcement officers' determinations of probable cause] are not reliable enough to justify an entry into a person's home to arrest him without a warrant, or a search of a home for objects in the absence of a search warrant. We see no reason to depart from this settled course when the search of a home is for a person rather than an object." 451 U.S. 204, 213, 101 S.Ct. 1642, 1648, 68 L.Ed.2d 38, 46.

Welsh v. Wisconsin (1984). "[A]n important factor to be considered when determining whether any exigency exists is the gravity of the underlying offense for which the arrest is being made. Moreover, although no exigency is created simply because there is probable cause to believe that a serious crime has been committed . . . application of the exigent-circumstances exception in the context of a home entry should rarely be sanctioned when there is probable cause to believe that only a minor offense . . . has been committed." 466 U.S. 740, 753, 104 S.Ct. 2091, 2099, 80 L.Ed.2d 732, 745.

Minnesota v. Olson (1990). "[A] warrantless intrusion may be justified by hot pursuit of a fleeing felon, or imminent destruction of evidence . . . or the need to prevent a suspect's escape, or the risk of danger to the police or to other persons inside or outside the dwelling." 436 N.W.2d at 97. Furthermore, "in the absence of hot pursuit there must be at least probable cause to believe that one or more of the other factors justifying the entry were present and that in assessing the risk of danger, the gravity of the crime and likelihood that the suspect is armed should be considered." 495 U.S. 91, 100, 110 S.Ct. 1684, 1690, 109 L.Ed.2d 85, 95–96.

Warden v. Hayden (1967). Police officers without a warrant in hot pursuit of an armed robbery suspect "acted reasonably when they entered the house and began to search for a man of the description they had been given and for weapons which he had used in the robbery or might use against them. The Fourth Amendment does not require police officers to delay in the course of an investigation if to do so would gravely endanger their lives or the lives of others." 387 U.S. 294, 298–99, 87 S.Ct. 1642, 1646, 18 L.Ed.2d 782, 787.

United States v. Santana (1976). Law enforcement officers who attempt an arrest in a public place may, under the *Hayden* "hot pursuit" rule, follow the person to be arrested into a dwelling in order to effectuate the arrest. 427 U.S. 38, 96 S.Ct. 2406, 49 L.Ed.2d 300.

Miller v. United States (1958). "The requirement of prior notice of authority and purpose before forcing entry into a home is deeply rooted in our heritage, and should not be given grudging application. . . . Every householder, the good and the bad, the guilty and the innocent, is entitled to the protection designed to secure the common interest against unlawful invasion of the house. The petitioner could not be lawfully arrested in his home by officers breaking in without first giving him notice of their authority and purpose. Because the petitioner did not receive that notice before the officers broke the door to invade his home, the arrest was unlawful, and the evidence seized should have been suppressed." 357 U.S. 301, 313–14, 78 S.Ct. 1190, 1198, 2 L.Ed.2d 1332, 1340–41.

Sabbath v. United States (1968). "An unannounced intrusion into a dwelling . . . is no less an unannounced intrusion whether officers break down a door, force open a chain lock on a partially open door, open a locked door by use of a passkey, or . . . open a closed but unlocked door." 391 U.S. 585, 590, 88 S.Ct. 1755, 1758, 20 L.Ed.2d 828, 834.

Gerstein v. Pugh (1975). "Whatever procedure a State may adopt, it must provide a fair and reliable determination of probable cause as a condition for any significant pretrial restraint of liberty, and this determination must be made by a judicial officer either before or promptly after arrest." 420 U.S. 103, 124–25, 95 S.Ct. 854, 868–89, 43 L.Ed.2d 54, 71–72.

County of Riverside v. McLaughlin (1991). "[A] jurisdiction that provides judicial determinations of probable cause within 48 hours of arrest will, as a general matter, comply with the promptness requirement of *Gerstein.* . . . Such a hearing may nonetheless violate *Gerstein* if the arrested individual can prove that his or her probable cause determination was delayed unreasonably." 500 U.S. 44, 56–57, 111 S.Ct. 1661, 1670, 114 L.Ed.2d 49, 63.

Washington v. Chrisman (1982). "[I]t is not 'unreasonable' under the Fourth Amendment for a police officer, as a matter of course, to monitor the movements of an arrested person, as his judgement dictates, following the arrest. The officer's need to ensure his own safety—as well as the integrity of the arrest—is compelling. Such surveillance is not an impermissible invasion of the privacy or personal liberty of an individual who has been arrested." 455 U.S. 1, 7, 102 S.Ct. 812, 817, 70 L.Ed.2d 778, 785.

Illinois v. Lafayette (1983). "It is evident that a stationhouse search of every item carried on or by a person who has lawfully been taken into custody by the police will amply serve the important and legitimate governmental interests involved." 462 U.S. 640, 648, 103 S.Ct. 2605, 2610, 77 L.Ed.2d 65, 72.

United States v. Edwards (1974). "[O]nce the accused is lawfully arrested and is in custody, the effects in his possession at the place of detention that were subject to search at the time and place of his arrest may lawfully be searched and seized without a warrant even though a substantial period of time has elapsed between the arrest and subsequent administrative processing, on the one hand, and the taking of the property for use as evidence, on the other." 415 U.S. 800, 807, 94 S.Ct. 1234, 1239, 39 L.Ed.2d 771, 778.

Frisbie v. Collins (1952). "[T]he power of a court to try a person for crime is not impaired by the fact that he had been brought within the court's jurisdiction by reason of a 'forcible abduction.' . . . [D]ue process of law is satisfied when one present in court is convicted of crime after having been fairly apprised of the charges against him and after a fair trial in accordance with constitutional procedural safeguards. There is nothing in the Constitution that requires a court to permit a guilty person rightfully convicted to escape justice because he was brought to trial against his will." 342 U.S. 519, 522, 72 S.Ct. 509, 511–12, 96 L.Ed. 541, 545–46.

Brown v. Illinois (1975). "The *Miranda* warnings are an important factor, to be sure, in determining whether the confession is obtained by exploitation of illegal arrest. But they are not the only factor to be considered. The temporal proximity of the arrest and the confession, the presence of intervening circumstances, . . . and, particularly, the purpose and flagrancy of the official misconduct are all relevant." 422 U.S. 590, 603–04, 95 S.Ct. 2254, 2261–62, 45 L.Ed.2d 416, 427.

New York v. Harris (1990). "Where the police have probable cause to arrest a suspect, the exclusionary rule does not bar the State's use of a statement made by the defendant outside of his home, even though the statement is taken after an arrest made in the home in violation of *Payton.*" 495 U.S. 14, 21, 110 S.Ct. 1640, 1644–45, 109 L.Ed.2d 13, 22.

Review and Discussion Questions

1. Is it possible to formally arrest an insane or extremely mentally retarded person? Explain.

2. Name several ways in which a law enforcement officer or officers can prevent a routine encounter with a person on the street from being considered a seizure tantamount to arrest.

3. Give three practical reasons why a law enforcement officer should obtain an arrest warrant if possible.

   takes discretion away from determin PC

4. How is a law enforcement officer's authority to arrest affected by time?

5. Is it valid to say that if an officer has strong probable cause to arrest someone, the officer may arrest the person anywhere in the country? Explain.

6. Under what circumstances may a law enforcement officer use deadly force, and what are the potential consequences of an illegal use of deadly force? Name several

circumstances under which little or no force should be used to make an arrest.

7. Do law enforcement officers have a broader right to self-defense when they are assaulted while making an arrest than when they are assaulted while simply walking or cruising their beat?

8. Assume that a law enforcement officer has probable cause to arrest a defendant for armed assault and probable cause to believe that the person is hiding in a third person's garage, which is attached to the house. What warrants, if any, does the officer need to enter the garage to arrest the defendant? What if the officer is in hot pursuit of the defendant? What if the defendant is known to be injured and unarmed?

9. Give reasons to support an argument that a law enforcement officer should never have to knock and announce before entering a dwelling to arrest a dangerous felon or a drug offender.

10. If a law enforcement officer has probable cause to arrest, does the officer have to make an arrest? If not, what alternatives to arrest are available, and under what circumstances should they be used?

REAL-LIFE FACT SITUATIONS

1. At the hearing on Alex's motion to suppress, Special Agent Robert Johnson with the Drug Enforcement Agency's (DEA) Atlanta Airport Task Force testified. Agent Johnson had twenty-five years of experience with DEA, including the past ten years during which he had worked drug interdiction at the Atlanta airport. Agent Johnson received information from a "cooperating individual at the airport" that an "individual flying under the name of Matthew Alex was traveling from Los Angeles, California, to Atlanta and continuing on to Mobile, Alabama, on a cash one-way ticket." Reservations had been made in Los Angeles late on the evening of July 6, 1994, for a 12:10 A.M. flight to Atlanta on July 7, with continuation on to Mobile, Alabama. Based on his experience, Agent Johnson was aware that Los Angeles was a "source city" for cocaine and marijuana; that it was common for drug couriers to make quick trips, due to the "spur of the moment type of demand business" done, and to pay cash for their tickets because no identification is required for such a purchase. Also common to the trade is the use of a call-back number which is not that of the traveler. Agent Johnson further testified that his partner, Agent Perry, called the call-back number and told Agent Johnson that the party answering the phone did not know Matthew Alex.

The officers went to the Mobile gate and asked the agent to page Alex so they could identify him, which they did. They approached, wearing civilian clothing with no weapons in evidence, identified themselves as police, and asked to speak with Alex. It was five to ten minutes prior to boarding for Alex's flight to Mobile, and boarding usually begins twenty to thirty minutes before takeoff. Johnson asked to see Alex's ticket, which Alex gave to him. The ticket was in Alex's name, but Agent Johnson saw and felt that no baggage claim tickets had been attached to the ticket, which is Delta's practice when baggage is checked. When asked for identification, Alex responded that "I lost my ID in Los Angeles. I was [using the bathroom] and I laid my ID on the counter next to me and when I was through it was gone."

When asked if he had anything else with identification on it, Alex replied negatively. He told the agents if they found his identification, he wanted it back. Johnson also knew from experience that it is common for couriers to travel without identification. Likewise, nervousness such as that displayed by Alex's trembling hands when the agents asked to see his ticket is also common with intercepted couriers. Asked about his lack of luggage, Alex said he had sent his ahead by "Federal Express or Western Union."

These events took only a matter of minutes. His ticket was returned to Alex, and he placed it in the left front pocket of his jacket. As he did so, Johnson noticed an "unusual bulge in his right front pocket." Alex was also wearing loose-fitting pants and jacket. Couriers carrying drugs on their body do this in order to conceal any bulges. When asked what was in his right front pocket, Alex responded by tapping this pocket and said it was his ticket, which Johnson knew was incorrect. Alex was then advised that the two officers were narcotics agents and asked if he would consent to a search of his person. He stated he had to catch his flight, and "[h]is voice was cracking, he was breathing very, very heavily." At this point, the officers concluded that the totality of circumstances suggested that Alex was carrying a controlled substance.

Alex turned to walk off, at which time the agents told him he was going to be detained while they attempted to obtain a search warrant. Alex then pushed past the agents, and when they repeated that he was being detained, Alex shoved Johnson with his forearm and was placed under arrest for simple battery. The agents then obtained the warrant and searched Alex, finding 1,197 grams (about half a kilo) of crack cocaine taped under his armpit with duct tape. Was the arrest of Alex legal? *Alex v. State,* 470 S.E.2d 305 (Ga.App. 1996).

2. In January 1988, Jennifer Dillon, who had mutual acquaintances with Clopton, agreed to cooperate with law enforcement officials by buying cocaine from Clopton, while she and Clopton were under surveillance. Dillon, who did not know where else to locate Clopton, went to the Flora-Bama lounge, which is located in Florida, just across the state line from Baldwin County, Alabama. There, Dillon found Clopton, and he agreed to sell her cocaine. Dillon then lured Clopton from the Flora-Bama into Baldwin County, where Clopton sold her one-eighth of an ounce of cocaine as, by prearrangement with Dillon, a Baldwin County Sheriff's Department investigator, A. D. Long, and a Gulf Shores police officer, Steve Stewart, observed the transaction.

Clopton was not arrested at the time. It is undisputed that Clopton did not thereafter evade arrest and that he was unaware that a Baldwin County grand jury had indicted him on November 4, 1988, in pertinent part, for the unlawful distribution of a controlled substance. Additionally, Clopton was unaware that a capias warrant had been issued for his arrest on the day of the indictment.

Dillon believed that Clopton lived in Florida. Based on that information, months before the indictment Officer Stewart had "'used the NCIC computer' to check an address for [Clopton] in Florida." Officer Stewart did not find a current physical address for Clopton but determined that Clopton had post office boxes in Baldwin County. Officer Stewart then abandoned efforts to locate Clopton. The record reveals no subsequent attempts by the State to locate Clopton.

In late 1991, as Clopton was returning from a foreign vacation, customs officials discovered the outstanding capias warrant from November 1988 and detained Clopton for arrest. The capias warrant was executed by the Baldwin County Sheriff's Department on October 9, 1991. On October 24, 1991, Clopton filed a motion to dismiss this case on the ground that the State's delay in his arrest had violated his right to a speedy trial as guaranteed by the Sixth Amendment to the United States Constitution. Should Clopton's motion be granted? *Ex Parte Clopton,* 656 So.2d 1243 (Ala. 1995).

3. On March 15, 1996, police officers received a call about a man dressed in a brown and black striped shirt and black pants selling contraband to pedestrians and persons in cars in the 1300 block of South Dorgenois Street in front of the Fast Stop Grocery Store. Officer Joe Belisle and his partner established a surveillance and saw the defendant reach into his shoe area, pull out an object, and hand it to the other individual. The defendant stood in front of the store after the transaction until he saw a police car turn the corner and drive toward him. He then placed his hands into his pockets and walked into the store. Officer Belisle, who was dressed in plain clothes, followed him into the store where the defendant purchased a bottle of water and then exited the store. The defendant walked to the corner of South Dorgenois and Erato Streets where he was detained by Officer Belisle and two other officers, Officers Butler and Carroll. The officers informed the defendant of his Miranda rights and told him he was being detained in conjunction with a narcotics investigation. They then patted down the defendant for their safety and asked him to remove his shoe. When the defendant complied, the officers saw a piece of foil sitting on top of his foot. Inside the foil was a white powdery substance later determined to be heroin. Was the defendant legally arrested so that the search and seizure of the foil could be valid as a search incident to arrest? *State v. Butler,* 700 So.2d 224 (La.App. 4. Cir. 1997).

4. On January 21, 1995, uniformed officers Ken Zbeiegien and Ken Butsey of the Mentor Police Department drove to appellant's home in a marked police car to serve an arrest warrant upon him. According to Zbeiegien's testimony, he approached appellant's home and spoke with a woman who told him that appellant was in the workshop behind the house. Butsey had already proceeded to the workshop, where he had walked in after knocking on the door, which was slightly ajar. Butsey radioed Zbeiegien to come to the workshop, which he did without knocking on the closed door or announcing his identity. Appellant, however, testified that the officers walked in together and that the door was closed. Allegedly, the door has an automatic door closer on it to prevent heat from escaping.

The officers informed appellant that a warrant had been issued for his arrest; however, neither had a copy of the warrant because it was department policy not to carry warrants. Appellant was not initially told of the nature of the charge he was being arrested for because the officers did not have that information. However, they testified that they called the station to determine the charge filed against appellant and notified him thereof. Appellant denies that the officers ever told him that he was under arrest and/or called the station.

According to the officers' testimonies, they told appellant several times that he was under arrest, but he refused to go with them. He asked to speak to his attorney, and they said he could do so from the station. After the officers tried to gain voluntary compliance for approximately five minutes, appellant became verbally combative and aggressive. He ordered the officers to leave and tried to push Zbeiegien out of the door. Butsey pushed Zbeiegien back inside and pepper-sprayed appellant to stop his behavior. Although he calmed down for several seconds, he once again became aggressive, at which time Butsey sprayed him again. At that point, Zbeiegien held his left side and Butsey held his right side. A physical struggle ensued, during which the officers were dragged several feet. Finally, they were able to handcuff appellant.

According to appellant, he agreed to go to the station with the officers but asked if he could call his attorney first. When he asked them to wait a minute, they handcuffed him and said they "did not have time to 'F' with you * * * and he sprayed me with mace right then and there." He denies that any commotion or struggle occurred and stated that he never resisted, used force, or touched Zbeiegien. He testified that he was running around the shop trying to look for a rag to wipe his eyes from the pepper spray and that the officers hit him with something, sprayed him twice more, and clubbed him with a flashlight. Zbeiegien testified that he never struck appellant or used excessive force against him. Butsey denied that he hit appellant with his flashlight, asp (collapsible club), or baton.

Upon arriving at the police station, appellant complained of having heart-attack-like symptoms and a sore shoulder. He was taken to the hospital but released. Butsey and Zbeiegien followed appellant to the hospital and gave him a copy of his warrant. Appellant claims that his motion for acquittal on the charge of resisting arrest should have been granted because his arrest was unlawful since the officers failed to "knock and announce" before entering the workshop and failed to inform him of the charge against him. Should the motion for acquittal be granted? *State v. Campana*, 678 N.E.2d 626 (Ohio.App. 11 Dist. 1996).

5. The defendant was initially arrested on March 27, 1991, for a robbery at a grocery store at gunpoint which occurred on March 25, 1991, based upon information provided by his alleged accomplice. However, when an eyewitness was unable to identify the defendant in a lineup, that arrest was voided. On April 1, 1991, the defendant was identified from a photographic array as a perpetrator of a robbery which occurred on March 27, 1991, at another grocery store. On April 2, 1991, the defendant was arrested. At 8:15 P.M., and 8:19 P.M., respectively, the two victims of the March 27, 1991, robbery viewed the defendant in a lineup, but were unable to identify him. However, at 8:20 P.M., the victim of a robbery at another grocery store on March 15, 1991, viewed the lineup and identified the defendant as one of the perpetrators. Within the next hour, the defendant was identified from the lineup by four other robbery victims of three separate robberies, with some similarity in modus operandi. At 9:55 P.M. the defendant was identified from

the lineup by yet another victim of a robbery which occurred at a bodega on December 31, 1990. The hearing court, after a hearing, suppressed these lineup identifications, holding that once the victims of the March 27, 1991, robbery were unable to identify the defendant, their photographic identification "could no longer provide a legal basis to detain him," and the police should have voided his arrest and immediately released him. Was the hearing court correct? *People v. Sainsbury*, 647 N.Y.S.2d 823 (A.D. 2 Dept. 1996).

6. On May 3, 1993, the Hillside police were investigating a series of alleged armed robberies. Three armed robberies had occurred at fast-food restaurants in Hillside, New Jersey. A fourth armed robbery was alleged to have occurred in Union, New Jersey. The Hillside police had received a tip that Gadsden was involved in a series of armed robberies in the area and were informed by Union police that a black Cadillac had been used in the Union armed robbery.

With this information, Hillside police officers travelled to Gadsden's residence in contiguous Newark. At some point during the day, they ran a motor-vehicle check on the license number of a black Cadillac which was outside his residence and determined that the vehicle belonged to defendant. Upon returning to the Hillside Police Department, Hillside officers telephoned the Union Police Department and gave them defendant's name, along with two other names, as possible suspects in the Union armed robbery. Later that same day, a photograph of Gadsden was shown to three of the alleged victims/witnesses of the Hillside armed robberies. Gadsden's photograph was positively identified by one of the individuals. On May 3, 1993, an arrest warrant for Gadsden was obtained from the Hillside Municipal Court.

Hillside officers went to Gadsden's residence in Newark and arrested him. He was taken to the Hillside Police Station where he was later charged with the offenses in the four indictments. Defendant's car was seized and impounded at the Hillside Police Department.

On May 4, 1993, Gadsden gave oral and written statements to the Hillside police implicating himself and Vernon Harris in the February 20, March 20, and April 11, 1993, armed robberies in Hillside. The following day, May 5, 1993, he gave oral and written statements to the Union Police implicating himself and Harris in the May 1, 1993, armed robbery in Union. Separate photographic arrays containing Gadsden's and Harris's photographs were shown to victims/witnesses in the other Hillside armed robberies. Comparisons of Gadsden's and Harris's fingerprints with fingerprints found at the scene of the Union armed robbery were positive.

The defense argued that the Hillside police were clearly in violation of N.J.S.A. 40A:14-152, which limits police jurisdiction to the boundaries of their own municipality. The defense contended that the Hillside police should have enlisted the assistance of the Newark Police Department, the Essex County Sheriff and the Essex County Prosecutor's Office in order to effectuate the arrests of Gadsden and Harris in Newark. The defense contended that because the Hillside police officers had no jurisdiction to arrest Gadsden and Harris in Newark, these arrests were illegal and that the United States Constitution and the New Jersey Constitution require suppression of all evidence obtained as a result of these illegal arrests. The defense further argued that the warrant was illegally obtained because it was based upon extrajurisdictional observations of Gadsden's home by Hillside police and that probable cause did not exist to issue the warrant. Should the motion to suppress be granted? *State v. Gadsden*, 697 A.2d 187 (N.J. Super. A.D. 1997).

CHAPTER FIVE

Search Warrants

OBJECTIVES

1. Know the general history of the development of the Fourth Amendment and of the development of the law of electronic surveillance.

2. Know how to obtain a search warrant, including the following:
   a. Who issues search warrants
   b. Grounds for issuance
   c. What may be seized
   d. How to describe the person or place to be searched and the things to be seized

3. Know how to execute a search warrant, including the following:
   a. Who may execute a search warrant
   b. When a search warrant may be executed, allowable delays, and how long the search may last
   c. Gaining entry to premises
   d. Authority to search persons not named in the warrant
   e. Allowable scope of the search and seizure
   f. Duties after the search is completed

4. Know the differences between an administrative search warrant and a criminal search warrant.

5. Know the meaning of and rationale justifying "special needs" searches.

6. Have a general understanding of Title III of the Omnibus Crime Control and Safe Streets Act of 1968, including the following:
   a. Familiarity with the conflicting demands for more effective law enforcement and individual privacy rights
   b. Knowledge of several ways in which Title III provides for judicial supervision of electronic surveillance
   c. An understanding of the similarities and differences between an interception order under Title III and an ordinary search warrant
   d. A knowledge of specific ways in which Title III protects individual rights, especially privacy rights
   e. An understanding of the types of interceptions of wire, oral, or electronic communications that are excepted from the coverage of Title III

OUTLINE

L ike the law of arrest, the law governing search warrants is based on guarantees in the Fourth Amendment to the U.S. Constitution.

> The right of the people to be secure in their persons, houses, papers and effects, against unreasonable searches and seizures, shall not be violated, and no Warrants shall issue, but upon probable cause, supported by Oath or affirmation, and particularly describing the place to be searched and the persons or things to be seized. U.S. Const., Amend. 4.

Whereas the main concern of the previous chapter on arrest was the **seizure** of the *person,* this chapter's concern is with a broader array of matters including the search of persons *and* places and the seizure of a variety of things. A **search** can be defined as an examination or inspection of a location, vehicle, or person by a law enforcement officer or other authorized person for the purpose of locating objects or substances relating to or believed to relate to criminal activities or wanted persons. In recent years, courts have increasingly analyzed search and seizure issues in terms of violation of the right of privacy and have expanded the definition of search to include any official intrusion into matters and activities as to which a person has exhibited a reasonable expectation of privacy. The U.S. Supreme Court definitions of search and seizure, set out in Chapter 3, are repeated here for emphasis.

> A "search" occurs when an expectation of privacy that society is prepared to consider reasonable is infringed. A "seizure" of property occurs when there is some meaningful interference with an individual's possessory interests in that property. *United States v. Jacobsen,* 466 U.S. 109, 113, 104 S.Ct. 1652, 1656, 80 L.Ed.2d 85, 94 (1984).

Probable cause, which is a common aspect of both arrest and search and seizure law, is discussed in detail in Chapter 6. ∎

History

The Fourth Amendment to the Constitution was adopted in response to abuses of governmental search and seizure authority originating in England in the seventeenth and eighteenth centuries. The early development of legally authorized searches and seizures under English common law is somewhat obscure. It appears that search warrants were first used in cases involving stolen property. The use of warrants to recapture stolen goods became widespread and increasingly violative of citizens' privacy. Eventually, the use of warrants was extended to the enforcement of other laws. For example, in the eighteenth century, the government issued general warrants to enforce strict libel laws. A general warrant is one that fails to specify the person or place to be searched or the person or item to be seized, and that leaves the time and manner of the search to the discretion of the searching officer. Law enforcement officers abused these general warrants, and soon no person or property was free from unlimited search conducted at the whim of an officer on the mere suspicion that the person possessed literature critical of the king or others in high places.

Despite their unpopularity with the citizenry, these abusive practices were transplanted to the American colonies. In the mid-eighteenth century, Parliament enacted legislation authorizing general searches, called **writs of assistance,** to be conducted against the colonists to enforce the Trade Acts. Writs of assistance authorized royal customs officers to search houses and ships at will to discover and seize smuggled goods or goods on which the required duties had not been paid. The colonists' reaction against the writs of assistance was strong and was one of the major causes of the American Revolution. As stated in the 1886 U.S. Supreme Court case of *Boyd v. United States:*

> The practice had obtained in the colonies of issuing writs of assistance to the revenue officers, empowering them, in their discretion, to search suspected places for smuggled goods, which James Otis pronounced "the worst instrument of arbitrary power, the most destructive of English liberty and the fundamental principles of law, that ever was found in an English law book"; since they placed "the liberty of every man in the hands of every petty officer." This was in February, 1761, in Boston, and the famous debate in which it occurred was perhaps the most prominent event which inaugurated the resistance of the colonies to the oppressions of the mother country. "Then and there," said John Adams, "then and there was the first scene of the first act of opposition to the arbitrary claims of Great Britain. Then and there the child Independence was born." 116 U.S. 616, 625, 6 S.Ct. 524, 529, 29 L.Ed. 746, 749 (1886).

The experiences of the Founding Fathers with general warrants and writs of assistance caused them to insist on including in the basic charters of the states and nation suitable guarantees against unreasonable searches and seizures. A prohibition against searches conducted at the whim of a law enforcement officer without any restrictions on the person or place to be searched or the person or item to be seized was first embodied in the Virginia Bill of Rights, adopted in 1776. By the close of the Revolutionary War, most of the states had adopted similar provisions. The present Fourth Amendment to the Constitution, with its emphasis on the protection of warrants issued upon probable cause, was included in the Bill of Rights in 1791. Today, every state's constitution contains a similar provision.

The policy underlying the warrant requirement of the Fourth Amendment was stated by the U.S. Supreme Court:

> The point of the Fourth Amendment, which often is not grasped by zealous officers, is not that it denies law enforcement the support of the usual inferences which reasonable men draw from evidence. Its protection consists in requiring that those inferences be drawn by a neutral and detached magistrate instead of being judged by the officer engaged in the often competitive enterprise of ferreting out crime. Any assumption that evidence sufficient to support a magistrate's disinterested determination to issue a search warrant will justify the officers in making a search without a warrant would reduce the Amendment to a nullity and leave the people's homes secure only in the discretion of police officers. . . . When the right of privacy must reasonably yield to the right of search is, as a rule, to be decided by a judicial officer, not by a policeman or Government enforcement agent. *Johnson v. United States,* 333 U.S. 10, 13–14, 68 S.Ct. 367, 369, 92 L.Ed. 436, 440 (1948).

Although several exceptions to the warrant requirement have been established over the years (see Part 3 of this book), warrants are clearly preferred and reviewing courts will accept evidence of a less "judicially competent or persuasive character than would have justified an officer in acting on his own without a warrant." *Jones v. United States,* 362 U.S. 257, 270, 80 S.Ct. 725, 736, 4 L.Ed.2d 697, 708 (1960).

The Fourth Amendment's drafting history shows that its purpose was to protect the people of the United States against arbitrary action by their own government and not to restrain the federal government's actions against aliens outside U.S. territory.

"The people" protected by the Fourth Amendment and several other amendments "refers to a class of persons who are part of a national community or who have otherwise developed sufficient connection with this country to be considered part of that community." *United States v. Verdugo-Urquidez,* 494 U.S. 259, 265, 110 S.Ct. 1056, 1061, 108 L.Ed.2d 222, 233 (1990). The *Verdugo-Urquidez* case held that the Fourth Amendment does not apply to a search and seizure by U.S. agents of property owned by a nonresident alien and located in a foreign country. The Fourth Amendment does, however, protect legal, resident aliens from unreasonable searches and seizures conducted on U.S. soil, since legal, resident aliens enjoy substantially the same constitutional rights as do U.S. citizens. *Yick Wo v. Hopkins,* 188 U.S. 356, 6 S.Ct. 1064, 30 L.Ed. 220 (1886). Whether illegal aliens enjoy the protection of the Fourth Amendment is a matter open to dispute.

Definition

A **search warrant** is (1) an order in writing, (2) issued by a proper judicial authority, (3) in the name of the people, (4) directed to a law enforcement officer, (5) commanding the officer to search for certain personal property, and (6) commanding the officer to bring that property before the judicial authority named in the warrant. A search warrant is similar to an arrest warrant, which is an order to take a *person* into custody and bring the person before the proper judicial authority. In this chapter, the terms of the preceding definition are clarified, and important relationships between search warrants and arrest warrants are highlighted.

Obtaining a Search Warrant

Law enforcement officers must conform to established laws and procedures in applying for a search warrant. Otherwise, the application will be denied or, if a warrant is issued, the warrant will be invalidated later by a court. In either instance, valuable evidence will be unavailable to be used in the prosecution of a criminal case. Search warrant procedures vary in different jurisdictions and are found in various statutes, rules, and court decisions. The laws and procedures common to most jurisdictions are summarized and discussed in this chapter.

Who May Issue Search Warrants

Only judicial officers who have been specifically authorized to do so may issue search warrants. Most jurisdictions give this authority to judicial officers such as clerks of court, magistrates, complaint justices, justices of the peace, and judges. Law enforcement officers need to know which judicial officers are authorized to issue search warrants in their jurisdictions. These judicial officers may be different from those authorized to issue arrest warrants. A search warrant issued by a person without authority is of no legal effect, and a search made under such a warrant is illegal. For convenience, the term **magistrate** is used in this chapter to designate an official authorized to issue search warrants.

In *Shadwick v. City of Tampa,* 407 U.S. 345, 92 S.Ct. 2119, 32 L.Ed.2d 783 (1972), the U.S. Supreme Court, rejecting the notion that all warrant authority must reside exclusively in a lawyer or judge, upheld a city charter provision authorizing municipal court clerks to issue arrest warrants for municipal ordinance violations. The Court concluded that "an issuing magistrate must meet two tests. He must be neutral and detached, and he must be capable of determining whether probable cause exists for the requested arrest or search." 407 U.S. at 350, 92 S.Ct. at 2123, 32 L.Ed.2d at 788. In other cases, the Court found that the following persons were *not* sufficiently "neutral and detached" to issue warrants:

- A state attorney general who was also the state's chief investigator and was later to be the chief prosecutor at trial. *Coolidge v. New Hampshire,* 403 U.S. 443, 91 S.Ct. 2022, 29 L.Ed.2d 564 (1971).

- A magistrate who received a fee for issuing a search warrant but received nothing for denying a warrant application. *Connally v. Georgia,* 429 U.S. 245, 97 S.Ct. 546, 50 L.Ed.2d 444 (1977).

- A magistrate who participated in a search, helping officers in determining what to seize. *Lo-Ji Sales, Inc. v. New York,* 442 U.S. 319, 99 S.Ct. 2319, 60 L.Ed.2d 920 (1979).

Grounds for Issuance

Before issuing a search warrant, the magistrate must have probable cause to believe that items subject to seizure are in a particular place or on a particular person at the time of the issuance of the warrant. A law enforcement officer applying for a search warrant must supply the magistrate with the grounds for issuance of the warrant. This is done by means of an **affidavit,** which is merely a written declaration or statement of facts sworn to before the magistrate. Exhibit 5.1 is a typical form for an affidavit for a search warrant.

If a law enforcement officer knowingly and intentionally, or with reckless disregard for the truth, makes false statements in an affidavit supporting a request for a search warrant, the warrant may not issue or evidence seized under the warrant may be suppressed. In *Franks v. Delaware,* 438 U.S. 154, 98 S.Ct. 2674, 57 L.Ed.2d 667 (1978), the U.S. Supreme Court held that a defendant may challenge the veracity of an affidavit used by the police to obtain a search warrant. The Court said:

> [W]here the defendant makes a substantial preliminary showing that a false statement knowingly and intentionally, or with reckless disregard for the truth, was included by the affiant in the warrant affidavit, and if the allegedly false statement is necessary to the finding of probable cause, the Fourth Amendment requires that a hearing be held at the defendant's request. In the event that at the hearing the allegation of perjury or reckless disregard is established by the defendant by a preponderance of the evidence, and, with the affidavit's false material set to one side, the affidavit's remaining content is insufficient to establish probable cause, the search warrant must be voided and the fruits of the search excluded to the same extent as if probable cause was lacking on the face of the affidavit. 438 U.S. at 155–56, 98 S.Ct. at 2676–77, 57 L.Ed.2d at 672.

In *United States v. Johns,* 851 F.2d 1131 (9th Cir. 1988), the court found that a *Franks* hearing was required where the defendants made a substantial preliminary showing that they never engaged in any activities at a storage unit that could have

AO 106 (Rev. 7/87) Affidavit for Search Warrant

United States District Court

_____ DISTRICT OF _____

In the Matter of the Search of
(Name, address or brief description of person, property or premises to be searched)

APPLICATION AND AFFIDAVIT
FOR SEARCH WARRANT

CASE NUMBER: _____

I _____ being duly sworn depose and say:

I am a(n) _____ and have reason to believe
Official Title

that ☐ on the person of or ☐ on the property or premises known as (name, description and/or location)

in the _____ District of _____
there is now concealed a certain person or property, namely (describe the person or property to be seized)

which is (state one or more bases for search and seizure set forth under Rule 41(b) of the Federal Rules of Criminal Procedure)

concerning a violation of Title _____ United States code, Section(s)_____.
The facts to support a finding of Probable Cause are as follows:

Continued on the attached sheet and made a part hereof.   ☐ Yes   ☐ No

_____
Signature of Affiant

Sworn to before me, and subscribed in my presence

_____ at _____
Date   City and State

_____   _____
Name and Title of Judicial Officer   Signature of Judicial Officer

EXHIBIT 5.1   A Typical Affidavit for a Search Warrant

produced the odors the officers allegedly smelled. Two expert witnesses swore the officer's affidavit was necessarily false because it was scientifically impossible to smell what the officers claimed to have smelled given the contents of the storage space searched under the warrant. Without the alleged falsities, the probable cause support for the search warrant collapsed because the remainder of the affidavit merely described the location and ownership of the storage unit. In *United States v. Pace*, 898 F.2d 1218 (7th Cir. 1990), the court found that the rule of the *Franks* case also prohibits the officer from deliberately or recklessly *omitting* material information from the application. That court held, however, that the failure to advise the magistrate that another magistrate had denied the warrant was not a material fact where the affidavit was sufficient to show probable cause and the second magistrate was neutral and detached. In addition, if a warrant application is so lacking in indicia of probable cause as to render official belief in its existence unreasonable, the officer making the application may be held liable for damages in a civil suit. *Malley v. Briggs,* 475 U.S. 335, 106 S.Ct. 1092, 89 L.Ed.2d 271 (1986). The following discussion covers in detail the information that must be presented to the magistrate to establish grounds for the issuance of a search warrant.

PROBABLE CAUSE. Some jurisdictions require that an affidavit contain *all* the information upon which a magistrate is to base a finding of probable cause to issue a search warrant. *Valdez v. State,* 476 A.2d 1162 (Md. 1984). Other jurisdictions allow supplementation of a defective or incomplete affidavit by sworn oral testimony given before the magistrate. *State v. Hendricks,* 328 N.E.2d 822 (Ohio 1974). Several jurisdictions permit issuance of search warrants over the telephone but still require that the information telephoned by the affiant to the magistrate be taken under oath and recorded. For example, Rule 41(c)(2)(C) of the *Federal Rules of Criminal Procedure* authorizes the issuance of warrants based on sworn testimony communicated by telephone or other appropriate means, including facsimile transmission, "[if] the circumstances make it reasonable to dispense, in whole or in part, with a written affidavit." Exhibit 5.3, appearing later in the chapter, is a typical form for a search warrant upon oral testimony.

Writing all the information on which probable cause is based in the affidavit is preferred. It forces the law enforcement officer to think carefully about the case before applying for a warrant, and it provides a complete record for a court to review the magistrate's decision if the warrant is later challenged. This chapter proceeds on the assumption that a written affidavit is the exclusive vehicle for applying to a magistrate for a search warrant.

An affidavit for a search warrant should inform a magistrate (1) that a criminal offense has been or is being committed and (2) that seizable evidence relating to that offense is in a particular place at a particular time. The amount of proof required to persuade the magistrate to issue a search warrant is essentially the same as that required for the issuance of an arrest warrant or that required before an officer may arrest without a warrant for a felony. The constitutional term used to describe this amount of proof is **probable cause.** (Probable cause is discussed in Chapter 3 and in further detail in Chapter 6.) In applying for a search warrant, the essential requirement is that the underlying facts and circumstances on which probable cause is based must be stated in the affidavit. These facts and circumstances must show "a fair probability that contraband or evidence of a crime will be found in a particular place." *Illinois v. Gates,* 462 U.S. 213, 238, 103 S.Ct. 2317, 2332, 76 L.Ed.2d 527, 548 (1983). An officer's mere conclusions, beliefs, or opinions will not suffice to establish probable cause.

Probable cause to search differs in two important respects from probable cause to arrest. First, probable cause to search and probable cause to arrest will usually arise out of different sets of facts. To find probable cause to arrest, a magistrate must find sufficient facts to show that an offense was committed and that a particular suspect committed it. Probable cause to search requires sufficient facts to show that particular items are connected with criminal activity and that they will be found in a particular place. Therefore, the same set of facts and circumstances might provide probable cause to arrest, but not probable cause to search, and vice versa.

Another difference between probable cause to arrest and probable cause to search is that time is a very important factor in determining probable cause to search. If there is too long a delay between the time when the information on which probable cause is based is gathered and the time when the search is executed, there may no longer be good reason to believe that the property is still at the same location. Probable cause is said to be "stale" in this situation.

> Staleness is not measured merely on the basis of the maturity of the information but in relation to (1) the nature of the suspected criminal activity (discrete crime or "regenerating conspiracy"), (2) the habits of the suspected criminal ("nomadic" or "entrenched"), (3) the character of the items to be seized ("perishable" or "of enduring utility"), and (4) the nature and function of the premises to be searched ("mere criminal forum" or "secure operational base"). *United States v. Bucuvalas*, 970 F.2d 937 (1st Cir. 1992).

In *United States v. Wagner*, 989 F.2d 69 (2d Cir. 1993), the information supporting probable cause to search the suspect's home was (1) a single small purchase of marijuana from the suspect in her home more than six weeks before the search, (2) a recorded statement of the suspect as to who was her source for that marijuana, and (3) an unsubstantiated assertion that the suspect's home was owned by the source. On these facts, the court could not find that the suspect engaged in continuing criminal activity in her home as a member of the source's drug distribution network. Therefore, since marijuana is the type of property that is likely to disappear or be moved, probable cause was found to be stale at the time the warrant was issued and the search conducted.

The length of time that an item of property is likely to remain at a given location depends on the nature of the property, the nature of the criminal activity, the duration of the criminal activity, the criminal suspects, and many other factors. In *United States v. Laury*, 985 F.2d 1293 (5th Cir. 1993), probable cause to search a suspected bank robber's home for instrumentalities and evidence of the crime was found not to be stale although nearly two months had passed since the date of the robbery. In that case, the affiant, an expert in bank robbery investigation, stated that bank robbers tend to keep evidence of the crime in their homes for a long time, sometimes several years.

Evidence of continuing crimes, especially white-collar crimes, is also likely to stay in one place for a long time. The U.S. Supreme Court found that business records of an illegal real estate scheme would probably remain at their location for an extended period of time after the business transactions had taken place.

> The business records sought were prepared in the ordinary course of petitioner's business in his law office or that of his real estate corporation. It is eminently reasonable to expect that such records would be maintained in those offices for a period of time and surely as long as the three months required for the investigation of a complex real estate scheme. *Andresen v. Maryland*, 427 U.S. 463, 479 n.9, 96 S.Ct. 2737, 2747 n.9, 49 L.Ed.2d 627, 641 n.9 (1976).

Other examples of continuing crimes, evidence of which is likely to stay in one place for a long time, are the cultivation and distribution of illegal drugs (*United States v. McKeever*, 5 F.3d 863 [5th Cir. 1993]) and gun control violations (*United States v. Maxim*, 55 F.3d 394 [8th Cir. 1995]).

ITEMS SUBJECT TO SEIZURE. Laws and court rules authorizing a warrant to be issued to search for and seize certain types of property vary in different jurisdictions. Rule 41(b) of the *Federal Rules of Criminal Procedure* is typical and is reproduced here:

(b) ***Property or Persons Which May Be Seized With a Warrant.*** *A warrant may be issued under this rule to search for and seize any (1) property that constitutes evidence of the commission of a criminal offense; or (2) contraband, the fruits of crime, or things otherwise criminally possessed; or (3) property designed or intended for use or which is or has been used as the means of committing a criminal offense; or (4) person for whose arrest there is probable cause, or who is unlawfully restrained.*

Categories 1 and 4 of Rule 41(b) require further discussion. Examples of "(1) property that constitutes evidence of the commission of a criminal offense" are clothing, blood, hair, fingerprints, or business records. Evidence of crime was added to the list of seizable items in response to the U.S. Supreme Court decision in *Warden v. Hayden,* 387 U.S. 294, 87 S.Ct. 1642, 18 L.Ed.2d 782 (1967). That case abolished the former rule that search warrants could not be used as a means of gaining access to a person's house or office and papers solely for the purpose of searching for mere evidence to be used against the person in a criminal proceeding.

One limitation on the seizure of mere evidence is that the evidence to be seized must be nontestimonial. This requirement protects persons from being compelled to be witnesses against themselves in violation of Fifth Amendment rights. It was originally assumed that private personal papers and business records could not be seized under this limitation because of their testimonial nature. The U.S. Supreme Court held, however, that a seizure of personal papers or business records from persons under a search warrant does not necessarily compel those persons to be witnesses against themselves. *Andresen v. Maryland,* 427 U.S. 463, 96 S.Ct. 2737, 49 L.Ed.2d 627 (1976). The Court quoted an earlier case stating that "'a party is privileged from producing the evidence, but not from its production.'" 427 U.S. at 473, 96 S.Ct. at 2745, 49 L.Ed.2d at 638. The Court held that the defendant in the *Andresen* case was not compelled to be a witness against himself because he was not required to say or to do anything during the search. If law enforcement authorities had attempted to subpoena the records, however, the defendant could have refused to give up the records by exercising his Fifth Amendment rights. The Court said:

> [A]lthough the Fifth Amendment may protect an individual from complying with a subpoena for the production of his personal records in his possession because the very act of production may constitute a compulsory authentication of incriminating information, . . . a seizure of the same materials by law enforcement officers differs in a crucial respect—the individual against whom the search is directed is not required to aid in the discovery, production, or authentication of incriminating evidence. 427 U.S. at 473–74, 96 S.Ct. at 2745, 49 L.Ed.2d at 638.

Bank records have even less protection. In *United States v. Miller,* 425 U.S. 435, 96 S.Ct. 1619, 48 L.Ed.2d 71 (1976), the U.S. Supreme Court held that a person's bank records are not private papers of the kind protected against compulsory production by the Fifth Amendment. Also, by choosing to deal with a bank, people lose their expectation of Fourth Amendment protection against government investigation:

> The checks are not confidential communications but negotiable instruments to be used in commercial transactions. All of the documents obtained, including financial statements and deposit slips, contain only information voluntarily conveyed to the banks and exposed to their employees in the ordinary course of business. 425 U.S. at 442, 96 S.Ct. at 1624, 48 L.Ed.2d at 79.

The *Miller* case concerned a subpoena, but either a search warrant or subpoena could be used to obtain a person's bank records without violating the person's Fifth

Amendment right against compulsory self-incrimination. Note that the *Miller* case does not automatically grant unrestricted access to bank records. Access may be restricted by state or federal statute.

Both the *Andresen* and *Miller* cases serve to highlight a basic principle regarding the obtaining of papers as evidence in criminal cases: "There is no special sanctity in papers, as distinguished from other forms of property, to render them immune from search and seizure, if only they fall within the scope of the principles of the cases in which other property may be seized, and if they be adequately described in the affidavit and warrant." *Gouled v. United States,* 255 U.S. 298, 309, 41 S.Ct. 261, 265, 65 L.Ed. 647, 652 (1921). Nevertheless, officers seizing items such as business records or personal papers under a warrant may request the defendant's assistance but may not compel assistance in any way. Otherwise the evidence may be suppressed because of a violation of the defendant's Fifth Amendment rights.

Another limitation on the seizure of mere evidence of crime is that the evidence must aid in a particular apprehension or conviction. The reason for this requirement was stated by the Supreme Court:

> The requirements of the Fourth Amendment can secure the same protection of privacy whether the search is for "mere evidence" or for fruits, instrumentalities or contraband. There must, of course, be a nexus—automatically provided in the case of fruits, instrumentalities or contraband—between the item to be seized and criminal behavior. Thus, in the case of "mere evidence" probable cause must be examined in terms of cause to believe that the evidence sought will aid in a particular apprehension or conviction. In doing so, consideration of police purposes will be served. *Warden v. Hayden,* 387 U.S. 294, 306–07, 87 S.Ct. 1642, 1650, 18 L.Ed.2d 782, 792 (1967).

The U.S. Supreme Court held that law enforcement officers may seize "mere evidence" of a separate crime under a warrant authorizing "seizure of fruits, instrumentalities and evidence of crime at this (time) unknown" if the evidence of a separate crime can be used to show intent to commit the crime for which the warrant was issued. *Andresen v. Maryland,* 427 U.S. 463, 96 S.Ct. 2737, 49 L.Ed.2d 627 (1976).

An affidavit for a search warrant should indicate, for each item of property sought in the warrant, the type of seizable property under which the item is classified according to the law of the jurisdiction. This informs the magistrate that the items sought are connected with criminal activity. For the remainder of this chapter, items of property allowed to be seized under state or federal law are referred to as "items subject to seizure" or "seizable items."

Category 4 of Rule 41(b) deals with the search for and seizure of persons. This provision authorizing a search warrant to issue for a "person for whose arrest there is probable cause" covers the situation, discussed in Chapter 4 ("Arrest"), in which the person to be arrested is in the home of a third person. Officers must apply for a search warrant to satisfy the requirement of *Steagald v. United States,* 451 U.S. 204, 101 S.Ct. 1642, 68 L.Ed.2d 38 (1981), that a search warrant be obtained to justify entry into the home of any person other than the person to be arrested. Even when a search warrant would not be required to enter a place to search for a person, category 4 makes the warrant procedure available. Law enforcement officers are thus encouraged to resort to the preferred alternative of acquiring an objective judicial predetermination of probable cause that the person sought is at the place to be searched.

The provision making it possible for a search warrant to issue for a person "who is unlawfully restrained" is designed to provide the authorization of a warrant to search for victims of crimes like kidnapping and criminal restraint. Although exigent circumstances, especially the need to act promptly to protect the life or well-being of the victim, will often justify an immediate warrantless search for the victim, this will not inevitably be the case.

PARTICULAR DESCRIPTION OF PLACE OR PERSON. The affidavit supporting a request for a search warrant for a *place* must contain a description of the premises to be searched that points directly to a definitely ascertainable place to the exclusion of all others. The U.S. Supreme Court stated that "[i]t is enough if the description is such that the officer with a search warrant can with reasonable effort ascertain and identify the place intended." *Steele v. United States,* 267 U.S. 498, 503, 45 S.Ct. 414, 416, 69 L.Ed. 757, 760 (1925).

A correct street address is sufficient to identify the place to be searched. For example, in *United States v. Dancy,* 947 F.2d 1232 (5th Cir. 1991), officers executed a search warrant that described the place to be searched only as 5121 Rapido Drive, Houston, Texas. The court held:

> A correct street address in a search warrant, even if no other description is given, is particular enough to withstand constitutional scrutiny. The warrant must describe the place to be searched in enough detail for the executing officer (1) to locate the premises with reasonable effort, and (2) to be sure that the wrong premises are not mistakenly searched. . . . A correct street address meets both prongs of the test. 947 F.2d at 1234.

In *United States v. Turner,* 770 F.2d 1508, 1509–10 (9th Cir. 1985), the affidavit for search warrant and the search warrant itself described the house as follows:

> 2762 Mountain View, Escondido, California, and further described as a beige two-story stucco and adobe house with an attached two-car garage. The garage has entry doors on either side of a large garage door. The entry door located on the south side of the garage door has a brass-plated deadbolt lock installed. On the south side of this door are two windows covered by tinfoil. The doors and trim of the house are painted brown. The entry to the residence is located on the south side of the residence and the garage entry faces west. The driveway to the residence off of Mountain View Drive leads north from Mountain View Drive and is marked by three mailboxes numbered 2800, 2810 and 2756. This driveway leads past these three residences, the last identified by a residence marker of 2756, D.A. Mieir. The driveway then turns to concrete and dead ends at the 2762 Mountain View Drive residence. There is a farm road leading past 2762 Mountain View Drive and into an avocado grove. The driveway leads north from Mountain View Drive. Entry to the 2762 Mountain View Drive residence is located on the south side.

The description of the suspect house turned out to be correct except for the street number. The house that the agents had surveilled, intended to search, and actually did search was 2800 Mountain View Drive. Number 2762 Mountain View Drive was located approximately two-tenths of a mile away in a location that the agents did not know existed, and it did not resemble the description of the suspect house. The court held that the description in the search warrant was sufficiently particular despite the wrong street address. The court said:

> The verbal description contained in the warrant described the house to be searched with great particularity; no nearby house met the warrant's detailed description; the address in the warrant was reasonable for the location intended; the house had been under surveillance before the warrant was sought; the warrant was executed by an officer who had participated in applying for the warrant

and who personally knew which premises were intended to be searched; and the premises that were intended to be searched were those actually searched. Under these circumstances, there was virtually no chance that the executing officer would have any trouble locating and identifying the premises to be searched, or that he would mistakenly search another house. 770 F.2d at 1511.

Officers should include detailed descriptions of the place to be searched (such as the one in the *Turner* case) in their affidavits to avoid errors and ensure that the particularity requirement is satisfied. In *United States v. Ellis,* 971 F.2d 701 (11th Cir. 1992), the warrant described the place to be searched as the "third mobile home on the north side" without any further description of its physical characteristics or mention of its occupant's name. The court found the description insufficiently particular.

The location of rural property is more difficult to describe, but there is also less chance that an error will be made in locating a particular piece of rural property. Therefore, a description of a farm or other rural property by the owner's name, the dwelling's color and style, and general directions will usually suffice. *Gatlin v. State,* 559 S.W.2d 12 (Ark. 1977).

When the place to be searched is a multiple-occupancy dwelling such as an apartment house, hotel, or rooming house, the affidavit must go beyond merely stating the location of the premises. In *Manley v. Commonwealth,* 176 S.E.2d 309 (Va. 1970), the affidavit on which the warrant was based read as follows:

> Place to be searched: 313 West 27th Street, a dwelling. The apartment of Melvin Lloyd Manley.

The defendant objected to the search on the ground that the apartment to be searched was not sufficiently described in the affidavit and warrant. The court held that the defendant's apartment was sufficiently described for the searching officers to locate it with very little effort:

> It has been generally held that a search warrant directed against a multiple-occupancy structure is invalid if it fails to describe the particular sub-unit to be searched with sufficient definiteness to preclude search of other units located in the larger structure and occupied by innocent persons. But there are exceptions to the general rule. Even though a search warrant against a multiple-occupancy structure fails to describe the particular sub-unit to be searched, it will ordinarily not be held invalid where it adequately specifies the name of the occupant of the sub-unit against which it is directed and provides the searching officers with sufficient information to identify, without confusion or excessive effort, such apartment unit. 176 S.E.2d at 314.

Whenever possible, however, information like room number, apartment number, and floor should be included in the affidavit. If necessary, a diagram showing the location should be attached to the affidavit.

In another case involving a multiple-occupancy dwelling, the description in the warrant of the place to be searched (a four-building apartment complex) gave a wrong street address but correctly stated the apartment number. Since there was only one apartment with that number in the entire complex, the court held that the description was sufficient:

> [T]he determining factor as to whether a search warrant describes the premises to be searched with sufficient particularity is not whether the description is technically accurate in every detail but rather whether the description is sufficient to enable the executing officer to locate and identify the premises with reasonable effort, and whether there is any reasonable probability that another premises

might be mistakenly searched which is not the one intended to be searched under the search warrant. *United States v. Darensbourg,* 520 F.2d 985, 987 (5th Cir. 1975).

To obtain sufficiently descriptive information, an officer may need to view the premises, examine floor plans, or make inquiries of landlords, tenants, or others to determine the correct limits of the place to be searched. The U.S. Supreme Court said that "[t]he validity of the warrant must be assessed on the basis of the information that the officers disclosed, or had a duty to discover and to disclose, to the issuing magistrate." *Maryland v. Garrison,* 480 U.S. 79, 85, 107 S.Ct. 1013, 1018, 94 L.Ed.2d 72, 81 (1987). Nevertheless, the sufficiency of the description will be judged in light of the information available to the officer at the time he or she prepared the affidavit. The later discovery of facts demonstrating that a warrant was unnecessarily broad does not retroactively invalidate the warrant. In short, if an officer is diligent in gathering the information on which his or her description of the place to be searched is based, the warrant will be valid even though hindsight reveals that honest mistakes were made.

A warrant may be issued for the search of the premises of an innocent third party who is not suspected of any crime. In a case involving the search of newspaper offices, the U.S. Supreme Court said that search warrants are not directed at persons but at the seizure of things. "The critical element in a reasonable search is not that the owner of the property is suspected of crime but that there is reasonable cause to believe that the specific 'things' to be searched for and seized are located on the property to which entry is sought." *Zurcher v. The Stanford Daily,* 436 U.S. 547, 556, 98 S.Ct. 1970, 1977, 56 L.Ed.2d 525, 535 (1978). The *Zurcher* case involved a warrant to search a newsroom to obtain photographs of demonstrators who had injured several police officers. Note that Congress, in the Privacy Protection Act (1980), 42 U.S.C.A. § 2000aa, provided extensive protection against searches and seizures of not only the news media and news people but also others engaged in disseminating communications to the public, unless there is probable cause to believe the person possessing the materials has committed or is committing the criminal offense to which the materials relate.

A search warrant may also be issued to search a *person* for particular items of evidence, although the more common procedure is to arrest the person and conduct a search incident to arrest (see Chapter 8). Again, the standard for determining the validity of a warrant to search a person is whether the warrant describes the person to be searched with sufficient particularity to enable identification with reasonable certainty. Even though a person's name is unknown or incorrectly stated, a warrant may still be valid if a description of the person is included. *United States v. Ferrone,* 438 F.2d 381 (3d Cir. 1971). A law enforcement officer applying for a warrant for the search of a person should not only state the person's name, if known, but also give a complete description including weight, height, age, race, clothing, address, and any aliases. *State v. Tramantano,* 260 A.2d 128 (Conn. Super. 1969). If the name in the affidavit is incorrect, the supporting information will still enable the person to be identified.

Some courts hold that any search of a person that requires surgery is prohibited by the Fourth Amendment. *Adams v. State,* 299 N.E.2d 834 (Ind. 1973). Other courts require additional information in the affidavit to justify the issuance of a search warrant requiring surgery. The U.S. Supreme Court case of *Winston v. Lee,* 470 U.S. 753, 105 S.Ct. 1611, 84 L.Ed.2d 662 (1985), discussed the interests that must be balanced in determining whether a search requiring surgery is constitutional.

The reasonableness of surgical intrusions beneath the skin depends on a case-by-case approach, in which the individual's interests in privacy and security are weighed against society's interests in conducting the procedure. In a given case, the question whether the community's need for evidence outweighs the substantial privacy interests at stake is a delicate one admitting of few categorical answers. 470 U.S. at 760, 105 S.Ct. at 1616, 84 L.Ed.2d at 669.

Among the factors to be weighed are the extent to which the procedure may threaten the safety or health of the individual and the extent of intrusion on the individual's dignitary interests in personal privacy and bodily integrity. Balanced against these individual interests is the community's interest in fairly and accurately determining guilt or innocence, the seriousness of the crime, the relevance and importance of the evidence sought, the likelihood of surgery's producing the evidence, and the available alternatives to surgery. In addition, a defendant may be entitled to an adversary hearing and an opportunity to appeal an order directing surgery. *United States v. Crowder*, 543 F.2d 312 (D.C.Cir. 1976).

The U.S. Supreme Court has established exceptions to the warrant requirement allowing warrantless searches of motor vehicles under limited circumstances. (See Chapter 11.) However, the basic rule is that a warrant is required for the search of a motor vehicle. Since vehicles are considered *places* for search and seizure purposes, an affidavit is required to contain a description of the vehicle to be searched that is sufficiently particular that the vehicle can be located with reasonable certainty. Some courts have held that only the license plate number is necessary to sufficiently describe a motor vehicle for purposes of issuance of a warrant. "A vehicle search warrant ordinarily should include the license plate number on its face, but when this is not practicable a detailed description of the vehicle or a narrow geographical limit to the search may provide the requisite check on police discretion." *United States v. Vaughn*, 830 F.2d 1185 (D.C.Cir. 1987). A detailed description would include information such as the make, body style, color, year, location, and owner or operator of the vehicle.

Mail may also be considered a *place* for search and seizure purposes. Courts have ruled that first-class domestic mail may not be lawfully opened without a warrant. (Domestic mail is any letter or package traveling wholly within the United States.) Therefore, law enforcement officers must follow the same procedures to obtain a warrant to search first-class domestic mail as to search places, persons, and vehicles.

If a search warrant is sought to install a tracking device such as a beeper, a problem arises in describing the place to be searched, because the location of a place is usually what is sought to be discovered. The U.S. Supreme Court responded to this issue as follows:

> [I]t will still be possible to describe the object into which the beeper is to be placed, the circumstances that led agents to wish to install the beeper, and the length of time for which beeper surveillance is requested. In our view, this information will suffice to permit issuance of a warrant authorizing beeper installation and surveillance. *United States v. Karo*, 468 U.S. 705, 718, 104 S.Ct. 3296, 3305, 82 L.Ed.2d 530, 543 (1984).

PARTICULAR DESCRIPTION OF THINGS. The affidavit supporting a request for a search warrant must contain a particular description of the items to be seized. The U.S. Supreme Court explained the reason for this requirement:

> The requirement that warrants shall particularly describe the things to be seized makes general searches under them impossible and prevents the seizure of one thing under a warrant describing another. As to what is to be taken, nothing is left to the discretion of the officer executing the warrant. *Marron v. United States*, 275 U.S. 192, 196, 48 S.Ct. 74, 76, 72 L.Ed. 231, 237 (1927).

In general, the items to be seized must be described with sufficient particularity so that the officer executing the warrant (1) can identify the items with reasonable certainty and (2) is left with no discretion as to which property is to be taken. The primary concern of courts evaluating descriptions of things to be seized in affidavits for search warrants is to ensure that a person will not be deprived of lawfully possessed property by a seizure made under an imprecise warrant.

A description of items merely as "stolen goods," "obscene materials," or "other articles of merchandise too numerous to mention" is inadequate because it is imprecise. *Marcus v. Search Warrant,* 367 U.S. 717, 81 S.Ct. 1708, 6 L.Ed.2d 1127 (1961). When an item can be described in detail, all available information about it should be included in the affidavit. For example, number, size, color, weight, condition, brand name, and other distinguishing features of an item to be seized should be a part of the description where applicable. The affidavit should also indicate how the item is connected with criminal activity by stating the category of items subject to seizure within which the item falls.

A more general description may be allowed when specificity is impossible or difficult. For example, in a case involving the robbery of a post office, the court found sufficiently specific the description in a warrant directing the seizure of "a variety of items, including 'currency' and 'United States postage stock (stamps; envelopes; checks).'" The court said:

> At the time of the application and issuance of the warrant in the instant case, a more precise description of the stamps and currency taken during the robbery was unascertainable. Although the postal inspectors knew that stamps and currency had been stolen, no further information was available to more particularly describe the items in the warrant. We find that the description of the stamps and currency by generic classes was reasonably specific under the circumstances of this case. *United States v. Porter,* 831 F.2d 760, 764 (8th Cir. 1987).

A more general description may also be allowed when a large number of items to be seized are of a common nature and not readily distinguishable. In a case involving a stolen shipment of women's clothing, a search warrant authorized the seizure of "[c]artons of women's clothing, the contents of those cartons, lists identifying the contents of the cartons, and control slips identifying the stores intended to receive these cartons, such items being contraband and evidence of a violation of Title 18, United States Code, Section 659, Possession of Goods Stolen from Interstate Shipments." The court said:

> We recognize . . . that the overriding principle of the Fourth Amendment is one of reasonableness and on occasion have accepted general descriptions in warrants, holding that such descriptions are not always constitutionally infirm. . . . Such general descriptions are permissible only in "special contexts in which there [is] substantial evidence to support the belief that the class of contraband [is] on the premises and in practical terms the goods to be described [can] not be precisely described" [citation omitted]. In *United States v. Klein,* 565 F.2d 183 (1st Cir. 1977), we set forth two tests which in particular circumstances may help to illuminate whether this principle is satisfied: first, the degree to which the evidence presented to the magistrate establishes reason to believe that a large collection of similar contraband is present on the premises to be searched, and, second, the extent to which, in view of the possibilities, the warrant distinguishes, or provides the executing agents with criteria for distinguishing, the contraband from the rest of an individual's possessions. *United States v. Fuccillo,* 808 F.2d 173, 176 (1st Cir. 1987).

The court found that government agents could have but did not obtain specific information, for presentment to the magistrate and inclusion in the warrant, that would have enabled the agents executing the search to differentiate contraband cartons of women's clothing from legitimate ones. The warrants were invalidated for failure to specify as nearly as possible the distinguishing characteristics of the goods to be seized.

Courts also allow a relaxation of the particularity requirement for search warrants seeking business records of businesses "permeated with fraud."

> [W]here there is probable cause to believe that a business is "permeated with fraud," either explicitly stated in the supporting affidavit or implicit from the evidence therein set forth, a warrant may authorize the seizure of all documents relating to the suspected criminal area but may not authorize the seizure of any severable portion of such documents relating to legitimate activities. *United States v. Oloyede,* 982 F.2d 133, 141 (4th Cir. (1991).

A general description will usually not be allowed if a more specific description is possible. In *United States v. Townsend,* 394 F.Supp. 736 (E.D. Mich. 1975), a search warrant commanded the seizure of "Stolen firearms, app. ten (10), which are stored in the basement of the above location, and in bedrooms, and any and all other stolen items, contraband." The court held that the phrase "any and all other stolen items" was impermissibly vague. With respect to the description "10 firearms," the court said:

> Firearms may be easily characterized by color, length, type and other defining attributes. Therefore, further description in the instant case is far from a "virtual impossibility," and the generic description in combination with the other defects in particularity, constitutes a violation of defendant's Fourth Amendment Guarantee. 394 F.Supp. at 747. . . .

Courts generally allow greater leeway in descriptions of contraband material.

> If the purpose of the search is to find a specific item of property, it should be so particularly described in the warrant as to preclude the possibility of the officer seizing the wrong property; whereas, on the other hand, if the purpose is to seize not a specific property, but any property of a specified character, which by reason of its character is illicit or contraband, a specific particular description of the property is unnecessary and it may be described generally as to its nature or character. *People v. Schmidt,* 473 P.2d 698, 700 (Colo. 1970).

In *United States v. Spears,* 965 F.2d 262 (7th Cir. 1992), the warrant authorized a search for and seizure of "controlled substances and other drug related paraphernalia, and materials for packaging controlled substances." The court held:

> The terms "controlled substances" and "materials for packaging controlled substances" are sufficiently specific on their face. The catch-all term "other drug related paraphernalia" also passes constitutional muster in that such items are easily identifiable and quickly found by drug law enforcement officers. A search warrant delineating those items generally, in combination with named contraband, sufficiently limits an officer's discretion to execute the warrant. 965 F.2d at 277.

In *United States v. Appoloney,* 761 F.2d 520, 524 (9th Cir. 1985), the court found the following description sufficient: "'wagering paraphernalia' such as betting slips, bottom sheets and owe sheets, and journals and schedules of sporting events."

General descriptions will not be allowed, however, if the items to be searched for or seized are books, films, recordings, or other materials that have not yet been adjudged obscene. Because these materials are presumed protected by the First Amendment, a very high degree of particularity is required in both the affidavit and the warrant. As the U.S. Supreme Court stated, "[T]he constitutional requirement that warrants must particularly describe the 'things to be seized' is to be accorded the most scrupulous exactitude when the 'things' are books, and the basis for their seizure is the ideas which they contain. . . . No less a standard could be faithful to First Amendment freedoms." *Stanford v. Texas,* 379 U.S. 476, 485–86, 85 S.Ct. 506, 511–12, 13 L.Ed.2d 431, 437 (1965). Therefore, in a case in which a magistrate viewed two films from the defendant's adult book store, concluded they were obscene, and issued a warrant authorizing the seizure of all other obscene materials, the U.S. Supreme Court held that the warrant was a prohibited general warrant:

> [T]he warrant left it entirely to the discretion of the officials conducting the search to decide what items were likely obscene and to accomplish their seizure. The Fourth Amendment does not permit such action. . . . Nor does the Fourth Amendment countenance open-ended warrants, to be completed while a seizure is being conducted and items seized or after the seizure has been carried out. *Lo-Ji Sales, Inc. v. New York,* 442 U.S. 319, 325, 99 S.Ct. 2319, 2324, 60 L.Ed.2d 920, 927–28 (1979).

On the other hand, a court found a warrant authorizing a search for child pornography materials sufficiently particular where

- the warrant quoted the statute that particularly described the sexually explicit conduct depicted in the materials that was prohibited, and
- there was only a small possibility that materials depicting child pornography could be protected by the First Amendment. *United States v. Koelling,* 992 F.2d 817 (8th Cir. 1993).

MULTIPLE AFFIDAVITS. A law enforcement officer applying for a search warrant may submit more than one affidavit to the magistrate. The additional or supplemental affidavits may be prepared by the officer or someone else.

> Since the object of the proceedings before the magistrate is to establish probable cause to justify issuance of a search warrant, law enforcement officers should not be hindered in their efforts to describe the basis for probable cause in supporting affidavits. So long as these affidavits are satisfactorily incorporated to all related documents necessary to the application for the warrant . . . the reviewing court will be assured of the simultaneous presence of these documents before the magistrate, and the search may be subjected to authoritative judicial review. *State v. Gamage,* 340 A.2d 1, 7 (Me. 1975).

The essential requirement is that all "affidavits are satisfactorily incorporated to all related documents necessary to the application for the warrant." The following procedure is suggested to ensure proper incorporation:

1. Entitle the first or primary affidavit "Affidavit and Request for Search Warrant."
2. Entitle all additional affidavits "Supplemental Affidavit 1," "Supplemental Affidavit 2," and so forth.
3. Include the following statement in the first or primary affidavit: "This request is also based on the information in the sworn statements in Supplemental Affidavit 1, Supplemental Affidavit 2, . . . which are attached." (The law requires that clear reference be made to all supplemental affidavits).

4. Securely attach all supplemental affidavits to the primary affidavit. Use a stapler or other semipermanent method of binding. A paper clip would be unsatisfactory because of its tendency to slip off.

By following these simple steps, the officer ensures that the magistrate will be simultaneously presented with all the information on which probable cause is to be based and that the appellate court will be able to effectively review the magistrate's decision.

Securing of Dwelling While Warrant Is Being Sought

When officers have probable cause to believe that evidence of criminal activity is in a dwelling, a temporary securing of the dwelling to prevent removal or destruction of evidence while a search warrant is being sought is not an unreasonable seizure of either the dwelling or its contents. The U.S. Supreme Court said:

> [T]he home is sacred in Fourth Amendment terms not primarily because of the occupants' *possessory* interests in the premises, but because of their *privacy* interests in the activities that take place within. . . . [A] seizure affects only possessory interests, not privacy interests. Therefore, the heightened protection we accord privacy interests is simply not implicated where a *seizure* of premises, not a search, is at issue. *Segura v. United States,* 468 U.S. 796, 810, 104 S.Ct. 3380, 3388, 82 L.Ed.2d 599, 612 (1984).

Furthermore, the *Segura* case held that insofar as the *seizure* of the premises is concerned, it made no difference whether the premises were secured by stationing officers within the premises or by establishing a perimeter stakeout after a security check of the premises revealed that no one was inside. Under either method, officers control the premises pending arrival of the warrant. Both an internal securing and a perimeter stakeout interfere to the same extent with the possessory interests of the owners.

State courts have further refined the circumstances justifying the securing of a dwelling while a warrant is being sought. For example, the Virginia Court of Appeals held:

> To determine whether a warrantless entry for the limited purpose of securing the premises is reasonable, we must balance the law enforcement need to preserve evidence and protect its officers against the individual's privacy interest in maintaining the sanctity of the home. We find that the balance is weighted in favor of entry when, based on the totality of the circumstances, the following factors are present: (1) police officers have probable cause to believe evidence is on the premises; (2) delaying entry would create a substantial risk that evidence will be lost or destroyed or the critical nature of the circumstances prevents the use of any warrant procedure; and (3) the police must not be responsible for creating their own exigencies. . . .
>
> Once an entry has been justified under the three-pronged test enunciated above, in order to determine if anyone is present who might destroy evidence or pose a threat to police safety, police officers may conduct a limited security check in those areas where individuals could hide. If this security check reveals that no one is on the premises, the police have no legitimate reason to remain on the premises and should leave once they have secured the premises. If police suspect that others may soon arrive who would destroy evidence, they should then set up an external stakeout, which constitutes a lesser form of intrusion. *Crosby v. Commonwealth,* 367 S.E.2d 730, 735–36 (Va.App. 1988).

Anticipatory Search Warrants

An **anticipatory search warrant,** also called a **prospective search warrant,** is a warrant to search a particular place for a particular seizable item that has not yet arrived at the place where the search is to be executed. In recent years, law enforcement officers have applied for anticipatory search warrants in increasing numbers, especially in cases involving contraband in the mails and those involving informants or undercover officers. In general, courts have held that anticipatory warrants, if issued under proper circumstances, upon a proper showing, and with proper safeguards, do not violate the Fourth Amendment.

> [W]hen law enforcement personnel offer a magistrate reliable, independent evidence indicating that a delivery of contraband will very likely occur at a particular place, and when the magistrate conditions the warrant's execution for the search of that place on that delivery, the warrant, if not overbroad or otherwise defective, passes constitutional muster. That the contraband has not yet reached the premises to be searched at the time the warrant issues is not, in constitutional terms, an insuperable obstacle. *United States v. Ricciardelli,* 998 F.2d 8, 11 (1st Cir. 1993).

Although anticipatory search warrants are not constitutionally forbidden, a warrant conditioned on a future event presents a potential for abuse above and beyond that which exists in more traditional settings. Officers executing these warrants are inevitably called on to determine when and whether the triggering event specified in the warrant has actually occurred. Therefore, magistrates who are asked to issue anticipatory warrants must be particularly vigilant in ensuring that opportunities for exercising unfettered discretion are eliminated. To satisfy these concerns, the magistrate must set conditions governing the execution of an anticipatory warrant that are "explicit, clear, and narrowly drawn so as to avoid misunderstanding or manipulation by government agents." *United States v. Garcia,* 882 F.2d 699, 703–04 (2nd Cir. 1989).

> There are two particular dimensions in which anticipatory warrants must limit the discretion of government agents. First, the magistrate must ensure that the triggering event is both ascertainable and preordained. The warrant should restrict the officers' discretion in detecting the occurrence of the event to almost ministerial proportions, similar to a search party's discretion in locating the place to be searched. Only then, in the prototypical case, are the ends of explicitness and clarity served. Second, the contraband must be on a sure and irreversible course to its destination, and a future search of the destination must be made expressly contingent upon the contraband's arrival there. Under such circumstances, a number of courts have found anticipatory search warrants to be valid. *United States v. Ricciardelli,* 998 F.2d 8, 12 (1st Cir. 1993).

A search warrant was held invalid in *State v. Vitale,* 530 P.2d 394 (Ariz.App. 1975), because of failure to satisfy the "sure and irreversible course" requirement. In that case, a warrant to search the defendant's pawn shop was issued on the basis that a reliable informant had agreed to sell a stolen television set to the defendant at the pawn shop. The police had the television in their possession at the time they applied for the warrant. After the sale, the warrant was executed and the television was seized. The court held that there was no probable cause that a crime had been committed at the time the warrant was issued.

> The informant had not yet approached appellant regarding the television set at the time the . . . search warrant was issued; also there had not been any recent dealings between the informant and appellant. . . .

In the instant case, no crime was in progress and it was a matter of speculation whether one would be committed in the future. The course of events strongly suggests that the duty to determine probable cause was improperly shifted from the magistrate to the police. 530 P.2d at 397–98.

If there had been some deal or arrangement between the informant and the defendant before the police applied for the warrant, the court might have found the warrant valid on the ground that a crime was in progress or at least was very likely to occur.

To ensure that a magistrate is provided with sufficient information to justify the issuance of an anticipatory search warrant, law enforcement officers should present strong evidence in an affidavit that the continuation of a process *already initiated* will result in seizable items arriving at a particular place at a particular time. To guard against premature execution of the warrant, the affidavit should carefully specify the time when the item to be seized will arrive at the place where the search is to occur and the time thereafter when the execution of the warrant is planned. This information will help satisfy the magistrate that the warrant will not be executed prematurely.

Redaction of Search Warrants

Search warrants may contain some clauses that are constitutionally sufficient and some that are not. Should courts suppress all evidence under these warrants, or only the evidence seized under the constitutionally insufficient clauses? To avoid the severe remedy of total suppression of all evidence under these warrants, many courts have adopted the theory of **redaction,** also called **partial suppression** and **severability.** Redaction involves invalidating clauses in a warrant that are constitutionally insufficient for lack of probable cause or particularity while preserving clauses that satisfy the Fourth Amendment.

Not all courts have adopted the concept of redaction, and the U.S. Supreme Court has not yet spoken on the issue. Those that have adopted redaction point out that it is not inconsistent with the deterrent effect of the exclusionary rule. Illegally seized evidence is still suppressed, thereby discouraging law enforcement officials from attempting to evade Fourth Amendment requirements and preventing the government from benefiting from its own wrongdoing. Yet redaction mitigates the heavy social costs of unnecessarily excluding legally seized evidence. As a further constitutional safeguard, courts have been careful not to use redaction when "the warrant, when read with the affidavit, is essentially general in character but as to some tangential items meets the requirement of particularity." *United States v. Cook,* 657 F.2d 730, 735 n.6 (5th Cir. 1981).

The Third Circuit Court of Appeals found that redaction is consistent with all five purposes of the warrant requirement:

> First, with respect to the search and seizure conducted pursuant to the valid portion of the redacted warrant, the intrusion into personal privacy has been justified by probable cause to believe that the search and seizure will serve society's need for law enforcement. Second, because it is a duly issued warrant that is being redacted, the objective of interposing a magistrate between law enforcement officials and the citizen has been attained. Third, even though it may not be coterminous with the underlying probable cause showing, the scope of a search pursuant to a particularized, overbroad warrant is nevertheless limited by the terms of its authorization. In the case of a warrant containing some invalid general clauses, redaction neither exacerbates nor ratifies the unwarranted intrusions conducted pursuant to the general clauses, but merely preserves the evidence

seized pursuant to those clauses particularly describing items to be seized. Fourth, as to the valid portions of the warrant salvaged by redaction, the individual whose property is to be searched has received notification of the lawful authority of the executing officer, his need to search, and the limits of his power to search. Fifth, redaction does not affect the generation of a record susceptible to subsequent judicial review. *United States v. Christine,* 687 F.2d 749, 758 (3d Cir. 1982)

KEY POINTS

1. An issuing magistrate for a search warrant must be neutral and detached and must be capable of determining whether probable cause exists for the requested search.

2. Before issuing a search warrant, the magistrate must have probable cause to believe that items subject to seizure are in a particular place or on a particular person at the time of the issuance of the warrant.

3. If a law enforcement officer knowingly and intentionally, or with reckless disregard for the truth, makes false statements in an affidavit supporting a request for a search warrant, the warrant may not issue or evidence seized under the warrant may be suppressed.

4. Probable cause to search for certain objects may become stale if there is too long a delay between the time when the information on which probable cause is based is gathered and the time when the search is executed. Depending on the nature of the object, the nature of the criminal activity, the criminal suspects, and other factors, there may no longer be good reason to believe that the property is still at the same location.

5. Generally, the types of property allowed to be seized under a search warrant are evidence of crime, contraband, fruits of crime, things otherwise criminally possessed, and instrumentalities of crime.

6. The affidavit supporting a request for a search warrant for a place must contain a description of the premises to be searched that points directly to a definitely ascertainable place to the exclusion of all others.

7. The affidavit supporting a request for a search warrant must contain a particular description of the items to be seized.

8. When law enforcement officers have probable cause to believe that evidence of criminal activity is in a dwelling, a temporary securing of the dwelling to prevent removal or destruction of evidence while a search warrant is being sought is not an unreasonable seizure of either the dwelling or its contents.

9. An *anticipatory* or *prospective* search warrant is a warrant to search a particular place for a particular seizable item that has not yet arrived at the place where the search is to be executed.

10. *Redaction* of search warrants, also called *partial suppression* and *severability,* involves invalidating clauses in a warrant that are constitutionally insufficient for lack of probable cause or particularity while preserving clauses that satisfy the Fourth Amendment.

Contents of the Warrant

Although search warrants vary in different jurisdictions, most search warrants contain the following information:

- The caption of the court or division of the court from which the warrant issues
- A particular description of the place or person to be searched
- A particular description of the property to be seized
- The names of persons whose affidavits have been taken in support of the warrant
- A statement of grounds for issuance of the warrant

AO 93 (Rev. 6/92) Search Warrant

United States District Court

_____ DISTRICT OF _____

In the Matter of the Search of
(Name, address or brief description of person or property to be searched)

SEARCH WARRANT

CASE NUMBER:

TO: _____ and any Authorized Officer of the United States

Affidavit(s) having been made before me by _____ who has reason to
                                                        Affiant

believe that ☐ on the person of or ☐ on the premises known as (name, description and/or location)

in the_____ District of _____ there is now
concealed a certain person or property, namely (describe the person or property)

I am satisfied that the affidavit(s) and any recorded testimony establish probable cause to believe that the person
or property so described is now concealed on the person or premises above-described and establish grounds for
the issuance of this warrant.

YOU ARE HEREBY COMMANDED to search on or before _____
                                                                         Date

(not to exceed 10 days) the person or place named above for the person or property specified, serving this warrant
and making the search (in the daytime — 6:00 A.M. to 10:00 P.M.) (at any time in the day or night as I find
reasonable cause has been established) and if the person or property be found there to seize same, leaving a copy
of this warrant and receipt for the person or property taken, and prepare a written inventory of the person or property seized and promptly return this warrant to _____
as required by law.   U.S. Judge or Magistrate Judge

_____   at   _____
Date and Time Issued   City and State

_____   _____
Name and Title of Judicial Officer   Signature of Judicial Officer

EXHIBIT 5.2A   A Typical Search Warrant Form, Page 1

- The name of the officer or officers to whom the warrant is directed together with
  a command to search the person or place named for the property specified
- A specification of the time during the day when the search may be conducted
- The name of the judicial officer to whom the warrant is to be returned

AO 93A (Rev. 5/85) Search Warrant Upon Oral Testimony

RETURN

DATE WARRANT RECEIVED	DATE AND TIME WARRANT EXECUTED	COPY OF WARRANT AND RECEIPT FOR ITEMS LEFT WITH

INVENTORY MADE IN THE PRESENCE OF

INVENTORY OF PERSON OR PROPERTY TAKEN PURSUANT TO THE WARRANT

CERTIFICATION

I swear that this inventory is a true and detailed account of the person or property taken by me on the warrant.

_____

Subscribed, sworn to, and returned before me this date.

_____   _____
U.S. Judge or Magistrate Judge   Date

EXHIBIT 5.2B   A Typical Search Warrant Form, Page 2

- The date of issuance
- The signature of the issuing magistrate together with a statement of the magistrate's official title

Exhibits 5.2 and 5.3 are typical search warrant forms.

AO 93A (Rev. 5/85) Search Warrant Upon Oral Testimony

United States District Court

DISTRICT OF

In the Matter of the Search of

(Name, address or brief description of person or property to be searched)

SEARCH WARRANT UPON ORAL TESTIMONY

CASE NUMBER:

TO: _____ and any Authorized Officer of the United States

Sworn oral testimony has been communicated to me by _____
 Affiant

that ☐ on the person of or ☐ on the premises known as (name, description and/or location)

in the_____ District of _____ there is now
concealed a certain person or property, namely (describe the person or property)

I am satisfied that the circumstances are such as to make it reasonable to dispense with a written affidavit and that
there is probable cause to believe that the property or person so described is concealed on the person or premises
above described and that grounds for application for issuance of the search warrant exist as communicated orally to
me in a sworn statement which has been recorded electronically, stenographically, or in longhand and upon the return
of the warrant, will be transcribed, certified as accurate and attached hereto.

YOU ARE HEREBY COMMANDED to search on or before _____
 Date

the person or place named above for the person or property specified, serving this warrant and making the search
(in the daytime — 6:00 AM to 10:00 PM) (at anytime in the day or night as I find reasonable cause has been
established) and if the person or property be found there to seize same, leaving a copy of this warrant and receipt for
the person or property taken, and prepare a written inventory of the person or property seized and promptly
return this warrant to _____
as required by law.   U.S. Judge or Magistrate Judge

_____ at _____
Date and Time Issued   City and State

_____ _____
Name and Title of Judicial Officer   Signature of Judicial Officer

I certify that on _____ at _____ ,
 Date   Time
_____ orally authorized the
 U.S. Judge or Magistrate Judge
issuance and execution of a search warrant conforming to all the foregoing terms.

_____ _____ _____
Name of affiant   Signature of affiant   Exact time warrant executed

EXHIBIT 5.3A A Typical Form for a Search Warrant upon Oral Testimony, Page 1

Execution of the Warrant

The execution (also called service) of a search warrant is essentially the carrying out
of the command or commands appearing on the face of the warrant itself. The U.S.
Supreme Court stated that "the Fourth Amendment confines an officer executing a

AO 93A (Rev. 5/85) Search Warrant Upon Oral Testimony

RETURN

DATE WARRANT RECEIVED	DATE AND TIME WARRANT EXECUTED	COPY OF WARRANT AND RECEIPT FOR ITEMS LEFT WITH

INVENTORY MADE IN THE PRESENCE OF

INVENTORY OF PERSON OR PROPERTY TAKEN PURSUANT TO THE WARRANT

CERTIFICATION

I swear that this inventory is a true and detailed account of the person or property taken by me on the warrant.

_____

Subscribed, sworn to, and returned before me this date.

_____   _____
U.S. Judge or Magistrate Judge   Date

EXHIBIT 5.2B   A Typical Form for a Search Warrant upon Oral Testimony, Page 2

---

search warrant strictly within the bounds set by the warrant. . . .” *Bivens v. Six Unknown Named Agents,* 403 U.S. 388, 394 n.7, 91 S.Ct. 1999, 2004 n.7, 29 L.Ed.2d 619, 625 n.7 (1971). Furthermore, “a search which is reasonable at its inception may violate the Fourth Amendment by virtue of its intolerable intensity and scope. . . . The scope of the search must be ‘strictly tied to and justified by’ the circumstances which rendered its initiation permissible.” *Terry v. Ohio,* 392 U.S. 1, 18, 88 S.Ct. 1868, 1878, 20 L.Ed.2d 889, 903–04 (1968). Although officers can determine many of their duties from simply reading the warrant, several aspects of the execution of search warrants need further explanation.

Who May Execute

A search warrant is directed to a particular officer or class of officers. Only the named officer or a member of the named class of officers may execute or serve the warrant. If a warrant is directed to a particular officer such as a sheriff, a deputy may execute the warrant and the sheriff need not be present. Private persons may be enlisted to help in the execution of a warrant, but an officer to whom the warrant is directed must be personally present at the search scene.

Time Considerations

Three different aspects of time affect a law enforcement officer in the execution of a search warrant. First is the allowable delay between the warrant's issuance and its execution. In jurisdictions with no time limit fixed by statute, court rule, or judicial decision, a warrant must be executed within a reasonable time after issuance. Reasonableness depends on the facts and circumstances of each case.

The chief concern of the courts is that probable cause does not become stale before execution of the warrant. Some jurisdictions require that a search warrant be executed and returned within ten days after its date of issuance. Some of these jurisdictions *also* require that the warrant be executed "forthwith." To resolve this apparent ambiguity, courts require that the warrant be executed within a reasonable time after issuance, so long as it is executed within the statutory period. *United States v. Harper,* 450 F.2d 1032 (5th Cir. 1971). *Therefore, even though an officer executed the warrant within the statutory ten-day period, the search could still be held unlawful if there had been unnecessary delay resulting in legal prejudice to the defendant.*

Unnecessary delay is determined from the facts and circumstances of each case. In a case interpreting a statute with both a "ten-day" provision and a "forthwith" provision, a warrant for the seizure of equipment used to manufacture LSD was executed six days after its issuance. The court held that the execution was timely, as the premises were under daily surveillance, and no activity was noted until after the first five days. The court said:

> While it is desirable that police be given reasonable latitude to determine when a warrant should be executed, it is also necessary that search warrants be executed with some promptness in order to lessen the possibility that the facts upon which probable cause was initially based do not become dissipated.
>
> We adopt the reasoning of the Second Circuit in *Dunnings* to the effect that "forthwith" means any time within 10 days after the warrant is issued, provided that the probable cause recited in the affidavit continues until the time of execution, giving consideration to the intervening knowledge of the officers and the passage of time. *United States v. Nepstead,* 424 F.2d 269, 271 (9th Cir. 1970).

There are many justifications for delaying the execution of a search warrant. For example, weather conditions, long travel distances, traffic problems, and similar obstacles may prevent the prompt execution of the warrant. Delays may be necessary to gather sufficient human resources for the search, to protect the safety of the searching officers, to prevent the destruction of evidence, and to prevent the flight of a suspect. When the warrant is for the search of both a person and premises, the search may be delayed until the person is present on the premises. *People v. Stansberry,* 268 N.E.2d 431 (Ill. 1971).

Another aspect of time affecting the execution of a search warrant is the time of day during which the warrant may be executed. In general, search warrants should be executed in the daytime. Courts have always frowned on nighttime searches. The U.S. Supreme Court said that "it is difficult to imagine a more severe invasion of privacy than the nighttime intrusion into a private home. . . ." *Jones v. United States,* 357 U.S. 493, 498, 78 S.Ct. 1253, 1257, 2 L.Ed.2d 1514, 1519 (1958). Furthermore, nighttime searches are more likely to be met with armed resistance. *State v. Brock,* 633 P.2d 805 (Or.App. 1981). As a result, to obtain a warrant authorizing a nighttime search, some jurisdictions require the affidavit to set forth specific facts showing a necessity for a nighttime search. Justification for a nighttime search has been found where a nighttime delivery of contraband was expected, where the property to be seized was likely to be removed promptly, and where part of a criminal transaction was to take place at night. *United States v. Curry,* 530 F.2d 636 (5th Cir. 1976).

Courts differ in their interpretations of when daytime and nighttime begin and end. A rule of thumb is that it is daytime when there is sufficient natural light to recognize a person's features. Otherwise, it is nighttime. Even if a nighttime search is not authorized, the execution of a search warrant that was begun in the daytime may be continued into the nighttime if it is a reasonable continuation of the daytime search. An officer is not required to cut short the reasonable execution of a daytime search warrant just because it becomes dark outside. *United States v. Joseph,* 278 F.2d 504 (3d Cir. 1960).

The third aspect of time, as it relates to the execution of a search warrant, is the amount of time allowed for the law enforcement officer to perform the search *once it is initiated.* The general rule was stated by the New Hampshire Supreme Court: "The police, in executing a search warrant for a dwelling, may remain on the premises only so long as it is reasonably necessary to conduct the search." *State v. Chaisson,* 486 A.2d 297, 303 (N.H. 1984). Furthermore, as stated by the Tenth Circuit Court of Appeals, "once a search warrant has been fully executed and the fruits of the search secured, the authority under the warrant expires and further governmental intrusion must cease." *United States v. Gagnon,* 635 F.2d 766, 769 (10th Cir. 1980). Therefore, after all the objects described in a warrant have been found, the warrant provides no authorization to search further. If, however, the executing officers have found some but not necessarily all of the described items, the search may lawfully continue.

Knock-and-Announce Requirement

Similar considerations apply to the entry of dwellings to search as apply to the entry of dwellings to arrest, as discussed in Chapter 4 under "Forced Entry." Law enforcement officers should knock and announce their authority and purpose before entering premises to execute a search warrant. Usually an announcement of identity as a law enforcement officer together with a statement that the officer has a search warrant is sufficient. A person may not refuse entry to an officer executing a warrant but must submit voluntarily. *State v. Valentine,* 504 P.2d 84 (Or. 1972). If entry is refused, the officer may enter using force, including breaking open doors and windows. The occupant must be given a brief opportunity to respond before entry is forced. But failure to respond or other behavior inconsistent with voluntary compliance is equivalent to refusal. Unoccupied premises may be entered, forcefully if reasonably necessary, as if officers had been refused entry. The sound of footsteps, whispers, or flushing toilets, indicating possible escape or destruction of evidence, may create exigent circumstances justifying an immediate forcible entry. *United States v. Mitchell,* 783 F.2d 971 (10th Cir. 1986).

The purposes of the so-called knock-and-announce requirements are as follows:

- To prevent violence to the police or other persons on the premises
- To protect the privacy of the occupants of the premises from unexpected intrusions
- To prevent property damage
- To provide the occupant an opportunity to examine the warrant and point out a possible mistaken address or other errors

"Although a search or seizure of a dwelling might be constitutionally defective if police officers enter without prior announcement, law enforcement interests may also establish the reasonableness of an unannounced entry." *Wilson v. Arkansas,* 514 U.S. 927, 936, 115 S.Ct. 1914, 1919, 131 L.Ed.2d 976, 984 (1995). For example, the *Wilson* case recognized that the knock-and-announce requirement could give way under circumstances presenting a threat of physical violence or where law enforcement officers have reason to believe that evidence would likely be destroyed or concealed if advance notice were given. In *Richards v. Wisconsin,* 520 U.S. 385, 117 S.Ct. 1416, 137 L.Ed.2d 615 (1997), however, the Court refused to allow a blanket exception to the knock-and-announce requirement in felony drug cases. The Court said:

> [T]he fact that felony drug investigations may frequently present circumstances warranting a no-knock entry cannot remove from the neutral scrutiny of a reviewing court the reasonableness of the police decision not to knock and announce in a particular case. Instead, in each case, it is the duty of a court confronted with the question to determine whether the facts and circumstances of the particular entry justified dispensing with the knock-and-announce requirement. 520 U.S. at ___, 117 S.Ct. at 1421, 137 L.Ed.2d at 624.

The Court then established a "reasonable suspicion" standard for determining exceptions to the knock-and-announce requirement.

> In order to justify a "no-knock" entry, the police must have a reasonable suspicion that knocking and announcing their presence, under the particular circumstances, would be dangerous or futile, or that it would inhibit the effective investigation of the crime by, for example, allowing the destruction of evidence. This standard— as opposed to a probable cause requirement—strikes the appropriate balance between the legitimate law enforcement concerns at issue in the execution of search warrants and the individual privacy interests affected by no-knock entries. . . . This showing is not high, but the police should be required to make it whenever the reasonableness of a no-knock entry is challenged. 520 U.S. at ___, 117 S.Ct. at 1421, 137 L.Ed.2d at 624.

In *United States v. Fields,* 113 F.3d 313 (2d Cir. 1997), the court found that officers had reasonable suspicion to justify a forcible unannounced entry where police had been informed by a "known and reliable" informant that the defendant was engaged in a cocaine-bagging operation and would be leaving his premises soon, the defendant had a known potential for violence, the defendant had been alerted that police were in his rear yard, and the defendant could have easily disposed of the drug evidence.

In *United States v. Ramirez,* ___ U.S. ___, ___, 118 S.Ct. 992, 996, 140 L.Ed.2d 191, ___ (1998), the U.S. Supreme Court held that "whether a 'reasonable suspicion' exists depends in no way on whether police must destroy property in order to enter." In that case, officers executing a no-knock search warrant broke a single pane of glass in the defendant's garage because they had been informed that a violent prison escapee was on the premises and might have access to a stash of weapons reported to be kept in the garage. The Court held that this police conduct was clearly reasonable and therefore did not violate the Fourth Amendment. Nevertheless, the Court cautioned that the reasonableness standard governs the method of execution of warrants. "Excessive or unnecessary destruction of property in the course of a search may violate the Fourth Amendment, even though the entry itself is lawful and the fruits of the search not subject to suppression." ___ U.S. at ___, 118 S.Ct. at 996, 140 L.Ed.2d at ___.

Some courts allow an exception to the knock-and-announce requirement when entry is achieved by ruse or deception. In *United States v. Contreras-Ceballos,* 999 F.2d 432 (9th Cir. 1993), an officer executing a search warrant for drugs knocked on the defendant's door and replied "Federal Express" when asked who was there. When the door was opened, the officer pushed his way in and announced his authority and purpose. The court held that the use of force to keep the door open and to enter did not violate the knock-and-announce requirement because there was no "breaking." "To rule otherwise would dictate a nonsensical procedure in which the officers, after having employed a permissible ruse to cause the door to be opened, must permit it to be shut by the occupants so that the officers could then knock, reannounce, and open the door forcibly if refused admittance." 999 F.2d at 435.

Finally, knocking and announcing "is excused when the officers are justifiably and virtually certain that the occupants already know their purpose." *United States v. Eddy,* 660 F.2d 381, 385 (8th Cir. 1981). In *United States v. Tracy,* 835 F.2d 1267 (8th Cir. 1988), the court held that the officers' failure to announce their purpose after knocking did not invalidate the search. Surveillance of the premises to be searched for drugs revealed attempts to fortify the premises and indications that the occupants were monitoring the surrounding area. Under these circumstances, the officers could have justifiably believed that the defendants were anticipating their arrival and knew their purpose. Announcing their purpose would have been a useless gesture and, in addition, could have resulted in the destruction of evidence. Nevertheless, since compliance with the knock-and-announce requirement is simple and effortless, it is seldom wise for an officer to assume a defendant's knowledge and risk having evidence excluded because of noncompliance with the requirement. A defendant may know the officer's authority and purpose but may not know of the existence of a warrant.

Note that some states have enacted "no-knock" laws that permit magistrates to issue search warrants specifically authorizing officers to enter premises without knocking and announcing their authority and purpose. The officer applying for the warrant must convince the magistrate that unannounced entry is necessary to prevent destruction of evidence or to prevent harm to the executing officer or others. These no-knock warrants have been criticized on the ground that exigent circumstances can only be determined at the time of executing the warrant and cannot be prejudged at the time of applying for the warrant. *Parsley v. Superior Court,* 513 P.2d 611 (Cal. 1973).

A separate issue is whether law enforcement officers executing a search warrant may lawfully gain access to the area to be searched by entering areas not particularly described in the warrant. In general, courts have approved any means of gaining entry that was both reasonable and necessary. In *Dalia v. United States,* the U.S. Supreme Court approved a covert entry into a dwelling by officers attempting to install electronic surveillance equipment pursuant to a warrant. The Court said that it is generally left to the discretion of the executing officers to determine the details of conducting the search under the warrant. The Court added:

Often in executing a warrant the police may find it necessary to interfere with privacy rights not explicitly considered by the judge who issued the warrant. For example, police executing an arrest warrant commonly find it necessary to enter the suspect's home in order to take him into custody, and they thereby impinge on both privacy and freedom of movement. . . . Similarly, officers executing search warrants on occasion must damage property in order to perform their duty. 441 U.S. 238, 257–58, 99 S.Ct. 1682, 1693–94, 60 L.Ed.2d 177, 193 (1979).

Therefore, officers executing a search warrant may use whatever method is reasonably necessary to gain access to premises to be searched, even to the extent of damaging property, if no reasonable alternative is available.

Search and Seizure of Third Persons and Their Property

When a search warrant is issued for the search of a named person or a named person *and* premises, officers executing the warrant clearly can detain and search the person named. However, may a person on the premises but not named in the warrant be detained or searched? *The general rule is that the search warrant for premises gives a law enforcement officer no authority to search a person not named in the warrant who merely happens to be on the premises.* In *Ybarra v. Illinois,* 444 U.S. 85, 100 S.Ct. 338, 62 L.Ed.2d 238 (1979), the defendant was a mere patron in a bar and the police had a warrant to search the bar and the bartender. The U.S. Supreme Court held that the search of the defendant was illegal because the police did not have probable cause particularized with respect to the defendant.

> [A] person's mere propinquity to others independently suspected of criminal activity does not, without more, give rise to probable cause to search that person. . . . Where the standard is probable cause, a search or seizure of a person must be supported by probable cause particularized with respect to that person. This requirement cannot be undercut or avoided by simply pointing to the fact that coincidentally there exists probable cause to search or seize another or to search the premises where the person may happen to be. The Fourth and Fourteenth Amendments protect the "legitimate expectations of privacy" of persons, not places. 444 U.S. at 91, 100 S.Ct. at 342, 62 L.Ed.2d at 245.

The Court said that a warrant to search a place cannot normally be construed to authorize a search of each person in that place. Therefore, if an officer wishes to search a place and also specific persons expected to be at that place, the officer should obtain a search warrant to search the place and each specific person. To obtain such a warrant, the officer must establish in the affidavit probable cause to search the place and each specific individual.

Detention of persons present on premises to be searched under a warrant may be allowed in certain circumstances, however. In *Michigan v. Summers,* 452 U.S. 692, 101 S.Ct. 2587, 69 L.Ed.2d 340 (1981), the U.S. Supreme Court held that officers executing a valid search warrant for contraband may detain the occupants of the premises while the search is being conducted. The Court said that "[i]f the evidence that a citizen's residence is harboring contraband is sufficient to persuade a judicial officer that an invasion of the citizen's privacy is justified, it is constitutionally reasonable to require that citizen to remain while officers of the law execute a valid warrant to search his home." 452 U.S. at 704–05, 101 S.Ct. at 2595, 69 L.Ed.2d at 351. In explaining the justification for the detention, the Court emphasized the limited additional intrusion represented by the detention once a search of the home had been authorized by a warrant. The Court went on to say:

In assessing the justification for the detention of an occupant of premises being searched for contraband pursuant to a valid warrant, both the law enforcement interest and the nature of the "articulable facts" supporting the detention are relevant. Most obvious is the legitimate law enforcement interest in preventing flight in the event that incriminating evidence is found. Less obvious, but sometimes of greater importance, is the interest in minimizing the risk of harm to the officers. Although no special danger to the police is suggested by the evidence in this record, the execution of a warrant to search for narcotics is the kind of transaction that may give rise to sudden violence or frantic efforts to conceal or destroy evidence. The risk of harm to both the police and the occupants is minimized if the officers routinely exercise unquestioned command of the situation. . . . Finally, the orderly completion of the search may be facilitated if the occupants of the premises are present. Their self-interest may induce them to open locked doors or locked containers to avoid the use of force that is not only damaging to property but may also delay the completion of the task at hand. 452 U.S. at 702–03, 101 S.Ct. at 2594, 69 L.Ed.2d at 349–50.

An officer also has authority to conduct a limited patdown search or frisk for weapons of any person at the search scene who the officer reasonably believes is dangerous. The officer must be able to justify the frisk with specific facts and circumstances to support the belief that a particular person was dangerous. A mere suspicion or hunch that a person was dangerous will not justify a protective frisk. (See Chapter 7 for details on conducting protective searches.)

If an officer at a search scene obtains information constituting probable cause to make a felony arrest, or if a crime is being committed in the officer's presence, the officer may arrest the offender and search him or her incident to the arrest. (See Chapter 8 for details on search incident to arrest.)

Similar rules apply to the search and seizure of the *property* of third persons on the premises described in a warrant. For purposes of this discussion, a third person is a person who is not the target of the warrant and is not a resident of the target premises. In general, when a law enforcement officer executing a search warrant knows or reasonably should know that personal property located within the described premises belongs to a third person, the officer may not search or seize the property under authority of the warrant. In *State v. Lambert,* 710 P.2d 693 (Kan. 1985), a police officer executing a warrant for an apartment and its *male* occupant discovered three *women* in the kitchen of the apartment. The officers searched a purse lying on the kitchen table and found drugs. The court invalidated the search, finding that the officer had no reason to believe that the purse either belonged to the occupant of the premises or was part of the premises described in the search warrant. However, where officers neither know nor have reason to believe that property belongs to a third person, a search or seizure of the property will be upheld. In *Carman v. State,* 602 P.2d 1255 (Alaska 1979), the court upheld the search of a purse because the court found that the police did not know whether the purse belonged to a permanent resident of the apartment or a visitor.

Scope of the Search

A search warrant authorizing the search of particularly described premises justifies a search of the described land, all of the buildings on the land, and other things attached to or annexed to the land. *United States v. Meyer,* 417 F.2d 1020 (8th Cir. 1969). Courts have generally also allowed a search of any vehicles owned or controlled by the owner of the premises and found on the premises. *United States v. Percival,* 756 F.2d

600 (7th Cir. 1985). Searches of areas neighboring or adjacent to the particularly described premises are usually not allowed. However, if neighboring or adjacent areas are only nominally separate and actually used as a single living or commercial area, courts may allow the search of the entire area despite a limited warrant description. In *United States v. Elliott,* 893 F.2d 220 (9th Cir. 1990), the court held that the search of a storeroom behind an apartment did not exceed the scope of the warrant authorizing the search of the apartment. The storeroom was accessible through a hole cut in the wall of the suspect's bathroom and covered by a burlap bag. The court found that the unconventional means of access did not sever the room from the rest of the apartment. And in *United States v. Principe,* 499 F.2d 1135 (1st Cir. 1974), a search of a cabinet in a hallway several feet away from the apartment described in the search warrant was justified where the owner testified that the cabinet "went with the apartment."

Officers executing a search warrant may look only where the items described in the warrant might be concealed. The U.S. Supreme Court stated the general rule: "A lawful search of fixed premises generally extends to the entire area in which the object of the search may be found and is not limited by the possibility that separate acts of entry or opening may be required to complete the search." *United States v. Ross,* 456 U.S. 798, 820–21, 102 S.Ct. 2157, 2170–71, 72 L.Ed.2d 572, 591 (1982). The Court provided the following useful examples of the application of the rule:

> [A] warrant that authorizes an officer to search a home for illegal weapons also provides authority to open closets, chests, drawers, and containers in which the weapon might be found. A warrant to open a footlocker to search for marijuana would also authorize the opening of packages found inside. A warrant to search a vehicle would support a search of every part of the vehicle that might contain the object of the search. When a legitimate search is under way, and when its purpose and its limits have been precisely defined, nice distinctions between closets, drawers, and containers, in the case of a home, or between glove compartments, upholstered seats, trunks and wrapped packages, in the case of a vehicle, must give way to the interest in the prompt and efficient completion of the task at hand. 456 U.S. at 821–22, 102 S.Ct. at 2171, 72 L.Ed.2d at 591.

An inaccurate description of the premises to be searched may cause officers to exceed the scope of a warrant, especially with respect to multiple-occupancy dwellings. In *Maryland v. Garrison,* 480 U.S. 79, 107 S.Ct. 1013, 94 L.Ed.2d 72 (1987), officers obtained and executed a warrant to search the person of Lawrence McWebb and "the premises known as 2036 Park Avenue third floor apartment." The officers reasonably believed, on the basis of the information available, that only one apartment was located on the third floor. In fact, the third floor was divided into two apartments, one occupied by McWebb and one by the defendant. Before the officers discovered that they were in the wrong person's apartment, they had discovered contraband that led to the defendant's conviction.

The Court concluded that the officers had made a reasonable effort to ascertain and identify the place intended to be searched and that their failure to realize the overbreadth of the warrant was objectively understandable and reasonable. Nevertheless, the Court said:

> If the officers had known, or should have known, that the third floor contained two apartments before they entered the living quarters on the third floor, and thus had been aware of the error in the warrant, they would have been obligated to limit their search to McWebb's apartment. Moreover . . . they were required to discontinue the search of respondent's apartment as soon as they dis-

covered that there were two separate units on the third floor and therefore were put on notice of the risk that they might be in a unit erroneously included within the terms of the warrant. 480 U.S. at 86–87, 107 S.Ct. at 1017–18, 94 L.Ed.2d at 82.

Therefore, although some latitude is allowed for honest mistakes in executing search warrants, officers may not rely blindly on the descriptions in a warrant but must make a reasonable effort to determine that the described place to be searched is the place *intended* to be searched.

Officers executing a search warrant must use only reasonable force in conducting the search. An otherwise reasonable search may be rendered unreasonable by the manner in which it is conducted. A search warrant gives officers authority to break into a house or other objects of search and to damage property if reasonably necessary to execute the warrant properly. In *United States v. Becker,* 929 F.2d 442 (9th Cir. 1991), the court found that the jackhammering of a concrete slab to execute a search warrant for drugs was reasonable, based on an examination of all the facts and circumstances: (1) officers had found evidence of the manufacture of methamphetamine in the shop next to the slab, (2) the concrete slab had been poured within the preceding forty-five days, and (3) the shop appeared to have been recently and hastily repainted and repaired. In a case involving a search of a vehicle for contraband, the U.S. Supreme Court said:

> An individual undoubtedly has a significant interest that the upholstery of his automobile will not be ripped or a hidden compartment within it opened. These interests must yield to the authority of a search, however. . . . *United States v. Ross,* 456 U.S. 798, 823, 102 S.Ct. 2157, 2172, 72 L.Ed.2d 572, 593 (1982).

Nevertheless, officers must exercise great care to avoid unnecessary damage to premises or objects. They must conduct a search in a manner designed to do the least damage possible, while still making a thorough examination of the premises. They should carefully replace objects that were necessarily moved or rearranged during the search. Generally, "[i]n executing a search warrant, to the extent possible, due respect should be given to the property of the occupants of the premises searched." *State v. Sierra,* 338 So.2d 609, 616 (La. 1976).

Finally, common decency mandates that officers executing a search warrant avoid any unnecessary injury to the feelings of persons present at the premises searched.

Seizure of Items Not Named in the Warrant

In *Coolidge v. New Hampshire,* the U.S. Supreme Court said that "[a]n example of the applicability of the 'plain view' doctrine is the situation in which the police have a warrant to search a given area for specific objects, and in the course of the search come across some other article of incriminating character." 403 U.S. 443, 465, 91 S.Ct. 2022, 2037, 29 L.Ed.2d 564, 582 (1971). This situation presented itself in *Cady v. Dombrowksi,* 413 U.S. 433, 93 S.Ct. 2523, 37 L.Ed.2d 706 (1973), when police were investigating a possible homicide. The defendant informed the police that he believed there was a body lying near his brother's farm. The police found the body and the defendant's car at the farm. Looking in through the window of the car, the police observed a pillowcase, backseat, and briefcase covered with blood. Police then obtained a warrant to search the car for those items. While executing the warrant, police discovered, in "plain view" in the car, a blood-covered sock and floormat, which they seized. The defendant claimed that the sock and the floormat taken from his car were illegally seized since they were not specifically listed in the affidavit for the search warrant.

The Court held that the seizure of the items was constitutional. Since the warrant was validly issued and the car was the item designated to be searched, the police were authorized to search the car. Although the sock and floormat were not listed in the warrant, the officers discovered these items in plain view in the car while executing the warrant and therefore could constitutionally seize them without a warrant.

The U.S. Supreme Court did not elaborate on this decision. However, decisions of many courts since the *Dombrowski* decision have established the rule that *a law enforcement officer lawfully executing a valid search warrant may seize items not particularly described in the warrant that are found at the searched premises, if the seizure satisfies all the requirements of the plain view doctrine.* (See Chapter 10 for a complete discussion of the plain view doctrine.)

Duties After the Search Is Completed

Proper execution of a search warrant entails several duties after the actual search is completed. Most jurisdictions require that the officer conducting the search inventory all the property seized and leave a copy of the warrant and inventory with the occupants, or on the premises if no occupant is present. The warrant, together with a copy of the inventory, must be returned to the magistrate designated in the warrant. A typical form for the return and inventory (which is usually on the back of the search warrant) appears in Exhibits 5.2(b) and 5.3(b).

Courts unanimously hold that these postsearch duties are ministerial acts and that failure to perform them will not result in suppression unless the defendant demonstrates legal prejudice or shows that the failure was intentional or in bad faith. *United States v. Marx*, 635 F.2d 436 (5th Cir. 1981).

KEY POINTS

11. In general, a search warrant should be executed in the daytime within a reasonable time after its issuance, and officers should remain on the searched premises only so long as is reasonably necessary to conduct the search.

12. Before law enforcement officers may lawfully force their way into a dwelling to execute a search warrant, they must first knock on the door, announce their authority and purpose, and then demand admittance. To justify an exception to this requirement, officers must have a reasonable suspicion that knocking and announcing their presence, under the particular circumstances, would be dangerous or futile or that it would inhibit the effective investigation of the crime by, for example, allowing the destruction of evidence.

13. A search warrant for premises gives a law enforcement officer no authority to *search* a person not named in the warrant who merely happens to be on the premises, but an officer may *detain* such a person under certain circumstances.

14. A search warrant authorizing the search of particularly described premises justifies a search of the described land, all of the buildings on the land, and other things attached or annexed to the land.

15. A search authorized by a warrant for a particular object allows a search of the entire area in which the object may be found and allows the opening of closets, chests, drawers, and containers in which the object might be found.

16. A law enforcement officer lawfully executing a valid search warrant may seize items not particularly described in the warrant that are found at the searched premises, if the seizure satisfies all the requirements of the plain view doctrine.

Administrative Search Warrants

An **administrative search** is a routine inspection of a home or business by governmental authorities responsible for determining compliance with various statutes and regulations. An administrative search seeks to enforce fire, health, safety, and housing codes, licensing provisions, and the like. It differs from a criminal search in that a criminal search is directed toward gathering evidence to convict a person of a crime. An administrative search ordinarily does not result in a criminal prosecution.

Before 1967, courts consistently held that administrative searches were not subject to the restrictions of the Fourth Amendment and that a search warrant was not needed to inspect residential or commercial premises for violations of regulatory and licensing provisions. In 1967, in *Camara v. Municipal Court,* 387 U.S. 523, 87 S.Ct. 1727, 18 L.Ed.2d 930, involving the safety inspection of a dwelling, and *See v. City of Seattle,* 387 U.S. 541, 87 S.Ct. 1737, 18 L.Ed.2d 943, involving inspection of business premises for fire safety reasons, the U.S. Supreme Court reversed earlier decisions and held that administrative inspections were subject to the warrant requirement of the Fourth Amendment. The basis for both the *Camara* and *See* decisions was the Court's belief that a person's right of privacy should not be determined by the nature of the search. In *Camara,* the Court said, "It is surely anomalous to say that the individual and his private property are fully protected by the Fourth Amendment only when the individual is suspected of criminal behavior." 387 U.S. at 530, 87 S.Ct. at 1732, 18 L.Ed.2d at 936. In *See,* the Court said that a "businessman, like the occupant of a residence, has a constitutional right to go about his business free from unreasonable official entries upon his private commercial property. . . ." 387 U.S. at 543, 87 S.Ct. at 1739, 18 L.Ed.2d at 946. Nevertheless, the Court held that, because administrative searches differ in nature and purpose from criminal searches, the probable cause standard for administrative searches differs in nature and is less stringent than the standard for criminal searches.

> The warrant procedure is designed to guarantee that a decision to search private property is justified by a reasonable governmental interest. But reasonableness is still the ultimate standard. If a valid public interest justifies the intrusion contemplated, then there is probable cause to issue a suitably restricted search warrant. 387 U.S. at 539, 87 S.Ct. at 1736, 18 L.Ed.2d at 941.

The Court further explained the less stringent probable cause standard in *Marshall v. Barlow's, Inc.,* 436 U.S. 307, 320–21, 98 S.Ct. 1816, 1824–25, 56 L.Ed.2d 305, 316 (1978), a case involving a search of a business for occupational safety reasons.

> Probable cause in the criminal law sense is not required. For purposes of an administrative search such as this, probable cause justifying the issuance of a warrant may be based not only on specific evidence of an existing violation but also on a showing that "reasonable legislative or administrative standards for conducting an . . . inspection are satisfied with respect to a particular [establishment]" [citing *Camara*]. A warrant showing that a specific business has been chosen for an OSHA search on the basis of a general administrative plan for the enforcement of the Act derived from neutral sources such as, for example, dispersion of employees in various types of industries across a given area, and the desired frequency of searches in any of the lesser divisions of the area, would protect an employer's Fourth Amendment rights.

Exceptions to Warrant Requirement

Despite the less stringent probable cause standard, the U.S. Supreme Court and other courts have carved out various exceptions to the warrant requirement for administrative searches. Exceptions based on emergency, consent, plain view, and open fields are similar to exceptions to the warrant requirement for criminal searches discussed in Part 3 of this book, but the standards are generally less stringent than those required for criminal searches. Another exception, allowing warrantless inspection of certain *licensed and closely regulated enterprises,* has been recognized by the Supreme Court. In *United States v. Biswell,* 406 U.S. 311, 92 S.Ct. 1593, 32 L.Ed.2d 87 (1972), the Court upheld a warrantless search of a storeroom of a gun dealer licensed under the Gun Control Act of 1968. The Court said:

> [I]f inspection is to be effective and serve as a credible deterrent, unannounced, even frequent, inspections are essential. In this context, the prerequisite of a warrant could easily frustrate inspection; and if the necessary flexibility as to time, scope and frequency is to be preserved, the protections afforded by a warrant would be negligible.
>
> It is also plain that inspections for compliance with the Gun Control Act pose only limited threats to the dealer's justifiable expectations of privacy. When a dealer chooses to engage in this pervasively regulated business and to accept a federal license, he does so with the knowledge that his business records, firearms, and ammunition will be subject to effective inspection. 406 U.S. at 316, 92 S.Ct. at 1596, 32 L.Ed.2d at 92–93.

The Supreme Court held that inspections of licensed and closely regulated enterprises are reasonable only if they satisfy three criteria:

- a "substantial" government interest must support the regulatory scheme under which the inspection is made,

- the warrantless inspections must be necessary to further the regulatory scheme, and

- the regulatory statute must provide a constitutionally adequate substitute for a warrant by advising the owner of commercial premises that the search is being made pursuant to the law and has a properly defined scope and by limiting the discretion of the inspecting officers. *New York v. Burger,* 482 U.S. 691, 107 S.Ct. 2636, 96 L.Ed.2d 601 (1987).

In the *Burger* case, the Court found that a New York statute allowing warrantless inspection of automobile junkyards satisfied these criteria. The state had a substantial interest in regulating the automobile junkyard industry because motor vehicle theft had increased in the state and was associated with this industry. Warrantless inspections were necessary because frequent and unannounced inspections provide an element of surprise crucial to regulating the market in stolen cars and parts. Finally, the statute gave adequate notice to automobile junkyard operators and authorized inspections only during business hours and within a narrowly defined scope.

Distinction Between Administrative and Criminal Search

Administrative search warrants and exceptions to the warrant requirement are not discussed in further detail because administrative searches are not conducted for purposes of the criminal law. However, the line between an administrative and a criminal search can sometimes become blurred. When an administrative search begins to take on the characteristics of a criminal search, the stricter standards applicable to criminal searches come into play. If these standards are not satisfied, any evidence obtained will be inadmissible in a criminal prosecution.

The line between administrative and criminal searches often becomes blurred in fire investigation cases, because several different purposes may be served by a fire investigation and fire scenes present varying degrees of emergency. In addition, reasonable privacy expectations may remain in fire-damaged premises, thereby affecting the necessity to obtain a warrant.

> Privacy expectations will vary with the type of property, the amount of fire damage, the prior and continued use of the premises, and in some cases the owner's efforts to secure it against intruders. Some fires may be so devastating that no reasonable privacy interests remain in the ash and ruins, regardless of the owner's subjective expectations. The test essentially is an objective one: whether "the expectation [is] one that society is prepared to recognize as 'reasonable.'" . . . If reasonable privacy interests remain in the fire-damaged property, the warrant requirement applies, and any official entry must be made pursuant to a warrant in the absence of consent or exigent circumstances. *Michigan v. Clifford,* 464 U.S. 287, 292–93, 104 S.Ct. 641, 646, 78 L.Ed.2d 477, 483 (1984).

If a warrant is necessary, the purpose of the search determines the type of warrant required. If the primary purpose is to determine the cause and origin of a recent fire, only an administrative warrant is needed. To obtain an administrative warrant, "fire officials need show only that a fire of undetermined origin has occurred on the premises, that the scope of the proposed search is reasonable and will not intrude unnecessarily on the fire victim's privacy, and that the search will be executed at a reasonable and convenient time." *Michigan v. Clifford,* 464 U.S. 287, 294, 104 S.Ct. 641, 647, 78 L.Ed.2d 477, 484 (1984). If the primary purpose of the search is to gather evidence of criminal activity, a criminal search warrant may be obtained only on a showing of probable cause to believe that particularly described seizable property will be found in the place to be searched.

If evidence of criminal activity is discovered during the course of a valid administrative search, it may be seized under the plain view doctrine and used to establish probable cause to obtain a criminal search warrant. Fire officials may not, however, rely on this evidence to expand the scope of their administrative search without first satisfying an independent judicial officer that probable cause exists. The purpose of the search is important even if exigent circumstances exist.

> Circumstances that justify a warrantless search for the cause of a fire may not justify a search to gather evidence of criminal activity once that cause has been determined. If, for example, the administrative search is justified by the immediate need to ensure against rekindling, the scope of the search may be no broader than reasonably necessary to achieve its end. A search to gather evidence of criminal activity not in plain view must be made pursuant to a criminal warrant upon a traditional showing of probable cause. *Michigan v. Clifford,* 464 U.S. 287, 294–95, 104 S.Ct. 641, 647, 78 L.Ed.2d 477, 484–85 (1984).

An administrative search took on the characteristics of a criminal search in *Michigan v. Tyler,* 436 U.S. 499, 98 S.Ct. 1942, 56 L.Ed.2d 486 (1978), a case involving a late-night fire in a furniture store leased by the defendant. When the fire was reduced to smoldering embers, the fire chief, while investigating the cause of the fire, discovered two plastic containers of flammable liquid. The detective took several pictures, but because visibility was hindered by darkness, steam, and smoke, the investigators departed the scene at 4:00 A.M. and returned shortly after daybreak to continue the investigation. More evidence of arson was found and seized at that time. About a month later, a state police arson investigator made several visits to the fire scene and obtained evidence that was used at trial in convicting the defendant. At no time was any warrant or consent to search obtained.

The Court held that the investigative activity on the date of the fire was legal but that the evidence-gathering activity a month after the fire was an illegal search and seizure.

> [W]e hold that an entry to fight a fire requires no warrant, and that once in the building, officials may remain there for a reasonable time to investigate the cause of the blaze. Thereafter, additional entries to investigate the cause of the fire must be made pursuant to the warrant procedures governing administrative searches. . . . Evidence of arson discovered in the course of such investigations is admissible at trial, but if the investigating officials find probable cause to believe that arson has occurred and require further access to gather evidence for a possible prosecution, they may obtain a warrant only upon a traditional showing of probable cause applicable to searches for evidence of crime. 436 U.S. at 511–12, 98 S.Ct. at 1951, 56 L.Ed.2d at 500.

Once a search is directed toward gathering evidence for a criminal prosecution, a criminal search warrant must be obtained. This requirement cannot be avoided by using other governmental officials to conduct searches under the guise of an administrative or regulatory inspection.

KEY POINTS

17. An administrative search is a routine inspection of a home or business to determine compliance with various statutes and regulations, not to gather evidence for a criminal prosecution. Administrative searches are subject to the warrant requirement of the Fourth Amendment.

18. Because administrative searches differ in nature and purpose from criminal searches, the probable cause standard for administrative searches differs in nature and is less stringent than the standard for criminal searches.

19. Exceptions to the administrative warrant requirement based on emergency, consent, plain view, and open fields have less stringent standards than corresponding exceptions for criminal searches. Warrantless searches are also allowed for certain licensed and closely regulated enterprises.

20. If evidence of criminal activity is discovered during the course of a valid administrative search, it may be seized under the plain view doctrine and used to establish probable cause to obtain a criminal search warrant.

"Special Needs" Searches

The U.S. Supreme Court has also recognized an exception to warrant and probable cause requirements of the Fourth Amendment where "special needs" of the government, "beyond the normal need for law enforcement, make the warrant and probable-cause requirement impracticable." *Griffin v. Wisconsin,* 483 U.S. 868, 873, 107 S.Ct. 3164, 3168, 97 L.Ed.2d 709, 717 (1987). Under this exception, searches are evaluated under the "reasonableness" standard of the Fourth Amendment.

To be reasonable under the Fourth Amendment, a search ordinarily must be based on individualized suspicion of wrongdoing. . . . But particularized exceptions to the main rule are sometimes warranted based on "special needs, beyond the normal need for law enforcement." . . . When such "special needs"—concerns other than crime detection—are alleged in justification of a Fourth Amendment intrusion, courts must undertake a context-specific inquiry, examining closely the competing private and public interests advanced by the parties. *Chandler v. Miller,* 520 U.S. 305, ___, 117 S.Ct. 1295, 1301, 137 L.Ed.2d 513, 522–23 (1997).

This requires balancing the nature and quality of the intrusion on the individual's Fourth Amendment interests against the importance of the governmental interests alleged to justify the intrusion.

Searches of Students

The U.S. Supreme Court created an exception to the warrant requirement, based on "special needs" for searches of students conducted by school officials. In *New Jersey v. T.L.O.,* 469 U.S. 325, 105 S.Ct. 733, 83 L.Ed.2d 720 (1985), the Court held that school officials carrying out searches and other functions pursuant to disciplinary policies act as representatives of the state and not merely as surrogates for parents and that they are therefore subject to the Fourth Amendment. However, in attempting to balance the students' legitimate privacy rights against the substantial interests of teachers and administrators in maintaining discipline in the classroom and on school grounds, the Court held that school officials need not obtain a warrant before searching students under their authority. The warrant requirement would unduly interfere with the maintenance of the swift and informal disciplinary procedures needed in the schools. Furthermore, rather than insist on strict adherence to the requirement that a search be based on probable cause to believe that the subject of the search has violated or is violating the law, "the legality of a search of a student should depend simply on the reasonableness, under all the circumstances, of the search." 469 U.S. at 341, 105 S.Ct. at 742, 83 L.Ed.2d at 734.

Determining the reasonableness of any search involves an inquiry into (1) whether the action was justified at its inception and (2) whether the search as actually conducted was reasonably related in scope to the circumstances that justified the interference in the first place. The Court said:

Under ordinary circumstances, a search of a student by a teacher or other school official will be "justified at its inception" when there are *reasonable grounds for suspecting* that the search will turn up evidence that the student has violated or is violating either the law or the rules of the school. Such a search will be permissible in its scope when the measures adopted are reasonably related to the objectives of the search and not excessively intrusive in light of the age and sex of the student and the nature of the infraction. 469 U.S. at 341–42, 105 S.Ct. at 744, 83 L.Ed.2d at 734–35. (Emphasis supplied.)

As indicated in the preceding quote, the school search approved in the *T.L.O.* case, while not based on probable cause, *was* based on individualized *suspicion* of wrongdoing. The Fourth Amendment, however, imposes no irreducible requirement of individualized suspicion. In *Vernonia School District 47J v. Acton,* 515 U.S. 646, 115 S.Ct. 2386, 132 L.Ed.2d 564 (1995), the Court held that a public school's interest in deterring drug use by students constituted a "special need" justifying *suspicionless* random drug testing of students participating in interscholastic athletics. The Court found that students in public schools have a decreased expectation of privacy because of the temporary custody, supervision, and control required to be exercised by the school. Furthermore, student athletes have even less of a legitimate privacy expectation, because of the inherent elements of communal undress, physical examinations, and special rules regulating their conduct.

> Somewhat like adults who choose to participate in a "closely regulated industry," students who voluntarily participate in school athletics have reason to expect intrusions upon normal rights and privileges, including privacy. 515 U.S. at 657, 115 S.Ct. at 2393, 132 L.Ed.2d at 577.

Looking next to the character of the intrusion, the Court found that the search procedures were relatively unobtrusive, the conditions for the urine testing being nearly identical to those typically encountered in public restrooms. Furthermore, the tests looked only for standard drugs, not medical conditions, and the test results were released to a limited group.

Finally, the Court found that deterring drug use by schoolchildren was clearly an important concern, noting that this program was directed more narrowly to drug use by school athletes, where the risk of immediate physical harm to the drug user or other players is particularly high. As to the efficacy of the program for addressing the problem the Court found it "self evident that a drug problem largely fueled by the 'role model' effect of athletes' drug use, and of particular danger to athletes, is effectively addressed by making sure that athletes do not use drugs." 515 U.S. at 663, 115 S.Ct. at 2395–96, 132 L.Ed.2d at 581.

The Court noted that the most significant element in approving this drug testing policy was that it was "undertaken in furtherance of the government's responsibilities, under a public school system, as guardian and tutor of children entrusted to its care." 515 U.S. at 665, 115 S.Ct. at 2396, 132 L.Ed.2d at 582. The Court cautioned against the assumption that suspicionless drug testing would readily pass constitutional muster in other contexts.

Searches of Government Employees

In *O'Connor v. Ortega,* 480 U.S. 709, 107 S.Ct. 1492, 94 L.Ed.2d 714 (1987), the Supreme Court held that "special needs" may justify the search of a public employee's office by the employee's supervisor. The Court said that, in the case of searches conducted by a public employer, the invasion of the employee's legitimate expectations of privacy must be balanced against the government's need for supervision, control, and the efficient operation of the workplace. No search warrant is required for such searches.

> [R]equiring an employer to obtain a warrant whenever the employer wished to enter an employee's office, desk, or file cabinets for a work-related purpose would seriously disrupt the routine conduct of business and would be unduly burdensome. Imposing unwieldy warrant procedures in such cases upon supervisors, who would otherwise have no reason to be familiar with such procedures, is simply unreasonable. 480 U.S. at 722, 107 S.Ct. at 1500, 94 L.Ed.2d at 726.

The Court applied a reasonableness standard rather than a probable cause standard.

> [T]he "special needs, beyond the normal need for law enforcement make the . . . probable-cause requirement impracticable," . . . for legitimate work-related, non-investigatory intrusions as well as investigations of work-related misconduct. A

standard of reasonableness will neither unduly burden the efforts of government employers to ensure the efficient and proper operation of the workplace, nor authorize arbitrary intrusions upon the privacy of public employees. We hold, therefore, that public employer intrusions on the constitutionally protected privacy interests of government employees for noninvestigatory, work-related purposes, as well as for investigations of work-related misconduct, should be judged by the standard of reasonableness under all the circumstances. Under this reasonableness standard, both the inception and the scope of the intrusion must be reasonable. . . . 480 U.S. at 725–26, 107 S.Ct. at 1502, 94 L.Ed.2d at 728.

The Court said that, given the great variety of work environments in the public sector, the question of whether an employee has a reasonable expectation of privacy must be determined on a case-by-case basis.

Governmental Drug Testing

The Court also used the "special needs" analysis to uphold warrantless governmental drug testing. *Skinner v. Railway Labor Executives' Ass'n.*, 489 U.S. 602, 109 S.Ct. 1402, 103 L.Ed.2d 639 (1989), upheld governmental regulations requiring railroad companies to test the blood and urine of employees involved in major train accidents and employees who violate particular safety rules. The Court found that the tests were not significant intrusions and that railroad workers have a diminished expectation of privacy because they work in a heavily regulated industry. The searches were held to be reasonable, despite the absence of individualized suspicion, because the government's significant special need to ensure public safety outweighed the employee's diminished privacy interest.

National Treasury Employees Union v. Von Raab, 489 U.S. 656, 109 S.Ct. 1384, 103 L.Ed.2d 685 (1989), upheld Customs Service regulations requiring employees seeking transfers or promotions to certain sensitive positions with the service to submit to urinalysis. The Court found that the government's special need to deter drug use outweighed the diminished privacy interests of the employees. Specifically, the Court emphasized the public interest in "ensuring that front-line interdiction personnel are physically fit, and have unimpeachable integrity and judgment" [and in] "prevent[ing] the promotion of drug users to positions that require the incumbent to carry a firearm, even if the incumbent is not engaged directly in the interdiction of drugs." 489 U.S. at 670, 109 S.Ct. at 1393, 103 L.Ed.2d at 705.

In *Chandler v. Miller*, 520 U.S. 305, 117 S.Ct. 1295, 137 L.Ed.2d 513 (1997), however, the U.S. Supreme Court struck down as unconstitutional a Georgia statute requiring candidates for designated state offices to certify that they have taken a drug test within thirty days prior to qualifying for nomination or election and that the test result was negative. The Court found that the alleged incompatibility of unlawful drug use with holding high state office was not sufficiently important to qualify as a special need for drug testing of candidates for state office.

[T]he proffered special need for drug testing must be substantial—important enough to override the individual's acknowledged privacy interest, sufficiently vital to suppress the Fourth Amendment's normal requirement of individualized suspicion. 520 U.S. at ___, 117 S.Ct. at 1303, 137 L.Ed.2d at 526.

The need to deter unlawful drug users from attaining high state office was not considered a concrete danger demanding departure from the Fourth Amendment's main rule.

- There was no evidence of a drug problem among the state's elected officials.
- Those officials did not perform high-risk, safety-sensitive tasks.
- The required certification of nondrug use did not immediately aid any drug interdiction effort.

The court, therefore, concluded that "where . . . public safety is not genuinely in jeopardy, the Fourth Amendment precludes the suspicionless search, no matter how conveniently arranged." 520 U.S. at ___, 117 S.Ct. at 1305, 137 L.Ed.2d at 529.

Searches of Probationers

In *Griffin v. Wisconsin,* 483 U.S. 868, 107 S.Ct. 3164, 97 L.Ed.2d 709 (1987), the Supreme Court upheld a warrantless search of a probationer's home by probation officers under the authority of Wisconsin's probation regulation. The Court found that the probation system's necessity for nonadversarial supervision of probationers is a "special need" justifying lessened Fourth Amendment protection for the probationer. This special need makes the warrant requirement impracticable and justifies replacement of the probable cause standard by a "reasonable grounds" standard, as defined by the Wisconsin Supreme Court. The Court said:

> A warrant requirement would interfere to an appreciable degree with the probation system, setting up a magistrate rather than the probation officer as the judge of how close a supervision the probationer requires. Moreover, the delay inherent in obtaining a warrant would make it more difficult for probation officials to respond quickly to evidence of misconduct . . . and would reduce the deterrent effect that the possibility of expeditious searches would otherwise create. . . . 483 U.S. at 876, 107 S.Ct. at 3170, 97 L.Ed.2d at 719.

KEY POINTS

21. An exception to the warrant and probable cause requirements of the Fourth Amendment exists where "special needs" of the government, beyond the normal need for law enforcement, make the warrant and probable cause requirement impracticable.

22. "Special needs" exceptions are evaluated under the "reasonableness" standard of the Fourth Amendment requiring the balancing of the nature and quality of the intrusion on the individual's Fourth Amendment interests against the importance of the governmental interests alleged to justify the intrusion.

Warrants for Electronic Surveillance

Electronic surveillance through the use of wiretaps, bugs, or other devices to overhear conversations or obtain other kinds of information is a relatively recent concern of criminal and constitutional law. Certainly the Founding Fathers could not have even imagined the possibilities for gathering information on crime created by the marvels of twentieth-century technology. Nor could they, when they drafted the Constitution, have contemplated the potential invasions of privacy brought about by the new technology. It is not surprising, then, that the Constitution gives little guidance for balancing privacy interests against the need for effective law enforcement in the area of electronic surveillance.

On the one hand, electronic listening, tracking, and recording devices provide a very powerful tool for law enforcement officials in investigating and prosecuting crime. On the other hand, the potential for the abuse of individual rights can be far greater with electronic surveillance than with any ordinary search or seizure. The task of resolving these competing interests has fallen on state legislatures, the United States Congress, and, ultimately, the courts. This section traces the early development of the law of electronic surveillance; examines legislative and judicial responses to the problem; and concludes with a discussion of Title III of the Omnibus Crime Control and Safe Streets Act of 1968, which provided authority for electronic surveillance pursuant to warrant.

History

Although electronic eavesdropping has been used as an information-gathering technique since the mid-1800s, the U.S. Supreme Court did not decide its first electronic eavesdropping case until 1928. In *Olmstead v. United States,* 277 U.S. 438, 48 S.Ct. 564, 72 L.Ed. 944 (1928), a case involving interception of telephone conversations by means of a wiretap, the Court held that wiretapping was not covered by the Fourth Amendment. One reason for this decision, as discussed in Chapter 3 under "Privacy," was that there was no search so long as there was no physical trespass into the defendant's premises. The other reason was that all the evidence had been obtained by hearing only, and since the Fourth Amendment referred only to the seizure of tangible items, the interception of a conversation could not qualify as a seizure. As shown in Chapter 3, the *Katz* case rendered invalid the first rationale of the *Olmstead* decision by changing the focus of Fourth Amendment analysis from a "property" approach to a "privacy" approach. The second rationale of the *Olmstead* decision has been disposed of by *Berger v. New York,* 388 U.S. 41, 87 S.Ct. 1873, 18 L.Ed.2d 1040 (1967), which held that conversations were protected by the Fourth Amendment and that the use of electronic devices to capture conversations was a search within the meaning of the Fourth Amendment.

Given the premise that electronic surveillance is a search and seizure within the meaning of the Fourth Amendment, it became necessary for the U.S. Supreme Court to decide what kinds of electronic surveillance the Fourth Amendment allows, to what extent electronic surveillance is allowed, and what kinds of electronic surveillance are prohibited, if any. The guidelines for these constitutional limits on electronic surveillance were worked out in a series of decisions in the mid-1960s.

This discussion begins with Justice William J. Brennan's dissent in *Lopez v. United States,* 373 U.S. 427, 83 S.Ct. 1381, 10 L.Ed.2d 462 (1963). In that dissent, Justice Brennan echoed the fears of law enforcement officials that if wiretaps were subjected to Fourth Amendment analysis, they would be completely prohibited, because they would be seen as inherently unreasonable searches. Brennan stated, "For one thing, electronic surveillance is almost inherently indiscriminate, so that compliance with the requirement of particularity in the Fourth Amendment would be difficult." 373 U.S. at 463, 83 S.Ct. at 1401, 10 L.Ed.2d at 485. He continued:

> If in fact no warrant could be devised for electronic searches, that would be a
> compelling reason for forbidding them altogether. The requirements of the
> Fourth Amendment . . . are the bedrock rules without which there would be no
> effective protection of the right to personal liberty. . . . Electronic searches cannot

be tolerated in the name of law enforcement if they are inherently unconstitutional. 373 U.S. at 464, 83 S.Ct. at 1401, 10 L.Ed.2d at 485.

Despite his strong language, it is clear that Brennan left open the possibility that some forms of electronic surveillance might be constitutionally permissible.

The Supreme Court first explicitly considered the constitutionality of electronic surveillance conducted under authority of a warrant three years later in *Osborn v. United States*, 385 U.S. 323, 87 S.Ct. 429, 17 L.Ed.2d 394 (1966). In that case, federal law enforcement officials had information that labor leader Jimmy Hoffa's attorney was trying to bribe a prospective juror. The officials obtained a warrant authorizing an undercover agent with a concealed tape recorder to record a specific conversation with the attorney. The tape of the conversation was admitted at trial, and the attorney was convicted of attempting to bribe a juror. The Court upheld the conviction, emphasizing that "[t]he issue here is . . . the permissibility of using such a device under the most precise and discriminate circumstances. . . ." 385 U.S. at 329, 87 S.Ct. at 432–33, 17 L.Ed.2d at 399.

The Supreme Court's limited grant of constitutional permissibility for electronic surveillance was tested again the next year in *Berger v. New York*, 388 U.S. 41, 87 S.Ct. 1873, 18 L.Ed.2d 1040 (1967). In *Berger*, the issue was the constitutionality of a New York statute that authorized electronic surveillance pursuant to a judicial warrant. The New York law provided as follows:

> An ex parte order for eavesdropping . . . may be issued by any justice . . . or judge . . . upon oath or affirmation of a district attorney, or of the attorney-general or of an officer above the rank of sergeant of any police department of the state . . . that there is reasonable ground to believe that evidence of crime may be thus obtained, and particularly describing the person or persons whose communications or discussions are to be overheard or recorded and the purpose thereof, and, in the case of a telegraphic or telephonic communication, identifying the particular telephone number or telegraph line involved. In connection with the issuance of such an order the justice or judge may examine on oath the applicant and any other witness he may produce and shall satisfy himself of the existence of reasonable grounds for the granting of such application. Any such order shall be effective for the time specified therein but not for a period of more than two months unless extended or renewed by the justice or judge who signed and issued the original order upon satisfying himself that such an extension or renewal is in the public interest. . . . N.Y.Code Crim.Proc. § 813–a.

The U.S. Supreme Court held the New York statute unconstitutional, primarily because it did not properly limit the nature, scope, or duration of the electronic surveillance. In so holding, the Court emphasized that the availability of an initial two-month surveillance period was "the equivalent of a series of intrusions, searches, and seizures pursuant to a single showing of probable cause." 388 U.S. at 59, 87 S.Ct. at 1883, 18 L.Ed.2d at 1052. The Court also stressed that the statute placed no termination requirement on the eavesdrop, even after the desired conversation had been obtained. Furthermore, the statute had two major deficiencies with respect to probable cause. First, an eavesdropping warrant could be issued without probable cause that a particular crime had been committed and without a particular description of "the property" (conversations in this context) to be seized. Second, an eavesdropping order could be extended or renewed without a showing of probable cause for continuation of the eavesdrop. Finally, in contrast to conventional search warrant procedures, the statute permitted electronic eavesdropping without prior notice or a showing of exigency excusing notice.

The Court's concern with the overbroad authorization of the New York statute is reflected in its comparison of the electronic search in the *Berger* case with the search in the *Osborn* case discussed earlier:

> The invasion [in *Osborn*] was lawful because there was sufficient proof to obtain a search warrant to make the search for the limited purpose outlined in the order of the judges. Through these "precise and discriminate" procedures the order authorizing the use of the electronic device afforded similar protections to those that are present in the use of conventional warrants authorizing the seizure of tangible evidence. Among other safeguards, the order described the type of conversation sought with particularity, thus indicating the specific objective of the Government in entering the constitutionally protected areas and the limitations placed upon the officer executing the warrant. Under it the officer could not search unauthorized areas; likewise, once the property sought, and for which the order was issued, was found the officer could not use the order as a passkey to further search. In addition, the order authorized one limited intrusion rather than a series or a continuous surveillance. And, we note that a new order was issued when the officer sought to resume the search and probable cause was shown for the succeeding one. Moreover, the order was executed by the officer with dispatch, not over a prolonged and extended period. In this manner no greater invasion of privacy was permitted than was necessary under the circumstances. Finally the officer was required to and did make a return on the order showing how it was executed and what was seized. Through these strict precautions the danger of an unlawful search and seizure was minimized. 388 U.S. at 57, 87 S.Ct. at 1882–83, 18 L.Ed.2d at 1051.

Despite the Supreme Court's disapproval of the New York statute in the *Berger* case, the possibility that a properly circumscribed warrant procedure for electronic surveillance could be created was left open. This possibility was given further credence by the landmark case of *Katz v. United States* (discussed in Chapter 3). In that case, FBI agents attached an electronic listening device to a public telephone booth and recorded the defendant's calls. The Court held that the interception was an unlawful search and seizure because there was no warrant. In discussing the warrant requirement, the Court said:

> [T]he surveillance was limited, both in scope and in duration, to the specific purpose of establishing the contents of the petitioner's unlawful telephonic communications. The agents confined their surveillance to the brief periods during which he [Katz] used the telephone booth, and they took great care to overhear only the conversation of the petitioner himself.
>
> Accepting this account of the Government's actions as accurate, it is clear that this surveillance was so narrowly circumscribed that a duly authorized magistrate, properly notified of the need for such investigation, specifically informed of the basis on which it was to proceed, and clearly apprised of the precise intrusion it would entail, could constitutionally have authorized, with appropriate safeguards, the very limited search and seizure that the Government asserts in fact took place. 389 U.S. 347, 354, 88 S.Ct. 507, 512–13, 19 L.Ed.2d 576, 583–84 (1967).

The possibility that a constitutionally permissible warrant procedure for electronic surveillance could be set up paved the way for congressional action in this area. In the year following the *Berger* and *Katz* opinions, Congress enacted the Omnibus Crime Control and Safe Streets Act of 1968. Title III of that act superseded earlier statutory prohibitions against intercepted communications and provided authorization for electronic surveillance pursuant to warrant.

Title III of the Omnibus Crime Control and Safe Streets Act of 1968

The passage of Title III of the Omnibus Crime Control and Safe Streets Act of 1968, following so closely on the heels of the *Berger* and *Katz* decisions, was not simply a result of Congress enacting legislation in response to the constitutional guidelines set out in those decisions. Concern had long been expressed about the inadequacy of existing electronic surveillance legislation. Besides the issues raised in various Supreme Court cases, defense lawyers and civil libertarians complained of governmental violations of the privacy rights of American citizens. On the other side, proponents of electronic surveillance argued that wiretapping and bugging were essential tools for law enforcement officials to combat the modern sophisticated criminal, especially in the area of organized crime. In fact, the belief that electronic surveillance was the only way to deal with the unique problems of investigating and prosecuting organized crime prompted the President's Crime Commission to recommend legislation authorizing electronic surveillance. Another impetus leading to the passage of Title III in 1968 was the political pressures that were exerted in the context of a national climate of fear brought about by intense social unrest and the assassinations of Martin Luther King, Jr., and Robert F. Kennedy and exemplified by the "law and order" presidential campaign of Richard M. Nixon. The result was a bipartisan effort to balance modern society's conflicting demands for privacy and more effective law enforcement.

The discussion now turns to an examination of Title III and cases interpreting it. Because of the length of the law, it is not possible to reproduce Title III's provisions verbatim. Therefore, the discussion is necessarily general in nature.

JUDICIAL SUPERVISION. One important characteristic of Title III, designed to protect against governmental abuses of citizens' privacy rights, is the law's provision for judicial supervision of all aspects of electronic surveillance. Federal law enforcement officials may not intercept wire, oral, or electronic communications without prior judicial approval. Before discussing the details of judicial supervision of electronic surveillance, definitions of important terms are necessary:

- **Intercept** is defined as "the aural or other acquisition of the contents of any wire, electronic, or oral communication through the use of any electronic, mechanical, or other device." 18 U.S.C.A. § 2510(4). (The 1986 amendments to Title III extended the law's coverage to include all forms of electronic communications and not just spoken conversations transmitted by telephone or overheard electronically.)

- **Wire communication** is defined as "any aural transfer made in whole or in part through the use of facilities for the transmission of communications by the aid of wire, cable, or other like connection between the point of origin and the point of reception (including the use of such connection in a switching station) furnished or operated by any person engaged in providing or operating such facilities for the transmission of interstate or foreign communications or communications affecting interstate or foreign commerce and such term includes any electronic storage of such communication." 18 U.S.C.A. § 2510(1).

- An **aural transfer** is defined as "a transfer containing the human voice at any point between and including the point of origin and the point of reception." 18 U.S.C.A. § 2510(18).

- **Oral communication** is defined as "any oral communication uttered by a person exhibiting an expectation that such communication is not subject to interception under circumstances justifying such expectation, but such term does not include any electronic communication." 18 U.S.C.A. § 2510(2).

- **Electronic communication** is defined as "any transfer of signs, signals, writing, images, sounds, data, or intelligence of any nature transmitted in whole or in part by a wire, radio, electromagnetic, photoelectronic or photooptical system that affects interstate or foreign commerce but does not include (A) any wire or oral communication; (B) any communication made through a tone-only paging device; (C) any communication from a tracking device . . . ; or (D) electronic funds transfer information stored by a financial institution in a communications system used for the electronic storage and transfer of funds." 18 U.S.C.A. § 2510(12).

A court may issue an interception order only for specified crimes including espionage, treason, labor racketeering, murder, kidnapping, robbery, extortion, bribery of public officials, gambling, drug trafficking, escape, and counterfeiting. Note that the 5th Circuit has held that, for jurisdictional purposes, an interception of a wiretap takes place at both the location of the tapped telephone and the original listening post. Therefore, judges in either jurisdiction have authority under Title III to issue interception orders. *United States v. Denman,* 100 F.3d 399 (5th Cir. 1996). Before issuing an interception order, the court must find all of the following:

- Probable cause to believe that the person whose communication is to be intercepted has committed, is committing, or is about to commit one of the specified crimes. "The probable cause showing required . . . for electronic surveillance does not differ from that required by the fourth amendment for a search warrant." *United States v. Macklin,* 902 F.2d 1320, 1324 (8th Cir. 1990).

- Probable cause to believe that particular communications concerning that offense will be obtained through the interception

- That normal investigative procedures have been tried and have failed, or reasonably appear to be unlikely to succeed if tried, or reasonably appear to be too dangerous. This condition is often referred to as the "necessity requirement" and is intended to ensure that electronic surveillance is not used unless normal investigative procedures are inadequate. For example, in *United States v. Wagner,* 989 F.2d 69 (1993), the necessity for a wiretap was established because (1) the rural location of the house and the presence of dogs made surveillance difficult, (2) the confidential informant was unable to determine the source of supply and method of delivery of marijuana, and (3) the government did not think it could infiltrate the marijuana distribution network with undercover agents.

- Probable cause to believe that the facilities from which, or the place where, the wire, oral, or electronic communications are to be intercepted are being used or are about to be used in connection with the commission of the specified offense, or are leased to, listed in the name of or commonly used by the suspect.

Other aspects of judicial supervision of electronic surveillance are the court's power to require, at any time, reports on the progress of the interception toward the achievement of authorized objectives, the requirement of court approval for any extension of the surveillance, and the requirement that the recordings of any communications be sealed under directions of the court immediately upon the order's expiration.

Judicial sanctions for violations of Title III include criminal penalties, penalties for contempt of court, and awards of civil damages. In addition, 18 U.S.C.A. § 2515 provides for the exclusion of evidence obtained in violation of Title III. In *United States v. Spadaccino*, 800 F.2d 292 (2d Cir. 1986), the court held that the good-faith exception to the exclusionary rule did not apply to violations of Title III. The court said that, where the legislature has spoken clearly on the issue, "it is appropriate to look to the terms of the statute and the intentions of the legislature, rather than to invoke judge-made exceptions to judge-made rules." 800 F.2d at 296.

PROCEDURES. Title III establishes specific procedures for the application for, the issuance of, and the execution of court orders for the interception of wire, oral, or electronic communications.

Application. Application procedures for interception orders are governed by 18 U.S.C.A. § 2518(1), which is quoted here:

> **§ 2518. Procedure for interception of wire, oral, or electronic communications**
> (1) *Each application for an order authorizing or approving the interception of a wire, oral, or electronic communication under this chapter shall be made in writing upon oath or affirmation to a judge of competent jurisdiction and shall state the applicant's authority to make such application. Each application shall include the following information:*
>
> (a) *the identity of the investigative or law enforcement officer making the application, and the officer authorizing the application;*
>
> (b) *a full and complete statement of the facts and circumstances relied upon by the applicant, to justify his belief that an order should be issued, including (i) details as to the particular offense that has been, is being, or is about to be committed, (ii) except as provided in subsection (11) [roving taps], a particular description of the nature and location of the facilities from which or the place where the communication is to be intercepted, (iii) a particular description of the type of communications sought to be intercepted, (iv) the identity of the person, if known, committing the offense and whose communications are to be intercepted;*
>
> (c) *a full and complete statement as to whether or not other investigative procedures have been tried and failed or why they reasonably appear to be unlikely to succeed if tried or to be too dangerous;*
>
> (d) *a statement of the period of time for which the interception is required to be maintained. If the nature of the investigation is such that the authorization for interception should not automatically terminate when the described type of communication has been first obtained, a particular description of facts establishing probable cause to believe that additional communications of the same type will occur thereafter;*
>
> (e) *a full and complete statement of the facts concerning all previous applications known to the individual authorizing and making the application, made to any judge for authorization to intercept, or for approval of interceptions of, wire, oral, or electronic communications involving any of the same persons, facilities or places specified in the application, and the action taken by the judge on each such application; and*
>
> (f) *where the application is for the extension of an order, a statement setting forth the results thus far obtained from the interception, or a reasonable explanation of the failure to obtain such results.*

Only the U.S. attorney general or other federal attorneys specified by Title III may authorize an application for a federal interception order. Only a federal investigative or law enforcement officer, as defined by Title III, or an attorney authorized to prosecute Title III offenses, may make an application for a federal interception order. With respect to the requirement of identifying the person whose communications are to be intercepted, the U.S. Supreme Court held that the applicant must name all persons who the government has probable cause to believe are committing the offense for which the application is made. *United States v. Donovan,* 429 U.S. 413, 97 S.Ct. 658, 50 L.Ed.2d 652 (1977). The *Donovan* case also held, however, that failure to comply with this identification requirement did not require the exclusion of evidence obtained by the interception.

Section 2518(11) allows law enforcement officials to apply for authorization to conduct "roving taps." A roving tap targets a particular suspect's communications wherever they are made and dispenses with the normal requirement that interceptions be limited to a fixed location. *United States v. Petti,* 973 F.2d 1441 (9th Cir. 1991), held that roving taps do not violate the particularity requirement of the Fourth Amendment if the surveillance is limited to communications involving an identified speaker and relates to crimes in which the speaker is a suspected participant.

Issuance. If, on the basis of the application, the judge makes the required findings, the judge may issue an order authorizing or approving the interception of wire, oral, or electronic communications. Each order must specify all of the following:

- The identity, if known, of the person whose communications are to be intercepted
- The nature and location of the communications facilities as to which, or the place where, authority to intercept is granted
- A particular description of the type of communication sought to be intercepted, and a statement of the particular offense to which the communication relates
- The identity of the agency authorized to intercept the communications, and the identity of the person authorizing the application
- The period of time during which the interception is authorized, including a statement as to whether or not the interception shall automatically terminate when the described communication has been first obtained

Execution. Every order to intercept wire, oral, or electronic communications must be executed "as soon as practicable." In *United States v. Martino,* 664 F.2d 860 (2d Cir. 1981), however, the court held that delay in the execution of an interception order did not require the suppression of evidence obtained if the delay was not willful and if the information on which probable cause was based had not become stale. In *United States v. Gallo,* 863 F.2d 185 (2d Cir. 1988), the court held that suppression of the intercepted communications was not required because of a five-month delay in installing the interception devices, where the government adequately explained that the installation was extremely difficult and the crime was one of continuing conduct, in which probable cause was "freshened" by visual surveillance.

Title III requires that authorized interceptions be conducted in such a way as to minimize the interception of communications not otherwise subject to interception under Title III. This minimization effort must be objectively reasonable under the circumstances. In *Scott v. United States,* 436 U.S. 128, 98 S.Ct. 1717, 56 L.Ed.2d 168 (1978), the U.S. Supreme Court held an interception reasonable although only 40 percent of the intercepted conversations related to crimes specified in the order, because the remaining conversations were ambiguous and brief. *United States v. Smith*, 909 F.2d 1164 (8th Cir. 1990), held that minimization efforts were reasonable despite failure to minimize the defendant's sister's phone conversations with his ex-girlfriend, because the officers suspected the defendant's family of aiding in drug activities but did not know which family members.

When a law enforcement officer intercepts communications relating to offenses other than those specified in the interception order, the officer must apply as soon as possible for judicial approval to disclose the evidence in court. Without judicial approval, the evidence may not be disclosed. In *United States v. Van Horn*, 789 F.2d 1492 (11th Cir. 1986), the court held that the judicial approval could take the form of the judge's granting of an extension order after receiving progress reports and applications for extensions describing the nature of the conversations being intercepted.

Authorized interceptions must terminate upon attainment of the authorized objective, or in any event in thirty days. In *United States v. Carneiro*, 861 F.2d 1171 (9th Cir. 1988), the court held that suppression of communications intercepted after the discovery of a drug source was not required, because the objective of the wiretap was to investigate the entire drug operation, not merely to discover a drug source. Extensions of an interception order may be granted, but only upon reapplication in accordance with the same procedures as for an original application.

Immediately upon the expiration of an interception order, recordings are required to be delivered to the judge issuing the order and to be sealed under the judge's directions. The purposes of this requirement are to prevent tampering, aid in establishing the chain of custody, protect confidentiality, and establish judicial control over the surveillance. The statutory term *immediately* has been interpreted to mean without unnecessary or unreasonable delay. Failure to deliver the recordings or unjustifiable or unexplained late delivery may cause the recordings to be excluded from evidence. Before ordering suppression, however, courts will examine all the circumstances, including whether the defendant has been prejudiced by tampering or other governmental misconduct. *United States v. Rodriguez*, 786 F.2d 472 (2d Cir. 1986). If there is a delay in sealing, the "Government must explain not only why a delay occurred but also why it is excusable." *United States v. Ojeda Rios*, 495 U.S. 257, 265, 110 S.Ct. 1845, 1850, 109 L.Ed.2d 224, 236 (1990). Courts consider the following factors in determining whether the government has presented a satisfactory explanation for its failure to seal or delay in sealing:

> the length of any delay before sealing, the care taken in handling the recordings, prejudice to the defendants, any tactical advantage accruing to the government, and whether deliberate or gross dereliction of duty or honest mistake caused the failure to file. *United States v. Suarez*, 906 F.2d 977, 982 (4th Cir. 1990).

Finally, within a reasonable time, but not later than ninety days after the termination of the period of an order, an *inventory* must be served upon the persons named in the order and upon such other parties to intercepted communications as the judge may determine in the interest of justice. This inventory must also be served after emergency interceptions are carried out. It must include a notice of the fact of the order, the date of approval of the application, the period of the authorized interception, and a statement of whether or not wire, oral, or electronic communications were intercepted during the period. Failure to serve the inventory is not grounds for suppression unless the failure causes actual, incurable prejudice. *United States v. Harrigan*, 586 F.2d 860, 865 (1st Cir. 1978).

APPLICABILITY TO THE STATES. Title III specifically authorizes state law enforcement officials to apply for, obtain, and execute orders authorizing or approving the interception of wire, oral, or electronic communications. The procedures are similar to those governing federal interception orders. The primary difference is that the state procedure must be authorized by a separate state statute. If a state statute so authorizes, the principal prosecuting attorney of the state, or of a political subdivision of the state, may apply to a state court judge of competent jurisdiction for an interception order. In granting the order, the judge must comply with both the applicable state statute and Title III. The interception order may be granted only when the interception may provide

> evidence of the commission of the offense of murder, kidnapping, gambling, robbery, bribery, extortion, or dealing in narcotic drugs, marihuana or other dangerous drugs, or other crime dangerous to life, limb, or property, and punishable by imprisonment for more than one year, designated in any applicable State statute authorizing such interception, or any conspiracy to commit any of the foregoing offenses. 18 U.S.C.A. § 2516(2).

"Generally speaking, insofar as wiretapping is concerned, states are free to superimpose more rigorous requirements upon those mandated by the Congress . . . but not to water down federally-devised safeguards." *United States v. Mora,* 821 F.2d 860, 863 n.3 (1st Cir. 1987). Federal courts are not obliged to adhere to more restrictive state laws, however, and will generally admit evidence that violates such a law, so long as the evidence was not obtained in violation of Title III. For example, in *United States v. Daniel,* 667 F.2d 783 (9th Cir. 1982), an interception of a conversation without a search warrant violated state law. Nevertheless, the evidence was held admissible in federal court because Title III does not require a warrant when one of the parties to the intercepted conversation consents to the interception.

SUPPRESSION. No contents of or evidence derived from electronic surveillance "may be received in evidence in any trial, hearing, or other proceeding in or before any court, grand jury, department, officer, agency, regulatory body, legislative committee, or other authority of the United States, a State, or a political subdivision thereof if the disclosure of that information would be in violation of this chapter." 18 U.S.C.A. § 2515. "Any aggrieved person in any trial, hearing, or proceeding in or before any court, department, officer, agency, regulatory body, or other authority of the United States, a State, or a political subdivision thereof may move to suppress" the contents of or evidence derived from intercepts under Title III. 18 U.S.C.A. § 2518(10)(a). An **aggrieved person** is "a person who was a party to any intercepted wire, oral, or electronic communication or a person against whom the interception was directed." 18 U.S.C.A. § 2510(11).

The U.S. Supreme Court held that the term *aggrieved person* should be construed in accordance with existent standing rules. Therefore, "any petitioner would be entitled to the suppression of government evidence originating in electronic surveillance violative of his own Fourth Amendment right to be free of unreasonable searches and seizures. Such violation would occur if the United States unlawfully overheard conversations of a petitioner himself or conversations occurring on his premises, whether or not he was present or participated in those conversations." *Alderman v. United States,* 394 U.S. 165, 176, 89 S.Ct. 961, 968, 22 L.Ed.2d 176, 188 (1969). A violation of Title III does not require suppression of evidence, however, if the provision violated is not central to the statute's underlying purpose of guarding against unwarranted use of wiretapping or electronic surveillance. *United States v. Chavez,* 416 U.S.

562, 94 S.Ct. 1849, 40 L.Ed.2d 380 (1974). Therefore, suppression is seldom imposed for inadvertent, unavoidable, or unintentional violations.

EXCEPTIONS TO TITLE III. Many types of interceptions of wire, oral, or electronic communications are either not covered by provisions of Title III or specifically excepted from coverage. Some of the more important exceptions to Title III's requirement of an interception order are discussed here in general terms.

A party to an oral communication who has no reasonable expectation of privacy with respect to the communication is not protected by either Title III or the Fourth Amendment. In *State v. Salisbury,* 662 F.2d 738 (11th Cir. 1981), the court held that a party to a conversation has no legitimate expectation that another party to the conversation will not record the conversation or reveal its contents to authorities. In *United States v. Harrelson,* 754 F.2d 1153 (5th Cir. 1985), the court held that surreptitiously recorded conversations between a prison inmate and his wife did not qualify as oral conversations. The court found that the couple suspected eavesdropping and therefore could have had no reasonable expectation of privacy. "Mistaking the degree of intrusion of which probable eavesdroppers are capable is not at all the same thing as believing there are no eavesdroppers." 754 F.2d at 1170.

Sections 2511(2)(c) and 2511(2)(d) exclude consent surveillance from the regulatory scheme established by Title III for court-ordered surveillance. Therefore, when one party to a communication consents to the interception of the communication, neither Title III nor the Fourth Amendment prevents the use of the communication in court against another party to the communication. Thus, a law enforcement officer or a private citizen who is a party to a communication may intercept the communication or permit a law enforcement official to intercept the communication without violating Title III or the Fourth Amendment. This exception allows a law enforcement officer or agent to wear a body microphone, act as an undercover agent without being wired, or eavesdrop on a telephone conversation with the permission of the person receiving the call, without the knowledge of the person making the call. For example, in *United States v. Capo,* 693 F.2d 1330 (11th Cir. 1982), the government's interception of a conversation between a consenting informant and the defendant was held not to be a violation of the Fourth Amendment, since the defendant willingly projected his voice outside the privacy of his home and his voice was intercepted at the other end. A private citizen, however, may not intercept a communication "for the purpose of committing any criminal or tortious act in violation of the Constitution or laws of the United States or of any state." The absence of federal regulation or preemption regarding consent surveillance has left the states free to fashion their own approaches by statute or court decision.

Title III does not apply to the use of electronic devices emitting signals that enable law enforcement officials to track the location of objects and persons. Use of these devices, sometimes called transmitters or beepers, is governed solely by the Fourth Amendment. Since most of the legal issues involving these devices relate to the attachment of the devices to vehicles and containers, discussion of these issues appear in Chapter 11 dealing with the warrantless search of vehicles and containers.

Similarly, Title III does not apply to trap-and-trace devices and pen registers. A trap-and-trace device traces the source of calls made *to* a particular telephone number. A pen register records all numbers dialed *from* a particular telephone number. In *Smith v. Maryland,* 442 U.S. 735, 99 S.Ct. 2577, 61 L.Ed.2d 220 (1979), the U.S. Supreme Court held that the installation and use of a pen register is not a search and is therefore not subject to the Fourth Amendment. The Court reasoned that the defendant had no reasonable expectation of privacy in the destination of his outgoing phone calls because the telephone company routinely monitors these calls to check billing, detect fraud, and prevent other violations of law. Federal courts have not yet addressed the Fourth Amendment implications of the use of trap-and-trace devices. Because telephone companies do not routinely monitor incoming calls, the rationale of the *Smith* case may not apply to the use of those devices. Since the *Smith* decision, Congress has enacted legislation (18 U.S.C.A. §§ 3121–3126) prohibiting the installation or use of a pen register or a trap-and-trace device except by court order.

Although law enforcement officials must obtain a judicial order to intercept wire, oral, or electronic communications, neither Title III nor the Fourth Amendment requires them to obtain judicial authorization to covertly enter premises to install a listening device. In *Dalia v. United States,* 441 U.S. 238, 99 S.Ct. 1682, 60 L.Ed.2d 177 (1979), a federal court authorized the interception of all oral communications concerning an interstate stolen-goods conspiracy at the defendant's office. Although the interception order did not explicitly authorize entry into the defendant's office, FBI agents secretly entered the office and installed a listening device in the ceiling. Six weeks later, after the surveillance had terminated, the agents reentered the office and removed the device. The defendant was convicted, partly on the basis of intercepted conversations. The Supreme Court considered the legislative history of Title III and concluded as follows:

> [O]ne simply cannot assume that Congress, aware that most bugging requires covert entry, nonetheless wished to except surveillance requiring such entries from the broad authorization of Title III, and that it resolved to do so by remaining silent on the subject. On the contrary, the language and history of Title III convey quite a different explanation for Congress' failure to distinguish between surveillance that requires covert entry and that which does not. Those considering the surveillance legislation understood that, by authorizing electronic interception of oral communications in addition to wire communications, they were necessarily authorizing surreptitious entries. 441 U.S. at 252, 99 S.Ct. at 1691, 60 L.Ed.2d at 189.

With respect to the Fourth Amendment, the Court found that nothing in the language of the Fourth Amendment or the Court's decisions suggested that search warrants must include a specification of the precise manner in which those warrants must be executed. "On the contrary, it is generally left to the discretion of the executing officers to determine the details of how best to proceed with the performance of a search authorized by warrant—subject of course to the general Fourth Amendment protection 'against unreasonable searches and seizures.'" 441 U.S. at 257, 99 S.Ct. at 1693, 60 L.Ed.2d at 192.

Finally, Title III provides authority for designated federal or state officials to intercept wire, oral, or electronic communications without a prior interception order if (1) an emergency situation exists that involves immediate danger of death or serious physical injury to any person, conspiratorial activities threatening the national security interest, or conspiratorial activities characteristic of organized crime; and (2) an interception order cannot be obtained in sufficient time. The determination of emergency must be made by the U.S. attorney general or other governmental official specified in Title III. The law enforcement officer carrying out the emergency surveillance must apply for an interception order under § 2518 within forty-eight hours after the interception has occurred or begins to occur. If an order is not obtained, the interception must immediately terminate when the sought-after communication is obtained or when the application is denied, whichever is earlier.

23. Electronic surveillance by agents of the government is a search and seizure governed by the Fourth Amendment.

24. Electronic surveillance is permissible only if conducted pursuant to the authority of a warrant affording protections similar to those present in the use of conventional warrants authorizing the seizure of tangible evidence.

25. A warrant procedure authorizing electronic surveillance must carefully circumscribe the search in nature, scope, and duration and must not permit a trespassory invasion of the home or office by general warrant, contrary to the command of the Fourth Amendment.

26. Title III of the Omnibus Crime Control and Safe Streets Act balances the need to use electronic surveillance for more effective law enforcement against the need to protect the privacy rights of individuals by providing for judicial supervision of all aspects of electronic surveillance and establishing warrant procedures similar to those required for the search and seizure of tangible objects.

27. Although a judicially issued interception order is required to intercept wire, oral, or electronic communications, judicial approval is not required to covertly enter premises to install a listening device.

Effect of Illegal Search and Seizure

The most important effect of an illegal search or seizure is the exclusion of the evidence obtained from use in court against the person whose rights were violated. (The exclusionary rule is discussed in detail in Chapter 3.) When crucial evidence is suppressed, the prosecution's case may be lost, and the person charged with the crime may go free.

Another possible effect of an illegal search and seizure is the civil or criminal liability of the officer conducting the search and seizure. As with an illegal arrest, the consequences for the officer depend on the circumstances of each case, including the officer's good faith, the degree of care used, the seriousness of the violation, and the extent of injury or intrusion suffered by the defendant.

Summary

The general rule is that all searches and seizures conducted without a warrant are unreasonable and violate the Fourth Amendment to the U.S. Constitution. Although there are many well-defined exceptions to this rule, searches made under the authority of a warrant not only are greatly preferred by the courts but also give the law enforcement officer greater protection from liability.

A search warrant is a written order issued by a proper judicial authority (the magistrate) commanding a law enforcement officer to search for certain personal property and bring it before the judicial authority named in the warrant. An officer may obtain a search warrant by submitting to a magistrate a written application in the form of a sworn affidavit. The affidavit must state underlying facts and circumstances supporting probable cause to believe that particularly described items are located in a particularly described place or on a particularly described person. Only items connected with criminal activity, such as stolen property, contraband, and instrumentalities and evidence of crime, may be seized.

If a magistrate finds probable cause to search, he or she will issue a search warrant directing an officer or class of officers to execute the warrant. Officers must conduct the search within a reasonable time after the warrant's issuance and within any time period specified by law or court rule. Before entering premises by force to execute the warrant, officers must knock and announce their authority and purpose, unless this notice will result in the loss or destruction of evidence, the escape of a suspect, or danger to an officer or others. Persons on the premises may not be searched, unless the search warrant authorizes the search of a particular person. Property of persons who are not the target of the warrant and not residents of the target premises may not be seized. If officers are executing a warrant to search for contraband, persons on the premises may be detained during the course of the search. Any person on the premises whom officers reasonably believe to be dangerous may be frisked for weapons.

A search under authority of a search warrant may extend to the entire premises described in the warrant, but only to those parts of the premises where the items to be seized might be concealed. The search must be conducted in a manner to avoid unnecessary damage to the premises or objects. Items not named in the warrant may be seized if all elements of the plain view doctrine are satisfied. After the search is completed, the officer must leave at the searched premises a copy of the warrant and a receipt for property taken. The officer must return the warrant along with a written inventory of property seized to the judicial officer designated in the warrant.

An administrative search is a routine inspection of a home or business to determine compliance with codes and licensing provisions dealing with fire, health, safety, housing, and so on. Although administrative searches are not directed toward convicting a person of a crime, they are still subject to the warrant requirement of the Fourth Amendment. The probable cause standard for administrative searches is less stringent than the standard for criminal searches. If, however, an administrative search takes on the characteristics of a criminal search, the traditional probable cause standard applies. Exceptions to the administrative search warrant requirement are similar to the exceptions for a criminal search warrant with less stringent standards. Also, warrantless searches are allowed for certain licensed and closely regulated enterprises.

An exception to the warrant and probable cause requirements of the Fourth Amendment exists where "special needs" of the government, beyond the normal need for law enforcement, make the warrant and probable cause requirement impracticable. "Special needs" exceptions are evaluated under the "reasonableness" standard of the Fourth Amendment.

Electronic surveillance was originally considered beyond the coverage of the Fourth Amendment because it involved no trespass into the defendant's premises and no seizure of tangible items. In a series of U.S. Supreme Court decisions in the mid-1960s, the Court reversed this approach and held that electronic surveillance by agents of the government is a search and seizure governed by the Fourth Amendment. The leading case adopting this new approach was *Katz v. United States*, which held that the Fourth Amendment protects people, not places, thereby shifting the focus of the Fourth Amendment from property to privacy. In addition, the Court held that electronic surveillance is permissible only if conducted pursuant to a warrant that carefully limits the surveillance in nature, scope, and duration. In 1968, Congress enacted Title III of the Omnibus Crime Control and Safe Streets Act, which attempts to balance the need to use electronic surveillance for more effective law enforcement against the need to protect individuals' privacy rights. Title III provides for judicial supervision of all aspects of electronic surveillance and establishes warrant procedures similar to those required for the search and seizure of tangible objects. These procedures are designed to limit who can authorize an application for an interception order, who can apply for an order, the duration of electronic surveillance allowed, and various aspects of the execution of an interception order.

The coverage of Title III has many exceptions. Title III does not protect a party to a conversation who has no reasonable expectation of privacy with respect to that conversation. Furthermore, if one party to a conversation consents to the interception of that conversation, the conversation may be used against the other party. Finally, Title III does not apply to the use of electronic devices such as beepers, trap-and-trace devices, and pen registers. Although an interception order is required to intercept wire, oral, or electronic communications, judicial approval is not required to covertly enter premises to install a listening device. Neither is an interception order required to intercept wire, oral, or electronic communications in emergencies involving immediate danger of death or serious physical injury, or conspiracies threatening national security or involving organized crime, although an interception order must be applied for within forty-eight hours of the emergency interception.

An illegal search and seizure, whether caused by a failure to comply with warrant procedures or by a failure to satisfy one of the exceptions to the warrant requirement, will result in application of the exclusionary rule. The evidence seized during the search will be inadmissible in court, a situation often resulting in termination of the prosecution and release of the person charged. Furthermore, officers conducting an illegal search may be civilly or criminally liable for their actions.

Key Holdings from Major Cases

United States v. Jacobsen (1984). "A 'search' occurs when an expectation of privacy that society is prepared to consider reasonable is infringed. A 'seizure' of property occurs when there is some meaningful interference with an individual's possessory interests in that property." 466 U.S. 109, 113, 104 S.Ct. 1652, 1656, 80 L.Ed.2d 85, 94.

Johnson v. United States (1948). "The point of the Fourth Amendment, which often is not grasped by zealous officers, is not that it denies law enforcement the support of the usual inferences which reasonable men draw from evidence. Its protection consists in requiring that those inferences be drawn by a neutral and detached magistrate instead of being judged by the officer engaged in the often competitive enterprise of ferreting out crime." 333 U.S. 10, 13–14, 68 S.Ct. 367, 369, 92 L.Ed. 436, 440.

Shadwick v. City of Tampa (1972). "[A]n issuing magistrate must meet two tests. He must be neutral and detached, and he must be capable of determining whether probable cause exists for the requested arrest or search." 407 U.S. 345, 350, 92 S.Ct. 2119, 2123, 32 L.Ed.2d 783, 788.

Franks v. Delaware (1978). "[W]here the defendant makes a substantial preliminary showing that a false statement knowingly and intentionally, or with reckless disregard for the truth, was included by the affiant in the warrant affidavit, and if the allegedly false statement is necessary to the finding of probable cause, the Fourth Amendment requires that a hearing be held at the defendant's request. In the event that at the hearing the allegation of perjury or reckless disregard is established by the defendant by a preponderance of the evidence, and, with the affidavit's false material set to one side, the affidavit's remaining content is insufficient to establish probable cause, the search warrant must be voided and the fruits of the search excluded to the same extent as if probable cause was lacking on the face of the affidavit." 438 U.S. 154, 155–56, 98 S.Ct. 2674, 2676–77, 57 L.Ed.2d 667, 672.

Andresen v. Maryland (1976). "[A]lthough the Fifth Amendment may protect an individual from complying with a subpoena for the production of his personal records in his possession because the very act of production may constitute a compulsory authentication of incriminating information, . . . a seizure of the same materials by law enforcement officers differs in a crucial respect—the individual against whom the search is directed is not required to aid in the discovery, production, or authentication of incriminating evidence." 427 U.S. 463, 473–74, 96 S.Ct. 2737, 2745, 49 L.Ed.2d 627, 638.

Gouled v. United States (1921). "There is no special sanctity in papers, as distinguished from other forms of property, to render them immune from search and seizure, if only they fall within the scope of the principles of the cases in which other property may be seized, and if they be adequately described in the affidavit and warrant." 255 U.S. 298, 309, 41 S.Ct. 261, 265, 65 L.Ed. 647, 652.

Warden v. Hayden (1967). "The requirements of the Fourth Amendment can secure the same protection of privacy whether the search is for 'mere evidence' or for fruits, instrumentalities or contraband. There must, of course, be a nexus—automatically provided in the case of fruits, instrumentalities or contraband—between the item to be seized and criminal behavior. Thus, in the case of 'mere evidence' probable cause must be examined in terms of cause to be-

lieve that the evidence sought will aid in a particular apprehension or conviction. In doing so, consideration of police purposes will be served." 387 U.S. 294, 206–07, 87 S.Ct. 1642, 1650, 18 L.Ed.2d 782, 792.

Steele v. United States (1925). "It is enough if the description [of the place to be searched] is such that the officer with a search warrant can with reasonable effort ascertain and identify the place intended." 267 U.S. 498, 503, 45 S.Ct. 414, 416, 69 L.Ed. 757, 760.

Zurcher v. The Stanford Daily (1978). "The critical element in a reasonable search is not that the owner of the property is suspected of crime but that there is reasonable cause to believe that the specific 'things' to be searched for and seized are located on the property to which entry is sought." 436 U.S. 547, 556, 98 S.Ct. 1970, 1977, 56 L.Ed.2d 525, 535.

Marron v. United States (1927). "The requirement that warrants shall particularly describe the things to be seized makes general searches under them impossible and prevents the seizure of one thing under a warrant describing another. As to what is to be taken, nothing is left to the discretion of the officer executing the warrant." 275 U.S. 192, 196, 48 S.Ct. 74, 76, 72 L.Ed. 231, 237.

Stanford v. Texas (1965). "[T]he constitutional requirement that warrants must particularly describe the 'things to be seized' is to be accorded the most scrupulous exactitude when the 'things' are books, and the basis for their seizure is the ideas which they contain." 379 U.S. 476, 485, 85 S.Ct. 506, 511–12, 13 L.Ed.2d 431, 437.

Segura v. United States (1984). "[W]here officers, having probable cause, enter premises, and with probable cause, arrest the occupants who have legitimate possessory interests in its contents and take them into custody and, for no more than the period here involved [nineteen hours], secure the premises from within to preserve the status quo while others, in good faith, are in the process of obtaining a warrant, they do not violate the Fourth Amendment's proscription against unreasonable seizures." 468 U.S. 796, 798, 104 S.Ct. 3380, 3382, 82 L.Ed.2d 599, 604.

"[S]ecuring a dwelling, on the basis of probable cause, to prevent the destruction or removal of evidence while a search warrant is being sought is not itself an unreasonable seizure of either the dwelling or its contents. . . . [A]bsent exigent circumstances, a warrantless search . . . is illegal." 486 U.S. at 810, 104 S.Ct. at 3388, 82 L.Ed.2d at 612.

Bivens v. Six Unknown Named Agents (1971). "[T]he Fourth Amendment confines an officer executing a search warrant strictly within the bounds set by the warrant. . . ." 403 U.S. 388, 394 n.7, 91 S.Ct. 1999, 2004 n.7, 29 L.Ed.2d 619, 625 n.7.

Jones v. United States (1958). "[I]t is difficult to imagine a more severe invasion of privacy than the nighttime intrusion into a private home. . . ." 357 U.S. 493, 498, 78 S.Ct. 1253, 1257, 2 L.Ed.2d 1514, 1519.

Richards v. Wisconsin (1997). "In order to justify a 'no-knock' entry, the police must have a reasonable suspicion that knocking and announcing their presence, under the particular circumstances, would be dangerous or futile, or that it would inhibit the effective investigation of the crime by, for example, allowing the destruction of evidence." 520 U.S. 385, ___, 117 S.Ct. 1416, 1421, 137 L.Ed.2d 615, 624.

Dalia v. United States (1979). "Often in executing a warrant the police may find it necessary to interfere with privacy rights not explicitly considered by the judge who issued the warrant. For example, police executing an arrest warrant commonly find it necessary to enter the suspect's home in order to take him into custody, and they thereby impinge on both privacy and freedom of movement. . . . Similarly, officers executing search warrants on occasion must damage property in order to perform their duty." 441 U.S. 238, 257–58, 99 S.Ct. 1682, 1693–94, 60 L.Ed.2d 177, 193.

Ybarra v. Illinois (1979). "[A] person's mere propinquity to others independently suspected of criminal activity does not, without more, give rise to probable cause to search that person." 444 U.S. 85, 91, 100 S.Ct. 338, 342, 62 L.Ed.2d 238, 245.

Michigan v. Summers (1981). "If the evidence that a citizen's residence is harboring contraband is sufficient to persuade a judicial officer that an invasion of the citizen's privacy is justified, it is constitutionally reasonable to require that citizen to remain while officers of the law execute a valid warrant to search his home." 452 U.S. 692, 704–05, 101 S.Ct. 2587, 2595, 69 L.Ed.2d 340, 351.

United States v. Ross (1982). "A lawful search of fixed premises generally extends to the entire area in which the object of the search may be found and is not limited by the possibility that separate acts of entry or opening may be required to complete the search." 456 U.S. 798, 820–21, 102 S.Ct. 2157, 2170–71, 72 L.Ed.2d 572, 591.

Coolidge v. New Hampshire (1971). "An example of the applicability of the 'plain view' doctrine is the situation in which the police have a warrant to search a given area for specific objects, and in the course of the search come across some other article of incriminating character." 403 U.S. 443, 465, 91 S.Ct. 2022, 2037, 29 L.Ed.2d 564, 582.

Camara v. Municipal Court (1967). "The [administrative] warrant procedure is designed to guarantee that a decision to search private property is justified by a reasonable governmental interest. But reasonableness is still the ultimate standard. If a valid public interest justifies the intrusion contemplated, then there is probable cause to issue a suitably restricted search warrant." 387 U.S. 523, 539, 87 S.Ct. 1727, 1736, 18 L.Ed.2d 930, 941.

Michigan v. Clifford (1984). To obtain an administrative warrant to determine the cause and origin of a recent fire, fire officials need show only that "a fire of undetermined origin has occurred on the premises, that the scope of the proposed search is reasonable and will not intrude unnecessarily on the fire victim's privacy, and that the search will be executed at a reasonable and convenient time." 464 U.S. 287, 294, 104 S.Ct. 641, 647, 78 L.Ed.2d 477, 484.

"Circumstances that justify a warrantless search for the cause of a fire may not justify a search to gather evidence of criminal activity once that cause has been determined. . . . A search to gather evidence of criminal activity not in plain view must be made pursuant to a criminal warrant upon a traditional showing of probable cause." 464 U.S. at 294–95, 104 S.Ct. at 647, 78 L.Ed.2d at 484–85.

Chandler v. Miller (1997). "To be reasonable under the Fourth Amendment, a search ordinarily must be based on individualized suspicion of wrongdoing. . . . But particularized exceptions to the main rule are sometimes warranted based on 'special needs, beyond the normal need for law enforcement.' . . . When such 'special needs'—concerns other than crime detection—are alleged in justification of a Fourth Amendment intrusion, courts must undertake a context-specific inquiry, examining closely the competing private and public interests advanced by the parties." 520 U.S. 305, ___, 117 S.Ct. 1295, 1301, 137 L.Ed.2d 513, 522–23.

"[W]here . . . public safety is not genuinely in jeopardy, the Fourth Amendment precludes the suspicionless search, no matter how conveniently arranged." 520 U.S. at ___, 117 S.Ct. at 1305, 137 L.Ed.2d at 529.

New Jersey v. T.L.O. (1985). "[T]he legality of a search of a student should depend simply on the reasonableness, under all the circumstances, of the search." 469 U.S. 325, 341, 105 S.Ct. 733, 742, 83 L.Ed.2d 720, 734.

"Under ordinary circumstances, a search of a student by a teacher or other school official will be 'justified at its inception' when there are reasonable grounds for suspecting that the search will turn up evidence that the student has violated or is violating either the law or the rules of the school. Such a search will be permissible in its scope when the measures adopted are reasonably related to the objectives of the search and not excessively intrusive in light of the age and sex of the student and the nature of the infraction." 469 U.S. at 341–42, 105 S.Ct. at 744, 83 L.Ed.2d at 734–35.

Vernonia School District 47J v. Acton (1995). "Somewhat like adults who choose to participate in a 'closely regulated industry,' students who voluntarily participate in school athletics have reason to expect intrusions upon normal rights and privileges, including privacy." 515 U.S. 646, 657, 115 S.Ct. 2386, 2393, 132 L.Ed.2d 564, 577.

Berger v. New York (1967). A warrant procedure authorizing electronic surveillance must carefully circumscribe the search in nature, scope, and duration and must not permit "a trespassory invasion of the home or office, by general warrant, contrary to the command of the Fourth Amendment." 388 U.S. 41, 64, 87 S.Ct. 1873, 1886, 18 L.Ed.2d 1040, 1055.

Alderman v. United States (1969). "[A]ny petitioner would be entitled to the suppression of government evidence originating in electronic surveillance violative of his own Fourth Amendment right to be free of unreasonable searches and seizures. Such violation would occur if the United States unlawfully overheard conversations of a petitioner himself or conversations occurring on his premises, whether or not he was present or participated in those conversations." 394 U.S. 165, 176, 89 S.Ct. 961, 968, 22 L.Ed.2d 176, 188.

Review and Discussion Questions

1. Why is time a more important factor in determining probable cause to search than it is in determining probable cause to arrest?

2. Formulate a set of circumstances in which there is probable cause to search but not probable cause to arrest; in which there is probable cause to arrest but not probable cause to search; in which there is probable cause both to arrest and to search.

3. Name three kinds of property that are *unlikely* to remain in a particular place for longer than a week. Name three kinds of property that are *likely* to remain in a particular place for longer than a week.

4. Why should law enforcement officers executing a search warrant refrain from asking the person against whom the search is directed to assist them in any way?

5. Assume that you are a law enforcement officer attempting to obtain a search warrant for urban premises, rural premises, a multiple-unit dwelling, and a motor vehicle. Describe, as you would in the affidavit, one of each of these places that is familiar to you. (For example, describe for purposes of a search warrant application a friend's farm in the country.)

6. Discuss three ways in which a search warrant and an arrest warrant are differently affected by time.

7. Law enforcement officers have a search warrant to search a house for heroin and to search the person of the houseowners' eighteen-year-old daughter. When the officers arrive at the house to execute the warrant, the following persons are present:

   a. The owners

   b. The eighteen-year-old daughter

   c. The daughter's fifteen-year-old brother, who appears extremely nervous

   d. The daughter's boyfriend, whom the officers recognize as a local gang member who is known to carry a knife

   e. An unidentified elderly couple

To what extent may the officers search or detain each person present?

8. A law enforcement officer has a search warrant to search the defendant's house for cameras stolen from a particular department store. May the officer

   a. Look in desk drawers?

   b. Search the defendant's body?

   c. Seize a brown paper bag containing a white powder resembling heroin, found in a desk drawer?

   d. Search the defendant's garage?

   e. Look in the defendant's wife's jewelry box?

   f. Break open a locked wall safe?

   g. Seize a portable radio found on a table with a tag from the department store attached to it?

9. Is each of the following descriptions in a search warrant of items to be seized sufficiently particular?

   a. An unknown-make .38-caliber, blue steel, with wood grips, revolver. See *United States v. Wolfenbarger,* 696 F.2d 750 (10th Cir. 1982).

   b. Videotape and equipment used in a copyright infringement. See *United States v. Smith,* 686 F.2d 234 (5th Cir. 1982).

   c. All doctor's files concerning an accident patient. See *United States v. Hershenow,* 680 F.2d 847 (1st Cir. 1982).

   d. Plaques, mirrors, and other items. See *United States v. Apker,* 705 F.2d 293 (8th Cir. 1983).

   e. Items related to the smuggling, packing, distribution, and use of controlled substances. See *United States v. Ladd,* 704 F.2d 134 (4th Cir. 1983).

   f. Business papers that are evidence and instrumentalities of a violation of a general tax fraud statute. See *United States v. Cardwell,* 680 F.2d 75 (9th Cir. 1982).

10. Does a warrant to search a house authorize a search of a tent set up on the premises near the house? Does a war-

rant authorizing the seizure of stolen typewriters authorize the seizure of nonstolen typewriters commingled with them? Is the seizure of an entire book of accounts permissible when only two or three pages of the book are relevant to the specifications of the search warrant?

1. This case arises out of a search of an apartment at 53R Centre Street in Middleboro. The police conducted the search pursuant to a warrant authorizing a search of the designated apartment, the tenant of the apartment, and "any person present" who may be found to have under his control or on his person controlled substances or related materials. The search warrant was part of a police effort to uncover a drug sale operation targeted at junior and senior high school students. During execution of the search warrant, the defendant, a forty-three year old adult male, entered the premises. A state police officer at the scene identified himself to the defendant, pat frisked him, and then searched him. The officer found a small caliber derringer in the defendant's right pocket and marijuana seeds in his left front pocket.

The defendant contends that the search of his person pursuant to the "any person present" language of the warrant violated his rights under the Fourth and Fourteenth Amendments to the United States Constitution, art. 14 of the Massachusetts Declaration of Rights, and G.L. c. 276, S 1. The defendant argues that the facts stated in the affidavit do not provide a basis for the "any person present" language and that, as applied to him, the search warrant was constitutionally defective as a general warrant. The warrant, affidavit, and circumstances fail to support the pat frisk and search of his person, the defendant claims, because he entered the premises while the search was in progress, did not fit the description of the alleged occupants or marihuana purchasers described in the affidavit, and did nothing to suggest that he was armed or engaged in criminal conduct. Is the defendant correct? *Commonwealth v. Souza,* 675 N.E.2d 432 (Mass.App.Ct. 1997).

2. In January 1995, two officers of the Cortland County Sheriff's Department applied for a search warrant, enabling them to search defendant and his residence and outbuildings located in the Town of Freetown, Cortland County. The application was granted by County Court and the warrant was executed on January 27, 1995, resulting in the seizure from defendant's premises of marihuana, various firearms including a pistol, seven rifles and six shotguns, and the utterance of oral admissions by defendant. The description set forth on the warrant stated "Rusty D. Davenport and residence at Ingram Road, Town of Freetown, Cortland County, N.Y." The police officers' affidavits submitted in support of the warrant application set forth a detailed description of the property to be searched including its distance from the intersection of two named roads, its distinctive coloration and a description of the residence as a trailer. A review of these documents also discloses that the authors of the affidavits (who also conducted the search) were fully familiar with the location of the premises, having previously conducted surveillance there. Defense counsel moved to suppress marijuana and firearms seized from defendant's residence as well as defendant's oral admissions. A suppression hearing was held before County Court, resulting in a determination that the search warrant was facially defective due to its failure "to particularly describe" defendant's residence by setting forth, inter alia, its street number or tax map number, the size, style and color of the residence or the nature thereof (i.e., whether it was a house, a trailer, or an apartment). County Court accordingly directed that the physical evidence seized from defendant's residence, as well as the oral admissions made by defendant to police officers, be suppressed. Was the County Court correct? *People v. Davenport,* 647 N.Y.S.2d 306 (A.D. 3 Dept. 1996).

3. On November 30, 1994, Police Officer Bruce Hammonds appeared in Supreme Court, Kings County, to seek a warrant to search "apartment 6C, in the premises located at 3101 Foster Avenue, Kings County." In his affidavit in support of the application, Officer Hammonds stated, inter alia, that the defendants were using "apartment 6C in the premises located at 3101 Foster Avenue, Kings County" for illegal purposes. The affidavit further stated that "the premises of 3101 Foster Avenue, Kings County is a six story brick faced residential * * * building." Prior to signing the warrant, the Supreme Court conducted a brief examination of Officer Hammonds at which Hammonds stated that he had been in the building located at 3101 Foster Avenue, Kings County, although he had never been in apartment 6C. Based upon this information the Supreme Court issued the warrant. However, although the warrant stated that there was probable cause for believing that contraband would be found in "apartment 6C in the premises of 3101 Foster Avenue, Kings County," it directed an immediate search of "apartment 6C in the premises of 3101 Wilson Avenue, Kings County, occupied by [the defendants]" (emphasis added). Thereafter Hammonds executed the warrant at

apartment 6C, 3101 Foster Avenue, Kings County, recovered drugs and a weapon, and arrested the defendants.

Based upon the error contained on the face of the warrant, the defendants moved to suppress the tangible evidence seized from the apartment. Should the evidence be suppressed? *People v. Graham*, 633 N.Y.S.2d 334 (A.D. 2 EDept. 1995).

4. At 11:05 A.M. on January 26, 1995, Officer Buddy Wilson and several other Kauai Police Department (KPD) officers went to Pila's apartment to execute a search warrant issued on suspected drug activity. As the officers approached the apartment, they saw Uilani Huddy seated at a picnic table about fifteen to twenty feet from the apartment's front door. Officer Wilson believed Huddy lived with Pila based on information obtained from a confidential informant and from KPD Detective Wesley Kaui. Officer Wilson acknowledged Huddy, identified himself as a police officer, and stated that he had a search warrant.

The officers then approached the closed front door of the apartment. Officer Wilson knocked on the door and announced "police, search warrant," but did not expressly demand entrance. The officers heard no suspicious sound or movement inside the apartment. Within two seconds of the announcement, Officer Wilson opened the unlocked door, and the officers entered the apartment. Upon entry, the officers saw Defendants and Reynaldo Abrigo seated around a coffee table. On the table were two clear plastic packets containing what appeared to be crystal methamphetamine, a small spoon, a gram scale, and other drug-related paraphernalia, all of which were seized. Before trial, Defendants and Abrigo jointly moved to suppress the seized evidence on statutory and constitutional grounds. Should the evidence be suppressed? *State v. Monay*, 943 P.2d 908 (Hawaii 1997).

5. On the evening of December 14, 1994, Portsmouth police executed a search warrant for the defendant's residence. The affidavit of Detective Tammy Early given in support of the warrant, together with Early's independent investigation, established that a confidential and reliable informant had observed "Debbie" distribute cocaine from the premises within the immediately preceding seventy-two hours. The informant further advised that "Debbie" distributed cocaine daily to "various persons" and "may possibly be in possession of a .38 handgun," was "known to have a .38."

Defendant's son, Duane, reportedly was her cocaine supplier and resided within "one city block." Duane frequently "stay[ed]" with defendant, often walking to her residence, and had recently been arrested for discharging a firearm into an unoccupied vehicle. When the warrant was executed, police were unable to determine if Duane was present on the property. Confronted with the

"threat of two weapons," Early concluded that execution of the warrant by "knocking and announcing" would imperil the police officers and, therefore, authorized a "no-knock" entry, utilizing a "ramming" device.

Upon entering the residence, police observed defendant running from the living room into the kitchen. She was detained, and the ensuing search revealed cocaine, marijuana, and related paraphernalia throughout the home. Defendant moved to suppress all evidence obtained during the search, arguing that it was the fruit of an improper no-knock entry. Should the evidence be suppressed? *Spivey v. Commonwealth,* 479 S.E.2d 543 (Va.App. 1997).

6. On September 13, 1993, Chicago Police Officer Salvatore Inglima sought a search warrant for an alleged drug dealer named "Jose" and the premises at 3417 West Evergreen, Chicago. The complaint for search warrant was based upon a tip from a reliable confidential informant that the informant had purchased cocaine from Jose at that address. The complaint further stated that, following the exchange, Jose "placed the remaining bags of cocaine * * * into a box." A warrant was issued authorizing a search of the "person of 'Jose,' a male, white Hispanic, dark, wavy hair, dark eyes, olive complexion, approximately 6'0", 160–170 lbs., thin build and the 2nd floor rear apartment at 3417 West Evergreen Street, Chicago, Cook County, Illinois."

The warrant further authorized seizure of the following instruments, articles, and things:

"Cocaine, Cocaine paraphernalia, co-mingled United States Currency, proof of residency and any other items in direct violation of Illinois Controlled Substance Act or any items which have been used in the commission of, or which constitute evidence of the offense of ILLINOIS COMPILED STATUTES, Chapter 720 S 570/402, Possession of a Controlled Substance."

On September 14, 1993, Officer Inglima and other members of the Chicago Police Department Organized Crime Division Task Force staked out the two-story apartment building located at 3417 West Evergreen in preparation to execute the search warrant. While on the stakeout the officers observed the defendant carry a gray metal box into the building. Some 15 minutes later, the officers entered the apartment building and proceeded to the second floor. There they encountered Jose Gonzalez exiting the rear apartment. The officers placed him in custody and began to search the apartment. The defendant was found seated at the kitchen table with the closed tool box on the table in front of him. Officer Inglima performed a protective pat down search of defendant, then opened the tool box and recovered from it a brick-shaped package containing approximately one kilogram of cocaine. Should the cocaine in the toolbox be suppressed? *People v. Llanos,* 681 N.E.2d 598 (Ill.App. 1 Dist. 1997).

CHAPTER SIX

Probable Cause

OBJECTIVES

1. Be able to define probable cause to search and to arrest.

2. Know the indications of criminal activity that support probable cause.

3. Understand the two-pronged test of the *Aguilar* case for establishing probable cause through the use of an informant's information.

4. Understand how an informant's information can be bolstered by corroboration in order to establish probable cause.

5. Understand what is required by the *Gates* "totality-of-the-circumstances" test for determining probable cause.

OUTLINE

1. Definition
2. Information obtained through the officer's own senses
   a. Indications of criminal activity supporting probable cause
      (1) Flight
      (2) Furtive conduct
      (3) Real or physical evidence
      (4) Admissions
      (5) False or implausible answers
      (6) Presence at a crime scene or in a high-crime area
      (7) Association with other known criminals
      (8) Past criminal conduct
      (9) Failure to protest
      (10) Facts arising during investigation or temporary detention
3. Information obtained by the officer through informants
   a. *Illinois v. Gates*
   b. *Aguilar v. Texas*
      (1) Prong 1: Informant's basis of knowledge
      (2) Prong 2: Informant's veracity
4. Corroboration
   a. *Spinelli v. United States*
   b. *Dawson v. State*
5. Totality-of-the-circumstances test
   a. The *Gates* decision
   b. Application of the test

Probable cause is discussed to a limited extent in Chapter 3, as one of the basic underlying concepts of criminal procedure. It is also referred to in Chapters 4 and 5 as an essential element of the law dealing with arrests and search warrants. This chapter attempts to impart a practical working knowledge of all aspects of probable cause as it concerns both arrest and search and seizure. This chapter is therefore important for a complete understanding of Chapters 4 and 5 as well as of the following chapters in Part 3 on exceptions to the search warrant requirement. ■

Definition

Two different but similar definitions of probable cause are quoted here, one for search and one for arrest, because different types of information are required to establish probable cause in each instance. An often-quoted definition of probable cause to *search* is that found in *Carroll v. United States,* 267 U.S. 132, 45 S.Ct. 280, 69 L.Ed. 543 (1925), in which the U.S. Supreme Court said that probable cause exists when "the facts and circumstances within their [the officers'] knowledge and of which they had reasonably trustworthy information [are] sufficient in themselves to warrant a man of reasonable caution in the belief that [seizable property would be found in a particular place or on a particular person]." (Bracketed material supplied.) 267 U.S. at 162, 45 S.Ct. at 288, 69 L.Ed. at 555. Paraphrasing the *Carroll* case, the Court defined probable cause to *arrest* in *Brinegar v. United States,* 338 U.S. 160, 175–76, 69 S.Ct. 1302, 1310–11, 93 L.Ed. 1879, 1890 (1949):

> Probable cause exists where the "facts and circumstances within their [the officers'] knowledge and of which they had reasonably trustworthy information [are] sufficient in themselves to warrant a man of reasonable caution in the belief that" an offense has been or is being committed [by the person to be arrested].

These definitions differ only in that the facts and circumstances that would justify an arrest may be different from those that would justify a search. This chapter is primarily concerned with the part of the definition of probable cause that is common to both arrests and searches—namely, the nature, quality, and amount of information necessary to establish probable cause. In this regard, another U.S. Supreme Court definition of probable cause may be helpful.

> "[T]he term 'probable cause,' according to its usual acceptation, means less than evidence which would justify condemnation. . . ." Finely-tuned standards such as proof beyond a reasonable doubt or by a preponderance of the evidence, useful in formal trials, have no place in the magistrate's decision. While an effort to fix some general, numerically precise degree of certainty corresponding to "probable cause" may not be helpful, it is clear that "only the probability, and not a prima facie showing, of criminal activity is the standard of probable cause." *Illinois v. Gates,* 462 U.S. 213, 235, 103 S.Ct. 2317, 2330, 76 L.Ed.2d 527, 546 (1983).

This chapter is designed to clarify the meaning of terms in this definition while concentrating on specific examples of information that law enforcement officers must have before they may arrest or search, with or without a warrant. *Effective criminal investigation and prosecution depends on the quality and quantity of the facts and circumstances gathered by law enforcement officers and their ability to communicate this information via reports, affidavits, and testimony.*

Information on which probable cause may be based can come to the attention of a law enforcement officer in two ways: (1) the officer may perceive the information, or (2) someone else may perceive the information and relay it to the officer. These information sources are treated differently by the courts and are discussed separately here.

KEY POINTS

1. Probable cause exists where the facts and circumstances within a law enforcement officer's knowledge and of which the officer has reasonably trustworthy information are sufficient in themselves to warrant a person of reasonable caution in the belief that a crime has been or is being committed by a particular person or that seizable property would be found in a particular place or on a particular person.

2. Only the probability, and not a prima facie showing, of criminal activity is the standard of probable cause.

Information Obtained Through the Officer's Own Senses

Law enforcement officers applying for an arrest or search warrant must state *in writing* in the complaint or affidavit the underlying facts on which probable cause for the issuance of the warrant is based (see Chapters 4 and 5). All warrantless arrests and most warrantless searches must also be based on probable cause. Although no written document is required, officers must be prepared to justify a warrantless arrest or search with underlying facts if its validity is later challenged. Therefore, whether or not a warrant is sought, officers must have sufficient information supporting probable cause in their minds *before* conducting an arrest or search.

One type of information used to support probable cause is information from the officer's own senses. This includes what an officer perceives through the senses of sight, hearing, smell, touch, and taste. Furthermore, an officer's perceptions may be given additional credence because of personal experience or expertise in a particular area.

> [I]n some situations a police officer may have particular training or experience that would enable him to infer criminal activity in circumstances where an ordinary observer would not. . . . In such situations, when an officer's experience and expertise is relevant to the probable cause determination, the officer must be able to explain sufficiently the basis of that opinion so that it "can be understood by the average reasonably prudent person." *State v. Demeter,* 590 A.2d 1179, 1183–84 (N.J. 1991).

Indications of Criminal Activity Supporting Probable Cause

A law enforcement officer's perceptions of a crime being committed in his or her presence clearly provide probable cause to arrest the person committing the crime. Crimes are seldom committed in an officer's presence, however, and usually an officer must develop probable cause over time from perceptions of a variety of facts and circumstances. The following discussion focuses on specific facts and circumstances indicative of criminal activity, together with court cases explaining their relative importance in the probable cause equation.

FLIGHT. "[D]eliberately furtive actions and flight at the approach of strangers or law officers are strong indicia of mens rea, and when coupled with specific knowledge on the part of the officer relating the suspect to the evidence of crime, they are proper factors to be considered in the decision to make an arrest." *Sibron v. New York,* 392 U.S. 40, 66–67, 88 S.Ct. 1889, 1904–05, 20 L.Ed.2d 917, 937 (1968). In *United States v. Bell,* 892 F.2d 959 (10th Cir. 1989), the court found that the following facts gave a narcotics officer reasonable suspicion that the suspect was transporting illegal drugs, justifying his detention for investigation: The suspect disembarked a plane from Hawaii and repeatedly went to a group of phones but did not appear to be talking; he had no luggage besides his shoulder bag and appeared visibly nervous; he met another person carrying a package and walked with him around the airport. The court held that, when the suspect dropped his bag and ran down the concourse in response to detention and questioning, the officer had probable cause to arrest him. Thus, flight *plus* other indications of criminal activity may provide probable cause to arrest.

Flight by itself, however, does not support a finding of probable cause. In *Wong Sun v. United States,* 371 U.S. 471, 83 S.Ct. 407, 9 L.Ed.2d 441 (1963), federal officers arrested a man named Hom Way at two o'clock in the morning and found narcotics in his possession. Hom Way told the officers that he had purchased an ounce of heroin from a person named Blackie Toy. At six o'clock that same morning, the officers went to a laundry operated by James Wah Toy. When Toy answered the door, one officer identified himself, whereupon Toy slammed the door and ran to his living quarters at the rear of the building. The officers broke in and followed Toy to his bedroom, where they arrested him.

The U.S. Supreme Court held that the arrest was made without probable cause. First, the officers had no basis in experience for confidence in the reliability of Hom Way's information. (More is said about reliability of informants later.) Second, the mere fact of Toy's flight did not provide a justification for a warrantless arrest without further information.

> Toy's refusal to admit the officers and his flight down the hallway thus signified a guilty knowledge no more clearly than it did a natural desire to repel an apparently unauthorized intrusion. . . .
> A contrary holding here would mean that a vague suspicion could be transformed into probable cause for arrest by reason of ambiguous conduct which the arresting officers themselves have provoked. 371 U.S. at 483–84, 83 S.Ct. at 415, 9 L.Ed.2d at 452–53.

FURTIVE CONDUCT. Law enforcement officers frequently observe persons engaged in secretive or furtive conduct, arousing suspicion of impending criminal activity or concealment of evidence of criminal activity. Usually, this conduct at least justifies an officer's further investigation to determine whether a crime is being or is about to be committed. (See Chapter 7 on stop and frisk.) Furtive conduct by itself, however, is usually insufficient to establish probable cause to arrest because the observed person may be making a totally innocent gesture, exhibiting a physical or mental problem, or reacting in fear to an officer's presence. A person's nervousness in the presence of a law enforcement officer does not alone amount to probable cause. The Supreme Court of Colorado stated that "[i]t is normal for law-abiding persons, as well as persons guilty of criminal activity, to be nervous when stopped by a policeman for a traffic offense." *People v. Goessl,* 526 P.2d 664, 665 (Colo. 1974). A person should not be subject to arrest or search on the basis of a mistaken interpretation of an innocent action.

In *United States v. Ingrao,* 897 F.2d 860 (7th Cir. 1990), the defendant was arrested because he carried a bag down a gangway previously used in a suspicious transaction and furtively looked around while crossing the street. The court held that, while furtive gestures are relevant to probable cause, more specific information connecting the defendant to criminal activity was needed to establish probable cause in that case.

When police have additional specific incriminating information, furtive conduct may be the deciding factor in determining probable cause to arrest. In *United States v. McCarty,* 862 F.2d 143 (7th Cir. 1988), officers had corroborated information from informants that the defendant was a convicted felon, that he was driving a tan compact car with Michigan license plates bearing the number 278, and that he was likely to be carrying a gun. While on routine patrol, officers saw the described car and followed it. The car attempted to evade the officers, and, when stopped, the driver was observed leaning to the right as if to hide something under the passenger seat. The officers arrested the defendant and seized a handgun found in his car. The court found probable cause to arrest the defendant for possession of a firearm by a convicted felon. "The fact that McCarty tried to evade [the officers] while they were following him, and his furtive gesture when he was stopped, reinforced the reasonableness of the officers' belief that McCarty had committed or was committing a crime." 862 F.2d at 147. Furtive conduct, therefore, is relevant to probable cause but must be evaluated in light of all the facts and circumstances, including time of day, setting, weather conditions, persons present, and nature of the crime.

REAL OR PHYSICAL EVIDENCE. Officers may establish probable cause by the observation and evaluation of real or physical evidence. In *State v. Heald,* 314 A.2d 820 (Me. 1973), officers were summoned at 2:00 A.M. to a store that had recently been burglarized. The officers discovered two sets of footprints in fresh-fallen snow leading from the store to the tire tracks of an automobile. Since the tire tracks were identifiable by a distinctive tread, the officers followed them. After a short distance, the officers met another officer who had found a checkbook belonging to the store owner in the road. Farther down the road the officers found a bag containing electrical parts. Then the officers came upon a car parked in the middle of the road with its lights off—the only other vehicle the officers had seen since leaving the scene of the crime, except a vehicle driven by a person known to the officers. As the patrol car approached the parked car, the parked car's lights came on and the car was driven away. The officers stopped the car and arrested its two occupants for breaking and entering.

The court held that the items of real evidence found and the reasonable inferences drawn from the evidence, together with the highly suspicious circumstances, provided probable cause to arrest the defendants. The court added that "although the possibility of mistake existed, as it invariably does in a probable cause situation, they would have been remiss in their duty if they had not arrested the defendants promptly." 314 A.2d at 825.

ADMISSIONS. A person's admission of criminal conduct to a law enforcement officer may provide probable cause to arrest. In *Rawlings v. Kentucky,* 448 U.S. 98, 100 S.Ct. 1556, 65 L.Ed.2d 633 (1980), a law enforcement officer, under authority of a search warrant, ordered the defendant's female companion (Cox) to empty the contents of her purse. Among those contents was a large quantity and variety of controlled substances. Upon pouring out these items, Cox told the defendant to take what was his. The defendant immediately claimed ownership of some of the controlled substances. The Court held that "[o]nce petitioner admitted ownership of the sizable quantity of drugs found in Cox's purse, the police clearly had probable cause to place the petitioner under arrest." 448 U.S. at 111, 100 S.Ct. at 2564, 65 L.Ed.2d at 645.

FALSE OR IMPLAUSIBLE ANSWERS. False or implausible answers to routine questions may be considered in determining probable cause, but usually they do not provide probable cause standing alone. In *United States v. Velasquez,* 885 F.2d 1076 (3d Cir. 1989), the court found that the following facts provided probable cause to arrest the defendant for interstate smuggling of contraband: (1) the defendant and her companion were on a long-distance trip from Miami, a major drug importation point, to the New York area; (2) the defendant and her companion had given the officer conflicting stories about the purpose of their trip and their relationship; (3) the defendant and her companion appeared nervous when answering the officer's questions; (4) the defendant had told the officer that the automobile she was driving belonged to her "cousin," but she could not give her cousin's name; and (5) the automobile she was driving had a false floor in its trunk and appeared specially modified to carry contraband in a secret compartment.

In *United States v. Anderson,* 676 F.Supp. 604 (E.D.Pa. 1987), the court held that police had probable cause to seize money found in a legally stopped car, based partially on the defendant's implausible statements.

> The officers knew that defendants were driving towards New York on a known drug route in a car owned by someone else, a procedure used by drug dealers to avoid forfeiture. The officers had found a large sum of money in small denominations, wrapped with rubber bands in small bundles. These bundles were in three bags. At the time of the stop, defendant Anderson stated that they won the money in Atlantic City and were on their way to Chester, however, the location where they were stopped and the way the money was packaged were not consistent with this story. Finally, a Chester police officer relayed that defendants were known drug pushers. Based on these facts, the police had probable cause to believe defendants were engaged in drug activity and that the money was drug-related. The money, therefore was properly confiscated. 676 F.Supp. at 608.

PRESENCE AT A CRIME SCENE OR IN A HIGH-CRIME AREA. Mere presence at a crime scene or in a high-crime area does not alone constitute probable cause to arrest. In *Ker v. California,* 374 U.S. 23, 83 S.Ct. 1623, 10 L.Ed.2d 726 (1963), however, the Supreme Court found probable cause to arrest the wife of a drug suspect based on her presence at an apartment that she shared with her husband and that was being used as the base for his narcotics operation.

> Probable cause for the arrest of petitioner Diane Ker, while not present at the time the officers entered the apartment to arrest her husband, was nevertheless present at the time of her arrest. Upon their entry and announcement of their identity, the officers were met not only by George Ker but also by Diane Ker, who was emerging from the kitchen. Officer Berman immediately walked to the doorway from which she emerged and, without entering, observed the brick-shaped package of marijuana in plain view. Even assuming that her presence in a small room with the contraband in a prominent position on the kitchen sink would not alone establish a reasonable ground for the officers' belief that she was in joint possession with her husband, that fact was accompanied by the officers' information that Ker had been using his apartment as a base of operations for his

narcotics activities. Therefore, we cannot say that at the time of her arrest there were not sufficient grounds for a reasonable belief that Diane Ker, as well as her husband, was committing the offense of possession of marijuana in the presence of the officers. 374 U.S. at 3637, 83 S.Ct. at 1631–32, 10 L.Ed.2d at 740.

Presence near the scene of a *recent* crime also provides a strong indication of probable cause. In *State v. Mimmovich,* 284 A.2d 282 (Me. 1971), an officer received a radio report that a break-in was in progress at a certain building. When the officer arrived at the building, he discovered that the rear window had been broken and metal bars over the window spread wide enough to permit the entrance of a person. He observed no suspects at the scene but heard voices coming from the second-floor porch of an adjoining building. The officer entered this building and went up to the roof, where he found the defendants, lightly clad on a cold night, attempting to conceal themselves. He arrested them, frisked them for weapons, and found coins that were later admitted into evidence. The court found that the radio warning that a break-in was in progress, the observations of the officer at the scene, the presence of the defendants near the scene of the crime, lightly clad on a cold winter night, and the defendants' attempt to conceal themselves were sufficient to give the officer probable cause to arrest the defendants.

Suspicious activity in a high-crime area may contribute to probable cause. For example, in *United States v. Green,* 670 F.2d 1148 (D.C.Cir. 1981), the court identified four factors that should be assayed in determining whether the "totality of the circumstances" provides probable cause in a drug case: (1) the presence of a suspect in a neighborhood notorious for drug trafficking or other crimes; (2) suspects engaging in a sequence of events typical of a drug transaction; (3) a suspect's flight after being confronted by police; and (4) a suspect's attempt to conceal the subject of his activities.

ASSOCIATION WITH OTHER KNOWN CRIMINALS. Association of a suspect with other known criminals may be considered in determining probable cause, but it is not alone sufficient to provide probable cause. In *United States v. Di Re,* 332 U.S. 581, 68 S.Ct. 222, 92 L.Ed. 210 (1948), the U.S. Supreme Court held that the defendant's presence in a car with others who illegally possessed counterfeit ration coupons did not provide probable cause to arrest the defendant, because no other information linked him to the crime.

> The argument that one who "accompanies a criminal to a crime rendezvous" cannot be assumed to be a bystander, forceful enough in some circumstances, is farfetched when the meeting is not secretive or in a suspicious hide-out but in broad daylight, in plain sight of passersby, in a public street of a large city, and where the alleged substantive crime is one which does not necessarily involve any act visibly criminal. If Di Re had witnessed the passing of papers from hand to hand, it would not follow that he knew they were ration coupons, and if he saw that they were ration coupons, it would not follow that he would know them to be counterfeit. . . . Presumptions of guilt are not lightly to be indulged from mere meetings. 332 U.S. at 593, 68 S.Ct. at 228, 92 L.Ed. at 219–20.

In *United States v. Lima,* 819 F.2d 687 (7th Cir. 1987), however, the court found probable cause to arrest a defendant who arrived on the scene of a drug transaction shortly after the other participants in the deal, parked directly behind the car of one of the known participants, and conversed with one of the participants who walked over to his car while the transaction was taking place. The court added that "any innocent interpretation is further undermined by the fact that neither [of the other principals] called off or postponed the delivery of the drugs despite [the defendant's] presence." 819 F.2d at 690.

An officer may use his or her experience, training, and knowledge in determining that probable cause connecting a defendant with criminal activity exists. *Texas v. Brown,* 460 U.S. 730, 103 S.Ct. 1535, 75 L.Ed.2d 502 (1983). For example, in *United States v. Munoz,* 738 F.Supp. 800 (S.D.N.Y. 1990), the court found that FBI agents' observations, knowledge, and assumptions that a kidnapper would take several people along for security when he went to pick up ransom money were enough to establish probable cause to arrest an accomplice who was "observed doing nothing but sitting as a passenger in the Jeep." 738 F.Supp. at 802.

PAST CRIMINAL CONDUCT. The mere fact that a suspect has a known criminal record does not alone provide probable cause to arrest.

> We do not hold that the officer's knowledge of the petitioner's physical appearance and previous record was either inadmissible or entirely irrelevant upon the issue of probable cause. . . . But to hold that knowledge of either or both of these facts constituted probable cause would be to hold that anyone with a previous criminal record could be arrested at will. *Beck v. Ohio,* 379 U.S. 89, 97, 85 S.Ct. 223, 228, 13 L.Ed.2d 142, 148 (1964).

As the Court stated, however, prior criminal activity of a suspect is relevant to the determination of probable cause. In *United States v. McGlory,* 968 F.2d 309 (3d Cir. 1992), officers observed the defendant drive up to the residence of a known drug dealer. When the dealer entered the defendant's vehicle and handed the defendant money, the officers arrested the defendant. The court noted that the mere observation of the money exchange was not sufficient to support probable cause to arrest. However, the court still found probable cause to arrest because one of the arresting officers had personally observed the defendant's participation in a narcotics transaction nine months before.

FAILURE TO PROTEST. An arrested person's failure to protest an arrest cannot be used to infer probable cause to support that arrest.

> It is the right of one placed under arrest to submit to custody and to reserve his defenses for the neutral tribunals erected by the law for the purpose of judging his case. An inference of probable cause from a failure to engage in discussion of the merits of the charge with arresting officers is unwarranted. Probable cause cannot be found from submissiveness, and the presumption of innocence is not lost or impaired by neglect to argue with a policeman. It is the officer's responsibility to know what he is arresting for, and why, and one in the unhappy plight of being taken into custody is not required to test the legality of the arrest before the officer who is making it. *United States v. Di Re,* 332 U.S. 581, 594–95, 68 S.Ct. 222, 228, 92 L.Ed. 210, 220 (1948).

FACTS ARISING DURING INVESTIGATION OR TEMPORARY DETENTION. Probable cause to arrest or search may arise during routine investigation or questioning of a person. An officer may initially only be seeking information or investigating suspicious circumstances. Yet during the course of investigation, other facts may come to the officer's attention, either from the words or actions of a temporarily detained person or from other sources. For example, the detained person may give evasive answers, attempt to flee, or act in a furtive manner, or the officer may perceive any of the other indications of possible criminal activity discussed earlier. If the combination of facts and circumstances is sufficient to establish probable cause to arrest or search, the officer may act accordingly.

The most important case on this subject is the U.S. Supreme Court case of *Terry v. Ohio,* 392 U.S. 1, 88 S.Ct. 1868, 20 L.Ed.2d 889 (1968), the leading case on stop and frisk. (In Chapter 7, the *Terry* case and other stop-and-frisk cases illustrate how probable cause to arrest or search may arise from routine investigation and questioning.)

KEY POINTS

3. Information perceived by a law enforcement officer through any of the five senses may support probable cause.

4. An officer's perceptions may be given additional credence because of the officer's personal experience or expertise in a particular area.

5. The following facts and circumstances may be considered in determining probable cause: flight of a suspect; furtive conduct; physical evidence connecting a person with criminal activity; a suspect's admission of criminal conduct; false or implausible answers to routine questions; presence at a crime scene or in a high-crime area; association with other known criminals; past criminal conduct.

Information Obtained by the Officer Through Informants

Most crimes are committed out of the presence of law enforcement officers. Therefore, officers must usually rely on information from sources other than their own perceptions to establish probable cause to arrest or search. This information must come from ordinary citizen informants or criminal informants who have themselves personally perceived indications of criminal activity. (The term **informant** is used in this chapter to refer to any person from whom a law enforcement officer obtains information on criminal activity.) The problem with using information from informants is ensuring that the information is trustworthy enough to be acted on. Over the years, courts have developed elaborate rules and procedures for establishing probable cause when the information comes from informants.

Illinois v. Gates

The method of establishing probable cause through the use of an informant's information is sometimes referred to as the **hearsay method,** as opposed to the direct observation method discussed previously. The hearsay method was the subject of a landmark decision by the U.S. Supreme Court in 1983. That decision, *Illinois v. Gates,* 462 U.S. 213, 103 S.Ct. 2317, 76 L.Ed.2d 527, abandoned an approach to determining probable cause through the use of informants that had been established by two previous Supreme Court decisions, *Aguilar v. Texas,* 378 U.S. 108, 84 S.Ct. 1509, 12 L.Ed.2d 723 (1964), and *Spinelli v. United States,* 393 U.S. 410, 89 S.Ct. 584, 21 L.Ed.2d 637 (1969). The *Aguilar* and *Spinelli* decisions had established specific requirements for law enforcement officers to follow in preparing complaints or affidavits when using information received from informants. The *Gates* decision abandoned rigid adherence to these specific requirements in favor of a "totality of the circumstances" approach to determining probable cause.

Despite the changes brought about by the *Gates* decision, there are good reasons for discussing the *Aguilar* and *Spinelli* decisions in detail. First, the underlying rationales of these decisions and other cases interpreting them retain their vitality and help in analyzing the totality of the circumstances under *Gates*. Second, several states have rejected the *Gates* decision based on their state constitutions or statutes. These states still require complaints and affidavits to be prepared according to the *Aguilar* and *Spinelli* requirements. For example, in *People v. Griminger*, 529 N.Y.S.2d 55, 524 N.E.2d 409 (N.Y. 1988), the New York Court of Appeals held that, as a matter of state law, the *Aguilar-Spinelli* two-pronged test should be employed in determining the sufficiency of an affidavit submitted in support of a search warrant application. The court specifically found that the *Gates* test did not offer a satisfactory alternative to the *Aguilar-Spinelli* inquiry's satisfactory method of providing reasonable assurance that probable cause determinations are based on information derived from a credible source with firsthand information.

> Given the deference paid to the Magistrate's probable cause finding, and given the somewhat subjective nature of the probable cause inquiry, the aims of predictability and precision are again well served by providing the Magistrate with *Aguilar-Spinelli* concrete, structured guidelines. More importantly, this will also prevent the disturbance of the rights of privacy and liberty upon the word of an unreliable hearsay informant, a danger we perceive under the *Gates* totality-of-the-circumstances test. 529 N.Y.S.2d at 58, 524 N.E.2d at 412.

Therefore, this discussion of the hearsay method of determining probable cause begins with a detailed analysis of the *Aguilar-Spinelli* line of cases. It then evaluates the effect of the *Gates* totality-of-the-circumstances approach to the hearsay method of determining probable cause. The discussion concentrates on the situation in which a law enforcement officer is applying for a search warrant based on information from informants. This approach is used to help focus the discussion and to emphasize again that the officer should *write down,* in the complaint or affidavit, all the information on which probable cause is based. The same probable cause considerations are involved in arrest warrants and warrantless arrests and searches, except that the information need not be written down in the warrantless situation.

Aguilar v. Texas

Before the *Gates* decision, the leading case on establishing probable cause under the hearsay method was the U.S. Supreme Court case of *Aguilar v. Texas,* 378 U.S. 108, 84 S.Ct. 1509, 12 L.Ed.2d 723 (1964). The *Aguilar* case set out a *two-pronged test* for determining probable cause when the information in an affidavit was either entirely or partially obtained from an informant:

1. The affidavit must describe underlying circumstances from which a neutral and detached magistrate may determine that the informant had a sufficient basis for his or her knowledge and that the information was not the result of mere rumor or suspicion.

2. The affidavit must describe underlying circumstances from which the magistrate may determine that the informant was credible or that the informant's information was reliable.

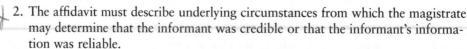

Both prongs of the *Aguilar* test had to be satisfied to establish probable cause. Each prong of the *Aguilar* test is discussed separately here, emphasizing the duties of the law enforcement officer in each case.

PRONG 1: INFORMANT'S BASIS OF KNOWLEDGE. A law enforcement officer must demonstrate to the magistrate in the affidavit underlying circumstances enabling the magistrate to independently evaluate the accuracy of an informant's conclusion. This is usually done by showing how the informant knows the supplied information. To satisfy this requirement, the affidavit must show either that

- the informant personally perceived the information given to the officer or
- the informant's information came from another source, but there is good reason to believe it.

Informant's Information Is Firsthand. If the informant came upon the information by personal perception, the law enforcement officer should have few problems in satisfying the first prong of the *Aguilar* test. The officer merely has to state, in the affidavit, *how, when,* and *where* the informant obtained the information furnished to the officer. In *State v. Daniels,* 200 N.W.2d 403 (Minn. 1972), the officer stated in the affidavit:

> For approximately the past two months I have received information from an informant whose information has recently resulted in narcotic arrests and convictions that a Gregory Daniels who resides at 929 Logan N, (down) has been selling marijuana, hashish and heroin. My informant further states that he has seen Daniels sell drugs, namely: heroin and further that he has seen Daniels with heroin on his person. The informant has seen heroin on the premises of 929 Logan N, (down) within the past 48 hours. 200 N.W.2d at 404.

The court said, "There seems to be no dispute that such personal observation satisfies that part of the *Aguilar* test which requires that the affidavit contain facts to enable the magistrate to judge whether the informant obtained his knowledge in a reliable manner." 200 N.W.2d at 406.

Stating in the affidavit the *time* when the informant obtained the information is very important, especially in applications for search warrants, because probable cause to search can become stale with time. In *United States v. Huggins,* 733 F.Supp. 445 (D.D.C. 1990), the court said, "[T]here is nothing in the affidavit from which the date of the controlled purchase can be determined and accordingly there was no way for the judicial officer to determine whether the information was stale. The controlled purchase could have occurred 'a day, a week, or months before the affidavit.'" 733 F.Supp. at 447.

Despite painstaking care by a law enforcement officer in establishing the basis of an informant's knowledge, courts will not find probable cause when errors in the informant's information result in serious injustice. In *United States v. Mackey,* 387 F.Supp. 1121 (D. Nev. 1975), officers detained the defendant for hitchhiking and sent his name through the computer at the National Crime Information Center (NCIC), a national clearinghouse for law enforcement agencies administered by the FBI. The computer reported that the defendant was wanted in another city for a parole violation. The officers arrested the defendant and subsequently found a gun in his possession. The NCIC report was later found to be false; the defendant had satisfied the parole violation five months earlier. The court ordered the suppression of all evidence resulting from the defendant's arrest.

[A] computer inaccuracy of this nature and duration, even if unintended, amounted to a capricious disregard for the rights of the defendant as a citizen of the United States. The evidence compels a finding that the government's action was equivalent to an arbitrary arrest, and that an arrest on this basis deprived defendant of his liberty without due process of law. 387 F.Supp. at 1125.

Therefore, although the officers acted properly in all respects, the evidence was ruled inadmissible through no fault of their own. Note that "information received from the NCIC computer bank has been routinely accepted in establishing probable cause for a valid arrest." *United States v. Hines,* 564 F.2d 925 (10th Cir. 1977). Officers should ordinarily feel free to act on such information so long as they do so in good faith.

Informant's Information Is Hearsay. If the informant's information comes from a third person, that person and his or her information must satisfy both prongs of the *Aguilar* test. The officer preparing the affidavit must show how the third person knows the information furnished to the informant. For example, if the third person saw criminal activity taking place at a particular time, a statement in the affidavit to that effect would be sufficient to satisfy the first prong of the *Aguilar* test. The officer must, however, also satisfy prong 2 of the *Aguilar* test with respect to *both* the informant *and* the third person. (Prong 2 of *Aguilar* is discussed later in this chapter.)

Detailing Informant's Information. Courts recognize one other method of satisfying the first prong of the *Aguilar* test besides stating how, when, and where the informant came by the information provided. In the U.S. Supreme Court case of *Spinelli v. United States,* 393 U.S. 410, 89 S.Ct. 584, 21 L.Ed.2d 637 (1969), the Court said:

> In the absence of a statement detailing the manner in which the information was gathered, it is especially important that the tip describe the accused's criminal activity in sufficient detail that the magistrate may know that he is relying on something more substantial than a casual rumor circulating in the underworld or an accusation based merely on an individual's general reputation. 393 U.S. at 416, 89 S.Ct. at 589, 21 L.Ed.2d at 644.

The *Spinelli* case cited another Supreme Court case, *Draper v. United States,* 358 U.S. 307, 79 S.Ct. 329, 3 L.Ed.2d 327 (1959), as an example of sufficient use of detail to satisfy the first prong of the *Aguilar* test. In the *Draper* case, the informant did not state the manner in which he had obtained his information. The informant did, however, report that the defendant had gone to Chicago the day before by train and that he would return to Denver by train with three ounces of heroin on one of two specified mornings. The informant went on to describe, with minute particularity, the clothes that the defendant would be wearing and the bag he would be carrying upon arrival at the Denver station. The Supreme Court said that "[a] magistrate, when confronted with such detail, could reasonably infer that the informant had gained his information in a reliable way." 393 U.S. at 417, 89 S.Ct. at 589, 21 L.Ed.2d at 644.

In *Soles v. State,* 299 A.2d 502 (Md.Spec.App. 1973), probable cause to conduct a warrantless search of an automobile was found even though the officer was unable to tell how, when, or where the informant obtained his information. The court held that the information given by the informant was sufficiently detailed to indicate that he had gained his information in a reliable way. Relevant parts of the officer's testimony at the motion to suppress hearing are quoted as follows, because the testimony indicates the type of detail that courts require to show that an informant spoke from personal knowledge.

The informant described the appellant in the following detail:

"A. The source described Mr. Soles. He gave—told me that the name of the subject was Soles. He didn't know any other name. Just Soles. He described Mr. Soles as being approximately five foot eight inches in height, approximately 160 pounds, as being a Negro male, approximately in his early 30s. I believe one age was 35 years of age. He said he had a receding hairline slightly, a small bush cut. He said his hair wasn't a big bush. He said it was short. He said he had a goatee and he was light skinned."

The informant described the appellant's automobile in the following detail:

"A. It was a late model blue convertible with a white top bearing New York tags, I believe WQ 9579, something like that; WX 9579. My recollection isn't real good on that."

The informant described the operation generally and the cocaine specifically in the following detail:

"THE WITNESS: The source called me at home and related to me that he had information about a male subject from New York who was a major distributor of cocaine to several known narcotics dealers in Washington. He related to me that this source was named Soles. He also indicated to me that he had given the tag number of Soles' car to my partner, Officer Robert Polzin, earlier that week, and in the conversation with this source he related to me that Soles had in excess of an eighth of a kilo of cocaine in his trunk of his car inside a briefcase. He said this cocaine would be inside a glass jar. He stated that Soles had several thousand dollars in cash on him, which were the assets from the sale of part of the cocaine he brought down from New York. He stated he was armed with a pistol, and stated that he would be leaving Washington for New York before three o'clock that evening."

The trial judge, "when confronted with such detail, could reasonably infer that the informant had gained his information in a reliable way," . . . that is, via first-hand observation. Upon our independent review, we draw such an inference. 299 A.2d at 507–08.

In summary, if a law enforcement officer does not know how, when, or where an informant obtained information, the officer can still satisfy the first prong of the *Aguilar* test by obtaining as much detail as possible from the informant and stating all of it in the affidavit.

PRONG 2: INFORMANT'S VERACITY. The second prong of *Aguilar* requires that the officer demonstrate to the magistrate in the affidavit underlying circumstances to convince the magistrate of the informant's veracity (that is, that the informant is credible or that the informant's information is reliable). In one of the few cases dealing with the reliability of an informant's information, the court found that information supplied by an unnamed street drug seller to one of his clients about a future drug "drop" was "reliable." The court said:

> Though from the criminal milieu, to be sure, he was not, wittingly at least, working with the police. He was not in the position of the "common informant . . . hidden behind a cloak of immunity from prosecution for his own misdeeds." . . . This street seller was, so far as he knew, engaged in a purely commercial venture for his own profit. He was dealing with a regular and presumably valued customer. Being unable initially to satisfy his customer's demand, it was to his every advantage to assure the prompt return of that customer as soon as fresh merchandise was available for sale. He simply had no purpose in misleading his own

clientele. The circumstances in which the seller passed on the information to a customer and confidant are replete, we think, with reasonable assurances of trustworthiness. Upon our constitutionally-mandated independent review, we believe the information furnished by this secondary informant to have been reliable, notwithstanding his utter lack of demonstrated credibility. *Thompson v. State,* 298 A.2d 458, 462 (Md. 1973).

Most cases have dealt with the "credibility" aspect of the informant's veracity rather than with the reliability of the informant's information. The amount and type of information required to establish credibility depends on whether the informant is an ordinary citizen informant or a criminal informant.

Ordinary Citizen Informant. An ordinary citizen informant is usually presumed credible and no further evidence of credibility need be stated in the affidavit beyond the informant's name and address and his or her status as a victim of, or witness to, a crime.

> One cannot approach the problem of informants whose information may or may not be sufficient to create "probable cause" as if there was only two classes: reliable informants whose information has previously been tested by the police and "all others." A multitude of cases . . . attest to the fact that information from a citizen who purports to be the victim of or to have witnessed a crime may, under certain circumstances, provide a sufficient basis for an arrest. *People v. Griffin,* 58 Cal.Rptr. 707, 711 (Cal.App. 1967).

The reason behind this rule was stated by the Supreme Court of Wisconsin:

> [A]n ordinary citizen who reports a crime which has been committed in his presence, or that a crime is being or will be committed, stands on much different ground than a police informer. He is a witness to criminal activity who acts with an intent to aid the police in law enforcement because of his concern for society or for his own safety. He does not expect any gain or concession for his information. An informer of this type usually would not have more than one opportunity to supply information to the police, thereby precluding proof of his reliability by pointing to previous accurate information which he has supplied. *State v. Paszek,* 184 N.W.2d 836, 843 (Wis. 1971).

Another reason for accepting the credibility of an ordinary citizen is the average person's fear of potential criminal or civil action for deliberately or negligently providing false information. *People v. Hicks,* 378 N.Y.S.2d 660, 341 N.E.2d 227 (N.Y. 1975).

Nevertheless, some courts have required more information to establish the credibility of an ordinary citizen informant. For example, in *State v. White,* 396 S.E.2d 601, 603 (Ga.App. 1990), the court stated:

> This court has always given the concerned citizen informer a preferred status insofar as testing the credibility of his information. . . . However, before an anonymous tipster can be elevated to the status of "concerned citizen," thereby gaining entitlement to the preferred status regarding credibility concomitant with that title, there must be placed before the magistrate facts from which it can be concluded that the anonymous tipster is, in fact, a "concerned citizen." . . . The affidavit in the case at bar contained no information from which it could be gleaned that the tipster was, in fact, a "concerned citizen." The magistrate was given nothing other than the affiant's conclusory statement that the tipster was a concerned citizen. That will not suffice.

In contrast, the Supreme Court of Virginia found an ordinary citizen informant credible where the affidavit stated that although the informant had not previously furnished information to the police concerning violations of the narcotics laws, he was steadily employed, was a registered voter, enjoyed a good reputation in his neighborhood, and had expressed concern for young people involved with narcotics. *Brown v. Commonwealth,* 187 S.E.2d 160 (Va. 1972). In another Virginia case, an officer's affidavit for a search warrant stated that the officer had known the ordinary citizen informant and his family for many years and that the informant was known to be credible. The court said:

> Although more extensive background information would be highly desirable, "a common sense and realistic" interpretation of the affidavit . . . leads us to the conclusion that it contains information reported by a first time citizen informer whose name was withheld by the affiant.
>
> Public-spirited citizens should be encouraged to furnish to the police information of crimes. Accordingly, we will not apply to citizen informers the same standard of reliability as is applicable when police act on tips from professional informers or those who seek immunity for themselves, whether such citizens are named . . . or, as here, unnamed. *Guzewicz v. Commonwealth,* 187 S.E.2d 144, 148 (Va. 1972).

These cases indicate that the more information provided in the affidavit about an ordinary citizen informant, the more likely the informant will be found to be credible. If, however, the informant appears in person before the magistrate and testifies under oath, subject to a charge of perjury if the information provided is false, no further evidence of credibility is needed. Personally testifying "provides powerful indicia of veracity and reliability." *United States v. Elliott,* 893 F.2d 220, 223 (9th Cir. 1990).

For certain crimes, the law enforcement officer must show not only that the informant is credible but also that the informant has some expertise in recognizing that a crime has been committed. In *United States v. Hernandez,* 825 F.2d 846 (5th Cir. 1987), the informant (Marone) told the police that the defendant (Hernandez) had attempted to pass a counterfeit twenty-dollar note. The court said:

> Generally, the reliability of an identified bystander or victim who witnesses crime need not be established. Hernandez challenges not Marone's motivation to tell the truth, but argues more narrowly that the Government has not shown that Marone possessed expertise in recognizing a bill as counterfeit. Nevertheless, it was known to the police that Marone was a carnival vendor who necessarily dealt with currency. Further, by immediately rejecting the bill once proffered and promptly notifying the police, Marone displayed confidence in his own ability to recognize the instant bill as counterfeit. Marone further conveyed this confidence by reporting to the police that the proffered paper was "an obviously counterfeit twenty dollar bill." We uphold the district court's determination that the circumstances would justify a reasonable law enforcement officer in believing there was a fair probability that a counterfeit note had been passed. 825 F.2d at 849–50.

Criminal Informant. Unlike the ordinary citizen's credibility, which may sometimes be presumed, the criminal informant's credibility must always be established by a statement of underlying facts and circumstances. Criminal informants may be professional police informants, persons with a criminal record, accomplices in a crime, or persons seeking immunity for themselves. Usually, criminal informants do not want their identities disclosed in an affidavit. The U.S. Supreme Court held that an informant's identity need not be disclosed if his or her credibility is otherwise satisfactorily established. In *McCray v. Illinois,* 386 U.S. 300, 306–07, 87 S.Ct. 1056, 1060, 18 L.Ed.2d 62, 68 (1967), the Court quoted the New Jersey Supreme Court with approval:

> "If a defendant may insist upon disclosure of the informant in order to test the truth of the officer's statement that there is an informant or as to what the informant related or as to the informant's reliability, we can be sure that every defendant will demand disclosure. He has nothing to lose and the prize may be the suppression of damaging evidence if the State cannot afford to reveal its source, as is so often the case. And since there is no way to test the good faith of a defendant who presses the demand, we must assume the routine demand would have to be routinely granted. The result would be that the State could use the informant's information only as a lead and could search only if it could gather adequate evidence of probable cause apart from the informant's data. Perhaps that approach would sharpen investigatorial techniques, but we doubt that there would be enough talent and time to cope with crime upon that basis. Rather we accept the premise that the informer is a vital part of society's defensive arsenal. The basic rule protecting his identity rests upon that belief."

Whether or not the informant's identity is disclosed in the affidavit, a statement of underlying facts and circumstances supporting credibility must be included. The following facts and circumstances are relevant.

1. Informant has given accurate information in the past. The usual method of establishing the credibility of a criminal informant is by showing that the informant has in the past given accurate information that has led to arrests, convictions, recovery of stolen property, or some like accomplishment. A law enforcement officer may not merely state in the affidavit the conclusion that the informant is credible because of proven credibility. The officer must state facts demonstrating that the informant has given accurate information in the past. This is sometimes referred to as establishing the informant's "track record."

Magistrates are required to evaluate affidavits that attempt to establish the credibility of informants in a commonsense manner and not with undue technicality. *United States v. Ventresca,* 380 U.S. 102, 85 S.Ct. 741, 13 L.Ed.2d 684 (1965). The main concern of the magistrate is the *accuracy* of the information supplied by the informant in the past. In *People v. Lawrence,* 273 N.E.2d 637 (Ill.App. 1971), the court found the informant credible even though none of his prior tips had resulted in convictions.

> Convictions, while corroborative of an informer's reliability, are not essential in establishing his reliability. Arrests, standing alone, do not establish reliability, but information that has been proved accurate does. Arrestees may not be prosecuted; if prosecuted they may not be indicted; if indicted they may not be tried; if tried they may not be convicted. If a case is tried, the informer may never testify; his credibility may never be passed upon in court. The true test of his reliability is the accuracy of his information. 273 N.E.2d at 639.

In *United States v. Dunnings,* 425 F.2d 836, 839 (2d Cir. 1969), the court found sufficient a statement that the informant had "furnished reliable and accurate information on approximately 20 occasions over the past four years." In *State v. Daniels,* 200 N.W.2d 403, 406–07 (Minn. 1972), the court held that the credibility of the informant was sufficiently shown where the affidavit stated that the informant's information "has recently resulted in narcotic arrests and convictions." In *United States v.*

Smith, 462 F.2d 456, 458 (8th Cir. 1972), the informant's credibility was established by an affidavit that specified:

> The informant has previously provided reliable information to agents of the Bureau of Narcotics and Dangerous Drugs. On one occassion [*sic*] within the last two weeks a search warrant was issued pursuant to the informants [*sic*] information and narcotics were seized. On another occassion [*sic*] within the last month the informant introduced me to an individual who he said was a dealer. I purchased heroin from the individual.

Generally, the more information provided about an informant's track record, the more likely the magistrate will find the informant credible. Types of information considered relevant are as follows:

- The time when previous information was furnished by the informant
- Specific examples of verification of the accuracy of the informant's information
- A description of how the informant's information helped in bringing about an arrest, conviction, or other result
- Documentation of the informant's consistency in providing accurate information
- Details of the informant's "general background, employment, personal attributes that enable him to observe and relate accurately, position in the community, reputation with others, personal connection with the suspect, any circumstances which suggest the probable absence of any motivation to falsify, the apparent motivation for supplying the information, the presence or absence of a criminal record or association with known criminals, and the like." *United States v. Harris,* 403 U.S. 573, 600, 91 S.Ct. 2075, 2090, 29 L.Ed.2d 723, 743 (1971) (dissenting opinion).

If an officer has no *personal* knowledge of circumstances demonstrating that an informant is credible, the officer may state in the affidavit information about the informant's credibility received from other law enforcement officers. *State v. Lambert,* 363 A.2d 707 (Me. 1976). The officer should state the names of other law enforcement officers and describe in detail how those officers acquired personal knowledge of the informant's credibility.

A dog trained to react to controlled substances may also be considered an informant. The dog's credibility can also be established by demonstrating the track record of the dog and its handler. In *United States v. Race,* 529 F.2d 12 (1st Cir. 1976), a dog reacted positively to two wooden crates in an airline warehouse containing some three hundred crates. The dog's reaction provided the basis for probable cause to arrest the defendant. The court said:

> We do not, of course, suggest that any dog's excited behavior could, by itself, be adequate proof that a controlled substance was present, but here the government laid a strong foundation of canine reliability and handler expertise. Murphy [the dog's handler] testified that the dog had undergone intensive training in detecting drugs in 1971, that he had at least four hours a week of follow-up training since then, as well as work experience, and that the strong reaction he had to the crates was one that in the past had invariably indicated the presence of marijuana, hashish, heroin or cocaine. 529 F.2d at 14.

2. Informant made admissions or turned over evidence against the informant's own penal interest. In *United States v. Harris,* 403 U.S. 573, 91 S.Ct. 2075, 29 L.Ed.2d

723 (1971), the U.S. Supreme Court held that an admission made by an informant against the informant's own penal interest is sufficient to establish the credibility of the informant.

> People do not lightly admit a crime and place critical evidence in the hands of the police in the form of their own admissions. Admissions of crime, like admissions against proprietary interests, carry their own indicia of credibility—sufficient at least to support a finding of probable cause to search. That the informant may be paid or promised a "break" does not eliminate the residual risk and opprobrium of having admitted criminal conduct. 403 U.S. at 583–84, 91 S.Ct. at 2082, 29 L.Ed.2d at 734.

In *State v. Appleton,* 297 A.2d 363 (Me. 1972), the court held that an informant's turning over criminal evidence against the informant's penal interest was also strongly convincing evidence of credibility. The informant purchased certain drugs at the defendant's apartment and the same day brought those drugs to the police to be tested. A law enforcement officer applied for a warrant to search the defendant's apartment, stating both that the informant had purchased the drugs and that he had delivered them to the police. The court held that the informant's actions justified a belief in the credibility of his story. "An informant is not likely to turn over to the police such criminal evidence unless he is certain in his own mind that his story implicating the persons occupying the premises where the sale took place will withstand police scrutiny." 297 A.2d at 369.

KEY POINTS

6. Probable cause may be based on information supplied to a law enforcement officer by ordinary citizen informants or criminal informants who have themselves personally perceived indications of criminal activity.

7. Under the *Aguilar* two-pronged test for determining probable cause when the information in an affidavit was either entirely or partially obtained from an informant, (1) the affidavit must describe underlying circumstances from which a neutral and detached magistrate may determine that the informant had a sufficient basis for his or her knowledge and that the information was not the result of mere rumor or suspicion, and (2) the affidavit must describe underlying circumstances from which the magistrate may determine that the informant was credible or that the informant's information was reliable.

8. An ordinary citizen informant is usually presumed credible, and no further evidence of credibility need be stated in the affidavit beyond the informant's name and address and his or her status as a victim or witness to crime.

9. A criminal informant's credibility is never presumed but must be established, usually by demonstrating the informant's "track record" of having given accurate information in the past.

10. A criminal informant's identity need not be disclosed if his or her credibility is otherwise satisfactorily established.

11. A dog trained to react to controlled substances may be considered an informant, and its credibility can be established by demonstrating the "track record" of the dog and its handler.

Corroboration

An officer with insufficient information to satisfy either or both prongs of the *Aguilar* test may be able to bolster that information by **corroboration.** Corroboration means strengthening or confirming the information supplied by the informant by stating in the affidavit supporting information obtained by law enforcement officers. For example, an officer may receive a tip from an informant about criminal activity. In addition, through surveillance or independent investigation, the officer or fellow officers may personally perceive further indications of criminal activity. By writing this corroborating information in the affidavit in addition to the information directed toward satisfying the *Aguilar* test, the officer enables a magistrate to consider all facts that may bear upon probable cause, no matter what the source of the information.

The corroborative information provided by the law enforcement officer in the affidavit may work in three possible ways:

- The information obtained by the officer may *in itself* provide probable cause independent of the informant's information. (See "Indications of Criminal Activity Supporting Probable Cause" earlier in this chapter.) Corroborating information of this degree provides probable cause to search even if neither prong of the *Aguilar* test is met.

- The officer's information may confirm or verify the information provided by the informant. For example, if an officer cannot satisfy prong 2 of the *Aguilar* test, the corroborating information may provide the necessary verification of the informant's report. In other words, if some significant details of the informant's information are shown to be true by the independent observation of a law enforcement officer, the magistrate is more likely to be convinced of the informant's veracity.

- The officer's information may be added to an informant's information that meets *Aguilar* standards. Although neither standing alone is sufficient to establish probable cause, a combination of all the information may be sufficient.

Therefore, to ensure that a magistrate is presented with sufficient information on which to base a determination of probable cause, the affidavit should include the following:

- All information directed toward satisfying the *Aguilar* two-pronged test
- All information perceived by law enforcement officers that corroborates the informant's information
- All additional corroborating information perceived by law enforcement officers relating to the criminal activity for which the search warrant is being sought

To illustrate how courts deal with corroboration, two cases with similar fact situations but different results are discussed in detail.

Spinelli v. United States

The U.S. Supreme Court case of *Spinelli v. United States,* 393 U.S. 410, 89 S.Ct. 584, 21 L.Ed.2d 637 (1969), is the leading case on corroboration. In that case, the defendant was convicted of traveling to St. Louis, Missouri, from a nearby Illinois suburb with the intention of conducting gambling activities prohibited by Missouri law. On appeal, the defendant challenged the validity of a search warrant that was used to obtain incriminating evidence against him. The affidavit in support of the search warrant contained the following allegations:

1. The FBI had kept track of the defendant's movements during five days in August 1965. On four of the five days, the defendant was seen crossing a bridge from Illinois to St. Louis between 11 A.M. and 12:15 P.M. and was seen parking his

car in a lot used by residents of a certain apartment house between 3:30 P.M. and 4:45 P.M. On one day, the defendant was followed further and was seen to enter a particular apartment in the building.

2. An FBI check with the telephone company revealed that this apartment contained two telephones listed under the name of Grace Hagen and carried two different numbers.

3. The defendant was known to the officer preparing the affidavit (the affiant) and to federal law enforcement agents and local law enforcement agents as a "bookmaker, an associate of bookmakers, a gambler, and an associate of gamblers." 393 U.S. at 414, 89 S.Ct. at 588, 21 L.Ed.2d at 642.

4. The FBI had been informed by a confidential reliable informant that the defendant was operating a handbook and accepting wagers and disseminating wagering information by means of telephones assigned the same numbers as the phones in the previously mentioned apartment.

The Court first discussed in detail allegation 4, the information obtained from the informant. The Court said:

> The informer's report must first be measured against *Aguilar*'s standards so that its probative value can be assessed. If the tip is found inadequate under *Aguilar,* the other allegations which corroborate the information contained in the hearsay report should then be considered. 393 U.S. at 415, 89 S.Ct. at 588, 21 L.Ed.2d at 643.

The Court found that prong 2 of *Aguilar* was not satisfied because the affiant merely stated that he had been informed by a "confidential reliable informant." This was a mere conclusion or opinion of the affiant, because no *underlying circumstances* were stated to show the magistrate that the informant was credible.

Nor was prong 1 satisfied. The affidavit failed to state sufficient *underlying circumstances* from which the informant concluded that the defendant was running a bookmaking operation. There was no statement as to how, when, or where the informant received his information—whether he personally observed the defendant at work or whether he ever placed a bet with him. If the informant obtained his information from third persons, there was no explanation as to why these sources were credible or how they obtained their information.

Finally, the affidavit did not describe the defendant's alleged criminal activity in sufficient detail to convince a magistrate that the information was more than mere rumor or suspicion. The only facts supplied were that the defendant was using two specified telephones to conduct gambling operations. As the Court said, this meager report could easily have been obtained from an offhand remark at a neighborhood bar.

The Supreme Court then considered allegations 1 and 2 of the affidavit to see whether they provided sufficient corroboration of the informant's information or probable cause in themselves. The Court found that these two items contained no suggestion of criminal conduct. The defendant's travels to and from the apartment building and his entry into a particular apartment could not be taken as indicative of gambling activity. And certainly nothing was unusual about an apartment containing two separate telephones. The Court, therefore, concluded:

> At most, these allegations indicated that Spinelli could have used the telephones specified by the informant for some purpose. This cannot by itself be said to support both the inference that the informer was generally trustworthy and that he had made his charge against Spinelli on the basis of information obtained in a reliable way. 393 U.S. at 417, 89 S.Ct. at 589, 21 L.Ed.2d at 644.

Finally, the Court considered allegation 3—that the defendant was "known" to the FBI and others as a gambler. The Court called this a bald and unilluminating assertion of police suspicion and said that it may not be used to give additional weight to allegations that would otherwise be insufficient.

Since the *Spinelli* decision, the Supreme Court has decided that the alleged criminal reputation of a suspect *may* be considered by a magistrate in evaluating an affidavit for a search warrant. *United States v. Harris,* 403 U.S. 573, 91 S.Ct. 2075, 29 L.Ed.2d 723 (1971). The Court said that criminal reputation could not be used in *Spinelli,* because *Spinelli* contained no factual indication of the defendant's past criminal activities to back up the assertion. The affiant in the *Harris* case stated in the affidavit that the defendant had a reputation for four years as a trafficker in illegal whiskey, that the officer had received information from all types of persons as to the defendant's activities, and that during this period a sizable stash of illegal whiskey had been found in an abandoned house under the defendant's control. The Court held that, when criminal reputation is supported by factual statements indicating prior criminal conduct, reputation can be considered along with other allegations.

The *Spinelli* case is instructive because it traces through all the *Aguilar* requirements for establishing probable cause using an informant's information and gives reasons why each test was not met by the affidavit. It then considers other information in the affidavit as corroboration of the informant's information and gives specific reasons why the corroborative information is inadequate.

Dawson v. State

Dawson v. State, 276 A.2d 680 (Md.Spec.App. 1971), is a case similar to the *Spinelli* case, except that the search warrant in *Dawson* was found to be valid. The discussion of the *Dawson* case centers on the differences between the two cases that caused the court in the *Dawson* case to reach a different conclusion.

In the *Dawson* case, the defendant was convicted of unlawfully maintaining premises for the purpose of selling lottery tickets and unlawfully betting, wagering, or gambling on the results of horse races. He appealed, claiming among other things that the search warrant of his home was illegal because probable cause was lacking. The affidavit for the warrant contained nine paragraphs. The first paragraph listed the investigative experience of the affiant and ended with his conclusion that gambling activities were at that time being conducted at the defendant's premises. The third through ninth paragraphs contained the direct observations of the affiant officer. (These paragraphs are considered later.) The second paragraph dealt with an informant's information and is quoted here:

> That on Thursday April 17, 1969 your affiant interviewed a confidential source of information who has given reliable information in the past relating to illegal gambling activities which has resulted in the arrest and conviction of persons arrested for illegal gambling activities and that the source is personally known to your affiant. That this source related that there was illegal gambling activities taking place at 8103 Legation Road, Hyattsville Prince George's County, Maryland by a one Donald Lee Dawson. That the source further related that the source would call telephone #577-5197 and place horse and number bets with Donald Lee Dawson. 276 A.2d at 685.

The court analyzed the second paragraph using the two-pronged *Aguilar* test. Considering the informant's basis of knowledge first, the court found that *Aguilar* was satisfied. The affidavit stated that the informant had personally called the phone number

577-5197 and had placed horse and number bets with the defendant. In contrast, in the *Spinelli* case, nothing was said about how the informant obtained his information.

The court found in *Dawson* that the information supplied about the credibility of the informant was barely sufficient. The affidavit stated that both arrests and convictions had resulted from the informant's information in the past, which was more than a mere conclusion or opinion of the affiant. The affidavit also went further to establish the informant's credibility than did the affidavit in *Spinelli,* where the informant was merely described as a "confidential reliable informant." The court implied that more specific information on the informant's credibility would have been desirable, but said:

> It may well be that the facts here recited are enough to establish the credibility of the informant. In view of the strong independent verification hereinafter to be discussed, however, it is unnecessary for the State to rely exclusively on such recitation. 276 A.2d at 686.

The court assumed for purposes of discussion that the credibility of the informant had *not* been adequately established and proceeded to discuss *corroboration,* making a concerted effort to compare the affidavit in this case with that in *Spinelli.*

Paragraphs 3 through 9 of the *Dawson* affidavit stated that a surveillance of the defendant's activities had been conducted during a six-day period in April 1969 and that the following information was obtained:

- The defendant was observed to be engaged in no apparent legitimate employment during the period.
- The defendant had two telephones in his residence with two separate lines, both of which had silent listings.
- One of the defendant's silent listings had been picked up in the course of a raid on a lottery operation three years earlier in another town.
- On each day of observation, the defendant was observed purchasing an Armstrong Scratch Sheet, which gives information about horses running at various tracks that day.
- On each morning of observation, the defendant was observed to leave his house between 9:02 and 10:20 A.M., to return to his house between 11:20 A.M. and 12:06 P.M., and to remain in his house until after 6:00 P.M. The affiant, who was experienced and expert in gambling investigations, stated that during the hours between noon and 6:00 P.M., horse and number bets can be placed and the results of betting become available.
- On each day of observation, the defendant was observed during his morning rounds stopping at a number of places, including liquor stores and restaurants, for very short periods. He never purchased anything from any of the stores, nor did he eat or drink at the restaurants. The affiant stated that such brief regular stops are classic characteristics of the pickup-man phase of a gambling operation: "He picks up the 'action' (money and/or list of bets) from the previous day or evening from prearranged locations—'drops.' At the same time, he delivers cash to the appropriate locations for the payoff of yesterday's successful players." 276 A.2d at 689.
- On one of the days, the defendant was observed in close association all day with another person who was known to have been arrested for alleged gambling violations three years before.
- Finally, the defendant had been arrested and convicted of gambling violations about three years before.

The court considered each allegation in detail. Although each allegation, taken separately, could admittedly have been consistent with innocent conduct on the defendant's part, the court refused to consider each allegation separately. Instead, the court said:

> [P]robable cause emerges not from any single constituent activity but, rather, from the overall pattern of activities. Each fragment of conduct may communicate nothing of significance, but the broad mosaic portrays a great deal. The whole may, indeed, be greater than the sum of its parts. 276 A.2d at 687.

Furthermore, the court relied heavily on the officer's experience in investigating gambling activities and the interpretations he was able to place on the defendant's conduct. The court, therefore, concluded:

> In reviewing the observations, the ultimate question for the magistrate must be What is revealed by the whole pattern of activity? In the case at bar, the various strands of observation, insubstantial unto themselves, together weave a strong web of probable guilt. 276 A.2d at 689.

The court compared this case with the *Spinelli* case and explained why the affidavit here was sufficient to provide probable cause while the one in *Spinelli* was not.

- In *Spinelli,* there were no observations of the pickup-man type of activity.
- In *Spinelli,* there was no observed association with a previously arrested gambler.
- In *Spinelli,* there was no daily purchase of an Armstrong Scratch Sheet to evidence some daily interest in horse races.
- In *Spinelli,* neither Spinelli's nor Grace Hagen's phone number had been previously picked up in a raided gambling headquarters.
- In *Spinelli,* Spinelli was not a convicted gambler.
- Finally, and perhaps most important, the confidential informant's information in *Spinelli* was so inadequate under *Aguilar* as to lend *no* additional light or interpretation to the direct observations. In contrast, the confidential informant's information in the *Dawson* case was very substantial and significantly enhanced the direct observations.

> The hearsay information may, of course, reinforce the direct observation just as the direct observation may reinforce the hearsay information. There is no one-way street from direct observation to hearsay information. Rather, each may simultaneously cross-fertilize and enrich the other. 276 A.2d at 690.

The court's emphasis on analyzing the overall pattern of activities and the totality of facts and circumstances in the *Dawson* case was an early harbinger of the approach to probable cause taken in the landmark decision of the U.S. Supreme Court in *Illinois v. Gates.*

KEY POINTS

12. *Corroboration* means strengthening the information supplied by the informant in the affidavit by stating supporting information obtained by the independent investigation of law enforcement officers.

13. Corroboration is a two-way street—direct observation of law enforcement officers may reinforce the hearsay information provided by the informant, and vice versa.

Totality-of-the-Circumstances Test

In the 1983 case of *Illinois v. Gates,* the U.S. Supreme Court abandoned the *Aguilar-Spinelli* two-pronged test for determining probable cause through the use of informants for a totality-of-the-circumstances test. More correctly, the Court abandoned a rigid adherence to the *Aguilar-Spinelli* test, since the elements of the *Aguilar-Spinelli* test remain important considerations under the new *Gates* test. This discussion of the *Gates* test begins with the facts of the case.

The *Gates* Decision

On May 3, 1978, the Bloomingdale, Illinois, Police Department received an anonymous letter that included statements that the defendants, a husband and wife, made their living selling drugs, that the wife would drive their car to Florida on May 3 and leave it to be loaded up with drugs, that the husband would fly down in a few days to drive the car back loaded with over $100,000 worth of drugs, and that the defendants had over $100,000 worth of drugs in the basement of their home. Acting on the tip, a police officer obtained the defendants' address and learned that the husband had made a reservation for a May 5 flight to Florida. The officer then made arrangements with a Drug Enforcement Administration (DEA) agent for surveillance of the May 5 flight. The surveillance revealed that the husband took the flight, stayed overnight in a motel room registered to his wife, and the next morning headed north with an unidentified woman toward Bloomingdale in a car bearing Illinois license plates issued to the husband. A search warrant for the defendants' residence and automobile was obtained, based on these facts and the anonymous letter. When the defendants arrived home, the police searched the car and the residence and found marijuana.

The Illinois Supreme Court found that the *Aguilar-Spinelli* two-pronged test had not been satisfied. First, the "veracity" prong was not satisfied because there was no basis for concluding that the anonymous person who wrote the letter to the police department was credible. Second, the "basis of knowledge" prong was not satisfied because the letter gave no information on how its writer knew of the defendants' activities. The court therefore concluded that no showing of probable cause had been made.

The U.S. Supreme Court said:

> We agree with the Illinois Supreme Court that an informant's "veracity," "reliability" and "basis of knowledge" are all highly relevant in determining the value of his report. We do not agree, however, that these elements should be understood as entirely separate and independent requirements to be rigidly exacted in every case, which the opinion of the Supreme Court of Illinois would imply. Rather . . . they should be understood simply as closely intertwined issues that may usefully illuminate the commonsense, practical question whether there is "probable cause" to believe that contraband or evidence is located in a particular place. *Illinois v. Gates,* 462 U.S. at 230, 103 S.Ct. at 2327–28, 76 L.Ed.2d at 543.

In effect, the Court said that the elements of the *Aguilar-Spinelli* two-pronged test are important considerations in determining the existence of probable cause, but they should be evaluated only as part of the ultimate commonsense determination and not as rigid rules to be applied mechanically. The Court believed that this totality-of-the-circumstances approach was more in keeping with the nature of probable cause as a fluid concept, which depends on probabilities arising from varying fact situations, and does not lend itself to a neat set of legal rules. The Court reiterated the following quotation from *Brinegar v. United States,* 338 U.S. 160, 175, 69 S.Ct. 1302, 1310, 93 L.Ed. 1879, 1890 (1949):

> In dealing with probable cause . . . as the very name implies, we deal with probabilities. These are not technical; they are the factual and practical considerations of everyday life on which reasonable and prudent men, not legal technicians, act.

The Supreme Court suggested that originally the two prongs of the *Aguilar-Spinelli* test were intended simply as guides to a magistrate's determination of probable cause, not as inflexible, independent requirements applicable in every case. The two prongs should be understood as

> relevant considerations in the totality of circumstances that traditionally has guided probable cause determinations: a deficiency in one may be compensated for, in determining the overall reliability of a tip by a strong showing as to the other, or by some other indicia of reliability. *Illinois v. Gates,* 462 U.S. at 233, 103 S.Ct. at 2329, 76 L.Ed.2d at 545.

The entire process of determining probable cause could, therefore, be simplified as follows:

> The task of the issuing magistrate is simply to make a practical, common-sense decision whether, given all the circumstances set forth in the affidavit before him, including the "veracity" and "basis of knowledge" of persons supplying hearsay information, there is a fair probability that contraband or evidence of a crime will be found in a particular place. And the duty of a reviewing court is simply to ensure that the magistrate had a "substantial basis for . . . conclud[ing]" that probable cause existed. 462 U.S. at 238–39, 103 S.Ct. at 2332, 76 L.Ed.2d at 548.

The *Gates* totality-of-the-circumstances test should cause little change in procedure for law enforcement officers applying for search warrants. If officers follow the advice in this chapter for preparing affidavits under the *Aguilar-Spinelli* test, the affidavits will have as good a chance or a better chance of satisfying the *Gates* test. The *Gates* emphasis on the value of corroborating information should, however, make it less difficult to obtain a search warrant based partially on information from an anonymous informant. As the *Gates* opinion indicated, overly rigid application of the two-pronged test tended to reject anonymous tips, because ordinary citizens generally do not provide extensive recitations of the basis of their everyday observations, and because the veracity of anonymous informants is largely unknown and unknowable. The Court said:

> [A]nonymous tips seldom could survive a rigorous application of either of the . . . prongs. Yet, such tips, particularly when supplemented by independent police investigation, frequently contribute to the solution of otherwise "perfect crimes." While a conscientious assessment of the basis for crediting such tips is required by the Fourth Amendment, a standard that leaves virtually no place for anonymous citizen informants is not. 462 U.S. at 237–38, 103 S.Ct. at 2332, 76 L.Ed.2d at 548.

With respect to the anonymous letter in the *Gates* case, the Supreme Court said that the corroboration of predictions that the defendants' car would be in Florida, that the husband would fly to Florida in a few days, and that the husband would drive the car back to Illinois indicated that the informant's other assertions were also true. The letter's accurate predictions of the defendants' future actions, especially, made it more likely that the informant also had access to reliable information of the defendants' alleged illegal activities. Although the tip was corroborated only as to the defendants' seemingly innocent behavior, and although it by no means indicated with certainty that illegal drugs would be found, the Court believed that it sufficed

> for the practical, common-sense judgment called for in making a probable cause determination. It is enough, for purposes of assessing probable cause, that "corroboration through other sources of information reduced the chances of a reckless or prevaricating tale," thus providing "a substantial basis for crediting the hearsay." 462 U.S. at 244, 103 S.Ct. at 2335, 76 L.Ed.2d at 552.

Application of the Test

The following quotations from two drug cases illustrate the kind of information courts look for in determining probable cause under the totality-of-the-circumstances standard. The first case, *United States v. Cruz,* did not involve an informant.

> [W]e conclude that the law enforcement officers had probable cause to arrest Cruz at the time they stopped his truck on the New Jersey Turnpike. The determination of whether probable cause to arrest exists can be based on the collective knowledge of all of the officers involved in the surveillance efforts because the various law enforcement officers in this investigation were in communication with each other. . . . The information that the agents had available to them at the time of arrest included the results of the prior surveillance efforts of the DEA [Drug Enforcement Administration] agent which suggested that Cesar Cruz was involved with narcotics activity. In addition, the agents had observed the loading of the four heavy boxes into the trailer portion of the tractor trailer truck from Florida; the extensive construction activity performed on the trailer that led the agents to believe that a hiding place for the boxes was being prepared; the suspects' preoccupation with ensuring that the lights of the truck were functioning properly, thus lessening the chances of being stopped by the police; Cruz's suspicious behavior in stopping his truck one mile after he had entered the New Jersey Turnpike, then turning off the truck's lights and standing by the cab of his truck for several minutes while he intently watched oncoming traffic; and Cruz's evasive driving when the police attempted to stop his truck. Although no single fact was sufficient by itself to establish probable cause, the totality of the circumstances as appraised by experienced drug enforcement agents was sufficient to support Cruz's arrest at the time the truck was stopped. 834 F.2d 47, 51 (2d Cir. 1987).

The second case, *United States v. De Los Santos,* did involve an informant.

> We believe that the officers had probable cause to believe that contraband would be found, and therefore they properly stopped and arrested De Los Santos. First, [DEA Special Agent] Castro knew that De Los Santos had dealt in heroin on previous occasions. He then received a tip from an informant who Castro knew and who had provided reliable information in the past. The informant told Castro that De Los Santos would travel to a certain area to store drugs and would pick them up the next day at a certain time. As predicted by the informant, the next morning De Los Santos arrived in the neighborhood in the same vehicle he had been in before. The agents observed him go to a residence and stay there for only two to four minutes. This surveillance, therefore, corroborated information provided by the informant.

Moreover, Castro testified *in camera* as to other information that the informant supplied. This information also is supportive of probable cause. As in *McCray*:

> the officer[s] in this case described with specificity "what the informer actually said, and why the officer thought the information was credible." . . . The testimony of each of the officers informed the court of the "underlying circumstances from which the informant concluded that the narcotics were where he claimed they were, and some of the underlying circumstances from which the officer concluded that the informant . . . was 'credible' or his information 'reliable.'"

McCray, 386 U.S. at 304, 87 S.Ct. at 1059 (citations omitted). Thus, under the totality of the circumstances test, "[t]here can be no doubt upon the basis of the circumstances related by [Castro], that there was probable cause to sustain the arrest. . . ." 810 F.2d 1326, 1336 (5th Cir. 1987).

This case illustrates the continuing validity of the elements of the *Aguilar-Spinelli* two-pronged test in determining probable cause using information supplied by an informant.

In contrast, the *Gates* test was not satisfied in *United States v. Campbell,* 920 F.2d 793 (11th Cir. 1990):

> Here, we must first decide if there was probable cause to search Campbell's pickup truck when it was stopped at the Union 76 Truck Stop. Probable cause exists "when the facts and circumstances would lead a reasonably prudent [person] to believe that the vehicle contains contraband." . . . The Supreme Court echoed this analysis when it adopted the totality of the circumstances test for determining when information provided by an informant rises to the level of probable cause. *Illinois v. Gates,* 462 U.S. 213, 230, 103 S.Ct. 2317, 2328, 76 L.Ed.2d 527, 543 (1983). The totality of the circumstances do not suggest that the Montgomery police had probable cause to arrest the defendants, much less search the vehicle when they first encountered it at the truck stop. The district court found that the confidential informant was not reliable, but still found that the officers had probable cause to arrest the occupants of the pickup based on reliability of the information provided by the informant. The key to the district court's conclusion was that the informant provided the police with the approximate time of the vehicle's arrival and the location where it would stop. Campbell concedes that when the agents observed the pickup truck enter the Union 76 Truck Stop "they had reasonable suspicion to conduct a valid investigatory stop under *Terry v. Ohio,* 392 U.S. 1, 88 S.Ct. 1868, 20 L.Ed.2d 889 (1968) and its progeny." . . . Thus, under the holding of *Alabama v. White,* 496 U.S. 325, 110 S.Ct. 2412, 110 L.Ed.2d 301 (1990), the most that the Montgomery police had was a reasonable suspicion of illegal activity. In *White* the police kept the suspect under surveillance in order to corroborate the information. There was not the type of corroboration of criminal activity . . . to elevate it to the level of probable cause. 920 F.2d at 796–97.

See Chapter 7 for a discussion of *Terry v. Ohio* and *Alabama v. White.*

In *United States v. Brown,* 744 F.Supp. 558 (S.D.N.Y. 1990), the court held that, under the *Gates* standard, probable cause for the issuance of a search warrant could be based almost entirely on information received from a single confidential informant. In that case, the informant had provided highly reliable information in the past, had been providing information on the defendant for over a month, and had personal knowledge about the premises to be searched. The court said:

The clear implication from the affidavit is that the informant had had a long relationship with law enforcement officials which had proved very reliable in the past. This information alone goes a long way to satisfying the totality of the circumstances test outlined in *Gates*. 744 F.Supp. at 567.

KEY POINTS

14. Under the *Gates* totality-of-the-circumstances test, the task of the issuing magistrate is to make a practical, commonsense decision whether, given all the circumstances set forth in the affidavit, there is a fair probability that contraband or evidence of crime will be found in a particular place.

15. The elements of the *Aguilar-Spinelli* two-pronged test are important considerations in determining the existence of probable cause but should be evaluated only

as part of the ultimate commonsense determination and not as rigid rules to be applied mechanically.

16. Corroboration of the details of an informant's tip by independent police investigation reduces the chances of a reckless or prevaricating tale and is a valuable means of satisfying the *Gates* totality-of-the-circumstances test for determining probable cause.

Summary

Probable cause exists when the facts and circumstances within a law enforcement officer's knowledge and of which the officer has reasonably trustworthy information are sufficient in themselves to warrant a person of reasonable caution in the belief either that

- a particular person has committed or is committing a crime or
- seizable items are located at a particular place or on a particular person.

Probable cause does not require certainty or proof beyond a reasonable doubt, but it does require something beyond mere suspicion. It is a practical, nontechnical, commonsense concept dealing with probabilities arising out of the varying facts and circumstances of everyday life. The U.S. Supreme Court has used the term "fair probability" to describe the probable cause standard.

Information on which probable cause is to be based may come to a law enforcement officer's attention in two possible ways:

- Through the officer's own perceptions
- Through the perceptions of an informant who relays the information to the officer

Some indications of criminal activity that may contribute to probable cause are as follows:

- Flight
- Furtive conduct

- Real or physical evidence such as fingerprints or weapons
- Incriminating admissions
- False or implausible answers
- Presence at a crime scene or in a high-crime area
- Association with other known criminals
- Past criminal conduct
- Facts arising during investigation or temporary detention

Standing alone, none of these indications of criminal activity may be sufficient to establish probable cause. However, when combined with other indications, each is a relevant factor in determining whether an arrest or a search is justified. Before law enforcement officers act, either to apply for a warrant or to conduct a warrantless arrest or search (in the proper circumstances), they should make sure that they have sufficient information on which to base their actions and that they can justify their actions before a magistrate or judge.

When information about criminal activity comes from an informant, an officer must satisfy the totality-of-the-circumstances test set out in the case of *Illinois v. Gates*. That test simply requires the officer to provide underlying facts and circumstances indicating a substantial basis for a magistrate to determine that probable cause to arrest or search exists. Highly relevant to this determination are the elements of the *Aguilar-Spinelli* two-pronged test. To satisfy this test, the officer must provide underlying circumstances indicating the basis of the informant's knowledge about the criminal activity and underlying circumstances from which the officer concluded that the informant was credible or that the information was reliable. These requirements need not be applied in a rigid, technical manner, but mere conclusions or opinions of the officer will not suffice to establish probable cause. The magistrate must be satisfied that the informant's information is not mere rumor, suspicion, or reckless or malicious fabrication. Corroboration of the details of an informant's tip by independent police work is a valuable means of satisfying the totality-of-the-circumstances test for determining probable cause.

Law enforcement officers applying for a warrant should write down in the affidavit, in an orderly manner, the following:

- All information directed toward satisfying the *Aguilar-Spinelli* two-pronged test

- All information perceived by law enforcement officers to corroborate the informant's information

- All additional corroborating information perceived by law enforcement officers with respect to the criminal activity for which the search warrant is being sought

---

Key Holdings from Major Cases

Carroll v. United States (1925). Probable cause exists when "the facts and circumstances within their [the officers'] knowledge and of which they had reasonably trustworthy information [are] sufficient in themselves to warrant a man of reasonable caution in the belief that [seizable property would be found in a particular place or on a particular person]." (Bracketed material supplied.) 267 U.S. 132, 162, 45 S.Ct. 280, 288, 69 L.Ed. 543, 555.

Brinegar v. United States (1949). "In dealing with probable cause . . . as the very name implies, we deal with probabilities. These are not technical; they are the factual and practical considerations of everyday life on which reasonable and prudent men, not legal technicians, act." 338 U.S. 160, 175, 69 S.Ct. 1302, 1310, 93 L.Ed. 1879, 1890.

"Probable cause exists where the 'facts and circumstances within their [the officers'] knowledge and of which they had reasonably trustworthy information [are] sufficient in themselves to warrant a man of reasonable caution in the belief that' an offense has been or is being committed [by the person to be arrested]." (Bracketed material supplied.) 338 U.S. at 175–76, 69 S.Ct. at 1310–11, 93 L.Ed. at 1890.

United States v. Di Re (1948). "The argument that one who 'accompanies a criminal to a crime rendezvous' cannot be assumed to be a bystander, forceful enough in some circumstances, is farfetched when the meeting is not secretive or in a suspicious hide-out but in broad daylight, in plain sight of passersby, in a public street of a large city, and where the alleged substantive crime is one which does not necessarily involve any act visibly criminal. . . . Presumptions of guilt are not lightly to be indulged from mere meetings." 332 U.S. 581, 593, 68 S.Ct. 222, 228, 92 L.Ed. 210, 219–20.

"It is the right of one placed under arrest to submit to custody and to reserve his defenses for the neutral tribunals erected by the law for the purpose of judging his case. An inference of probable cause from a failure to engage in discussion of the merits of the charge with arresting officers is unwarranted. Probable cause cannot be found from submis-

siveness, and the presumption of innocence is not lost or impaired by neglect to argue with a policeman. It is the officer's responsibility to know what he is arresting for, and why, and one in the unhappy plight of being taken into custody is not required to test the legality of the arrest before the officer who is making it." 332 U.S. 581, 594–95, 68 S.Ct. 222, 228, 92 L.Ed. 210, 220.

Aguilar v. Texas (1964). "Although an affidavit may be based on hearsay information and need not reflect the direct personal observations of the affiant . . . the magistrate must be informed of some of the underlying circumstances from which the informant concluded that the narcotics were where he claimed they were, and some of the underlying circumstances from which the officer concluded that the informant, whose identity need not be disclosed . . . was 'credible' or his information 'reliable.' Otherwise, 'the inferences from the facts which lead to the complaint' will be drawn not 'by a neutral and detached magistrate,' as the Constitution requires, but instead, by a police officer 'engaged in the often competitive enterprise of ferreting out crime' . . . or, as in this case, by an unidentified informant." 378 U.S. 108, 114–15, 84 S.Ct. 1509, 1514, 12 L.Ed.2d 723, 729.

Note: This approach to determining probable cause when the information in an affidavit was either entirely or partially obtained from an informant is referred to as the *Aguilar* two-pronged test. Rigid adherence to this test was abandoned in favor of a totality-of-the-circumstances test in *Illinois v. Gates.*

Spinelli v. United States (1969). "The informer's report must first be measured against *Aguilar*'s standards so that its probative value can be assessed. If the tip is found inadequate under *Aguilar,* the other allegations which corroborate the information contained in the hearsay report should then be considered." 393 U.S. 410, 415, 89 S.Ct. 584, 588, 21 L.Ed.2d 637, 643.

Illinois v. Gates (1983). "We agree with the Illinois Supreme Court that an informant's 'veracity,' 'reliability' and 'basis of knowledge' are all highly relevant in determining the value of his report. We do not agree, however, that these elements should be understood as entirely separate and independent requirements to be rigidly exacted in every case. . . . Rather . . . they should be understood simply as closely intertwined issues that may usefully illuminate the common-sense, practical question whether there is 'probable cause' to believe that contraband or evidence is located in a particular place." 462 U.S. 213, 230, 103 S.Ct. 2317, 2327–28, 76 L.Ed.2d 527, 543.

The two prongs of *Aguilar* "are better understood as relevant considerations in the totality of circumstances that traditionally has guided probable cause determinations: a deficiency in one may be compensated for, in determining the overall reliability of a tip by a strong showing as to the other, or by some other indicia of reliability." 462 U.S. at 233, 103 S.Ct. at 2329, 76 L.Ed.2d at 545.

"'The term "probable cause," according to its usual acceptation, means less than evidence which would justify condemnation. . . .' Finely tuned standards such as proof beyond a reasonable doubt or by a preponderance of the evidence, useful in formal trials, have no place in the magistrate's deci-

sion. While an effort to fix some general, numerically precise degree of certainty corresponding to 'probable cause' may not be helpful, it is clear that 'only the probability, and not a prima facie showing, of criminal activity is the standard of probable cause.'" 462 U.S. at 235, 103 S.Ct. at 2330, 76 L.Ed.2d at 546.

"[I]t is wiser to abandon the 'two-pronged test' established by our decisions in *Aguilar* and *Spinelli*. In its place we reaffirm the totality of the circumstances analysis that traditionally has informed probable cause determinations. The task of the issuing magistrate is simply to make a practical, common-sense decision whether, given all the circumstances set forth in the affidavit before him, including the 'veracity' and 'basis of knowledge' of persons supplying hearsay information, there is a fair probability that contraband or evidence of a crime will be found in a particular place. And the duty of a reviewing court is simply to ensure that the magistrate had a 'substantial basis for . . . conclud[ing]' that probable cause existed." 462 U.S. at 238–39, 103 S.Ct. at 2332, 76 L.Ed.2d at 548.

Review and Discussion Questions

1. Why is it important for a law enforcement officer to write down in a complaint or affidavit the facts and circumstances on which probable cause is based?

2. Give an example of a strong indication of probable cause to *arrest* that is arrived at through each of the five senses: sight, hearing, smell, taste, and touch.

3. Give an example of a strong indication of probable cause to *search* that is arrived at through each of the five senses: sight, hearing, smell, taste, and touch.

4. List three possible strong indications of probable cause to *arrest* for each of the following crimes:

   a. Theft

   b. Assault

   c. Arson

   d. Breaking and entering

   e. Rape

   f. Driving to endanger

5. Discuss the significance in the probable cause context of the phrase "conduct innocent in the eyes of the untrained may carry entirely different 'messages' to the experienced or trained . . . observer." *Davis v. United States*, 409 F.2d 458, 460 (D.C.Cir. 1969). Discuss specifically in terms of drug offenses and gambling offenses.

6. Must law enforcement officers know exactly the elements and name of the specific crime for which they are arresting or searching to have probable cause? See *People v. Georgev*, 230 N.E.2d 851 (Ill. 1967).

7. What does *corroboration* mean, and why is it important to a law enforcement officer in establishing probable cause through the use of informants?

8. How did the U.S. Supreme Court case of *Illinois v. Gates* change the requirements for establishing probable cause through the use of informants? Does the *Gates* decision make the law enforcement officer's task easier or harder?

9. Mr. A walks into a police station, drops three wristwatches on a table, and tells an officer that Mr. B robbed a local jewelry store two weeks ago. Mr. A will not say anything else in response to police questioning. A quick investigation reveals that the three watches were among a number of items stolen in the jewelry store robbery. Do the police have probable cause to do each of the following?

   a. Arrest Mr. A.

   b. Arrest Mr. B.

   c. Search Mr. A's home.

   d. Search Mr. B's home.

10. If you answered no to any of the items in question 9, explain why in detail. If you answered yes to any of them, draft the complaint or affidavit for a warrant, or explain why a warrant is not needed.

1. The affidavit submitted to the magistrate by Officer Carmichael stated as follows:

On September 29, 1995, I received an anonymous call from a concerned citizen regarding possible narcotics sales taking place at 1030 NE 7th Av[.] # 8. The caller stated that they observed heavy pedestrian and vehicular traffic coming to and from a two story apartment building.

During the week of October 7, through 11, 1995 Clay Barrett (1157), and I met with a confidential informant. This C.I. has been proven trustworthy and honest in the past and I have personally used this C.I. on prior investigations and he/she has always been accurate and reliable. The C.I. was then briefed as to the activity occurring at 1030 NE 7th Av[.] # 8. The C.I. then agreed to attempt a purchase of illegal narcotics from the suspect location under controlled conditions.

The C.I. was first searched and found to be free of any narcotics, currency, or any other contraband. The C.I. was then fitted with a Unitel listening device which Det. Barrett and I monitored. The C.I. was then given one twenty dollar bill. . . . The C.I. was then dropped off nearby the suspect location. It was at this point that we were unable [sic] maintain visual contact with the C.I. Pursuant to my instruction, The C.I. traveled directly to the suspect location.

The C.I. met a B/M subject as he walked up to apartment # 8. The B/M said "WHAT YOU WANT?" The C.I. said "I NEED A DIME" (street slang for a $10 piece of crack cocaine). The B/M said "COME ON." The B/M walked to apartment # 8 and went inside. The B/M brought back one cocaine rock. The C.I. looked at the rock and said "THAT'S SMALL." The B/M said "O.K. MAN, TAKE THESE" and gave the C.I. three smaller cocaine rocks. The C.I. gave the B/M the twenty dollar bill in exchange for the three cocaine rocks. The B/M then gave the C.I. a ten dollar bill . . . in change. The B/M told the C.I. "I'm ALWAYS HERE DOG, COME ON BACK." The C.I. then walked directly back to the undercover vehicle, and upon physical contact with me he/she surrendered three cocaine rocks. The C.I. was then transported away from the suspect location and searched again. The C.I. was found to be free of any narcotics, contraband and currency. This includes the previously issued investigative funds.

During the aforementioned series of events, the C.I. made no stops and did not come into contact with anyone other than the persons involved in the transaction. The suspect cocaine [tested] positive for the presence of cocaine.

Based upon the recitations in the affidavit, the magistrate issued the search warrant. Thereafter, the defendant was arrested and cocaine was found in her home. The defendant moved to suppress the evidence.

At the hearing on the motion, Officer Carmichael testified that he lost sight of the confidential informant as the informant approached the apartment building. However, Carmichael explained that he could see the building, but because his vehicle was known, he was forced to secrete himself. Although Carmichael did not see the informant enter the apartment, the entire transaction was heard via the wire. Moreover, Carmichael did not believe that there was enough time between the drop off and the buy for the informant to have gone elsewhere to purchase the cocaine. The court granted the motion to suppress, ruling that because the officer did not see the informant go into or come out of the apartment, there could not be probable cause to search the specific apartment listed. Was the court correct? *State v. Badgett,* 695 So.2d 468 (Fla.App. 4 Dist. 1997).

2. Hampton Police Detective Olen Payne, assisted by Detectives John Decker and others, was pursuing an arrest of Clyde Boyce on "outstanding murder warrants." Planning to entice Boyce into custody, police enlisted an informant to telephone Boyce, a known narcotics dealer, and solicit a drug purchase from him. After the informant confirmed the contact with Boyce, the detectives secreted themselves in and about the informant's mobile home and awaited Boyce's arrival to consummate the transaction. Boyce reputedly delivered drugs "moments" after a "call," and, within a "few minutes," an automobile arrived and defendant exited and entered the trailer.

Hidden in the rear of the residence, Detective Payne observed defendant and heard him declare, "This better not be no set up," to someone in the kitchen area. Although Payne had never before seen either Boyce or the defendant, the defendant's appearance was consistent with the physical description of Boyce, which, together with the attendant circumstances, prompted Payne to mistakenly identify the defendant as Boyce. Intending to then effect an arrest of Boyce, Payne, assisted by other officers, forced the defendant to the floor and hand-cuffed him. Immediately thereafter, police discovered a "small bag" of cocaine on the kitchen floor, "right at that point where [the defendant] initially was standing." A "similar bag" was found by Detective Burton in the defendant's trouser pocket during a search incident to arrest. Was the arrest of the defendant legal? *Shears v. Commonwealth,* 477 S.E.2d 309 (Va.App. 1996).

3. An unidentified citizen came in person to the Cumming Police Department and reported that he had seen a man walking along a local highway and removing mail from a mailbox. He gave a detailed description of the man and his clothing. This information was dispatched by radio to a patrol officer who observed a man, later identified as Redd, walking along the highway in the location reported. According to the officer, Redd fit the description given by the dispatcher "to a tee." The officer notified the dispatcher that he had located the individual and turned his vehicle around to speak to Redd, but Redd turned and began walking in the opposite direction.

The officer called to Redd and asked him what he was doing, but, according to the officer, "He really didn't answer me." The officer explained to Redd that he had stopped him to inquire about someone taking mail from mailboxes and that "we could clear the problem up real quick if he'd give me consent to search him." According to the officer, Redd appeared very nervous, backed away from the car, then turned and walked away. The officer testified that he would have conducted a limited protective search for weapons had Redd allowed him to approach, but "that never ever happened because he never let me get close enough to search him."

When the officer called out to him to come back, Redd responded, "'I'm not going to be arrested, and I'm not coming back.'" When the officer repeated his request for Redd to stop and talk to him, Redd did not answer but jumped over a guardrail beside the highway and disappeared into nearby woods. Other city and county law enforcement officers arrived in response to the officer's earlier call and surrounded the wooded area that Redd had entered. Another officer encountered Redd coming out of the woods, identified himself, and ordered Redd not to move. Redd did not obey but turned away and reached into his pocket. The officer drew his service revolver and ordered Redd not to move and to put his hands in the air; Redd first discarded a "small, black case" he was holding in his hand and then obeyed. The case contained two syringes and a white powdery substance later shown to be methamphetamine.

At the hearing, Redd gave a substantially different version of his encounter with the first officer, contending that he responded completely and fully to the officer's questions and told the officer that he lived "right up the road." He testified that he explained to the officer he

was simply checking his own mailbox. He then declined to be searched. When the officer continued to follow him in his car, Redd testified he became fearful that the officer was going to run him over, jumped over the railing, slipped, and fell down a hill into the woods. But Redd agreed that he later disobeyed the arresting officer's instructions not to move in order to discard the black case from his pocket.

On appeal, Redd contends there was no basis for the arrest which led to the discovery of the methamphetamine. While acknowledging that the officer had a right to approach him and talk to him, he contends that the officer lacked probable cause to arrest him after their encounter. Did the officer have probable cause to arrest? *Redd v. State,* 494 S.E.2d 31 (Ga.App. 1997).

4. At 10:50 P.M., on July 20, 1995, Beloit police received an anonymous telephone tip that "four or five black males," not otherwise described, were selling drugs to motorists at a certain intersection. Two officers arrived at the location about thirty minutes later and saw Ford and three other black males seated on the hood of a car about seventy-five to a hundred feet from the intersection. One of the officers approached Ford, whom he knew, and as he did so, the officer smelled marijuana. He told Ford that he "smelled like marijuana."

The officer then ordered Ford off the car, had him place his hands on the hood, and began patting him down. He did the pat down because he was investigating possible drug trafficking, he smelled marijuana, and it is his routine practice to conduct pat downs during street interrogations for safety reasons. During the initial pat down, the officer felt a large square wad of soft material in Ford's front pants pocket. When asked what it was, Ford said that it was money. Ford became "jumpy" whenever the officer's hands approached the front of Ford's waist, and Ford even grabbed the officer's hand as it approached that area. Since Ford was not cooperating with the pat down and gave the impression that he intended to run, the officer took Ford in a "full Nelson" hold to his squad car, where he placed Ford's hands behind his back and handcuffed him.

Upon resuming the pat down, Ford was still "jumpy" whenever the officer approached the waistband of his boxer shorts, which was visible above Ford's jeans. The officer testified that it was a "common place for people to put guns and other contraband[,] down the front of their shorts." Although he had not felt a weapon or contraband, the officer asked Ford if he could look inside Ford's shorts. In response, Ford took a step back, whereupon the officer pulled out the waistband about one and one-half inches and shined a flashlight into Ford's underwear. The officer discovered two plastic bags of marijuana wedged between Ford's thigh and genitals. The officer removed the bags of marijuana and arrested Ford for possession of a controlled substance.

Ford moved to suppress the marijuana, but the trial court concluded that the officer had probable cause to search Ford's boxer shorts and denied the motion. Ford then entered a guilty plea and was convicted of possession of THC, as a second offense.

Ford does not contend that either the investigatory stop or the initial pat down frisk were unreasonable. . . . The State, in turn, acknowledges that the officer's actions in pulling out the waistband of Ford's boxer shorts and shining a flashlight into them exceeded the scope of a Terry frisk. . . . The record supports both concessions. Thus, the only issue in this case is whether the officer's search can be justified on the basis that the officer had probable cause, under all of the facts and circumstances known to him, to conduct a more intrusive search of Ford's person. Did the officer have probable cause for the search? *State v. Ford*, 565 N.W.2d 286 (Wis.App. 1997).

5. A confidential informant told Special Agent Randy Reeves of the United States Immigration and Naturalization Service that he had spoken to the defendant on the telephone and that he had ordered two ounces of heroin. The informant further described the defendant as an Asian male, and indicated that he knew the defendant as "David." The informant said that the heroin delivery would take place that day outside a doughnut shop on Morton Street in the Roxbury section of Boston between 3:30 and 4 P.M., and that the defendant would deliver the heroin alone in a black Mercedes-Benz automobile. The informant had previously been arrested; this was the first time that the informant had provided any information to the police.

Special Agent Reeves then talked with Detective Thomas Morrissey and Detective Russell Grant of the Boston police department. The three then planned a stakeout near the doughnut shop. At approximately 4 P.M., the defendant appeared alone in a black Mercedes-Benz in front of the doughnut shop. He pulled in front of the doughnut shop and, although he slowed down, he did not come to a complete stop but instead proceeded down Morton Street. Detective Morrissey and Detective Grant followed. When the defendant stopped at a red light, Detective Grant ran in front of the defendant's automobile and displayed his badge. As Detective Grant approached, the defendant stepped out of his vehicle and put his right hand into his upper left pocket. Detective Morrissey, who had also left his vehicle, then drew his weapon, and the defendant removed his hand from his pocket. On searching the defendant the police officers found two large plastic bags containing a "tannish" colored powder; laboratory testing revealed that the substance was heroin. Was the search of the defendant legal? *Commonwealth v. Joe*, 682 N.E.2d 586 (Mass. 1997).

6. In 1994, Roy A. Grannis was living at his mother's house. In June, his sister, Toni Cobain, borrowed a videotape from his bedroom. When Cobain viewed the tape, she discovered it contained two scenes relevant here, each apparently filmed with a home video camera. The first scene involves minor girls playing in a park. The camera focuses on their clothed genitalia and buttocks and on one girl's breast area as she bends over. As far as the record shows, no adult initiated, contributed to, or otherwise influenced the girls' conduct. The second scene shows a minor girl taking a bath. It is taken from a vantage point located outside the bathroom, through "what appears to be a crack in the wall." At one point, the girl looks around and the camera moves away. The camera then returns to focus on the girl, showing her unclothed breasts and pubic area. As far as the record shows, no adult initiated, contributed to, or otherwise influenced the girl's conduct while bathing.

Several months after borrowing the tape, Cobain turned it over to the Aberdeen Police Department. The next day, officers of that department presented the tape and an accompanying affidavit to a magistrate. The affidavit incorporated the tape and stated that Grannis's mother owned a home video camera that Grannis knew how to operate. The magistrate issued a search warrant for Grannis's mother's house, and officers executing the warrant found two more videotapes that have relevance here.

The State charged Grannis with possessing visual or printed matter depicting a minor engaged in sexually explicit conduct, based on the videotape that Cobain had borrowed and then taken to the police. Did the tape borrowed by Cobain give the magistrate probable cause to believe that evidence of a crime would be found in Grannis's mother's house? *State v. Grannis*, 930 P.2d 327 (Wash.App. Div. 2 1997).

Exceptions to the Search Warrant Requirement

CHAPTER SEVEN

Stop and Frisk

OBJECTIVES

1. Understand the law's preference for search warrants and the reasons for the allowance of exceptions to the warrant requirement.

2. Know the distinctions between a stop, a formal arrest, a seizure tantamount to an arrest, and minimal nonintrusive contact between a citizen and a law enforcement officer.

3. Know the distinctions between a frisk and a full search.

4. Understand the competing interests that need to be balanced in determining the reasonableness of a stop and frisk.

5. Know the circumstances that justify a law enforcement officer in stopping a person and the extent of the interference with the person's freedom of action permitted by the law.

6. Know the circumstances that justify a law enforcement officer in frisking a person and the scope of the search permitted by the law.

7. Be able to apply the legal principles governing stop and frisk to analogous situations such as detentions and examinations of luggage, mail, and other containers.

OUTLINE

1. History
2. *Terry, Sibron,* and *Peters*
   a. *Terry v. Ohio*
   b. *Sibron v. New York*
   c. *Peters v. New York*
3. The reasonableness standard
4. Determination of whether to stop
   a. What is a stop?
   b. Authority to stop
   c. Information from informants
   d. Facts and circumstances determining reasonableness
   e. Extent of stop
      (1) Ordering driver and passengers out of vehicle
      (2) Reasonable investigative methods
      (3) Time
      (4) Force
5. Determination of whether to frisk
   a. Limited authority
   b. Scope of search
6. Specific circumstances in stop and frisk
   a. Observation of bulge or heavy object
   b. Hand concealed in clothing; force
   c. Innocent conduct
   d. Admission by defendant
   e. Traffic stops and roadblocks
   f. Violent crime
   g. Objects felt in frisk
   h. Collective knowledge of police
   i. High-crime area
   j. Association with known criminals
   k. Other suspicious circumstances
7. Miscellaneous issues in stop and frisk
   a. Stop and frisk and *Miranda*
   b. Frisking of persons of the opposite sex
   c. Containers and other property

The early chapters of this book emphasize the law's preference for warrants based on probable cause as the chief means of balancing the need for efficient and effective law enforcement against the need to protect the rights of individual citizens to be secure against unreasonable searches and seizures. In *Aguilar v. Texas*, 378 U.S. 108, 84 S.Ct. 1509, 12 L.Ed.2d 723 (1964), the U.S. Supreme Court stated that the preference for warrants is so strong that less persuasive evidence will justify the issuance of a warrant than would justify a warrantless search or warrantless arrest.

> [W]hen a search is based upon a magistrate's, rather than a police officer's determination of probable cause, the reviewing courts will accept evidence of a less "judicially competent or persuasive character than would have justified an officer in acting on his own without a warrant," . . . and will sustain the judicial determination so long as "there was a substantial basis for [the magistrate] to conclude that [seizable evidence was] probably present. . . ." 378 U.S. at 111, 84 S.Ct. at 1512, 12 L.Ed.2d at 726.

The warrant procedure is preferred because it places responsibility for deciding the delicate question of probable cause with a neutral and detached judicial officer. Law enforcement is served, because law enforcement officers may search certain persons or places and seize certain persons or things when the officers can show reasonable grounds that a person, place, or thing is significantly connected with criminal activity. The Fourth Amendment rights of citizens are also served, because the decision to allow a search and seizure is removed from the hurried judgment of overzealous law enforcement officers engaged in the competitive enterprise of investigating crime.

Nevertheless, in practice, situations often arise in which the time and effort needed to obtain a warrant would unjustifiably frustrate enforcement of the laws. To ensure that the delicate balance between individual rights and law enforcement is maintained, courts have carved out various exceptions to the warrant requirement and have allowed warrantless searches and seizures in certain situations. One important exception is a stop and frisk.

In Chapter 4, a formal arrest was defined as "the taking of a person into custody for the commission of an offense as the prelude to prosecuting him for it." Also discussed were seizures tantamount to arrest, in which, although an officer has no intention of taking a person into custody and charging the person with a crime, the circumstances surrounding the detention are indistinguishable from an arrest in important respects. Stop and frisk involves an even less intrusive seizure of a person and a limited search of that person.

As a preliminary definition, **stop and frisk** is a police practice involving the temporary detention, questioning, and limited search of a person suspected of criminal activity. A **stop** may be initiated on a reasonable suspicion of crime amounting to less than probable cause for the purposes of crime prevention and investigation. A **frisk** is allowed for the protection of the law enforcement officer carrying out the investigation.

Stop and frisk should be distinguished from the common situation, also described in Chapter 4, in which the law enforcement officer approaches a person in a public place and asks whether the person is willing to answer questions. In this situation, the officer needs no justification or level of suspicion to approach the person, and the officer has no authority to detain the person, even momentarily, whether or not the person agrees to cooperate. However, if an initially friendly and neutral encounter somehow provides the officer with reason to suspect criminal activity or danger, the officer may be justified in making the more significant intrusion of a stop and frisk. ■

History

The law enforcement officer's power to detain and question suspicious persons dates back to the common law of England. Ancient statutes and court decisions gave constables the power to detain suspicious persons overnight to investigate their suspicious activities. In the United States, until the mid-1960s, police-initiated contacts with citizens short of arrests were generally left to the discretion of individual officers and not subject to constitutional protections or judicial oversight. In the mid-1960s, a period of expanding constitutional rights for citizens, reformers called for the extension of constitutional protections to all police-citizen encounters and review of these encounters by the courts. This resulted in formalized procedures for many aspects of prearrest procedure and stirred up a controversy that continues to this day. Police and their supporters argued that, because of their experience and professionalism, street encounters should be subject to their discretion rather than formal rules. On the other hand, civil libertarians argued that a free society requires that constitutional safeguards protect each citizen, especially minorities and dissidents, at all places and all times. In response, the U.S. Supreme Court adopted formal guidelines governing street encounters amounting to less than arrests or full searches in three cases decided in 1968. In those cases (*Terry v. Ohio, Sibron v. New York,* and *Peters v. New York*), the Court attempted to resolve the conflicting interests by applying a balancing test under the reasonableness clause of the Fourth Amendment.

Terry, Sibron, and *Peters*

We begin our discussion of stop and frisk with summaries of *Terry v. Ohio,* 392 U.S. 1, 88 S.Ct. 1868, 20 L.Ed.2d 889 (1968), and *Terry*'s companion cases, *Sibron v. New York* and *Peters v. New York,* 392 U.S. 40, 88 S.Ct. 1889, 20 L.Ed.2d 917 (1968).

Terry v. Ohio

In the *Terry* case, a police detective with thirty-nine years' experience observed two men alternately pacing back and forth five or six times in front of a store window, each time peering into the store and returning to a corner to confer. The two men were joined briefly by a third man. When he walked away, the first two resumed their pacing, peering, and conferring. When the third man rejoined them again, the detective, suspecting that the men were casing the store for an armed robbery, approached them, identified himself, and asked their names. When the men "mumbled something," the detective grabbed Terry, spun him around to place him between the other two suspects and himself, and patted down the outside of his clothing. Feeling a pistol in Terry's coat pocket, the officer seized it. He patted down the outer clothing of the other two men and found one more weapon. Terry and the other man were arrested and convicted of carrying concealed weapons. They appealed, claiming that the weapons were obtained by means of an unreasonable search and should not have been admitted into evidence at their trial.

The U.S. Supreme Court affirmed the convictions. The Court said that, even though *stop and frisk* represented a lesser restraint than a traditional *arrest and search,* the procedure is still governed by the Fourth Amendment. However, stop and frisk is not subject to as stringent a limitation as is a traditional full arrest and search. Instead of applying the **probable cause** standard to stop and frisk, the Court applied the fundamental test of the Fourth Amendment: the **reasonableness** in all the circumstances of the particular governmental invasion of a citizen's personal security.

In discussing the reasonableness of the officer's actions in this case, the Court first mentioned the long tradition of armed violence of American criminals and the number of law enforcement officers killed or wounded in action. In light of this, the Court recognized law enforcement officers' need to protect themselves when suspicious circumstances indicate possible criminal activity by potentially dangerous persons, but when probable cause for an arrest is lacking. In these situations, the Court felt it would be unreasonable to deny an officer the authority to take necessary steps to determine whether a suspected person is armed and to neutralize the threat of harm. The Court concluded that

> where a police officer observes unusual conduct which leads him reasonably to conclude in light of his experience that criminal activity may be afoot and that the persons with whom he is dealing may be armed and presently dangerous, where in the course of investigating this behavior he identifies himself as a policeman and makes reasonable inquiries, and where nothing in the initial stages of the encounter serves to dispel his reasonable fear for his own or other's safety, he is entitled for the protection of himself and others in the area to conduct a carefully limited search of the outer clothing of such persons in an attempt to discover weapons which might be used to assault him. 392 U.S. at 30, 88 S.Ct. at 1884–85, 20 L.Ed.2d at 911.

Sibron v. New York

In the *Sibron* case, the facts were stated by the Court:

> At the hearing on the motion to suppress, Officer Martin testified that while he was patrolling his beat in uniform on March 9, 1965, he observed Sibron "continually from the hours of 4:00 P.M. to 12:00, midnight . . . in the vicinity of 742 Broadway." He stated that during this period of time he saw Sibron in conversation with six or eight persons whom he (Patrolman Martin) knew from past experience to be narcotics addicts. The officer testified that he did not overhear any of these conversations, and that he did not see anything pass between Sibron and any of the others. Late in the evening Sibron entered a restaurant. Patrolman Martin saw Sibron speak with three more known addicts inside the restaurant. Once again, nothing was overheard and nothing was seen to pass between Sibron and the addicts. Sibron sat down and ordered pie and coffee, and as he was eating, Patrolman Martin approached him and told him to come outside. Once outside, the officer said to Sibron, "You know what I am after." According to the officer, Sibron "mumbled something and reached into his pocket." Simultaneously, Patrolman Martin thrust his hand into the same pocket, discovering several glassine envelopes, which, it turned out, contained heroin.

Sibron was convicted of unauthorized possession of narcotics and appealed on the basis that the seizure was made in violation of his Fourth Amendment rights.

The Supreme Court found that the police officer in the *Sibron* case did not have probable cause to make an arrest and therefore could not justify the search as incident to arrest. The officer knew nothing of the conversations between Sibron and the others, and he saw nothing pass between them. All he had to go on was the fact that the others were addicts. This was not enough. "The inference that persons who talk to narcotics addicts are engaged in criminal traffic in narcotics is simply not the sort of reasonable inference required to support an intrusion by the police upon an individual's personal security." 392 U.S. at 62, 88 S.Ct. at 1902, 20 L.Ed.2d at 934. There was no basis to arrest until after the unlawful search.

Moreover, nothing in the record gave the slightest indication that the officer thought Sibron might be armed and dangerous. The officer, therefore, could not justify his actions on the grounds of self-protection. The *Terry* case did not authorize a routine frisk of everyone seen on the street or encountered by an officer. The officer in *Sibron* was apparently after narcotics and nothing else. His search was therefore unreasonable under the standards announced in the *Terry* case. Since there was neither probable cause to arrest nor sufficient justification to frisk, the heroin seized by the officer was not admissible in evidence, and the conviction of Sibron was reversed.

Peters v. New York

In the *Peters* case, an off-duty patrol officer heard a noise outside his apartment door. He saw two men tiptoeing furtively about the hallway, neither of whom he recognized although he had lived in the building for twelve years. After telephoning the police, he entered the hallway with his gun drawn, slamming the door behind him. The two suspects fled down the stairs and the officer gave chase. He caught up with the defendant, questioned him, and patted down his clothing. In the course of the frisk, the officer discovered a hard object that he believed could be a weapon. The object was an envelope containing burglar's tools. Peters was convicted of possessing burglar's tools.

The Supreme Court affirmed the conviction of Peters. The Court did not examine the officer's actions from a stop-and-frisk standpoint but rather found probable cause to arrest and sufficient authority to search incident to the arrest. The Court's decision emphasized the defendant's furtive action and his flight in establishing probable cause.

> It is difficult to conceive of stronger grounds for an arrest, short of actual eyewitness observation of criminal activity. . . . [D]eliberately furtive actions and flight at the approach of strangers or law officers are strong indicia of *mens rea* [criminal intent], and when coupled with specific knowledge on the part of the officer relating the suspect to the evidence of crime, they are proper factors to be considered in the decision to make an arrest. 392 U.S. at 66–67, 88 S.Ct. at 1904, 20 L.Ed.2d at 937.

The remainder of this chapter discusses in detail the powers of and limitations on a law enforcement officer in conducting a stop and frisk.

The Reasonableness Standard

Stop-and-frisk procedures are serious intrusions on an individual's privacy. They are governed by the Fourth Amendment to the Constitution, which prohibits unreasonable searches and seizures.

> It is quite plain that the Fourth Amendment governs "seizures" of the person which do not eventuate in a trip to the station house and prosecution for crime— "arrests" in traditional terminology. It must be recognized that whenever a police

officer accosts an individual and restrains his freedom to walk away, he has "seized" that person. And it is nothing less than sheer torture of the English language to suggest that a careful exploration of the outer surfaces of a person's clothing all over his or her body in an attempt to find weapons is not a "search." Moreover, it is simply fantastic to urge that such a procedure performed in public by a policeman while the citizen stands helpless, perhaps facing a wall with his hands raised, is a "petty indignity." It is a serious intrusion upon the sanctity of the person, which may inflict great indignity and arouse strong resentment, and it is not to be undertaken lightly. *Terry v. Ohio,* 392 U.S. at 16–17, 88 S.Ct. at 1877, 20 L.Ed.2d at 903.

Nevertheless, because a stop is more limited in scope than an arrest and because a frisk is more limited in scope than a full search, a stop and frisk may be judged by a less rigid standard than the probable cause standard applicable to an arrest and search. The *Terry* case made clear that stop and frisk is governed not by the warrant clause of the Fourth Amendment but by the reasonableness clause.

[W]e deal here with an entire rubric of police conduct—necessarily swift action based upon the on-the-spot observations of the officer on the beat—which historically has not been, and as a practical matter could not be, subjected to the warrant procedure. Instead, the conduct involved in this case must be tested by the Fourth Amendment's general proscription against unreasonable searches and seizures. 392 U.S. 1, 20, 88 S.Ct. 1868, 1879, 20 L.Ed.2d 889, 905.

The question for the law enforcement officer then becomes whether it is reasonable, in a particular set of circumstances, for the officer to seize a person and subject the person to a limited search when there is no probable cause to arrest.

The determination of reasonableness involves a consideration of the competing interests involved in a stop-and-frisk situation. On one side are the individual's right to privacy and the individual's right to be free from unreasonable searches and seizures. As the Supreme Court said in *Terry,* "Even a limited search of the outer clothing for weapons constitutes a severe, though brief, intrusion upon cherished personal security, and it must surely be an annoying, frightening, and perhaps humiliating experience." 392 U.S. at 24–25, 88 S.Ct. at 1881–82, 20 L.Ed.2d at 908.

On the other side are the governmental interests involved. One of these is effective crime prevention and detection. The other governmental interest, with which the Court in *Terry* was most concerned, is the interest of police officers in taking steps to assure themselves that the person with whom they are dealing is not armed with a weapon that could unexpectedly be used against them:

Certainly it would be unreasonable to require that police officers take unnecessary risks in the performance of their duties. American criminals have a long tradition of armed violence, and every year in this country many law enforcement officers are killed in the line of duty, and thousands more are wounded. 392 U.S. at 23, 88 S.Ct. at 1881, 20 L.Ed.2d at 907.

Balancing these competing interests in a particular situation requires a consideration of

- whether *any* police interference at all is justified by the circumstances, and
- if so, *how extensive* an interference those circumstances justify.

In the following discussion, the stop aspect and the frisk aspect are considered separately because the stop and the frisk each have different purposes, different sets of circumstances that justify them, and different consequences for the person who is subjected to the procedure.

1. The determination of the reasonableness of a stop and frisk involves balancing the individual's right to privacy and right to be free from unreasonable searches and seizures against the governmental interests of effective crime prevention and detection and the safety of law enforcement officers and others.

Determination of Whether to Stop

The U.S. Supreme Court recognized that stopping persons for the purpose of investigating possible criminal activity is necessary to the government's interest in effective crime prevention and detection:

> [I]t is this interest which underlies the recognition that a police officer may in appropriate circumstances and in an appropriate manner approach a person for purposes of investigating possibly criminal behavior even though there is no probable cause to make an arrest. *Terry v. Ohio*, 392 U.S. at 22, 88 S.Ct. at 1880, 20 L.Ed.2d at 906–07.

What Is a Stop?

Not every approach of a person by a law enforcement officer for purposes of investigating possible criminal activity will be considered a stop. In the *Terry* case, the Supreme Court noted:

> Obviously not all personal intercourse between policemen and citizens involves "seizures" of persons. Only when the officer, by means of physical force or show of authority, has in some way restrained the liberty of a citizen may we conclude that a "seizure" has occurred. 392 U.S. at 19 n.16, 88 S.Ct. at 1879 n.16, 20 L.Ed.2d at 905 n.16.

A stop is the least intrusive type of seizure of the person governed by the Fourth Amendment. (More intrusive types of seizures—formal arrests and seizures tantamount to arrest—are discussed in Chapter 4.)

In *United States v. Mendenhall*, 446 U.S. 544, 100 S.Ct. 1870, 64 L.Ed.2d 497 (1980), the U.S. Supreme Court developed a test to be applied in determining whether a person has been seized within the meaning of the Fourth Amendment.

> [A] person has been "seized" within the meaning of the Fourth Amendment only if, in view of all of the circumstances surrounding the incident, a reasonable person would have believed that he was not free to leave. Examples of circumstances that might indicate a seizure even where the person did not attempt to leave, would be the threatening presence of several officers, the display of a weapon by an officer, some physical touching of the person of the citizen, or the use of language or tone of voice indicating that compliance with the officer's request might

be compelled. . . . In the absence of some such evidence, otherwise inoffensive contact between a member of the public and the police cannot, as a matter of law, amount to a seizure of that person. 446 U.S. at 554–55, 100 S.Ct. at 1877, 64 L.Ed.2d at 509.

In the *Mendenhall* case, the Court found no seizure (and therefore no stop) on the following facts:

> The events took place in the public concourse. The agents wore no uniforms and displayed no weapons. They did not summon the respondent to their presence, but instead approached her and identified themselves as federal agents. They requested, but did not demand to see the respondent's identification and ticket. Such conduct without more, did not amount to an intrusion upon any constitutionally protected interest. The respondent was not seized simply by reason of the fact that the agents approached her, asked her if she would show them her ticket and identification and posed to her a few questions. Nor was it enough to establish a seizure that the person asking the questions was a law enforcement official. In short, nothing in the record suggests that the respondent had any objective reason to believe that she was not free to end the conversation in the concourse and proceed on her own way, and for that reason we conclude that the agents' initial approach to her was not a seizure. 446 U.S. at 555, 100 S.Ct. at 1877–78, 64 L.Ed.2d at 510.

Cases since *Mendenhall* have established that, even when law enforcement officers have no basis for suspecting a particular person, they may ask questions of that person, including requests to examine identification or search luggage, and there is no seizure "as long as the police do not convey the message that compliance with their requests is required." *Florida v. Bostick,* 501 U.S. 429, 435, 111 S.Ct. 2382, 2386, 115 L.Ed.2d 389, 398–99 (1991).

"*Mendenhall* establishes that the test for existence of a 'show of authority' is an objective one: not whether the citizen perceived that he was being ordered to restrict his movement, but whether the officer's words and actions would have conveyed that to a reasonable person." *California v. Hodari D.,* 499 U.S. 621, 628, 111 S.Ct. 1547, 1551, 113 L.Ed.2d 690, 698 (1991). Application of this objective test was the basis for the Supreme Court's decision in *Michigan v. Chesternut,* 486 U.S. 567, 108 S.Ct. 1975, 100 L.Ed.2d 565 (1988). In that case, the Court said:

> The [*Mendenhall*] test is necessarily imprecise, because it is designed to assess the coercive effect of police conduct, taken as a whole, rather than to focus on particular details of that conduct in isolation. Moreover, what constitutes a restraint on liberty prompting a person to conclude that he is not free to "leave" will vary, not only with the particular police conduct at issue, but also with the setting in which the conduct occurs. 486 U.S. at 573, 108 S.Ct. at 1979, 100 L.Ed.2d at 572.

In the *Chesternut* case, officers in a patrol car chased the defendant after they observed the defendant run when he saw the patrol car. The chase consisted of a brief acceleration to catch up with the defendant followed by a short drive alongside the defendant. The Court held that no stop occurred, because the defendant could not have reasonably believed that he was not free to disregard the police presence and go about his business. The Court noted that the police did not activate a siren or flasher, did not command the defendant to halt, did not display any weapons, and did not operate the patrol car in an aggressive manner to block the defendant's course or otherwise control the direction or speed of the defendant's movement. The Court recognized that "[w]hile the very presence of a police car driving parallel to a running pedestrian could be somewhat intimidating, this kind of police presence does not, standing alone, constitute a seizure." 486 U.S. at 575, 108 S.Ct. at 1980, 100 L.Ed.2d at 573.

United States v. Dockter, 58 F.3d 1284 (8th Cir. 1995), held that defendants were not seized within the meaning of Fourth Amendment when a deputy sheriff pulled his vehicle behind their automobile, which was parked off the traveled portion of the road and had its parking lights on, and activated his amber warning lights. The deputy sheriff did not block their vehicle in any manner to preclude them from leaving, did not draw his weapon, and spoke to them in a tone that was inquisitive rather than coercive. Nor was there a seizure when, in a different case, two law enforcement officers walked up to the defendant, who was seated on a bus, asked him a few questions, and asked whether they could search his bags. The U.S. Supreme Court said that, although the defendant may not have felt free to leave, his freedom of movement was restricted by a factor independent of police conduct.

[T]he mere fact that Bostick did not feel free to leave the bus does not mean that the police seized him. Bostick was a passenger on a bus that was scheduled to depart. He would not have felt free to leave the bus even if the police had not been present. Bostick's movements were "confined" in a sense, but this was the natural result of his decision to take the bus; it says nothing about whether or not the police conduct at issue was coercive. *Florida v. Bostick,* 501 U.S. 429, 436, 111 S.Ct. 2382, 2387, 115 L.Ed.2d 389, 399 (1991).

The Court stated:

[I]n order to determine whether a particular encounter constitutes a seizure, a court must consider all the circumstances surrounding the encounter to determine whether the police conduct would have communicated to a reasonable person that the person was not free to decline the officers' requests or otherwise terminate the encounter. That rule applies to encounters that take place on a city street or in an airport lobby, and it applies equally to encounters on a bus. 501 U.S. at 439–40, 111 S.Ct. at 2389, 115 L.Ed.2d at 401–02.

Note that, for purposes of the Fourth Amendment, a seizure requires an *intentional* acquisition of physical control. For example, if a parked and unoccupied police car slips its brake and pins a passerby against a wall, it is likely that a tort has occurred but not a violation of the Fourth Amendment. And the situation would not change if the passerby happened, by lucky chance, to be a serial murderer for whom there was an outstanding arrest warrant—even if, at the time he was thus pinned, he was in the process of running away from two pursuing police officers. In *Brower v. County of Inyo,* 489 U.S. 593, 596–97, 109 S.Ct. 1378, 1381, 103 L.Ed.2d 628, 635 (1989), the Court said:

[A] Fourth Amendment seizure does not occur whenever there is a governmentally caused termination of an individual's freedom of movement (the innocent passerby), nor even whenever there is a governmentally caused and governmentally *desired* termination of an individual's freedom of movement (the fleeing felon), but only when there is a governmental termination of freedom of movement *through means intentionally applied.*

If the "show of authority" by a law enforcement officer does not result in a halting or submission by the person being confronted, there is no seizure. In *California v. Hodari D.,* 499 U.S. 621, 111 S.Ct. 1547, 113 L.Ed.2d 690 (1991), the defendant, who was fleeing the approach of an unmarked police car, was surprised when he confronted an officer on foot pursuing him from another direction. The defendant immediately tossed away a small rock and was soon thereafter tackled by the officer. The rock was recovered and proved to be crack cocaine. The Court held that, in the absence of any physical contact or submission to the officer's show of authority, the defendant was not seized until he was tackled. The cocaine abandoned while he was running was, therefore, not the fruit of a *seizure* and not subject to exclusion.

Authority to Stop

A law enforcement officer may stop and briefly detain a person for investigative purposes if the officer has a *reasonable suspicion* supported by articulable facts that criminal activity "may be afoot," even if the officer lacks probable cause. (Indications of criminal activity are discussed in Chapter 6.) Reasonable suspicion is "considerably less than proof of wrongdoing by a preponderance of the evidence" and "is obviously less demanding than that for probable cause." *United States v. Sokolow,* 490 U.S. 1, 7, 109 S.Ct. 1581, 1585, 104 L.Ed.2d 1, 10 (1989). The concept of reasonable suspicion, like probable cause, is not "readily, or even usefully, reduced to a neat set of legal rules." *Illinois v. Gates,* 462 U.S. 213, 232, 103 S.Ct. 2317, 2329, 76 L.Ed.2d 527, 544 (1983). In evaluating the validity of a stop, courts will consider the totality of the circumstances—the whole picture.

> [T]he totality of the circumstances—the whole picture—must be taken into account. Based upon that whole picture the detaining officers must have a particularized and objective basis for suspecting the particular person stopped of criminal activity. . . . The analysis proceeds with various objective observations, information from police reports, if such are available, and consideration of the modes or patterns of operation of certain kinds of lawbreakers. From these data, a trained officer draws inferences and makes deductions—inferences and deductions that might well elude an untrained person.
>
> The process does not deal with hard certainties, but with probabilities. Long before the law of probabilities was articulated as such, practical people formulated certain common-sense conclusions about human behavior; jurors as factfinders are permitted to do the same—and so are law enforcement officers. *United States v. Cortez,* 449 U.S. 411, 417–18, 101 S.Ct. 690, 695, 66 L.Ed.2d 621, 629 (1981).

The officer must be able to give reasons to justify any stop. As the Supreme Court said in *Terry,* "[I]n justifying the particular intrusion the police officer must be able to point to specific and articulable facts which, taken together with rational inferences from those facts, reasonably warrant that intrusion." 392 U.S. at 21, 88 S.Ct. at 1880, 20 L.Ed.2d at 906. A court will not accept an officer's mere statement or conclusion that criminal activity was suspected. The officer must be able to back up the conclusion by reciting the specific facts that led to that conclusion. For example, in *United States v. Pavelski,* 789 F.2d 485 (7th Cir. 1986), the court held that an officer who testified to a "gut feeling that things were really wrong" failed to articulate any objective facts indicative of criminal activity.

Furthermore, the officer's decision to initiate a stop will be judged against the following objective standard: "[W]ould the facts available to the officer at the moment of the seizure or the search 'warrant a man of reasonable caution in the belief' that the action taken was appropriate?" *Terry v. Ohio,* 392 U.S. at 21–22, 88 S.Ct. at 1880, 20 L.Ed.2d at 906. This objective standard is similar to the standard imposed on law enforcement officers in traditional search and seizure or arrest situations. For example, assume that an officer is attempting to obtain a warrant for a person's arrest. Since probable cause is required to obtain the warrant, the officer must produce specific facts sufficient to support a reasonable belief *that a specific crime has been or is being committed.* In the stop-and-frisk situation, no crime may have been committed—there is only a possibility that criminal activity is under way, perhaps only in the planning stage. However, the officer must still have specific facts indicating a *possibility of impending criminal activity* to justify the initial intrusion. The common element in the two situations is that officers must be able to justify their action with specific facts. The only difference is in the nature of the information to be given, and for an investigative stop, the officer need only show facts indicating the possibility that criminal behavior is afoot.

The officer's authority to stop is not limited to crimes about to be committed or crimes in the process of being committed. The U.S. Supreme Court has authorized the stop of a person whom officers suspected of being involved in a *completed* felony. The Court said:

> [W]here police have been unable to locate a person suspected of involvement in a past crime, the ability to briefly stop that person, ask questions, or check identification in the absence of probable cause promotes the strong government interest in solving crimes and bringing offenders to justice. Restraining police action until after probable cause is obtained would not only hinder the investigation, but might also enable the suspect to flee in the interim and to remain at large. Particularly in the context of felonies or crimes involving a threat to public safety, it is in the public interest that the crime be solved and the suspect detained as promptly as possible. The law enforcement interests at stake in these circumstances outweigh the individual's interest to be free of a stop and detention that is no more extensive than permissible in the investigation of imminent or ongoing crimes. *United States v. Hensley,* 469 U.S. 221, 229, 105 S.Ct. 675, 681, 83 L.Ed.2d 604, 612 (1985).

Note that an officer has the duty to discontinue the investigation and not make a *Terry*-type stop of a person when, by the time of the intended stop, justification for the initial suspicion has disappeared.

> The scope of a policeman's inquiry and the permissibility of continuing to press the on-going investigation necessarily depend upon the continuing flow of information coming to the officer's attention after the start of the originally undertaken investigation. If the officer discovers additional evidence of possible wrongdoing, he may expand his inquiry as suggested by this new information. . . . The converse proposition also holds true. An officer cannot continue to press his investigation when he discovers new evidence demonstrating that his original interpretation of his suspect's actions was mistaken. *State v. Garland,* 482 A.2d 139, 144 (Me. 1984)

Information from Informants

In *Adams v. Williams,* 407 U.S. 143, 92 S.Ct. 1921, 32 L.Ed.2d 612 (1972), a law enforcement officer on patrol in his cruiser was approached by a person known to him and was told that a man seated in a nearby vehicle had a gun at his waist and was carrying narcotics. The officer approached the vehicle, tapped on the window, and asked the occupant (the defendant) to open the door. When the defendant rolled down the window instead, the officer reached in, removed a pistol from the defendant's waistband, and then arrested the defendant. The U.S. Supreme Court held that the officer acted justifiably in responding to the informant's tip:

> The informant was known to him personally and had provided him with information in the past. This is a stronger case than obtains in the case of an anonymous telephone tip. The informant here came forward personally to give information that was immediately verifiable at the scene. Indeed, under Connecticut law, the informant herself might have been subject to immediate arrest for making a false complaint had Sgt. Connolly's investigation proven the tip incorrect. Thus, while the Court's decisions indicate that this informant's unverified tip may have been insufficient for a narcotics arrest or search warrant, the information carried enough indicia of reliability to justify the officer's forcible stop of Williams.
>
> In reaching this conclusion, we reject respondent's argument that reasonable cause for a stop and frisk can only be based on the officer's personal observation, rather than on information supplied by another person. Informants' tips, like all other clues and evidence coming to a policeman on the scene, may vary greatly in their value and reliability. One simple rule will not cover every situation. Some tips, completely lacking in indicia of reliability, would either warrant no police response or require further investigation before a forcible stop of a suspect would be authorized. But in some situations—for example, when the victim of a street crime seeks immediate police aid and gives a description of his assailant, or when a credible informant warns of a specific impending crime— the subtleties of the hearsay rule should not thwart an appropriate police response. 407 U.S. at 146–47, 92 S.Ct. at 1923–24, 32 L.Ed.2d at 617–18.

Under *Adams v. Williams,* an officer may stop a person based on an informant's tip if the tip carries "enough indicia of reliability" to provide reasonable suspicion of criminal activity. This standard is less than the probable cause standard discussed in Chapter 6. Nevertheless, the officer must be able to give specific reasons why the tip was believed to be reliable. As the quoted material indicates, an anonymous telephone tip might not be sufficiently reliable without corroboration.

Alabama v. White, 496 U.S. 325, 110 S.Ct. 2412, 110 L.Ed.2d 301 (1990), illustrates the level of corroboration needed to support an anonymous tip and provide reasonable suspicion to justify an investigatory stop. In that case, police received an anonymous telephone tip that the defendant would be leaving a particular apartment at a particular time in a particular vehicle, that she would be going to a particular motel, and that she would be in possession of cocaine. Police went immediately to the apartment building and saw a vehicle matching the caller's description. They observed the defendant leave the building and enter the vehicle, and they followed her along the most direct route to the motel, stopping her vehicle just short of the motel. A consensual search of the vehicle revealed marijuana, and after the defendant was arrested, cocaine was found in her purse.

The U.S. Supreme Court held that the anonymous tip, as corroborated by independent police work, exhibited sufficient indicia of reliability to provide reasonable suspicion to make the investigatory stop. The Court referred to the totality of the circumstances approach of *Illinois v. Gates* (see Chapter 6) in determining whether an informant's tip establishes probable cause.

> *Gates* made clear . . . that those factors that had been considered critical under *Aguilar* and *Spinelli*—an informant's "veracity," "reliability," and "basis of knowledge"—remain "highly relevant in determining the value of his report." . . . These factors are also relevant in the reasonable suspicion context,

although allowance must be made in applying them for the lesser showing required to meet that standard. 496 U.S. at 328–29, 110 S.Ct. at 2415, 110 L.Ed.2d at 308.

The anonymous tip in this case, like the one in *Gates,* provided virtually nothing from which one might conclude that the caller is either honest or has reliable information, nor did the tip give any indication of the basis for the caller's predictions regarding the defendant's activities. As in *Gates,* however, in this case there was more than the tip itself. And although the tip was not as detailed and the corroboration not as complete, also as in *Gates,* the required degree of suspicion was not as high. The Court's rather lengthy discussion of reasonable suspicion is worthy of quotation:

> Reasonable suspicion is a less demanding standard than probable cause not only in the sense that reasonable suspicion can be established with information that is different in quantity or content than that required to establish probable cause, but also in the sense that reasonable suspicion can arise from information that is less reliable than that required to show probable cause. . . . Reasonable suspicion, like probable cause, is dependent upon both the content of information possessed by police and its degree of reliability. Both factors—quantity and quality are considered in the "totality of the circumstances—the whole picture," . . . that must be taken into account when evaluating whether there is reasonable suspicion. Thus, if a tip has a relatively low degree of reliability, more information will be required to establish the requisite quantum of suspicion than would be required if the tip were more reliable. The *Gates* Court applied its totality of the circumstances approach in this manner, taking into account the facts known to the officers from personal observation, and giving the anonymous tip the weight it deserved in light of its indicia of reliability as established through independent police work. The same approach applies in the reasonable suspicion context, the only difference being the level of suspicion that must be established. Contrary to the court below, we conclude that when the officers stopped the respondent, the anonymous tip had been sufficiently corroborated to furnish reasonable suspicion that respondent was engaged in criminal activity and that the investigative stop therefore did not violate the Fourth Amendment. 496 U.S. at 330–31, 110 S.Ct. at 2416, 110 L.Ed.2d at 309.

To better understand how corroboration works to supplement an anonymous tip in providing reasonable suspicion, it is worthwhile to discuss in detail the Court's analysis of corroboration. First, although not every detail mentioned by the tipster was verified—such as the name of the woman leaving the building or the precise apartment from which she left—the officers did corroborate that a woman left the building and got into the particularly described vehicle. Given that the officers proceeded to the building immediately after the call and that the defendant emerged not too long thereafter, it also appears that the defendant's departure was within the time frame predicted by the caller. Furthermore, since her four-mile route was the most direct way to the motel but nevertheless involved several turns, the caller's prediction of the defendant's destination was significantly corroborated even though she was stopped before she reached the motel. Moreover, the caller's ability to predict the defendant's future behavior demonstrated inside information—a special familiarity with her affairs. When significant aspects of the caller's predictions were verified, the officers had reason to believe not only that the caller was honest but also that he was well informed. Under the totality of the circumstances, the anonymous tip, as corroborated, exhibited sufficient indicia of reliability to justify the investigatory stop of the defendant's car.

Officers may rely on a police radio dispatch to obtain facts to justify the stop of a person or vehicle. If, however, it is later determined that the person relaying the information over the radio had no factual foundation for the message, the stop will be ruled illegal. In *United States v. Robinson*, 536 F.2d 1298 (9th Cir. 1976), the court said:

> We recognize that effective law enforcement cannot be conducted unless police officers can act on directions and information transmitted by one officer to another and that officers, who must often act swiftly, cannot be expected to cross-examine their fellow officers about the foundation for the transmitted information. The fact that an officer does not have to have personal knowledge of the evidence supplying good cause for a stop before he can obey a direction to detain a person or a vehicle does not mean that the Government need not produce evidence at trial showing good cause to legitimate the detention when the legality of the stop is challenged. If the dispatcher himself had had founded suspicion, or if he had relied on information from a reliable informant who supplied him with adequate facts to establish founded suspicion, the dispatcher could properly have delegated the stopping function to Officer Holland. But if the dispatcher did not have such cause, he could not create justification simply by relaying a direction to a fellow officer to make the stop. 536 F.2d at 1299–1300.

Facts and Circumstances Determining Reasonableness

In *State v. King*, 499 N.W.2d 190 (Wis.App. 1993), the Wisconsin Supreme Court neatly summarized the types of facts and circumstances relevant in determining the reasonableness of a stop in its discussion of *State v. Guzy*, 407 N.W.2d 548 (Wis. 1987).

> The reasonableness of an investigatory stop . . . depends on all the facts and circumstances that are present at the time of the stop. . . . In *Guzy*, the police were alerted to a robbery committed by a suspect described as a white male, five feet five to five feet eight inches tall, with dark, shoulder-length hair and a beard, a slim build, wearing sunglasses and a blue vest with red stripes. Shortly thereafter, two officers followed a truck which caught their attention because the passenger appeared to be a male with dark, shoulder-length hair, as described in the report. The only other specific and articulable fact known to the officers was that the truck was spotted in the location at a time that would be consistent with a vehicle fleeing the crime scene.
>
> In concluding that the officers acted reasonably by stopping the vehicle to further investigate, the *Guzy* court adopted Professor LaFave's six factor analysis for use in making the determination of reasonableness:
>
> (1) the particularity of the description of the offender or the vehicle in which he fled; (2) the size of the area in which the offender might be found, as indicated by such facts as the elapsed time since the crime occurred; (3) the number of persons about in that area; (4) the known or probable direction of the offender's flight; (5) observed activity by the particular person stopped; and (6) knowledge or suspicion that the person or vehicle stopped has been involved in other criminality of the type presently under investigation. . . .
>
> The court also noted the following additional circumstances relevant in the determination of reasonableness: (1) alternative means available to the officer to investigate short of making the stop; (2) the opportunity for further investigation, if action was not taken immediately; and (3) whether the description of the

individual known to the officer would allow him to quickly identify the individual so that there would be minimal intrusion. . . . Additionally, the severity or inherently dangerous nature of the criminal activity reported is a relevant consideration. 499 N.W.2d at 192–93.

Extent of Stop

Once an officer determines that the circumstances justify stopping an individual to investigate possible criminal activity, to what extent do those circumstances allow the officer to interfere? In other words, how long may the person be detained, how much force may be used, and how much questioning may the person be subjected to? In *Florida v. Royer,* 460 U.S. 491, 500, 103 S.Ct. 1319, 1325, 75 L.Ed.2d 229, 238 (1983), the U.S. Supreme Court said:

> The predicate permitting seizures on suspicion short of probable cause is that law enforcement interests warrant a limited intrusion on the personal security of the suspect. The scope of the intrusion permitted will vary to some extent with the particular facts and circumstances of each case. This much, however is clear: an investigative detention must be temporary and last no longer than is necessary to effectuate the purpose of the stop. Similarly, the investigative methods employed should be the least intrusive means reasonably available to verify or dispel the officer's suspicion in a short period of time. . . . It is the State's burden to demonstrate that the seizure it seeks to justify on the basis of a reasonable suspicion was sufficiently limited in scope and duration to satisfy the conditions of an investigative seizure.

See pages 108–109 for a detailed discussion of the *Royer* case.

An investigative stop can range from a friendly encounter with minimal intrusion to an angry confrontation accompanied by the use of force. Officers must be able to point to specific facts and circumstances to indicate that the extent of the interference with an individual was reasonable. This reasonableness determination involves a "weighing of the gravity of the public concerns served by the seizure, the degree to which the seizure advances the public interest, and the severity of the interference with individual liberty." *Brown v. Texas,* 443 U.S 47, 51, 99 S.Ct. 2637, 2640, 61 L.Ed.2d 357, 362 (1979).

ORDERING DRIVER AND PASSENGERS OUT OF VEHICLE. An officer who has lawfully stopped a motor vehicle may, for personal safety reasons, order the driver out of the vehicle, even though he or she has no reason to suspect foul play from the particular driver at the time of the stop. The U.S. Supreme Court said:

> We think this additional intrusion can only be described as de minimis. The driver is being asked to expose to view very little more of his person than is already exposed. The police have already lawfully decided that the driver shall be briefly detained; the only question is whether he shall spend that period sitting in the driver's seat of his car or standing alongside it. Not only is the insistence of the police on the latter choice not a "serious intrusion upon the sanctity of the person," but it hardly rises to the level of a "'petty indignity.'" . . . What is at most a mere inconvenience cannot prevail when balanced against legitimate concerns for the officer's safety. *Pennsylvania v. Mimms,* 434 U.S. 106, 111, 98 S.Ct. 330, 333, 54 L.Ed.2d 331, 337 (1977).

Once the driver is out of the car, the officer may

- conduct a frisk, if the officer has reason to believe that the person is armed and dangerous, and

- request consent to search the car, whether or not the officer has a subjective intention to arrest or issue a traffic ticket. *Ohio v. Robinette,* 519 U.S. 33, 117 S.Ct. 417, 136 L.Ed.2d 347 (1996).

In *Maryland v. Wilson,* 519 U.S. 408, ___, 117 S.Ct. 882, 886, 137 L.Ed.2d 41, 48 (1997), the Court extended the rule of the *Mimms* case by holding that "an officer making a traffic stop may order *passengers* to get out of the car pending completion of the stop" (emphasis supplied). The Court found that the danger to an officer from a traffic stop is likely to be greater when there are passengers in addition to the driver in the stopped car. While there is not the same basis for ordering the passengers out of the car as there is for ordering the driver out, the additional intrusion on the passenger is minimal.

> [A]s a practical matter, the passengers are already stopped by virtue of the stop of the vehicle. The only change in their circumstances which will result from ordering them out of the car is that they will be outside of, rather than inside of, the stopped car. Outside the car, the passengers will be denied access to any possible weapon that might be concealed in the interior of the passenger compartment. It would seem that the possibility of a violent encounter stems not from the ordinary reaction of a motorist stopped for a speeding violation, but from the fact that evidence of a more serious crime might be uncovered during the stop. And the motivation of a passenger to employ violence to prevent apprehension of such a crime is every bit as great as that of the driver. 519 U.S. at ___, 117 S.Ct. at 886, 137 L.Ed.2d at 47–48.

Once the passenger is outside the car, if the officer has sufficient specific facts to support a belief that a dangerous situation exists, the officer may frisk the traffic offender's passengers for weapons. In *United States v. Tharpe,* 536 F.2d 1098 (5th Cir. 1976), the court found sufficient facts to justify such a frisk under the following circumstances: (1) the driver showed the officer a false license, (2) the driver admitted being the "bad check" suspect of whom the officer had just been informed by radio, (3) the officer recognized the two passengers as burglary suspects, (4) the officer was alone, and (5) the encounter occurred late at night.

REASONABLE INVESTIGATIVE METHODS. An officer's initial questioning of a suspect may assure the officer that no further investigation is necessary. For example, a law enforcement officer in a patrol car observed a young man, carrying a flashlight and a small box, walking on the sidewalk of a residential street at 2:40 A.M. The officer drove past the young man and then stopped to ask him what he was doing. The young man replied that he was collecting nightcrawlers for fishing bait. The officer wished him luck and drove on.

On the other hand, the answers given by the stopped person may cause the officer to believe more strongly that something is amiss. In this situation, the officer is permitted to investigate further or, if probable cause exists, to arrest the person. For example, in *State v. Davis,* 517 A.2d 859 (N.J. 1986), an officer lawfully stopped the defendant and his companion on bicycles based on a reliable informant's tip that the men had been hanging around a closed gas station earlier at around midnight. The officer asked them whether they had been at the gas station and what their purpose was. After receiving implausible answers, the officer asked for identification, and the companion produced a third person's automobile registration. After further implausible answers to the officer's questions, the officer got out of his police car and noticed a registration tag on one of the bicycles. When the officer radioed to determine whether the bicycles were stolen, both men admitted that they were stolen, and the officer arrested them. The court found that the officer's investigative techniques were reasonable under the circumstances.

> Once Officer D'Andrea stopped the individuals, he acted by using reasonably unintrusive techniques in a manner calculated to either verify or dispel his suspicions in a short period of time. He asked questions limited to the circumstances surrounding their presence at the gas station. Officer D'Andrea merely sought to ascertain if defendant and his companion had been "hanging around" the closed gas station at approximately midnight, as reported . . . and, if so, what they had been doing there. . . . As the questioning unfolded, Officer D'Andrea received answers that tended to strengthen his suspicions that the suspects were up to no good. For defendant and his compatriot not only failed miserably to dispel the officer's suspicions, they effectively talked themselves into the arrest at issue.
>
> Officer D'Andrea, as a reasonable police officer, could not have allowed defendant and his companion to pass, without, at the very least, asking them if they had been at the gas station, and, if so, why. He conducted the stop and the questioning in an efficient and unobtrusive manner. Hence, we conclude his conduct in stopping and questioning the defendant was reasonable and did not violate defendant's rights . . . to be free of unreasonable searches and seizures. 517 A.2d at 868–69.

During a traffic stop, "reasonable investigation includes asking for the driver's license and registration, requesting that the driver sit in the patrol car, and asking the driver about his destination and purpose." *United States v. Bloomfield,* 40 F.3d 910, 915 (8th Cir. 1994). Likewise, an officer may engage in similar routine questioning of the vehicle's passengers to verify information provided by the driver. Moreover, "if the responses of the detainee and the circumstances give rise to suspicions unrelated to the traffic offense, an officer may broaden his inquiry and satisfy those suspicions." *United States v. Barahona,* 990 F.2d 412, 416 (8th Cir. 1993). Once the purposes of an initial traffic stop are completed, however, the officer may not further detain the vehicle or its occupants unless something that occurs during the traffic stop generates necessary reasonable suspicion to justify further detention. *United States v. Mesa,* 62 F.3d 159 (6th Cir. 1995).

When a situation being investigated requires immediate action, extraordinary investigative methods are sometimes upheld by the courts. In *State v. Burgess,* 716 P.2d 948 (Wash.App. 1986), officers discovered an abandoned pickup truck about a block from an animal clinic that had sounded a silent alarm. By running a registration check, they discovered that the pickup belonged to the defendant and that he had burglarized the same animal clinic on a previous occasion. The officers flattened the vehicle's tires to secure it while they continued their investigation. The defendant argued that the officers had made an unreasonable "seizure" by deflating the tires of his truck. The court said:

> [T]he detention of the truck in this manner was valid as a reasonably limited intrusion into Burgess's right "to be secure" in his "effects" protected by the Fourth Amendment against "unreasonable searches and seizures." Warrantless seizures may be justified where police officers are faced with emergencies or exigencies which do not permit reasonable time and delay for a judicial officer to evaluate and act upon an application for a warrant. . . . Here, the officers deflated

the truck tires during the time when several of them were in pursuit of a burglary suspect they believed was Burgess. The deflation of his truck tires, unaccompanied by any exploratory search at that time, was reasonably restricted in time and place and necessary to prevent the suspect from fleeing the scene of the burglary. If the officers had not deflated the tires, they would have been faced with the possibility that Burgess would remove the truck, taking its contents with him. 495 N.W.2d at 640.

TIME. "[T]he brevity of the invasion of the individual's Fourth Amendment interests is an important factor in determining whether the seizure is so minimally intrusive as to be justifiable on reasonable suspicion." *United States v. Place,* 462 U.S. 696, 709, 103 S.Ct. 2637, 2645, 77 L.Ed.2d 110 (1983). An investigative stop is not subject to any rigid time limitation, but at some point an extended stop that has not developed probable cause can no longer be justified as reasonable. In determining the reasonableness of the duration of a stop, courts consider the law enforcement purposes to be served by the stop as well as the time reasonably needed to effectuate those purposes. The U.S. Supreme Court said:

> In assessing whether a detention is too long in duration to be justified as an investigative stop, we consider it appropriate to examine whether the police diligently pursued a means of investigation that was likely to confirm or dispel their suspicions quickly, during which time it was necessary to detain the defendant. . . . A court making this assessment should take care to consider whether the police are acting in a swiftly developing situation and in such cases the court should not indulge in unrealistic second-guessing. . . . The question is not simply whether some other alternative was available, but whether the police acted unreasonably in failing to recognize or to pursue it. *United States v. Sharpe,* 470 U.S. 675, 686–87, 105 S.Ct. 1568, 1575–76, 84 L.Ed.2d 605, 615–16 (1985).

In the *Sharpe* case, the Court approved a twenty-minute detention of a driver made necessary by the driver's own evasion of a drug agent and the decision of a state police officer, who had been called to assist in making the stop, to hold the driver until the agent could arrive on the scene. The Court found that it was reasonable for the state police officer to hold the driver for the brief period pending the drug agent's arrival because (1) the state police officer could not be certain that he was aware of all of the facts that had aroused the drug agent's suspicions, and, (2) as a highway patrolman, he lacked the agent's training and experience in dealing with narcotics investigations.

United States v. Hardy, 855 F.2d 753 (11th Cir. 1988), held that a canine sniff is the kind of brief, minimally intrusive investigation technique that may justify a *Terry* stop. The court noted that "a canine sniff does not require the opening of luggage and does not reveal intimate but noncontraband items to public view. . . . Nor does a canine sniff involve the time-consuming disassembly of luggage or an automobile frequently required in a thorough search for contraband." 855 F.2d at 759.

Other reasons that might justify an officer in prolonging the detention of a suspect are that the officer is attempting to obtain further information over the police radio or from other persons, summoning assistance, traveling to the scene of suspected criminal activity, caring for injured persons or responding to other emergency circumstances, and dealing with evasive tactics or other delays caused by the suspect. In *United States v. Quinn,* 815 F.2d 153 (1st Cir. 1987), the court held that the detention of the defendant for investigation for twenty to twenty-five minutes did not transform the initial lawful *Terry* stop of the defendant into a seizure tantamount to arrest. Although several police officers were present, they made no threats, displayed no weapons, and exerted no physical restraint on the defendant. Moreover, the officers had a strong suspicion of criminal activity, and there was no way they could have greatly shortened the inquiry. Note that twenty to twenty-five minutes is probably the outside time limit beyond which a stop becomes a seizure tantamount to arrest, requiring a justification of probable cause.

Under ordinary circumstances, an officer who has a reasonable suspicion that a person may be engaged in criminal activity should initiate a stop of the person immediately. Nevertheless, a short delay in making the stop may be justified in certain situations. For example, in *State v. Cyr*, 501 A.2d 1303 (Me. 1985), an officer had grounds to stop a truck parked in an area of recent burglaries after observing the person in the driver's seat duck down to avoid detection. However, because the officer was transporting an arrested person, he continued driving slowly past the truck. In his rearview mirror, the officer observed the truck leave its parking place and follow his cruiser. After being informed that no other police unit was available to intercept the truck, the officer stopped the truck some two to three minutes after the first observation.

The court held that the suspicion had not evaporated because of the delay, since the truck remained within the officer's sight at all times and the delay resulted from the presence of an arrested person in the officer's vehicle. A longer delay, however, may cause a stop to be held illegal. For example, in *United States v. Posey*, 663 F.2d 37 (7th Cir. 1981), the court held that suspicion had evaporated where the defendant was stopped fifteen minutes after suspicion arose and fifteen miles away from the place where the defendant was originally seen.

FORCE. When law enforcement officers make an investigative stop, they may take such steps as are "reasonably necessary to protect their personal safety and to maintain the status quo during the course of the stop." *United States v. Hensley*, 469 U.S. 221, 235, 105 S.Ct. 675, 684, 83 L.Ed.2d 604, 616 (1985). Use of force in making a stop is governed by the Fourth Amendment standard of reasonableness, judged from the perspective of a reasonable officer on the scene rather than from hindsight. The nature and quality of the intrusion on the suspect's Fourth Amendment interests must be balanced against the countervailing governmental interests at stake. The reasonableness inquiry is an objective one—"whether the officers' actions are 'objectively reasonable' in light of the facts and circumstances confronting them, without regard to their underlying intent or motivation." *Graham v. Connor*, 490 U.S. 386, 397, 109 S.Ct. 1865, 1872, 104 L.Ed.2d 443, 456 (1989). Facts and circumstances that may be considered include the severity of the crime at issue, whether the suspect poses an immediate threat to the safety of the officers or others, and whether the suspect is actively resisting or attempting to evade the investigatory stop. Furthermore, "[t]he calculus of reasonableness must embody allowance for the fact that police officers are often forced to make split-second judgments—in circumstances that are tense, uncertain, and rapidly evolving—about the amount of force that is necessary in a particular situation." 490 U.S. at 396–97, 109 S.Ct. at 1872, 104 L.Ed.2d at 455–56.

The Eighth Circuit Court of Appeals listed factors to be considered in determining whether the amount and kind of force used was reasonable and consistent with an investigative stop. These include

(1) the number of officers and police cars involved, (2) the nature of the crime and whether there is reason to believe the suspect is armed, (3) the strength of the officer's articulable, objective suspicions, (4) the need for immediate action by the officer, (5) the presence or lack of suspicious behavior or movement by the person under observation, and (6) whether there was an opportunity for the

	STOP	**FORMAL ARREST**
Justification	Reasonable suspicion supported by articulable facts that criminal activity may be afoot.	Probable cause to believe that the person to be arrested has committed or is committing a crime.
Warrant	Not needed.	Preferred but not needed for arrests in public places. Arrest warrant is needed to enter suspect's home to arrest the suspect. Search warrant is needed to enter a third person's home to arrest the suspect.
Notice	None required.	Officer must give notice that the person is under arrest, notice of the officer's authority to arrest, and notice of the cause of arrest.
Force	Officer may use a reasonable degree of force judged from the perspective of a reasonable officer on the scene. Officer may never use deadly force. Officer must use the least intrusive methods reasonably available to confirm or dispel the officer's suspicions of criminal activity.	Officer may use any reasonably necessary nondeadly force to arrest for a felony or misdemeanor. Officer may use deadly force to arrest for a felony if the officer has probable cause to believe that the suspect poses a threat of serious physical harm either to the officer or others. Officer may never use deadly force to arrest for a misdemeanor.
Time limit	Must be temporary and last no longer than is necessary to effectuate the purpose of the stop.	Whatever time is reasonably needed to effectuate the arrest and bring the person into custody.
Search allowed	Protective patdown frisk of outer clothing for weapons, only if officer has reason to believe he or she is dealing with an armed and dangerous individual.	Full body search for weapons and evidence of arrestee and of the area into which the arrestee might reach in order to grab a weapon or evidentiary items.

EXHIBIT 7.1   Comparison of a Stop and a Formal Arrest

officer to have made the stop in less threatening circumstances. *United States v. Seelye,* 815 F.2d 48, 50 (8th Cir. 1987).

In *United States v. Bullock,* 71 F.3d 171 (5th Cir. 1995), the court held that law enforcement officers were justified in drawing their weapons on the defendant after stopping his vehicle for speeding. The officers had been informed over the radio that the defendant was a suspect in a bank robbery committed just hours before, and the officers were familiar with the defendant from previous encounters and knew him to be a dangerous man, one who had previously resisted arrest and threatened police. In *United States v. Melendez-Garcia,* 28 F.3d 1046, 1053 (10th Cir. 1994), however, the court held that it was unreasonable, after stopping drug suspects' vehicles, for officers to aim their guns at the suspects and handcuff them "when they outnumbered the defendants, executed the stop on an open highway during the day, had no tips or observations that the suspects were armed or violent, and the defendants had pulled their cars to a stop off the road and stepped out of their cars in full compliance with police orders."

See Exhibit 7.1 for a comparison of a stop and a formal arrest.

KEY POINTS

2. A person has been "seized" within the meaning of the Fourth Amendment only if, in view of all of the circumstances surrounding the incident, a reasonable person would have believed that he or she was not free to leave. A "stop" is the least intrusive type of seizure of the person governed by the Fourth Amendment.

3. A Fourth Amendment seizure occurs only when there is a governmental termination of freedom of movement through means *intentionally* applied.

4. A law enforcement officer may stop and briefly detain a person for investigative purposes if the officer has a reasonable suspicion supported by articulable facts that criminal activity may be afoot.

5. A law enforcement officer's decision to initiate a stop will be judged against the objective standard: Would the facts available to the officer at the moment of the seizure or the search warrant a person of reasonable caution in the belief that the action taken was appropriate?

6. A law enforcement officer may stop a person based on an informant's tip if, under the totality of the circumstances, the tip, plus any corroboration of the tip by independent police investigation, carries enough indicia of reliability to provide reasonable suspicion of criminal activity.

7. Reasonable suspicion is a less demanding standard than probable cause, not only in the sense that reasonable suspicion can be established with information that is different in quantity or content than that required to establish probable cause, but also in the sense that reasonable suspicion can arise from information that is less reliable than that required to show probable cause.

8. An investigative stop must last no longer than reasonably necessary and must use the least intrusive methods reasonably available, to confirm or dispel the officer's suspicions of criminal activity.

9. An officer who has lawfully stopped a motor vehicle may order both the driver and passengers out of the vehicle pending completion of the stop.

10. An officer making an investigatory stop may use an objectively reasonable degree of force or threat of force to effect the stop.

Determination of Whether to Frisk

The law enforcement officer's determination of whether to frisk a suspect is a separate issue from the determination of whether to stop. It involves a different governmental interest to be served and a different set of factors to be considered by the officer. The governmental interest served by giving police the authority to frisk is that of protecting the officer and others from possible violence by persons being investigated for crime. "[W]e cannot blind ourselves to the need for law enforcement officers to protect themselves and other prospective victims of violence in situations where they may lack probable cause for an arrest." *Terry v. Ohio*, 392 U.S. at 24, 88 S.Ct. at 1881, 20 L.Ed.2d at 907–08.

Balanced against this interest is the citizen's right to privacy, which would necessarily be invaded by giving police the right to frisk suspects. The Supreme Court said, "We must still consider, however, the nature and quality of the intrusion on individual rights which must be accepted if police officers are to be conceded the right to search for weapons in situations where probable cause to arrest for crime is lacking." 392 U.S. at 24, 88 S.Ct. at 1881, 20 L.Ed.2d at 908. As noted earlier, the Court considers the stop-and-frisk procedure to be a serious intrusion on a person's rights, possibly inflicting great indignity and arousing strong resentment.

The Supreme Court considered these competing interests and set out a limited authority for a protective frisk by law enforcement officers in the following terms:

> Our evaluation of the proper balance that has to be struck in this type of case leads us to conclude that there must be a narrowly drawn authority to permit a reasonable search for weapons for the protection of the police officer, where he has reason to believe that he is dealing with an armed and dangerous individual, regardless of whether he has probable cause to arrest the individual for a crime. 392 U.S. at 27, 88 S.Ct. at 1883, 20 L.Ed.2d at 909.

Limited Authority

The law enforcement officer's authority to frisk is a limited and narrowly drawn authority. An officer may not frisk everyone that the officer stops to investigate possible criminal activity. Before deciding to conduct any frisk, an officer must have "reason to believe that he is dealing with an armed and dangerous individual." The courts call this standard "reasonable suspicion." The officer need not be absolutely certain that the individual is armed. Rather, the issue, as stated in *Terry*, is "whether a reasonably prudent man in the circumstances would be warranted in the belief that his safety or that of others was in danger." 392 U.S. at 27, 88 S.Ct. at 1883, 20 L.Ed.2d at 909. Thus, frisks are governed by an objective standard similar to the standard governing stops. An officer must be able to justify a search or frisk of a person by pointing to specific facts and "specific reasonable inferences which he is entitled to draw from the facts in light of his experience." 392 U.S. at 27, 88 S.Ct. at 1883, 20 L.Ed.2d at 909.

Many factors may be considered in deciding whether it is appropriate to frisk a person. Some factors will carry more weight with one officer than with another because of differences in the officers' experience and knowledge. The following is a partial list of considerations in deciding to frisk a person:

- The suspected crime involves the use of weapons.
- The suspect is nervous or edgy about being stopped.
- There is a bulge in the suspect's clothing.
- The suspect's hand is concealed in his or her clothing.
- The suspect does not present satisfactory identification or an adequate explanation for suspicious behavior.

- The area the officer is operating in is known to contain armed persons.
- The suspect exhibits belligerent behavior upon being stopped.
- The officer believes that the suspect may have been armed on a previous occasion.

Justification to frisk usually requires a combination of one or more of these factors or others, evaluated in the light of an officer's experience and knowledge.

Scope of Search

The U.S. Supreme Court requires a frisk to be "a *reasonable* search for weapons for the protection of the police officer" (emphasis supplied). *Terry v. Ohio,* 392 U.S. at 27, 88 S.Ct. at 1883, 20 L.Ed.2d at 909. Since the *only* justifiable purpose of a frisk is the protection of the officer and others, the search must be strictly "limited to that which is necessary for the discovery of weapons which might be used to harm the officer or others nearby." 392 U.S. at 26, 88 S.Ct. at 1882, 20 L.Ed.2d at 908. If the protective search goes beyond what is necessary to determine if the suspect is armed, it is no longer valid under *Terry,* and its fruits will be suppressed.

Therefore, the frisk must initially be limited to a patdown of the *outer* clothing. An officer has no authority to reach inside clothing or into pockets in the *initial* stages of a frisk. During the patdown, if the officer detects an object that feels like a weapon, the officer may then reach inside the clothing or pocket and seize it. If the object is not a weapon but is some other implement of crime (such as a burglar's tool), that implement is admissible in evidence for the crime to which it relates (for example, attempted burglary). The general principle under *Terry* is that, if the officer feels no weaponlike object during the course of the patdown, the officer can no longer have a reasonable fear that the person is armed. Any further search without probable cause would exceed the purpose of the frisk—namely, the protection of the officer and others—and would be unreasonable under the Fourth Amendment. Any evidence obtained from the search would be inadmissible.

The Supreme Court has approved an extension of the permissible scope of a protective search for weapons beyond the person of the suspect to include the passenger compartment of an automobile. In *Michigan v. Long,* 463 U.S. 1032, 103 S.Ct. 3469, 77 L.Ed.2d 1201 (1983), two police officers patrolling at night observed a car traveling erratically and at excessive speed. When the car swerved into a ditch, the officers stopped to investigate. The defendant, who was the only occupant of the car, met the officers at the rear of the car. He did not respond to initial requests to produce his license and registration, but after the request was repeated, he began walking toward the car to obtain the papers. Note that at this point, while the officers had sufficient grounds for a *Terry* stop, they did *not* have sufficient grounds to conduct a frisk for weapons. However, as the officers approached the car, they saw a hunting knife on the floorboard of the driver's side of the car. The Supreme Court held that the officers then had sufficient grounds to conduct a patdown search of the driver and a limited search of the passenger compartment of the car for weapons.

> [T]he search of the passenger compartment of an automobile, limited to those areas in which a weapon may be placed or hidden, is permissible if the police officer possesses a reasonable belief based on 'specific and articulable facts which, taken together with the rational inferences from those facts, reasonably warrant' the officers in believing that the suspect is dangerous and the suspect may gain

immediate control of weapons. 463 U.S. at 1049, 103 S.Ct. at 3480, 77 L.Ed.2d at 1220 (1983).

In reaching this decision, the Court recognized that roadside encounters between police and suspects are especially hazardous and that danger may arise from the possible presence of weapons in the area surrounding a suspect. The Court emphasized, however, that its decision does not mean that the police may conduct automobile searches whenever they conduct an investigative stop. Since the sole justification for a *Terry* search is the protection of police officers and others nearby, officers may conduct such a search only when they have a reasonable suspicion that the suspect is dangerous. Unlike a warrantless search incident to a lawful arrest (see Chapter 8), a *Terry* search is not justified by any need to prevent the disappearance or destruction of evidence of crime.

However, "[i]f, while conducting a legitimate *Terry* search of the interior of the automobile, the officer should . . . discover contraband other than weapons, he clearly cannot be required to ignore the contraband, and the Fourth Amendment does not require its suppression in such circumstances." *Michigan v. Long,* 463 U.S. 1032, 1050, 103 S.Ct. 3469, 3481, 77 L.Ed.2d 1201, 1220 (1983). In the *Long* case, one of the officers shined a flashlight into the car and saw a pouch protruding from under the armrest of the front seat. Since the pouch could have contained a weapon, the officer was justified in lifting the armrest, revealing an open pouch containing marijuana. Having discovered the marijuana pursuant to a legitimate *Terry* frisk, the officer was justified in seizing the marijuana under the plain view doctrine. Under that doctrine, if police are lawfully in a position from which they view an object, if its incriminating character is immediately apparent, and if the officers have a lawful right of access to the object, they may seize it without a warrant. If, however, the police lack probable cause to believe that an object in plain view is contraband without conducting some further search of the object, the plain view doctrine cannot justify its seizure. The plain view doctrine is discussed in Chapter 10.

Relying on the plain view doctrine, the Supreme Court has also approved a so-called plain touch (or plain feel) exception to the rule allowing only the seizure of weapons or weaponlike objects in the course of a frisk. That exception allows the seizure of nonthreatening contraband if its identity as contraband is immediately apparent to the sense of touch as the result of the patdown search. *Minnesota v. Dickerson,* 508 U.S. 366, 113 S.Ct. 2130, 124 L.Ed.2d 334 (1993). This plain touch exception is discussed on pages 367–369.

KEY POINTS

11. A law enforcement officer may conduct a reasonable limited protective search (frisk) for weapons where the officer has reasonable suspicion that he or she is dealing with an armed and dangerous person, regardless of whether the officer has probable cause to arrest.

12. A frisk must initially be limited to a patdown of the outer clothing. If a weaponlike object is detected or if a nonthreatening object's identity as contraband is immediately apparent to the officer's sense of touch, the officer may reach inside the clothing or pocket and seize the object.

13. An officer may search the passenger compartment of a motor vehicle for weapons, if the officer has a reasonable, articulable suspicion that the vehicle's occupant is dangerous and that the occupant may gain immediate control of weapons. The officer may also seize contraband discovered in plain view during the course of such a search.

Specific Circumstances in Stop and Frisk

Stop and frisk encompasses an infinite variety of possible situations. A mere statement of general guidelines may not be sufficient to clearly indicate what behavior is or is not appropriate for a law enforcement officer in a given situation. Therefore, specific situations involving stop and frisk are presented here to show how courts throughout the United States deal with stop and frisk. Actual court decisions are discussed, and emphasis is placed on analyzing the courts' evaluations of the reasonableness of the actions of law enforcement officers. The cases are grouped under various headings indicating major factors influencing the courts' decisions.

Observation of Bulge or Heavy Object

In *State v. Simmons,* 818 P.2d 787 (Idaho App. 1991), a sheriff's department notified local pawn shops to be alert for a described person suspected of burglary of a home and stealing silver dollars. When a pawn shop reported a person matching the description trying to sell silver dollars, detectives went to the pawn shop and saw the suspect apparently attempting to sell coins. He was wearing a long wool coat that seemed out of place for the weather of the day, appeared nervous, and was sweating. One detective observed a bulge in an exterior pocket of the suspect's coat, and when the other detective frisked the suspect, he felt a hard object in the coat pocket that possibly felt like a small gun or knife. He reached his hand in and pulled out a pipe that appeared to be one used for smoking illegal drugs.

The court upheld both the stop and the frisk. The court found that the facts gave the detectives an articulable basis to believe that the person in the store was the burglar of the home. Consequently, they had sufficient grounds to make an investigative *Terry* stop of the suspect to inquire and confirm or dispel their suspicions. When they noticed the bulge in the suspect's overcoat pocket, they had reasonable grounds to be concerned for their safety and to conduct a frisk for weapons. The defendant claimed that wearing a long wool coat on a warm day and being nervous were not suspicious behavior and that the officers had no reason to fear him. Nevertheless, the court said that "taken together . . . all of the information the police had about the case generated a reasonable, articulable suspicion, and a concern for their safety which warranted the intrusion." 818 P.2d at 792.

In *United States v. Barnes,* 909 F.2d 1059 (7th Cir. 1990), the court upheld the seizure of a pistol discovered as the result of a patdown search of a person lawfully stopped for having altered temporary license plates. The frisk was justified by the officer's observation of a "heavy object" protruding from the person's jacket and the person's attempt to reach for his pocket during the initial patdown.

Hand Concealed in Clothing; Force

In *United States v. Laing,* 889 F.2d 281 (D.C. Cir. 1989), a police emergency response team went to an apartment building shortly after midnight to execute a warrant to search apartment 202. From information supporting the warrant, the police believed the occupants were drug dealers armed with automatic weapons. Also, they recognized the apartment's neighborhood as a high-crime area. As police approached the building, they observed the defendant shove his hand into the front of his pants and run from the lobby to apartment 202. The officers reached him outside the apartment, and when he refused their order to lie down, they forced him to the floor and ordered him to remove his hand from his pants. When he refused that order, they forcibly removed his hand and ordered him to stretch out on the floor. When he complied, his pant legs rose up, revealing bags of cocaine in plain view.

The court found adequate justification for both the stop and the frisk of the defendant and found the use of force reasonable.

> The amount of force used to carry out the stop and search must be reasonable, but may include using handcuffs or forcing the detainee to lie down to prevent flight . . . or drawing guns where law officers reasonably believe they are necessary for their protection. . . . Factors that may justify an investigative stop, a search for weapons, or the escalated use of force include the time of day, the "high-crime" nature of the area, an informant's tips that persons might be armed, furtive hand movements, flight or attempted flight by the person sought to be detained, and a pressing need for immediate action. . . .
>
> The officers' treatment of Laing clearly falls within the *Terry* doctrine. Laing's hand movements and flight toward apartment 202, coupled with the time of day and the officers' knowledge of the area and their belief that those in the apartment were heavily armed, make it clear that the officers' actions were motivated by a genuine and well-founded fear that Laing was armed and were reasonable under the circumstances. 889 F.2d at 285.

Innocent Conduct

A series of individual lawful acts may provide reasonable suspicion of criminal activity sufficient to justify a stop, if the overall pattern of those acts is indicative of criminal activity. In *Reid v. Georgia,* the U.S. Supreme Court found no such overall pattern from the following facts: (1) the defendant had arrived from Fort Lauderdale, which a Drug Enforcement Administration (DEA) agent testified is a principal place of origin of cocaine sold elsewhere in the country; (2) the defendant arrived in the early morning, when law enforcement activity is diminished; (3) he and his companion appeared to the agent to be trying to conceal the fact that they were traveling together; and (4) they apparently had no luggage other than their shoulder bags.

> We conclude that the agent could not as a matter of law, have reasonably suspected the petitioner of criminal activity on the basis of these observed circumstances. Of the evidence relied on, only the fact that the petitioner preceded another person and occasionally looked backward at him as they proceeded through the concourse relates to their particular conduct. The other circumstances describe a very large category of presumably innocent travelers, who would be subject to virtually random seizures were the Court to conclude that as little foundation as there was in this case could justify a seizure. Nor can we agree, on this record, that the manner in which the petitioner and his companion walked through the airport reasonably could have led the agent to suspect them of wrongdoing. Although there could, of course, be circumstances in which wholly lawful conduct might justify the suspicion that criminal activity was afoot . . . this is not such a case. The agent's belief that the petitioner and his companion were attempting to conceal the fact that they were traveling together, a belief that was more an "inchoate and unparticularized suspicion or 'hunch,'" . . . than a fair inference in the light of his experience, is simply too

slender a reed to support the seizure in this case. *Reid v. Georgia,* 448 U.S. 438, 441, 100 S.Ct. 2752, 2754, 65 L.Ed.2d 890, 894 (1980).

In *United States v. Sokolow,* 490 U.S. 1, 109 S.Ct. 1581, 104 L.Ed.2d 1 (1989), however, the Court found an overall pattern indicating criminal activity from a similar but more specific and detailed set of facts. In that case, the defendant was stopped by DEA agents upon his arrival at Honolulu International Airport. The agents found 1,063 grams of cocaine in his carry-on luggage. When the defendant was stopped, the agents knew that (1) he paid $2,100 for two airplane tickets from a roll of $20 bills; (2) he traveled under a name that did not match the name under which his telephone number was listed; (3) his original destination was Miami, a source city for illicit drugs; (4) he stayed in Miami for only forty-eight hours, even though a round-trip flight from Honolulu to Miami takes twenty hours; (5) he appeared nervous during his trip; and (6) he checked none of his luggage. The Court found reasonable suspicion to justify the stop, even though there was no evidence of ongoing criminal activity. Applying a totality of the circumstances test, the Court said that "[a]ny of these factors is not by itself proof of any illegal conduct and is quite consistent with innocent travel. But we think taken together they amount to reasonable suspicion." 490 U.S. at 9, 109 S.Ct. at 1586, 104 L.Ed.2d at 11.

In *United States v. Martinez,* 808 F.2d 1050 (5th Cir. 1987), the defendant purchased several chemicals, each with a legitimate use other than the manufacture of illegal drugs. A DEA officer stopped the defendant's car based on the officer's knowledge that there was no legitimate use for the particular *combination* of chemicals. The court held that the stop of the vehicle was justified and that, when the officer smelled an odor he recognized as characteristic of illegal drug manufacture, his temporary detention of the occupants of the car for further investigation was also justified. Therefore, the perception of totally innocent activity may provide to an officer with experience and knowledge about a particular type of crime a reasonable and articulable suspicion of criminal activity sufficient to justify a stop.

Admission by Defendant

The defendant's vehicle was stopped by a police officer for speeding. After stopping the vehicle, the officer walked up to it and the defendant got out, holding his right hand in the pocket of his knee-length coat. The pocket was baggy and sagging. The officer grabbed the defendant's arm and asked him whether he had a gun. The defendant answered yes. The officer then removed the gun and arrested the defendant.

The court assumed without discussion that the stop was reasonable because it was a routine traffic stop. In dealing with the frisk, the court cited *Terry v. Ohio:*

> *Terry v. Ohio* . . . tells us that when a police officer has reason to believe that he is dealing with an armed individual he has a right to search for weapons regardless of whether he has probable cause to arrest that individual for a crime. Here the officer did not merely think he was dealing with an armed person—he knew he was. *State v. Hall,* 476 P.2d 930, 931 (Or.App. 1970).

Traffic Stops and Roadblocks

[A] traffic stop is valid under the Fourth Amendment if the stop is based on an observed traffic violation or if the police officer has reasonable articulable suspicion that a traffic or equipment violation has occurred or is occurring. It is irrelevant, for purposes of Fourth Amendment review, "whether the stop in question is sufficiently ordinary or routine according to the general practice of the police department or the particular officer making the stop." . . . It is also irrelevant that the officer may have had other subjective motives for stopping the vehicle. Our sole inquiry is whether this particular officer had reasonable suspicion that this particular motorist violated "any one of the multitude of applicable traffic and equipment regulations" of the jurisdiction. *United States v. Botero-Ospina,* 71 F.3d 783, 787 (10th Cir. 1995).

Random stops of vehicles, based on whim, hunch, or rumor, to check licenses, registrations, or equipment are not allowed, however. In *Delaware v. Prouse,* 440 U.S. 648, 663, 99 S.Ct. 1391, 1401, 59 L.Ed.2d 660, 673 (1979), the U.S. Supreme Court held

> that except in those situations in which there is at least articulable and reasonable suspicion that a motorist is unlicensed or that an automobile is not registered, or that either the vehicle or an occupant is otherwise subject to seizure for violation of law, stopping an automobile and detaining the driver in order to check his driver's license and the registration of the automobile are unreasonable under the Fourth Amendment.

The Court expressed its concern that random vehicle checks presented a potential danger of arbitrary or discriminatory enforcement of the law. Nevertheless, the Court's decision specifically held open the possibility for states to develop methods for spot checks that involve less intrusion or that do not involve the unconstrained exercise of discretion. The Court suggested as one possible alternative the questioning of all oncoming traffic at roadblock-type stops.

In *Michigan Department of State Police v. Sitz,* 496 U.S. 444, 110 S.Ct. 2481, 110 L.Ed.2d 412 (1990), the Supreme Court approved a highway sobriety checkpoint program with guidelines governing checkpoint operations, site selection, and publicity. During the only operation of the checkpoint at the time of the Court decision, 126 vehicles had passed through the checkpoint, the average delay per vehicle was twenty-five seconds, and two drivers were arrested for driving under the influence.

The Court found that a Fourth Amendment "seizure" occurs when a vehicle is stopped at a checkpoint. The Court used the balancing test of *United States v. Martinez-Fuerte,* 428 U.S. 543, 96 S.Ct. 3074, 49 L.Ed.2d 1116 (1976) and *Brown v. Texas,* 443 U.S. 47, 99 S.Ct. 2637, 61 L.Ed.2d 357 (1979), to determine the reasonableness of such seizures under the Fourth Amendment. That test involves balancing "the gravity of the public concerns served by the seizure, the degree to which the seizure advances the public interest, and the severity of the interference with individual liberty." 443 U.S. at 51, 99 S.Ct. at 2640, 61 L.Ed.2d at 362. The Court found the magnitude of the drunken driving problem beyond dispute. In analyzing "the degree to which the seizure advances the public interest" the Court found in *Sitz* that this balancing factor was "not meant to transfer from politically accountable officials to the courts the decision as to which among reasonable alternative law enforcement techniques should be employed to deal with a serious public danger." 496 U.S. at 453, 110 S.Ct. at 2487, 110 L.Ed.2d at 422. That choice remains with the governmental officials who have a unique understanding of and a responsibility for limited public resources, including a finite number of police officers.

The Supreme Court found that the "objective" intrusion, measured by the duration of the seizure and the intensity of the investigation, was minimal. With respect to the "subjective" intrusion, the Court referred to the following language in *United*

States v. Ortiz, 422 U.S. 891, 894–95, 95 S.Ct. 2585, 2587–88, 45 L.Ed.2d 623, 628 (1975).

> [T]he circumstances surrounding a checkpoint stop and search are far less intrusive than those attending a roving-patrol stop. Roving patrols often operate at night on seldom-traveled roads, and their approach may frighten motorists. At traffic checkpoints the motorist can see that other vehicles are being stopped, he can see visible signs of the officers' authority, and he is much less likely to be frightened or annoyed by the intrusion.

The Court noted that the "fear and surprise" to be considered are not the natural fear of one who has been drinking over the prospect of being stopped at a sobriety checkpoint but, rather, the fear and surprise engendered in law-abiding motorists by the nature of the stop. Other factors considered by the courts in determining whether a roadblock is reasonable are the following:

> (1) The degree of discretion, if any, left to the officer in the field; (2) the location designated for the roadblock; (3) the time and duration of the roadblock; (4) standards set by superior officers; (5) advance notice to the public at large; (6) advance warning to the individual approaching motorist; (7) maintenance of safety conditions; (8) degree of fear or anxiety generated by the mode of operation; (9) average length of time each motorist is detained; (10) physical factors surrounding the location, type and method of operation; (11) the availability of less intrusive methods for combating the problem; (12) the degree of effectiveness of the procedure; and (13) any other relevant circumstances which might bear upon the test. *State v. Deskins,* 673 P.2d 1174, 1185 (Kan. 1983).

Violent Crime

In *People v. Anthony,* 86 Cal.Rptr. 767 (Cal.App. 1970), police officers on patrol received a radio report of an armed robbery in their vicinity. The report came in at about 3:30 A.M., minutes after the robbery happened. The officers had seen only one moving car in the vicinity. They approached the car and noticed that one of the passengers fit the description of the robber given to them over the radio. The car was stopped and the two occupants were instructed to get out. No questions were asked, but one of the officers immediately began a patdown search of the defendant for weapons. Bullets were found, and the defendant was arrested.

The court held that both the stop and the frisk were justified.

> It is well established that circumstances short of probable cause to make an arrest may justify an officer's stopping motorists for questioning, and if the circumstances warrant it, the officer may in self-protection request a suspect to alight from an automobile and to submit to a superficial search for concealed weapons. . . . If the reason for the stop is an articulate suspicion of a crime of violence, and the officer has reason to fear for his personal safety, he may immediately proceed to make a pat-down search for weapons without asking any prior questions. . . . "'There is no reason why an officer, rightfully but forcibly confronting a person suspected of a serious crime, *should have to ask one question and take the risk that the answer might be a bullet.'*" 86 Cal.Rptr. at 773.

To summarize, an officer is not required to ask questions before frisking a suspect if the nature of the crime being investigated is violent and if the officer has a reasonable fear for his or her own safety.

Objects Felt in Frisk

In *People v. Navran,* 483 P.2d 228 (Colo. 1971), police had a certain residence under surveillance as a receiving point for marijuana shipments and had probable cause to arrest the occupant of the residence, although he was absent at the time. The defendants entered the driveway of the residence in a car, proceeded up the driveway, and were attempting to back out when the police stopped them. The officers knew that the defendants were not occupants of the residence, nor were they subjects of the investigation. Nevertheless, the officers caused the defendants to be spread-eagled against their car and searched. One of the officers patted down the defendants' outer and inner clothing. During the frisk of one defendant, the officer felt a lump in a shirt pocket. This lump was later disclosed to be a plastic bag containing marijuana seeds and a package of cigarette rolling papers. The court approved the stop:

> Admittedly the police officers would have been derelict in their duty had they not stopped the defendants' vehicle to determine whether the occupant of the residence, or any other known subject of the investigation, was in the car. Likewise, the officers could have detained the defendants long enough to ascertain why they were on the premises. 483 P.2d at 230.

However, the court found the *frisk* unreasonable:

> It is apparent that the search conducted herein was not the "reasonable search for weapons" contemplated by the *Terry* case. . . . The right to "stop and frisk" is not an open invitation to conduct an unlimited search incident to arrest or a means to effect a search to provide grounds for an arrest. Rather, it is a right to conduct a limited search for weapons. . . . The seeds and cigarette papers seized were not shown by any evidence produced at the hearing to have been taken from the defendants under circumstances which would permit a search for weapons. 483 P.2d at 232.

In another case involving objects felt in a frisk, an officer received a radio report that a murder had just been committed. The officer proceeded to the scene of the crime and observed the defendant, who fit the description that the officer had received on the radio. The officer stopped the defendant and conducted a frisk for weapons. Just after the officer started the search around the defendant's waistband, the defendant abruptly grabbed his outside upper jacket pocket. The officer moved the defendant's hand away from the pocket and from the outside felt a round cylindrical object that the officer surmised was a twelve-gauge shotgun shell. He reached into the pocket and removed the object, at the same time pulling out a marijuana cigarette. The cylindrical object was revealed to be a lipstick container. The defendant was convicted of unauthorized possession of marijuana.

The reasonableness of the stop was not in question. The officer clearly had a duty to investigate the defendant on the basis of the description given over the police radio. With respect to the reasonableness of the frisk, the court found that the officer could have reasonably believed that his safety was in danger and that the frisk was justified:

> Though there is some confusion in the record it is susceptible of the inference that at the moment the officer had not yet eliminated the possibility that defendant was hiding a relatively short shotgun under his jacket. In any event a shotgun was not necessarily the only object which, in combination with a shell, could be used as a weapon. The officer could reasonably believe that any sharp object could be used as a detonator. . . . Hindsight may suggest that, in order to combine maximum personal safety for the officer with a minimum invasion of

defendant's privacy, the officer should first have ascertained what else defendant was carrying. We do not believe, however, that under the circumstances the officer was required to proceed in the coldly logical sequence which may suggest itself after the event. It appears from the record that his reaching into the pocket was almost a reflexive motion, provoked by defendant's sudden gesture toward the pocket and his own feeling of the contents. We cannot say that under all of the circumstances defendant's constitutional rights were violated. *People v. Atmore,* 91 Cal.Rptr. 311, 313–14 (Cal.App. 1970).

Collective Knowledge of Police

A law enforcement officer may stop a person on the basis of a wanted flyer indicating that another law enforcement agency has a reasonable suspicion that the person is or was involved in a crime. In *United States v. Hensley,* 469 U.S. 221, 232, 105 S.Ct. 675, 683–84, 83 L.Ed.2d 604, 614 (1985), the U.S. Supreme Court said: "[I]f a flyer or bulletin has been issued on the basis of articulable facts supporting a reasonable suspicion that the wanted person has committed an offense, then reliance on that flyer or bulletin justifies a stop to check identification . . . to pose questions to the person, or to detain the person briefly while attempting to obtain further information."

The *Hensley* case emphasized that, since criminal suspects are increasingly mobile and increasingly likely to flee across jurisdictional boundaries, police in one jurisdiction should be able to act promptly in reliance on information from another jurisdiction. If a flyer has been issued in the absence of a reasonable suspicion, however, a stop in objective reliance on it would violate the Fourth Amendment, although the officers making the stop would have a good-faith defense to any civil suit arising from the incident. Moreover, a stop made in reliance on a wanted flyer must not be significantly more intrusive than would have been permitted the agency that issued the flyer.

In *United States v. Rodriguez,* 831 F.2d 162 (7th Cir. 1987), the DEA was investigating a drug distribution network and had adequate suspicion to stop the defendant's car to check his identification. A DEA agent asked the state police to conduct the stop, and a state police officer did so. The defendant claimed that the state police officer who stopped his car had inadequate information to justify the stop. The court held as follows:

> [T]he officer making the investigatory stop might reasonably rely on the request of another investigator. The requesting DEA agent had good grounds for articulable suspicion and the detaining officer had a reasonable basis for believing the request to be well-founded—even though she did not personally know the facts giving rise to the suspicion. Unlike *Hensley,* here the automobile to be stopped with its occupant was pointed out specifically by the requesting officer, and the detaining officer knew the requesting officer was coordinating a large investigation with local agencies. The state trooper was therefore merely acting as an "extension" or agent of the DEA agent and she could act on the DEA agent's suspicions. 831 F.2d at 166.

High-Crime Area

In *Brown v. Texas,* 443 U.S. 47, 99 S.Ct. 2637, 61 L.Ed.2d 357 (1979), police on patrol in an area with a high incidence of drug traffic stopped the defendant in an alley while he was walking away from another person. The officer later testified that the situation "looked suspicious and we had never seen that subject in that area before." The U.S. Supreme Court held the stop illegal.

> The fact that appellant was in a neighborhood frequented by drug users, standing alone, is not a basis for concluding that appellant himself was engaged in criminal conduct. In short, the appellant's activity was no different from the activity of other pedestrians in that neighborhood. 443 U.S. at 52, 99 S.Ct. at 2641, 61 L.Ed.2d at 362–63.

Presence in a high-crime area combined with other specific suspicious information, however, may provide a legally justifiable basis for a stop. In *United States v. Stanley*, 915 F.2d 54 (1st Cir. 1990), the court held that an officer was justified in making an investigatory stop of a suspect who was alone in his car, after midnight, in an area frequently used for illegal drug activities. The suspect was leaning over the car's center console, which was slightly illuminated, and appeared to be attempting to hide something when he saw the officer approaching. The court specifically stated that the reputation of the area was an appropriate factor in determining the reasonableness of an investigatory stop. The court also said that the circumstances of the case "are to be viewed through the eyes of a reasonable and cautious police officer on the scene, guided by his experience and training." 915 F.2d at 56.

Association with Known Criminals

In *United States v. Cruz*, 909 F.2d 422 (11th Cir. 1989), the court found adequate grounds, based partially on the suspect's association with known drug dealers, for both a stop and frisk of the suspect under the following circumstances:

> First, the appellant was seen walking together with a known drug dealer who had negotiated with one of the agents for the delivery of fifteen grams of cocaine. Second, the agents certainly understood that the crime of drug trafficking has a particularly violent nature. Finally, the appellant's male companion was seen speaking to one of the dealers whom the agents knew was present to exchange a kilogram of cocaine. While none of these factors, by themselves, necessarily justifies an investigative stop, they are each relevant in the determination of whether the agents had reasonable suspicion to stop the appellant. . . . Thus under all the circumstances known to the officers at the time of the stop, we hold that the officers had reasonable suspicion to stop the appellant who had walked away from the scene of the original arrests.
>
> Because the detective had reasonable suspicion to stop the appellant, she also had the right to make a limited protective search for concealed weapons in order to secure the safety of herself and the safety of those around her. The factors articulated above indicated that the appellant was likely involved in narcotics trafficking and, as is judicially recognized, such individuals are often armed. . . . In addition, in an area known for heavy drug trafficking, the appellant was walking down the street and stopping before a car of known dealers who were at the scene to exchange some cocaine. Under these circumstances, a limited protective search, including a search of the purse, was reasonable. 909 F.2d at 424.

Other Suspicious Circumstances

In *Modesto v. State*, 258 A.2d 287 (Del.Super. 1969), after a high-speed chase, a law enforcement officer stopped the defendant's vehicle for speeding. The officer asked the defendant to get out of the vehicle. The defendant turned toward the officer and proceeded to take off his coat while he was still seated in the car. As he got out of the car, he dropped the coat on the passenger seat where he had been sitting. The officer thought it was peculiar for the defendant to remove his coat on a cold November night, so the officer grabbed the coat as the defendant was getting out. The officer noticed a pistol on the passenger seat, which had been covered by the coat, and the officer seized the pistol.

The court analyzed the reasonableness of both the stop and the frisk:

> The question then becomes whether or not the policeman acted legally when he reached into the car and picked up the defendant's coat. It should be noted that this case involves an incident where the police had a duty to act in stopping the vehicle. It is not a case of general exploratory investigation. Since the police had a duty to act, they also had a right to take reasonable measures to see that their safety was not endangered. . . . In view of the lateness of the hour, the high speed chase, the number of men in the car [3], the fact that the men had been drinking, the police acted reasonably in self protection in asking the gentlemen to get out of the car. Moreover, under these facts, it was reasonable for the police to conduct a limited patdown search for weapons. A person cannot avoid such a search of his clothing by removing his clothing when it necessarily remains in the general vicinity where he is to remain. The police do not have to risk watching three men to make sure that they did not at any time go back to the clothing left in the car. And the mere fact that the coat was removed is another circumstance justifying a self protection frisk search. 258 A.2d at 288.

In another case, two police officers received information over the police radio that a shooting had occurred. The suspects were described as two black men in dark clothing and one Puerto Rican in light clothing. The officers proceeded to the scene of the shooting and observed a black man in dark clothing and a Puerto Rican in light clothing walking together near the scene, acting normally. The only reasons the police had to connect the two men with the reported shooting were that they were walking in the general area and they fit the limited description police had been given. The police had no information about the physical makeups or characteristics of the men they were seeking. The officers stopped the two men, frisked them on the spot, and found a gun in the defendant's belt.

The court discussed the stop and frisk aspects of the case together:

> A policeman may legally stop a person and question him. But he may not without a warrant restrain that person from walking away and "search" his clothing, unless he has "probable cause" to arrest that person or he observes such unusual and suspicious conduct on the part of the person who is stopped and searched that the policeman may reasonably conclude that criminal activity may be afoot, and that the person with whom he is dealing may be armed and dangerous. *Commonwealth v. Berrios*, 263 A.2d 342, 343 (Pa. 1970).

The court found that the circumstances of this case would *not* warrant a reasonably prudent person in the belief that his or her safety or the safety of others was in danger:

> If the policemen were constitutionally justified in searching Berrios under these circumstances, then every Puerto Rican wearing light clothing and walking with a negro in this area could likewise be validly searched. This, we cannot accept. 263 A.2d at 344.

In *United States v. $37,590.00,* 736 F.Supp. 1272 (S.D.N.Y. 1990), the court held that the mere facts that a person clutched his shoulder bags, refused to answer inquiries about them, and reached for them when asked what they contained, provided neither grounds for a stop nor an objective, reasonable, particularized suspicion that the person was armed and dangerous.

KEY POINTS

14. A series of individual lawful acts may provide reasonable suspicion of criminal activity sufficient to justify a stop, if the overall pattern of those acts is indicative of criminal activity.

15. A law enforcement officer may not stop a motor vehicle and detain the driver to check license and registration unless the officer has reasonable, articulable suspicion of criminal activity or unless the stop is conducted in accordance with a properly conducted highway checkpoint program.

16. The test to determine the reasonableness of the stop of a vehicle at a highway checkpoint involves balancing the gravity of the public concerns served by the

seizure, the degree to which the seizure advances the public interest, and the severity of the interference with individual liberty.

17. If a stop is made on a reasonable, articulable suspicion of a crime of violence, and the officer has reason to fear for his or her personal safety, the officer may immediately proceed to make a patdown search for weapons without asking any prior questions.

18. A law enforcement officer may stop a person on the basis of a wanted flyer indicating that another law enforcement agency has a reasonable suspicion that the person is or was involved in a crime.

Miscellaneous Issues in Stop and Frisk

This section discusses the following issues related to stop and frisk: whether *Miranda* warnings are required in the typical stop-and-frisk situation, what considerations are raised by frisking persons of the opposite sex, and how the principles already discussed apply to the investigative detention of containers and other property.

Stop and Frisk and *Miranda*

As discussed in Chapter 13, the *Miranda* warnings must be given before any interrogation of a person in custody or otherwise deprived of freedom of action in any significant way. Are the warnings required to be given before questioning in connection with a stop and frisk? The U.S. Supreme Court said no, holding that the ordinary *Terry*-type investigative stop and the ordinary traffic stop are noncustodial and do not require the administration of *Miranda* warnings. (See pages 445–446.)

If, however, circumstances develop out of an ordinary stop that create a coercive and compelling atmosphere resulting in a significant deprivation of a person's freedom of action, *Miranda* warnings would be required. For example, if the police outnumber the suspects, questioning is sustained and accusatory, force is used, or other coercive factors are present, alone or in combination, then it is very likely the warnings will be required. In other words, in determining custody for *Miranda* purposes, "the ultimate inquiry is simply whether there is a 'formal arrest or restraint on freedom of movement' of the degree associated with a formal arrest." *California v. Beheler,* 463 U.S. 1121, 1125, 103 S.Ct. 3517, 3520, 77 L.Ed.2d 1275, 1279 (1983). Since a stop is by definition a seizure of a lesser degree than a formal arrest, *Miranda* warnings are not required before questioning in connection with a stop.

Frisking of Persons of the Opposite Sex

The frisking of a person of the opposite sex presents a delicate situation for which few specific guidelines are available. On the one hand, in many situations a law enforcement officer could reasonably fear that a person of the opposite sex presented a danger to the officer or to other persons. On the other hand, if routine frisk procedures are used on a person of the opposite sex, an officer may be subjected to charges of assault or sexual misconduct. Therefore, an examination of the outer clothing of a person of the opposite sex should not be undertaken without some degree of certainty that the person is armed. The officer may ask a person to remove an overcoat or other covering, and the officer may squeeze handbags, shoulder bags, or other containers. Containers should not be opened unless a weaponlike object is felt. If the person is arrested, the search and seizure of clothing, pockets, bags, and bundles is governed by the law of search incident to arrest (see Chapter 8).

Containers and Other Property

The general rule regarding the investigatory detention of property was stated by the U.S. Supreme Court:

> Although the Fourth Amendment may permit the detention for a brief period of property on the basis of only "reasonable, articulable suspicion" that it contains contraband or evidence of criminal activity . . . it proscribes—except in certain well-defined circumstances—the search of that property unless accomplished pursuant to judicial warrant issued upon probable cause. *Smith v. Ohio,* 494 U.S. 541, 542, 110 S.Ct. 1288, 1289, 108 L.Ed.2d 464, 467 (1990).

In *United States v. Place,* 462 U.S. 696, 103 S.Ct. 2637, 77 L.Ed.2d 110 (1983), the Supreme Court held that the principles of the *Terry* case apply to the warrantless seizure and limited investigation of personal luggage. In that case, based on information from law enforcement officers in Miami, DEA agents at a New York airport believed that the defendant might be carrying narcotics. Upon the defendant's arrival at the airport, the agents approached him, informed him of their suspicion, and requested and received identification from him. When the defendant refused to consent to a search of his luggage, one of the agents told him that they were going to take the luggage to a federal judge to try to obtain a search warrant. The agents then took the luggage to another airport, where they subjected it to a "sniff test" by a trained narcotics detection dog, and the dog reacted positively to one of the bags. At this point, approximately ninety minutes had elapsed since the seizure of the luggage. The agents later obtained a search warrant for the luggage and, upon opening the luggage, discovered a large quantity of cocaine.

As in the *Terry* case, the Court balanced the nature and quality of the intrusion on the individual's Fourth Amendment interests against the importance of the governmental interests alleged to justify the intrusion. The court found a substantial governmental interest in detecting drug trafficking, a unique problem because it is highly organized and conducted by sophisticated criminal syndicates, the profits are enormous, and drugs are easily concealed. The Court said:

> The context of a particular law enforcement practice, of course, may affect the determination whether a brief intrusion on Fourth Amendment interests on less than probable cause is essential to effective criminal investigation. Because of the inherently transient nature of drug courier activity at airports, allowing police to

make brief investigative stops of persons at airports on reasonable suspicion of drug-trafficking substantially enhances the likelihood that police will be able to prevent the flow of narcotics into distribution channels. 462 U.S. at 704, 103 S.Ct. at 2643, 77 L.Ed.2d at 119.

With respect to the intrusion on Fourth Amendment rights, the Court found that seizures of property can vary in intrusiveness and that some brief detentions of personal effects may be so minimally intrusive that strong, countervailing governmental interests will justify a seizure based only on specific, articulable facts that the property contains contraband or evidence of a crime. The Court held that

> when an officer's observations lead him reasonably to believe that a traveler is carrying luggage that contains narcotics, the principles of *Terry* and its progeny would permit the officer to detain the luggage briefly to investigate the circumstances that aroused his suspicion, provided that the investigative detention is properly limited in scope. 462 U.S. at 706, 103 S.Ct. at 2644, 77 L.Ed.2d at 120.

In addition, the Court specifically found that the brief investigation of the luggage could include a "canine sniff" by a well-trained narcotics detection dog. This procedure was found to be uniquely limited in nature because it does not require opening the luggage, it does not expose noncontraband items to view, and it discloses only the presence or absence of narcotics, a contraband item.

Nevertheless, the Court found that the scope of the investigative detention of the luggage in the *Place* case exceeded the limits established in the *Terry* case, primarily because of the length of the detention. The Court said:

> Although the 90-minute detention of respondent's luggage is sufficient to render the seizure unreasonable, the violation was exacerbated by the failure of the agents to accurately inform respondent of the place to which they were transporting his luggage, of the length of time he might be dispossessed, and of what arrangements would be made for return of the luggage if the investigation dispelled the suspicion. In short, we hold that the detention of respondent's luggage in this case went beyond the narrow authority possessed by police to detain briefly luggage reasonably suspected to contain narcotics. 462 U.S. at 710, 103 S.Ct. at 2646, 77 L.Ed.2d at 122.

Although the Court did not establish any rigid time limitation on an investigative detention, it clearly indicated that efforts of officers to minimize the intrusion on Fourth Amendment rights would be considered in determining the reasonableness of the detention. Time limitations on investigative detentions are discussed earlier under "Extent of Stop."

Note that courts look differently upon detaining a person than detaining (or holding for further examination) an object. When, however, the object is something such as a person's passport, airline ticket, luggage, or driver's license, the person is not really free to leave, even though technically it is the object, not the person, being detained. Courts will more carefully scrutinize detentions of objects that actually detain persons.

In *United States v. Van Leeuwen,* 397 U.S. 249, 90 S.Ct. 1029, 25 L.Ed.2d 282 (1970), a case in which a person was not detained, a postal clerk advised a police officer that he was suspicious of two packages of coins that had just been mailed. The police officer immediately noted that the return address was fictitious and that the person who mailed the packages had Canadian license plates. Later investigation disclosed that the addresses on both packages (one in California, the other in Tennessee) were under investigation for trafficking in illegal coins. On this basis, a search warrant for both packages was obtained, but not until the packages had been detained for slightly more than a day. The defendants were convicted of trafficking in illegal coins.

The Court upheld the warrantless detention of the packages while the investigation was made, recognizing nevertheless that a detention of mail could at some point become an unreasonable seizure of "papers" or "effects" within the meaning of the Fourth Amendment. The Court emphasized, however, that the investigation was conducted promptly and that most of the delay was attributable to the fact that the Tennessee authorities could not be reached until the following day because of a time zone differential. As in the *Place* case, the length of time of the detention was an important determinant of the detention's reasonableness.

In *State v. Phaneuf,* 597 A.2d 55 (Me. 1991), the court held that a detention for several hours of a first-class package at the post office to allow a warrantless canine sniff to detect the presence of drugs was not so intrusive as to be unreasonable. In its decision, the court discussed *United States v. Thomas,* 757 F.2d 1359 (2d Cir. 1985), which excluded from evidence fruits of a search conducted under a warrant based on information obtained from a dog sniff of a door of a suspected drug dealer's apartment. In *Thomas,* the court found that a heightened expectation of privacy in residences prevented officers from bringing a trained dog to the door of the defendant's apartment to sniff for drugs. The Maine court, however, allowed the dog sniff of the package, rejecting the defendant's contention that the Fourth Amendment creates a *heightened* expectation of privacy in the mail akin to that in one's domicile.

Detention and search of carry-on luggage at airline security checkpoints are a special case because of the severe danger presented by allowing weapons or explosives on an airplane.

> Routine security searches at airport checkpoints pass constitutional muster because the compelling public interest in curbing air piracy generally outweighs their limited intrusiveness. . . . Consequently, all carry-on luggage can be subjected to initial x-ray screening for weapons and explosives without offending the Fourth Amendment. In the event the initial x-ray screening is inconclusive as to the presence of weapons or explosives, the luggage may be hand-searched as reasonably required to rule out their presence. . . . Other contraband inadvertently discovered during a routine checkpoint search for weapons and explosives may be seized and introduced in evidence at trial even though unrelated to airline security. *United States v. Doe,* 61 F.3d 107, 109–10 (1st Cir. 1995).

On the other hand, lawful airline security searches of carry-on luggage may not be enlarged or tailored systemically to detect contraband (for instance, narcotics) unrelated to airline security. For example, in *United States v. $124,570 U.S. Currency,* 873 F.2d 1240, 1243–45 (9th Cir. 1989), the court upheld suppression of contraband unrelated to airline security where screeners were rewarded monetarily by law enforcement authorities for detecting such contraband in carry-on luggage.

KEY POINTS

19. *Miranda* warnings are not required before questioning in connection with an ordinary *Terry*-type investigative stop or an ordinary traffic stop.

20. A law enforcement officer may detain property for a brief time if the officer has a reasonable, articulable suspicion that the property contains contraband or evidence of criminal activity. The officer may not search the property without a search warrant but may subject the property to a properly conducted "canine sniff."

Summary

A law enforcement officer may intrude on a person's freedom of action and *stop* the person for purposes of investigating possible criminal behavior even though the officer does not have probable cause to arrest the person. A stop is the least intrusive type of seizure of a person governed by the Fourth Amendment. Under that amendment, a person has been seized only if, in view of all the circumstances surrounding the incident, a reasonable person would have believed that he or she was not free to leave.

The officer making a stop must be able to justify the stop with specific facts and circumstances indicating possibly criminal behavior. This is sometimes called "reasonable, articulable suspicion of criminal activity." The investigative detention must last no longer than necessary to achieve its purpose, and the investigative methods used must be the least intrusive means reasonably available to verify or dispel the officer's suspicion. An officer who has lawfully stopped a motor vehicle may order both the driver and passengers out of the vehicle pending completion of the stop.

A law enforcement officer may, upon less than probable cause, intrude on a person's privacy for purposes of conducting a protective search for weapons, also called a *frisk*. A frisk is not automatically authorized whenever there is a stop. The officer must be able to demonstrate, by specific facts and circumstances, reasonable suspicion that the person might be armed and dangerous. Furthermore, the frisk must be very strictly limited to a protective purpose and, therefore, will initially consist of a patdown search of outer clothing. If a weaponlike object is detected, or if a nonthreatening object's identity as contraband is immediately apparent to the officer's sense of touch, the officer may reach inside the clothing or pocket and seize the object. Evidence of crime seized as the result of a properly conducted frisk will be admissible in court.

The standard to be applied for both the stop and the frisk is whether the action taken by the officer was reasonable at its inception and limited in scope to what was minimally necessary for the accomplishment of the lawful purpose. This standard was developed by the U.S. Supreme Court as a result of a careful balancing of the needs of the police to prevent and investigate crime and to protect themselves and others from danger against the constitutional rights of individuals to their privacy, security, and freedom of action. Achieving an equitable balance in the infinite variety of encounters between police and citizens requires a careful consideration of the totality of the facts and circumstances.

Key Holdings from Major Cases

Terry v. Ohio (1968). "It is quite plain that the Fourth Amendment governs 'seizures' of the person which do not eventuate in a trip to the station house and prosecution for crime—'arrests' in traditional terminology. It must be recognized that whenever a police officer accosts an individual and restrains his freedom to walk away, he has 'seized' that person. And it is nothing less than sheer torture of the English language to suggest that a careful exploration of the outer surfaces of a person's clothing all over his or her body in an attempt to find weapons is not a 'search.' Moreover, it is simply fantastic to urge that such a procedure performed in public by a policeman while the citizen stands helpless, perhaps facing a wall with his hands raised, is a 'petty indignity.' It is a serious intrusion upon the sanctity of the person, which may inflict great indignity and arouse strong resentment, and it is not to be undertaken lightly." 392 U.S. 1, 16–17, 88 S.Ct. 1868, 1877, 20 L.Ed.2d 889, 903.

"Obviously not all personal intercourse between policemen and citizens involves 'seizures' of persons. Only when the officer, by means of physical force or show of authority, has in some way restrained the liberty of a citizen may we conclude that a 'seizure' has occurred." 392 U.S. at 19 n.16, 88 S.Ct. at 1879 n.16, 20 L.Ed.2d at 905 n.16.

"[W]e deal here with an entire rubric of police conduct—necessarily swift action based upon the on-the-spot observations of the officer on the beat—which historically has not been, and as a practical matter could not be, subjected to the warrant procedure. Instead, the conduct involved in this case must be tested by the Fourth Amendment's general proscription against unreasonable searches and seizures." 392 U.S. at 20, 88 S.Ct. at 1879, 20 L.Ed.2d at 905.

"[I]n justifying the particular intrusion the police officer must be able to point to specific and articulable facts which, taken together with rational inferences from those facts, reasonably warrant that intrusion." 392 U.S. at 21, 88 S.Ct. at 1880, 20 L.Ed.2d at 906.

The police officer's decision to initiate a stop will be judged against the following objective standard: "[W]ould the facts available to the officer at the moment of the seizure or the search 'warrant a man of reasonable caution in the belief' that the action taken was appropriate?" 392 U.S. at 21–22, 88 S.Ct. at 1880, 20 L.Ed.2d at 906.

"[I]t is this interest [crime prevention and detection] which underlies the recognition that a police officer may in appropriate circumstances and in an appropriate manner approach a person for purposes of investigating possibly criminal behavior even though there is no probable cause to make an arrest." 392 U.S. at 22, 88 S.Ct. at 1880, 20 L.Ed.2d at 906–07.

"Certainly it would be unreasonable to require that police officers take unnecessary risks in the performance of their duties. American criminals have a long tradition of armed violence, and every year in this country many law enforcement officers are killed in the line of duty, and thousands more are wounded." 392 U.S. at 23, 88 S.Ct. at 1881, 20 L.Ed.2d at 907.

"[W]e cannot blind ourselves to the need for law enforcement officers to protect themselves and other prospective victims of violence in situations where they may lack probable cause for an arrest." 392 U.S. at 24, 88 S.Ct. at 1881, 20 L.Ed.2d at 907–08.

"Even a limited search of the outer clothing for weapons constitutes a severe, though brief, intrusion upon cherished personal security, and it must surely be an annoying, frightening, and perhaps humiliating experience." 392 U.S. at 24–25, 88 S.Ct. at 1881–82, 20 L.Ed.2d at 908.

"Our evaluation of the proper balance that has to be struck in this type of case leads us to conclude that there must be a narrowly drawn authority to permit a reasonable search for weapons for the protection of the police officer, where he has reason to believe that he is dealing with an armed and dangerous individual, regardless of whether he has probable cause to arrest the individual for a crime." 392 U.S. at 27, 88 S.Ct. at 1883, 20 L.Ed.2d at 909.

The issue in determining an officer's authority to frisk is "whether a reasonably prudent man in the circumstances would be warranted in the belief that his safety or that of others was in danger." 392 U.S. at 27, 88 S.Ct. at 1883, 20 L.Ed.2d at 909.

An officer must be able to justify a search or frisk of a person by pointing to specific facts and "specific reasonable inferences which he is entitled to draw from the facts in light of his experience." 392 U.S. at 27, 88 S.Ct. at 1883, 20 L.Ed.2d at 909.

"[W]here a police officer observes unusual conduct which leads him reasonably to conclude in light of his experience that criminal activity may be afoot and that the persons with whom he is dealing may be armed and presently dangerous, where in the course of investigating this behavior he identifies himself as a policeman and makes reasonable inquiries, and where nothing in the initial stages of the encounter serves to dispel his reasonable fear for his own or other's safety, he is entitled for the protection of himself and others in the area to conduct a carefully limited search of the outer clothing of such persons in an attempt to discover weapons which might be used to assault him." 392 U.S. at 30, 88 S.Ct. at 1884–85, 20 L.Ed.2d at 911.

Sibron v. New York (1968). "The inference that persons who talk to narcotics addicts are engaged in criminal traffic in narcotics is simply not the sort of reasonable inference required to support an intrusion by the police upon an individual's personal security." 392 U.S. 40, 62, 88 S.Ct. 1889, 1902, 20 L.Ed.2d 917, 934.

United States v. Mendenhall (1980). "[A] person has been 'seized' within the meaning of the Fourth Amendment only if, in view of all of the circumstances surrounding the incident, a reasonable person would have believed that he was not free to leave. Examples of circumstances that might indicate a seizure even where the person did not attempt to leave, would be the threatening presence of several officers, the display of a weapon by an officer, some physical touching of the person of the citizen, or the use of language or tone of voice indicating that compliance with the officer's request might be compelled. . . . In the absence of some such evidence, otherwise inoffensive contact between a member of the public and the police cannot, as a matter of law, amount to a seizure of that person." 446 U.S. 544, 554–55, 100 S.Ct. 1870, 1877, 64 L.Ed.2d 497, 509.

California v. Hodari D. (1991). "*Mendenhall* establishes that the test for existence of a 'show of authority' is an objective one: not whether the citizen perceived that he was being ordered to restrict his movement, but whether the officer's words and actions would have conveyed that to a reasonable person." 499 U.S. 621, 628, 111 S.Ct. 1547, 1551, 113 L.Ed.2d 690, 698.

Michigan v. Chesternut (1988). "The [*Mendenhall*] test is necessarily imprecise, because it is designed to assess the coercive effect of police conduct, taken as a whole, rather than to focus on particular details of that conduct in isolation. Moreover, what constitutes a restraint on liberty prompting a person to conclude that he is not free to 'leave' will vary, not only with the particular police conduct at issue, but also with the setting in which the conduct occurs." 486 U.S. 567, 573, 108 S.Ct. 1975, 1979, 100 L.Ed.2d 565, 572.

"While the very presence of a police car driving parallel to a running pedestrian could be somewhat intimidating, this kind of police presence does not, standing alone, constitute a seizure." 486 U.S. at 575, 108 S.Ct. at 1980, 100 L.Ed.2d at 573.

Florida v. Bostick (1991). "[N]o seizure occurs when police ask questions of an individual, ask to examine the individual's identification, and request consent to search his or her luggage—so long as the officers do not convey a message that compliance with their requests is required." 501 U.S. 429, 437, 111 S.Ct. 2382, 2388, 115 L.Ed.2d 389, 400.

"[I]n order to determine whether a particular encounter constitutes a seizure, a court must consider all the circumstances surrounding the encounter to determine whether the police conduct would have communicated to a reasonable person that the person was not free to decline the officers' requests or otherwise terminate the encounter. That rule applies to encounters that take place on a city street or in an airport lobby, and it applies equally to encounters on a bus." 501 U.S. at 439–40, 111 S.Ct. at 2389, 115 L.Ed.2d at 401–02.

Brower v. County of Inyo (1989). "[A] Fourth Amendment seizure does not occur whenever there is a governmentally caused termination of an individual's freedom of movement . . . nor even whenever there is a governmentally caused and governmentally *desired* termination of an individual's freedom of movement . . . but only when there is a governmental termination of freedom of movement *through means intentionally applied.*" 489 U.S. 593, 596–97, 109 S.Ct. 1378, 1381, 103 L.Ed.2d 628, 635.

United States v. Sokolow (1989). Reasonable suspicion is "considerably less than proof of wrongdoing by a preponderance of the evidence" [and] "is obviously less demanding than that for probable cause." 490 U.S. 1, 7, 109 S.Ct. 1581, 1585, 104 L.Ed.2d 1, 10.

United States v. Hensley (1985). "[W]here police have been unable to locate a person suspected of involvement in a past crime, the ability to briefly stop that person, ask questions, or check identification in the absence of probable cause promotes the strong government interest in solving crimes and bringing offenders to justice. Restraining police action until after probable cause is obtained would not only hinder the investigation, but might also enable the suspect to flee in the interim and to remain at large. Particularly in the context of felonies or crimes involving a threat to public safety, it is in the public interest that the crime be solved and the suspect detained as promptly as possible. The law enforcement interests at stake in these circumstances outweigh the individual's interest to be free of a stop and detention that is no more extensive than permissible in the investigation of imminent or ongoing crimes." 469 U.S. 221, 229, 105 S.Ct. 675, 681, 83 L.Ed.2d 604, 612.

"[I]f a flyer or bulletin has been issued on the basis of articulable facts supporting a reasonable suspicion that the wanted person has committed an offense, then reliance on that flyer or bulletin justifies a stop to check identification . . . to pose questions to the person, or to detain the person briefly while attempting to obtain further information." 469 U.S. at 232, 105 S.Ct. at 683–84, 83 L.Ed.2d at 614.

Alabama v. White (1990). "*Gates* made clear . . . that those factors that had been considered critical under *Aguilar* and *Spinelli*—an informant's 'veracity,' 'reliability,' and 'basis of knowledge'—remain 'highly relevant in determining the value of his report.' . . . These factors are also relevant in the reasonable suspicion context, although allowance must be made in applying them for the lesser showing required to meet that standard." 496 U.S. 325, 328–29, 110 S.Ct. 2412, 2415, 110 L.Ed.2d 301, 308.

"Reasonable suspicion is a less demanding standard than probable cause not only in the sense that reasonable suspicion can be established with information that is different in quantity or content than that required to establish probable cause, but also in the sense that reasonable suspicion can arise from information that is less reliable than that required to show probable cause. . . . Reasonable suspicion, like probable cause, is dependent upon both the content of information possessed by police and its degree of reliability. Both factors—quantity and quality are considered in the 'totality of the circumstances—the whole picture,' . . . that must be taken into account when evaluating whether there is reasonable suspicion. Thus, if a tip has a relatively low degree of reliability, more information will be required to establish the requisite quantum of suspicion than would be required if the tip were more reliable. The *Gates* Court applied its totality of the circumstances approach in this manner, taking into account the facts known to the officers from personal observation, and giving the anonymous tip the weight it deserved in light of its indicia of reliability as established through independent police work. The same approach applies in the reasonable suspicion context, the only difference being the level of suspicion that must be established. Contrary to the court below, we conclude that when the officers stopped the respondent, the anonymous tip had been sufficiently corroborated to furnish reasonable suspicion that respondent was engaged in criminal activity and that the investigative stop therefore did not violate the Fourth Amendment." 496 U.S. at 330–31, 110 S.Ct. at 2416, 110 L.Ed.2d at 309.

Florida v. Royer (1983). "[A]n investigative detention must be temporary and last no longer than is necessary to effectuate the purpose of the stop. Similarly, the investigative methods employed should be the least intrusive means reasonably available to verify or dispel the officer's suspicion in a short period of time. . . . It is the State's burden to demonstrate that the seizure it seeks to justify on the basis of a reasonable suspicion was sufficiently limited in scope and duration to satisfy the conditions of an investigative seizure." 460 U.S. 491, 500, 103 S.Ct. 1319, 1325, 75 L.Ed.2d 229, 238.

Pennsylvania v. Mimms (1977). The additional intrusion of ordering the driver of a lawfully stopped vehicle out of the vehicle "can only be described as de minimis. The driver is being asked to expose to view very little more of his person than is already exposed. The police have already lawfully decided that the driver shall be briefly detained; the only question is whether he shall spend that period sitting in the driver's seat of his car or standing along side it. Not only is the insistence of the police on the latter choice not a 'serious intrusion upon the sanctity of the person,' but it hardly rises to the level of a '"petty indignity."' . . . What is at most a mere inconvenience cannot prevail when balanced against legitimate concerns for the officer's safety." 434 U.S. 106, 111, 98 S.Ct. 330, 333, 54 L.Ed.2d 331, 337.

Maryland v. Wilson (1997). "[A]n officer making a traffic stop may order passengers to get out of the car pending completion of the stop." 519 U.S. 408, ___, 117 S.Ct. 882, 886, 137 L.Ed.2d 41, 48.

United States v. Sharpe (1985). "In assessing whether a detention is too long in duration to be justified as an investigative stop, we consider it appropriate to examine whether the police diligently pursued a means of investigation that was likely to confirm or dispel their suspicions quickly, during which time it was necessary to detain the defendant. . . . A court making this assessment should take care to consider whether the police are acting in a swiftly developing situation and in such cases the court should not indulge in unrealistic second-guessing. . . . The question is not simply whether some other alternative was available, but whether the police acted unreasonably in failing to recognize or to pursue it." 470 U.S. 675, 686–87,105 S.Ct. 1568, 1575–76, 84 L.Ed.2d 605, 615–16.

Graham v. Connor (1989). "The calculus of reasonableness must embody allowance for the fact that police officers are often forced to make split-second judgments—in circumstances that are tense, uncertain, and rapidly evolving—about the amount of force that is necessary in a particular situation." 490 U.S. 386, 396–97, 109 S.Ct. 1865, 1872, 104 L.Ed.2d 443, 455–56.

"[T]he 'reasonableness' inquiry in an excessive force case is an objective one: the question is whether the officers' actions are 'objectively reasonable' in light of the facts and circumstances confronting them, without regard to their underlying intent or motivation." 490 U.S. at 397, 109 S.Ct. at 1872, 104 L.Ed.2d at 456.

Michigan v. Long (1983). "[T]he search of the passenger compartment of an automobile, limited to those areas in which a weapon may be placed or hidden, is permissible if the police officer possesses a reasonable belief based on 'specific and articulable facts which, taken together with the rational inferences from those facts, reasonably warrant' the officers in believing that the suspect is dangerous and the suspect may gain immediate control of weapons." 463 U.S. 1032, 1049, 103 S.Ct. 3469, 3480, 77 L.Ed.2d 1201, 1220.

"If, while conducting a legitimate *Terry* search of the interior of the automobile, the officer should . . . discover contraband other than weapons, he clearly cannot be required to ignore the contraband, and the Fourth Amendment does not require its suppression in such circumstances." 463 U.S. at 1050, 103 S.Ct. at 3481, 77 L.Ed.2d at 1220.

Delaware v. Prouse (1979). "[E]xcept in those situations in which there is at least articulable and reasonable suspicion that a motorist is unlicensed or that an automobile is not

registered, or that either the vehicle or an occupant is otherwise subject to seizure for violation of law, stopping an automobile and detaining the driver in order to check his driver's license and the registration of the automobile are unreasonable under the Fourth Amendment." 440 U.S. 648, 663, 99 S.Ct. 1391, 1401, 59 L.Ed.2d 660, 673.

California v. Beheler (1983). "Although the circumstances of each case must certainly influence a determination of whether a suspect is 'in custody' for purposes of receiving *Miranda* protection, the ultimate inquiry is simply whether there is a 'formal arrest or restraint on freedom of movement' of the degree associated with a formal arrest." 463 U.S. 1121, 1125, 103 S.Ct. 3517, 3520, 77 L.Ed.2d 1275, 1279.

Smith v. Ohio (1990). "Although the Fourth Amendment may permit the detention for a brief period of property on the basis of only 'reasonable, articulable suspicion' that it contains contraband or evidence of criminal activity . . . it proscribes—except in certain well-defined circumstances—the search of that property unless accomplished pursuant to judicial warrant issued upon probable cause." 494 U.S. 541, 542, 110 S.Ct. 1288, 1289, 108 L.Ed.2d 464, 467.

United States v. Place (1983). "The context of a particular law enforcement practice, of course, may affect the determination whether a brief intrusion on Fourth Amendment interests on less than probable cause is essential to effective criminal investigation. Because of the inherently transient nature of drug courier activity at airports, allowing police to make brief investigative stops of persons at airports on reasonable suspicion of drug-trafficking substantially enhances the likelihood that police will be able to prevent the flow of narcotics into distribution channels." 462 U.S. 696, 704, 103 S.Ct. 2637, 2643, 77 L.Ed.2d 110, 119.

"[W]hen an officer's observations lead him reasonably to believe that a traveler is carrying luggage that contains narcotics, the principles of Terry and its progeny would permit the officer to detain the luggage briefly to investigate the circumstances that aroused his suspicion, provided that the investigative detention is properly limited in scope." 462 U.S. at 706, 103 S.Ct. at 2644, 77 L.Ed.2d at 120.

"Although the 90-minute detention of respondent's luggage is sufficient to render the seizure unreasonable, the violation was exacerbated by the failure of the agents to accurately inform respondent of the place to which they were transporting his luggage, of the length of time he might be dispossessed, and of what arrangements would be made for return of the luggage if the investigation dispelled the suspicion. In short, we hold that the detention of respondent's luggage in this case went beyond the narrow authority possessed by police to detain briefly luggage reasonably suspected to contain narcotics." 462 U.S. at 710, 103 S.Ct. at 2646, 77 L.Ed.2d at 122.

United States v. Van Leeuwen (1970). "The rule of our decision certainly is not that first-class mail can be detained

29 hours after mailing in order to obtain the search warrant needed for its inspection. We only hold that on the facts of this case—the nature of the mailings, their suspicious character, the fact that there were two packages going to separate destinations, the unavoidable delay in contacting the more distant of the two destinations, the distance between Mt. Vernon and Seattle—a 29-hour delay between the mailings and the service of the warrant cannot be said to be 'unreasonable'

within the meaning of the Fourth Amendment. Detention for this limited time was, indeed, the prudent act rather than letting the packages enter the mails and then, in case the initial suspicions were confirmed, trying to locate them en route and enlisting the help of distant federal officials in serving the warrant." 397 U.S. 249, 253, 90 S.Ct. 1029, 1032–33, 25 L.Ed.2d 282, 286.

Review and Discussion Questions

1. Name some of the factors that might distinguish a *Terry*-type investigative stop from a seizure tantamount to an arrest.

2. In determining whether he or she has a reasonable suspicion that criminal activity is afoot, must an officer have a particular crime in mind?

3. Is less evidence required to support an investigative stop for a suspected violent crime than for a minor misdemeanor?

4. Can a lawfully stopped suspect be transported by the police to a crime scene for identification by victims or witnesses? Or would this action convert the stop into a seizure tantamount to arrest?

5. How does the indicia of reliability test for evaluating an informant's tip in the stop-and-frisk situation differ from the totality-of-the-circumstances test of the *Gates* case discussed in Chapter 6? Why should there be different tests?

6. Must there be an immediate possibility of criminal activity to justify a *Terry*-type investigative stop, or would a possibility of criminal activity at some time in the future suffice?

7. Assuming that a frisk of a person is warranted, how extensive a search is permitted? Can the officer look for razor blades, nails, vials of acid, or mace containers? Can the officer look into briefcases, shopping bags, purses, hatbands, and other containers?

8. Should an officer conducting a roadblock-type stop to check licenses and registrations be allowed to order every driver stopped out of his or her vehicle? What factors might provide justification to frisk a driver or passengers in this situation?

9. Assuming that a law enforcement officer reasonably believes that a suspect is dangerous and may gain immediate control of weapons from an automobile, how extensive a protective search of the automobile may be made? May the officer look into suitcases and other containers?

10. If law enforcement officers have a reasonable suspicion that a package contains contraband, does the length of time that they may detain the package for investigation depend upon whether a person is carrying the package?

REAL-LIFE FACT SITUATIONS

1. Roane County Deputy Sheriff Jack Stockton testified that he worked for the Harriman Police Department on September 29, 1993, and conducted surveillance of a house where drugs were reportedly being distributed. While conducting the surveillance, he saw a car drop the defendant off in the street in front of the house. He said that the defendant entered the house for a couple of minutes and then returned to the street. He said that the defendant was standing in the middle of the road and that he thought she saw him. He recalled that he decided

to approach the defendant to get her out of the way before the people in the house discovered the surveillance. He said that he shined his flashlight on her as he was approaching her and that he noticed a shiny object in her right front pocket. He admitted that he did not know what the object was immediately, but when he got close to her, he recognized that it was a pipe used to smoke crack cocaine. He said that the defendant was nervous and fidgety and that he grabbed the object from her pocket and then frisked her. He recalled finding a small piece of crack cocaine in her pocket. He said that after he took the pipe and cocaine from the defendant, her ride arrived, and he allowed her to leave. Approximately twenty days later, Officer Stockton obtained a warrant against the defendant for possession of cocaine.

On cross-examination, Officer Stockton admitted that he did not stop any of the other people he had seen enter and leave the house that night and reiterated that he approached the defendant because she was a threat to his surveillance. He recalled that the pipe was sticking out of her pocket an inch when he noticed it. He admitted that he first thought that the shiny object was a weapon and that he realized it was a pipe used to smoke crack cocaine when he frisked her. However, he also stated that he recognized that the object was used to smoke crack cocaine when he got close enough to the defendant. The officer testified that, after he confiscated the pipe, he continued to search the defendant for drugs, not for weapons.

On redirect examination, Officer Stockton clarified that he removed the pipe from the defendant's pocket because he recognized what it was when he approached her. During recross-examination, the officer testified that he did not recall whether he told the defendant to stop when he approached her but said that he ran up to her and that she knew she could not go anywhere because she knew who he was and that he wanted her. Should the defendant's motion to suppress the cocaine be granted? *State v. Moore*, 949 S.W.2d 704 (Tenn.Cr.App. 1997).

2. At 1:15 A.M., on May 21, 1993, Manchester Police Officers Robert Oxley and George Baker saw the defendant emerge from 184 Cedar Street. The officers knew that building as a place where drug sales occurred at "all hours of the night." Each officer had made a number of drug arrests in the building. Because of this fact, the officers were suspicious of anyone leaving that building at 1:15 A.M., so they monitored the defendant's movements.

After leaving the building, the defendant walked in the direction of the police cruiser. He looked at the cruiser, then reversed his direction and started walking in the opposite direction. Officer Baker drove the cruiser around the block, expecting to see the defendant walking toward him as the cruiser approached. Instead, however, the defendant was walking in the same direction he had been when he left the building. This time, he was walking "in a hurried fashion." The defendant entered the front passenger seat of a car that was parked in front of 162 Cedar Street. Two other people were in the car, the driver and a person in the back seat.

Officer Baker drove the cruiser behind the other car and illuminated it with the cruiser's exterior "takedown" lights. Once the vehicle was illuminated, the officers observed the defendant acting "very nervous," looking back and forth, and leaning toward the floor. Both offi-

cers left the cruiser and Officer Oxley asked the defendant to get out of the car. When he complied, the officer saw a small plastic bag on the floor in front of the defendant's seat. Officer Oxley recognized the white substance in the bag as cocaine. He arrested the defendant after a field test confirmed the presence of cocaine in the bag. Should the defendant's motion to suppress the cocaine be granted? *State v. Vadnais*, 677 A.2d 155 (N.H. 1996).

3. Harris was arrested at approximately 2:15 P.M. on August 17, 1994, when two police officers observed him dancing in the street near the 900 block of Muncie Avenue. When the squad car pulled alongside Harris, the officers noticed that he had a metal object in his hand that they described as being consistent with a crack pipe made from antennas that have been broken off vehicles. The officers began questioning Harris and formed the opinion that he was intoxicated based on his actions. When they asked him what he was holding in his left hand, he opened his hand to display the item and said, "My medicine stick." The police officers arrested him for possession of drug paraphernalia and for further investigation of his intoxication. During a search incident to arrest, an officer found a pill bottle in Harris's pocket that contained twenty-three rocks of crack cocaine. Harris contends that the officers did not have adequate facts in their possession to justify a temporary investigative detention, and so the contraband obtained as a result of the search was improperly admitted into evidence. Is Harris correct? *Harris v. State*, 913 S.W.2d 706 (Tex.App.—Texarkana 1995).

4. In early August, 1996, police officers in Plaquemines Parish received information that "Mattie" Clausen was selling cocaine and LSD in large amounts. However, the officers were unable to confirm this information during the next two months. On October 1, 1996, the officers received information from a known and reliable informant that Clausen was driving to New Orleans that evening to buy some LSD. The officers established a surveillance and followed Clausen from Plaquemines Parish to the French Quarter in New Orleans, where they observed him enter a building on Dumaine Street. A short time later Clausen left the building, reentered his car, and drove back toward Plaquemines Parish. The officers followed, and sometime after he had entered the parish, the officers saw him make a left turn without using his turn signal. In addition, the officer could see he was not wearing a seat belt.

The officers stopped Clausen, asked him to exit his car, and advised him he was under investigation for narcotics activity. Officer Mike Buras did a quick patdown frisk of the defendant and felt something square inside one of his pockets. The officer admitted he could not tell what the object was. He testified he asked Clausen what was in his pocket, and Clausen pulled out a small wooden box with a lid which the officer recognized as drug paraphernalia. The officer testified, however, that there was only an odor or at most a residue of marijuana inside the box. The officer seized the box. He also produced a form for consent to search Clausen's car, which Clausen signed. However, there is no indication from the transcript that any evidence was seized from the car.

Other officers arrived, and one of those officers searched Clausen. Inside one pocket of Clausen's pants the officer found two baggies containing a total of twenty "hits" of LSD. Should the evidence obtained in the two searches of Clausen be suppressed? *State v. Clausen,* 697 So.2d 1066 (La.App. 4.Cir. 1997).

5. On May 16, 1995, at approximately 4:30 P.M., Officer Jones saw defendant, Gilbert Avila, walking across a parking lot. The officer observed defendant littering. Moreover, the officer noted that defendant's manner while littering was "suspicious." Defendant first walked to the passenger side of a truck, then to the driver's side, then back to the front of the truck with his hand directly in front of his body. Finally, he dropped a white envelope from his waist. Officer Jones contacted defendant while the defendant was standing in the open driver's side door of the truck. The officer told defendant that he had observed him littering and asked defendant for identification. The defendant provided a driver's license in the name of Joseph Vargas. While the officer was talking to the defendant, he observed what appeared to be two containers of alcohol on the front seat of the truck. From where the officer was standing, he could not tell if they were full or empty.

Next, the officer observed "a long black metal object" that was similar to a "Mag" flashlight, approximately eight to ten inches from the defendant's left hand, behind the defendant in the truck. The officer became concerned for his safety and inquired as to the nature of the object. Without turning around, the defendant said that he did not know what the object was. Defendant further stated that the truck did not belong to him but belonged to a friend of his. The defendant stated that he had illegal alcohol in the truck but that he did not have any weapons.

The officer told the defendant to walk to the back of the truck. The defendant complied, and when he reached the rear of the truck he "assumed the position" without being asked to. The officer then conducted a pat-down search of the defendant's person for weapons. While patting down defendant, the officer felt a bulky and somewhat hard object at defendant's ankle. The officer asked what the object was, and the defendant's reply was unclear. The officer repeated his question, and the defendant said, "'It is meth.'" After finding two more bulges,

the officer handcuffed the defendant and removed three baggies of methamphetamine. The defendant was placed under arrest, and later more methamphetamine and a gun were found in his vehicle.

The defendant contends the trial court erroneously denied his suppression motion because (1) the officer was not justified in performing a pat-down search for weapons under the circumstances, and (2) even if the pat-down search was justified, the officer's inquiry into the nature of the lump exceeded the limits of a pat-down search. Is the defendant correct? *People v. Avila,* 68 Cal.Rptr 432 (Cal.App. 4 Dist. 1997).

6. While conducting surveillance of the 2100 block of Main Street in the City of Lynchburg, Investigator Thomas observed two men conducting what he believed to be drug transactions in front of the residence at 2110 Main Street. The general area was known to the officers as an open air drug market, and the residence at 2110 Main Street was a reputed crack house. Thomas relayed his observation and a description of the two suspects to members of a narcotics strike force who were waiting in a staging area nearby. During his surveillance, Thomas observed appellant standing among a group of eight other individuals on the sidewalk in front of the residence. Thomas testified that appellant had been standing near the residence for at least fifteen minutes but that he had not been involved in the apparent drug dealing. Thomas further stated that appellant had no contact with the two men Thomas suspected of drug dealing and that appellant had done nothing "except stand there."

Officer Duff was one of four members of the strike force responding to Thomas' call. Thomas informed Duff that the two suspects had joined the group of individuals standing in front of the residence. Duff testified that, in addition to the group on the sidewalk, approximately three other individuals were seated in a van parked at the curb and four or five others occupied the front porch area of the residence. Duff knew the area was an open air drug market, he knew shots had been fired there in the past, and, on a previous occasion, Duff had seen a pellet gun in a mailbox located only a few feet from the group on the sidewalk.

Duff testified that "[d]ue to the nature and reputation of the area and my experience with the area and, also, some of the people that I had observed there it was our decision to place all of the people that were on the sidewalk on the ground in a prone position momentarily for our safety and their safety. . . . We were going to secure the two target suspects and then make the scene secure, either by having people leave or making sure that there were no weapons with the people that decided to stay."

As he approached the scene, Duff ordered the individuals on the sidewalk, including appellant, to lie on the ground in a prone position and extend their arms. Duff testified that the officers would not have pursued anyone who chose to leave the scene other than the two suspects. He acknowledged, however, that no one left or was told they could leave. The appellant immediately assumed a prone position as Duff ordered, but he kept his hands underneath his torso. Duff approached the appellant, again ordering him to extend his arms. Appellant complied as Duff grabbed his arm and rolled him onto his right side. In search of a weapon, Duff found no weapons on the ground under the appellant. Still concerned about his safety and the possibility of finding a weapon, Duff conducted a pat-down search of appellant's waistline and of the left front of his pants. As a result of the search, Duff seized the cocaine used to support appellant's conviction. The trial court denied appellant's motion to suppress the cocaine, finding "that the police officers . . . acted properly and had reasonable probability or reasonable basis to believe that the area involved was very dangerous; that it was a high crime area." Should the appellant's motion to suppress the cocaine be granted? *Welshman v. Commonwealth*, 491 S.E.2d 294 (Va.App. 1997).

CHAPTER EIGHT

Search Incident to Arrest

OBJECTIVES

1. Understand the allowable purposes of a search incident to arrest as set forth in the holding of *Chimel v. California*.

2. Know the limits on the allowable scope of a search incident to arrest with respect to the following:

    a. Property that may be searched for and seized

    b. Search and seizure of the arrestee's body and items in or on the body or associated with or carried on the body

    c. Search of the area into which the arrestee might reach

        (1) Motor vehicles

        (2) Other persons

    d. Search of other areas of the premises

3. Be familiar with other requirements of a valid search incident to arrest such as the following:

    a. Lawful custodial arrest

    b. Contemporaneousness of arrest and search

    c. Who may conduct the search

    d. Limitations on use of force

OUTLINE

Chimel v. California

Another important exception to the Fourth Amendment warrant requirement is a
search incident to arrest. Since 1969, the law of search incident to arrest has been controlled by the U.S. Supreme Court case of *Chimel v. California*. In that case, law enforcement officers arrived at the defendant's home with a warrant for his arrest for the
burglary of a coin shop. The defendant was not at home, but his wife let the officers
in to wait for him. When the defendant arrived, the officers handed him the warrant
and asked whether they could look around. He objected, but the officers searched the
entire house anyway on the basis of the lawful arrest. The officers found coins and
other items that were later used in court to obtain a conviction against the defendant.
The U.S. Supreme Court found the search of the entire house unreasonable.

> When an arrest is made, it is reasonable for the arresting officer to search the
> person arrested in order to remove any weapons that the latter might seek to use
> in order to resist arrest or effect his escape. Otherwise, the officer's safety might
> well be endangered, and the arrest itself frustrated. In addition, it is entirely rea-
> sonable for the arresting officer to search for and seize any evidence on the ar-
> restee's person in order to prevent its concealment or destruction. And the area
> into which an arrestee might reach in order to grab a weapon or evidentiary
> items must, of course, be governed by a like rule. A gun on a table or in a
> drawer in front of one who is arrested can be as dangerous to the arresting offi-
> cer as one concealed in the clothing of the person arrested. There is ample justi-
> fication, therefore, for a search of the arrestee's person and the area "within his
> immediate control"—construing that phrase to mean the area from within
> which he might gain possession of a weapon or destructible evidence.
>
> There is no comparable justification, however, for routinely searching any
> room other than that in which an arrest occurs—or, for that matter, for search-
> ing through all the desk drawers or other closed or concealed areas in that room
> itself. Such searches, in the absence of well-recognized exceptions, may be made
> only under the authority of a search warrant. 395 U.S. 752, 762–63, 89 S.Ct.
> 2034, 2040, 23 L.Ed.2d 685, 694.

The *Chimel* decision drastically changed the area allowed to be searched incident
to arrest from that allowed under previous law. Under pre-*Chimel* law, an officer was
allowed to search incident to arrest the area considered to be in the "possession" or
under the "control" of the arrested person. These vague standards were interpreted
by the courts to include areas that were not necessarily under the defendant's "physical control" but were within his or her "constructive possession." Under this interpretation, law enforcement officers could search an entire residence incident to an arrest made in the residence, and they had almost free reign in deciding what would be
searched. Furthermore, because neither a written application for a warrant nor a
demonstration of probable cause before a magistrate was required, the search incident to arrest was administratively more convenient and heavily used by law enforcement officers.

Although a warrant or probable cause is still not needed to conduct a search incident to arrest, *Chimel* has made it much more difficult for officers to obtain admissible evidence as a result of such a search. This chapter discusses various ramifications
of the limitations *Chimel* places on a law enforcement officer's power to search incident to arrest.

Scope

The allowable scope of a search incident to arrest depends largely on the allowable purposes of a such a search. *Chimel* allows a law enforcement officer to search a person incident to arrest for only two purposes:

- To search for and remove weapons that the arrestee might use to resist arrest or effect an escape
- To search for and seize evidence to prevent its concealment or destruction. The following types of property may be seized:

  (1) property that constitutes evidence of the commission of a criminal offense; or (2) contraband, the fruits of crime, or things otherwise criminally possessed; or (3) property designed or intended for use or which is or has been used as the means of committing a criminal offense. F.R.Crim.P. 41(b).

In addition, an officer may seize evidence of crimes other than the crime for which the arrest was made. In *United States v. Simpson,* 453 F.2d 1028 (10th Cir. 1972), the defendant was arrested under a warrant for possessing and transporting explosives. During a search incident to the arrest, the arresting officer found a third person's Selective Service Certificate and Classification Card, the possession of which was illegal. The court held that the certificate and card were admissible in court, even though they did not relate to the offense of possessing explosives.

> The general rule is that incident to a lawful arrest, a search without a warrant may be made of portable personal effects in the immediate possession of the person arrested. The discovery during a search of a totally unrelated object which provides grounds for prosecution of a crime different than that which the accused was arrested for does not render the search invalid. 453 F.2d at 1031.

Search of the Arrestee's Body

The *Chimel* case gives few guidelines as to the allowable extent of the search of an arrestee's body. However, the later cases of *United States v. Robinson,* 414 U.S. 218, 94 S.Ct. 467, 38 L.Ed.2d 427 (1973), and *Gustafson v. Florida,* 414 U.S. 260, 94 S.Ct. 488, 38 L.Ed.2d 456 (1973), held that a law enforcement officer may conduct a *full* search of a person's body incident to the custodial arrest of the person. In each case, the U.S. Supreme Court upheld an inspection of the contents of a cigarette package seized incident to the arrest of the defendant for a traffic violation. Illegal drugs were found in both cases. In the *Robinson* case, the Court said:

A police officer's determination as to how and where to search the person of a suspect whom he has arrested is necessarily a quick ad hoc judgment which the Fourth Amendment does not require to be broken down in each instance into an analysis of each step in the search. The authority to search the person incident to a lawful custodial arrest, while based upon the need to disarm and to discover evidence, does not depend on what a court may later decide was the probability in a particular arrest situation that weapons or evidence would in fact be found upon the person of the suspect. A custodial arrest of a suspect based on probable cause is a reasonable intrusion under the Fourth Amendment; that intrusion being lawful, a search incident to the arrest requires no additional justification. It is the fact of the lawful arrest which establishes the authority to search, and we hold that in the case of lawful custodial arrest a full search of the person is not only an exception to the warrant requirement of the Fourth Amendment, but is also a "reasonable" search under that Amendment. 414 U.S. at 235, 94 S.Ct. at 477, 38 L.Ed.2d at 441.

This language was quoted with approval in the *Gustafson* decision, 414 U.S. at 263–64, 94 S.Ct. at 491, 38 L.Ed.2d at 460. Therefore, under the *Robinson-Gustafson* rule, whenever an officer makes a lawful custodial arrest, the officer may make a full search of the arrestee's body incident to the arrest.

Full Search

What constitutes a full search of the arrestee's body? The following principles can be derived from court decisions dealing with this question.

- A full search of the arrestee's body allows the seizure of evidence on or in the body. Relatively nonintrusive seizures such as obtaining hair samples and fingernail clippings will usually be upheld if reasonable and painless procedures are employed. In *Commonwealth v. Tarver*, 345 N.E.2d 671 (Mass. 1975), the court upheld a seizure of hair samples from the head, chest, and pubic area of a person incident to arrest of that person for murder and sexual abuse of a child. More intrusive searches and seizures, such as obtaining blood samples or comparable intrusions into the body, require stricter limitations. *Schmerber v. California* (discussed in Chapter 4) teaches that a more intrusive search and seizure will be upheld only if (1) the process was a reasonable one performed in a reasonable manner (in *Schmerber*, blood was taken from a person arrested for drunk driving by a physician in a hospital environment according to accepted medical practices); (2) there was a clear indication in advance that the evidence sought would be found; and (3) there were exigent circumstances (in *Schmerber*, the blood test had to be taken before the percentage of alcohol in the blood diminished). If the purpose of obtaining blood had been to determine blood type, drawing the blood without a warrant would not have been permissible because there would be no exigent circumstances. *United States ex rel. Parson v. Anderson*, 354 F.Supp. 1060 (D.Del. 1972), order affirmed 481 F.2d 94 (3d Cir. 1973).

- A full search of the arrestee's body allows the *seizure* and *search* of items of evidence or weapons immediately associated with the arrestee's body, such as clothing, billfolds, jewelry, wristwatches, and weapons strapped or carried on the person. In this context, "immediately associated" means attached in a permanent or semipermanent way to the arrestee's body or clothing. In *State v. Smith*, 203

N.W.2d 348 (Minn. 1972), the court held that the seizure of the defendant's boots at the time of booking was a valid seizure incident to arrest. A search of items seized might include going through the pockets of clothing; examining clothing for bloodstains, hair, or dirt; and examining weapons for bloodstains, fingerprints, or serial numbers. In *United States v. Molinaro,* 877 F.2d 1341 (7th Cir. 1989), the 7th Circuit Court of Appeals agreed with several other U.S. courts of appeals in holding that a person's wallet may be validly seized and its contents immediately searched incident to the arrest of the person, to prevent the destruction or concealment of evidence. In *United States v. Chan,* 830 F.Supp. 531 (N.D.Cal. 1993), Drug Enforcement Administration (DEA) agents arrested the defendant, seized an electronic pager in his possession, and, within minutes, searched the pager by activating its memory and retrieving certain telephone numbers stored in the pager. The court upheld the search as a valid search incident to arrest.

- A full search of the arrestee's body allows the *seizure* and *search* of other personal property and containers that are *not* immediately associated with the arrestee's body but that the arrestee is carrying or otherwise has under his or her immediate control. *United States v. Johnson,* 846 F.2d 279 (5th Cir. 1988). Property that might be seized and searched includes luggage, attache cases, bundles, or packages.

Remoteness of Search

In *United States v. Chadwick,* 433 U.S. 1, 97 S.Ct. 2476, 53 L.Ed.2d 538 (1977), the U.S. Supreme Court held that the *search* of seized luggage or other personal property not immediately associated with the arrestee's body would not be allowed where the search is remote in time and place from the arrest, or where there is no exigency. In the *Chadwick* case, the defendants arrived in Boston from San Diego by train and loaded a large, double-locked footlocker, which they had transported with them, into the trunk of their waiting car. Federal narcotics agents, who had probable cause to arrest and to search the footlocker but no warrants, arrested the defendants. The agents took exclusive control over the footlocker and transported it and the defendants to the federal building in Boston. An hour and a half later, the agents, without the defendants' consent and without a search warrant, opened the footlocker and found large amounts of marijuana. The U.S. Supreme Court held that the search of the footlocker was illegal.

> The potential dangers lurking in all custodial arrests make warrantless searches of items within the "immediate control" area reasonable without requiring the arresting officer to calculate the probability that weapons or destructible evidence may be involved. [citing *United States v. Robinson* and *Terry v. Ohio*] However, warrantless searches of luggage or other property seized at the time of an arrest cannot be justified as incident to that arrest either if the "search is remote in time and place from the arrest," . . . or no exigency exists. Once law enforcement officers have reduced luggage or other personal property not immediately associated with the person of the arrestee to their exclusive control, and there is no longer any danger that the arrestee might gain access to the property to seize a weapon or destroy evidence, a search of that property is no longer an incident of the arrest.
>
> Here the search was conducted more than an hour after federal agents had gained exclusive control of the footlocker and long after respondents were securely

in custody; the search therefore cannot be viewed as incidental to the arrest or as justified by any other exigency. Even though on this record the issuance of a warrant by a judicial officer was reasonably predictable, a line must be drawn. In our view, when no exigency is shown to support the need for an immediate search, the Warrant Clause places the line at the point where the property to be searched comes under the exclusive dominion of police authority. Respondents were therefore entitled to the protection of the Warrant Clause with the evaluation of a neutral magistrate, before their privacy interests in the contents of the footlocker were invaded. 433 U.S. at 14–16, 97 S.Ct. at 2485–86, 53 L.Ed.2d at 550–51.

Footnotes to the *Chadwick* opinion indicate that the Court's decision was based in large part on its belief that the defendants' legitimate privacy interests were violated. In footnote 10 the Court said:

Unlike searches of the person, *United States v. Robinson,* 414 U.S. 218 (1973); *United States v. Edwards,* 415 U.S. 800 (1974), searches of possessions within an arrestee's immediate control cannot be justified by any reduced expectations of privacy caused by the arrest. Respondents' privacy interest in the contents of the footlocker was not eliminated simply because they were under arrest. 433 U.S. at 16 n.10, 97 S.Ct. at 2486 n.10, 53 L.Ed.2d at 551 n.10.

In footnote 8 the Court said:

Respondents' principal privacy interest in the footlocker was, of course, not in the container itself, which was exposed to public view, but in its contents. A search of the interior was therefore a far greater intrusion into Fourth Amendment values than the impoundment of the footlocker. Though surely a substantial infringement with respondents' use and possession, the seizure did not diminish respondents' legitimate expectation that the footlocker's contents would remain private. 433 U.S. at 13–14 n.8, 97 S.Ct. at 2485 n.8, 53 L.Ed.2d at 550 n.8.

To summarize, law enforcement officers may seize and search incident to arrest luggage and other personal property not immediately associated with the arrestee's body if that property is within the arrestee's immediate control and if the search is not remote in time and place from the arrest. Once officers have the property under their exclusive control, however, and there is no further danger that the arrestee might gain access to the property to seize a weapon or destroy evidence, officers may not search the property without a warrant or consent.

Emergencies

Of course, there may be other justifications for a warrantless search of luggage taken from a suspect at the time of his arrest; for example, if officers have reason to believe that luggage contains some immediately dangerous instrumentality, such as explosives, it would be foolhardy to transport it to the station house without opening the luggage and disarming the weapon. *United States v. Chadwick,* 433 U.S. 1, 15 n.9, 97 S.Ct. 2476, 2485 n.9, 53 L.Ed.2d 538, 551 n.9 (1977).

In *United States v. Johnson,* 467 F.2d 630 (2d Cir. 1972), police officers were notified by a reliable informant that a recent arrestee's suitcase containing a shotgun could be found near the rear door of an apartment building. The officers knew that the building was located in a transient and high-crime area and that the suitcase was probably visible to passersby. The officers rushed to the apartment building, opened the suitcase, and found the shotgun. The court upheld both the seizure and search of the suitcase.

> [I]n opening the suitcases, the police were not acting in violation of the Fourth Amendment. The "exigencies of the situation made that course imperative." . . . The officers were holding a suitcase which they had probable cause to believe contained a contraband sawed-off shotgun. There was a substantial possibility the gun was loaded. As they stood in that transient and high crime area, their own safety and the safety of others required that they know whether they were holding a dangerous weapon over which they had no control. . . . Under these circumstances, we cannot hold that the police were required to carry the suitcase, unopened, to the police station to obtain a warrant or that an officer should have stood near or held the unopened suitcase as a warrant was obtained. The police were entitled to know what they were holding in their possession. 467 F.2d at 639.

State Departures from the *Robinson-Gustafson* Rule

The *Robinson* case has been criticized on the ground that it facilitates "pretext" or "subterfuge" arrests for minor offenses and searches incident to those arrests for evidence of more serious crimes for which probable cause to arrest is lacking. In *Whren v. United States,* 517 U.S. 806, 116 S.Ct. 1769, 135 L.Ed.2d 89 (1996), the U.S. Supreme Court clearly stated that an officer's ulterior motives do not invalidate the officer's conduct that is justifiable on the basis of probable cause to believe that a violation of law has occurred. Furthermore, such conduct is valid under the Fourth Amendment regardless of whether a "reasonable officer" would have been motivated to engage in such conduct. In short, if police conduct is justified by probable cause, subjective intent or pretext is irrelevant for Fourth Amendment purposes. The Court went on to say that

> of course . . . the Constitution prohibits selective enforcement of the law based on considerations such as race. But the constitutional basis for objecting to intentionally discriminatory application of laws is the Equal Protection Clause, not the Fourth Amendment. Subjective intentions play no role in ordinary, probable-cause Fourth Amendment analysis. 517 U.S. at 813, 116 S.Ct. at 1774, 135 L.Ed.2d at 98.

Nevertheless, based on interpretations of their state constitutions, some state courts have refused to follow the *Robinson-Gustafson* rule allowing a full-body search incident to a lawful custodial arrest. Several states, including Alaska, Colorado, Hawaii, and Oregon, have placed various limitations on the *Robinson-Gustafson* rule. The Supreme Court of Hawaii limited the warrantless search of an arrestee's person incident to a lawful custodial arrest (1) to disarming the arrested person when there is reason to believe from the facts and circumstances that the person may be armed and (2) to discovering evidence related to the crime *for which the person was arrested. State v. Kaluna,* 520 P.2d 51, 60 (Hawaii 1974). Under this more restrictive rule, officers may not search for *evidence* incident to offenses that would not produce evidence (such as loitering and minor traffic offenses), and officers may not search for weapons unless they can point to specific facts and circumstances indicating the likelihood that the arrested person was armed and dangerous.

The California Supreme Court also refused to go along with the U.S. Supreme Court's decisions in the *Robinson* and *Gustafson* cases. In California, an officer may not conduct a full-body search of an arrested person when the arrest will be disposed of by a mere citation or the arrested person will be transported in a law enforcement vehicle to a police facility where the opportunity to post bond is available. Officers may, however, conduct a patdown frisk for weapons before placing an arrested person in a law enforcement vehicle for transportation to the station house. The court recognized the increased danger to law enforcement officers in this situation. *People v. Longwill,* 123 Cal.Rptr. 297, 538 P.2d 753 (Cal. 1975).

KEY POINTS

2. The allowable purposes of a search incident to arrest are (1) to search for and remove weapons that the arrestee might use to resist arrest or effect an escape and (2) to search for and seize evidence to prevent its concealment or destruction.

3. A law enforcement officer may conduct a full search of a person's body incident to the arrest of the person.

4. A full search of the arrestee's body allows the *seizure* and *search* of weapons or evidence on, in, or immediately associated with the body.

5. A full search of the arrestee's body allows the *seizure* and *search* of other personal property *not* immediately associated with the arrestee's body but under the immediate control of the arrestee. This property may not be searched, however, if the search is remote in time and place from the arrest or no exigency exists.

6. If police conduct is justified by probable cause to believe that a violation of law has occurred, subjective intent or pretext is irrelevant for Fourth Amendment purposes.

Search of Area into Which the Arrestee Might Reach

And the area into which an arrestee might reach in order to grab a weapon or evidentiary items must, of course, be governed by a like rule. A gun on a table or in a drawer in front of one who is arrested can be as dangerous to the arresting officer as one concealed in the clothing of the person arrested. There is ample justification, therefore, for a search of the arrestee's person and the area "within his immediate control"—construing that phrase to mean the area from within which he might gain possession of a weapon or destructible evidence. 395 U.S. at 763, 89 S.Ct. at 2040, 23 L.Ed.2d at 694.

This quotation from the *Chimel* case (also quoted at the start of this chapter) gives definite guidelines as to the extent of the area around an arrestee that is "within his immediate control" and is therefore subject to search by an officer. This determination of the permissible area of search depends on several factors such as the size and shape of the room, the size and agility of the arrestee, whether the arrestee was handcuffed or otherwise subdued, the size and type of evidence being sought, the number of people arrested, and the number of officers present. This area is sometimes called the arrestee's "wingspan," "wingspread," or "grabbing distance."

The following cases illustrate the *Chimel* guidelines. In *James v. Louisiana,* 382 U.S. 36, 86 S.Ct. 151, 15 L.Ed.2d 30 (1965), the defendant, a suspected possessor of narcotics, was lawfully arrested on a downtown street corner. The officers then took him to his home some distance away and conducted an intensive search that yielded narcotics. The Court held the search unreasonable:

> In the circumstances of this case . . . the subsequent search of the petitioner's home cannot be regarded as incident to his arrest on a street corner more than two blocks away. A search "can be incident to an arrest only if it is substantially contemporaneous with the arrest and is confined to the immediate vicinity of the arrest." 382 U.S. at 37, 86 S.Ct. at 151, 15 L.Ed.2d at 31 (1965).

For the same reason, the search of an arrestee's vehicle located a substantial distance from the doorstep of his home where he was arrested could not be justified as a search incident to arrest. *United States v. Lasanta,* 978 F.2d 1300 (2d Cir. 1992).

United States v. Tarazon, 989 F.2d 1045 (9th Cir. 1993), held that the drawers of the desk at which the defendant was sitting when he was arrested were clearly within the defendant's control and could be searched incident to the arrest moments after the arrest. In *People v. Spencer,* 99 Cal.Rptr. 681 (Cal.App. 1972), officers went to the defendant's trailer home to arrest him for participating in an armed robbery. They found him lying in bed. One officer immediately searched under the blankets for a gun as other officers attempted to subdue the defendant, who was resisting. Two revolvers were found in a box at the foot of the bed. The court held that this box was within the area of the defendant's reach and that the revolvers were admissible in evidence.

If it is necessary for an arrested person to go into a different area of the premises from that in which he or she was arrested, the officer may, for protective purposes, accompany the person and search if necessary. The following quotation from *Washington v. Chrisman* (discussed in Chapter 4) is worthy of repetition:

> [I]t is not "unreasonable" under the Fourth Amendment for a police officer, as a matter of course, to monitor the movements of an arrested person, as his judgement dictates, following the arrest. The officer's need to ensure his own safety—as well as the integrity of the arrest—is compelling. Such surveillance is not an impermissible invasion of the privacy or personal liberty of an individual who has been arrested. 455 U.S. 1, 7, 102 S.Ct. 812, 817, 70 L.Ed.2d 778, 785 (1982).

In *Giacalone v. Lucas,* 445 F.2d 1238, 1247 (6th Cir. 1971), an arrest under warrant for conspiracy to commit extortion took place early in the morning when the arrested person was in his bedclothes. An officer suggested that the defendant change into street clothes before leaving for the station. The defendant agreed and went to his bedroom, followed by the officers. As the defendant went to a chest of drawers to obtain clothing, one officer searched the drawer and found a blackjack and several other weapons. The defendant was convicted of illegal possession of a blackjack. The court held the search was lawful:

> Certainly, if immediately after a lawful arrest, the arrestee reads the arrest warrant and without coercion consents to go to his bedroom to change into more appropriate clothing, the arresting officers—incident to that arrest—may search the areas upon which the arrestee focuses his attention and are within his reach to gain access to a weapon or to destroy evidence. 445 F.2d at 1247.

Officers may not, however, deliberately move an arrested person near an object or place they want to search in order to activate the incident-to-arrest exception. *United States v. Perea,* 986 F.2d 633 (2d Cir. 1993).

Search of Motor Vehicles

In *New York v. Belton,* 453 U.S. 454, 460–61, 101 S.Ct. 2860, 2864, 69 L.Ed.2d 768, 775 (1981), the U.S. Supreme Court held:

> [W]hen a policeman has made a lawful custodial arrest of the occupant of an automobile, he may, as a contemporaneous incident of that arrest, search the passenger compartment of that automobile.
>
> It follows from this conclusion that the police may also examine the contents of any containers found within the passenger compartment, for if the passenger compartment is within the reach of the arrestee, so also will containers in it be within his reach. . . . Such a container may, of course, be searched whether it is open or closed, since the justification for the search is not that the arrestee has no privacy interest in the container, but that the lawful custodial arrest justifies the infringement of any privacy interest the arrestee may have.

In a footnote, the Court defined a container as any object capable of holding another object. A container thus includes "closed or open glove compartments, consoles or other receptacles located anywhere within the passenger compartment, as well as luggage, boxes, bags, clothing, and the like." 453 U.S. at 460–61 n.4, 101 S.Ct. at 2684 n.4, 69 L.Ed.2d at 775 n.4. The Court also pointed out that only the interior of the passenger compartment of an automobile, and not the trunk, may be searched incident to arrest.

In *United States v. White,* 871 F.2d 41 (6th Cir. 1989), the court upheld a search of the defendant's automobile incident to his arrest *in his vehicle,* even though he was handcuffed and placed in the back seat of a police cruiser at the time of the search. The court said that

> even after the arrestee has been separated from his vehicle and is no longer within reach of the vehicle or its contents, the *Belton* rule allowing a police officer to search a vehicle incident to a lawful arrest applies, and such a search is valid. 871 F.2d at 44.

United States v. Strahan, 984 F.2d 159 (6th Cir. 1993), held that the *Belton* rule applies only where the police initiate contact while the defendant is within his automobile. In that case, the search of the vehicle incident to arrest was not allowed where the defendant was initially arrested not while within his vehicle but approximately thirty feet from his vehicle.

The *Belton* case deals only with the search incident to arrest exception to the warrant requirement and has nothing to do with the so-called automobile exception under the *Carroll* doctrine. (See Chapter 11.) The U.S. Supreme Court specifically referred to the *Chimel* case, stating that articles inside the relatively narrow compass of the passenger compartment of an automobile are in fact generally, even if not inevitably, within "the area into which an arrestee might reach in order to grab a weapon or evidentiary item." 395 U.S. at 763, 89 S.Ct. at 2040, 23 L.Ed.2d at 694. Therefore, the holding in the *Belton* case does not apply unless there has been a custodial arrest of the occupant of an automobile. And it is the custodial arrest that provides the justification for examining the contents of containers seized from the passenger compartment of the automobile. Moreover, as the previously quoted passage from the *Belton* case indicates, the searching of any containers found in the automobile must be substantially contemporaneous with the arrest of the automobile's occupant. If a container is seized and searched some time later, after it is in the exclusive control of the police, the *Chadwick* case requires that a warrant be obtained.

Search of Persons Other Than the Arrestee

When an arrest is made, other persons besides the arrested person are often in the vicinity. Courts generally allow a limited search or frisk of an arrestee's companion or companions in the immediate area of the arrest, when the arresting officer reasonably believes that these persons may present a danger or may destroy evidence. (See "Determination of Whether to Frisk" in Chapter 7.) The allowed search is limited to a patdown search of the companion's body and a search of the area within his or her immediate control for weapons or destructible evidence. "[A] search of items within the area of immediate control of a person who is present during a custodial arrest for a recent crime in which guns were used is reasonable when an objective probability of danger to law enforcement exists under the circumstances." *United States v. Simmons,* 567 F.2d 314, 320 (7th Cir. 1977).

Some courts apply a totality of the circumstances test in determining whether a search of an arrestee's companions is justified. In *United States v. Flett,* 806 F.2d 823 (8th Cir. 1986), the court upheld a patdown search of an arrestee's companion, even though the companion made no threatening moves toward the officer and the officer noticed no bulge in the companion's clothing. The court said that the focus of the judicial inquiry was not whether the officer had an indication that the person was armed and dangerous but rather "whether the officer reasonably perceived the subject of the frisk as potentially dangerous." 806 F.2d at 828. The court found that the patdown search was justified by the following circumstances:

- The arrestee was the subject of an arrest warrant for narcotics violations.
- The arrestee was a known member of a national motorcycle gang with violent propensities.
- The arrestee was the "enforcer" of the local chapter of the motorcycle gang and had been previously charged with a firearms violation.
- The companion was in the arrestee's house, was dressed in attire similar to that of gang members, and physically resembled known gang members.
- The officer had fifteen years' experience in law enforcement.

The area within the reach of the defendant's companions is also subject to search. In *United States v. Lucas,* 898 F.2d 606 (8th Cir. 1990), the court held that a search of a cabinet in a small kitchen, immediately after officers had handcuffed the defendant and while they were removing him from the kitchen, was a valid search incident to arrest. The defendant had attempted to reach the cabinet door immediately before his struggle with the arresting officers. The court particularly noted that two of the defendant's friends, who had not been handcuffed, were still at the kitchen table when the search took place. A revolver found in the cabinet was held admissible in evidence against the defendant.

KEY POINTS

7. When a law enforcement officer has made a lawful custodial arrest of an automobile's occupant, the officer may contemporaneously search the passenger compartment of that automobile and may also examine the contents of any containers found within the passenger compartment, whether the containers are open or closed.

8. A law enforcement officer may conduct a limited search or frisk of an arrestee's companion or companions in the immediate area of the arrest, when the arresting officer reasonably believes that these persons may present a danger or may destroy evidence.

Search of Other Areas of the Premises

Under the rule of the *Chimel* case, officers may not conduct a full search of any areas of the premises other than the limited area within the arrestee's immediate control. Officers may, however, conduct a quick and limited search of a premises incident to an arrest to protect their own safety and the safety of others. This is sometimes referred to as a "protective sweep." Officers also may have to go through other rooms in entering or leaving the premises. These movements into other areas of the premises are not considered full-blown searches, because the officers are not looking for weapons or incriminating evidence. Nevertheless, an officer who observes a weapon or other seizable item lying open to view may seize it, and that item will be admissible in court if the requirements of the plain view doctrine are satisfied (see Chapter 10).

In *Maryland v. Buie,* 494 U.S. 325, 110 S.Ct. 1093, 108 L.Ed.2d 276 (1990), two men, one of whom was wearing a red running suit, committed an armed robbery. The same day, police obtained an arrest warrant for the defendant and his suspected accomplice and executed the warrant for the defendant at his house. After the defendant was arrested upon emerging from the basement, one of the officers entered the basement "in case there was someone else" there and seized a red running suit lying in plain view.

In determining the reasonableness of the search of the basement leading to the plain view seizure, the U.S. Supreme Court balanced the officer's need to search against the invasion entailed by the search. Possessing an arrest warrant and probable cause to believe the defendant was in his home, the officers were entitled to enter and search anywhere in the house in which the defendant might be found. Once he was found, however, the search for him was over, and the officers no longer had that particular justification for entering any rooms that had not yet been searched. Those rooms, however, were not immune from entry simply because of the defendant's expectation of privacy with respect to them. That privacy interest must be balanced against the

> interest of the officers in taking steps to assure themselves that the house in which a suspect is being or has just been arrested is not harboring other persons who are dangerous and who could unexpectedly launch an attack. The risk of danger in the context of an arrest in the home is as great as, if not greater than, it is in an on-the-street or roadside investigatory encounter. 494 U.S. at 333, 110 S.Ct. at 1098, 108 L.Ed.2d at 285.

The Court held that the police officers had a limited right to conduct a protective sweep for their own protection.

> [A]s an incident to the arrest the officers could, as a precautionary matter and without probable cause or reasonable suspicion, look in closets and other spaces immediately adjoining the place of arrest from which an attack could be immediately launched. Beyond that, however, . . . there must be articulable facts which, taken together with the rational inferences from those facts, would warrant a reasonably prudent officer in believing that the area to be swept harbors an individual posing a danger to those on the arrest scene. 494 U.S. at 334, 110 S.Ct. at 1098, 108 L.Ed.2d at 286.

Thus, the standard to justify a protective sweep in conjunction with an in-home arrest is the same as the standard to justify an investigatory *Terry*-type stop: reasonable suspicion based on specific and articulable facts. The Supreme Court emphasized that a protective sweep of areas beyond the area immediately adjoining the place of arrest permits only a cursory inspection of those spaces where a person may be found; it does not permit a full search of the premises. The sweep may last no longer than is necessary to dispel the reasonable suspicion of danger and in any event no longer than it takes to complete the arrest and depart from the premises.

In *United States v. Soria,* 959 F.2d 855 (10th Cir. 1992), the court held a protective sweep of the defendant's auto shop proper when the defendant was arrested during a drug transaction close to the shop. The officers believed that drug-dealing activities had taken place in the shop and that others may have been hiding inside. In *United States v. Hogan,* 38 F.3d 1148 (10th Cir. 1994), however, a protective sweep of the defendant's residence was held invalid where the defendant was arrested outside his residence. He was not home when the police first arrived, and the only possible danger to the police was the hypothetical possibility that the defendant's accomplice to the murder committed a month earlier might be in the residence.

Sometimes the events and circumstances surrounding an arrest will justify officers going into other parts of an arrestee's residence for reasons unrelated to their safety. In a bank robbery case, the defendant was arrested in his girlfriend's apartment. At the time of his arrest, the defendant was nude and the apartment was dark. An officer went to get clothing for the defendant and found two jackets of the type that had been described as having been worn by the bank robbers. On the way out of the apartment, an officer turned on the kitchen light so he could see his way. Money taken during the robbery was observed on the kitchen floor.

The court held that both the jackets and the money were admissible in evidence. Finding no violation of the *Chimel* rule, the court said:

> Since they were bound to find some clothing for Titus rather than take him nude to FBI headquarters on a December night, the fatigue jackets were properly seized under the "plain view" doctrine. Welch was entitled to turn on the kitchen lights, both to assist his own exit and to see whether the other robber might be about; when he saw the stolen money, he was permitted to seize it. Everything the agents took was in their "plain view" while they were where they had a right to be; there was no general rummaging of the apartment. *United States v. Titus,* 445 F.2d 577, 579 (2d Cir. 1971).

KEY POINTS

9. Law enforcement officers may not conduct a *full* search of any areas of the premises other than the limited area within the arrestee's immediate control.

10. Incident to an arrest, the arresting officer may look in closets and other spaces immediately adjoining the place of arrest from which an attack could be immediately launched.

11. The Fourth Amendment permits a properly limited "protective sweep" in conjunction with an in-home arrest when the searching officer possesses a reasonable suspicion based on specific and articulable facts that the area to be swept harbors an individual posing a danger to those on the arrest scene.

Other Requirements for a Valid Search Incident to Arrest

Several other requirements for a valid search incident to arrest have been touched on in the previous discussion. This section treats each of these requirements in further detail.

Lawful Custodial Arrest

To justify a full search incident to arrest, an arrest must be a lawful **custodial arrest.** The word *custodial* is important here because in some states the term *arrest* is applied to situations in which an officer stops a person and issues a ticket, citation, or notice to appear in court, instead of taking the person into custody and transporting the person to a police station or other place to be dealt with according to the law. A full search would not be authorized in situations in which the officer merely issued a ticket, citation, or notice to appear. In other words, the officer must take the arrested person into custody to justify a full search. In *United States v. Parr,* 843 F.2d 1228 (9th Cir. 1988), the court found that where the defendant was stopped on suspicion of driving with a suspended driver's license and placed briefly in a patrol car, without any other restraint or questioning, there was no custodial arrest. And, therefore, the search of the defendant's car could not be justified as a search incident to arrest. The court observed that "sitting in the patrol car for several minutes was merely a normal part of traffic police procedure for identifying delinquent drivers and did not constitute custodial arrest." 843 F.2d at 1230. The rule requiring a *custodial* arrest is based on the U.S. Supreme Court's observation

> that the danger to an officer is far greater in the case of the extended exposure which follows the taking of a suspect into custody and transporting him to the police station than in the case of the relatively fleeting contact resulting from the typical *Terry*-type stop. . . . *United States v. Robinson,* 414 U.S. 218, 234–35, 94 S.Ct. 467, 476, 38 L.Ed.2d 427, 440.

No further justification beyond that of a lawful custodial arrest is necessary to validate the seizure of an item in conjunction with a search incident to arrest. As stated by the 9th Circuit Court of Appeals, "For an item to be validly seized during a search incident to arrest, the police need not have probable cause to seize the item, nor do they need to recognize immediately the item's evidentiary nature." *United States v. Holzman,* 871 F.2d 1496, 1505 (9th Cir. 1989).

Contemporaneousness

A search "can be incident to an arrest only if it is substantially contemporaneous with the arrest and is confined to the immediate vicinity of the arrest." *James v. Louisiana,* 382 U.S. 36, 37, 86 S.Ct. 151, 151, 15 L.Ed.2d 30, 31 (1965). (The *James* case is discussed on pages 304–305.) To be contemporaneous, a search must be conducted as close in time to the arrest as practically possible. The reason for this rule is that officers may search incident to arrest only (1) to protect themselves and (2) to prevent the destruction or concealment of evidence. A delayed search indicates that the officers were not concerned about either of these possibilities and that the search was conducted for another, impermissible, purpose.

Sometimes circumstances prevent an officer from conducting an immediate search incident to arrest. For example, body cavity searches and searches of persons of the opposite sex must usually be delayed. In these situations, the officer should remove the arrested person from the scene and conduct the search as soon as favorable circumstances prevail. In *United States v. Miles,* 413 F.2d 34 (3d Cir. 1969), an arrest for an armed bank robbery took place in a crowded hotel lobby, which was lit only by candles because of a power failure. The court held that under these circumstances it was proper for officers to make a cursory search for weapons at the hotel and to make a more thorough search later at the station.

Even though it is feasible to search an arrested person at the time of arrest, courts will allow a delay between the arrest and search under certain circumstances. The U.S. Supreme Court made such an exception to the general rule in the case of *United States v. Edwards,* 415 U.S. 800, 94 S.Ct. 1234, 39 L.Ed.2d 771 (1974). In that case, the defendant was arrested shortly after 11:00 P.M. for attempting to break into a building. The defendant was taken to jail. Law enforcement officials had probable cause to believe that the defendant's clothing contained paint chips from the crime scene. Since the police had no substitute clothing for the defendant, they waited until the next morning to seize his clothing without a warrant. Paint chips matching those at the break scene were found on the clothing.

The Court held that, despite the delay, the clothing was lawfully seized incident to the defendant's arrest. The administrative process and the mechanics of arrest had not yet come to a halt the next morning. The police had custody of the defendant and the clothing and could have seized the clothing at the time of arrest. It was reasonable to delay the seizure until substitute clothing was available.

> [O]nce the accused is lawfully arrested and is in custody, the effects in his possession at the place of detention that were subject to search at the time and place of his arrest may lawfully be searched and seized without a warrant even though a substantial period of time has elapsed between the arrest and subsequent administrative processing, on the one hand, and the taking of the property for use as evidence on the other. 415 U.S. at 807, 94 S.Ct. at 1239, 39 L.Ed.2d at 778.

The *Edwards* case does *not* allow law enforcement officers to delay a search incident to arrest for as long as they wish. Nor does the case sanction *all* delays in searching and seizing evidence incident to arrest. Officers must be able to provide good reasons for delaying a search incident to arrest, and the duration of a delay must be reasonable under the circumstances. Otherwise the search and seizure may be declared illegal.

The U.S. Supreme Court stated that "an incident search may not precede an arrest and serve as part of its justification." *Sibron v. New York,* 392 U.S. 40, 63, 88 S.Ct. 1889, 1902, 20 L.Ed.2d 917, 934–35 (1968). The Court reiterated this principle in *Smith v. Ohio,* holding that the exception for searches incident to arrest "does not permit the police to search any citizen without a warrant or probable cause so long as an arrest immediately follows." 494 U.S. 541, 543, 110 S.Ct. 1288, 1290, 108 L.Ed.2d 464, 468 (1990). This does not necessarily mean that the arrest must always precede the search, although that is the usual sequence. The search may precede the arrest and still be a valid search incident to arrest, if

- probable cause to *arrest* existed at the time of the search and did not depend on the fruits of the search, and
- the "formal arrest followed quickly on the heels of the challenged search." *Rawlings v. Kentucky,* 448 U.S. 98, 111, 100 S.Ct. 2556, 2564, 65 L.Ed.2d 633, 645 (1980).

Who May Conduct the Search

If possible, the law enforcement officer making the arrest should conduct the search incident to the arrest. If an officer makes an arrest and does not search the arrested person right away but later allows another officer to search the person, the later search may be held unlawful. It would not meet the requirement of contemporaneousness, nor would it indicate a concern for the protection of the officer or the prevention of the destruction or concealment of evidence.

	FRISK	SEARCH INCIDENT TO ARREST
Justification	Officer must have reason to believe that the person to be searched is an armed and dangerous person.	Officer must make a lawful custodial arrest of the person to be searched.
Purpose	Protection of the officer and other prospective victims of violence.	1. To search for and remove weapons that the arrestee might use to resist arrest or effect an escape. 2. To search for and seize evidence in order to prevent its concealment or destruction.
Extent of search of person	Carefully limited search or patdown of the outer clothing in order to discover weapons that might be used to assault the officer.	Full body search and search of the area into which an arrestee might reach in order to grab a weapon or evidentiary item.
Extent of search of vehicle	Areas in the passenger compartment in which a weapon may be placed or hidden.	The entire passenger compartment and the contents of any containers found within the passenger compartment.
Items that may be seized	Weapons or weapon-like objects and nonthreatening contraband if its identity as contraband is immediately apparent to the touch.	Weapons and evidence.
Use of force	Only the force reasonably necessary to protect the officer and others.	Only the force reasonably necessary to protect the officer and others, to prevent the escape of the arrestee, and to prevent the destruction or concealment of evidence.

EXHIBIT 8.1   Comparison of a Frisk and a Search Incident to Arrest

Nevertheless, if the arresting officer transfers an arrested person to the custody of another officer, the second officer may again search the arrested person. This second search is allowed because the second officer is entitled to take personal safety measures and need not rely on the assumption that the arrestee has been thoroughly searched for weapons by the arresting officer. *United States v. Dyson*, 277 A.2d 658 (D.C.App. 1971).

Use of Force

Law enforcement officers searching a person incident to arrest may use the degree of force reasonably necessary to protect themselves, prevent escape, and prevent the destruction or concealment of evidence. Courts will review the use of force strictly, and officers should use as little force as is necessary to accomplish their legitimate purpose. In *Salas v. State,* 246 So.2d 621 (Fla.Dist.Ct.App. 1971), a seizure of drugs incident to arrest was upheld even though the arresting officer put a choke hold on the arrestee and forced him to spit out drugs he was attempting to swallow. However, before more intrusive measures are taken, such as pumping the stomach or probing body cavities, the following conditions must be satisfied:

- The officer must have good reason to believe that the person's body contains evidence that should be removed. For example, in *People v. Jones,* 97 Cal.Rptr. 492 (Cal.App. 1971), officers observed the defendant thrust drug capsules into his mouth and quickly swallow them.

- If possible, the procedure should be performed by a doctor working under sanitary conditions and in a medically approved manner.

- Only the amount of force reasonably necessary to make the person submit to the examination may be used. *Blackford v. United States,* 247 F.2d 745 (9th Cir. 1957).

Exhibit 8.1 shows a comparison of a frisk and a search incident to arrest.

KEY POINTS

12. The lawful custodial arrest that justifies a full-body search incident to arrest is an arrest that involves taking the person into custody and transporting him or her to a police station or other place to be dealt with according to the law.

13. In general, a search incident to arrest must be contemporaneous with the arrest and confined to the immediate vicinity of the arrest.

14. A search incident to arrest may not precede an arrest and serve as part of the arrest's justification.

15. Law enforcement officers searching a person incident to arrest may use the degree of force reasonably necessary to protect themselves, prevent escape, and prevent the destruction or concealment of evidence.

Search Incident to Detention

In *Cupp v. Murphy,* 412 U.S. 291, 93 S.Ct. 2000, 36 L.Ed.2d 900 (1973), the U.S. Supreme Court decided that a law enforcement officer may conduct a limited warrantless search of a person merely *detained* for investigation. In that case, the defendant was notified of his wife's strangulation and then voluntarily came to the police headquarters and met his attorney there. Police noticed a dark spot on the defendant's finger and asked whether they could take a scraping from his fingernails. The defendant refused. Under protest and without a warrant, police proceeded to take the samples, which turned out to include particles of skin and blood of the defendant's wife and fabric from her clothing. The evidence was admitted at trial, and the defendant was convicted of second-degree murder.

The Court held that the momentary detention of the defendant to get the fingernail scrapings constituted a seizure governed by the Fourth Amendment. The Court, citing the *Chimel* case, also recognized that under prescribed conditions, warrantless searches incident to an arrest are constitutionally valid. In this case, however, without an arrest or search warrant, a full *Chimel* search of the defendant's body and the area within his immediate control would not have been permissible. Nevertheless, the Court validated the search under a limited application of the *Chimel* rule based on the unique facts of the case:

- The defendant was not arrested but was detained only long enough to take the fingernail scrapings.

- The search was very limited in extent, involving only the scraping of fingernails. (The Court was careful to point out that a full *Chimel* search would not have been justified without an arrest. The officers therefore could not have searched the defendant's body and the area within his immediate control.)

- The evidence—blood and skin on the fingernails—was readily destructible.

- The defendant made attempts to destroy the evidence, creating exigent circumstances.

- The officers had probable cause to arrest the defendant, even though he was not actually arrested.

All five of these conditions were essential to the Court's decision and must be satisfied to make a search incident to detention legal. Otherwise a warrant must be obtained before a search is conducted.

Summary

Search incident to arrest is a recognized exception to the warrant requirement of the Fourth Amendment. The U.S. Supreme Court case of *Chimel v. California* permits the search of a person who has been subjected to a lawful custodial arrest for the purposes of removing weapons and preventing the concealment or destruction of evidence. A full search for weapons and seizable evidence is permitted, whether or not there is any likelihood of danger or any reason to believe evidence will be found.

A search incident to arrest must be substantially contemporaneous with the arrest and may extend to the arrestee's body and to the area, and to all items and containers, within his or her immediate control—the area from which the arrestee might gain possession of a weapon or destructible evidence. Any weapon or seizable evidence found within this area may be seized. If, however, the item seized is luggage or other personal property not immediately associated with the person of the arrestee, a delayed search of the property, after it has come within the exclusive control of the police, may not be conducted without a warrant or exigent circumstances. A search incident to the arrest of an occupant of a motor vehicle may extend to the passenger area of the vehicle and may include a search of containers found in the vehicle, if the search is contemporaneous with the arrest.

Patdown searches of persons in the vicinity of the arrested person and searches of the areas within their immediate control may be conducted incident to the arrest, if reasonably necessary to remove weapons and prevent the concealment or destruction of evidence. Full searches of areas of the premises beyond the immediate control of the arrestee or companions may not be conducted. Nevertheless, an officer may look in closets and other spaces immediately adjoining the place of arrest from which an attack could be immediately launched. Also, an officer may conduct a properly limited protective sweep of the area beyond the spaces immediately adjoining the place of arrest when the officer reasonably suspects, based on specific and articulable facts, that the area to be swept harbors a person posing a danger to those on the arrest scene. Under the plain view doctrine, if police are lawfully in a position from which they view an object, if its incriminating character is apparent, and if the officers have a lawful right of access to the object, they may seize it without a warrant. Searches incident to arrest may be delayed in a variety of circumstances, but there must be good reason for a delay and the duration of the delay must be reasonable under the circumstances.

The U.S. Supreme Court has approved a limited warrantless search of a person merely detained for investigation. Law enforcement officers may conduct such a search, however, only if they have probable cause to arrest the suspect and if there is an imminent danger that crucial evidence will be destroyed if the search is not made immediately.

Key Holdings from Major Cases

Chimel v. California (1969). "When an arrest is made, it is reasonable for the arresting officer to search the person arrested in order to remove any weapons that the latter might seek to use in order to resist arrest or effect his escape. Otherwise, the officer's safety might well be endangered, and the arrest itself frustrated. In addition, it is entirely reasonable for the arresting officer to search for and seize any evidence on the arrestee's person in order to prevent its concealment or destruction. And the area into which an arrestee might reach in order to grab a weapon or evidentiary items must, of course, be governed by a like rule. A gun on a table or in a drawer in front of one who is arrested can be as dangerous to the arresting officer as one concealed in the clothing of the person arrested. There is ample justification, therefore, for a search of the arrestee's person and the area 'within his immediate control'—construing that phrase to mean the area from within which he might gain possession of a weapon or destructible evidence." 395 U.S. 752, 762–63, 89 S.Ct. 2034, 2040, 23 L.Ed.2d 685, 694.

United States v. Robinson (1973). "It is the fact of the lawful arrest which establishes the authority to search, and we hold that in the case of lawful custodial arrest a full search of the person is not only an exception to the warrant requirement of the Fourth Amendment, but is also a 'reasonable' search under that Amendment." 414 U.S. 218, 235, 94 S.Ct. 467, 477, 38 L.Ed.2d 427, 441.

United States v. Chadwick (1977). "Once law enforcement officers have reduced luggage or other personal property not immediately associated with the person of the arrestee to their exclusive control, and there is no longer any danger that the arrestee might gain access to the property to seize a weapon or destroy evidence, a search of that property is no longer an incident of the arrest." 433 U.S. 1, 15, 97 S.Ct. 2476, 2485, 53 L.Ed.2d 538, 551.

Whren v. United States (1996). An officer's ulterior motives do not invalidate the officer's conduct that is justifiable on the basis of probable cause to believe that a violation of law has occurred. 517 U.S. 806, 116 S.Ct. 1769, 135 L.Ed.2d 89.

New York v. Belton (1981). "[W]hen a policeman has made a lawful custodial arrest of the occupant of an automobile, he may, as a contemporaneous incident of that arrest, search the passenger compartment of that automobile."

"It follows from this conclusion that the police may also examine the contents of any containers found within the passenger compartment, for if the passenger compartment is within the reach of the arrestee, so also will containers in it be within his reach. . . . Such a container may, of course, be searched whether it is open or closed, since the justification for the search is not that the arrestee has no privacy interest in the container, but that the lawful custodial arrest justifies the infringement of any privacy interest the arrestee may have." 453 U.S. 454, 460–61, 101 S.Ct. 2860, 2864, 69 L.Ed.2d 768, 775.

Maryland v. Buie (1990). "[A]s an incident to the arrest the officers could, as a precautionary matter and without probable cause or reasonable suspicion, look in closets and other spaces immediately adjoining the place of arrest from which an attack could be immediately launched. Beyond that, however, . . . there must be articulable facts which, taken together with the rational inferences from those facts, would warrant a reasonably prudent officer in believing that the area to be swept harbors an individual posing a danger to those on the arrest scene." 494 U.S. 325, 334, 110 S.Ct. 1093, 1098, 108 L.Ed.2d 276, 286.

"The Fourth Amendment permits a properly limited protective sweep in conjunction with an in-home arrest when the searching officer possesses a reasonable belief based on specific and articulable facts that the area to be swept harbors an individual posing a danger to those on the arrest scene." 494 U.S. at 337, 110 S.Ct. at 1099–100, 108 L.Ed.2d at 288.

James v. Louisiana (1965). "A search 'can be incident to an arrest only if it is substantially contemporaneous with the arrest and is confined to the immediate vicinity of the arrest.'" 382 U.S. 36, 37, 86 S.Ct. 151, 151, 15 L.Ed.2d 30, 31.

United States v. Edwards (1974). "[O]nce the accused is lawfully arrested and is in custody, the effects in his possession at the place of detention that were subject to search at the time and place of his arrest may lawfully be searched and seized without a warrant even though a substantial period of time has elapsed between the arrest and subsequent administrative processing, on the one hand, and the taking of the property for use as evidence on the other." 415 U.S. 800, 807, 94 S.Ct. 1234, 1239, 39 L.Ed.2d 771, 778.

Cupp v. Murphy (1973). "Where there is no formal arrest, as in the case before us, a person might well be less hostile to the police and less likely to take conspicuous, immediate steps to destroy incriminating evidence on his person. Since he knows he is going to be released, he might be likely instead to be concerned with diverting attention away from himself. Accordingly, we do not hold that a full *Chimel* search would have been justified in this case without a formal arrest and without a warrant. But the respondent was not subjected to such a search.

"At the time Murphy was being detained at the station house, he was obviously aware of the detectives' suspicions. Though he did not have the full warning of official suspicion that a formal arrest provides, Murphy was sufficiently apprised of his suspected role in the crime to motivate him to attempt to destroy what evidence he could without attracting further attention. Testimony at trial indicated that after he refused to consent to the taking of fingernail samples, he put his hands behind his back and appeared to rub them together. He then put his hands in his pockets, and a 'metallic sound, such as keys or change rattling' was heard. The rationale of *Chimel,* in these circumstances, justified the police in subjecting him to the very limited search necessary to preserve the highly evanescent evidence they found under his fingernails. . . . On the facts of this case, considering the existence of probable cause, the very limited intrusion undertaken incident to the station house detention, and the ready destructibility of the evidence, we cannot say that this search violated the Fourth and Fourteenth Amendments." 412 U.S. 291, 296, 93 S.Ct. 2000, 2004, 36 L.Ed.2d 900, 906.

Review and Discussion Questions

1. Assume that while riding in the first-class section of an airplane, a person is legally arrested for transporting illegal drugs. Can the arresting officers immediately conduct searches of the following items and places incident to the arrest?

   a. The person's clothing

   b. The person's suitcase

   c. The entire first-class section of the airplane

   d. The person's body cavities

   If you approved any of the preceding searches, consider whether each search *should* be made and what are the possible alternatives.

2. If a defendant is arrested in an automobile for stealing the automobile, may the arresting officer search other passengers in the automobile incident to the defendant's arrest?

3. In a typical search incident to arrest situation, the arrest is followed by a search and then by a seizure. Is a search followed by a seizure and then by an arrest valid? Is a seizure followed by an arrest and then by an additional search valid?

4. What search incident to an arrest problems are presented when the person arrested is a person of the opposite sex?

5. Does the nature of the offense arrested for have any effect on the scope of a search incident to arrest?

6. Assume that a defendant is arrested in his kitchen for the armed robbery of a bank earlier that day. The arresting officers have an arrest warrant but no search warrant. The defendant is one of three persons wanted in the robbery. The defendant's automobile, the suspected getaway car, is parked in his driveway. Indicate the full extent of the arresting officers' authority to search the defendant, his premises, and his automobile.

7. Assume the same facts as in question 6 except that the defendant is arrested while running from his house to his automobile. Indicate the full extent of the arresting officers' authority to search the defendant, his premises, and his automobile. What if the officers have only a search warrant for the defendant's house, and no arrest warrant? What if it is raining heavily?

8. Is the scope of a search incident to arrest affected by any of the following circumstances?

   a. The defendant is handcuffed and chained to a pole.

   b. The defendant is unconscious.

   c. The defendant is surrounded by a group of friends.

   d. The defendant is arrested on a dark street.

9. Since the search of containers in the passenger compartment of an automobile is now allowed incident to a custodial arrest under the ruling in *New York v. Belton,* should law enforcement officers wait until a defendant is in an automobile before making an arrest, when possible? Should officers make custodial arrests for offenses for which they would ordinarily not make custodial arrests?

10. Discuss the meaning of the statement "It is not at all clear that the 'grabbing distance' authorized in the *Chimel* case is conditioned upon the arrested person's continued capacity 'to grab.'" *People v. Fitzpatrick,* 346 N.Y.S.2d 793, 797, 300 N.E.2d 139, 143 (N.Y. 1973).

1. At approximately 10 P.M. on September 19, 1995, Trooper Ron Nordman of the Washington State Patrol stopped Timothy Thomas for speeding on State Route 395. His check of the status of Mr. Thomas' driver's license revealed it was revoked. Trooper Nordman arrested Mr. Thomas for first degree driving while license revoked, searched his person, and placed him in the back of the patrol car. Trooper Connelly was in his vehicle traveling ahead of Trooper Nordman when Trooper Nordman stopped Mr. Thomas. He returned to the location to assist. Trooper Connelly approached Ms. Parker, who was sitting in the front passenger seat of Mr. Thomas' vehicle. He observed an open container on the passenger side. He decided to run a breath test on Ms. Parker before he released the car to her. She voluntarily exited the vehicle, took the test and passed it.

Trooper Nordman conducted a search of the passenger compartment of Mr. Thomas' automobile after Ms. Parker got out of it. He did not begin this search until some 15 to 20 minutes after he had placed Mr. Thomas in the back of his patrol car. Trooper Nordman testified there was an open purse with a large amount of cash lying loosely on top of it in the front passenger seat. Trooper Nordman also testified the car contained a "felony forest"—there were "a large number of Christmas tree shaped air fresheners in the passenger area hanging from the vents in the passenger area, as well as in the purse in the passenger's seat." He observed a handheld scanner under the armrest. He did not explain whether these items are typically used in the drug trade, nor did he indicate they played any role in his decision to examine the contents of the purse.

Trooper Nordman asked Ms. Parker about the money, and she answered she had received it from the purchaser of a car she had sold. When he separately asked Mr. Thomas about the money, he answered it was his, and stated he placed it on Ms. Parker's purse after the stop. Mr. Thomas later explained he knew he was driving with a revoked license; he expected the trooper would arrest him for that offense, and he placed the cash on top of the purse because he knew Ms. Parker would need bail money to obtain his release. Ms. Parker then admitted the money belonged to Mr. Thomas.

Trooper Nordman removed the purse from the car and placed it on the trunk. He asked Ms. Parker if Mr. Thomas had placed anything else in her purse. She said, "no." He proceeded to examine the contents of the purse. Inside he found a small closed coin purse. He opened it and discovered the methamphetamine in a plastic baggie. The state charged Ms. Parker with possession of methamphetamine. She moved to suppress the

evidence. Should her motion to suppress be granted? *State v. Parker,* 944 P.2d 1081 (Wash.App. Div. 3 1997).

2. On February 19, 1994, in Seattle at approximately 10:42 P.M. Officer Jason Chittenden of the Seattle Police Department observed Petitioner Travis Lee Rife, a pedestrian, alight from a public transit bus and cross Aurora Avenue near 85th Street outside a crosswalk and against a traffic signal. The officer stopped petitioner, informed him he was stopping him for jaywalking, obtained identification from him, and made a radio check for outstanding warrants. The officer did not present a notice of infraction to the petitioner for his signature. Nor was any notice even issued.

The officer testified the Seattle Police Department does not have a policy requiring officers to run a check for outstanding warrants for pedestrians or drivers stopped for traffic violations but that he normally runs a check anyway. The petitioner was cooperative at all times after he was stopped by the officer. The warrant check lasted five to ten minutes, with verification taking an additional five to ten minutes. Petitioner was not free to leave during this period. The officer did not cite him for the traffic infraction ("jaywalking") for which he was stopped but formally arrested him for two outstanding warrants determined in the warrant check.

At the police station, in a search incident to the petitioner's arrest under the outstanding warrants, Officer Chittenden discovered a bundle of heroin in the petitioner's pocket. Based upon this discovery, petitioner was charged by the King County Prosecuting Attorney in the King County Superior Court on February 24, 1994, with violation of the Uniform Controlled Substances Act. The petitioner moved to suppress the heroin. Should his motion be granted? *State v. Rife,* 943 P.2d 266 (Wash. 1997).

3. On March 15, 1996, police officers received a call about a man dressed in a brown and black striped shirt and black pants selling contraband to pedestrians and persons in cars in the 1300 block of South Dorgenois Street in front of the Fast Stop Grocery Store. Officer Joe Belisle and his partner established a surveillance and saw the defendant reach into his shoe area, pull out an object, and hand it to the other individual. The defendant stood in front of the store after the transaction until he saw a police car turn the corner and drive toward him. He then placed his hands into his pockets and walked into the store. Officer Belisle, who was dressed in plain clothes, followed him into the store where the defendant purchased a bottle of water and then exited the store.

The defendant walked to the corner of South Dorgenois and Erato Streets where he was detained by Officer Belisle and two other officers, Officers Butler and Carroll. The officers informed the defendant of his *Miranda* rights and told him he was being detained in conjunction with a narcotics investigation. They then patted down the defendant for their safety and asked him to remove his shoe. When the defendant complied, the officers saw a piece of foil sitting on top of his foot. Inside the foil was a white powdery substance. The officers arrested the defendant and charged him with intent to distribute heroin. Officer Belisle testified that the area was known for drug trafficking. Should the defendant's motion to suppress the evidence be granted? *State v. Butler,* 700 So.2d 224 (La.App. 4 Cir. 1997).

4. An officer from the City of Norcross Police Department responded to a call that a white male with stringy hair was attempting to enter a black truck near room 219 of the Apartment Inn. The officer arrived at the address and saw a man fitting that description run from a black truck into room 215. The officer went to room 215, knocked on the door and waited two or three minutes until Sprinkles and another woman opened the door. When the officer asked where the man was, the women denied that any man had run into their room. Noticing that the bathroom door was closed, the officer asked if the man was in the bathroom. The women replied that he was. The officer advised the women that he was investigating a report that someone matching the description of the man he saw run into their room had been attempting to enter a black truck in the parking lot. After stating that the truck was hers, Sprinkles told the officer that she wanted to leave. The officer told Sprinkles she could not leave until he confirmed the truck was hers, met with the man in the bathroom, and talked to the person who called the police. Within "a couple of minutes," a second officer arrived and the man came out of the bathroom. As they waited for the arrival of the person who called police, Sprinkles took her purse and an overnight bag, pushed the second officer out of the doorway, and began walking down the sidewalk. One of the officers told Sprinkles that if she did not come back so he could complete his investigation, she would be arrested for obstruction. Sprinkles stated she was leaving and kept walking. The officer advised her that she was under arrest and grabbed her arm in order to handcuff her. Sprinkles began yelling at and fighting the officers. They forced her to the ground, handcuffed her, and placed her in the back of the police car. While she was in the police car, one of the officers looked in Sprinkles' purse for identification and, finding none, looked in her luggage. In it, he found envelopes containing $3,000 in cash and plastic bags containing substances which later tested positive for methamphetamine and marijuana.

Should the defendant's motion to suppress the evidence found in her luggage be suppressed? *Sprinkles v. State,* 488 S.E.2d 492 (Ga.App. 1997).

5. On December 27, 1993, four Salt Lake County police officers went to appellant's home to execute drug-related arrest warrants for the appellant and his girlfriend, Kelly Jensen. One of the officers, Detective Russo, knew the appellant. While Detective Russo stood out of view, another officer knocked on a rear sliding glass door. When appellant appeared at the door, the officer asked if "he were Steve Wells, or if he lived there." The appellant replied that "no Steve is here." Detective Russo then made a positive identification of the appellant. The appellant also recognized Detective Russo and immediately ran downstairs.

Detective Russo announced that the officers had arrest warrants, but the appellant refused to open the door. Thus, to gain entry, Detective Russo picked up a nearby shovel and shattered the sliding glass door. Deputy Sterner entered the home first and ran downstairs, where he was bitten by the appellant's dog. Deputy Sterner testified he arrested the appellant at the bottom of the stairs immediately after the officers had subdued the dog. Jensen was found hiding in a downstairs closet and was also placed under arrest. While sitting with Jensen in a bedroom adjacent to where she was arrested, Deputy Sterner observed a baggie containing a substance he believed to be marijuana. As he went to retrieve the baggie, Deputy Sterner also noticed two marijuana pipes on the floor. Deputy Sterner testified that he then asked Jensen "where the cocaine was." In response, Jensen explained that the appellant had hidden marijuana in a vacuum cleaner and cocaine in the lining of a leather jacket lying on a bed. Detective Russo recognized the jacket as belonging to the appellant. Subsequently, the officers retrieved the cocaine from the lining of the jacket. The record reflects that both suspects were handcuffed and in custody when the cocaine was seized. Detective Russo testified that, although the appellant attempted to elude the officers before their entry, the officers handcuffed him soon after entering the home. Detective Russo further testified that Jensen was "[p]robably handcuffed" when she directed the officers to the appellant's jacket. Should the motion to suppress the cocaine found in the jacket be granted? *State v. Wells,* 928 P.2d 386 (Utah App. 1996).

6. On December 13, 1994, shortly after midnight, Officer Shannon Planck ("Planck") of the Butler Police Department responded to a dispatch from DeKalb County regarding a 911 call from a female indicating that someone was going to kill her. When Planck arrived, DeLong was standing beside his truck, outside the home. Ronda Rowe ("Rowe"), DeLong's girlfriend, came out of the

house and began yelling profanities at the police and telling them not to arrest DeLong. Rowe and DeLong both indicated that they had been fighting over the volume of the television. While DeLong was still outside by his truck, Planck spoke to Rowe inside the house and she indicated that she had been struck and pushed by DeLong. Planck observed bruising, redness, and a small amount of blood. Planck left the house and advised DeLong that he was being placed under arrest for battery. By the time Planck arrested DeLong, three additional police officers were at the scene. DeLong asked Planck for permission to leave his jacket at the house because it was a nice jacket. Planck allowed DeLong to remove the jacket and Planck placed the jacket on the trunk of the police car. Planck then searched, handcuffed, and placed DeLong in the backseat of his police car. Planck grabbed the jacket and started towards the house to leave the jacket with Rowe. Planck indicated he felt a hard, cylindrically shaped object in the jacket and believed there could have been a weapon. Planck testified that after he felt something in the jacket, he did not want to hand it back to Rowe in her state of mind without checking it for officer safety. Planck reached inside the pocket of the jacket and pulled out a plastic baggie which contained a white powdered substance. Planck returned to his police car with the jacket, removed DeLong, and read him his *Miranda* rights. Planck kept the jacket in his custody until he arrived at the jail and could search the entire jacket. Should DeLong's motion to suppress the evidence found in the jacket be granted? *DeLong v. State,* 670 N.E.2d 56 (Ind.App. 1996).

CHAPTER NINE

Consent Searches

OBJECTIVES

1. Be able to explain the benefits, to the law enforcement officer and to the person being searched, of a consent search.

2. Understand the circumstances that are considered in determining whether a consent search is voluntary.

3. Understand the difference between a consent to enter premises and a consent to search the premises.

4. Understand how the scope of a consent search is limited by
   a. the person giving consent,

b. the area to which consent to search is given,
   c. time, and
   d. the object searched for.

5. Understand when a third person may be authorized to consent to a search of a person's property and how third-party consent is affected by the person's reasonable expectation of privacy.

OUTLINE

1. Introduction—benefits of consent searches
2. Voluntariness requirement
   a. Force or threat of force
   b. Submission to a fraudulent or mistaken claim of authority
   c. Misrepresentation or deception
   d. Arrest or detention
   e. Knowledge of right to refuse consent
   f. Informing suspect that he or she is free to go
   g. Suspect's attitude about the likelihood of discovering evidence
   h. Clearness and explicitness of consent
   i. Notification of counsel
   j. Physical, mental, emotional, and educational factors
3. Scope
   a. Consent merely to enter

   b. Area of search
   c. Time
   d. Object of search
   e. Revocation of consent
4. Who may give consent
   a. Persons having equal rights or interests in property
   b. Landlord-tenant
   c. Hotel manager—hotel guest
   d. Host-guest
   e. Employer-employee
   f. School official—student
   g. Principal-agent
   h. Husband-wife
   i. Parent-child
   j. Bailor-bailee
   k. Voluntary production of evidence
   l. Reasonable expectation of privacy

Another well-established exception to the search warrant requirement is the **consent search.** A consent search occurs when a person voluntarily waives his or her Fourth Amendment rights and allows a law enforcement officer to search his or her body, premises, or belongings. The consenting person relinquishes any right to object to the search on constitutional grounds, and any evidence seized as a result of the search is admissible in court, even though there was no warrant and no probable cause to search. A consent search can benefit a consenting party who is innocent of any wrongdoing.

> If the search is conducted and proves fruitless, that in itself may convince the police that an arrest with its possible stigma and embarrassment is unnecessary, or that a far more extensive search pursuant to a warrant is not justified. In short, a search pursuant to consent may result in considerably less inconvenience for the subject of the search, and, properly conducted, is a constitutionally permissible and wholly legitimate aspect of effective police activity. *Schneckloth v. Bustamonte,* 412 U.S. 218, 228, 93 S.Ct. 2041, 2048, 36 L.Ed.2d 854, 863 (1973).

Law enforcement officers use the consent search frequently because it is faster than warrant procedures and does not require the often difficult determination of whether there is probable cause, either to search or to arrest. Consent searches, however, present many opportunities for abuse of a person's Fourth Amendment rights by law enforcement officers. To protect those rights, courts closely examine the circumstances surrounding every consent search to determine whether the consent was truly voluntary. The U.S. Supreme Court said:

> [T]he Fourth and Fourteenth Amendments require that consent not be coerced, by explicit or implicit means, by implied threat or covert force. For, no matter how subtly the coercion were applied, the resulting "consent" would be no more than a pretext for the unjustified police intrusion against which the Fourth Amendment is directed. . . .
>
> The problem of reconciling the recognized legitimacy of consent searches with the requirement that they be free from any aspect of official coercion cannot be resolved by any infallible touchstone. To approve such searches without the most careful scrutiny would sanction the possibility of official coercion; to place artificial restrictions upon such searches would jeopardize their basic validity. Just as was true with confessions the requirement of "voluntary" consent reflects a fair accommodation of the constitutional requirements involved. In examining all the surrounding circumstances to determine if in fact the consent to search was coerced, account must be taken of subtly coercive police questions, as well as the possibly vulnerable subjective state of the person who consents. Those searches that are the product of police coercion can thus be filtered out without undermining the continuing validity of consent searches. In sum, there is no reason for us to depart in the area of consent searches, from the traditional definition of "voluntariness." *Schneckloth v. Bustamonte,* 412 U.S. 218, 228–29, 93 S.Ct. 2041, 2048–49, 36 L.Ed.2d 854, 864 (1973).

When the prosecuting attorney attempts to introduce into court evidence obtained as a result of a consent search, the court requires proof by "clear and convincing evidence" that the consent was voluntary and not the result of duress or coercion, express or implied. *United States v. Gonzales,* 842 F.2d 748, 754 (5th Cir. 1988). The prosecutor's proof will consist almost entirely of the law enforcement officer's testimony about the circumstances surrounding the obtaining of the consent and the conducting of the search. The remainder of this chapter is devoted to explaining in detail the meaning of the voluntariness requirement and providing guidelines for the law enforcement officer in conducting consent searches. ■

Voluntariness Requirement

There are no set rules for determining whether a consent to search is voluntary. Courts will examine all the circumstances surrounding the giving of the consent in making this decision. The following examples illustrate the circumstances courts consider important in deciding the question of voluntariness of consent.

Force or Threat of Force

Courts usually find consent involuntary if law enforcement officers used force or threats of force in obtaining the consent. In *United States v. Al-Azzawy,* 784 F.2d 890 (9th Cir. 1985), the defendant gave permission to search his trailer as he was approached by numerous police officers with guns drawn while the defendant knelt outside his trailer with his hands on his head. The court found that, under these coercive conditions, the consent to search was not voluntary. And in *United States v. Hatley,* 999 F.2d 392 (9th Cir. 1993), the court found the defendant's consent to search not voluntary where it was given after the officer threatened to take the defendant's child into custody. Lack of voluntary consent was also found where officers told the defendant that if he did not consent, the officers could and would get a search warrant that would allow them to tear the paneling off his walls and ransack his house. *United States v. Kampbell,* 574 F.2d 962 (8th Cir. 1978).

A mere statement by police that they will attempt to obtain a warrant if consent is withheld is usually not considered coercion, however, especially if the officer indicates that he or she must apply for the warrant from a neutral and detached judicial authority and if the statement that a warrant can be obtained is well founded.

> One factor to be considered is whether a threat to obtain a search warrant will invalidate a subsequent consent. Courts have drawn distinctions where, on one hand, an officer merely says that he will attempt to obtain a search warrant or whether, on the other hand, he says he can obtain the search warrant, as if it were a foregone conclusion. However, consent is not likely to be held invalid where an officer tells a defendant that he could obtain a search warrant if the officer had probable cause upon which a warrant could issue. *United States v. Kaplan,* 895 F.2d 618, 622 (9th Cir. 1990).

Sometimes the initial encounter between a law enforcement officer and a suspect requires the officer to use force or threat of force for personal or public safety. Despite the coercive nature of the initial confrontation, an officer may still obtain a valid consent to search if the consent itself is obtained without coercion. In *United States v. Alfonso,* 759 F.2d 728 (9th Cir. 1985), police with guns drawn arrested the defendant in his motel room. After determining that no weapons or other persons were in the room, the officers holstered their guns. The officers informed the defendant of the purpose of their investigation, and the defendant, who was not handcuffed, responded that he had "nothing to hide." The court held that the defendant's consent to a search of his luggage was voluntary, despite the initial armed confrontation.

Submission to a Fraudulent or Mistaken Claim of Authority

A subtler form of coercion is a law enforcement officer's assertion of a right to search when no such right exists. A person's submitting to a false assertion of authority and allowing a search does not constitute a voluntary consent. Rather than an act of free will, it is merely a mistaken demonstration of respect for the law. It matters not whether the officer's assertion of authority was mistaken or was deliberately designed to deceive the person. In *Bumper v. North Carolina,* 391 U.S. 543, 88 S.Ct. 1788, 20 L.Ed.2d 797 (1968), officers went to the home of a rape suspect to look for evidence. The home was owned and occupied by the defendant's grandmother. The officers told the grandmother that they had a search warrant, and she let them in. During the course of their search, a rifle was found. At the hearing on the motion to suppress the rifle as evidence, the prosecutor relied on the grandmother's consent rather than on the warrant to support the legality of the search. (In fact, no warrant was ever returned, nor was there any information about the conditions under which it was issued.)

The U.S. Supreme Court held that a search cannot be justified on the basis of consent when that consent has been given only after an announcement by the officers conducting the search that they have a search warrant:

> When a prosecutor seeks to rely upon consent to justify the lawfulness of a search, he has the burden of proving that the consent was, in fact, *freely and voluntarily given.* This burden cannot be discharged by showing no more than acquiescence to a claim of lawful authority. A search conducted in reliance upon a warrant cannot later be justified on the basis of consent if it turns out that the warrant was invalid. The results can be no different when it turns out that the State does not even attempt to rely upon the validity of the warrant, or fails to show that there was, in fact, any warrant at all.
>
> When a law enforcement officer claims authority to search a home under a warrant, he announces in effect that the occupant has no right to resist the search. The situation is instinct with coercion—albeit colorably lawful coercion. Where there is coercion there cannot be consent. [Emphasis supplied.] 391 U.S. at 548–50, 88 S.Ct. at 1792, 20 L.Ed.2d at 802–03.

Misrepresentation or Deception

Coercion may also take the form of misrepresentation or deception on matters other than the officer's authority. A person's consent to search based on false impressions created by a law enforcement officer is not voluntary. In *Commonwealth v. Wright,* 190 A.2d 709 (Pa. 1963), officers arrested the defendant for robbery and murder and questioned him at police headquarters, but they obtained no incriminating statements. The next day officers, without a search warrant, went to the defendant's apartment to conduct a search. They falsely told the defendant's wife that the defendant had admitted the crime and had sent the police for the "stuff." The frightened and upset wife admitted the officers to the apartment and led them to money taken in the robbery. The court held that the consent given by the wife was not voluntary: "[I]t is well established that the consent may not be gained through stealth, deceit, or misrepresentation, and that if such exists this is tantamount to implied coercion." 190 A.2d at 709, 711.

If, however, the deceit is carried out by an undercover officer and concerns only the officer's identity as a governmental agent, a person's misplaced confidence in the agent will not make the person's consent involuntary.

> Entry of an undercover agent is not illegal if he enters a home for the "very purposes contemplated by the occupant." . . . If the occupant reveals private information to the visitor under such circumstances, he or she assumes the risk the visitor will reveal it. *United States v. Goldstein*, 611 F.Supp. 624, 626 (N.D. Ill. 1985).

In the *Goldstein* case, the undercover officer gained entrance to the defendant's home for the purpose understood by the defendant's wife: to discuss the possible purchase of a stolen emerald. The court held that the wife's voluntarily showing the officer the emerald was the result of her misplaced trust in the officer and did not implicate any Fourth Amendment privacy interest. "A government agent may obtain an invitation onto property by misrepresenting his identity, and if invited, does not need probable cause nor warrant to enter so long as he does not exceed the scope of his invitation." *United States v. Scherer*, 673 F.2d 176, 182 (7th Cir. 1982).

Arrest or Detention

The custodial circumstances surrounding the encounter are important to the determination of whether a voluntary consent was given. In *United States v. Watson*, 423 U.S. 411, 96 S.Ct. 820, 46 L.Ed.2d 598 (1976), the U.S. Supreme Court held that a consent to search is not involuntary solely because the person giving the consent is under arrest or otherwise in custody. Nevertheless, courts tend to examine very carefully any consent given under these circumstances. A person who has been taken into custody or arrested is believed to be "more susceptible to duress or coercion from the custodial officers." *United States v. Richardson*, 388 F.2d 842, 845 (6th Cir. 1968).

In general, it will be harder to prove a consent was voluntary when the person giving the consent was in custody than if the person was not. However, if the person in custody is subjected to additional coercive action by a law enforcement officer, such as handcuffing, display of weapons, or incarceration, or if the officer interrogates the person without giving *Miranda* warnings, a subsequent consent to search is likely to be considered involuntary. Evasive or uncooperative conduct on the part of the person in custody is also considered to indicate that the consent is not voluntary. In *United States v. Mendenhall*, 446 U.S. 544, 100 S.Ct. 1870, 64 L.Ed.2d 497 (1980), the U.S. Supreme Court held that a person subjected to a legal *Terry*-type stop was capable of giving a valid consent to search.

If the arrest or detention itself is illegal, courts will generally hold that any consent obtained by exploitation of the illegal conduct is "fruit of the poisonous tree" unless the causal chain between the illegal conduct and the obtaining of consent has been broken. In determining whether the causal chain has been broken, courts consider the time elapsed between the illegality and the giving of consent, the presence of intervening circumstances, and the purpose and flagrancy of the official conduct. *Brown v. Illinois,* 422 U.S. 590, 95 S.Ct. 2254, 45 L.Ed.2d 416 (1975). In *Florida v. Royer,* 460 U.S. 491, 103 S.Ct. 1319, 75 L.Ed.2d 229 (1983), the U.S. Supreme Court, after finding that the defendant was being illegally detained when he consented to the search of his luggage, held that the consent was tainted by the illegality and was ineffective to justify the search. In *United States v. Maez,* 872 F.2d 1444 (10th Cir. 1989), the consent to search was held invalid where the illegal arrest was such that it would cause surprise, fright, and confusion and where the defendant was in the custody of at least three officers for forty-five minutes between the arrest and the giving of consent. In *United States v. Wellins,* 654 F.2d 550 (9th Cir. 1981), however, despite an illegal arrest of the defendant, the court held that a consent to search obtained one and one-quarter hours after the illegal arrest was valid. Attenuating circumstances were found where the defendant was given *Miranda* warnings and allowed to consult with his attorney and codefendant before signing a consent form. Another court held that the passage of a significant amount of time and the lack of flagrant misconduct by police helped purge the taint of an illegal arrest. *United States v. Cherry,* 794 F.2d 201 (5th Cir. 1986).

Knowledge of Right to Refuse Consent

Before the U.S. Supreme Court decision in *Schneckloth v. Bustamonte* (discussed earlier), some courts held that, to prove voluntary consent to search, the prosecution had to show that the person giving consent knew of the right to refuse consent. Other courts ruled that knowledge of the right to refuse consent was only one factor to be considered in determining voluntariness. In *Schneckloth v. Bustamonte,* the Court adopted the latter view:

> [W]hen the subject of a search is not in custody and the State attempts to justify a search on the basis of his consent, the Fourth and Fourteenth Amendments require that it demonstrate that the consent was in fact voluntarily given, and not the result of duress or coercion, express or implied. Voluntariness is a question of fact to be determined from all the circumstances, and while the subject's knowledge of a right to refuse is a factor to be taken into consideration, the prosecution is not required to demonstrate such knowledge as a prerequisite to establishing a voluntary consent. 412 U.S. at 248–49, 93 S.Ct. at 2059, 36 L.Ed.2d at 875.

A law enforcement officer seeking to obtain a valid consent to search from a person not in custody need not give any warnings or otherwise ensure that the person is aware of the right to refuse consent.

Nevertheless, even though formal warnings are not required for noncustodial consent searches, the courts still consider a person's knowledge of the right to refuse consent as very persuasive evidence of voluntariness.

> [T]he . . . salutary practice of informing individuals that they are free to refuse consent to a search and to contact a lawyer . . . does not absolutely prove unco-erced consent, [but] it does in many instances assuage the fear of a court that an individual was intimidated into consent to a search. *United States v. Berry,* 670 F.2d 583, 597–98 (5th Cir. 1982).

For example, in *In re Joe R.,* 165 Cal.Rptr. 837, 612 P.2d 927 (Cal. 1980), the court found voluntary consent to search despite the presence of several officers with drawn guns, where officers had explained the right to refuse consent. But in *United States v.*

Jones, 846 F.2d 358 (6th Cir. 1988), the court found the consent involuntary in similar circumstances, where the police failed to apprise the defendant of his *Miranda* rights or his right to refuse consent. In that case, the defendant, who had no formal education, had been stopped initially by three police cars and led by police to believe he was under arrest. Therefore, an officer may give a person formal warning of this right to increase the chances that the consent will be voluntary. Furthermore, since the courts have not yet decided whether knowledge of the right to refuse consent is necessary for a valid consent when the consenting person is in custody, officers should so inform persons under arrest or otherwise in custody. The following warning should adequately inform a person of the right to refuse consent:

> I am a law enforcement officer. I would like to request permission from you to search your premises (person, belongings).
>
> You have an absolute right to refuse to grant permission for me to search unless I have a search warrant.
>
> If you do grant permission to search, anything found can be used against you in a court of law. If you refuse, I will not make a search at this time.

A consent to search given by a person after receiving such a warning is likely to be considered voluntary by a court, assuming the officer did not use coercion.

If an officer has clear indications that the consenting person already knows of the right to insist on a search warrant, there is no need for the officer to give any warnings. In *United States v. Manuel,* 992 F.2d 272 (10th Cir. 1993), the court held that the defendant's steadfast, repeated refusals to consent to the search of a gift-wrapped package demonstrated his knowledge of the right to refuse consent. When he finally did consent under noncoercive circumstances, the court found the consent voluntary.

Some state courts have refused to follow the *Schneckloth v. Bustamonte* totality-of-the-circumstances test and have required that consenting persons be aware of their right to refuse consent in addition to requiring that the consent be voluntary. The New Jersey Supreme Court held that the state constitution demands that

> the validity of a consent to search, even in a noncustodial situation, must be measured in terms of waiver; i.e., where the state seeks to justify a search on the basis of consent it has the burden of showing that the consent was voluntary, an essential element of which is knowledge of the right to refuse consent. *State v. Johnson,* 346 A.2d 66, 68 (N.J. 1975).

Likewise, *Case v. State,* 519 P.2d 523 (Okla.Crim.App. 1974), held that officers must give *Miranda* warnings before obtaining consent.

Informing Suspect That He or She Is Free to Go

In *Ohio v. Robinette,* 519 U.S. 33, 117 S.Ct. 417, 136 L.Ed.2d 347 (1996), the defendant was legally stopped for speeding and the officer asked for and was handed the defendant's license. The officer ran a computer check that indicated that the defendant had no previous violations. The officer then asked the defendant to step out of his car, turned on his mounted video camera, issued a verbal warning, and returned his license. After receiving a negative response to questions about the defendant's possession of drugs or weapons, the officer requested and received consent to search his car. In the car the officer found drugs. The defendant claimed that a lawfully seized defendant must be advised that he is "free to go" before his consent to search will be recognized as voluntary. The court held that it does not. "[I]t [would] be unrealistic to require police officers to always inform detainees that they are free to go before a consent to search may be deemed voluntary." 519 U.S. at ___, 117 S.Ct. at 421, 136 L.Ed.2d at 355.

Suspect's Attitude About the Likelihood of Discovering Evidence

In *United States v. Crespo,* 834 F.2d 267 (2d Cir. 1987), the court found a voluntary consent to search based largely on the trial judge's finding that "having observed Jose Crespo, I believe he is arrogant and self-assured and that it is quite likely that he believed that the agents would not find the materials which were in a closet on a shelf hidden in a bag." 834 F.2d at 272. And in *United States v. Gonzalez-Basulto,* 898 F.2d 1011 (5th Cir. 1990), one of the considerations that led the court to find a voluntary consent was that the defendant "may well have believed that no drugs would be found because the cocaine was hidden in boxes toward the front of the trailer and there was little crawl space in the trailer." 898 F.2d at 1013.

Clearness and Explicitness of Consent

Another issue in determining the voluntariness of consent is whether the expression of consent is clear, explicit, and unequivocal. Hesitation or ambiguity in the giving of consent could indicate that the consent is not voluntary.

Both written and oral consent to search are equally effective in waiving a person's right to object later to the search on constitutional grounds. A signed and witnessed writing or a tape-recorded oral statement provides the best proof of a clear, voluntary waiver of a known right. A written or recorded consent is also the best way to refute any challenges later raised by the defendant. Exhibit 9.1 is a suggested form for obtaining a written consent to search.

Consent need not be expressed in words but may be implied from a person's gestures or conduct. For example, in *United States v. Benitez,* 899 F.2d 995 (10th Cir. 1990), the defendant never verbally consented to a search of his vehicle. Nevertheless, valid consent was found where the defendant exited his vehicle, opened the trunk, and opened a suitcase contained in the trunk. And in *United States v. Williams,* 754 F.2d 672 (1985), the court found indicative of voluntariness that the defendant assisted the officer in opening the suitcase by twice setting the tumbler on its combination lock.

Notification of Counsel

A defendant has no Sixth Amendment right to counsel until after the initiation of adversary judicial criminal proceedings. *Kirby v. Illinois,* 406 U.S. 682, 92 S.Ct. 1877, 32 L.Ed.2d 411 (1972). Thus, before the filing of formal charges, police are not required to notify retained counsel before soliciting a person's consent, even if the person is under arrest. However, the refusal by police to allow a person to consult with counsel upon request may be relevant to the determination of voluntariness of consent. By the same token, consent given after consultation with counsel will very likely be found to be voluntary. *Cody v. Solem,* 755 F.2d 1323, 1330 (8th Cir. 1985). Furthermore, it has been suggested that where police have agreed with counsel (whenever retained) not to communicate with a suspect, a breach of that agreement may bar a valid consent. *Hall v. Iowa,* 705 F.2d 283, 289–90 (8th Cir. 1983).

CONSENT TO SEARCH

I, _____, have been requested to consent to a search of my _____, located at _____. I have also been advised of my constitutional rights to refuse consent and to require that a search warrant be obtained prior to any search. I have further been advised that if I do consent to a search, any evidence found as a result of the search can be seized and used against me in any court of law, and that I may withdraw my consent to search at any time prior to the conclusion of the search.

After having been advised of my constitutional rights as stated above, I hereby waive those rights and consent to a search and authorize _____ and _____ to conduct a complete search of the above-described _____. This consent to search is being given by me voluntarily and without threats or promises of any kind.

_____
Signature

_____
Location and Date

WITNESSES:

_____
Signature, Title and Date

_____
Signature, Title and Date

EXHIBIT 9.1   A Suggested Consent to Search Form

Physical, Mental, Emotional, and Educational Factors

Voluntariness of consent may be affected by the physical, mental, or emotional condition of the person giving consent. These personal characteristics must be balanced against police pressures and tactics used to induce cooperation; the length of the police contact; the general conditions under which the contact occurs; excessive physical or psychological pressure; and inducements, threats, or other methods used to compel a response. If a person is sick, injured, mentally ill, under the influence of alcohol or drugs, or otherwise impaired, that person's vulnerability to subtle forms of coercion may affect the voluntariness of consent. Likewise, if a person is immature, inexperienced, mentally retarded, illiterate, or emotionally upset, the impairment of perception and understanding may render any consent to search a mere submission to authority. *United States v. Gallego-Zapata,* 630 F.Supp. 665 (D.Mass. 1986).

The existence of any one of these conditions or states of mind alone usually does not invalidate an otherwise uncoerced consent. "[T]he mere fact that one has taken drugs, or is intoxicated, or mentally agitated, does not render consent involuntary."

United States v. Rambo, 789 F.2d 1289, 1297 (8th Cir. 1986). In *United States v. Gay,* 774 F.2d 368, 377 (10th Cir. 1985), the court said:

> The issue squarely put is whether Gay was so intoxicated that his consent to search was not the product of a rational intellect and a free will. . . . The question is one of mental awareness so that the act of consent was that of one who knew what he was doing. It is elementary that one must know he is giving consent for the consent to be efficacious.

In the *Gay* case, the court found voluntary consent to search the defendant's automobile glove compartment despite the defendant's intoxication, based on evidence that the defendant

- was able to answer questions addressed to him;
- produced his driver's license on request;
- responded when asked if he had been drinking;
- emptied his pockets upon request; and
- denied access to the automobile's trunk, which was found to contain cocaine in a later search.

Courts also consider a person's intelligence and educational level in determining the voluntariness of consent. In *United States v. Bates,* 840 F.2d 858 (11th Cir. 1988), the court found a valid consent where "[t]he defendant, an educated man, had 'been informed of [his] right to refuse to consent to such a search.'" 840 F.2d at 861. And in *United States v. Kaplan,* 895 F.2d 618 (9th Cir. 1990), one of the court's reasons for finding voluntary consent was that the defendant, a doctor, "was not a person lacking in education and understanding." 895 F.2d at 622.

Although a person's unfamiliarity with the English language is not an indication of intelligence or educational level, language barriers make determining voluntariness more difficult. In *State v. Xiong,* 504 N.W.2d 428, 432 (Wis.App. 1993), the court said:

> It is incumbent upon the police to effectively communicate their objectives when seeking consent to search. Merely providing an interpreter is not enough. The interpretation must convey what is intended to be communicated. Communication is effective only if it clearly and accurately relates all pertinent information to the listener. If effective communication is not provided, then that is a form of coercion.

KEY POINTS

3. Consent to search given in submission to force, threats of force, or other show of authority is not voluntary.

4. Consent to search obtained by misrepresentation or deception is not voluntary, except that a person's misplaced trust in an undercover police agent will not alone invalidate an otherwise voluntary consent.

5. Knowledge of the right to refuse consent is only one factor among others to be considered in determining the voluntariness of a consent search.

6. The Fourth Amendment does not require that a lawfully seized person be advised that he or she is "free to go" before the person's consent to search will be recognized as voluntary.

7. Voluntary consent to search may be given in writing, orally, or by a person's conduct so long as the expression of consent is clear and unequivocal.

8. Voluntariness of consent may be affected by the physical, mental, or emotional condition and the educational level of the person giving consent.

Scope

Determination of the allowable scope of a consent search involves issues of whether permission to actually search, rather than merely enter, has been given and what limits are placed on the search in terms of area, time, and object searched for. Also included in this section is a discussion of revocation of consent.

Consent Merely to Enter

Although a person may give a valid consent to an officer's requests, it may not be a consent to *search*. The best example of this is a person's consent to allow an officer to *enter* his or her home in compliance with the officer's request for an interview. This does *not* automatically give the officer a right to search. There is a vital distinction between the granting of admission to one's home for the purposes of conversation and the granting of permission to thoroughly search the home.

In *Duncan v. State,* 176 So.2d 840 (Ala. 1965), officers investigating a murder knocked on the defendant's hotel room door and were invited in by the defendant. The defendant was not advised that they were police officers, nor did the officers make any request to search the defendant's room. Nevertheless, a search was conducted and incriminating evidence was found.

The court held that the invitation to enter his room, extended by the defendant to the person who knocked on the door, did not constitute a consent to search his room. Quoting from another case, the court said:

> "To justify the introduction of evidence seized by a police officer within a private residence on the ground that the officer's entry was made by invitation, permission, or consent, there must be evidence of a statement or some overt act by the occupant of such residence sufficient to indicate his intent to waive his rights to the security and privacy of his home and freedom from unwarranted intrusions therein. An open door is not a waiver of such rights." 176 So.2d at 853.

Although an invitation to *enter* premises is not the equivalent of a consent to *search* the premises, an officer need not ignore contraband or other criminal evidence lying in plain view. Under the **plain view doctrine,** if police are lawfully in a position from which they view an object, if its incriminating character is apparent, and if the officers have a lawful right of access to the object, they may seize it without a warrant. In *Robbins v. Mackenzie,* 364 F.2d 45 (1st Cir. 1966), officers were investigating a robbery, and preliminary information led them to suspect a man named Albert. The officers went to Albert's apartment, knocked on the door, identified themselves, and were invited into the apartment by Albert, who opened the door and walked back into the room. The defendant was present in the apartment as a guest of Albert. While talking to the two men, the officers noticed various objects fitting the description of items stolen in the robbery lying in plain view. They arrested the two men and seized the evidence observed.

The court held that the evidence seized was admissible against the defendant (Albert's guest). Because the officers were rightfully in the room by Albert's invitation, they were also rightfully there with respect to the defendant. Seeing what was patently and obviously open to view was therefore not a search, and seizing the evidence was not a violation of the defendant's rights. (The plain view doctrine is discussed in detail in Chapter 10.)

Area of Search

Assuming that an officer obtains a valid consent not only to *enter* premises but also to *search* the premises, "the standard for measuring the scope of a suspect's consent under the Fourth Amendment is that of 'objective reasonableness'—what would the typical reasonable person have understood by the exchange between the officer and the suspect?" *Florida v. Jimeno,* 500 U.S. 248, 251, 111 S.Ct. 1801, 1803–04, 114 L.Ed.2d 297, 302 (1991). In *People v. Cruz,* 40 Cal.Rptr. 841, 395 P.2d 889 (Cal. 1964), an officer obtained permission to "look around" an apartment. The court held that this did not authorize the officer to open and search boxes and suitcases that he had been informed were the property of persons other than the person giving consent. In other words, an officer can search only the parts of premises over which the person giving consent has some possessory right or control, and not personal property that the officer knows belongs to some other person. In *State v. Johnson,* 427 P.2d 705 (Wash. 1967), valid consent was given to officers to search the trunk of a car. The court held that this consent did not extend to search of the passenger area of the car and that evidence found in the passenger area was inadmissible in court. In another case, a consent to search form that authorized officers to search the defendant's car and remove "whatever documents or items of property whatsoever, which they deem pertinent to the investigation," was held to grant authority for a general and exploratory search. Therefore, officers did not exceed the scope of the consent by opening an *unlocked* suitcase found in the car's trunk. *United States v. Kapperman,* 764 F.2d 786 (11th Cir. 1985).

The limitation on the area of search allowed by consent applies equally to searches of the person as to searches of premises. In a case involving both a nonverbal consent and a limitation on the area of the person allowed to be searched by consent, a police officer, while questioning the defendant with regard to narcotics, asked the defendant whether he was still using or carrying narcotics. When the defendant replied that he was not, the officer asked him whether he minded if he checked him for needle marks. The defendant said nothing but put his arms out sideways. The officer did not check the defendant's arms but instead patted down his coat and found marijuana cigarettes. The court held that the search went beyond the area to which the defendant had consented to allow a search:

> Bowen's putting out his arms sideways in response to a query whether he minded allowing the officer to check "if he had any marks on him" could hardly be said to be naturally indicative or persuasive of the giving of an intended consent to have the officer switch instead to a general search of his pockets—in which he had two marijuana cigarettes. *Oliver v. Bowens,* 386 F.2d 688, 691 (9th Cir. 1967).

As a general rule, if an officer asks for and obtains consent to search a specific area, whether in a place or on a person, the officer is limited to that specific area. If the search goes beyond that area, any evidence seized is likely to be held inadmissible in court.

Time

A consent to search may also be limited with respect to time. In *State v. Brochu,* 237 A.2d 418 (Me. 1967), officers investigating the death of the defendant's wife obtained a valid consent from the defendant to search his home. The officers conducted a search and found nothing. At that time, the defendant had not been accused of anything. However, later in the day, police received information giving them probable cause to arrest the defendant for his wife's murder and to obtain a search warrant for his premises. The defendant was arrested that evening, and the search warrant was executed the next day. The validity of the warrant was challenged, and the prosecution attempted to justify the second search on the basis that the defendant's earlier consent continued in effect after his arrest to the next day. The court rejected this contention.

The officers entered the defendant's home on the 5th under the protection of his consent. By nightfall, however, the defendant had ceased to be the husband assisting in the solution of his wife's death and had become the man accused of his wife's murder by poison (and) held under arrest for hearing.

> When the defendant became the accused, the protective cloak of the Constitution became more closely wrapped around him. . . .
>
> The consent of December 5 in our view should be measured on the morning of the 6th by the status of the defendant as the accused. There is no evidence whatsoever that the consent of the 5th was ever discussed with the defendant at or after his arrest, or that he was informed of the State's intent to enter and search his home on the 6th on the strength of a continuing consent. We conclude, therefore, that consent of the defendant had ended by December 6, and accordingly the officers were not protected thereby on the successful search of the 6th. 237 A.2d at 421.

If a significant period of time has passed since a consent to search was given, a new consent should be obtained before continuing to search, especially if intervening events suggest that a second consent might not be given so readily as the original consent. Otherwise, a search warrant should be obtained.

Object of Search

If the consenting person places no limit on the scope of a search, the scope is "generally defined by its expressed object." *Florida v. Jimeno,* 500 U.S. 248, 251, 111 S.Ct. 1801, 1804, 114 L.Ed.2d 297, 303 (1991). Therefore, a search may be as broad as the officer's previously acquired knowledge about the crimes likely to have been committed and the items of evidence likely to be discovered. *United States v. Sealey,* 630 F.Supp. 801 (E.D.Cal. 1986). In the *Jimeno case,* a police officer was following the defendant's car after overhearing the defendant arranging what appeared to be a drug transaction. The officer stopped the defendant's car for a traffic infraction and declared that he had reason to believe that the defendant was carrying narcotics in the car. The officer asked permission to search the car, the defendant consented, and the officer found cocaine inside a folded paper bag on the car's floorboard.

The Court held that a criminal suspect's Fourth Amendment right to be free from unreasonable searches is not violated when, after he gives a police officer permission to search his automobile, the officer opens a closed container found within the car that might reasonably hold the object. The Court said:

> We think that it was objectively reasonable for the police to conclude that the general consent to search respondent's car included consent to search containers within that car which might bear drugs. A reasonable person may be expected to know that narcotics are generally carried in some form of a container. 500 U.S. at 251, 111 S.Ct. at 1804, 114 L.Ed.2d at 303.

United States v. Rodney, 956 F.2d 295 (D.C.Cir. 1992), held that a request to conduct a body search for drugs reasonably includes a request to conduct some search of the crotch area. The court noted that drug dealers frequently hide drugs near their genitals.

Note that the "objective reasonableness" standard depends on the facts of each case. A general consent to search a vehicle does not necessarily allow the search of all containers in a vehicle. For example, a consent to search the trunk of a car may not include authorization to pry open a locked briefcase found inside the trunk. As the U.S. Supreme Court noted in the *Jimeno* case, "[i]t is very likely unreasonable to think that a suspect, by consenting to the search of his trunk, has agreed to the breaking open of a *locked* briefcase within the trunk, but it is otherwise with respect to a closed paper bag" (emphasis supplied). 500 U.S. at 251–52, 111 S.Ct. at 1804, 114 L.Ed.2d at 303.

Of course, the consenting person may specifically limit the scope of a consent search to a search for a particular object. In *People v. Superior Court (Arketa),* 89 Cal.Rptr. 316 (Cal.App. 1970), a person gave officers consent to search his premises for a crime suspect. The officers conducted a thorough search of the house and its closets for a crowbar without advising the person that they wanted to look for a crowbar. The court invalidated the search because it went beyond the scope of the consent granted. In a case in which an individual consented to a search of his person for *weapons,* the court held that "the scope of the search consented to must be limited to the scope of the right of search asserted, unless it should clearly appear that free and voluntary consent was given to a general and exploratory search." *People v. Rice,* 66 Cal.Rptr. 246, 249 (Cal.App. 1968). In *Rice,* the seizure of marijuana in a plastic bottle in the defendant's pocket was held illegal as beyond the scope of the consent granted. Law enforcement officers should confine their search to only those areas where the object for which they have consent to search could possibly be located, taking into consideration the size, shape, and character of the object.

Revocation of Consent

Consent to search may be revoked or withdrawn at any time after the search has been partially completed. In *State v. Lewis,* 611 A.2d 69 (Me. 1992), after arresting the defendant for drunk driving and releasing him on personal recognizance, a state trooper offered to drive the defendant to a nearby motel. When the defendant retrieved a carry-on bag from his car, the trooper asked and received permission to check the bag for guns. The trooper immediately observed two large brown bags inside the carry-on bag, smelled marijuana, and asked permission to examine the bags. The defendant refused and attempted to return the carry-on bag to his car. The trooper intervened and searched the brown bags, finding marijuana. The court found that the defendant had revoked his consent to search the carry-on bag before the trooper opened the brown bags.

> Even though defendant consented to the trooper's looking inside his carry-on bag, he at no time consented to the trooper's looking into the brown bags contained therein. Rather, by expressly terminating his consent when the trooper requested to open the brown bags and by seeking to return them to his car, defendant most certainly manifested a subjective expectation of privacy with respect to those inside bags. Because those bags were always closed and their contents shielded from the trooper's view, society would regard defendant's expectation of privacy in them to be reasonable. 611 A.2d at 70.

In *United States v. Bily,* 406 F.Supp. 726 (E.D.Pa. 1975), the defendant consented to a search of his house for pornographic films. After an investigation of approximately two hours, during which certain films were discovered, the defendant stated, "That's enough, I want you to stop." The court held that this was a revocation of consent that took immediate effect. Only the seizures of film that took place before the revocation were held valid.

In *United States v. Ibarra,* 731 F.Supp. 1037 (D.Wyo. 1990), the court held that a motorist's closing and locking the trunk of his car after a police officer's consensual search of the trunk constituted a revocation of that consent and barred any further search.

KEY POINTS

9. Although an invitation to *enter* premises is not the equivalent of a consent to *search* the premises, an officer invited onto premises need not ignore contraband or other criminal evidence lying in plain view.

10. The scope of a consent search depends on what the typical reasonable person would have understood by the exchange between the officer and the suspect.

11. A person giving consent to search may place a time limitation on the search.

12. If the consenting person places no limit on the scope of a consent search, the scope is generally defined by its expressed object.

13. Consent to search may be revoked or withdrawn at any time after the search has been partially completed.

Who May Give Consent

In general, the only person able to give a valid consent to a search is the person whose constitutional protection against unreasonable searches and seizures would be invaded by the search if it were conducted without consent. This means, for example, that when the search of a person's body or clothing is contemplated, only that person can consent to the search. The same rule applies to searches of property, except that when several people have varying degrees of interest in the same property, more than one person may be qualified to give consent to search.

In certain situations, the law recognizes authority in a third person to consent to a search of property even though he or she is not the person against whose interests the search is being conducted. In *United States v. Matlock,* 415 U.S. 164, 94 S.Ct. 988, 39 L.Ed.2d 242 (1974), the U.S. Supreme Court stated the test for determining whether a third person could consent to a search of premises or effects:

> [W]hen the prosecution seeks to justify a warrantless search by proof of voluntary consent, it is not limited to proof that consent was given by the defendant, but may show that permission to search was obtained from a third party who possessed *common authority over or other sufficient relationship to the premises or effects sought to be inspected.* [Emphasis supplied.] 415 U.S. at 171, 94 S.Ct. at 993, 39 L.Ed.2d at 249–50.

The Court then defined "common authority":

> Common authority is, of course, not to be implied from the mere interest a third party has in the property. The authority which justifies the third-party consent does not rest upon the law of property, with its attendant historical and legal refinements, . . . but rests rather on mutual use of the property by persons generally having joint access or control for most purposes, so that it is reasonable to

recognize that any of the co-inhabitants has the right to permit the inspection in his own right and that the others have assumed the risk that one of their number might permit the common area to be searched. 415 U.S. at 171 n.7, 94 S.Ct. at 993 n.7, 39 L.Ed.2d at 250 n.7.

Furthermore, a warrantless entry and search is valid when based on the consent of a third party whom the police, at the time of the entry, *reasonably believe* to possess common authority over the premises but who *in fact* does not. This does not suggest that law enforcement officers may always accept a person's invitation to enter premises.

> Even when the invitation is accompanied by an explicit assertion that the person lives there, the surrounding circumstances could conceivably be such that a reasonable person would doubt its truth and not act upon it without further inquiry. As with other factual determinations bearing upon search and seizure, determination of consent to enter must "be judged against an objective standard: would the facts available to the officer at the moment . . . 'warrant a man of reasonable caution in the belief'" that the consenting party had authority over the premises? . . . If not, then warrantless entry without further inquiry is unlawful unless authority actually exists. But if so, the search is valid. *Illinois v. Rodriguez,* 497 U.S. 177, 188–89, 110 S.Ct. 2793, 2801, 111 L.Ed.2d 148, 161 (1990).

The *Rodriguez* case has been construed as "appli[cable] to situations in which an officer would have had valid consent to search if the facts were as he reasonably believed them to be." *United States v. Whitfield,* 939 F.2d 1071, 1074 (D.C.Cir. 1991). *Rodriguez* would not validate, however, a search premised on an erroneous view of the law. For example, an investigator's erroneous belief that landladies are generally authorized to consent to a search of a tenant's premises could not provide the authorization necessary for a warrantless search.

Note that a person with common authority may consent to a search only in the absence of other persons with equal or superior authority. In *State v. Leach,* 782 P.2d 1035 (Wash. 1989), a co-owner of a travel agency consented to a search of the agency office. The defendant, the other owner of the agency with a superior interest, was arrested at the office and was present during the search. His consent to search the office was not sought, however. The court invalidated the search.

> Where the police have obtained consent to search from an individual possessing, at best, equal control over the premises, that consent remains valid against a cohabitant, who also possesses equal control, only while the cohabitant is absent. However, should the cohabitant be present and able to object, the police must also obtain the cohabitant's consent. Any other rule exalts expediency over an individual's Fourth Amendment guarantees. Accordingly, we refuse to beat a path to the door of exceptions. 782 P.2d at 1040.

Questions of who may give valid consent are often confusing and complicated, and courts tend to carefully scrutinize any waiver of a person's constitutional rights. The remainder of this chapter examines examples of consent search situations in which the person giving the consent is not the person against whose interests the search is being conducted.

Persons Having Equal Rights or Interests in Property

It is well settled that, when two or more persons have substantially equal rights of ownership, occupancy, or other possessory interest in property to be searched or seized, any one of the persons may legally authorize a search, and any evidence found may be used against any of the other persons. In *United States v. Kelley*, 953 F.2d 562 (9th Cir. 1992), the court found authority to consent to a search of the defendant's bedroom and closet under the following circumstances: the person giving consent had rented the apartment together with the defendant and had signed the lease; she described herself as the defendant's roommate; and she had joint access not only to the common areas of the apartment but also to the defendant's separate bedroom, where the apartment telephone was located.

In determining whether a person is a joint occupant of premises, courts will consider whether the person paid rent, how long the person stayed, whether the person left belongings on the premises, whether the person possessed a key, and whether there was any written or oral agreement among other parties as to the person's right to use and occupy the premises. In *Illinois v. Rodriguez*, 497 U.S. 177, 110 S.Ct. 2793, 111 L.Ed.2d 148 (1990), the U.S. Supreme Court held that the defendant's former cotenant did not have common authority to grant police consent to enter the defendant's premises without a warrant, even though she had some furniture and household effects in the premises and sometimes spent the night at the premises after moving out a month before the search at issue. Her name was not on the lease; she did not contribute to the rent; she was not allowed to invite others to the apartment on her own; she never went to the premises when the defendant was not at home; she had moved her clothing and that of her children from the premises; and she had taken a key to the premises without the defendant's knowledge.

Consent to search given by a person with common authority over the premises is not invalidated because that person gave consent with the expectation of receiving a reward. In *Bertolotti v. State,* 476 So.2d 130 (Fla. 1985), a woman who knew of the possibility of a reward through a crime watch program consented to a search of an apartment she shared with the defendant. The court said:

> A community-wide, regularly advertised program which rewards any citizen who provides information useful to the police in their criminal investigations is not tantamount to recruiting police agents; the state should not be penalized in the use of information so obtained. Mrs. Griest's consent to the search was not vitiated by the possibility of financial reward. 476 So.2d at 132.

In a case involving equal rights to *personal* property, the defendant, at his murder trial, objected to the introduction into evidence of clothing seized from his duffel bag. At the time of the seizure, the duffel bag was being used jointly by the defendant and his cousin and had been left in the cousin's home. When police arrested the cousin, they asked him whether they could have his clothing. The cousin directed them to the duffel bag, and both the cousin and his mother consented to its search. During the search, the officers came upon the defendant's clothing in the bag and seized it as well. The Court upheld the legality of the search over the defendant's objections.

> Since Rawls (the cousin) was a joint user of the bag, he clearly had authority to consent to its search. The officers therefore found evidence against petitioner while in the course of an otherwise lawful search [*plain view doctrine*]. . . . Petitioner argues that Rawls only had actual permission to use one compartment of the bag and that he had no authority to consent to a search of the other compartments. We will not, however, engage in such metaphysical subtleties in judging the efficacy of Rawls' consent. Petitioner, in allowing Rawls to use the bag and in leaving it in his house, must be taken to have assumed the risk that Rawls would allow someone else to look inside. We find no valid search and seizure

claim in this case. *Frazier v. Cupp,* 394 U.S. 731, 740, 89 S.Ct. 1420, 1425, 22 L.Ed.2d 684, 693–94 (1969).

A third party who has common authority to use premises may give consent to a search of the premises even if not *actually* using the premises at the time of the search. In *United States v. Cook,* 530 F.2d 145 (7th Cir. 1976), the defendant's landlady consented to a search of a poultry house on her property. The poultry house consisted of a large room in which the landlady had segregated an area with wire fence for her exclusive use. She gave the defendant permission to use the remaining space, but she retained the right to use the space if necessary. The defendant claimed that since neither the landlady nor her family *actually* used the defendant's area, there was no common authority. The court upheld the search, however, ruling that the defendant had assumed the risk that the landlady would permit others to inspect the premises.

A third party cannot consent to a search of more than that over which he or she has common authority. In *United States v. Gilley,* 608 F.Supp. 1065 (S.D.Ga. 1985), the court held that a consent to search a home given by the home's occupant did not authorize a search of a guest's travel bag found in the living room. The guest had done nothing that diminished his natural expectation of privacy in the contents of the bag. The host lacked common authority over the bag, as she had not been authorized to open or use the bag, and she had not in fact opened the bag.

Landlord-Tenant

A landlord has *no* implied authority to consent to a search of a tenant's premises or a seizure of the tenant's property during the period of the tenancy, even though the landlord has the authority to enter the tenant's premises for the limited purposes of inspection, performance of repairs, or housekeeping services. *Chapman v. United States,* 365 U.S. 610, 81 S.Ct. 776, 5 L.Ed.2d 828 (1961). Once the tenant has abandoned the premises or the tenancy has otherwise terminated, however, and the landlord has the primary right to occupation and control of the premises, the landlord may consent to a search of the premises, even though the former tenant has left personal belongings on the premises. *United States v. Sledge,* 760 F.2d 854 (9th Cir. 1981). Furthermore, since a landlord clearly has joint authority over, and access to, common areas of an apartment building, a landlord may give valid consent to search those areas. *United States v. Kelly,* 551 F.2d 760 (8th Cir. 1977).

Hotel Manager–Hotel Guest

The U.S. Supreme Court held that the principles governing a landlord's consent to a search of tenant's premises apply to consent searches of hotel rooms allowed by hotel managers. In *Stoner v. California,* 376 U.S. 483, 84 S.Ct. 889, 11 L.Ed.2d 856 (1964), police investigating a robbery went to the defendant's hotel. The defendant was not in his room, and police obtained permission from the hotel clerk to search the defendant's room. Items of evidence incriminating the defendant in the robbery were found in the room.

The Court held that the search was illegal and that the items seized could not be used against the defendant in court. The defendant's constitutional right was at stake here—not the clerk's or the hotel's. Therefore, only the defendant, either directly or through an agent, could waive that right. There was no evidence that the police had any basis whatsoever to believe that the night clerk had been authorized by the defendant to permit the police to search his room.

It is true . . . that when a person engages a hotel room he undoubtedly gives "implied or express permission" to "such persons as maids, janitors or repairmen" to enter his room "in the performance of their duties." . . . But the conduct of the night clerk and the police in the present case was of an entirely different order. . . .

No less than a tenant of a house, or the occupant of a room in a boarding house . . . a guest in a hotel room is entitled to constitutional protection against unreasonable searches and seizures. . . . That protection would disappear if it were left to depend upon the unfettered discretion of an employee of the hotel. 376 U.S. at 489–90, 84 S.Ct. at 893, 11 L.Ed.2d at 861.

When the term of a hotel guest's occupancy of a room expires, however, the guest loses his or her exclusive right to privacy in the room, whether or not the guest remains in the room. The hotel manager then has the right to enter the room and may consent to a search of the room and a seizure of items found in the room. *United States v. Larson,* 760 F.2d 852 (8th Cir. 1985).

Host-Guest

In general, the owner or primary occupant of the premises (the host) may validly consent to a search of the premises, and any evidence found would be admissible against a guest on the premises. In *United States v. Hall,* 979 F.2d 77 (6th Cir. 1992), the owner of a residence gave consent to search the room of the defendant, whom he had allowed to stay at his residence in exchange for farm work. The court held that the owner had authority to consent to the search where he owned all the furniture in the room, he had personal items stored in an adjacent room accessed through the defendant's room, the room was never locked, and there was no agreement between him and the defendant that he was not to go in the room.

If, however, the person against whom a search for evidence is directed is a long-term guest and has a section of the premises set aside for exclusive personal use, the host may not consent to a search of that area of the premises. *Reeves v. Warden,* 346 F.2d 915 (4th Cir. 1965). The host's authority to consent to a search of the guest's area of the premises depends on the length of time of the guest's stay, the exclusiveness of the guest's control of a particular area of the premises, and the guest's reasonable expectation of privacy in that area of the premises. Also, a host may not consent to a search of an item that is obviously the exclusive personal property of the guest. *State v. Edwards,* 570 A.2d 193 (Conn. 1990), held that although a lessee of an apartment could consent to a search of her apartment, she could not consent to a search of a guest's backpack:

As "a common repository for one's personal effects, and therefore . . . inevitably associated with the expectation of privacy" . . . luggage may be lawfully searched, in general, only pursuant to a warrant. . . . We can discern no intrinsic constitutional distinction between a backpack and luggage. 570 A.2d at 202.

Employer-Employee

In general, an employer may consent to a search of any part of the employer's premises over which the employer has authority and control. In *State v. Robinson,* 206 A.2d 779 (N.J.Super. 1965), the court held that an employer could validly consent to the search of an employee's locker in the employer's plant. The employer not only owned the premises, but under the terms of a contract between the employer and the employee's union, the employer retained a master key to all employee's lockers. In *United States v. Carter,* 569 F.2d 801 (4th Cir. 1977), an employer's consent to search a company vehicle in an employee's custody was held valid. The employer not only owned the vehicle but could tell the employee what and what not to do with it and could designate any other use of it.

However, an employer may not effectively consent to a search of an area set aside for use by an employee and within the employee's exclusive control. In *United States v. Blok,* 188 F.2d 1019 (D.C.Cir. 1951), the court held that an employee's boss could not validly consent to a search of a desk assigned for the employee's exclusive use.

> In the absence of a valid regulation to the contrary, appellee was entitled to, and did keep private property of a personal sort in her desk. Her superiors could not reasonably search the desk for her purse, her personal letters, or anything else that did not belong to the government and had no connection with the work of the office. Their consent did not make such a search by the police reasonable. 188 F.2d at 1021.

An employee's ability to consent validly to a search of the employer's premises depends on the scope of the employee's authority. The average employee, such as a clerk, janitor, maintenance person, driver, or other person temporarily in charge, may not give such consent. *United States v. Block,* 202 F.Supp. 705 (S.D.N.Y. 1962). If, however, the employee is a manager or other person of considerable authority who is left in complete charge for a substantial period of time, the employee probably would be able effectively to consent to a search of the employer's premises. *United States v. Antonelli Fireworks Co.,* 155 F.2d 631 (2d Cir. 1946). In *People v. Litwin,* 355 N.Y.S.2d 646 (N.Y.App.Div. 1974), the court held that a baby-sitter has insufficient authority over the premises of his or her employer to give a valid consent to search the premises.

School Official–Student

The search by police of a high school student's locker, when consented to by a school official, is valid because of the relationship between the school authorities and the students. The school authorities have an obligation to maintain discipline over students, and usually they retain partial access to the students' lockers so that neither has an exclusive right to use and possession of the lockers. Thus, in a case in which the locker of a student suspected of burglary was opened by police with the consent of school authorities and incriminating evidence was found, the court said:

> Although a student may have control of his school locker as against fellow students, his possession is not exclusive against the school and its officials. A school does not supply its students with lockers for illicit use in harboring pilfered property or harmful substances. We deem it a proper function of school authorities to inspect the lockers under their control and to prevent their use in illicit ways or for illegal purposes. We believe this right of inspection is inherent in the authority vested in school administrators and that the same must be retained and exercised in the management of our schools if their educational functions are to be maintained and the welfare of the student bodies preserved. *State v. Stein,* 456 P.2d 1, 3 (Kan. 1969).

Consent searches of college dormitory rooms are treated similarly to searches of hotel rooms. In *Commonwealth v. McCloskey,* 272 A.2d 271 (Pa.Super. 1970), police, aided by the dean of men, searched the defendant's room at a university and found marijuana. The evidence was held to be inadmissible in court.

> A dormitory room is analogous to an apartment or a hotel room. It certainly offers its occupant a more reasonable expectation of freedom from governmental intrusion than does a public telephone booth. The defendant rented the dormitory room for a certain period of time, agreeing to abide by the rules established by his lessor, the University. As in most rental situations, the lessor, Bucknell University, reserved the right to check the room for damages, wear and unauthorized appliances. Such right of the lessor does not mean McCloskey was not entitled to have a "reasonable expectation of freedom from governmental intrusion," or that he gave consent to the police search, or gave the University authority to consent to such search. 272 A.2d at 273.

Principal-Agent

A person clearly may give someone else authority to consent to a search of the person's property. The person giving the authority is called the **principal;** the person acting for the principal is called his or her **agent.** For example, an attorney may consent to a search of a client's premises if the attorney has been specifically authorized to do so by the client. In *Brown v. State,* 404 P.2d 428 (Nev. 1965), a search of the defendant's premises and a seizure of his farm animals were upheld because consent to search had been given by the defendant's attorney after consultation with the defendant. Without a specific authorization to give consent to search, however, the mere existence of an attorney-client relationship gives an attorney no authority to waive a client's personal rights. In another example, *State v. Kellam,* 269 S.E.2d 197 (N.C.App. 1980), homeowners gave their next-door neighbor the key to their house with instructions to "look after their house" while the owners were away. The court held that the neighbor's consent to search the house was valid.

A principal has the power to limit the authority of his or her agent with respect to the principal's property. Therefore, for example, an employer could limit an employee's authority to show business records to certain persons and not to others. A principal may not, however, limit an agent's authority for the purpose of obstructing justice. Therefore, in a case in which a doctor told his employee to take business records and hide them from the authorities, the court said that "when an employer gives an employee access to documents intentionally and knowingly in order to obstruct justice, that employee is a custodian of those records for the purposes of a valid subpoena or seizure." *United States v. Miller,* 800 F.2d 129, 135 (7th Cir. 1986).

Husband-Wife

"Where two persons, such as a husband and wife, have equal rights to the use and occupation of certain premises, either may give consent to a search, and the evidence thus disclosed can be used against either." *United States v. Ocampo,* 492 F.Supp. 1211, 1236 (E.D.N.Y. 1980). In *Roberts v. United States,* 332 F.2d 892 (8th Cir. 1964), officers questioned the defendant's wife as part of a murder investigation. The wife volunteered information that the defendant had fired a pistol into the ceiling of their home some time ago. She later validly consented to a search for and seizure of the bullet in the ceiling.

The court sustained the search on the basis that the consent was voluntary, the place of the search was the home of the defendant's wife, and the premises were under the wife's immediate and complete control at the time of the search. Furthermore, the bullet could not be considered a personal effect of the husband, over which the wife would have no power to consent to search.

It is not a question of agency, for a wife should not be held to have authority to waive her husband's constitutional rights. This is a question of the wife's own rights to authorized entry into premises where she lives and of which she had control. 332 F.2d at 896–97.

Some courts have even allowed estranged spouses to consent to the search of marital premises they have vacated. In *United States v. Long,* 524 F.2d 660 (9th Cir. 1975), the court held that an estranged wife, as a joint owner of a house she had vacated, could give consent to search the house even though her husband (the temporarily absent current occupant) had changed the locks on the doors.

Parent-Child

A parent's consent to search premises owned by the parent will usually be effective against a child who lives on those premises.

Hardy's father gave his permission to the officers to enter and search the house and the premises *which he owned* and in which his son lived with him. Under the circumstances presented here the voluntary consent of Hardy's father to search *his own* premises is binding on Hardy and precludes his claim of violation of constitutional rights. *Commonwealth v. Hardy,* 223 A.2d 719, 723 (Pa. 1966).

A parent may not consent to a search of an area of the parent's home occupied by the child, however, if the child uses the room exclusively, has sectioned it off, has furnished it with his or her own furniture, pays rent, or otherwise establishes an expectation of privacy. *State v. Peterson,* 525 S.W.2d 599 (Mo.App. 1975). Furthermore, parents may not consent to a search of a child's room in their home if the child has already refused to grant such consent. "Constitutional rights may not be defeated by the expedient of soliciting several persons successively until the sought-after consent is obtained." *People v. Mortimer,* 46 A.D.2d 275, 277, 361 N.Y.S.2d 955, 958 (N.Y. 1974).

The Supreme Court of Georgia identified the following factors to be considered in determining whether a minor's consent to search family premises is valid:

whether the minor lived on the premises; whether the minor had a right of access to the premises and the right to invite others thereto; whether the minor was of an age at which he or she could be expected to exercise at least minimal discretion; and whether officers acted reasonably in believing that the minor had sufficient control over the premises to give a valid consent to search. *Davis v. State,* 422 S.E.2d 546, 549 (Ga. 1992).

Bailor-Bailee

A bailee of personal property may consent to a search of the property if the bailee has full possession and control. (A bailee is a person in rightful possession of personal property by permission of the owner or bailor.) In *United States v. Eldridge,* 302 F.2d 463 (4th Cir. 1962), the defendant loaned his car to a friend for the friend's personal use. Police investigating a theft asked the friend for permission to search the trunk of the car. The friend opened the trunk, and the police found incriminating evidence against the defendant.

The court held that the search was legal and that the evidence found was admissible against the defendant. The friend had been given rightful possession and control over the automobile and could do with it whatever was reasonable under the circumstances. The defendant had reserved no exclusive right to the trunk when he gave his friend the key. The friend's opening of the trunk for the police was a reasonable exercise of his control over the car for the period during which he was permitted to use it.

If the bailee giving consent has only limited control over the property, such as for shipment, storage, or repair purposes, evidence found by law enforcement officers would not be admissible in court against the owner of the property. Thus, an airline could not consent to the search of a package that the defendant had wrapped, tied, and delivered to the airline solely for transportation purposes. *Corngold v. United States,* 367 F.2d 1 (9th Cir. 1966). Nor could the owner of a boat who had agreed to store certain of defendant's items on his boat give a valid consent to police to search and seize the items. *Commonwealth v. Storck,* 275 A.2d 362 (Pa. 1971). And *State v. Farrell,* 443 A.2d 438, 442 (R.I. 1982), held that "one who entrusts his automobile to another for the purposes of repair, or periodic inspection as required by law, does not confer the kind of mutual use or control which would empower that person to consent to a warrantless search and seizure."

In *United States v. Most,* 876 F.2d 191 (D.C.Cir. 1989), the court held that a store clerk who was asked by the defendant to watch a package could not give a legally valid consent to search the package. The court said, "We see no basis for holding that delivery people who *move* packages may not consent to a search, but that store clerks who *watch* packages may." 876 F.2d at 200 n.18.

Voluntary Production of Evidence

If a person voluntarily produces incriminating evidence, without any attempt by police to obtain consent and without coercion, deception, or other illegal police conduct, there is no search and seizure, and the evidence is admissible in court. In the U.S. Supreme Court case of *Coolidge v. New Hampshire,* 403 U.S. 443, 91 S.Ct. 2022, 29 L.Ed.2d 564 (1971), two officers went to the defendant's home, while the defendant was at the police station under investigation for murder, to check out the defendant's story with his wife. The officers asked the wife whether the defendant owned any guns, and she replied, "Yes, I will get them in the bedroom." She then took four guns out of a closet and gave them to the officers. The officers then asked her what her husband had been wearing on the night in question, and she produced several pairs of trousers and a hunting jacket. The police seized all this evidence, and it was used against the defendant in court.

The Court found no objection to the introduction of the previously described evidence in court. In fact, the Court found that the actions of the police did not even amount to a search and seizure. Because the Court discussed in detail the significance of the actions of the police, and because of the importance of the issue, the Court's opinion is quoted here at length:

> [I]t cannot be said that the police should have obtained a warrant for the guns and clothing before they set out to visit Mrs. Coolidge, since they had no intention of

rummaging around among Coolidge's effects or of dispossessing him of any of his property. Nor can it be said that they should have obtained Coolidge's permission for a seizure they did not intend to make. There was nothing to compel them to announce to the suspect that they intended to question his wife about his movements on the night of the disappearance or about the theft from his employer. Once Mrs. Coolidge had admitted them, the policemen were surely acting normally and properly when they asked her, as they asked those questioned earlier in the investigation, including Coolidge himself, about any guns there might be in the house. The question concerning the clothes Coolidge had been wearing on the night of the disappearance was logical and in no way coercive. Indeed, one might doubt the competence of the officers involved had they not asked exactly the questions they did ask. And surely when Mrs. Coolidge of her own accord produced the guns and clothes for inspection, rather than simply describing them, it was not incumbent on the police to stop her or avert their eyes. . . .

In assessing the claim that this course of conduct amounted to a search and seizure, it is well to keep in mind that Mrs. Coolidge described her own motive as that of clearing her husband, and that she believed that she had nothing to hide. She had seen her husband himself produce his guns for two other policemen earlier in the week, and there is nothing to indicate that she realized that he had offered only three of them for inspection on that occasion. The two officers who questioned her behaved, as her own testimony shows, with perfect courtesy. There is not the slightest implication of an attempt to coerce or dominate her, or for that matter, to direct her actions by the more subtle techniques of suggestion that are available to officials in circumstances like these. To hold that the conduct of the police here was a search and seizure would be to hold, in effect, that a criminal suspect has constitutional protection against the adverse consequences of a spontaneous, good-faith effort by his wife to clear him of suspicion. 403 U.S. at 488–90, 91 S.Ct. at 2049–50, 29 L.Ed.2d at 596.

Reasonable Expectation of Privacy

Since the U.S. Supreme Court decision in *Katz v. United States,* 389 U.S. 347, 88 S.Ct. 507, 19 L.Ed.2d 576 (1967), courts have considered a person's reasonable expectation of privacy as a major factor in determining whether consent to search that person's property could be given by a third person. In *United States v. Novello,* 519 F.2d 1078 (5th Cir. 1975), the defendant rented an enclosed storage area that was accessible only to the rental agent and to those working with the agent. The defendant stored his truck containing marijuana in the area. Law enforcement officers, acting on an informant's tip, obtained consent to enter the enclosed area from one of the persons having access and discovered marijuana in the truck. The court held that the defendant had no reasonable expectation of privacy in the storage area and upheld the search. It said, "One who knows that others have of right general and untrammeled access to an area, a right as extensive as his own, can scarcely have much expectation of secrecy in it or confidence about whom they may let inspect it." 519 F.2d at 1080.

The Oregon Court of Appeals relied on a defendant's reasonable expectation of privacy to invalidate the search of a bedroom in a private residence that the defendant occupied under a rental agreement. A father and his two daughters leased and occupied the residence along with the defendant. The defendant was the only occupant of a private room under an agreement with the father. One of the daughters gave consent to search the defendant's room, where incriminating evidence was found. The court held that the daughter could not consent to a search of the defendant's room.

The defendant had a reasonable expectation of privacy in the room because he rented it, was its sole occupant, and had never given anyone permission to enter it. *State v. Fitzgerald,* 530 P.2d 553 (Or.App. 1974).

KEY POINTS

14. In general, the only person able to give a valid consent to a search is the person whose constitutional protection against unreasonable searches and seizures would be invaded by the search if it were conducted without consent.

15. A person may specifically authorize another to consent to a search of the person's property.

16. Consent to search may be obtained from a third party whom the police, at the time of entry, reasonably believe to possess common authority over or other sufficient relationship to the premises or effects sought to be inspected.

17. If a person voluntarily produces incriminating evidence, without any attempt by police to obtain consent and without coercion, deception, or other illegal police conduct, there is no search and seizure, and the evidence is admissible in court.

18. If a person establishes a reasonable expectation of privacy in property, another person may not consent to a search of the property.

Summary

A consent search occurs when a person allows a law enforcement officer to search his or her body, premises, or belongings. Consent searches are convenient for law enforcement officers, requiring no justification such as probable cause or a warrant, but consent searches present many opportunities for abuse. For this reason, courts exercise a strong presumption against consents to search and place a heavy burden on prosecutors to prove that a consent to search was voluntary. Voluntariness depends on the totality of circumstances surrounding the giving of consent. Among the circumstances considered are the following:

- Force or threat of force by police

- Fraudulent or mistaken claim of police authority

- Misrepresentation or deception by police

- Arrest or detention of consenting person

- Consenting person's awareness of the right to refuse consent to search

- Consenting person's attitude about the likelihood of discovery of evidence

- Clearness and explicitness of consent

- Physical, mental, emotional, and educational status of consenting person

The Fourth Amendment does not require that a lawfully seized person be advised that he or she is free to go before the person's consent to search will be recognized as voluntary.

A consent to *enter* premises is not the equivalent of a consent to *search* the premises. If, however, an officer who has been invited to enter premises observes criminal evidence lying open to view, the officer may seize the evidence if he or she complies with the requirements of the plain view doctrine.

The standard for measuring the scope of a suspect's consent is that of "objective reasonableness": what would the typical reasonable person have understood by the exchange between the officer and the suspect? The scope of a consent search may be limited in area, in time, and by the object for which the search is allowed. If the consenting person places no limit on the scope of a search, the scope is generally defined by its expressed object. Consent to search may be revoked by the person giving it at any time.

The constitutional right to refuse to consent to a search is a personal right of the individual against whom the search is directed. A person other than the person against whose interests the search is being conducted cannot effectively consent to a search of property unless (1) the person has been specifically authorized to do so, or (2) the person possesses common authority over, or has other sufficient relationship to, the premises or effects sought to be inspected. If a person establishes an exclusive reasonable expectation of privacy in property, another person may not consent to a search of the property.

Key Holdings from Major Cases

Schneckloth v. Bustamonte (1973). "In situations where the police have some evidence of illicit activity, but lack probable cause to arrest or search, a search authorized by a valid consent may be the only means of obtaining important and reliable evidence. . . . And in those cases where there is probable cause to arrest or search, but where the police lack a warrant, a consent search may still be valuable. If the search is conducted and proves fruitless, that in itself may convince the police that an arrest with its possible stigma and embarrassment is unnecessary, or that a far more extensive search pursuant to a warrant is not justified. In short, a search pursuant to consent may result in considerably less inconvenience for the subject of the search, and, properly conducted, is a constitutionally permissible and wholly legitimate aspect of effective police activity." 412 U.S. 218, 228, 93 S.Ct. 2041, 2048, 36 L.Ed.2d 854, 863.

"[T]he Fourth and Fourteenth Amendments require that consent not be coerced, by explicit or implicit means, by implied threat or covert force. For, no matter how subtly the coercion were applied, the resulting 'consent' would be no more than a pretext for the unjustified police intrusion against which the Fourth Amendment is directed. . . .

"The problem of reconciling the recognized legitimacy of consent searches with the requirement that they be free from any aspect of official coercion cannot be resolved by any infallible touchstone. To approve such searches without the most careful scrutiny would sanction the possibility of official coercion; to place artificial restrictions upon such searches would jeopardize their basic validity. Just as was true with confessions the requirement of 'voluntary' consent reflects a fair accommodation of the constitutional requirements involved. In examining all the surrounding circumstances to determine if in fact the consent to search was coerced, account must be taken of subtly coercive police questions, as well as the possibly vulnerable subjective state of the person who consents. Those searches that are the product of police coercion can thus be filtered out without undermining the continuing validity of consent searches. In sum, there is no reason for us to depart in the area of consent searches, from the traditional definition of 'voluntariness.'" 412 U.S. at 228–29, 93 S.Ct. at 2048–49, 36 L.Ed.2d at 864.

"[W]hen the subject of a search is not in custody and the State attempts to justify a search on the basis of his consent, the Fourth and Fourteenth Amendments require that it demonstrate that the consent was in fact voluntarily given, and not the result of duress or coercion, express or implied. Voluntariness is a question of fact to be determined from all the circumstances, and while the subject's knowledge of a right to refuse is a factor to be taken into consideration, the prosecution is not required to demonstrate such knowledge as a prerequisite to establishing a voluntary consent." 412 U.S. at 248–49, 93 S.Ct. at 2059, 36 L.Ed.2d at 875.

Bumper v. North Carolina (1968). "When a prosecutor seeks to rely upon consent to justify the lawfulness of a search, he has the burden of proving that the consent was, in fact, freely and voluntarily given. This burden cannot be discharged by showing no more than acquiescence to a claim of lawful authority. A search conducted in reliance upon a warrant cannot later be justified on the basis of consent if it turns out that the warrant was invalid. The results can be no different when it turns out that the State does not even attempt to rely upon the validity of the warrant, or fails to show that there was, in fact, any warrant at all.

"When a law enforcement officer claims authority to search a home under a warrant, he announces in effect that the occupant has no right to resist the search. The situation is instinct with coercion—albeit colorably lawful coercion. Where there is coercion there cannot be consent." 391 U.S. 543, 548–50, 88 S.Ct. 1788, 1792, 20 L.Ed.2d 797, 802–03.

Ohio v. Robinette (1996). "[I]t [would] be unrealistic to require police officers to always inform detainees that they are free to go before a consent to search may be deemed voluntary." 519 U.S. 33, ___, 117 S.Ct. 417, 421, 136 L.Ed.2d 347, 355.

Florida v. Jimeno (1991). "[T]he standard for measuring the scope of a suspect's consent under the Fourth Amendment is that of 'objective reasonableness'—what would the typical reasonable person have understood by the exchange between the officer and the suspect?" 500 U.S. 248, 251, 111 S.Ct. 1801, 1803–04, 114 L.Ed.2d 297, 302.

"If the consenting person places no limit on the scope of a search, the scope is 'generally defined by its expressed object.'" 500 U.S. at 251, 111 S.Ct. at 1804, 114 L.Ed.2d at 303.

"[I]t was objectively reasonable for the police to conclude that the general consent to search respondent's car included consent to search containers within that car which might bear drugs. A reasonable person may be expected to know that narcotics are generally carried in some form of a container." 500 U.S. at 251, 111 S.Ct. at 1804, 114 L.Ed.2d at 303.

United States v. Matlock (1974). "[W]hen the prosecution seeks to justify a warrantless search by proof of voluntary consent, it is not limited to proof that consent was given by the defendant, but may show that permission to search was obtained from a third party who possessed common authority over or other sufficient relationship to the premises or effects sought to be inspected." 415 U.S. 164, 171, 94 S.Ct. 988, 993, 39 L.Ed.2d 242, 249–50.

"Common authority is . . . not to be implied from the mere interest a third party has in the property. The authority which justifies the third-party consent does not rest upon the law of property, with its attendant historical and legal refinements, . . . but rests rather on mutual use of the property by persons generally having joint access or control for most purposes, so that it is reasonable to recognize that any of the co-inhabitants has the right to permit the inspection in his own right and that the others have assumed the risk that one of their number might permit the common area to be searched." 415 U.S. at 171 n.7, 94 S.Ct. at 993 n.7, 39 L.Ed.2d at 250 n.7.

Illinois v. Rodriguez (1990). A warrantless entry and search is valid when based on the consent of a third party whom the police, at the time of the entry, *reasonably believe* to possess common authority over the premises, but who *in fact* does not. 497 U.S. 177, 110 S.Ct. 2793, 111 L.Ed.2d 148.

Chapman v. United States (1961). A landlord has no implied authority to consent to a search of a tenant's premises or a seizure of the tenant's property during the period of the tenancy, even though the landlord has the authority to enter the tenant's premises for the limited purposes of inspection, performance of repairs, or housekeeping services. 365 U.S. 610, 81 S.Ct. 776, 5 L.Ed.2d 828.

Stoner v. California (1964). "No less than a tenant of a house . . . a guest in a hotel room is entitled to constitutional protection against unreasonable searches and seizures. . . . That protection would disappear if it were left to depend upon the unfettered discretion of an employee of the hotel." 376 U.S. 483, 489–90, 84 S.Ct. 889, 893, 11 L.Ed.2d 856, 861.

Coolidge v. New Hampshire (1971). If a person voluntarily produces incriminating evidence, without any attempt by police to obtain consent and without coercion, deception, or other illegal police conduct, there is no search and seizure and the evidence is admissible in court. 403 U.S. 443, 91 S.Ct. 2022, 29 L.Ed.2d 564.

Review and Discussion Questions

1. If a person is deprived of freedom of action in a significant way by law enforcement officers, should the person be given warnings of the right to refuse consent before being asked for consent to search?

2. If a law enforcement officer asks a person for consent to search his or her home for stolen jewelry when the officer's real purpose is to look for marked money, is the consent voluntary?

3. Assume that law enforcement officers have obtained a valid consent to search an arrested defendant's automobile for drugs, and an initial search proves fruitless. Can the officers search the automobile again two hours later without obtaining a new consent to search? What about two days later? What about two weeks later? What changes in the defendant's status might render the initial consent no longer valid?

4. If, after giving consent to search, a person becomes nervous and revokes or limits the scope of the search, can this reaction be used by the officers as an indication of probable cause to obtain a search warrant?

5. Are third-party consents to search the defendant's premises valid in the following circumstances?

   a. A husband, out of anger at his wife, the defendant, invites the police into the house and points out evidence incriminating the wife.

   b. The defendant's girlfriend, who lives with him part-time, consents to a search of the defendant's apartment.

   c. A wife disobeys the instructions of her husband, the defendant, not to allow a search of their home. Does it matter whether the police know of the instructions?

6. Is it proper for a law enforcement officer to deliberately avoid attempting to obtain consent to search from the defendant and instead attempt to obtain consent from someone with equal authority over the defendant's premises? Does it matter whether the law enforcement officer had an opportunity to attempt to obtain consent from the defendant and deliberately failed to take it? What if the defendant was deliberately avoiding the police?

7. The dissenting opinion in *Florida v. Jimeno* stated, "Because an individual's expectation of privacy in a container is distinct from, and far greater than, his expectation of privacy in the interior of his car, it follows that an individual's consent to a search of the interior of his car cannot necessarily be understood as extending to containers in the car." 500 U.S. at 254, 111 S.Ct. at 1805, 114 L.Ed.2d at 305. Discuss.

8. Should a person be able to limit the number of officers conducting a consent search? Should a person be able to choose which officer or officers will conduct the consent

search? Should a person be allowed to follow around the officer conducting the search?

9. Can the following persons give a valid consent to search?

a. A highly intoxicated person

b. A five-year-old, a seven-year-old, or a ten-year-old child

c. A mentally retarded or senile person

d. An emotionally upset person

e. An uneducated person

10. Can the driver of a motor vehicle consent to a search of the vehicle even though a passenger objects? Can the owner of a store consent to a search of the store even though an employee objects? Can a parent consent to a search of his or her home even though a child objects?

REAL-LIFE FACT SITUATIONS

1. In 1992 appellant brought her 10-year-old niece Carla from Mexico to her home for the purpose of having her learn English, attend school, and baby-sit appellant's daughter. Carla never attended school. Instead, she cleaned the appellant's house and baby-sat, initially for one child and later two, five days a week from 7:00 A.M. to 3:00 P.M. Carla worked for appellant for approximately 18 months. During the last 12 months, the appellant hit Carla with her hands, an extension cord, a belt, a hammer, and a rock. The appellant also pulled Carla's ears, cut Carla with a knife, burned Carla with a spoon which she heated on the stove, pinched Carla's fingers with a pair of pliers, and dragged Carla back into the house when she tried to run away, hitting Carla's head against the door frame.

This abuse ended on June 19, 1994, when Carla left the appellant's house early in the morning and knocked on a neighbor's door in search of work. The neighbor called police. When police responded, they noticed Carla had a black eye, marks on her arms, and swollen fingers which were unable to bend. They took Carla to the station, where she was interviewed. Female officers examined Carla's body and reported that she had bruises and scarring on her back which appeared to have been made by a belt.

The evidence received during the hearing on the appellant's motion to suppress, and the inferences reasonably supported by the evidence, proved that after Carla was interviewed at the police station, officers went to the appellant's home in three or four police vehicles for the purpose of arresting the appellant. Carla was in one of the vehicles. Three officers, including Officer Reynaldo Perez, knocked on appellant's door. Officer Perez informed the appellant in Spanish that they were there to ask questions about Carla's whereabouts. It was his intent to determine whether the appellant was Carla's guardian. The appellant invited the officers into the apartment. They entered three to four feet into the living room area, where the appellant was attending to her two children. The appellant said Carla's natural parents were in Mexico. She also told police she did not know where Carla was but that Carla was upset and had left. While the appellant was being placed under arrest, Carla was summoned to the residence. She identified the appellant as the person who abused her. The appellant was taken from the apartment.

Officer Perez and a female officer remained in the apartment with Carla and the two young children. Officer Perez asked Carla if "we could search the house" for the items she had mentioned in her interview. Carla said yes and began walking toward the bathroom. Officer Perez followed Carla through the small apartment. Carla retrieved and handed to the officer the instruments with which appellant had abused her, including a pair of pliers from the bathroom, a spoon and a grinding stone from the kitchen, a belt from a hook in the hallway, and an extension cord from the living room. None of the items was hidden, and none was found within a private area such as a locked box or bureau drawers. Should the appellant's motion to suppress the evidence found in her home be granted? *People v. Santiago,* 64 Cal.Rptr.2d 794 (Cal.App. 2 Dist. 1997).

2. In October 1995 Marine Patrol Officer Brian Linscott went to the defendant's restaurant in Portland, after receiving reliable information that a lobsterman had sold short lobsters to the defendant. The restaurant was open for business and Linscott, who was dressed in his uniform, entered and asked to speak with the manager or the head chef. A bartender directed Linscott to go upstairs. Seeing no employees in the upstairs dining area, Linscott walked through the room and entered the kitchen, where he encountered a woman who appeared to be a cook. He identified himself as a marine patrol officer and asked her if he could speak to the manager or the head chef. She replied that the manager was not available and said, "I guess I'm in charge." Linscott asked the

woman if he could see where the lobsters were stored. She directed him to a lobster tank located in a cocktail area that was open to the public but not then in use, i.e., the lights were off and the room was empty. The woman led Linscott into the room and turned on the lights. Linscott began removing lobsters from the tank and measuring them. After he found one or two short lobsters, the woman brought Linscott a container to put them in. Within a few minutes the restaurant's head chef arrived and remained with Linscott while he checked the lobsters. Linscott would measure a lobster and, on a few occasions after finding a short lobster, would hand it to the head chef, who would also measure it and then place it in the container with the other short lobsters. At no time did anyone protest Linscott's actions. Linscott found 16 undersized lobsters and cited the defendant for possession of short lobsters in violation of 12 M.R.S.A. §6431. Should the defendant's motion to suppress the evidence collected by the officer be granted? *State v. Seamen's Club,* 691 A.2d 1248 (Me. 1997).

3. On April 27, 1994, at approximately 4:00 P.M., an individual named Sherrill walked into the Midtown South precinct and told Police Officer Joseph Gallo that he had been assaulted earlier in the day by a man he knew as "Will." Sherrill informed Gallo that Will was staying at 330 West 36th Street, apartment 708, and Sherrill led Gallo there.

When they arrived at the apartment, Gallo observed defendant inside through the wide-open front door. Sherrill pointed out the defendant as the man named Will who had assaulted him, and Gallo then knocked on the door and asked the defendant about the incident. The defendant admitted having had an argument with Sherrill. Gallo asked defendant for identification, and the defendant initially reached for his pocket, but then told Gallo he did not have it.

The defendant then began to walk toward a dresser inside the apartment. Gallo followed the defendant into the room to make sure that defendant did not produce a gun or knife from the dresser. Gallo testified that he wanted to see what the defendant was doing with his hands, and did not want the defendant to have his back to him in case he retrieved a weapon. Gallo's gun was holstered at all times, and he never touched the defendant.

The defendant removed one card from his wallet and then replaced it. He then produced a New York City welfare identification card, bearing his photograph and the name "Frank Mills." Gallo asked him to remove the first card, which turned out to be another welfare identification card, with the defendant's photo and the name "William Smith." Gallo asked the defendant what "the deal" was, and the defendant responded that the latter card was "old" and "no good." Defendant was then

placed under arrest. The defendant claims that the two identification cards should be suppressed because they were recovered pursuant to a warrantless entry and search of his home. Is the defendant correct? *People v. Smith,* 658 N.Y.S.2d 259 (A.D. 1 Dept. 1997).

4. Prior to 20 January 1995, Detective E. M. Ruiz of the Winston-Salem Police Department received information that the defendant possessed drugs at his residence. Detective Ruiz obtained this information from the defendant's girlfriend, Janet Abrams. On 20 January 1995, Abrams called Ruiz and informed Ruiz that the drugs were located in a black suitcase and a black trunk in the room Abrams shared with defendant. Detective Ruiz relayed this information to Detective J. D. Cooke, also with the Winston-Salem Police Department. The detectives concluded they did not have sufficient information to obtain a search warrant for the defendant's residence and decided to use a procedure known as "knock and talk."

The trial court made the following findings concerning the "knock and talk" procedure. The "knock and talk" procedure is a tactic used by law enforcement in Winston-Salem when they get information that a certain person has drugs in a residence but the officers do not have probable cause for a search warrant. The officers then proceed to the residence, knock on the door, and ask to be admitted inside. Thereafter gaining entry, the officers inform the person that they are investigating information that drugs are in the house. The officers then ask for permission to search and apparently are successful in many cases in getting the occupant's "apparent consent."

The trial court found that in the instant case Abrams told Ruiz in advance that she would give consent to search the bedroom she shared with the defendant. Detective Cooke and Detective Ruiz arrived at the defendant's residence with three additional officers and a K-9 dog. The trial court also made the following findings: That Detective Ruiz and Detective Cooke approached the door, knocked on the door. That a James Walters came to the door. The two officers were in plain clothes with a badge and guns in holsters and that the other three officers and the dog remained in the van in front of the house. That the officers asked Mr. Walters if they could come in rather than stand outside. That they then went inside. That Officer Ruiz advised Mr. Walters they were investigating drugs and had information that Kenneth Smith had the drugs there in that residence. That Officer Ruiz asked Mr. Walters if they could search, and he gave permission to search the common areas and said he had the bedroom in the basement where he slept on a couch.

Additional findings were that the other three officers and the K-9 dog then entered the house and conducted a search in these areas. No controlled substances were found. Detective Ruiz asked Abrams if the officers could search the bedroom she occupied with defendant, "to which she had already stated that she would give consent." The K-9 dog entered the room and indicated that drugs were in a suitcase and a black trunk located in the bedroom closet. A bag of marijuana was also found in the closet. Based on these findings, the trial court concluded that defendant's constitutional rights had been violated and granted defendant's motion to suppress. Was the trial court correct? *State v. Smith,* 488 S.E.2d 210 (N.C. 1997).

5. While driving his car in Salt Lake County, the defendant turned left at an intersection without signaling. Having observed the improper turn, Deputy David Broadhead pursued the defendant's car and activated his overhead lights to signal defendant to stop. As he pursued the vehicle, Deputy Broadhead saw the defendant make several "stuffing" movements toward the passenger side of the front seat. When the defendant finally pulled over about two blocks away, Deputy Broadhead saw him make another similar movement toward the same area of the car. The officer approached the car and asked the defendant, who appeared extremely nervous, why he had repeatedly moved toward the right side of the front seat. The defendant replied, "I didn't know that I was." When the officer asked defendant whether he had concealed any weapons or contraband under the seat, the defendant replied, "No, you're free to look if you want." The officer explained to the defendant that, because defendant appeared nervous and had made several "stuffing" movements toward the right side of the front seat, he was concerned that the defendant had hidden a weapon or contraband in that area. The officer then said that he would like to "check" under the front seat, and the defendant replied, "Go right ahead."

Deputy Broadhead looked under the front passenger seat and discovered a brown leather case sticking out from under the seat. When the officer opened the case and discovered drugs and drug paraphernalia, he confronted the defendant. The defendant said that the case was not his and that he did not know why it was in his car. The officer then arrested the defendant for unlawful possession of the controlled substances and drug paraphernalia.

Before trial, the defendant moved to suppress the evidence found in the leather case, arguing that the scope of his consent did not extend to the contents of the leather case. He emphasized that he gave Deputy Broadhead permission only to "look" under the front seat and that the officer never asked for permission to "search" but only to "check" under the front seat. The defendant argues that his consent to "look" or "check" for weapons or drugs did not reasonably include permission to look for those items in containers found under the seat. Should the defendant's motion to suppress the evidence be granted? *State v. Stephens,* 946 P.2d 734 (Utah App. 1997).

6. On November 2, 1995, at approximately 7:15 P.M., St. Petersburg police officers Mark Carr and J. DeLuca were on motorcycle patrol as part of the street level narcotics unit. They observed Parker walking down the street, and drove up behind her and asked if she would speak with them. She said she would. After Officer Carr asked Parker some questions about whether she had identification and what she was doing in the neighborhood, Officer DeLuca asked her if she had any narcotics on her person. Parker responded that she did not. Officer DeLuca asked her if she would show that she did not have any narcotics on her person, and, responding affirmatively, Parker pulled out her pockets. Officer DeLuca then asked Parker if she had any narcotics in her bra because, according to the officers, the bra is a common place for women to hide narcotics. Parker responded that she did not, and Officer DeLuca asked her if she would shake her shirt and bra in order to prove this. Parker complied, and a tissue fell to the ground. Parker placed her foot on the tissue and tried to stomp on it. Officer DeLuca grabbed her arm to prevent her from destroying evidence because in his experience and training crack cocaine is commonly placed in tissue. He retrieved the tissue and found that it in fact contained what later tested positive for crack cocaine. Should the defendant's motion to suppress the cocaine be granted? *Parker v. State,* 693 So.2d 92 (Fla.App. 2 Dist. 1997).

CHAPTER TEN

The Plain View Doctrine

OBJECTIVES

1. Understand why the plain view doctrine is not a true exception to the search warrant requirement.

2. Be able to distinguish the plain view doctrine from the law of search incident to arrest.

3. Be able to give examples of prior valid intrusions into constitutionally protected areas.

4. Understand how the plain view doctrine is affected by the reasonable expectation of privacy of the person against whom a search or observation is directed.

5. Understand the demarcations between
    a. a plain view observation and probable cause to believe that an item of evidence is in a certain place and
    b. a plain view observation and a search, especially with respect to closer examinations of items and examinations of containers.

6. Understand the so-called "plain touch" or "plain feel" doctrine.

OUTLINE

1. Introduction—distinction between plain view observation and search
2. Requirements of the plain view doctrine
    a. The officer, as the result of a prior valid intrusion, must be in a position in which he or she has a legal right to be
        (1) Effecting an arrest or search incident to arrest
        (2) Conducting a stop and frisk
        (3) Executing a search warrant
        (4) Making controlled deliveries
        (5) Pursuing a fleeing suspect
        (6) Responding to an emergency
    b. The officer must not unreasonably intrude on any person's reasonable expectation of privacy
    c. The incriminating character of the object to be seized must be immediately apparent to the officer
        (1) Probable cause
        (2) Mechanical or electrical aids
        (3) Shifting of position
        (4) Closer examination of items
    d. The discovery of the item of evidence by the officer need not be inadvertent
3. "Plain touch" or "plain feel"

T he **plain view doctrine** was simply stated in the U.S. Supreme Court decision in *Harris v. United States:* "It has been settled that objects falling in the plain view of an officer who has a right to be in a position to have that view may be introduced in evidence." 390 U.S. 234, 236, 88 S.Ct. 992, 993, 19 L.Ed.2d 1067, 1069 (1968). Under the doctrine, "if police are lawfully in a position from which they view an object, if its incriminating character is apparent, and if the officers have a lawful right of access to the object, they may seize it without a warrant." *Minnesota v. Dickerson,* 508 U.S. 366, 375, 113 S.Ct. 2130, 2136–37, 124 L.Ed.2d 334, 345 (1993).

The plain view doctrine permits law enforcement officers to observe and seize evidence without a warrant or other justification. It is a recognized exception to the warrant requirement of the Fourth Amendment, even though a plain view observation technically does not constitute a **search.** A search occurs only if there is an infringement of a person's reasonable expectation of privacy; a law enforcement officer's mere observation of an item of evidence from a position in which the officer has a right to be is ordinarily not an infringement of a person's privacy rights. But the Fourth Amendment prohibits unreasonable **seizures** as well as unreasonable searches.

> The right to security in person and property protected by the Fourth Amendment may be invaded in quite different ways by searches and seizures. A search compromises the individual interest in privacy; a seizure deprives the individual of dominion over his or her person or property. . . . The "plain view" doctrine is often considered an exception to the general rule that warrantless searches are presumptively unreasonable, but this characterization overlooks the important difference between searches and seizures. If an article is already in plain view, neither its observation nor its seizure would involve any invasion of privacy. . . . A seizure of the article, however, would obviously invade the owner's possessory interest. . . . If "plain view" justifies an exception from an otherwise applicable warrant requirement, therefore, it must be an exception that is addressed to the concerns that are implicated by seizures rather than by searches. *Horton v. California,* 496 U.S. 128, 133–34, 110 S.Ct. 2301, 2306, 110 L.Ed.2d 112, 120–21 (1990).

The theory of the plain view doctrine consists of extending to nonpublic places such as the home, where searches and seizures without a warrant are presumptively unreasonable, the long-standing authority of the police to make warrantless seizures in public places of incriminating objects such as weapons and contraband.

> [T]he practical justification for that extension is the desirability of sparing police, whose viewing of the object in the course of a lawful search is as legitimate as it would have been in a public place, the inconvenience and the risk—to themselves or to preservation of the evidence—of going to obtain a warrant. *Arizona v. Hicks,* 480 U.S. 321, 327, 107 S.Ct. 1149, 1153, 94 L.Ed.2d 347, 355 (1987).

Therefore, the plain view doctrine is not predicated on any sort of exigency but is permitted in the interest of police convenience.

> The reason so light and transient a justification as police convenience is deemed reasonable is because of the absolutely minimal risk posed by the Plain View Doctrine to either of the two traditional Fourth Amendment values or concerns. . . . In terms of the initial intrusion or breach into the zone of privacy, the Plain View Doctrine, by definition, poses no threat whatsoever. It does not authorize the crossing of a threshold or other initiation of an intrusion. It does not even come into play until the intrusion is already a valid fait accompli. . . .

In terms of the other traditional Fourth Amendment concern, preventing even a validly initiated search from degenerating into an exploratory fishing expedition or general rummaging about, the Plain View Doctrine, again by definition, poses no threat whatsoever, for it authorizes not even the most minimal of further searching. It authorizes only the warrantless seizure by the police of probable evidence already revealed to them, with no further examination or searching being involved. *State v. Jones*, 653 A.2d 1040, 1045 (Md.Spec.App. 1995). ■

Requirements of the Plain View Doctrine

Despite the apparent simplicity and obviousness of its basic concept, the plain view doctrine does not give law enforcement officers a license to look around anywhere, any time, and under any circumstances and to seize anything they wish. The doctrine has carefully prescribed requirements developed through court decisions over the years. These requirements can be summarized as follows:

- The officer, as the result of a prior valid intrusion, must be in a position in which he or she has legal right to be.
- The officer must not unreasonably intrude on any person's reasonable expectation of privacy.
- The incriminating character of the object to be seized must be immediately apparent to the officer.
- The discovery of the item of evidence by the officer need not be inadvertent.

Before the seizure of an item of evidence can be justified under the plain view doctrine, the law enforcement officer seizing the item must satisfy all four of these requirements. The remainder of this chapter is devoted to a discussion of these requirements.

The Officer, as the Result of a Prior Valid Intrusion, Must Be in a Position in Which He or She Has a Legal Right to Be

The situations in which a law enforcement officer is in a position in which he or she has a legal right to be are too numerous to present an exhaustive listing. The U.S. Supreme Court gave several examples in *Coolidge v. New Hampshire*:

> What the "plain view" cases have in common is that the police officer in each of them had a prior justification for an intrusion in the course of which he came . . . across a piece of evidence incriminating the accused. The doctrine serves to supplement the prior justification—whether it be a warrant for another object, hot pursuit, search incident to lawful arrest, or some other legitimate reason for being present unconnected with a search directed against the accused—and permits the warrantless seizure. 403 U.S. at 466, 91 S.Ct. at 2038, 29 L.Ed.2d at 583.

For purposes of this chapter, a prior valid intrusion or a prior justification for an intrusion simply means that a law enforcement officer has made a legal encroachment into a constitutionally protected area or has otherwise legally invaded a person's reasonable expectation of privacy. Stated otherwise, "[i]t is . . . an essential predicate to any valid warrantless seizure of incriminating evidence that the officer did not violate the Fourth Amendment in arriving at the place from which the evidence could be plainly viewed." *Horton v. California*, 496 U.S. 128, 136, 110 S.Ct. 2301, 2308, 110

L.Ed.2d 112, 123 (1990). This section discusses several examples in which this requirement of the plain view doctrine has been applied.

EFFECTING AN ARREST OR SEARCH INCIDENT TO ARREST. A law enforcement officer may lawfully seize an object that comes into view during a lawfully executed **arrest** or a **search incident to arrest.** The law of search incident to arrest and the plain view doctrine must be clearly distinguished. Under the rule of *Chimel v. California* (see Chapter 8), a law enforcement officer may search a person incident to arrest only for weapons or to prevent the destruction or concealment of evidence. The extent of the search is limited to the arrestee's body and the area within the arrestee's immediate control, "construing that phrase to mean the area from within which he might gain possession of a weapon or destructible evidence." 395 U.S. at 763, 89 S.Ct. at 2040, 23 L.Ed.2d at 694.

The plain view doctrine does not extend the permissible area of search incident to arrest. In the *Chimel* case, the Court specifically said:

> There is no comparable justification, however, for routinely searching any room other than that in which an arrest occurs—or for that matter, for searching through all the desk drawers or other closed or concealed areas in that room itself. Such searches, in the absence of well-recognized exceptions, may be made only under the authority of a search warrant. 395 U.S. at 763, 89 S.Ct. at 2040, 23 L.Ed.2d at 694.

Nevertheless, the law of search incident to arrest does not require a law enforcement officer to ignore or avert his or her eyes from objects readily visible in the room where the arrest occurs. If the arresting officer observes an item of evidence open to view but outside the area under the immediate control of the arrestee, the officer may seize it, so long as the observation was made in the course of a lawful arrest or an appropriately limited search incident to arrest. The item of evidence is admissible in court if all requirements of the plain view doctrine are satisfied. The same rule applies to items of evidence observed during the course of a properly limited protective sweep. (See Chapter 8.)

CONDUCTING A STOP AND FRISK. A seizable item observed by an officer during the course of a lawful **stop and frisk** may also be seized without a warrant. (See Chapter 7 for a discussion of stop and frisk.) Again, the plain view doctrine does not extend the area of search permissible under stop-and-frisk law, but it does give the officer authority to seize readily visible objects. This authority extends to the passenger compartment of an automobile.

> If while conducting a legitimate *Terry* search of the interior of the automobile, the officer should . . . discover contraband other than weapons, he clearly cannot be required to ignore the contraband, and the Fourth Amendment does not require its suppression in such circumstances. *Michigan v. Long,* 463 U.S. 1032, 1050, 103 S.Ct. 3469, 3481, 77 L.Ed.2d 1201, 1220 (1983).

EXECUTING A SEARCH WARRANT. In the case of *Cady v. Dombrowski,* 413 U.S. 433, 93 S.Ct. 2523, 37 L.Ed.2d 706 (1973), the U.S. Supreme Court held that an officer executing a valid **search warrant** could legally seize items of evidence lying in plain view even though they were not particularly described in the warrant. For purposes of this discussion, law enforcement officers executing a valid search warrant are in a position in which they have a legal right to be. Once officers have discharged their duties under a search warrant, however, the warrant no longer provides a legitimate justification for their presence on premises. Therefore, a seizure of items of evidence observed in plain view after a search warrant is fully executed is an illegal seizure. *United States v. Limatoc,* 807 F.2d 792 (9th Cir. 1987).

MAKING CONTROLLED DELIVERIES. The U.S. government has the right to inspect all incoming goods from foreign countries at the port of entry. In addition, common carriers have a common-law right to inspect packages they accept for shipment, based on their duty to refrain from carrying contraband. Although the sheer volume of goods in transit prevents systematic inspection of all or even a large percentage of these goods, common carriers and customs officials inevitably discover contraband in transit in a variety of circumstances. When such a discovery is made, it is routine procedure to notify the appropriate authorities, so that the authorities may identify and prosecute the person or persons responsible for the movement of the contraband. The arrival of law enforcement authorities on the scene to confirm the presence of contraband and to determine what to do with it does not convert the otherwise legal search by the common carrier or customs official into a government search subject to the Fourth Amendment. *United States v. Edwards,* 602 F.2d 458 (1st Cir. 1979). See also *United States v. Jacobsen,* 466 U.S. 109, 104 S.Ct. 1652, 80 L.Ed.2d 85 (1984).

Law enforcement authorities, rather than simply seizing the contraband and destroying it, will often make a so-called controlled delivery of the container, monitoring the container on its journey to the intended destination. The person dealing in the contraband can then be identified upon taking possession of and asserting control over the container. The typical pattern of a controlled delivery has been described as follows:

> They most ordinarily occur when a carrier, usually an airline, unexpectedly discovers what seems to be contraband while inspecting luggage to learn the identity of its owner, or when the contraband falls out of a broken or damaged piece of luggage, or when the carrier exercises its inspection privilege because some suspicious circumstance has caused it concern that it may unwittingly be transporting contraband. Frequently, after such a discovery, law enforcement agents restore the contraband to its container, then close or reseal the container, and authorize the carrier to deliver the container to its owner. When the owner appears to take delivery he is arrested and the container with the contraband is seized and then searched a second time for the contraband known to be there. *United States v. Bulgier,* 618 F.2d 472, 476 (7th Cir. 1980).

The U.S. Supreme Court, relying on the plain view doctrine, held that no protected privacy interest remains in contraband in a container once government officers have lawfully opened that container and identified its contents as illegal. Furthermore, the simple act of resealing the container to enable the police to make a controlled delivery does not operate to revive or restore the lawfully invaded privacy rights. The Court said:

> The plain view doctrine is grounded on the proposition that once police are lawfully in a position to observe an item first-hand, its owner's privacy interest in that item is lost; the owner may retain the incidents of title and possession but not privacy. . . . [O]nce a container has been found to a certainty to contain illicit drugs, the contraband becomes like objects physically within the plain view of the police, and the claim to privacy is lost. Consequently, the subsequent reopening of the container is not a "search" within the intendment of the Fourth Amendment. *Illinois v. Andreas,* 463 U.S. 765, 771–72, 103 S.Ct. 3319, 3324, 77 L.Ed.2d 1003, 1010 (1983).

In the *Andreas* case, the Court acknowledged that there are often unavoidable interruptions of control or surveillance of a container and that at some point after such an interruption, courts should recognize that the container may have been put to other uses, thereby reinstating the individual's legitimate expectation of privacy in the container. The Court decided that a workable, objective standard that limits the risk of intrusion on legitimate privacy interests when such an interruption occurs is whether there is a substantial likelihood that the contents of the container have been changed during the gap in surveillance. If there is no such likelihood, the officer may legally open the container without a warrant.

PURSUING A FLEEING SUSPECT. Law enforcement officers who are lawfully on premises in **hot pursuit** of a dangerous person may seize items of evidence observed open to their view. In *Warden v. Hayden,* 387 U.S. 294, 87 S.Ct. 1642, 18 L.Ed.2d 782 (1967), the police were informed that an armed robbery had taken place and that a suspect wearing a light cap and dark jacket had entered a certain house less than five minutes before the officers arrived. Several officers entered the house and began to search for the described suspect and weapons that he had used in the robbery and might use against them. One officer, while searching the cellar, found in a washing machine clothing of the type that the fleeing man was said to have worn. The Court held that the seizure of the clothing was lawful:

> [T]he seizures occurred prior to or immediately contemporaneous with Hayden's arrest, as part of an effort to find a suspected felon, armed, within the house into which he had run only minutes before the police arrived. The permissible scope of search must, therefore, at the least, be as broad as may reasonably be necessary to prevent the dangers that the suspect at large in the house may resist or escape. 387 U.S. at 299, 87 S.Ct. at 1646, 18 L.Ed.2d at 787.

If, however, the suspect had already been taken into custody when the officer looked into the washing machine, the seizure of the clothing would have been unlawful. There no longer would have been any danger of the fleeing suspect's using a weapon against the officers and, therefore, no reason to look for weapons in the washing machine.

To summarize, officers who enter a constitutionally protected area in hot pursuit of a fleeing suspect are in a position in which they have a legal right to be and may seize items of evidence observed lying open to view during the hot pursuit and the protective search for weapons. Note that hot pursuit does not necessarily involve a violent crime or a dangerous person. The U.S. Supreme Court held that there was a hot pursuit when officers chased the defendant, who the officers had probable cause to believe had just purchased illegal drugs, from her doorway into her house. *United States v. Santana,* 427 U.S. 38, 96 S.Ct. 2406, 49 L.Ed.2d 300 (1976).

RESPONDING TO AN EMERGENCY. Related to the hot pursuit situation is the situation in which an officer responds to an **emergency** and observes items of evidence open to view. In *United States v. Gillenwaters,* 890 F.2d 679 (4th Cir. 1989), a police officer responded to a report of a stabbing at the defendant's home. The victim was a visiting friend, and the officer arrived while paramedics were still tending the woman's wounds. The officer briefly questioned the woman and also observed several incriminating items open to view in the room where the victim lay. A search warrant was obtained partially on the basis of these observations. The court held that the observations were not an improper warrantless search.

> Hager [the officer] was responding to an emergency call; he arrived while the victim was still receiving emergency medical treatment on the scene; he at-

tempted to obtain evidence from her concerning her assailant. His presence was unquestionably justified by exigent circumstances, and his observations—made in the room where the victim lay bleeding—fall within the scope of the plain view doctrine. 890 F.2d at 682.

In *State v. Moulton,* 481 A.2d 155 (Me. 1984), police had probable cause to believe that a dangerous criminal suspect was on the premises of an auto repair complex. The officers believed that the suspect not only had stolen motor vehicles and parts but had driven one vehicle into a lake and had set another on fire. The auto repair complex was large, with many exits, making it difficult to secure. The likely presence of tools, vehicles, and flammable liquids added to the danger, and the hour was late, adding to the difficulty of obtaining a warrant. Under these exigent circumstances, the court found that the officers were justified in entering the building without a search warrant for the suspect. Once inside the building, officers observed criminal evidence lying in plain view and seized it. These warrantless seizures were held reasonable under the Fourth Amendment, and a subsequent search warrant, obtained in part on the basis of the items found in plain view, was valid.

Police may thus enter premises and search without a warrant for a dangerous criminal suspect if

- the police have probable cause to believe that the dangerous criminal suspect is on the premises, and
- there are exigent circumstances precluding police from securing the premises long enough to obtain a search warrant.

Once police have made a valid intrusion into the premises, they may seize items of evidence lying in plain view.

Law enforcement officers may be tempted to justify otherwise illegal searches by resorting to this combination of the plain view doctrine and response to an emergency. Courts will carefully examine these situations and will invalidate a search if a genuine emergency does not exist, or if a search goes beyond what is necessary to respond to the emergency. In *Arizona v. Hicks,* summarized on pages 361 and 363, the search went beyond what was necessary to respond to the emergency. Therefore, in the absence of probable cause to justify the additional search and in the absence of probable cause to seize the object, the plain view doctrine did not apply. The U.S. Supreme Court stated that "a warrantless search must be 'strictly circumscribed by the exigencies which justify its initiation,' . . ." *Mincey v. Arizona,* 437 U.S. 385, 393, 98 S.Ct. 2408, 2414, 57 L.Ed.2d 290, 300 (1978). In the *Mincey* case, the prosecution attempted to justify an extensive four-day warrantless search of a murder victim's apartment on the basis of a "murder scene exception" to the warrant requirement. The search occurred when there was no emergency threatening life or limb and after all persons in the apartment had been located.

The Court said that police may make warrantless entries on premises where they reasonably believe that a person within needs immediate aid. Police may also make a prompt warrantless protective search of the area to see whether other potentially dangerous persons are still on the premises. Any evidence observed in plain view during the course of these legitimate emergency activities may be seized. However, the Court held that absent an emergency, "the 'murder scene exception' . . . is inconsistent with the Fourth and Fourteenth Amendments—that the warrantless search of Mincey's apartment was not constitutionally permissible simply because a homicide had recently occurred there." 437 U.S. at 395, 98 S.Ct. at 2414, 57 L.Ed.2d at 302. In *Thompson v. Louisiana,* 469 U.S. 17, 105 S.Ct. 409, 83 L.Ed.2d 246 (1984), the Court reiterated that even a limited two-hour, general, nonemergency search of a murder scene remains a significant intrusion on a person's privacy and may not be conducted without a warrant.

1. The plain view doctrine allows the warrantless seizure of incriminating evidence observed after a prior justification for an intrusion, whether that justification be a warrant for another object, hot pursuit, search incident to arrest, an emergency, or some other legitimate reason.

2. Once police are lawfully in a position to observe an item firsthand, its owner's privacy interest in that item is lost, although the owner may retain the incidents of title and possession.

3. Absent a continuing emergency, a warrantless search of a murder scene is not constitutionally permissible simply because a homicide had recently occurred there.

The Officer Must Not Unreasonably Intrude on Any Person's Reasonable Expectation of Privacy

Not all observations made by law enforcement officers who are in a position in which they have a legal right to be will satisfy Fourth Amendment requirements. If an observation unreasonably intrudes on a person's reasonable expectation of privacy, it will be considered an illegal search unless it is supported by a warrant or falls within a recognized exception to the warrant requirement.

In a case illustrating this principle, a law enforcement officer observed the defendant and another man enter the men's room of a city park and remain there. After about five minutes, the officer entered the plumbing access area of the rest room and observed the men performing illegal sexual acts. The officer had observed no other suspicious acts by the defendant before the defendant entered the men's room. The court held that this was not a plain view observation by the officer but an illegal search.

> The People here urge us to hold that clandestine observation of doorless stalls in public rest rooms is not a "search" and hence is not subject to the Fourth Amendment's prohibition of unreasonable searches. This would permit the police to make it a routine practice to observe from hidden vantage points the rest room conduct of the public whenever such activities do not occur within fully enclosed toilet stalls and would permit spying on the "innocent and guilty alike." Most persons using public rest rooms have no reason to suspect that a hidden agent of the state will observe them. The expectation of privacy a person has when he enters a rest room is reasonable and is not diminished or destroyed because the toilet stall being used lacks a door.
>
> Reference to expectations of privacy as a Fourth Amendment touchstone received the endorsement of the United States Supreme Court in *Katz v. United States,* 389 U.S. 347, 88 S.Ct. 507, 19 L.Ed.2d 576 (1967). Viewed in the light of *Katz,* the standard for determining what is an illegal search is whether defendant's "reasonable expectation of privacy was violated by unreasonable governmental intrusion." *People v. Triggs,* 106 Cal.Rptr. 408, 412–13, 506 P.2d 232, 236–37 (Cal.1973).

If, however, a person has no reasonable expectation of privacy in a place or an object, plain view observations of the place or object by law enforcement officers violate no Fourth Amendment rights. In *New York v. Class,* 475 U.S. 106, 106 S.Ct. 960, 89 L.Ed.2d 81 (1986), a law enforcement officer stopped an automobile for a traffic infraction. After the driver voluntarily got out of the vehicle, the officer entered the vehicle and removed some papers from the dashboard in order to ascertain the vehicle identification number (VIN). (Federal law requires the VIN to be placed in the plain view of someone outside the automobile to facilitate the VIN's usefulness for various governmental purposes such as research, insurance, safety, theft prevention, and vehicle recall.)

The Court held that there was no reasonable expectation of privacy in the VIN because of the important role played by the VIN in the pervasive governmental regulation of the automobile and because of the efforts of the federal government to ensure that the VIN is placed in plain view. Furthermore, the placement of papers on top of the VIN was insufficient to create a privacy interest in the VIN, since efforts to restrict access to an area do not generate a reasonable expectation of privacy where none would otherwise exist. The mere viewing of the formerly obscured VIN was not, therefore, a violation of the Fourth Amendment. Moreover, since the officer's entry into the vehicle to uncover the VIN did not violate the Fourth Amendment, the officer had a legal right to be where he was when he saw a gun under the seat. The gun was thus in plain view, and, given the officer's probable cause that the gun was evidence of a crime, the officer could seize it under the plain view doctrine.

KEY POINTS

4. If a person has no reasonable expectation of privacy in a place or an object, plain view observations by law enforcement officers violate no Fourth Amendment rights.

The Incriminating Character of the Object to Be Seized Must Be Immediately Apparent to the Officer

This requirement of the plain view doctrine means that before an object may be seized, the police must have **probable cause** that the object is subject to seizure without conducting some further search of the object. *Arizona v. Hicks,* 480 U.S. 321, 107 S.Ct. 1149, 94 L.Ed.2d 347 (1987).

PROBABLE CAUSE. "If . . . the police lack probable cause to believe that an object in plain view is contraband without conducting some further search of the object—*i.e.,* if 'its incriminating character [is not] "immediately apparent,"' . . . the plain-view doctrine cannot justify its seizure." *Minnesota v. Dickerson,* 508 U.S. 366, 375, 113 S.Ct. 2130, 2137, 124 L.Ed.2d 334, 345 (1993). The term **contraband,** as used in this quote, should be interpreted to include the categories of property subject to seizure as listed in Chapter 5:

1. Property that constitutes evidence of the commission of a criminal offense;

2. Contraband, the fruits of crime, or things otherwise criminally possessed; or

3. Property designed or intended for use or that is or has been used as the means of committing a criminal offense.

In *Coolidge v. New Hampshire,* 403 U.S. 443, 466, 91 S.Ct. 2022, 2038, 29 L.Ed.2d 564, 583 (1971), the U.S. Supreme Court said that a seizure of an item in plain view is justified "only where it is *immediately apparent* to the police that they have evidence before them" (emphasis supplied). The term "immediately apparent" has been broadly interpreted to give officers a reasonable time within which to make the probable cause determination. For example, in *United States v. Johnston,* 784 F.2d 416 (1st Cir. 1986), the court held that an item's incriminating nature need not be determined by the first officer who observes the item, but may be based on the collective knowledge of all officers lawfully on the premises after all have observed the item. In the *Johnston* case, an officer came across torn pages from a notebook while executing a search warrant for narcotics. Probable cause to seize the pages as incriminating evidence did not develop, however, until the team of searching officers completed a search of the rest of the premises and discovered related evidence of narcotics violations. So long as the officers had probable cause to believe the items were incriminating by the time of completion of the execution of the search warrant, the *immediately apparent* requirement was held to be satisfied.

In *State v. Mosher,* 270 A.2d 451 (Me. 1970), a Massachusetts police officer arrested the defendant and two companions for trespassing with their automobile on private property. While waiting for assistance, the officer observed articles of clothing wrapped in cellophane lying inside the car. Later, after the car had been removed to the police station, the officer learned through police channels that similar clothing had recently been stolen in Maine. He obtained a search warrant and seized the clothing.

The court found the search warrant defective but upheld the seizure because the items of clothing were in the officer's plain view. The court said:

> Even where . . . no search is necessary, the accompanying seizure must be accompanied by probable cause or reasonable grounds to believe that the property falls within a category which warrants the seizure. 270 A.2d at 453.

When the officer seized the items, he had probable cause to believe that the articles of clothing were *stolen* based on the report that similar articles had been stolen in Maine. If the officer had seized the articles of clothing when he first observed them, the seizure would have been illegal. At that time, he had no reason to believe that they were stolen or that they came under any other category of seizable property. It was only after he received the report that similar clothing had been stolen in Maine that he had probable cause to believe the property was seizable.

Officers may use their background and experience to evaluate the facts and circumstances in arriving at a probable cause determination. In *Texas v. Brown,* 460 U.S. 730, 103 S.Ct. 1535, 75 L.Ed.2d 502 (1983), an officer stopped the defendant's automobile at night at a routine driver's license checkpoint, asked the defendant for his license, and shined a flashlight into the car. The officer observed an opaque green party balloon, knotted about one-half inch from the tip. After shifting his position, the officer also observed several small vials, quantities of loose white powder, and an open bag of party balloons in the open glove compartment. The U.S. Supreme Court held that the officer had probable cause to believe that the balloon contained an illicit substance:

> [The officer] testified that he was aware, both from his participation in previous narcotics arrests and from discussions with other officers, that balloons tied in the manner of the one possessed by [the defendant] were frequently used to carry narcotics. This testimony was corroborated by that of a police department

chemist who noted that it was "common" for balloons to be used in packaging narcotics. In addition, [the officer] was able to observe the contents of the glove compartment of [the defendant's] car, which revealed further suggestions that [the defendant] was engaged in activities that might involve possession of illicit substances. The fact that [the officer] could not see through the opaque fabric of the balloon is all but irrelevant: the distinctive character of the balloon itself spoke volumes as to its contents—particularly to the trained eye of the officer. 460 U.S. at 742–43, 103 S.Ct. at 1543, 75 L.Ed.2d at 514.

In *Shipman v. State,* 282 So.2d 700 (Ala. 1973), however, the object containing drugs was found to be insufficiently distinctive in character to justify its seizure. In that case, law enforcement officers detained several persons on a store owner's complaint that they were acting in an unruly manner. An officer observed one of the persons move an object to the top of his boot. The object, though clearly not a weapon, was seized and was later determined to contain heroin. The court held that, even though the object was in plain view, its seizure was illegal because the officer did not have probable cause to believe it was contraband.

The reason for this rule is apparent. If the rule were otherwise, an officer acting on mere groundless suspicion, could seize anything and everything belonging to an individual which happened to be in plain view on the prospect that on further investigation some of it might prove to have been stolen or to be contraband. It would open the door to unreasonable confiscation of a person's property while a minute examination of it is made in an effort to find something criminal. Such practice would amount to the "general exploratory search from one object to another until something incriminating at last emerges" which was condemned in *Coolidge v. New Hampshire.* . . . Ex post facto justification of a seizure made on mere groundless suspicion, is totally contrary to the basic tenets of the Fourth Amendment. . . .

For an item in plain view to be validly seized, the officer must possess some judgment at the time that the object to be seized is contraband and that judgment must be grounded upon probable cause. 282 So.2d at 704.

In certain instances, an officer may have occasion to *search* rather than *seize* items found in plain view. In *Arizona v. Hicks,* 480 U.S. 321, 107 S.Ct. 1149, 94 L.Ed.2d 347 (1987) (discussed in further detail later), an officer conducting an emergency search of an apartment after a shooting incident observed stereo equipment that he *suspected* was stolen. He searched the equipment, moving it for closer examination, and obtained the serial numbers. He determined that the equipment was stolen, and some was seized immediately and some was seized later under a warrant. The Court held that the same probable cause standard applies to plain view *searches* as applies to plain view *seizures.* Since the officer had only a *suspicion* that the stereo equipment was stolen, his search was not based on probable cause and was therefore unreasonable under the Fourth Amendment.

MECHANICAL OR ELECTRICAL AIDS. Although the plain view doctrine does not allow a law enforcement officer to conduct a further search of an object to determine its incriminating nature, it is well settled that an officer may use mechanical or electrical aids to assist in observing items of evidence. Of course, the officer must be in a position in which he or she has a legal right to be and must not intrude on someone's reasonable expectation of privacy. *Texas v. Brown,* 460 U.S. 730, 103 S.Ct. 1535, 75 L.Ed.2d 502 (1983). In *Marshall v. United States,* 422 F.2d 185 (5th Cir. 1970), when a law enforcement officer arrived at a drive-in restaurant, he was told that a car had been parked in the parking lot for an hour with its lights on and with a person lying in the backseat. The officer went over to the car to see whether anything was wrong. He shined a flashlight into the car and observed the defendant lying in the back with a sawed-off shotgun resting on the floorboard between his feet. He arrested the defendant and seized the shotgun.

The court held that the observation of the shotgun by the officer was not a search. The officer was in a position in which he had a legal right to be, and his use of the flashlight did not, in itself, make his observations unlawful:

> When the circumstances of a particular case are such that the police officer's observation would not have constituted a search had it occurred in daylight, then the fact that the officer used a flashlight to pierce the nighttime darkness does not transform his observation into a search. Regardless of the time of day or night, the plain view rule must be upheld where the viewer is rightfully positioned, seeing through eyes that are neither accusatory nor criminally investigatory. The plain view rule does not go into hibernation at sunset. 422 F.2d at 189.

Similarly, courts have generally approved of the use of binoculars to enhance natural observations so long as they are not used to see into an area that would otherwise be impossible to view with the naked eye. In *United States v. Grimes,* 426 F.2d 706 (5th Cir. 1970), an officer stationed himself in a field about fifty yards from the defendant's house and with the aid of binoculars watched the activities of the defendant, a known liquor violator. The officer observed the defendant place two large cardboard boxes (each of which contained six gallons of untaxed whiskey) into a 1961 Buick. The liquor was later found in the car while another person was driving the car on a public street. The court held that the officer's use of binoculars to observe the defendant's activities did not constitute an illegal search. A defendant's reasonable expectation of privacy was violated, however, in a case in which police looked into an eighth-floor window from a vantage point two to three hundred yards away using high-powered binoculars.

> We . . . view the test of validity of the surveillance as turning upon whether that which is perceived or heard is that which is conducted with a reasonable expectation of privacy and not upon the means used to view it or hear it. So long as that which is viewed or heard is perceptible to the naked eye or unaided ear, the person seen or heard has no reasonable expectation of privacy in what occurs. Because he has no reasonable expectation of privacy, governmental authority may use technological aids to visual or aural enhancement of whatever type available. However, the reasonable expectation of privacy extends to that which cannot be seen by the naked eye or heard by the unaided ear. While governmental authority may use a technological device to avoid detection of its own law enforcement activity, it may not use the same device to invade the protected right. *People v. Arno,* 153 Cal.Rptr. 624, 627 (Cal.App. 1979).

SHIFTING OF POSITION. In *Texas v. Brown,* 460 U.S. 730, 103 S.Ct. 1535, 75 L.Ed.2d 502 (1983), the U.S. Supreme Court held that a police officer's changing of position to get a better vantage point to look inside a vehicle did not invalidate an otherwise legal plain view observation.

> [T]he fact that [Officer] Maples "changed [his] position" and "bent down at an angle so [he] could see what was inside" Brown's car . . . is irrelevant to Fourth

Amendment analysis. The general public could peer into the interior of Brown's automobile from any number of angles; there is no reason Maples should be precluded from observing as an officer what would be entirely visible to him as a private citizen. There is no legitimate expectation of privacy . . . shielding that portion of the interior of an automobile which may be viewed from outside the vehicle by either inquisitive passersby or diligent police officers. In short, the conduct that enabled Maples to observe the interior of Brown's car and of his open glove compartment was not a search within the meaning of the Fourth Amendment. 460 U.S. at 740, 103 S.Ct. at 1542, 75 L.Ed.2d at 512–13.

CLOSER EXAMINATION OF ITEMS. A difficult issue is how far an officer may go in examining an item more closely before the examination constitutes a search rather than a mere plain view observation. The U.S. Supreme Court gave some guidelines in a case in which police, investigating a shooting, entered the defendant's apartment to search for the shooter, other victims, and weapons. One officer noticed stereo components and, suspecting they were stolen, read and recorded their serial numbers, moving some of the equipment in the process. After checking with headquarters and learning that the components were stolen, the officer seized some of the components and obtained warrants for others. The Court analyzed the officer's actions in terms of search and seizure law.

> [T]he mere recording of the serial numbers did not constitute a seizure. . . . [I]t did not "meaningfully interfere" with respondent's possessory interest in either the serial numbers or the equipment, and therefore did not amount to a seizure. . . . Officer Nelson's moving of the equipment, however, did constitute a "search" separate and apart from the search for the shooter, victims, and weapons that was the lawful objective of his entry into the apartment. Merely inspecting those parts of the turntable that came into view during the latter search would not have constituted an independent search because it would have produced no additional invasion of respondent's privacy interest. . . . But taking action, unrelated to the objectives of the authorized intrusion, which exposed to view concealed portions of the apartment or its contents, did produce a new invasion of respondent's privacy unjustified by the exigent circumstance that validated the entry. *Arizona v. Hicks,* 480 U.S. 321, 324–25, 107 S.Ct. 1149, 1152, 94 L.Ed.2d 347, 353–54 (1987).

The lesson of the *Hicks* case is that an officer's examination of an item of property will be a *search* rather than a *plain view observation* if

- the officer produces a new invasion of the person's property by taking action that exposes to view concealed portions of the premises or its contents; and
- the officer's action is unrelated to, and unjustified by, the objectives of his or her authorized intrusion.

In *United States v. Silva,* 714 F.Supp. 693 (S.D.N.Y. 1989), an officer executing a search warrant for fruits and instrumentalities of the crime of bank robbery discovered a notebook in plain view. The government argued that once the notebook was in plain view, the officer was justified in opening and reading it to ascertain its value as evidence. The court rejected that contention, specifically referring to the *Hicks* case.

> This court can hardly imagine a less intrusive action than moving a stereo turntable to view its serial number. By comparison, the opening of a notebook

or document is, if anything, a more significant intrusion since it is bound to reveal something of much greater personal value than the bottom of a turntable. Accordingly, the court is constrained to conclude that, after *Hicks,* even the minor investigation of a notebook beyond inspecting what is visible must constitute a search. 714 F.Supp. at 696.

The court further elaborated in a footnote:

> The court does not hold that an officer cannot read a document or book if it is plainly visible without opening or disturbing it in any way. The holding is limited to finding that if the incriminating nature of the document cannot be readily ascertained without moving or disturbing it, an officer may not, absent probable cause move or further search the book or document. 714 F.Supp. at 696 n.6.

Ordinarily, the opening and examination of a closed container by a government agent will be considered a search because of the serious invasion of privacy these actions usually entail. Nevertheless, courts have held these actions not to be searches where

- the contents of the container can be inferred from its outward appearance, distinctive configuration, transparency, or other characteristics (*United States v. Haley,* 669 F.2d 201 [4th Cir. 1982]); or
- the container has already been opened and its contents examined by a private party.

In *United States v. Eschweiler,* 745 F.2d 435 (7th Cir. 1984), the court held that the removal of a key from an envelope that said "safe-deposit box key" and had the name of the bank on it was not an additional search of the envelope, which was found in plain view.

> [A] container that proclaims its contents on the outside is not a private place. This point would be obvious if the envelope had been transparent; then its contents would have been literally in plain view. The inscription and other characteristics that unequivocally revealed its contents made it transparent in the contemplation of the law. 745 F.2d at 440.

In *United States v. Jacobsen,* 466 U.S. 109, 104 S.Ct. 1652, 80 L.Ed.2d 85 (1984), the U.S. Supreme Court allowed a warrantless examination of a partially closed container by government agents after the container had been opened and its contents examined by a private party. Employees of a freight carrier examined a damaged cardboard box wrapped in brown paper and found a white powdery substance in the innermost of four plastic bags that had been concealed in a tube inside the package. The employees notified the Drug Enforcement Administration (DEA), replaced the plastic bags in the tube, and placed the tube back in the box. A DEA agent arrived and removed the tube from the box and the plastic bags from the tube. When he saw the white powder, he opened the bags and removed a small amount of the white powder. He then subjected the powder to a field chemical test. The test indicated that the powder was cocaine.

The U.S. Supreme Court found that the initial invasion of the package by the freight carrier employees did not violate the Fourth Amendment, because it was a private rather than a governmental action. The Court then analyzed the additional invasions of privacy by the DEA agent in terms of the degree to which they exceeded the scope of the private search. The Court found that even if the white powder was not itself in plain view because it was enclosed in so many containers and covered with papers, the DEA agent could be virtually certain that nothing else of significance was in the package and that a manual inspection of the tube and its contents would not tell him anything more than the freight carrier employees had already told him. The agent's reexamination of the contents of the package merely avoided the risk of a flaw in the employees' recollection, rather than further infringing on someone's privacy. Had the DEA agent's conduct significantly exceeded that of the freight carrier's employees, then he would have conducted a new and different search that would have been subject to Fourth Amendment protections. The Court said:

> Respondents could have no privacy interest in the contents of the package, since it remained unsealed and since the Federal Express employees had just examined the package and had, of their own accord, invited the federal agent to their offices for the express purpose of viewing its contents. The agent's viewing of what a private party had freely made available for his inspection did not violate the Fourth Amendment. . . . Similarly, the removal of the plastic bags from the tube and the agent's visual inspection of their contents enabled the agent to learn nothing that had not previously been learned during the private search. It infringed no legitimate expectation of privacy and hence was not a "search" within the meaning of the Fourth Amendment. 466 U.S. at 119–20, 104 S.Ct. at 1659–60, 80 L.Ed.2d at 98.

The Court further held that the agent's assertion of dominion and control over the package and its contents was a seizure but that the seizure was reasonable, since it was apparent that the tube and plastic bags contained contraband and little else. The Court said that

> it is well-settled law that it is constitutionally reasonable for law enforcement officials to seize "effects" that cannot support a justifiable expectation of privacy without a warrant, based on probable cause to believe they contain contraband. 466 U.S. at 121–22, 104 S.Ct. at 1661, 80 L.Ed.2d at 99.

The Supreme Court then addressed the question of whether the additional intrusion occasioned by the field test, which had not been conducted by the freight carrier employees and therefore exceeded the scope of the private search, was an unlawful search or seizure within the meaning of the Fourth Amendment. The Court held that a chemical test that merely discloses whether or not a particular substance is cocaine, and no other arguably "private" fact, compromises no legitimate privacy interest. Furthermore, even though the test destroyed a quantity of the powder and thereby permanently deprived its owner of a protected possessory interest, the infringement was constitutionally reasonable. The Court reasoned that the law enforcement interests justifying the procedure were substantial and, because only a trace amount of material was involved, the seizure could have, at most, only a minimal effect on any protected property interest.

To summarize, a law enforcement officer may examine, without a warrant, a container whose contents are not open to view, if any privacy interest in the contents of the container has already been compromised by a private party and information about the contents has been made available to the officer by the private party. In addition, it is constitutionally permissible for the officer to seize the contents of the container, if the officer has probable cause to believe the contents are contraband, and to conduct a chemical field test so long as only a trace amount of the substance is destroyed by the test.

5. Before a law enforcement officer may seize an item of property that is observed open to view, the officer must have probable cause to believe that the property comes within one of the categories of property subject to seizure under state or federal law. An officer is allowed a reasonable time within which to make the probable cause determination, but the officer may not conduct a further search of the object to make the probable cause determination.

6. Law enforcement officers may use mechanical or electrical devices, such as binoculars and flashlights, to assist in observing items of evidence, so long as they do not intrude on someone's reasonable expectation of privacy.

7. An officer's examination of an item of property will be a *search* rather than a *plain view observation* if the officer produces a new invasion of the property by taking action that exposes to view concealed portions of the premises or its contents and the officer's action is unrelated to and unjustified by the objectives of his or her authorized intrusion.

8. A law enforcement officer may open and examine the contents of a closed container found in open view, if the contents of the container can be inferred from its outward appearance, distinctive configuration, transparency, or other characteristics.

9. A law enforcement officer may open and examine, without a warrant, a container whose contents are not open to view, if any privacy interest in the contents of the container has already been compromised by a private party and information about the contents has been made available to the officer by the private party.

The Discovery of the Item of Evidence by the Officer Need Not Be Inadvertent

In *Horton v. California*, 496 U.S. 128, 110 S.Ct. 2301, 110 L.Ed.2d 112 (1990), a police officer investigating an armed robbery determined that there was probable cause to search the defendant's home for the proceeds of, and weapons used in, the robbery. His affidavit for a search warrant referred to police reports that described both the weapons and the proceeds, but the warrant issued by the magistrate only authorized a search for the proceeds. In executing the warrant, the officer did not find the stolen property but did find the weapons in plain view and seized them. The officer testified that, while he was searching for the named stolen property, he was also interested in finding other evidence connecting the defendant to the robbery. Thus, the seized evidence was not discovered "inadvertently."

In holding that inadvertence was not a necessary condition of a legitimate plain view seizure, the Court discussed the 1971 case of *Coolidge v. New Hampshire*, 403 U.S. 443, 91 S.Ct. 2022, 29 L.Ed.2d 564. Justice Stewart's opinion in *Coolidge* stated that "the discovery of evidence in plain view must be inadvertent." 403 U.S. at 469, 91 S.Ct. at 2040, 29 L.Ed.2d at 585. Nevertheless, Justice Stewart's analysis of the plain view doctrine did not command a majority, and a plurality of the Court has since made clear that the discussion is not a binding precedent. Justice Stewart concluded that the inadvertence requirement was necessary to avoid a violation of the express constitutional requirement that a valid warrant must particularly describe the things to be seized. The Court in *Horton* found two flaws in this reasoning.

First, evenhanded law enforcement is best achieved by the application of objective standards of conduct, rather than standards that depend upon the subjective state of mind of the officer. The fact that an officer is interested in an item of evidence and fully expects to find it in the course of a search should not invalidate its seizure if the search is confined in area and duration by the terms of a warrant or a valid exception to the warrant requirement. If the officer has knowledge approaching certainty that the item will be found, we see no reason why he or she would deliberately omit a particular description of the item to be seized from the application for a search warrant. Specification of the additional item could only permit the officer to expand the scope of the search. On the other hand, if he or she has a valid warrant to search for one item and merely a suspicion concerning the second, whether or not it amounts to probable cause, we fail to see why that suspicion should immunize the second item from seizure if it is found during a lawful search for the first. . . .

Second, the suggestion that the inadvertence requirement is necessary to prevent the police from conducting general searches, or from converting specific warrants into general warrants, is not persuasive because that interest is already served by the requirements that no warrant issue unless it "particularly describ[es] the place to be searched and the persons or things to be seized," . . . and that a warrantless search be circumscribed by the exigencies which justify its initiation. . . . Scrupulous adherence to these requirements serves the interests in limiting the area and duration of the search that the inadvertence requirement inadequately protects. Once those commands have been satisfied and the officer has a lawful right of access, however, no additional Fourth Amendment interest is furthered by requiring that the discovery of evidence be inadvertent. If the scope of the search exceeds that permitted by the terms of a validly issued warrant or the character of the relevant exception from the warrant requirement, the subsequent seizure is unconstitutional without more. 496 U.S. at 138–40, 110 S.Ct. at 2308–09, 110 L.Ed.2d at 124–25.

In this case, the scope of the search was not enlarged in the slightest by the omission of any reference to the weapons in the warrant. In fact, if the items named in the warrant had been found or surrendered at the outset, no search for weapons could have taken place.

The prohibition against general searches and general warrants serves primarily as a protection against unjustified intrusions on privacy. But reliance on privacy concerns is misplaced when the inquiry concerns the scope of an exception that merely authorizes an officer with a lawful right of access to an item to seize it without a warrant.

Note that the great majority of state and federal courts adopted the inadvertence requirement in response to *Coolidge v. New Hampshire*. Although federal courts are bound by the *Horton* decision abandoning the inadvertence requirement, some state courts may retain the inadvertence requirement based on interpretations of their state constitutions. The reader must determine the state of the law in his or her state by consulting pertinent court decisions.

KEY POINTS

10. Even though a law enforcement officer is interested in an item of evidence and fully expects to find it in the course of a search, a plain view seizure of the item is not invalidated if the search is confined in its scope by the terms of a warrant or a valid exception to the warrant requirement.

"Plain Touch" or "Plain Feel"

In *Minnesota v. Dickerson*, 508 U.S. 366, 113 S.Ct. 2130, 124 L.Ed.2d 334 (1993), the U.S. Supreme Court applied the principles of the plain view doctrine to a situation in which a law enforcement officer discovered contraband through the sense of touch during an otherwise lawful search. In the *Dickerson* case, officers on patrol observed the defendant leaving a building known for cocaine traffic. When the defendant attempted to evade the officers, they stopped him and ordered him to submit to a patdown search. The search revealed no weapons, but the officer conducting the search felt a small lump in the defendant's jacket. The officer examined the lump with his fingers, it slid, and the officer believed it to be a lump of crack cocaine in cellophane. The officer then reached into the pocket and retrieved a small plastic bag of crack cocaine.

The Court said:

> We think that this [plain view] doctrine has an obvious application by analogy to cases in which an officer discovers contraband through the sense of touch during an otherwise lawful search. The rationale of the plain view doctrine is that if contraband is left in open view and is observed by a police officer from a lawful vantage point, there has been no invasion of a legitimate expectation of privacy and thus no "search" within the meaning of the Fourth Amendment— or at least no search independent of the initial intrusion that gave the officers their vantage point. . . . The warrantless seizure of contraband that presents itself in this manner is deemed justified by the realization that resort to a neutral magistrate under such circumstances would often be impracticable and would do little to promote the objectives of the Fourth Amendment. . . . The same can be said of tactile discoveries of contraband. If a police officer lawfully pats down a suspect's outer clothing and feels an object whose contour or mass makes its identity immediately apparent, there has been no invasion of the suspect's privacy beyond that already authorized by the officer's search for weapons; if the object is contraband, its warrantless seizure would be justified by the same practical considerations that inhere in the plain view context. 508 U.S. at 375–76, 113 S.Ct. at 2137, 124 L.Ed.2d at 345–46.

In this case, however, the Court held the seizure of the package of cocaine illegal, because the contraband contents of the defendant's pocket were not immediately apparent to the officer. Only after the officer squeezed, slid, and otherwise manipulated the pocket's contents did he determine that it was cocaine. The Court found that the facts of this case were very similar to those of *Arizona v. Hicks* (discussed on pages 361 and 363), in which the Court invalidated the warrantless seizure of stolen stereo equipment found by police while executing a valid search warrant for other evidence.

> Although the officer was lawfully in a position to feel the lump in respondent's pocket, because *Terry* entitled him to place his hands upon respondent's jacket, the court below determined that the incriminating character of the object was not immediately apparent to him. Rather, the officer determined that the item was contraband only after conducting a further search, one not authorized by *Terry* or by any other exception to the warrant requirement. Because this further search of respondent's pocket was constitutionally invalid, the seizure of the cocaine that followed is likewise unconstitutional. 508 U.S. at 379, 113 S.Ct. at 2139, 124 L.Ed.2d at 348.

Therefore, to paraphrase the plain view doctrine, if police are lawfully in a position from which they feel an object, if its incriminating character is *immediately apparent,* and if the officers have a lawful right of access to the object, they may seize it without a warrant. If, however, the police lack probable cause to believe that the object felt is subject to seizure without conducting some further search of the object, its seizure is not justified.

Some courts have further expanded the analogy to the plain view doctrine to the other senses of smell, taste, and hearing. For example, *United States v. Haley*, 669 F.2d 201 (4th Cir. 1982), held that "[a]nother characteristic [of a container] which brings the contents into plain view is the odor given off by those contents." 669 F.2d at 203. The U.S. Supreme Court has not dealt with the senses of smell, taste, or hearing in the context of the plain view doctrine, and the question remains open whether these senses would be treated similarly to the sense of touch.

KEY POINTS

11. If a law enforcement officer is lawfully in a position from which he or she *feels* an object, if the object's incriminating character is *immediately apparent,* and if the officer has a lawful right of access to the object, the officer may seize it without a warrant.

Summary

Under the plain view doctrine, an observation of items lying open to view by a law enforcement officer who has a right to be in a position to have that view is not a search, and the officer may seize the evidence without a warrant. The doctrine has four requirements, all of which must be satisfied before seizure of an item of evidence can be legally justified.

First, the officer, as a result of a prior valid intrusion, must be in a position in which he or she has a legal right to be. Some examples of situations in which an officer's intrusion is justified are effecting an arrest or search incident to an arrest, conducting a stop and frisk, executing a search warrant, making controlled deliveries, pursuing a fleeing suspect, and responding to an emergency.

Second, the officer must not unreasonably intrude on any person's reasonable expectation of privacy. To satisfy this requirement, the officer must use common sense to keep the investigation of crime within reasonable bounds.

Third, the incriminating character of the object to be seized must be immediately apparent to the officer. This simply means that before an object may be seized, the officer must have *probable cause* that the object is subject to seizure without conducting some further search of the object. An officer may use his or her experience and background to assist in determining whether a particular item is seizable. The officer may use mechanical or electrical aids, such as a flashlight or binoculars, to assist in observing an item, so long as this does not unreasonably intrude on someone's reasonable expectation of privacy. The officer may also examine items more closely, unless

- the officer produces a new invasion of the person's property by taking action that exposes to view concealed portions of the premises or its contents; and

- the officer's action is unrelated to, and unjustified by, the objectives of his or her authorized intrusion.

Furthermore, the opening of a container to determine whether incriminating evidence is inside is prohibited unless

- the contents of the container can be inferred from its outward appearance, distinctive configuration, transparency, or other characteristics; or

- any privacy interest in the container's contents has already been compromised by a private party and information about the contents has been made available to the officer by the private party.

Fourth, the discovery of the item of evidence by the officer need not be inadvertent. Nevertheless, even though the officer is interested in finding a particular item of evidence, the officer may not expand the scope of the search beyond the original justification for the search, whether that justification is a search warrant for other items of evidence, an exception to the search warrant requirement, or some other justification.

Analogizing to the plain view doctrine, the U.S. Supreme Court has allowed the seizure of an object discovered through "plain touch" rather than "plain view." Therefore, if police are lawfully in a position from which they feel an object, if its incriminating character is *immediately apparent,* and if the officers have a lawful right of access to the object, they may seize it without a warrant. If, however, the police lack probable cause to believe that the object felt is subject to seizure without conducting some further search of the object, its seizure is not justified.

Key Holdings from Major Cases

Harris v. United States (1968). "It has been settled that objects falling in the plain view of an officer who has a right to be in a position to have that view may be introduced in evidence. . . ." 390 U.S. 234, 236, 88 S.Ct. 992, 993, 19 L.Ed.2d 1067, 1069.

Coolidge v. New Hampshire (1971). "What the 'plain view' cases have in common is that the police officer in each of them had a prior justification for an intrusion in the course of which he came . . . across a piece of evidence incriminating the accused. The doctrine serves to supplement the prior justification—whether it be a warrant for another object, hot pursuit, search incident to lawful arrest, or some other legitimate reason for being present unconnected with a search directed against the accused—and permits the warrantless seizure. Of course, the extension of the original justification is legitimate only where it is immediately apparent to the police that they have evidence before them." 403 U.S. 443, 466, 91 S.Ct. 2022, 2038, 29 L.Ed.2d 564, 583.

Michigan v. Long (1983). "If while conducting a legitimate *Terry* search of the interior of the automobile, the officer should . . . discover contraband other than weapons, he clearly cannot be required to ignore the contraband, and the Fourth Amendment does not require its suppression in such circumstances." 463 U.S. 1032, 1050, 103 S.Ct. 3469, 3481, 77 L.Ed.2d 1201, 1220.

Illinois v. Andreas (1983). "The plain view doctrine is grounded on the proposition that once police are lawfully in a position to observe an item first-hand, its owner's privacy interest in that item is lost; the owner may retain the incidents of title and possession but not privacy. . . . [O]nce a container has been found to a certainty to contain illicit drugs, the contraband becomes like objects physically within the plain view of the police, and the claim to privacy is lost. Consequently, the subsequent reopening of the container is not a 'search' within the intendment of the Fourth Amendment." 463 U.S. 765, 771–72, 103 S.Ct. 3319, 3324, 77 L.Ed.2d 1003, 1010.

New York v. Class (1986). "Because of the important role played by the VIN [vehicle identification number] in the pervasive governmental regulation of the automobile and the efforts by the Federal Government to ensure that the VIN is placed in plain view . . . there was no reasonable expectation of privacy in the VIN. . . . [W]here the object at issue is an identification number behind the transparent windshield of an automobile driven upon the public roads, we believe that the placement of the obscuring papers was insufficient to create a privacy interest in the VIN. The mere viewing of the formerly obscured VIN was not, therefore, a violation of the Fourth Amendment." 475 U.S. 106, 114, 106 S.Ct. 960, 966, 89 L.Ed.2d 81, 90–91.

Police officers are not authorized "to enter a vehicle to obtain a dashboard-mounted VIN when the VIN is visible from outside the automobile. If the VIN is in the plain view of someone outside the vehicle, there is no justification for governmental intrusion into the passenger compartment to see it." 475 U.S. at 119, 106 S.Ct. at 968–69, 89 L.Ed.2d at 94.

Texas v. Brown (1983). "[T]he use of artificial means to illuminate a darkened area simply does not constitute a search, and thus triggers no Fourth Amendment protection." 460 U.S. 730, 740, 103 S.Ct. 1535, 1542, 75 L.Ed.2d 502, 512.

United States v. Jacobsen (1984). "[I]t is well-settled law that it is constitutionally reasonable for law enforcement officials to seize 'effects' that cannot support a justifiable expectation of privacy without a warrant, based on probable cause to believe they contain contraband." 466 U.S. 109, 121–22, 104 S.Ct. 1652, 1661, 80 L.Ed.2d 85, 99.

Horton v. California (1990). "[E]ven though inadvertence is a characteristic of most legitimate 'plain view' searches, it is not a necessary condition." 496 U.S. 128, 130, 110 S.Ct. 2301, 2304, 110 L.Ed.2d 112, 118–19.

"The fact that an officer is interested in an item of evidence and fully expects to find it in the course of a search should not invalidate its seizure if the search is confined in area and duration by the terms of a warrant or a valid exception to the warrant requirement." 496 U.S. at 138, 110 S.Ct. at 2308, 110 L.Ed.2d at 124.

Minnesota v. Dickerson (1993). "If a police officer lawfully pats down a suspect's outer clothing and feels an object whose contour or mass makes its identity immediately apparent, there has been no invasion of the suspect's privacy beyond that already authorized by the officer's search for weapons; if the object is contraband, its warrantless seizure would be justified by the same practical considerations that inhere in the plain view context." 508 U.S. 366, 375–76, 113 S.Ct. 2130, 2137, 124 L.Ed.2d 334, 346.

Review and Discussion Questions

1. The dissent in the *Horton* case said that "there are a number of instances in which a law enforcement officer might deliberately choose to omit certain items from a warrant application even though he has probable cause to seize them, knows they are on the premises, and intends to seize them when they are discovered in plain view." 496 U.S. at 146, 110 S.Ct. at 2313, 110 L.Ed.2d at 129. Give examples with reasons.

2. If law enforcement officers are in a place in which they have a right to be and they observe bottles that appear to contain illegal drugs, may they open the bottles and examine the contents further? May law enforcement officers use their sense of smell, taste, or touch to determine whether items are subject to seizure when they are not sure?

3. Assume that law enforcement officers have a warrant to arrest the defendant for having stolen guns four months ago. The officers suspect that the guns are at the defendant's home, but that suspicion is based on stale information insufficient to obtain a search warrant. May the officers seize guns found in plain view when they arrest the defendant? Would it make any difference if the officers could have easily found out whether the guns were still at the defendant's home by contacting a reliable informant?

4. May law enforcement officers take an item off the shelf in an antique store and examine it to determine whether it is stolen? May officers do the same thing in a private home into which they have been invited by a person who does not know they are law enforcement officers?

5. Discuss the meaning of the following statement of the U.S. Supreme Court: " 'Plain view' is perhaps better understood . . . not as an independent 'exception' to the warrant clause, but simply as an extension of whatever the prior justification for an officer's 'access to an object' may be." *Texas v. Brown,* 460 U.S. 730, 738–39, 103 S.Ct. 1535, 1540–41, 75 L.Ed.2d 502, 511 (1983).

6. What problems are presented by an officer executing a search warrant for specified obscene materials, who seizes some magazines that are in plain view and were not specified in the warrant?

7. What are the limits on protective searches? May officers routinely look throughout a house for other suspects whenever they make an arrest or search? May officers go into other buildings on the premises? May officers go into neighboring homes? If an arrest is made in the hallway of a motel, may officers conduct a protective search of all or any of the rooms of the motel?

8. Does the plain view doctrine authorize a warrantless entry into a dwelling to seize contraband visible from outside the dwelling? Why? What if an officer observes contraband from the hallway of a motel through the open door to one of the rooms? What if an officer observes contraband lying on the desk in someone's office?

9. Would it be proper for officers executing a search warrant for stolen property to bring along victims of the theft to aid the officers in seizing other stolen items not named in the warrant that might be in plain view? Why?

10. If law enforcement officers are legitimately on premises, may they record the serial numbers of any objects that they suspect are stolen property? May they take photographs of these objects?

REAL-LIFE FACT SITUATIONS

1. Pursuant to a writ of possession issued by a magistrate in Elmore County, Sheriff Rick Layher and Detective Greg Berry, of the Mountain Home Police Department, went to Myers' rented mobile home for the purpose of removing Myers and his possessions from the residence. After arriving, the sheriff knocked on the door, but he received no response. Layher and Berry were then informed by neighbors that no one had been living in the residence for quite some time. Sheriff Layher knocked on the door again. After discovering that the front door was unlocked, the sheriff and the detective entered the home to determine whether Myers was living in the residence. Initially, the officers believed that Myers had abandoned the home, leaving behind some of his personal belongings. As the officers walked through the home, they found a small baggie, containing a green leafy substance, on top of a television in a back bedroom. In a second bedroom, the officers discovered drug paraphernalia

lying against the wall and a second baggie, which contained numerous seeds, lying on top of another television. The substances in both of the baggies was marijuana. The contraband was not seized at this point.

Sheriff Layher and Detective Berry left the residence to discuss the situation with a local deputy prosecuting attorney. The deputy prosecuting attorney contacted the lawyer who was representing Myers' landlord, and it was determined that because the police had a legal right to be in the mobile home by virtue of the writ of possession, the evidence discovered could be seized. The sheriff and the detective then returned to Myers' residence. According to the record, the police were able to contact Myers indirectly to inform him that he needed to return to his mobile home to remove his personal belongings so the officers could turn possession of the premises over to the landlord pursuant to the civil writ.

When Myers arrived at the home, he found the police photographing the drug paraphernalia and the baggies. The officers again advised Myers to remove his personal property from the residence, at which time Myers indicated that the marijuana and the drug paraphernalia belonged to him. These items were then seized by the officers and Myers was charged with the misdemeanor offenses of possession of marijuana and possession of drug paraphernalia. Should Myers's motion to suppress the marijuana and drug paraphernalia be granted? *State v. Myers*, 942 P.2d 564 (Idaho App. 1997).

2. Officer Dwayne Scheuermann testified at the hearing on the motion to suppress that on January 10, 1994, at approximately 2:00 P.M., he and Chuck Husmeier, an agent of the Alcohol, Tobacco, and Firearms (ATF), were investigating a weapons violation by Kuwanda Smith of 268 North Robertson Street. Looking for a Smith and Wesson 0.9 mm handgun, the officers went to Ms. Smith's apartment and spoke to Ms. Smith's mother, who told them that Ms. Smith was not at home. Kuwanda Smith reportedly was out looking for the gun to turn it over to the police. The investigators looked for Ms. Smith in the neighborhood and then returned to the apartment. As they approached, they saw Kuwanda Smith standing with the defendant near a flight of stairs. When the defendant saw the officers, he ran up the stairs to Kuwanda Smith's apartment. Believing that the defendant might have a weapon, Agent Husmeier chased the defendant up the stairs and followed the defendant into the apartment where he saw the defendant discard a white object near a refrigerator. After Agent Husmeier detained the defendant, Officer Scheuermann recovered the piece of plastic containing several rocklike objects which appeared to be cocaine and placed the defendant under arrest, advising him of his *Miranda* rights. The defendant first said he had no knowledge of the cocaine but then he admitted possessing it and discarding it.

On appeal the defendant contends that the officers did not have reasonable suspicion to stop him, and did not have sufficient information to justify entering the apartment without a warrant, and the seizure was illegal because the police did not have probable cause to arrest him. The state argues that the police were justified to enter the apartment without a warrant based on exigent circumstances and probable cause to arrest. Who is correct, the defendant or the state? *State v. Laird*, 674 So.2d 425 (La.App. 4 Cir. 1996).

3. On November 1, 1996, at approximately 9:25 P.M., Officers Mark Nunemacher and Scott Oesterlin were on routine patrol when they observed a car with a severely shattered windshield, which they recognized as belonging to a suspected drug dealer, Joyce McDonald. The officers followed the car into the parking lot of an apartment complex known as a location for drug trafficking. After the car had been parked in Joyce McDonald's usual parking space, the officers activated the squad car's overhead lights. Both officers got out of the car and approached the vehicle. Officer Nunemacher asked the driver (respondent Varnado) if she was Joyce McDonald. Varnado replied that she was Beverly McDonald, Joyce's sister. Varnado was unknown to the officers. When asked for identification, Varnado replied that she did not have any with her.

Officer Nunemacher asked Varnado to step out of the car and sit in the back of the squad car while he checked her driving status on the computer. Before placing her in the squad car, Officer Nunemacher conducted a pat-down search of the defendant's bulky coat for weapons. During the search for weapons, the officer moved Varnado's coat and observed a large bulge in her jeans pocket. The officer patted down the pocket without manipulating its contents and felt textured objects that he recognized to be crack cocaine, as well as a smooth object. He asked Varnado if the drugs were hers, and she responded they were not. The officer then reached into her pocket and retrieved about $2,000 in cash and several plastic bags containing crack cocaine. Should Varnado's motion to suppress the evidence be granted? *State v. Varnado*, 1997 WL 749421 (Minn.App.).

4. On May 6, 1989, the Suffolk County Police Department, after an investigation and a controlled purchase of cocaine, obtained and executed a search warrant for an apartment in Bay Shore. The defendant, who was one of three persons inside the apartment at the time the warrant was executed, had been observed outside of the apartment earlier in the day in possession of a duffel bag. At the time that the warrant was executed, the duffel bag was outside the apartment, several feet to the immediate left of the front steps to the apartment. After se-

curing the apartment and the three individuals inside, an officer returned to the duffel bag where he observed a plastic "zip-lock" bag protruding from a side pocket of the duffel bag. Believing that the plastic bag contained drugs, the officer pulled back the flap of the pocket to get a better look. Upon doing so, he observed that the plastic bag contained what appeared to be a handgun. Upon removal of the plastic bag, he determined that it in fact contained a small automatic handgun. The trial court denied suppression of the handgun on the grounds that the search of the duffel bag was warranted by exigent circumstances incident to a lawful arrest and that the handgun was in plain view. Was the trial court correct in denying suppression of the handgun? *People v. Johnson*, 660 N.Y.S.2d 730 (A.D. 2 Dept. 1997).

5. Around 5:00 A.M. on June 1, 1995, a tenant of a Phoenix storage facility noticed smoke emanating from another unit in the building. The storage warehouse consists of three buildings built in a U shape, facing a common driveway. Each building is divided into separate units, but there is common attic space. Each unit has one large garage-type door, as well as a standard entrance door. Firefighters responding to the tenant's call first entered unit 4; after determining the fire's path, they cut the lock and forced open the door to unit 3, rented by Steven M. Mazen. The fire not only burned through the ceiling but was so hot it melted the solder on the water pipes; the resulting leak extinguished most of the fire in unit 3.

Upon opening the door to unit 3, the firefighters saw an elaborate system of grow lights and irrigation pipes trained on approximately fifteen singed marijuana plants. Because of his training as an emergency medical technician, the firefighter who opened the unit recognized the plants as probably being marijuana. The police were then called.

Police officers, who arrived during the cleanup operation, could clearly see the marijuana plants through the unit's open door. At approximately 6:30 A.M. the firefighters left and the arson investigator arrived. Shortly thereafter, detectives from the Drug Enforcement Bureau (DEB) arrived. The police officers and DEB detectives seized the growing equipment, the marijuana plants, and plastic garbage bags filled with marijuana. Mazen was later arrested and charged. Should Mazen's motion to suppress the evidence be granted? *Mazen v. State*, 940 P.2d 923 (Ariz. 1997).

6. On September 29, 1993, officers from the Asbury Park Police Department, in conjunction with an officer from the Bradley Beach police, were searching for an individual for whom an arrest warrant had been issued on a domestic violence complaint. The person was known to frequent the Clover Club bar in Asbury Park. After searching the main part of the bar, one of the officers went to see if the fugitive was in the restroom. He pushed against the door, meeting with some resistance. He then pushed the door again, and it opened. The officer could not tell what caused the resistance. He thought that there was a spring providing resistance designed to automatically close the door. No one testified that the door was locked, that the door had a lock that was not engaged, that an individual was holding the door shut, or that the door was not equipped with a lock at all.

In describing the bathroom itself, the officer said that it was approximately four feet deep by seven feet long with a toilet at the far end and a sink. When he opened the door, he saw the defendant and another individual facing each other. The defendant was holding a plastic bag, similar to a sandwich bag, in his hand, and a dollar bill was falling to the floor. Based on his experience involving over one thousand narcotics arrests, the dollar bill and plastic bag indicated to the officer that there was some type of narcotic activity taking place. The officer attempted to grab the bag out of defendant's hand. The defendant resisted, holding the bag to his midsection. A scuffle ensued. The officer was able to see a white powdery substance of an amount approximately the size of a golfball in the bag.

The defendant tried to raise the bag to his mouth. The officer prevented him from doing so by grabbing the defendant from behind. Noticing that the defendant's hand was dangerously close to the officer's weapon, the officer struck the defendant in the head two times, causing him to fall to the floor of the bathroom. From his knees, the defendant thrust the plastic bag into the toilet. Officers pulled the defendant away from the toilet and subdued him. The officer retrieved the bag from the toilet. The bag contained cocaine. Should the defendant's motion to suppress the cocaine be granted? *State v. Boynton*, 688 A.2d 145 (N.J. Super A.D. 1997).

CHAPTER ELEVEN

Search and Seizure of Vehicles and Containers

OBJECTIVES

1. Understand the rationale behind and the scope of search allowed under the *Carroll* doctrine or automobile exception to the search warrant requirement.

2. Understand what types of exigent circumstances will justify the search of a motor vehicle on probable cause.

3. Understand the differences between a motor vehicle and a movable container with respect to expectations of privacy and the ramifications of those differences for purposes of a warrantless search.

4. Understand the circumstances under which a motor vehicle may be impounded and the requirements that must be met before an inventory of the vehicle's contents may be conducted by law enforcement officers.

5. Be able to analyze any search and seizure situation involving a motor vehicle in terms of the reasonable expectation of privacy of the vehicle's owner and occupants.

OUTLINE

1. Introduction—unique nature of motor vehicles
2. The *Carroll* doctrine
   a. Probable cause
   b. Delay in search
   c. Exigent circumstances
   d. Entry on private premises
   e. Scope of search
      (1) Search of entire vehicle
      (2) Search of container found in vehicle
      (3) Search of container not found in vehicle
      (4) Other container searches
3. Impoundment and inventory of vehicles
   a. Impoundment
   b. Inventory
      (1) Standard procedures
      (2) Scope
      (3) Time
      (4) Plain view doctrine
4. Impoundment of vehicle under forfeiture statutes
5. Expectation of privacy
   a. Electronic beepers
   b. Searches by dogs

The same basic legal principles apply to the search of vehicles as apply to the search of fixed premises. For instance, it is well settled that an automobile is a personal effect, a place, or a thing within the meaning of the Fourth Amendment and is protected against unreasonable searches and seizures. Therefore, law enforcement officers should obtain a warrant whenever they want to search a motor vehicle unless the situation falls within one of the exceptions to the warrant requirement discussed in this chapter or in other chapters of this book. (Guidelines for obtaining a warrant can be found in Chapters 5 and 6.)

Courts have created exceptions to the warrant requirement for motor vehicles because of their unique nature. Among the unique characteristics of motor vehicles are their mobility, their use as transportation to and from crime scenes, and their employment in transporting dangerous weapons, stolen goods, contraband, and instrumentalities of crime. In addition, a person has a lesser expectation of privacy in a motor vehicle because it travels public thoroughfares where its occupants and contents are open to view, it seldom serves as a residence or permanent place for personal effects, it is required to be registered and its occupant is required to be licensed, it is extensively regulated with respect to the condition and manner in which it is operated on public streets and highways, it periodically undergoes an official inspection, and it is often taken into police custody in the interests of public safety. This chapter discusses the exceptions to the warrant requirement for searches and seizures of motor vehicles and also examines the search and seizure of movable containers, because similar considerations apply to both areas of the law. ■

The *Carroll* Doctrine

The *Carroll* **doctrine** holds that a warrantless search of a readily mobile motor vehicle by a law enforcement officer who has probable cause to believe that the vehicle contains items subject to seizure is not unreasonable under the Fourth Amendment. The *Carroll* doctrine originated in the case of *Carroll v. United States*, 267 U.S. 132, 45 S.Ct. 280, 69 L.Ed. 543 (1925), and is sometimes referred to as the **automobile exception** to the search warrant requirement. In the *Carroll* case, federal prohibition agents obtained information that the defendant and another person were bootleggers who frequently traveled a certain road in a certain automobile. The officers later unexpectedly encountered the two men driving on that road in that automobile. The officers pursued and stopped the automobile on the highway. They thoroughly searched the automobile, finding several bottles of illegal liquor concealed in its upholstery. No warrant had been obtained for the search.

The U.S. Supreme Court held:

> On reason and authority the true rule is that if the search and seizure without a warrant are made upon probable cause, that is upon a belief, reasonably arising out of circumstances known to the seizing officer, that an automobile or other vehicle contains that which by law is subject to seizure and destruction, the search and seizure are valid. The Fourth Amendment is to be construed in the light of what was deemed an unreasonable search and seizure when it was adopted, and in a manner which will conserve public interests as well as the interests and rights of individual citizens. 267 U.S. at 149, 45 S.Ct. at 283, 69 L.Ed. at 549.

Probable Cause

The controlling consideration in the search of a vehicle without a warrant is probable cause to believe that the vehicle contains items that are connected with criminal activity and thus are subject to seizure. This was emphasized in the *Carroll* decision:

> Having thus established that contraband goods concealed and illegally transported in an automobile or other vehicle may be searched for without a warrant, we come now to consider under what circumstances such search may be made. It would be intolerable and unreasonable if a prohibition agent were authorized to stop every automobile on the chance of finding liquor, and thus subject all persons lawfully using the highways to the inconvenience and indignity of such a search. Travellers may be so stopped in crossing an international boundary because of national self-protection reasonably requiring one entering the country to identify himself as entitled to come in, and his belongings as effects which may be lawfully brought in. But those lawfully within the Country, entitled to use the public highways, have a right to free passage without interruption or search unless there is known to a competent official, authorized to search, probable cause for believing that their vehicles are carrying contraband or illegal merchandise. 267 U.S. at 153–54, 45 S.Ct. at 285, 69 L.Ed. at 551–52.

Probable cause is discussed in detail in Chapters 3 and 6. In vehicle search and seizure cases, probable cause depends on the particular circumstances of each situation. The law enforcement officer's determination of probable cause must be based on objective facts that could justify the issuance of a warrant by a magistrate and not merely on the subjective good faith of the officer. Evidence seized from a vehicle that is not seized on the basis of probable cause will be inadmissible in court.

Delay in Search

If possible, warrantless searches under the *Carroll* doctrine should be conducted immediately at the scene where the vehicle is stopped. If, however, the surrounding circumstances make an immediate search on the highway unsafe or impractical, the vehicle may be removed to a more convenient location. If a search is conducted without unreasonable delay after the vehicle's arrival at the new location, the probable cause factor existing on the highway remains in force, and the warrantless search is constitutionally permissible.

In *Chambers v. Maroney,* 399 U.S. 42, 90 S.Ct. 1975, 26 L.Ed.2d 419 (1970), the police had information that armed robbers carrying the fruits of the crime had fled the robbery scene in a light blue compact station wagon. Four men were said to be in the vehicle, one wearing a green sweater and another wearing a trench coat. The police stopped a vehicle fitting the description, arrested the four occupants, and drove the vehicle to the police station. The vehicle was thoroughly searched at the station, and evidence was seized leading to the defendant's conviction.

The U.S. Supreme Court upheld the search:

> In enforcing the Fourth Amendment's prohibition against unreasonable searches and seizures, the Court has insisted upon probable cause as a minimum requirement for a reasonable search permitted by the Constitution. As a general rule, it has also required the judgment of a magistrate on the probable cause issue and the issuance of a warrant before a search is made. Only in exigent

circumstances will the judgment of the police as to probable cause serve as a sufficient authorization for a search. *Carroll* . . . holds a search warrant unnecessary where there is probable cause to search an automobile stopped on the highway; the car is movable, the occupants are alerted, and the car's contents may never be found again if a warrant must be obtained. Hence an immediate search is constitutionally permissible.

Arguably, because of the preference for a magistrate's judgment, only the immobilization of the car should be permitted until a search warrant is obtained; arguably, only the "lesser" intrusion is permissible until the magistrate authorizes the "greater." But which is the "greater" and which the "lesser" intrusion is itself a debatable question and the answer may depend on a variety of circumstances. For constitutional purposes, we see no difference between on the one hand seizing and holding a car before presenting the probable cause issue to a magistrate and on the other hand carrying out an immediate search without a warrant. Given probable cause to search either course is reasonable under the Fourth Amendment.

On the facts before us, the blue station wagon could have been searched on the spot when it was stopped since there was probable cause to search and it was a fleeting target for a search. The probable cause factor still obtained at the station house and so did the mobility of the car unless the Fourth Amendment permits a warrantless seizure of the car and the denial of its use to anyone until a warrant is secured. In that event there is little to choose in terms of practical consequences between an immediate search without a warrant and the car's immobilization until a warrant is obtained. 399 U.S. at 51–52, 90 S.Ct. at 1981, 26 L.Ed.2d at 428–29.

Michigan v. Thomas, 458 U.S. 259, 102 S.Ct. 3079, 73 L.Ed.2d 750 (1982), upheld a warrantless search of an automobile stopped on the road and taken into police custody, even though a prior search had already been made. *Florida v. Meyers*, 466 U.S. 380, 104 S.Ct. 1852, 80 L.Ed.2d 381 (1984), upheld a warrantless search of an impounded automobile eight hours after it had been impounded. And *United States v. Johns*, 469 U.S. 478, 105 S.Ct. 881, 83 L.Ed.2d 890 (1985), upheld a warrantless search of an impounded vehicle three days after the vehicle had been impounded. Officers should obtain a warrant for searches to be made more than three days after impounding a vehicle.

Exigent Circumstances

In the passage just quoted, the Supreme Court said that "[o]nly in exigent circumstances will the judgment of the police as to probable cause serve as a sufficient authorization for a search." Some lower courts have taken this to mean that the police must be able to demonstrate specific facts establishing exigent circumstances, in addition to probable cause, before searching a vehicle stopped on the road. The U.S. Supreme Court, however, has made it clear that this is not necessary. In *Michigan v. Thomas*, 458 U.S. 259, 261, 102 S.Ct. 3079, 3081, 73 L.Ed.2d 750, 753 (1982), the Court said:

In *Chambers v. Maroney* . . . we held that when police officers have probable cause to believe there is contraband inside an automobile that has been stopped on the road, the officers may conduct a warrantless search of the vehicle, even after it has been impounded and is in police custody. We firmly reiterated this holding in *Texas v. White*, 423 U.S. 67, 96 S.Ct. 304, 46 L.Ed.2d 209 (1975). . . . It is thus clear that the justification to conduct such a warrantless search does not vanish once the car has been immobilized; nor does it depend upon a reviewing court's assessment of the likelihood in each particular case that the car would have been driven away, or that its contents would have been tampered with, during the period required for the police to obtain a warrant.

In short, the requirement that exigent circumstances must exist before the police's judgment as to probable cause will justify a warrantless search is automatically satisfied in the case of a motor vehicle that is "readily mobile." "If a car is readily mobile and probable cause exists to believe it contains contraband, the Fourth Amendment . . . permits police to search the vehicle without more." *Pennsylvania v. Labron*, 518 U.S. 938, 940, 116 S.Ct. 2485, 2487, 135 L.Ed.2d 1031, 1036 (1996). Some state courts, however, may interpret their own constitutions to require stricter standards than those of the U.S. Supreme Court.

When a motor vehicle is not readily mobile, the law enforcement officer must satisfy the requirement of exigent circumstances in addition to the requirement of probable cause before conducting a warrantless search or seizure. Usually, exigent circumstances are established by demonstrating specific facts showing either that the vehicle may be moved to an unknown location or out of the jurisdiction, making a search under authority of a warrant impossible, or that items subject to seizure may be removed from the vehicle and concealed or destroyed.

For example, in *California v. Carney*, 471 U.S. 386, 105 S.Ct. 2066, 85 L.Ed.2d 406 (1985), Drug Enforcement Agency (DEA) agents had probable cause to search a mobile motor home parked in a lot in the downtown area of a large city. The Court applied the standard that a search of a vehicle is justified under the *Carroll* doctrine if the vehicle "is being used on the highways, or if it is readily capable of such use and is found stationary in a place not regularly used for residential purposes—temporary or otherwise." 471 U.S. at 392, 105 S.Ct. at 2070, 85 L.Ed.2d at 414. The warrantless search of this mobile home was upheld because the vehicle was readily mobile by the turn of the ignition key and was so situated that an objective observer would conclude that it was being used not as a residence but as a vehicle. In a footnote, the Court listed some factors that would indicate that a mobile home was being used as a residence. "Among the factors that might be relevant in determining whether a warrant would be required in such a circumstance is its location, whether the vehicle is readily mobile or instead, for instance, elevated on blocks, whether the vehicle is licensed, whether it is connected to utilities, and whether it has convenient access to a public road." 471 U.S. at 394 n.3, 105 S.Ct. at 2071 n.3, 85 L.Ed.2d at 415 n.3. In *United States v. Levesque*, 625 F.Supp. 428 (D.N.H. 1985), the court disallowed a warrantless search of a motor home that was not readily mobile:

> The trailer at issue . . . was situated in a trailer park and on a lot, objectively indicating that it was being used as a residence. Although the truck which tows the trailer was only a few feet from the trailer, the trailer was not readily mobile in light of the fact that one end of the trailer was elevated on blocks and that the trailer was connected to utilities at the campground, and also because of the three quarters of an hour lead time to connect the trailer and truck. The mobile home exception to the warrant requirement thus would appear to have no application herein. 625 F.Supp. 450–51.

In *United States v. Tartaglia*, 864 F.2d 837 (D.C.Cir. 1989), police had probable cause to search a train roomette for drugs. Analogizing the train roomette to the readily mobile motor home in the *Carney* case, the court found exigent circumstances justifying a warrantless search of the roomette:

> Because the police did not have sufficient time to procure a warrant before train 98 left Union Station and because there was more than a reasonable likelihood that the train, and therefore the roomette and its contents, would be moved before a warrant could be obtained, the warrantless search of defendant's roomette was justified under the exigent circumstances exception to the warrant requirement of the Fourth Amendment. 864 F.2d at 843.

In *Cardwell v. Lewis,* 417 U.S. 583, 94 S.Ct. 2464, 41 L.Ed.2d 325 (1974), the U.S. Supreme Court found exigent circumstances justifying the warrantless seizure of the defendant's automobile from a commercial parking lot in which the defendant had left it before his appearance at the police station, where he was arrested. The defendant had been fully aware that he was under investigation for several months, and he had told his attorney to see that his wife and family got the car. The Court based its finding of exigent circumstances on the possibility that the attorney or a family member might remove evidence from the car if the police delayed seizing it.

In *United States v. Forker,* 928 F.2d 365 (11th Cir. 1991), officers had probable cause to search a Cadillac for drugs and evidence of a drug distribution conspiracy. The Cadillac was parked in a motel parking lot, and police had recently arrested the defendant Forker, its driver. The court found that the following facts created exigent circumstances:

> The officers were not certain how many sets of keys to the Cadillac existed; they were not certain if the car would remain in the parking lot if they left to obtain a warrant. At the time Forker was stopped and arrested at the Holiday Inn parking lot, there were suspects in another hotel ten minutes away and Frawley, the suspected source of the cash as well as the known owner of the Cadillac driven by Forker, was inside the Holiday Inn. The agents had not apprehended all suspects and were not even aware of how many people were involved in the conspiracy. Further, the Cadillac was in the middle of a public parking lot, vulnerable to the efforts of cohorts of Forker's to seize the cash or destroy evidence. The agents were in the middle of a fast-moving series of events which prompted the search of the vehicle. The circumstances that prompted the search of the Cadillac were certainly exigent and as such, we find that the search of the vehicle was not violative of Forker and Frawley's fourth amendment rights. 928 F.2d at 369.

In a different case in which there were no indications of the potential mobility of an automobile, however, the court disallowed a warrantless search of a parked, unoccupied automobile:

> [A]ny search of an automobile that was parked, immobile and unoccupied at the time the police first encountered it in connection with the investigation of a crime must be authorized by a warrant issued by a magistrate or, alternatively, the prosecution must demonstrate that exigent circumstances other than the potential mobility of the automobile exist. Here, the prosecution failed to demonstrate any individualized exigent circumstances. *State v. Kock,* 725 P.2d 1285, 1287 (Or. 1986).

If a vehicle or its contents present a potential danger to the public safety if not searched immediately, the *exigent circumstances* requirement of the *Carroll* doctrine may be satisfied, even though the car is immobile. In *United States v. Cepulonis*, 530 F.2d 238 (1st Cir. 1976), a law enforcement officer observed, through the window of an automobile, a sawed-off shotgun protruding from beneath the front seat. The court upheld the immediate warrantless seizure of the shotgun, finding probable cause and also finding that someone other than the car's owner (who was in custody) could have moved the car. The court went on to say:

> Moreover, a legitimate concern for public safety counselled against leaving the car, with a loaded shotgun visible through the window, unguarded in the Motel parking lot and "vulnerable to intrusion by vandals." . . . Under the circumstances the agents were faced with a choice whether to seize and hold the car while securing a warrant or to carry out an immediate warrantless search. 530 F.2d at 243.

In *Coolidge v. New Hampshire*, 403 U.S. 443, 91 S.Ct. 2022, 29 L.Ed.2d 564 (1971), the U.S. Supreme Court indicated that the exigent circumstances requirement would not be satisfied if there were no real possibility that someone would remove the car and conceal or destroy evidence within it. In the *Coolidge* case, the police had known for some time of the probable role of the defendant's automobile in a crime. The police went to the defendant's home, arrested him inside his house, and escorted his wife and children to another town to spend the night. No other adults resided in the house. The vehicle was unoccupied and in the defendant's driveway. Police towed the vehicle to the station house and searched it there without a warrant.

The Court held that the search of the automobile could not be justified under the *Carroll* doctrine because the car was not movable, nor were there any other exigent circumstances to justify the search.

> [S]urely there is nothing in this case to invoke the meaning and purpose of the rule of *Carroll v. U.S.*—no alerted criminal bent on flight, no fleeting opportunity on an open highway after a hazardous chase, no contraband or stolen goods or weapons, no confederates waiting to move the evidence, not even the inconvenience of a special police detail to guard the immobilized automobile. In short, by no possible stretch of the legal imagination can this be made into a case where "it is not practicable to secure a warrant," . . . and the "automobile exception," despite its label, is simply irrelevant. 403 U.S. at 462, 91 S.Ct. at 2035–36, 29 L.Ed.2d at 580.

In *Lavicky v. Burnett*, 758 F.2d 468 (10th Cir. 1985), the automobile exception was held not to apply to the warrantless seizure and search of the defendant's truck, which was immobile because its engine was partially dismantled.

Entry on Private Premises

When law enforcement officers, acting on probable cause and following closely behind a vehicle, would have been authorized to stop and search the vehicle while on a public way, they may properly follow the vehicle onto private property and conduct the search there. In *Scher v. United States*, 305 U.S. 251, 59 S.Ct. 174, 83 L.Ed. 151 (1938), an informant's tip and careful surveillance gave police officers probable cause to believe that a certain automobile contained contraband. The officers followed the auto until the defendant parked it in his garage. The Court held the subsequent warrantless search of the car in the garage valid.

[I]t seems plain enough that just before he entered the garage, the following officers properly could have stopped petitioner's car and made search. . . .

Passage of the car into the open garage closely followed by the observing officer did not destroy this right. 305 U.S. at 255, 59 S.Ct. at 176, 83 L.Ed. at 154.

Scope of Search

The scope of the search of a vehicle under the *Carroll* doctrine depends on whether the searching officer has probable cause to search the entire vehicle or whether the officer has probable cause only to search a particular container found in the vehicle.

SEARCH OF ENTIRE VEHICLE. The permissible scope of a warrantless search of a motor vehicle under the *Carroll* doctrine has been defined in the case of *United States v. Ross,* 456 U.S. 798, 102 S.Ct. 2157, 72 L.Ed.2d 572 (1982), a case involving the legitimate stopping of an automobile by police officers who had probable cause to believe that the automobile contained narcotics. During the search of the car, the searching officer found and opened a closed brown paper bag and a zippered leather pouch, discovering heroin in the bag and a large amount of money in the pouch. In holding the search legal, the U.S. Supreme Court said:

[T]he scope of the warrantless search authorized by [the *Carroll*] exception is no broader and no narrower than a magistrate could legitimately authorize by warrant. If probable cause justifies the search of a lawfully stopped vehicle, it justifies the search of every part of the vehicle and its contents that may conceal the object of the search. 456 U.S. at 825, 102 S.Ct. at 2173, 72 L.Ed.2d at 594.

Emphasizing that the scope of a search under the *Carroll* doctrine depends entirely on the object of the search, the Supreme Court stated:

The scope of a warrantless search of an automobile thus is not defined by the nature of the container in which the contraband is secreted. Rather, it is defined by the object of the search and the places in which there is probable cause to believe that it may be found. Just as probable cause to believe that a stolen lawnmower may be found in a garage will not support a warrant to search an upstairs bedroom, probable cause to believe that undocumented aliens are being transported in a van will not justify a warrantless search of a suitcase. Probable cause to believe that a container placed in the trunk of a taxi contains contraband or evidence does not justify a search of the entire cab. 456 U.S. at 824, 102 S.Ct. at 2172, 72 L.Ed.2d at 593.

The scope of the warrantless search allowed under the *Carroll* doctrine may even extend to dismantling part of the vehicle. In *United States v. Zucco,* 71 F.3d 188 (5th Cir. 1995), police had probable cause to search an entire recreational vehicle because cocaine had been found in a cabinet in the vehicle as the result of a valid consent search. When a drug-sniffing dog alerted to another part of the vehicle, police were authorized to remove a wall panel, where they discovered a large cache of cocaine.

Furthermore, in *United States v. Johns,* 469 U.S. 478, 105 S.Ct. 881, 83 L.Ed.2d 890 (1985), the Court held that, where officers have probable cause to search a vehicle for a specific object, the search of a container in the vehicle that could contain that object need not be conducted at the same time as the seizure or search of the vehicle. Customs agents in the *Johns* case had seized and impounded a vehicle under the *Carroll* doctrine on the basis of probable cause to believe it contained marijuana. The

Court approved a warrantless search, conducted three days later, of plastic bags found in the vehicle.

If an officer obtains probable cause to search a container after the container has been removed from a vehicle, the *Carroll* doctrine does not apply, even if the container is in the process of being returned to the vehicle. The officer must have probable cause to believe that items subject to seizure are contained *somewhere inside the vehicle*. As stated by the Maine Supreme Judicial Court in a case in which the defendant voluntarily retrieved from his car a carry-on bag containing two bags, and an officer searched the two bags after smelling the odor of marijuana, "the fact that the bags came from the car and were in the process of being returned to the car does not trigger the automobile exception." *State v. Lewis,* 611 A.2d 69, 71 (Me. 1992).

Officers may not search the occupants of a vehicle under the *Carroll* doctrine. *United States v. Di Re,* 332 U.S. 581, 68 S.Ct. 222, 92 L.Ed. 210 (1948). However, passengers in a vehicle have no reasonable expectation of privacy in the interior area of the vehicle. Therefore, a warrantless search based on probable cause of areas such as the glove compartment, the spaces under the seats, and the trunk is permissible. Such a search invades no Fourth Amendment interest of the passengers, even if it turns up evidence implicating the passengers. *Rakas v. Illinois,* 439 U.S. 128, 99 S.Ct. 421, 58 L.Ed.2d 387 (1978). Also, if an officer has probable cause to arrest one or more occupants of the vehicle, the officer may search all arrested occupants and the passenger compartment incident to the arrest. (See the discussion of *New York v. Belton* in Chapter 8.)

To summarize, under the *Carroll* doctrine, if officers have probable cause to search an entire vehicle for a specific seizable item, they may search to the same extent as if they had a warrant to search for that item.

SEARCH OF CONTAINER FOUND IN VEHICLE. Where officers have probable cause only to search a particular container placed in a vehicle, however, they may search that container without a warrant but not the entire vehicle. In *California v. Acevedo,* 500 U.S. 565, 111 S.Ct. 1982, 114 L.Ed.2d 619 (1991), police observed the defendant leave an apartment known to contain marijuana with a brown paper package the same size as marijuana packages they had seen earlier. He placed the bag in the trunk of his car and started to drive away. Fearing the loss of evidence, officers in an unmarked car stopped him. They opened the trunk and the bag and found marijuana.

The Court held that the Fourth Amendment does not compel separate treatment for an automobile search that extends only to a container within the vehicle. The Court said:

> The interpretation of the *Carroll* doctrine set forth in *Ross* now applies to all searches of containers found in an automobile. In other words, the police may search without a warrant if their search is supported by probable cause. The Court in *Ross* put it this way:
>
> > "The scope of a warrantless search of an automobile . . . is not defined by the nature of the container in which the contraband is secreted. Rather, it is defined by the object of the search and the places in which there is probable cause to believe that it may be found." 456 U.S. at 824, 102 S.Ct. at 2172.
>
> It went on to note: "Probable cause to believe that a container placed in the trunk of a taxi contains contraband or evidence does not justify a search of the entire cab." *Ibid.* We affirm that principle. In the case before us, the police had probable cause to believe that the paper bag in the automobile's trunk contained

marijuana. That probable cause now allows a warrantless search of the paper bag. The facts in the record reveal that the police did not have probable cause to believe that contraband was hidden in any other part of the automobile and a search of the entire vehicle would have been without probable cause and unreasonable under the Fourth Amendment. 500 U.S. at 579–80, 111 S.Ct. at 1991, 114 L.Ed.2d at 634.

SEARCH OF CONTAINER NOT FOUND IN VEHICLE. The rationale justifying a warrantless search of an automobile believed to be transporting items subject to seizure arguably applies with equal force to any movable container believed to be carrying such an item. The U.S. Supreme Court, however, squarely rejected that argument. In *United States v. Chadwick*, 433 U.S. 1, 97 S.Ct. 2476, 53 L.Ed.2d 538 (1977), federal railroad officials became suspicious when they noticed that a large footlocker loaded onto a train was unusually heavy and leaking talcum powder, a substance often used to mask the odor of marijuana. Narcotics agents met the train at its destination, and a trained police dog signaled the presence of a controlled substance inside the footlocker. The agents did not seize the footlocker at that time. Instead, they waited until the defendant arrived and placed the footlocker in the trunk of his automobile. Before he started the engine, the officers arrested him and his two companions. The agents then removed the footlocker to a secure place, opened it without a warrant, and discovered a large quantity of marijuana.

The prosecution did not contend on appeal that the locker's brief contact with the automobile's trunk sufficed to make the *Carroll* doctrine applicable. Rather, the prosecution argued that the warrantless search was "reasonable" because a footlocker has some of the mobile characteristics that support warrantless searches of automobiles. The Supreme Court rejected the argument:

> The factors which diminish the privacy aspects of an automobile do not apply to respondents' footlocker. Luggage contents are not open to public view, except as a condition to a border entry or common carrier travel; nor is luggage subject to regular inspections and official scrutiny on a continuing basis. Unlike an automobile, whose primary function is transportation, luggage is intended as a repository of personal effects. In sum, a person's expectations of privacy in personal luggage are substantially greater than in an automobile. 433 U.S. at 13, 97 S.Ct. at 2484, 53 L.Ed.2d at 549.

The Court noted that the practical problems associated with the temporary detention of a piece of luggage during the period of time necessary to obtain a warrant are significantly less than those associated with the detention of an automobile. In holding the warrantless search of the footlocker unjustified, the Court reaffirmed the general principle that closed packages and containers may not be searched without a warrant. Thus, the Court declined to extend the rationale of the automobile exception to permit a warrantless search of any movable container found in a public place. *California v. Acevedo*, 500 U.S. 565, 111 S.Ct. 1982, 114 L.Ed.2d 619 (1991). (See also the discussion of the *Chadwick* case in Chapter 8.)

OTHER CONTAINER SEARCHES. Inventory searches of containers are discussed in Chapter 4 and in this chapter at pages 385–391. Investigatory detentions of containers are discussed in Chapter 7. Seizures and searches of containers incident to arrest are discussed in Chapter 8. Seizures and searches of containers under the plain view doctrine are discussed in Chapter 10. Seizures and searches of abandoned containers are discussed in Chapter 12.

1. Under the *Carroll* doctrine, if a car is readily mobile and probable cause exists to believe it contains contraband, the Fourth Amendment permits police to search the vehicle without additional justification.

2. The justification to search a motor vehicle under the *Carroll* doctrine does not vanish once the vehicle has been immobilized, impounded, and taken into police custody; nor does it depend on the likelihood that the vehicle would have been driven away or that its contents would have been tampered with during the period required for the police to obtain a warrant.

3. To conduct a warrantless search of a vehicle that is not readily mobile, law enforcement officers must demonstrate exigent circumstances in addition to probable cause. Exigent circumstances are established by showing that the vehicle may be moved or that evidence in the vehicle may be concealed or destroyed, making a search under authority of a warrant impossible.

4. If an officer has probable cause to search an entire vehicle for a particular object under the *Carroll* doctrine, the officer may look anywhere in the vehicle in which there is probable cause to believe the object may be found, including containers that could hold the object.

5. If an officer has probable cause to search only a particular container placed in a vehicle, the officer may search that container without a warrant but not the entire vehicle.

6. The *Carroll* doctrine does not permit the warrantless search of any movable container found in a public place, even if the searching officer has probable cause. Closed containers and packages may not be searched without a warrant or justification under some other exception to the warrant requirement.

Impoundment and Inventory of Vehicles

The police may impound motor vehicles for a variety of reasons. Accompanying the impoundment of a vehicle, police routinely inventory the contents of the vehicle for reasons of safety, liability, and convenience. This section explores the legal issues involved in impounding and inventorying motor vehicles.

Impoundment

> In the interests of public safety and as part of what the Court has called "community caretaking functions," . . . automobiles are frequently taken into police custody. Vehicle accidents present one such occasion. To permit the uninterrupted flow of traffic and in some instances to preserve evidence, disabled or damaged vehicles will often be removed from the highways or streets in caretaking and traffic control activities. Police will also frequently remove and impound automobiles which violate parking ordinances and which thereby jeopardize both the public safety and the efficient movement of vehicular traffic. The authority of police to seize and remove from the streets vehicles impeding traffic or threatening public safety and convenience is beyond challenge. *South Dakota v. Opperman*, 428 U.S. 364, 368–69, 96 S.Ct. 3092, 3096, 49 L.Ed.2d 1000, 1005 (1976).

Other reasons that may justify police **impoundment** of a vehicle are

- the driver has been arrested and taken into custody. *United States v. Lyles*, 946 F.2d 78 (8th Cir. 1991);

- the driver is incapacitated by intoxication, injury, illness or some other condition. *United States v. Ford*, 872 F.2d 1231 (6th Cir. 1989);
- the vehicle is seized as evidence of or an instrument of a crime. *United States v. Cooper*, 949 F.2d 737 (5th Cir. 1991);
- the vehicle is forfeited pursuant to a state or federal forfeiture law. *United States v. Bizzell*, 19 F.3d 1524 (4th Cir. 1994);
- the vehicle has been reported stolen.

Note that in many jurisdictions, the right of police to impound vehicles is defined by statute or departmental policy or both. If an officer impounds a vehicle in violation of statute or policy, or for some other illegitimate reason such as harassment of the driver or conducting an investigatory search, the impoundment may be held illegal. *United States v. Ibarra*, 955 F.2d 1405 (10th Cir. 1992).

Impoundment procedure usually involves the police taking possession of the vehicle and moving it to a garage or police lot for safekeeping. The main justification for impoundment is that the vehicle would otherwise be left unattended on a public street or highway and would be an easy target for theft or vandalism, leaving the police open to potential liability.

Law enforcement officers are not constitutionally required to offer a defendant the opportunity to make other arrangements for the safekeeping of his or her vehicle, nor must they always choose methods of dealing with a defendant's vehicle that are less intrusive than impoundment. As stated by the U.S. Supreme Court, "[t]he reasonableness of any particular governmental activity does not necessarily or invariably turn on the existence of alternative 'less intrusive' means." *Illinois v. Lafayette*, 462 U.S. 640, 647, 103 S.Ct. 2605, 2610, 77 L.Ed.2d 65, 72 (1983). Therefore, nothing prohibits the exercise of police discretion to impound a vehicle rather than to lock and park it in a safe place, for instance, "so long as that discretion is exercised according to standard criteria and on the basis of something other than suspicion of evidence of criminal activity." *Colorado v. Bertine*, 479 U.S. 367, 375, 107 S.Ct. 738, 743, 93 L.Ed.2d 739, 748 (1987).

Some states, however, require officers to consider reasonable alternatives to impoundment. "Although an officer is not required to exhaust all possibilities, the officer must at least consider alternatives; attempt, if feasible, to obtain a name from the driver of someone in the vicinity who could move the vehicle; and then reasonably conclude from this deliberation that impoundment is proper." *State v. Coss*, 943 P.2d 1126, 1130 (Wash.App. 1997). In the *Coss* case, impoundment of a stopped vehicle was found unreasonable and, therefore, unlawful where the driver had a suspended license but a properly licensed passenger could have driven the vehicle from the scene of the stop.

Inventory

Assuming that a vehicle has been lawfully impounded, may the vehicle then be searched for incriminating evidence without a warrant? Unless the situation satisfies the requirements of the *Carroll* doctrine, police have no authority to conduct a warrantless investigatory search of a lawfully impounded motor vehicle. In other words, police must obtain a search warrant to search an impounded vehicle unless they have probable cause to search the vehicle and

- the vehicle was readily mobile when originally stopped, or
- exigent circumstances make an immediate warrantless search necessary.

Nevertheless, in *South Dakota v. Opperman*, 428 U.S. 364, 96 S.Ct. 3092, 49 L.Ed.2d 1000 (1976), the U.S. Supreme Court approved a more limited search of a lawfully impounded motor vehicle: the routine practice of local police departments of securing and inventorying the vehicle's contents. This limited type of search is allowed to protect

- the owner's property while it remains in police custody;
- the police against claims or disputes over lost, stolen, or vandalized property; and
- the police from potential danger.

This **inventory** procedure is not considered to be a search for purposes of the Fourth Amendment because its object is not to find incriminating evidence as part of a criminal investigation. Rather, it is considered to be a routine administrative-custodial procedure and "must not be a ruse for a general rummaging in order to discover incriminating evidence." *Florida v. Wells*, 495 U.S. 1, 4, 110 S.Ct. 1632, 1635, 109 L.Ed.2d 1, 6 (1990). Nevertheless, an investigatory motive will not invalidate an inventory if there is also an administrative motive.

> It would be disingenuous of us to pretend that when the agents opened Judge's bag, they weren't hoping to find some more evidence to use against him. But, they could have also reasonably had an administrative motive, which is all that is required under *Bertine*. While there are undoubtedly mixed motives in the vast majority of inventory searches, the constitution does not require and our human limitations do not allow us to peer into a police officer's "heart of hearts." *United States v. Judge*, 864 F.2d 1144, 1147 n.5 (5th Cir. 1989).

STANDARD PROCEDURES. Each law enforcement agency must have standard procedures for inventorying impounded vehicles, or the inventories will be declared an illegal search. In upholding the validity of an inventory of an impounded car in *South Dakota v. Opperman*, the U.S. Supreme Court emphasized that the police were using a standard inventory form pursuant to standard police procedures. The Court said, "The decisions of this Court point unmistakably to the conclusion reached by both federal and state courts that inventories pursuant to standard police procedures are reasonable." 428 U.S. at 372, 96 S.Ct. at 3092, 49 L.Ed.2d at 1007. The Ninth Circuit Court of Appeals invalidated an inventory of a legally impounded automobile because the local police department did not have a standard procedure regarding the inventorying of an impounded vehicle's contents.

> [E]ven if an investigatory motive was not shown, our decision would be the same because the inventorying of impounded cars was not shown to be a routine practice and policy of *this* police department, as was the case in *Opperman*. . . . It is the inventorying practice and not the impounding practice that, if routinely followed and supported by proper noninvestigatory purposes, could render the inventory a reasonable search under *Opperman*. The fact that other police departments routinely follow such a practice may give support to the proposition that such a practice, if locally followed, is reasonable. It does not, however, render reasonable a search where the inventorying practice is not locally followed and the search, thus, is a departure from local practice. *United States v. Hellman*, 556 F.2d 442, 444 (9th Cir. 1977).

Standard inventory procedures need not be written. In *United States v. Feldman,* 788 F.2d 544 (9th Cir. 1986), the court approved a procedure under which officers are instructed orally that stolen vehicles must be impounded and their contents inventoried on a standard printed form.

SCOPE. Officers should follow standard departmental procedures as to the allowable scope of a vehicle inventory. The inventory should be restricted to accessible areas of the vehicle in which the owner's or occupant's personal belongings might be vulnerable to theft or damage. Areas covered by the inventory would usually include an unlocked glove compartment, an unlocked trunk, the sun visors, the front and rear seat areas, and other places where property is ordinarily kept. *People v. Andrews,* 85 Cal.Rptr. 908 (Cal.App. 1970). As a part of the inventory, a notation should be made of the vehicle identification number, the motor number, and the make, model, and license plate number of the car in order that the car may be easily identified later. *Cotton v. United States,* 371 F.2d 385 (9th Cir. 1967).

If officers dismantle the vehicle, look behind the upholstery, or in any other manner indicate that their purpose is other than to protect and secure the vehicle's contents, the courts will consider the inventory a pretext for a search designed to uncover evidentiary materials. The inventory will then be considered an illegal warrantless search, and the fruits of the search will be inadmissible in court. But when officers reasonably believe that the contents of an automobile or the contents of a locked compartment in an automobile present a danger to themselves or others, they may make as extensive a search as is necessary to end the danger.

The U.S. Supreme Court decision in *Colorado v. Bertine,* 479 U.S. 367, 107 S.Ct. 738, 93 L.Ed.2d 739 (1987), expanded the allowable scope of an inventory search to include the opening of closed containers found within the impounded vehicle and the examination of their contents. Standardized criteria must regulate the opening of containers found during inventory searches to narrow the latitude of individual police officers and prevent the inventory search from becoming a general rummaging to discover incriminating evidence.

> But in forbidding uncanalized discretion to police officers conducting inventory searches, there is no reason to insist that they be conducted in a totally mechanical "all or nothing" fashion. . . . A police officer may be allowed sufficient latitude to determine whether a particular container should or should not be opened in light of the nature of the search and characteristics of the container itself. Thus, while policies of opening all containers or of opening no containers are unquestionably permissible, it would be equally permissible, for example, to allow the opening of closed containers whose contents officers determine they are unable to ascertain from examining the containers' exteriors. The allowance of the exercise of judgment based on concerns related to the purposes of an inventory search does not violate the Fourth Amendment. *Florida v. Wells,* 495 U.S. 1, 4, 110 S.Ct. 1632, 1635, 109 L.Ed.2d 1, 6–7 (1990).

In *United States v. Khoury,* 901 F.2d 948 (11th Cir. 1990), the court held that a *second* examination of a diary found in a briefcase during an inventory of the defendant's impounded car was an illegal search. The officer's initial examination consisted of flipping through a notebook to look for items of value. He determined that it was a diary but *not* that it had evidentiary value. Subsequently, he further examined the notebook and decided that it did have evidentiary value. The court said:

[Agent] Simpkins' initial inspection of the notebook was necessary and proper to ensure that there was nothing of value hidden between the pages of the notebook. Having satisfied himself that the notebook contained no discrete items of value and having decided that the diary entries themselves would have intrinsic value to [the defendant], Simpkins had satisfied the requisites of the inventory search and had no purpose other than investigation in further inspecting the notebook. Such a warrantless investigatory search may not be conducted under the guise of an inventory. 901 F.2d at 959.

Note that, if the inventory of a vehicle is not completed, a court may consider it a mere subterfuge for an exploratory search and invalidate it. In *Bowen v. State,* 606 P.2d 589 (Okl.Cr. 1980), a so-called inventory of a vehicle by police was discontinued when a shotgun was found. The court said, "While the rationale for such procedures is to protect property from being stolen and to prevent false charges of theft against police officers, the search here was obviously not conducted for that purpose, since the spare tire, jack, battery, a blanket and other items in the trunk were not inventoried after the shotgun was removed." 606 P.2d at 592.

TIME. A vehicle inventory should be conducted as soon as possible after the impoundment, taking into consideration the police agency's human resources, facilities, workload, and other circumstances. An unreasonably delayed inventory indicates that police were not really concerned about safeguarding the owner's property or protecting themselves against claims or from danger but were primarily interested in looking for evidence.

[T]he Fourth Amendment requires that, without a demonstrable justification based upon exigent circumstances other than the mere nature of automobiles, the inventory be conducted either contemporaneously with the impoundment or as soon thereafter as would be safe, practical, *and* satisfactory in light of the objectives for which this exception to the Fourth Amendment warrant requirement was created. In other words, to be valid, there must be a sufficient temporal proximity between the impoundment and the inventory. When the inventory must be postponed, each passing moment detracts from the full effectuation of the objectives of the inventory, and indeed, disserves those objectives; at some point, the passage of time requires, to uphold the validity of the inventory, proof of some immediate and exigent circumstances (other than the mere nature of automobiles) the attention to which is more important than protecting the arrestee's property and protecting the police from false claims or danger associated with that property. *Ex parte Boyd,* 542 So.2d 1276, 1279 (Ala. 1989).

PLAIN VIEW DOCTRINE. Although an officer may not look for evidence of crime while conducting a bona fide inventory, if contraband or other items subject to seizure are observed open to view, those items may lawfully be seized and are admissible in evidence. Under the **plain view doctrine,** an officer lawfully conducting an inventory of a vehicle is in a position in which he or she has a legal right to be as the result of a prior valid intrusion. (See Chapter 10.) In both the *Opperman* and *Bertine* cases, officers discovered drugs in plain view while lawfully conducting inventories of impounded vehicles.

Exhibit 11.1 shows a comparison of a *Carroll* doctrine search and an inventory search.

	SEARCH UNDER *CARROLL* DOCTRINE	INVENTORY SEARCH
Justification	Probable cause to search vehicle combined with exigent circumstances. (Exigent circumstances requirement is satisfied if vehicle is readily mobile.)	Impoundment of vehicle by police.
Purpose	To obtain evidence of crime.	To protect the owner's property while it remains in police custody; to protect the police against claims or disputes over lost, stolen, or vandalized property; and to protect the police from potential danger.
Scope of search of entire vehicle	If there is probable cause to search the entire vehicle, the search may extend to every part of the vehicle and its contents that may conceal the object of the search, including the opening of containers. If there is probable cause to search only a container in the vehicle, then only the container and not the entire vehicle may be searched.	If standard departmental procedures are followed, inventory may extend to all areas of the vehicle in which the owner's or occupant's personal belongings might be vulnerable to theft or damage.
Scope of search of containers found in vehicle	If there is probable cause to search the entire vehicle, a container that may contain the object of the search may be searched. If there is probable cause to search only a container in a vehicle, then only the container may be searched.	If standard departmental procedures are followed, the inventory may include the opening of closed containers found within the vehicle and the examination of their contents.
Time	Search should be conducted without unreasonable delay, but vehicle may be removed to another location for the search, and searches up to three days later have been upheld.	Inventory should be conducted as soon as possible after the impoundment of the vehicle, taking into consideration the police agency's human resources, facilities, work load, and other circumstances, such as an emergency requiring the inventory to be delayed.
Plain view doctrine	If items subject to seizure other than the object of the search are observed open to view during a search under the *Carroll* doctrine, the items may be lawfully seized and are admissible in evidence. (The requirements of the plain view doctrine must be satisfied.)	If items subject to seizure are observed open to view during a bona fide inventory, the items may be lawfully seized and are admissible in evidence. (The requirements of the plain view doctrine must be satisfied.)

EXHIBIT 11.1 Comparison of a *Carroll* Doctrine Search and an Inventory Search

7. Police may impound motor vehicles when they impede traffic or threaten public safety and convenience, or when their drivers or owners are taken into custody or are incapacitated.

8. Police may inventory the contents of lawfully impounded vehicles according to standardized procedures to protect the owner's property; to protect the police against claims over lost, stolen, or vandalized property; and to protect the police from potential danger.

9. The allowable scope of an inventory search of an impounded vehicle extends to accessible areas of the vehicle in which the owner's or occupant's personal belongings might be vulnerable to theft or damage. It may include opening closed containers found within the vehicle and examining their contents.

10. Although an officer may not look for evidence of crime while conducting a bona fide inventory, if contraband or other items subject to seizure are observed open to view, those items may lawfully be seized under the plain view doctrine.

Impoundment of Vehicle Under Forfeiture Statutes

Another ground for allowing a warrantless search of a vehicle by law enforcement officers is the seizure and impoundment of the vehicle under a specific state forfeiture statute. In *Cooper v. California,* 386 U.S. 58, 87 S.Ct. 788, 17 L.Ed.2d 730 (1967), the defendant was arrested for selling heroin wrapped in brown paper to a police informer. At the time of the arrest, the defendant's car was seized and impounded pursuant to a state forfeiture statute. The statute required that any officer making an arrest for a narcotics offense involving the use of a vehicle must seize and hold the vehicle as evidence pending a judicial declaration of forfeiture or release. Evidence showed that the defendant used his vehicle in connection with his possession and transportation of narcotics. One week after the seizure, police searched the car and discovered a piece of brown paper in the glove compartment. The brown paper was later introduced at trial. The state had not acquired title to the car at the time of the search.

This search could not be justified under the *Carroll* doctrine because no exigent circumstances existed. The car had been in police custody for a week, during which time the police could easily have applied for a warrant. Nevertheless, the Court held the search legal, finding that the car was lawfully held by the police in connection with criminal activity under the state forfeiture statute. Because the car was to be held for a considerable period of time, and because the police could deny possession of the car to its owner, the police had possessory rights of their own for the limited purpose of searching the vehicle. Note that a delay of a week would not be allowed in the ordinary inventory of a lawfully impounded vehicle. The *Cooper* case allowed the delayed search because the car was to be lawfully held by the police for a substantial period of time pending litigation of the forfeiture issue.

The *Cooper* case allows law enforcement officers to conduct a warrantless search of a vehicle, in the absence of exigent circumstances, when all the following conditions are met:

• A state statute requires law enforcement officers to seize vehicles involved in certain offenses and hold them pending forfeiture proceedings.

- The officer seizes a vehicle in connection with an offense named in the state forfeiture statute and impounds it.

- The search of the car is closely related to the reason the defendant was arrested, the reason the vehicle was impounded, and the reason it is being retained.

- The officer expects that the car will be in police custody for a considerable time.

- The officer can legally deny possession of the car to the owner.

The *Cooper* decision does not require that officers have probable cause to search a car impounded under a forfeiture statute. Nevertheless, because of the general preference for warrants, if officers do have probable cause to search, they should obtain a search warrant.

Expectation of Privacy

In recent years, courts have begun to analyze warrantless searches and seizures of vehicles to determine whether they intrude upon a person's reasonable expectation of privacy. In *Cardwell v. Lewis*, 417 U.S. 583, 94 S.Ct. 2464, 41 L.Ed.2d 325 (1974), the U.S. Supreme Court held that where probable cause exists, a warrantless examination of the exterior of a car is not unreasonable under the Fourth and Fourteenth Amendments.

> One has a lesser expectation of privacy in a motor vehicle because its function is transportation and it seldom serves as one's residence or as the repository of personal effects. A car has little capacity for escaping public scrutiny. It travels public thoroughfares where both its occupants and its contents are in plain view. . . . This is not to say that no part of the interior of an automobile has Fourth Amendment protection; the exercise of a desire to be mobile does not, of course, waive one's right to be free of unreasonable governmental intrusion. But insofar as Fourth Amendment protection extends to a motor vehicle, it is the right to privacy that is the touchstone of our inquiry. 417 U.S. at 590–91, 94 S.Ct. at 2469–70, 41 L.Ed.2d at 335.

In *South Dakota v. Opperman*, 428 U.S. 364, 96 S.Ct. 3092, 49 L.Ed.2d 1000 (1976), the Court approved the warrantless inventory of an automobile impounded for parking violations. The Court said:

> Besides the element of mobility, less rigorous warrant requirements govern because the expectation of privacy with respect to one's automobile is significantly less than that relating to one's home or office. In discharging their varied responsibilities for ensuring the public safety, law enforcement officials are necessarily brought into frequent contact with automobiles. Most of this contact is distinctly noncriminal in nature. . . . Automobiles, unlike homes, are subjected to pervasive and continuing governmental regulation and controls, including periodic inspection and licensing requirements. As an everyday occurrence, police stop and examine vehicles when license plates or inspection stickers have expired, or if other violations, such as exhaust fumes or excessive noise, are noted, or if headlights or other safety equipment are not in proper working order. 428 U.S. at 367–68, 96 S.Ct. at 3096, 49 L.Ed.2d at 1004.

Furthermore, a person does not have a greater expectation of privacy in a vehicle merely because the vehicle is capable of functioning as a home.

In our increasingly mobile society, many vehicles used for transportation can be and are being used not only for transportation, but for shelter, i.e., as a "home" or "residence." To distinguish between respondent's motor home and an ordinary sedan for purposes of the vehicle exception would require that we apply the exception depending upon the size of the vehicle and the quality of its appointments. Moreover, to fail to apply the exception to vehicles such as a motor home ignores the fact that a motor home lends itself easily to use as an instrument of illicit drug traffic and other illegal activity. . . . We decline . . . to distinguish between "worthy" and "unworthy" vehicles which are either on the public roads and highways, or situated such that it is reasonable to conclude that the vehicle is not being used as a residence. *California v. Carney*, 471 U.S. 386, 393–94, 105 S.Ct. 2066, 2070, 85 L.Ed.2d 406, 414–15 (1985).

The quoted passages indicate that the courts are imposing fewer restrictions on law enforcement officers with regard to warrantless searches of vehicles. Nevertheless, even though the reasonable expectation of privacy in a vehicle is less than that in a home or office, law enforcement officers must not violate that expectation when conducting searches or inventories of vehicles. For example, the U.S. Supreme Court has stated that "a search, even of an automobile, is a substantial invasion of privacy. To protect that privacy from official arbitrariness, the Court always has regarded probable cause as the minimum requirement for a lawful search." *United States v. Ortiz*, 422 U.S. 891, 896, 95 S.Ct. 2585, 2588, 45 L.Ed.2d 623, 629 (1975).

Electronic Beepers

A **beeper** is a radio transmitter, usually battery operated, that emits periodic signals that can be picked up by a radio receiver. A beeper neither records nor transmits any sounds other than its signal, but the signal can be monitored by directional finders, enabling law enforcement officers to determine the beeper's location. The U.S. Supreme Court dealt with the Fourth Amendment implications of the use of beepers for the first time in *United States v. Knotts*, 460 U.S. 276, 103 S.Ct. 1081, 75 L.Ed.2d 55 (1983). With the consent of a chemical company, officers installed a beeper in a five-gallon container of chloroform, a substance used to manufacture illicit drugs. One of the defendants purchased the container of chloroform and transported it by automobile to a codefendant's secluded cabin in another state. Law enforcement officers monitored the progress of the automobile carrying the chloroform all the way to its destination. After three days of visual surveillance of the cabin, officers obtained a search warrant, searched the cabin, and found evidence of the illegal manufacture of drugs.

The Court held that the warrantless monitoring of the beeper by law enforcement officers to trace the location of the chloroform container did not violate the defendant's legitimate expectation of privacy:

The governmental surveillance conducted by means of the beeper in this case amounted principally to the following of an automobile on public streets and highways. . . . A person travelling in an automobile on public thoroughfares has no reasonable expectation of privacy in his movements from one place to another. When [the codefendant] travelled over the public streets he voluntarily conveyed to anyone who wanted to look the fact that he was travelling over particular roads in a particular direction, the fact of whatever stops he made, and the fact of his final destination when he exited from public roads onto private property. 460 U.S. at 281, 103 S.Ct. at 1085, 75 L.Ed.2d at 62.

Although the owner of the cabin and surrounding premises undoubtedly had a justifiable expectation of privacy within the cabin, the expectation did not extend to the visual observation of his codefendant's automobile arriving on his premises after leaving a public highway or to movements of objects such as the container of chloroform outside the cabin. That the officers relied not only on visual surveillance but also on the use of the beeper to locate the automobile did not alter the situation. "Nothing in the Fourth Amendment prohibited the police from augmenting the sensory faculties bestowed upon them at birth with such enhancement as science and technology afforded them in this case." 460 U.S. at 282, 103 S.Ct. at 1086, 75 L.Ed.2d at 63.

The Court emphasized the limited use the officers made of the signals from the beeper. There was no indication that the beeper signal was received or relied on after it had indicated that the chloroform container had ended its automotive journey at the defendant's camp. Moreover, there was no indication that the beeper was used in any way to reveal information as to the container's movement within the cabin or in any way that would not have been visible to the naked eye from outside the cabin.

The U.S. Supreme Court case of *United States v. Karo,* 468 U.S. 705, 104 S.Ct. 3296, 82 L.Ed.2d 530 (1984), addressed the question of whether the monitoring of a beeper in a private residence, a location not open to visual surveillance, violates the Fourth Amendment rights of those who have a justifiable interest in the privacy of the residence. In that case, government agents installed a beeper in a container of chemicals with the consent of the original owner, who sold the container to the defendant. The agents saw the defendant pick up the container from the owner, followed the defendant to his house, and determined that the container was inside the house where it was monitored. The Court found that the government's warrantless surreptitious use of an electronic device to obtain information it could not have obtained by observation from outside the curtilage of a house was the same, for purposes of the Fourth Amendment, as a law enforcement officer's warrantless surreptitious entry of the house to verify that the beeper was in the house. Even though the monitoring of a beeper inside a private residence is less intrusive than a full-scale search, it is illegal unless conducted under authority of a warrant. The Court said:

> Requiring a warrant will have the salutary effect of ensuring that use of beepers is not abused, by imposing upon agents the requirement that they demonstrate in advance their justification for the desired search. This is not to say that there are no exceptions to the warrant rule, because if truly exigent circumstances exist no warrant is required under general Fourth Amendment principles. 468 U.S. at 717–18, 104 S.Ct. at 3305, 82 L.Ed.2d at 543.

Therefore, the warrantless monitoring of a beeper is permissible only if the beeper or its container could have been observed from outside the curtilage of a house, or if there is an emergency. Otherwise, the monitoring of a beeper located in a place not open to visual surveillance is illegal without a warrant.

Searches by Dogs

In *United States v. Solis,* 536 F.2d 880 (9th Cir. 1976), the court held that the use of specially trained dogs to detect the smell of marijuana in a vehicle did not violate the reasonable expectation of privacy of the vehicle's owner. In that case, a drug agent suspected that marijuana was hidden in the floor of a certain semitrailer parked at the rear of a gas station. The agent went to the gas station and found the semitrailer with what appeared to be white talcum powder on its doors. The officer knew from his training and experience that marijuana was often smuggled in semitrailer floors and that talcum powder was often used to conceal marijuana's odor. The agent notified the customs office, which sent two customs officers with specially trained marijuana-sniffing dogs. The dogs, which were determined to be extremely reliable, reacted positively to marijuana in the semitrailer. A search warrant was obtained, and the marijuana was seized.

The court held that the use of the dogs to help the officers establish probable cause to search was reasonable and did not violate the defendant's reasonable expectation of privacy. The court said:

> The dogs' intrusion such as it was into the air space open to the public in the vicinity of the trailer appears to us reasonably tolerable in our society. There was no invasion of the "curtilage"—the trailer. No sophisticated mechanical or electronic devices were used. The investigation was not indiscriminate, but solely directed to the particular contraband. There was an expectation that the odor would emanate from the trailer. Efforts made to mask it were visible. The method used by the officers was inoffensive. There was no embarrassment to or search of the person. The target was a physical fact indicative of possible crime, not protected communications. We hold that the use of the dogs was not unreasonable under the circumstances and therefore was not a prohibited search under the fourth amendment. 536 F.2d at 882–83.

In *United States v. Stone,* 866 F.2d 359 (10th Cir. 1989), the court held that police use of a trained dog to sniff an automobile detained on reasonable suspicion that it contained narcotics was not a search. The court analogized the situation to the detention of luggage at airports.

> Upon reasonable suspicion, police may temporarily detain luggage at an airport. Under such circumstances, police use of a narcotics dog to sniff the luggage is not a search. . . . Likewise, we think police may employ a narcotics dog to sniff an automobile which they have stopped upon reasonable suspicion to believe it contains narcotics. Under these circumstances, police use of a narcotics dog is not a search requiring a search warrant or probable cause. 866 F.2d at 363.

Courts disagree over the search and seizure implications of the use of drug-detecting dogs. The safest procedure for law enforcement officers is to make sure drug-detecting dogs are reliable and to obtain a warrant before conducting a search based on a dog's reactions.

KEY POINTS

11. The reasonable expectation of privacy in a motor vehicle is less than that in a home or office because it travels public thoroughfares where its occupants and contents are open to view, it seldom serves as a residence or permanent place for personal effects, and it is subject to pervasive and continuing governmental regulation and controls.

12. The warrantless monitoring of a beeper in a motor vehicle to trace the movement of the vehicle over public thoroughfares does not violate the reasonable expectation of privacy of the occupant of the vehicle.

13. The use of specially trained dogs to detect the smell of drugs in a vehicle does not violate the reasonable expectation of privacy of the vehicle's owner.

Summary

Although the search and seizure of motor vehicles are generally governed by the warrant requirement of the Fourth Amendment, courts have created certain exceptions to the warrant requirement for motor vehicles, based on the differences between a motor vehicle and fixed premises. A motor vehicle is mobile and is used to transport criminals, weapons, and fruits and instrumentalities of crime. It seldom serves as a residence or a permanent repository of personal effects. Furthermore, a person has a reduced expectation of privacy in a motor vehicle because the vehicle travels public thoroughfares where its occupants and contents are open to view, and because the vehicle is subject to extensive governmental regulation, including periodic inspection and licensing.

The most important exception to the warrant requirement is the so-called automobile exception as embodied in the *Carroll* doctrine. Under the *Carroll* doctrine, law enforcement officers may conduct a warrantless search of a motor vehicle if they have probable cause to believe that the vehicle contains items subject to seizure and if exigent circumstances make obtaining a warrant impracticable. If the vehicle is readily mobile, the exigent circumstances requirement is automatically satisfied and the police need not provide supporting facts and circumstances to establish the existence of exigent circumstances. In addition, police may conduct a warrantless search of a vehicle that was readily mobile when originally encountered even after the vehicle has been impounded and is in police custody. The scope of the search is defined by the object of the search and the places in which there is probable cause to believe the object may be found. If police have probable cause to believe that a particular seizable item is located somewhere in a vehicle that is readily mobile, they may search the vehicle as if they had a search warrant for the item. This means they have the right to open and search closed, opaque containers, located inside the vehicle, in which the seizable item might be contained. If, however, police do not have probable cause to

search the entire vehicle but only probable cause to search a particular container inside the vehicle, they may search only that container but not the entire vehicle. Warrantless searches on probable cause of movable, closed, opaque containers *unassociated with a vehicle* are not allowed under the rationale of the *Carroll* doctrine. Closed, opaque containers may only be searched under authority of a warrant or some other exception to the warrant requirement. For example, if a closed, opaque container is seized incident to the arrest of an occupant of a motor vehicle, the search and seizure of the contents of the container are governed by the case of *New York v. Belton* (discussed in Chapter 8).

The inventory of an impounded vehicle may also be conducted without a warrant. This procedure is not considered to be a search for Fourth Amendment purposes, but merely an administrative procedure. The officer making the inventory may not look for incriminating evidence but may be concerned only with protecting the owner's property, protecting the police against claims or disputes over lost or stolen property, and protecting the police from potential danger. The inventory of a vehicle must be limited in scope and intensity by the purposes for which it is allowed and must conform to standard police procedures. Nevertheless, evidence of crime found in plain view during the inventory may be seized and will be admissible in court. Seizure and impoundment of a vehicle under a state forfeiture statute may also provide legal justification for a warrantless search of the vehicle.

Although courts are in disagreement, they generally approve the tracing of the location of a motor vehicle on public thoroughfares by means of an electronic beeper, and the detection of drugs in a motor vehicle by means of sniffing by specially trained dogs. Both these limited types of intrusion are allowed because of the reduced expectation of privacy in motor vehicles.

Key Holdings from Major Cases

Carroll v. United States (1925). "[I]f the search and seizure without a warrant are made upon probable cause, that is, upon a belief, reasonably arising out of circumstances known to the seizing officer, that an automobile or other vehicle contains that which by law is subject to seizure and destruction, the search and seizure are valid." 267 U.S. 132, 149, 45 S.Ct. 280, 283, 69 L.Ed.2d 543, 549.

Chambers v. Maroney (1970). "Carroll . . . holds a search warrant unnecessary where there is probable cause to search

an automobile stopped on the highway; the car is movable, the occupants are alerted, and the car's contents may never be found again if a warrant must be obtained. Hence an immediate search is constitutionally permissible.

"Arguably, because of the preference for a magistrate's judgment, only the immobilization of the car should be permitted until a search warrant is obtained; arguably, only the 'lesser' intrusion is permissible until the magistrate authorizes the 'greater.' But which is the 'greater' and which the 'lesser' intrusion is itself a debatable question and the answer may depend on a variety of circumstances. For constitutional purposes, we see no difference between on the one hand seizing and holding a car before presenting the probable cause issue to a magistrate and on the other hand carrying out an immediate search without a warrant. Given probable cause to search either course is reasonable under the Fourth Amendment." 399 U.S. 42, 51–52, 90 S.Ct. 1975, 1981, 26 L.Ed.2d 419, 428–29.

Michigan v. Thomas (1982). "In *Chambers v. Maroney* . . . we held that when police officers have probable cause to believe there is contraband inside an automobile that has been stopped on the road, the officers may conduct a warrantless search of the vehicle, even after it has been impounded and is in police custody. . . . It is thus clear that the justification to conduct such a warrantless search does not vanish once the car has been immobilized; nor does it depend upon a reviewing court's assessment of the likelihood in each particular case that the car would have been driven away, or that its contents would have been tampered with, during the period required for the police to obtain a warrant." 458 U.S. 259, 261, 102 S.Ct. 3079, 3081, 73 L.Ed.2d 750, 753.

Pennsylvania v. Labron (1996). "If a car is readily mobile and probable cause exists to believe it contains contraband, the Fourth Amendment . . . permits police to search the vehicle without more." 518 U.S. 938, 940, 116 S.Ct. 2485, 2487, 135 L.Ed.2d 1031, 1036.

California v. Carney (1985). A search of a vehicle (motor home) is justified under the *Carroll* doctrine if the vehicle "is being used on the highways, or if it is readily capable of such use and is found stationary in a place not regularly used for residential purposes—temporary or otherwise." 471 U.S. 386, 392, 105 S.Ct. 2066, 2070, 85 L.Ed.2d 406, 414.

Coolidge v. New Hampshire (1971). There were no exigent circumstances under the *Carroll* doctrine where there was "no alerted criminal bent on flight, no fleeting opportunity on an open highway after a hazardous chase, no contraband or stolen goods or weapons, no confederates waiting to move the evidence, not even the inconvenience of a special police detail to guard the immobilized automobile. In short, by no possible stretch of the legal imagination can this be made into a case where 'it is not practicable to secure a warrant,' . . . and the 'automobile exception,' despite its label, is simply irrelevant." 403 U.S. 443, 462, 91 S.Ct. 2022, 2035–36, 29 L.Ed.2d 564, 580.

United States v. Ross (1982). "[T]he scope of the warrantless search authorized by [the *Carroll*] exception is no broader and no narrower than a magistrate could legitimately authorize by warrant. If probable cause justifies the search of a lawfully stopped vehicle, it justifies the search of every part of the vehicle and its contents that may conceal the object of the search." 456 U.S. 798, 825, 102 S.Ct. 2157, 2172, 72 L.Ed.2d 572, 594.

United States v. Johns (1985). "*Ross* authorizes a warrantless search of packages several days after they were removed from vehicles that police officers had probable cause to believe contained contraband." 469 U.S. 478, 479, 105 S.Ct. 881, 883, 83 L.Ed.2d 890, 893–94.

United States v. Di Re (1948). Officers may not search the occupants of a vehicle under the *Carroll* doctrine. 332 U.S. 581, 68 S.Ct. 222, 92 L.Ed. 210.

California v. Acevedo (1991). "In the case before us, the police had probable cause to believe that the paper bag in the automobile's trunk contained marijuana. That probable cause now allows a warrantless search of the paper bag. The facts in the record reveal that the police did not have probable cause to believe that contraband was hidden in any other part of the automobile and a search of the entire vehicle would have been without probable cause and unreasonable under the Fourth Amendment." 500 U.S. 565, 580, 111 S.Ct. 1982, 1991, 114 L.Ed.2d 619, 634.

United States v. Chadwick (1977). "The factors which diminish the privacy aspects of an automobile do not apply to respondents' footlocker. Luggage contents are not open to public view, except as a condition to a border entry or common carrier travel; nor is luggage subject to regular inspections and official scrutiny on a continuing basis. Unlike an automobile, whose primary function is transportation, luggage is intended as a repository of personal effects. In sum, a person's expectations of privacy in personal luggage are substantially greater than in an automobile." 433 U.S. 1, 13, 97 S.Ct. 2476, 2484, 53 L.Ed.2d 538, 549.

Illinois v. Lafayette (1983). "The reasonableness of any particular governmental activity does not necessarily or invariably turn on the existence of alternative 'less intrusive' means." 462 U.S. 640, 647, 103 S.Ct. 2605, 2610, 77 L.Ed.2d 65, 72.

South Dakota v. Opperman (1976). "The authority of police to seize and remove from the streets vehicles impeding traffic or threatening public safety and convenience is beyond challenge.

"When vehicles are impounded, local police departments generally follow a routine practice of securing and inventorying the automobiles' contents. These procedures developed in response to three distinct needs: the protection of the owner's property while it remains in police custody, . . . the protection of the police against claims or disputes over lost or stolen property, . . . and the protection of the police from potential danger, ... The practice has been viewed as essential to respond to incidents of theft or vandalism. . . . In addition, police frequently attempt to determine whether a vehicle has been stolen and thereafter abandoned." 428 U.S. 364, 369, 96 S.Ct. 3092, 3096, 49 L.Ed.2d 1000, 1005.

Colorado v. Bertine (1987). "Nothing prohibits the exercise of police discretion to impound a vehicle rather than to park and lock it in a safe place, for instance, "so long as that discretion is exercised according to standard criteria and on the basis of something other than suspicion of evidence of criminal activity." 479 U.S. 367, 375, 107 S.Ct. 738, 743, 93 L.Ed.2d 739, 748.

The allowable scope of an inventory search of an impounded vehicle may include the opening of closed containers found within the vehicle and the examination of their contents. 479 U.S. 367, 107 S.Ct. 738, 93 L.Ed.2d 739.

Florida v. Wells (1990). "A police officer [conducting an inventory search] may be allowed sufficient latitude to determine whether a particular container should or should not be opened in light of the nature of the search and characteristics of the container itself. Thus, while policies of opening all containers or of opening no containers are unquestionably permissible, it would be equally permissible, for example, to allow the opening of closed containers whose contents officers determine they are unable to ascertain from examining the containers' exteriors. The allowance of the exercise of judgment based on concerns related to the purposes of an inventory search does not violate the Fourth Amendment." 495 U.S. 1, 3, 110 S.Ct. 1632, 1635, 109 L.Ed.2d 1, 6–7.

Cardwell v. Lewis (1974). "One has a lesser expectation of privacy in a motor vehicle because its function is transportation and it seldom serves as one's residence or as the repository of personal effects. A car has little capacity for escaping public scrutiny. It travels public thoroughfares where both its occupants and its contents are in plain view. . . . This is not to say that no part of the interior of an automobile has Fourth Amendment protection; the exercise of a desire to be mobile does not, of course, waive one's right to be free of unreasonable governmental intrusion. But insofar as Fourth Amendment protection extends to a motor vehicle, it is the right to privacy that is the touchstone of our inquiry." 417 U.S. 583, 590–91, 94 S.Ct. 2464, 2469–70, 41 L.Ed.2d 325, 335.

United States v. Knotts (1983). "The governmental surveillance conducted by means of the beeper [located inside the vehicle] in this case amounted principally to the following of an automobile on public streets and highways. . . . A person travelling in an automobile on public thoroughfares has no reasonable expectation of privacy in his movements from one place to another. When [the codefendant] travelled over the public streets he voluntarily conveyed to anyone who wanted to look the fact that he was travelling over particular roads in a particular direction, the fact of whatever stops he made, and the fact of his final destination when he exited from public roads onto private property." 460 U.S. 276, 281, 103 S.Ct. 1081, 1085, 75 L.Ed.2d 55, 62.

United States v. Karo (1984). "Requiring a warrant will have the salutary effect of ensuring that use of beepers is not abused, by imposing upon agents the requirement that they demonstrate in advance their justification for the desired search. This is not to say that there are no exceptions to the warrant rule, because if truly exigent circumstances exist no warrant is required under general Fourth Amendment principles." 468 U.S. 705, 717–18, 104 S.Ct. 3296, 3305, 82 L.Ed.2d 530, 543.

Review and Discussion Questions

1. Are there any situations in which a warrant is required to search a motor vehicle? In reality, isn't the warrant requirement the exception rather than the rule in automobile cases?

2. Do the legal principles in this chapter apply to vehicles such as bicycles, rowboats, motor homes, trains, or airplanes?

3. If a law enforcement officer has probable cause to believe a vehicle contains small concealable items such as drugs, jewels, or rare coins, to what extent can he or she search the vehicle without a warrant under the *Carroll* doctrine? Can the upholstery be ripped open? Can the vehicle be dismantled? Can the tires be taken off to look inside them? Can pillows, radios, clothing, and other potential containers be dismantled or ripped apart?

4. Under the *Carroll* doctrine, an officer with probable cause to search a motor vehicle has the choice to either conduct the search immediately or impound the vehicle and search it later at the station house. What factors should be considered in making this choice?

5. Describe three situations in which there are exigent circumstances and probable cause to search a vehicle that is *not* readily mobile.

6. If the postal service turns over to the police plastic bags believed to contain illegal drugs, may the police conduct chemical tests on the contents of the bags without a warrant?

7. Assume that a person is arrested for drunken driving late at night while driving alone on a city street. He tells the police that he does not want his car impounded and that a friend will pick up the car some time the next day. He says he will sign a statement absolving the police from any liability for any loss of or damage to the car or its contents. Can the police still impound the car? Should they?

8. Under the *Carroll* doctrine, must the police have probable cause to search the vehicle at the time it is stopped on the highway in order to search it later at the station? Suppose a person is arrested on the highway for drunk driving and is told to accompany officers to the station to post bond. A routine check at the station reveals that the vehicle is stolen. May the officers search it without a warrant?

9. If officers have probable cause to search a vehicle stopped on the highway but no probable cause to arrest the passengers of the vehicle, can they search the passengers also? Are the passengers "containers" under the ruling of the *Ross* case? Does the answer depend on the nature of the evidence the officers are looking for?

10. Is a warrantless installation of a beeper proper in each of the following circumstances?

   a. Attaching a beeper to the outside of an automobile

   b. Placing a beeper somewhere inside an automobile

   c. Opening a closed package or luggage to install a beeper

   d. Attaching a beeper to the outside of a package or luggage

   e. Placing a beeper with money taken in a bank robbery

REAL-LIFE FACT SITUATIONS

1. On June 9, 1996, a police officer for the City of Florence was on patrol when he saw a vehicle with a filing cabinet protruding from the trunk. The record varies as to whether this occurred at approximately 2:00 A.M. or 3:00 A.M. The officer followed the vehicle "to see if I could find something to stop it for." The officer testified that it appeared that when the driver realized she was being followed, the vehicle sped away. The officer chased the vehicle for approximately four blocks, activated his lights at some point, and stopped the vehicle at Ivey's driveway. The officer ordered the driver, Freda Compton, out of the car. Ivey was in the passenger seat, and an infant was in the backseat. The officer questioned Ivey and Ms. Compton about the filing cabinet in the trunk, but at the hearing on the motion to suppress he indicated that he was unsure whether he talked to Ivey before or after he searched the filing cabinet. The officer testified that he searched the filing cabinet because (1) the stop was made in the early morning hours, (2) the car sped away after noticing that the officer was following, and (3) Ivey's answers regarding the ownership of the filing cabinet were inconsistent. The officer testified that Ivey told him the filing cabinet was his and that it contained papers pertaining to the infant; Ivey also told him that he had found the filing cabinet on the street. The officer testified that the vehicle was speeding and attempting to elude him, but he did not issue a ticket to the driver. The officer searched the cabinet and found evidence that indicated that it belonged to the TVR Company. Upon making radio inquiry, the officer learned that this business had been burglarized shortly before he stopped the vehicle. He arrested Ivey and Ms. Compton. The officer testified that he did not ask permission to look into the filing cabinet and that before he learned of the burglary, he

did not have probable cause to arrest Ivey. Should Ivey's motion to suppress the contents of the filing cabinet be granted? *State v. Ivey,* 709 So.2d 502 (Ala.Crim.App. 1997).

2. In the early morning hours of August 24, 1994, Officer Paul Gill of the West Valley Police Department was dispatched to a local convenience store. The store clerk had summoned the police to investigate an "individual out front bothering customers, walking around in his underwear." Officer Gill arrived at the store at approximately 3:00 A.M. and was closely followed by West Valley Police Officer James Schmidt. The two officers discovered defendant standing next to a car in his "boxers." As the officers approached defendant, they observed him erratically pacing back and forth in front of the car, mumbling to himself, and exhibiting jerky body movements. Concerned about the defendant's mannerisms, Officer Gill asked defendant if he was "on" anything. Defendant responded by stating that he had "had a few beers and had smoked a joint." As Officer Gill tried to converse with the defendant, his condition progressively worsened. The officers noted that, in response to questions asked of him, defendant's answers were not in context, and the defendant was inattentive and unfocused on what was transpiring.

   The defendant was handcuffed and arrested for public intoxication. At that time, Officer Gill was concerned about the defendant's deteriorating condition and summoned medical assistance. Officer Gill also called West Valley Police Officer William McCarthy to the scene, who, according to Officer Gill, "was a little more educated on different types of effects of controlled substances or what might be going on with [defendant]."

When Officer McCarthy arrived, the defendant was still handcuffed and standing by Officer Gill's patrol car. Officer McCarthy recognized the defendant from prior encounters and approached him to determine whether he was all right. Officer McCarthy observed that the defendant was foaming at the mouth, displaying jittery movements, had dilated pupils, and had marks on his arms indicating that he was injecting substances intravenously. Officer McCarthy immediately asked defendant whether he had done some "cheve," which, according to Officer McCarthy, is a street term for heroin. The defendant responded in the affirmative.

After the defendant was placed in the back of Officer Gill's police cruiser, Officer Gill decided to impound the vehicle and began an inventory search of the passenger compartment. Scattered on the floorboard were dollar bills, and a syringe and a spoon were located between the center console and the passenger seat. Meanwhile, Officer McCarthy and Officer Schmidt were inventorying the trunk of the vehicle and, after lifting the carpet covering the trunk space, discovered five balloons containing heroin. At the suppression hearing, the state failed to demonstrate that the police department had standardized inventory procedures and what those procedures were. Should the heroin be suppressed? *State v. Montoya*, 937 P.2d 145 (Utah App. 1997).

3. Trooper Jack McMullin stopped the vehicle in which Patrick Lane was riding on Interstate 44 in Greene County, Missouri, for failure to signal a lane change. While checking the driver's vehicle registration and license, McMullin noted that Lane's eyes were bloodshot, a strong scent of deodorizer was emanating from the vehicle, and the driver appeared nervous. After completing the registration and driver's license check, McMullin asked the driver if the vehicle contained anything illegal such as guns or drugs. The driver denied having illegal matter in the vehicle. The driver originally rejected McMullin's request to search the vehicle. After McMullin informed the driver that the vehicle would be detained until a police dog could perform a "sniff search," the driver granted permission for the search. McMullin found two small bags of marijuana in a duffel bag and a gallon bag of marijuana in the driver's suitcase. McMullin placed the driver under arrest and asked Lane to drive the vehicle to Troop D headquarters. Lane agreed to do so.

After arriving at Troop D headquarters, McMullin resumed his search of the vehicle. He discovered the psilocybin mushrooms in a duffel bag bearing Lane's name. McMullin showed the contraband to the driver who asserted it belonged to Lane. Lane was arrested and charged with the class C felony of possessing psilocybin. Should Lane's motion to suppress the mushrooms be granted? *State v. Lane*, 937 S.W.2d 721 (Mo. banc 1997).

4. On July 21, 1994, a reliable informant notified Detective Barrett (Barrett), a Laramie County Sheriff's Department detective, that someone named "John," later identified as Gronski, had about eight pounds of marijuana at an apartment on Myers Court. The informant told Barrett that a woman named Jennifer Carroll (Carroll) showed him a greenish duffle bag with bags of marijuana in it and that Gronski and his girlfriend discussed leaving town while the informant was in the apartment.

The informant told Barrett he saw Gronski put the duffle bag in a blue Lincoln Continental and gave Barrett a partial license plate number of the car. Based on this information, Barrett believed he had probable cause to obtain a search warrant. Barrett asked other deputies to maintain surveillance on the apartment and the car while he obtained a search warrant for the apartment and the car.

Before Barrett reached the station to prepare the paperwork for the warrant, however, he received notice that two people were driving away from the apartment in the car. Officers followed the car in unmarked vehicles. The officers were going to stop the car as soon as a marked patrol car arrived to assist them. Before a marked patrol car could arrive, however, Gronski parked the car in a store parking lot, got out of the car and locked it. When Gronski and his passenger (Carroll) left the car, officers stopped them, separated them, questioned them and took Gronski's car keys and driver's license. Officers asked Gronski for permission to search the car, but Gronski refused to give them permission. An officer told Gronski to sit in a patrol car while police questioned Carroll. During questioning, Carroll told officers there was marijuana either in the car or in the trunk of the car. Barrett decided to search the car and the trunk for the duffle bag without a search warrant. The duffle bag was found in the trunk and searched. Officers found approximately eight pounds of marijuana in the duffle bag. Should Gronski's motion to suppress the marijuana be granted? *Gronski v. State*, 910 P.2d 561 (Wyo. 1996).

5. On June 27, 1996, at about 11:44 P.M., defendants Drummond, Kato, and Webster were sitting in a darkened car on the premises of the M & M Car Wash (M & M) on Sicklerville Road, in Monroe Township, Gloucester County. The car was in the exit lane area near a coin-operated air freshener machine. M & M is a "do-it-yourself" car wash. There is a coin-operated vacuum machine in the area outside of the wash bays.

Patrolman James Stellaccio, a fourteen and one-half year veteran of the Monroe Township police, was patrolling in uniform with his partner, Patrolman Steven

Farrell, in a marked police vehicle when they noticed a darkened car on the car wash property. Stellaccio believed that the car wash was closed as its lights were off. He could not tell whether the car was occupied. The judge found that the car wash was sufficiently illuminated for vision by the light from a streetlamp on Sicklerville Road. Deeming the presence of the darkened car in an apparently closed facility sufficiently suspicious to warrant "making an inquiry on property and life," the officers pulled up in front of the car. As they did, two defendants, Drummond and Kato, immediately left the parked car, moving towards its trunk and away from the police car. Concerned, the officers then left their vehicle and approached on foot in a "tactical move" calculated to "circle the area to get behind the individuals that made the move to the rear of the vehicle." As Stellaccio drew closer, he recognized Drummond and asked, "Michael, what are you doing?" At this point, Drummond discarded a Newport cigarette pack onto the ground. Retrieved by Stellaccio, it appeared to contain CDS. Drummond was arrested. The ensuing search of the vehicle revealed a large rock of crack cocaine in the front center console. Kato and Webster were then also arrested.

Should the evidence be suppressed? *State v. Drummond,* 701 A.2d 958 (N.J.Super.A.D. 1997).

6. On Wednesday evening, March 31, 1993, Caban visited friends, Fred and Denise Hollingsworth, at their apartment in the City of Janesville, Wisconsin. He parked his unlocked car on the public street, just south of the Hollingsworth driveway. Officers of the Rock County Metro Drug Unit, who were preparing to execute a search warrant of the Hollingsworth apartment, observed Caban enter the apartment building. Minutes later they executed the warrant. They placed Caban in hand restraints and made him lie on the floor. An officer searched him and found substantial cash on his person. The officer identified Caban as a person involved in a previous attempt to purchase "hash." He instructed another officer to search Caban's automobile. The officer searched the passenger compartment and the car's locked trunk. From the passenger compartment, she seized a plastic bag containing marijuana. The police then placed Caban under arrest. Should Caban's motion to suppress the seized evidence be granted? *State v. Caban,* 551 N.W.2d 24 (Wis.App. 1996).

CHAPTER TWELVE

Open Fields and Abandoned Property

OBJECTIVES

1. Understand the interrelationship of the concepts of "open fields," "curtilage," and "reasonable expectation of privacy" and discuss their importance to the law of search and seizure.

2. Be able to analyze a fact situation involving a description of a place and determine whether the place is located in the open fields or is within the curtilage.

3. Know the differences among the open fields doctrine, the plain view doctrine, and observations into the curtilage from a vantage point in the open fields or a public place.

4. Know the factors considered by courts in determining whether premises, objects, or vehicles have been abandoned and the significance of abandonment in the law of search and seizure.

OUTLINE

1. *Hester v. United States*
2. Open fields
   a. Determination of curtilage
      (1) Residential yard
      (2) Fences
      (3) Distance from the dwelling
      (4) Multiple-occupancy dwellings
      (5) Garages
      (6) Other outbuildings
      (7) Unoccupied tracts
   b. Reasonable expectation of privacy
   c. Plain view, open fields, and observations into constitutionally protected areas

     (1) Aerial observations
     (2) Driveways and other means of access to dwellings
3. Abandoned property
   a. Indications of intent to abandon property
      (1) Premises
      (2) Objects
      (3) Motor vehicles
   b. Lawfulness of police behavior
   c. Reasonable expectation of privacy in the property

The Fourth Amendment to the U.S. Constitution guarantees "the right of the people to be secure in their persons, *houses,* papers, and effects, against unreasonable *searches* and seizures . . ." (emphasis supplied). U.S. Const., Amend. 4. The words *houses* and *searches* are italicized because the meaning of open fields depends on court interpretation of the word *houses,* and the meaning of abandoned property depends on court interpretation of the word *searches.* The legal meanings of these terms and their interrelationships are introduced with a summary of *Hester v. United States,* 265 U.S. 57, 44 S.Ct. 445, 68 L.Ed. 898 (1924), which established the concepts of **open fields** and **abandoned property** in the law of search and seizure. ∎

Hester v. United States

In *Hester v. United States,* revenue officers investigating suspected bootlegging went to the house of Hester's father. As they approached, they saw Henderson drive up to the house. The officers concealed themselves and observed Hester come out of the house and hand Henderson a quart bottle. An alarm was given. Hester went to a nearby car and removed a gallon jug, and he and Henderson fled across an open field. One of the officers pursued, firing his pistol. Henderson threw away his bottle, and Hester dropped his jug, which broke, keeping about one quart of its contents. A broken jar, still containing some of its contents, was found outside the house. The officers examined the jug, the jar, and the bottle and determined that they contained illicitly distilled whiskey. The officers had neither a search warrant nor an arrest warrant.

The defendant was convicted of concealing distilled spirits and contended on appeal that the testimony of the two officers was inadmissible because their actions constituted an illegal search and seizure. The U.S. Supreme Court said:

> It is obvious that even if there had been a trespass, the above testimony was not obtained by an illegal search or seizure. The defendant's own acts, and those of his associates, disclosed the jug, the jar and the bottle—and there was no seizure in the sense of the law when the officers examined the contents of each after it had been *abandoned.* . . . The only shadow of a ground for bringing up the case is drawn from the hypothesis that the examination of the vessels took place upon Hester's father's land. As to that, it is enough to say that, apart from the justification, the special protection accorded by the Fourth Amendment to the people in their "persons, houses, papers and effects," is not extended to the *open fields.* The distinction between the latter and the house is as old as the common law. [Emphasis supplied.] 265 U.S. at 58–59, 44 S.Ct. at 446, 68 L.Ed. at 900.

The remainder of this chapter is devoted to a discussion of the law of search and seizure applied to open fields and abandoned property, as the law has developed since the *Hester* case.

Open Fields

The basic open fields doctrine was stated by the U.S. Supreme Court in the *Hester* case: "[T]he special protection accorded by the Fourth Amendment to the people in their 'persons, houses, papers and effects' is not extended to the open fields." 265 U.S. at 59, 44 S.Ct. at 446, 68 L.Ed. at 900. The open fields doctrine allows law enforcement officers to search for and seize evidence in the open fields without a warrant, probable cause, or any other legal justification. Even if officers trespass on the land of another while searching the open fields, the evidence they seize will not be inadmissible by reason of trespass. *Oliver v. United States,* 466 U.S. 170, 104 S.Ct. 1735, 80 L.Ed.2d 214 (1984). Furthermore, the officers themselves will not be held liable for trespass in a civil suit if the trespass was required in the performance of their duties. *Giacona v. United States,* 257 F.2d 450 (5th Cir. 1958).

The key issue under the open fields doctrine is the determination of where the area protected by the Fourth Amendment ends and the open fields begin. The answer is found in court decisions interpreting the word *houses* in the Fourth Amendment. This term has been given a very broad meaning by the courts. The Fourth Amendment has been held to protect people in their homes, whether owned, rented, or leased. The term *houses* has also been held to include any quarters in which a person is staying or living, whether permanently or temporarily. Examples of protected living quarters are hotel and motel rooms, apartments, rooming and boarding house rooms, and even hospital rooms.

Furthermore, the protection of the Fourth Amendment extends to places of business. *See v. City of Seattle,* 387 U.S. 541, 87 S.Ct. 1737, 18 L.Ed.2d 943 (1967). The protection extended to places of business is limited, however, to areas or sections that are not open to the public:

[A] private business whose doors are open to the general public is also to be considered open to entry by the police for any proper purpose not violative of the owner's constitutional rights—e.g., patronizing the place or surveying it to promote law and order or to suppress a breach of the peace. *State v. LaDuca,* 214 A.2d 423, 426 (N.J. Super. 1965).

For convenience, the word *house* is used in the remainder of this chapter to refer to either residential or commercial premises covered by the Fourth Amendment.

Courts have extended the meaning of *houses* under the Fourth Amendment to include the "ground and buildings immediately surrounding a dwelling house." *State v. Sindak,* 774 P.2d 895, 898 (Idaho 1989). This area is commonly known as the **curtilage.** The concept of curtilage is vital to the open fields doctrine because the open fields are considered to be all the space not contained within the curtilage. The following discussion focuses on the facts and circumstances that courts rely on in determining the extent of the curtilage.

Determination of Curtilage

To determine whether property to be searched falls within a house's curtilage, the law enforcement officer must consider "the factors that determine whether an individual reasonably may expect that an area immediately adjacent to the home will remain private." *Oliver v. United States,* 466 U.S. 170, 180, 104 S.Ct. 1735, 1742, 80 L.Ed.2d 214, 225 (1984). The Court described those factors in another case:

[W]e believe that curtilage questions should be resolved with particular reference to four factors: *the proximity of the area claimed to be curtilage to the home, whether the area is included within an enclosure surrounding the home, the nature of the uses to which the area is put, and the steps taken by the resident to protect the area from observation by people passing by.* [Emphasis supplied.] *United States v. Dunn,* 480 U.S. 294, 301, 107 S.Ct. 1134, 1139, 94 L.Ed.2d 326, 334–35 (1987).

These factors are not intended to produce a finely tuned formula but rather are useful analytical tools to help determine whether the area in question should be placed under the same Fourth Amendment protection as the home. The Court emphasized that "the primary focus is whether the area in question harbors those intimate activities associated with domestic life and the privacies of the home." 480 U.S. at 301 n.4, 107 S.Ct. at 1139 n.4, 94 L.Ed.2d at 335 n.4. The four factors are discussed here under various headings through an analysis of court decisions on the open fields doctrine.

RESIDENTIAL YARD. The backyard of a house has repeatedly been held to be within the curtilage of a house and thereby protected from a warrantless search under the Fourth Amendment. *United States v. Van Dyke,* 643 F.2d 992 (4th Cir. 1980). For example, in *United States v. Boger,* 755 F.Supp. 333, 338 (E.D.Wash. 1990), the court said:

> [I]t is clear that the area of Mr. Boger's backyard . . . is within the curtilage of the home. The area was enclosed with sight obscuring fences on the east and west, and by the house on the south. An unoccupied field was to the north. The area in question was obviously used by the resident as part of the home. An outside patio was located on the rear of the home and the backyard was in grass and landscaping. Clearly the resident had taken appropriate steps to protect the area from observation on three sides and an unoccupied open field was on the fourth side.

If, however, a residential yard is accessible to the public and the owner takes no steps to protect the area from observation, it may not qualify for Fourth Amendment protection. In *People v. Bradley,* 81 Cal.Rptr. 457, 460 P.2d 129 (Cal. 1969), an officer had received information that the defendant was growing marijuana under a fig tree outside his residence. The officer went to the defendant's residence to investigate. The premises were described by the court as a house that faced the street with a driveway that ran along the east of the house and terminated in a garage at the rear and east of the house. The defendant's residence was attached to the rear of the garage. The fig tree was about twenty feet from the defendant's door. The officer observed marijuana plants growing in a keg near the base of the tree, partially covered by the leaves and limbs of the tree. In finding the seizure of the plants legal, the court said:

> [T]hey were located a scant 20 feet from defendant's door to which presumably delivery men and others came, and the front house, as well as defendant's house, apparently had access to the yard. Under the circumstances it does not appear that defendant exhibited a subjective expectation of privacy as to the plants. Furthermore, any such expectation would have been unreasonable. *People v. Bradley,* 81 Cal.Rptr. 457, 459, 460 P.2d 129, 131 (Cal. 1969).

Law enforcement officers should treat the residential yard of a house as part of the curtilage unless there are clear indications that the person residing in the house allowed members of the public access to the yard and had no reasonable expectation of privacy in the yard.

FENCES. If the area immediately surrounding a house is enclosed by a fence, the area within the fence is usually defined as the curtilage. In *United States v. Swepston,* 987 F.2d 1510 (10th Cir. 1993), the court found that a chicken shed located a hundred feet from the defendant's house was within the curtilage of the house. The shed and the house were enclosed by a barbed wire fence and *no fence separated the two structures.* In addition, the defendant maintained a path between the house and the shed and visited the shed regularly, neither the house nor the shed could be seen from a public road or adjoining property, and there was no evidence that the shed was not being used for intimate activities of the home. In contrast, in the same case, marijuana gardens located about three hundred feet from the codefendant's house were found to be outside the curtilage.

> [A]lthough the gardens were encircled by a barbed wire fence, *they were outside the fence that encircled [the codefendant's] house, and they were separated from [his] house by the chain-link fence.* . . . [T]he area within the barbed wire fence contained numerous chickens and chicken huts and was used primarily for the raising of game chickens. These huts were visible to the . . . officers as they overflew the area, and indicated to them that the area was not being used for intimate activities of the home. Finally, [the codefendant] did little to protect the marijuana gardens from observation by those standing in the open fields surrounding [his] property. [Emphasis supplied.] 987 F.2d at 1515.

If a piece of land is already outside the curtilage, erecting fences around it or taking other steps to protect privacy in the land will not establish that the expectation of privacy in the land is legitimate and bring the land within the curtilage. In *Oliver v. United States,* to conceal their criminal activities, the defendants planted marijuana on secluded land and erected fences and "No Trespassing" signs around the property. The U.S. Supreme Court said:

> [I]t may be that because of such precautions, few members of the public stumbled upon the marijuana crops seized by the police. Neither of these suppositions demonstrates, however, that the expectation of privacy was *legitimate* in the sense required by the Fourth Amendment. The test of legitimacy is not whether the individual chooses to conceal asserted "private" activity. Rather, the correct inquiry is whether the government's intrusion infringes upon the personal and societal values protected by the Fourth Amendment. . . . [W]e find no basis for concluding that a police inspection of open fields accomplishes such an infringement. 466 U.S. at 182–83, 104 S.Ct. at 1743, 80 L.Ed.2d at 227.

Also, whether a fence defines the curtilage may depend on the nature of the fence. In *United States v. Brady,* 734 F.Supp. 923 (E.D.Wash. 1990), the court found that the fence was not sufficient to define the curtilage.

> There was no "no trespassing" sign posted on or near the gate. The fence was not a sight-obstructing fence. The fence did not completely enclose the property in that there was a wide gap on either side of the gate which could reasonably be construed to be a pedestrian path. The fence was not of a type which evidenced an intent to exclude strangers. 734 F.Supp. at 928.

DISTANCE FROM THE DWELLING. Some courts use a rule of thumb that the curtilage ends approximately 75 feet from the main dwelling. See *United States ex rel. Saiken v. Bensinger,* 546 F.2d 1292 (7th Cir. 1976). Other courts refuse to adopt a per se rule in determining the extent of the curtilage but use a totality of the circumstances approach, with the distance from the dwelling as one of many factors to be weighed in making the determination. For example, in *State v. Silva,* 509 A.2d 659 (Me. 1986), the court held that a marijuana patch located roughly 250 feet behind the defendant's house was within the curtilage and was entitled to Fourth Amendment protection. The marijuana patch was within a cultivated lawn extending from the house to a tree-studded bog just beyond the patch; a swath of trees stood between the patch and the house but was not long enough to cut the back lawn completely in half; and the lawn was dotted with fruit trees, fruit bushes, two gardens, a shed, and flowers.

MULTIPLE-OCCUPANCY DWELLINGS. Multiple-occupancy dwellings are treated differently from single-occupancy dwellings for purposes of determining the extent of curtilage. Most courts hold that the shared areas of multiple-occupancy buildings (such as common corridors, passageways, driveways, and yards) are not entitled to the protection of the Fourth Amendment because tenants do not have a reasonable expectation of privacy with respect to those areas. *United States v. Nohara,* 3 F.3d 1239 (9th Cir. 1993). Nevertheless, there are many different types of multiple-occupancy dwellings, and courts will examine all the facts and circumstances in determining the curtilage. In *Fixel v. Wainwright,* 492 F.2d 480 (5th Cir. 1974), two law enforcement officers who had been informed that narcotics were being sold on the defendant's premises observed the defendant's behavior at his residence in a four-unit apartment building. Over a forty-five-minute period, several people entered the defendant's apartment, and each time the defendant would go into his backyard and remove a shaving kit from beneath some rubbish under a tree. One officer then went into the backyard and seized the shaving kit while the other officer arrested the defendant. Chemical analysis revealed that the shaving kit contained heroin. The government argued that the defendant's backyard was an area common to, or shared with, other tenants and should not be entitled to the protection usually afforded the curtilage of a purely private residence. The court held, however, that the backyard was a protected area and that the seizure and search of the shaving kit were illegal:

> The backyard of Fixel's home was not a common passageway normally used by the building's tenants for gaining access to the apartments. . . . Nor is the backyard an area open as a corridor to salesmen or other businessmen who might approach the tenants in the course of their trade. . . . This apartment was Fixel's home, he lived there and the backyard of the building was completely removed from the street and surrounded by a chain link fence. . . . While the enjoyment of his backyard is not as exclusive as the backyard of a purely private residence, this area is not as public or shared as the corridors, yards or other common areas of a large apartment complex or motel. Contemporary concepts of living such as multi-unit dwellings must not dilute Fixel's right to privacy anymore than is absolutely required. We believe that the backyard area of Fixel's home is sufficiently removed and private in character that he could reasonably expect privacy. 492 F.2d at 484.

Porches and fire escapes outside a person's apartment or unit in a multiple-occupancy dwelling also fall within the curtilage of the apartment or unit.

> Unlike public halls or stairs which are public areas used in common by tenants and their guests or others lawfully on the property, a fire escape in a non-fireproof building is required outside of each apartment as a secondary means of egress for the occupants of that apartment. While it is true that in the event of fire others might have occasion to lawfully pass over the fire escape of another, this would be the only time that one might be lawfully on the fire escape of another. *People v. Terrell,* 53 Misc.2d 32, 38–39, 277 N.Y.S.2d 926, 933 (N.Y. 1967).

GARAGES. Garages are usually held to be part of the curtilage, especially if they are near or attached to the dwelling house and used in connection with it. Therefore, in *Commonwealth v. Murphy,* 233 N.E.2d 5 (Mass. 1968), a case in which a garage and a house were surrounded on three sides by a fence and the garage was close to the house, fifty to seventy-five feet from the street, the garage was held to be within the curtilage. A garage not used by its owner in connection with the owner's residence, however, was held to be outside the curtilage. *People v. Swanberg*, 22 A.D.2d 902, 255 N.Y.S.2d 267 (N.Y. 1964). Furthermore, a garage used in connection with a multiunit dwelling was held to be outside the curtilage because it was used in common by many tenants of the dwelling. *People v. Terry*, 77 Cal.Rptr. 460, 454 P.2d 36 (Cal. 1969).

OTHER OUTBUILDINGS. In determining whether an outbuilding is part of the curtilage, courts consider factors such as distance from the dwelling house, presence and location of fences, family use of the building, and attempts to protect the area from observation. In *United States v. Dunn*, 480 U.S. 294, 107 S.Ct. 1134, 94 L.Ed.2d 326 (1987), a barn located fifty yards from a fence surrounding a house and sixty yards from the house itself was held to be outside the curtilage. The U.S. Supreme Court found that the owner had done little to protect the barn area from observation by those standing in the open fields. The Court also found it especially significant that law enforcement officials possessed objective data indicating that the barn was not being used for intimate activities of the home. Rather, they knew that a truck carrying a container of phenylacetic acid was backed up to the barn, a strong odor of the acid emanated from the barn, and the sound of a pumplike motor could be heard from within the barn.

In *United States v. Calabrese*, 825 F.2d 1342 (9th Cir. 1987), the court found that a structure located some fifty feet from a main residence and its two *attached* garages was not within the curtilage. Most significant in the court's determination was law enforcement officials' knowledge, obtained during a previous legal search, that the detached structure was being used to manufacture methamphetamine and not for domestic activities.

In *United States v. Van Damme*, 823 F.Supp. 1552 (D.Mont. 1993), the court held that a greenhouse compound located more than 200 feet from the defendant's house and surrounded by a twelve-foot stockade fence was not part of the curtilage of the house.

> [B]ecause of the isolation of the greenhouse compound from the rest of the property, the lack of nearby buildings or facilities, and the absence of any indicia of activities commonly associated with domestic life, the investigating officers had no reason to deem the greenhouse compound as part of the Defendant's home. Additionally, the citizen informant's report provided the officers with some "objective data indicating that the [compound] was not being used for intimate activities of the home." 823 F.Supp. at 1558.

In contrast, a barn was held to be within the curtilage where a driveway ran between the house and the barn, tracks of vehicles and footprints were visible in the snow leading to both the house and the barn, and no barriers separated the house and the barn. *Rosencranz v. United States*, 356 F.2d 310 (1st Cir. 1966).

UNOCCUPIED TRACTS. An unoccupied, uncultivated, remote tract of land is almost always held to be outside the curtilage and in the open fields. The U.S. Supreme Court stated that

> the term "open fields" may include any unoccupied or undeveloped area outside of the curtilage. An open field need be neither "open" nor a "field" as those terms are used in common speech. For example . . . a thickly wooded area nonetheless may be an open field as that term is used in construing the Fourth Amendment. *Oliver v. United States*, 466 U.S. 170, 180 n.11, 104 S.Ct. 1735, 1742 n.11, 80 L.Ed.2d 214, 225 n.11 (1984).

In *Maine v. Thornton,* the companion case to *Oliver v. United States,* police officers, after receiving a tip that marijuana was being grown in the woods behind the defendant's residence, entered the woods by a path between the residence and a neighboring house. They followed a path through the woods until they reached two marijuana patches fenced with chicken wire and having "No Trespassing" signs. Later, the officers, upon determining that the patches were on the defendant's property, obtained a search warrant and seized the marijuana. The U.S. Supreme Court held that the officers' actions were not an unreasonable search and seizure, because the area was an open field. In another case, the Wisconsin Supreme Court held that the Fourth Amendment did not apply to a local sheriff's warrantless digging in a field about 450 feet from the defendant's house to find the body of the defendant's wife, who had disappeared.

> Under the "open fields" doctrine, the fact that evidence is concealed or hidden is immaterial. The area [the open field] is simply not within the protection of the Fourth Amendment. If the field where the body was found does not have constitutional protection, the fact that the sheriff, rather than observing the evidence that might have been in plain view, dug into the earth to find the body and committed a trespass in so doing does not confer protection. *Conrad v. State,* 218 N.W.2d 252, 257 (Wis. 1974).

A difficult question is presented if the unoccupied area searched is not completely vacant but is being used as a building lot. In *People v. Grundeis,* 108 N.E.2d 483 (Ill. 1952), law enforcement officers received a complaint that lumber, sacks of cement, and a cart had been stolen. Investigation led the officers to suspect the defendant. They went to the defendant's property, where the defendant was laying the foundation for a house, searched the property without a warrant, and found some of the stolen items. The court held that the area searched came within the category of open fields, even though a house was in the process of construction on it:

> If the lot had been left completely untouched, there could be no doubt that it would fall within the ruling of the *Hester* case. That a large quantity of building material has been brought upon the lot and a foundation for a house dug out, or even completely laid, does not change the nature of the place. Not even the broad policy of protection against "invasion of 'the sanctity of a man's home and the privacies of life,' " . . . is infringed by what took place here. Defendant's constitutional rights were not violated. 108 N.E.2d at 487.

Reasonable Expectation of Privacy

In determining the legality of the search in many of the cases discussed previously, courts have considered whether the person owning or inhabiting the premises had a reasonable expectation of privacy in the area searched. In this sense, reasonable expectation of privacy could be considered just another one of the facts and circumstances used to determine the extent of the curtilage. Since the U.S. Supreme Court decision in *Katz v. United States,* 389 U.S. 347, 88 S.Ct. 507, 19 L.Ed.2d 576 (1967), however, a person's reasonable expectation of privacy has taken on a whole new meaning and importance in the law of search and seizure.

In the *Katz* case, a landmark opinion involving electronic eavesdropping, the Supreme Court stated that "the Fourth Amendment protects people, not places." 389 U.S. at 351, 88 S.Ct. at 511, 19 L.Ed.2d at 582. A later court decision said that *Katz* "shifts the focus of the Fourth Amendment from 'protected areas' to the individual's expectations of privacy. Whether the government's activity is considered a 'search' depends upon whether the individual's reasonable expectations of privacy are disturbed." *Davis v. United States,* 413 F.2d 1226, 1232 (5th Cir. 1969).

In *Oliver v. United States,* a case involving a police seizure of marijuana from a secluded plot of land surrounded by fences and "No Trespassing" signs, the U.S. Supreme Court stated that "an individual may not legitimately demand privacy for activities conducted out of doors in fields, except in the area immediately surrounding the home." 466 U.S. at 178, 104 S.Ct. at 1741, 80 L.Ed.2d at 224. The Court went on to say:

> [O]pen fields do not provide the setting for those intimate activities that the [Fourth] Amendment is intended to shelter from government interference or surveillance. There is no societal interest in protecting the privacy of those activities such as the cultivation of crops, that occur in open fields. Moreover, as a practical matter these lands usually are accessible to the public and the police in ways that a home, an office or commercial structure would not be. It is not generally true that fences or "No Trespassing" signs effectively bar the public from viewing open fields in rural areas. And . . . the public and police lawfully may survey lands from the air. For these reasons, the asserted expectation of privacy in open fields is not an expectation that "society recognizes as reasonable." 466 U.S. at 179, 104 S.Ct. at 1741, 80 L.Ed.2d at 224.

Plain View, Open Fields, and Observations into Constitutionally Protected Areas

Law enforcement officers often confuse the open fields and plain view doctrines. The plain view doctrine states that if a law enforcement officer, as the result of a prior valid intrusion, is in a position in which he or she has a legal right to be, items of evidence lying open to view may be seized if their incriminating character is immediately apparent (see Chapter 10). Under the open fields doctrine, an officer need not be concerned with the validity of the prior intrusion into a constitutionally protected area. Open fields are not a constitutionally protected area, and therefore the officer may not only seize items that are open to view but may search for items hidden from view and seize them. Of course, all seizures must be based on probable cause that the items are property subject to seizure.

In addition, from a vantage point in the open fields or a public place, an officer may, without a warrant, make observations into constitutionally protected areas. "[A] law enforcement 'officer's observations from a public vantage point where he has a right to be' and from which the activities or objects he observes are 'clearly visible' do not constitute a search within the meaning of the Fourth Amendment." *United States v. Taylor,* 90 F.3d 903, 908 (4th Cir. 1996). These observations may be enhanced by electrical or mechanical means such as flashlights or binoculars. *United States v. Dunn,* 480 U.S. 294, 107 S.Ct. 1134, 94 L.Ed.2d 326 (1987). In *United States v. Taft,* 769 F.Supp. 1295 (D.Vt. 1991), the court found no constitutional violation where police, while standing in the open fields, observed the defendant's cabin from about fifty yards with the aid of binoculars. Information obtained from such observations may be used as a basis for probable cause to arrest or to obtain a search warrant.

Observations into constitutionally protected areas may not, however, violate the reasonable expectation of privacy of the person whose premises or activities are being observed. In *Raettig v. State,* 406 So.2d 1273 (Fla.App. 1981), a person in lawful possession of a camper truck was held to have established a reasonable expectation of privacy by painting over the windows, locking the doors, and refusing access to the police. That expectation was violated when an officer shined a flashlight through a minute crack to observe the contents of the truck. The defendant's failure to seal the crack "could hardly be regarded as an implied invitation to any curious passerby to take a look." 406 P.2d at 1278. Also in *State v. Ward,* 617 So.2d 568 (Hawaii 1980), the court held that

> [t]he constitution does not require that in all cases a person, in order to protect his privacy, must shut himself off from fresh air, sunlight and scenery. And as a corollary, neither does the constitution hold that a person, by opening his curtains, thereby opens his person, house, papers and effects to telescopic scrutiny by the government. 617 P.2d at 573.

In the *Ward* case, the court found that the viewing with binoculars of a crap game in a seventh-story apartment from a vantage point an eighth of a mile away was an illegal search. "[If] the purpose of the telescopic aid is to view that which could not be seen without it, it is a constitutional invasion." 617 P.2d at 573.

AERIAL OBSERVATIONS. In *California v. Ciraolo,* 476 U.S. 207, 106 S.Ct. 1809, 90 L.Ed.2d 210 (1986), the U.S. Supreme Court held that the Fourth Amendment was not violated by a warrantless aerial observation from an altitude of a thousand feet of a fenced-in backyard within the curtilage of a home. The Court, relying on *Katz v. United States,* 389 U.S. 347, 88 S.Ct. 507, 19 L.Ed.2d 576 (1967), analyzed the case by means of a two-part inquiry: First, has the individual manifested a subjective expectation of privacy in the object of the challenged search? Second, is society willing to recognize that expectation as reasonable?

The Court found that the defendant clearly manifested his own subjective intent and desire to maintain privacy by placing a ten-foot fence around his backyard. His expectation of privacy from observation from the air was found not to be reasonable, however.

> That the area is within the curtilage does not itself bar all police observation. The Fourth Amendment protection of the home has never been extended to require law enforcement officers to shield their eyes when passing by a home on public thoroughfares. Nor does the mere fact that an individual has taken measures to restrict some views of his activities preclude an officer's observations from a public vantage point where he has a right to be and which renders the activities clearly visible. 476 U.S. at 213, 106 S.Ct. at 1812, 90 L.Ed.2d at 216.

Because the observations took place from public navigable airspace, from which any member of the public flying in that airspace could have observed everything the officers observed, the defendant's expectation that his backyard was protected from observation was not an expectation that society was prepared to honor.

> In an age where private and commercial flight in the public airways is routine, it is unreasonable for respondent to expect that his marijuana plants were constitutionally protected from being observed with the naked eye from an altitude of 1,000 feet. The Fourth Amendment simply does not require the police traveling in the public airways at this altitude to obtain a warrant in order to observe what is visible to the naked eye. 476 U.S. at 215, 106 S.Ct. at 1813, 90 L.Ed.2d at 218.

Applying the same reasoning, the Supreme Court held that police observation of the defendant's greenhouse from a helicopter flying at four hundred feet did not violate the defendant's reasonable expectation of privacy and was therefore not a search.

[T]he helicopter in this case was *not* violating the law, and there is nothing in the record or before us to suggest that helicopters flying at 400 feet are sufficiently rare in this country to lend substance to respondent's claim that he reasonably anticipated that his greenhouse would not be subject to observation from that altitude. Neither is there any intimation here that the helicopter interfered with respondent's normal use of the greenhouse or of other parts of the curtilage. As far as this record reveals, no intimate details connected with the use of the home or curtilage were observed, and there was no undue noise, no wind, dust, or threat of injury. In these circumstances, there was no violation of the Fourth Amendment. *Florida v. Riley,* 488 U.S. 445, 451–52, 109 S.Ct. 693, 697, 102 L.Ed.2d 835, 843 (1989).

In *Dow Chemical Co. v. United States,* 476 U.S. 227, 106 S.Ct. 1819, 90 L.Ed.2d 226 (1986), the Court held that the Environmental Protection Agency's aerial photography of a chemical company's two thousand–acre outdoor industrial plant complex from navigable airspace was not a search prohibited by the Fourth Amendment.

[T]he open areas of an industrial plant complex with numerous plant structures spread over an area of 2,000 acres are not analogous to the "curtilage" of a dwelling for purposes of aerial surveillance; such an industrial complex is more comparable to an open field and as such it is open to the view and observation of persons in aircraft lawfully in the public airspace immediately above or sufficiently near the area for the reach of cameras. 476 U.S. at 239, 106 S.Ct. at 1827, 90 L.Ed.2d at 238.

DRIVEWAYS AND OTHER MEANS OF ACCESS TO DWELLINGS. In *Lorenzana v. Superior Court of Los Angeles County,* 108 Cal.Rptr. 585, 511 P.2d 33 (Cal. 1973), a narcotics officer investigating a tip about heroin dealing went to the place where the dealing was said to be occurring. The place was a single-family dwelling, seventy feet from the sidewalk, with access from the west. There were no doorways or defined pathways on the east side of the house, and a strip of land covered with grass and dirt separated the east side of the house from the driveway of the apartment next door. The officer went to the east side of the house, peeked through a two-inch gap under the partially drawn shade of a closed window, and observed indications of criminal activity.

The court held that the officer's observations constituted an illegal search. The court initially analyzed the problem in terms of whether the officer was standing on a part of the property surrounding the house that had been opened, expressly or impliedly, to public use. Under the facts, the officer was found to have made his observations from a position in which he had no right to be. Because neither a warrant nor one of the established exceptions to the warrant requirement justified the intrusion, the intrusion was unlawful.

The court went on to discuss the officer's actions at length, in terms of the defendant's reasonable expectation of privacy:

[T]he generic *Katz* rule permits the resident of a house to rely justifiably upon the privacy of the surrounding areas as a protection from the peering of the officer unless such residence is "exposed" to that intrusion by the existence of public pathways or other invitations to the public to enter upon the property. This justifiable reliance on the privacy of the property surrounding one's residence thus leads to the *particular* rule that searches conducted without a warrant from such parts of the property *always* are unconstitutional unless an exception to the warrant requirement applies. . . .

Pursuant to the principles of *Katz,* therefore, we do not rest our analysis exclusively upon such abstractions as "trespass" or "constitutionally protected areas" or upon the physical differences between a telephone booth and the land surrounding a residence; we do, however, look to the conduct of people in regard to these elements. Taking into account the nature of the area surrounding a private residence, we ask whether that area has been opened to public use; if so, the occupant cannot claim he expected privacy from all observations of the officer who stands upon that ground; if not, the occupant does deserve that privacy. Since the eavesdropping officer in the case before us stood upon private property and since such property exhibited no invitation to public use, we find that the officer violated petitioner Lorenzana's expectations of privacy, and hence his constitutional rights. 108 Cal.Rptr. at 594, 511 P.2d at 42.

In general, if an officer gathers information while situated in a public place or in a place where an ordinary citizen with legitimate business might be expected to be, the officer will not be invading anyone's reasonable expectation of privacy. Therefore, an officer's observations from an ordinary means of access to a dwelling, such as a front porch or side door, will not ordinarily violate a person's reasonable expectation of privacy. *People v. Willard,* 47 Cal.Rptr. 734 (Cal.App. 1965). Once officers are in a place in which they have a legitimate right to be, they may look around and peer through windows or other openings.

> Peering through a window or a crack in the door or a keyhole is not, in the abstract, genteel behavior, but the Fourth Amendment does not protect against all conduct unworthy of a good neighbor.... [I]t is the duty of a policeman to investigate, and *we cannot say that . . . the Fourth Amendment itself draws the blinds the occupant could have drawn and did not. People v. Berutko,* 77 Cal.Rptr. 217, 222, 453 P.2d 721, 726 (Cal. 1969).

Furthermore, so long as officers are where they have a right to be, they may listen at doors or gather evidence with their other senses. In *United States v. Perry,* 339 F.Supp. 209, 213 (S.D.Cal. 1972), the court said:

> The general rule is that information obtained by an officer using his natural senses, where the officer has a right to be where he is, is admissible evidence. The fact that the information is in the form of conversations emanating from a private space, such as a hotel room, is not a bar to its admissibility.

> Regardless of which sense an officer is using to detect criminal activity occurring in a constitutionally protected area, the officer does not have authority to enter into the area to make a search or seizure without a warrant. Only a search warrant gives this authority, unless there is an emergency or the situation falls within one of the other recognized exceptions to the search warrant requirement.

> An officer is not entitled to conduct a warrantless entry and seizure of incriminating evidence simply because he has seen the evidence from outside the premises. "Incontrovertible testimony of the senses that an incriminating object is on premises belonging to a criminal suspect may establish the fullest possible measure of probable cause. But even where the object is contraband, this Court has repeatedly stated and enforced the basic rule that the police may not enter and make a warrantless seizure," absent exigent circumstances. *United States v. Wilson,* 36 F.3d 205, 209 n. 4 (1st Cir. 1994).

In a case in which both probable cause and exigent circumstances were found, an officer approached the defendant's front door, looked through his picture window adjacent to the door, and observed a large amount of money and what appeared to him to be illegal drugs on the defendant's dining room table. As the officer was looking through the window, someone inside the house quickly closed the blinds. Under these circumstances, the officer "had a reasonable basis for concluding that there was probable cause to believe that criminal activity was in progress in the house and that there was an imminent danger that evidence would be destroyed unless the officers immediately entered the house and took possession of it." *United States v. Taylor,* 90 F.3d 903, 909–10 (4th Cir. 1996).

KEY POINTS

1. Law enforcement officers may search for items of evidence in the open fields without a warrant, probable cause, or any other legal justification and may seize items if they have probable cause to believe that the items are "property subject to seizure" under the law of the officers' jurisdiction.

2. Open fields is all the space that is not contained within the *curtilage* and need be neither "open" nor "fields." The curtilage is the area around the home that harbors those intimate activities associated with domestic life and the privacies of the home.

3. Whether an area falls within the curtilage is determined by considering four factors: the proximity of the area claimed to be curtilage to the home, whether the area is included within an enclosure surrounding the home, the nature of the uses to which the area is put, and the steps taken by the resident to protect the area from observation by people passing by.

4. Generally, if the area surrounding a house is enclosed by a fence, the area within the fence is defined as the curtilage.

5. Generally, the shared areas of multiple-occupancy buildings are not entitled to Fourth Amendment protection because the public has access to them.

6. Law enforcement officers may make warrantless observations into constitutionally protected areas from a vantage point in the open fields or the air, if the observations do not violate the reasonable expectation of privacy of the person whose premises or activities are being observed.

Abandoned Property

The meaning of the term *abandoned property* depends on the interpretation given to the word *searches* in the Fourth Amendment. As defined earlier, a search occurs "when an expectation of privacy that society is prepared to consider reasonable is infringed." *United States v. Jacobsen,* 466 U.S. 109, 113, 104 S.Ct. 1652, 1656, 80 L.Ed.2d 85, 94 (1984). It follows that no search occurs when a law enforcement officer observes, examines, or inspects property whose owner has "voluntarily discarded, left behind, or otherwise relinquished his interest in the property in question so that he could no longer retain a reasonable expectation of privacy with regard to it. . . ." *United States v. Colbert,* 474 F.2d 174, 176 (5th Cir. 1973). Because there is no search under the Fourth Amendment, officers may lawfully seize abandoned property without a warrant or probable cause and may use it as evidence in court.

The main difference between the abandonment doctrine and the plain view doctrine turns on the nature of the place from which the officer seizes an object. Under the plain view doctrine, if a law enforcement officer, as the result of a prior valid intrusion into a constitutionally protected area or a prior valid invasion of a reasonable expectation of privacy, is in a position in which he or she has a legal right to be, items of evidence lying open to view may be seized. The plain view doctrine is applicable only after the law enforcement officer has made such a lawful intrusion. On the other hand, if a law enforcement officer, acting lawfully, seizes objects that have been discarded on the street, in a public park, or in some other *situation not protected by the Fourth Amendment to the Constitution,* the seizure is legal under the abandonment doctrine. Note that the abandonment doctrine, unlike the plain view doctrine, involves no prior intrusion into a constitutionally protected area or prior invasion of a reasonable expectation of privacy. Law enforcement officers must learn this distinction because, for officers to lawfully seize items that have been discarded within a constitutionally protected area, all elements of the plain view doctrine must be satisfied or any item of evidence seized will be inadmissible in court. When law enforcement officers attempt to justify a seizure of property on the ground that it was abandoned, they must be prepared to prove abandonment.

The remainder of this chapter is devoted to a discussion of specific facts and circumstances bearing on the issue of abandonment, as illustrated by decisions of courts throughout the United States. These facts and circumstances can be classified into three broad categories:

- Indications of intent to abandon property
- Lawfulness of police behavior
- Reasonable expectation of privacy in the property

These categories are not intended to be a rigid classification scheme but are merely offered as a useful vehicle for organizing the discussion of individual court decisions on abandonment. Abandonment is a subtle and flexible concept and is not susceptible to finely tuned formulas or bright-line rules. Courts, therefore, must consider all the relevant facts and circumstances in determining whether abandonment has occurred in a given case.

Indications of Intent to Abandon Property

An important consideration of courts in determining whether property has been abandoned is the intent of the person vacating or discarding the property to relinquish all title, possession, or claim to that property. "[I]ntent may be inferred from words spoken, acts done, and other objective facts." *United States v. Colbert,* 474 F.2d 174, 176 (5th Cir. 1973). Sometimes intent to abandon is easy to establish, such as when a person voluntarily throws an object away, without any inducement by the police. In many situations, however, a person's intent to abandon property is not so easily established. The following discussion highlights the various indications of intent relied on by the courts in determining abandonment. The discussion is divided into three parts—premises, objects, and motor vehicles—because intent to abandon is determined in different ways for each kind of property.

PREMISES. In *Abel v. United States,* 362 U.S. 217, 80 S.Ct. 683, 4 L.Ed.2d 668 (1960), officers of the Immigration and Naturalization Service arrested the defendant in his hotel room, under an administrative arrest warrant, and charged him with illegally being in the United States. Before he was escorted out of his room, the defendant was permitted to pack his personal belongings. He packed nearly everything in the room except for a few things that he left on a windowsill and that he put in a wastebasket. He then checked out of the hotel, turned in his keys, and paid his bill. Shortly thereafter, an FBI agent, with the permission of the hotel management, searched the defendant's room without a warrant. In the wastebasket, the FBI agent found a hollow pencil containing microfilm and a block of wood containing a "cipher pad." The Court held that the search for and seizure of the pencil and block of wood were legal:

These two items were found by an agent of the F.B.I. in the course of a search he undertook of petitioner's hotel room, immediately after petitioner had paid his bill and vacated the room. They were found in the room's wastepaper basket, where petitioner had put them while packing his belongings and preparing to leave. No pretense is made that this search by the F.B.I. was for any purpose other than to gather evidence of crime, that is, evidence of petitioner's espionage. As such, however, it was entirely lawful, although undertaken without a warrant. This is so for the reason that at the time of the search petitioner had vacated the room. The hotel then had the exclusive right to its possession, and the hotel management freely gave its consent that the search be made. Nor was it unlawful to seize the entire contents of the wastepaper basket, even though some of its contents had no connection with crime. So far as the record shows, petitioner had abandoned these articles. He had thrown them away. So far as he was concerned, they were bona vacantia. There can be nothing unlawful in the Government's appropriation of such abandoned property. . . . The two items which were eventually introduced in evidence were assertedly means for the commission of espionage, and were themselves seizable as such. These two items having been lawfully seized by the Government in connection with an investigation of crime, we encounter no basis for discussing further their admissibility as evidence. 362 U.S. at 241, 80 S.Ct. at 698, 4 L.Ed.2d at 687–88.

In another case involving a hotel room, a court found that the defendant had abandoned a room he had rented on March 23, when he failed to pay his bill on March 28 and did not return to or communicate with the hotel before his arrest on April 8. At the time he rented the room, the defendant said he intended to stay only one night. A search of the defendant's baggage left in the room was therefore held not to violate his property rights. *United States v. Cowan,* 396 F.2d 83 (2d Cir. 1968). In *State v. Oken,* 569 A.2d 1218 (Me. 1990), the Maine Supreme Judicial Court found that, at 8:30 A.M. on November 17, when the police searched room 48 of the Coachman Motor Inn, the defendant had abandoned the room. Even though the defendant still retained the room key and checkout time was not until 11:00 A.M. on the 17th, the court based its conclusion of abandonment on the following observations of the motion justice:

> "[N]o later than five and one-half hours after he checked into the Coachman, he drove to Freeport and checked into the Freeport Inn. He left nothing in Room 48 except a bloody jersey, a half bottle of vodka and some orange juice. He left no luggage. According to the manager and according to common sense, this is consistent with a person who has left and does not intend to return. From the police logs at the scene of the crime, it is clear that defendant did not return to the Coachman prior to approximately 1:30 A.M. on the 17th. From the motel manager's observations, we know defendant was not at the Coachman at 4:45 A.M. There is no evidence that defendant returned to the Coachman between 1:30 A.M. and 4:45 A.M. The bed in Room 48 was not slept in. Defendant was still in Freeport at 10:00 A.M. on the 17th and was extending his stay." 569 A.2d at 1220–21.

In *United States v. Hoey,* 983 F.2d 890 (8th Cir. 1993), the court found that the following facts established abandonment of an apartment: the defendant personally told her landlord she was leaving, she was six weeks behind in her rent, she held a moving sale, and her neighbor saw her leave. Courts have found abandonment of an apartment even in cases in which the abandoning party had time left on the rental period:

Baggett quit his job, received pay for one day's work, told several people that he was going to New Orleans to get a job, paid all bills that he owed except one, told his friends in Little Rock good-bye on the 11th, turned the apartment keys over to the owner, and took all personal belongings to New Orleans with him. Of course, had he returned within the two days before his rent came due, he could not have gone into his apartment for Ballard [the landlord] had the keys. The fact that the rent was paid up for three days after Baggett left does not mean that the apartment had not been abandoned. *Baggett v. State*, 494 S.W.2d 717, 719 (Ark. 1973).

The following quotation from a case involving a warrantless search of a house illustrates other indications of intent to abandon:

[I]t was clearly established that even though the Mannings had rented the . . . house for thirty days, they departed after the first day leaving no personal belongings. The door was unlocked, food was on the table, and dishwater was in the sink. Thirty days later the same condition prevailed. Moreover, the decayed food created a stench, the grass was uncut, and the weeds had grown high.

These circumstances strongly indicate that the Mannings had abandoned the house. . . . *United States v. Manning*, 440 F.2d 1105, 1111 (5th Cir. 1971).

The nonpublic areas of a business office come within the Fourth Amendment's protection against unreasonable searches and seizures. If the office is abandoned by its occupant, however, it no longer has this protection. The indications of intent to abandon for an office are similar to those for a room or house. In *Mullins v. United States*, 487 F.2d 581 (8th Cir. 1973), U.S. postal inspectors, without a warrant, searched for and seized business records from an office that had previously been rented by the defendant. The defendant claimed that the search and seizure were illegal because he did not intend to abandon the office and the records kept there. The court found that the facts indicated an intent to abandon. The search and seizure were made on June 12, 1972. The defendant had rented the office from May 1, 1971, through October 31, 1971, but had left the state in August 1971. No rent had been paid for the office beginning November 1, 1971, nor did the defendant, his wife, or any business associate or employee visit the office after November 1, 1971. Finally, the office had been padlocked by the U.S. District Attorney during February 1972.

The mere absence of a person from the premises does not make the premises abandoned, unless the person had an intent to abandon the premises. Therefore, in a case in which the defendant's absence from his apartment was involuntary because of his arrest and incarceration, the court held that the prosecution should bear an especially heavy burden of showing that he intended to abandon it. The prosecution did not satisfy this burden by merely showing the defendant's absence without showing any other indications of intent to abandon. *United States v. Robinson*, 430 F.2d 1141 (6th Cir. 1970).

OBJECTS. Intent to abandon objects involves many of the same considerations as intent to abandon premises. For example, a strong indication of a person's intent to abandon an object is leaving the object unattended and unclaimed for a long period of time. In *United States v. Gulledge*, 469 F.2d 713 (5th Cir. 1972), two men left a U-Haul trailer at a service station, asking permission to leave it there for two or three days. The men stated that "everything we own is in the trailer." Ten days later, the men not having returned, the service station attendant called law enforcement authorities. The trailer was searched without a warrant, and stolen whiskey was found. The court held that the search was legal because the property had been abandoned.

Another indication of intent to abandon an object is the defendant's own words of disclaimer of ownership or possession. In *United States v. Lee,* 916 F.2d 814 (2d Cir. 1990), the defendant on three separate occasions told officers he was traveling without luggage. When informed that a maroon suitcase was sitting unclaimed in the baggage area, he adamantly denied that it was his. The court held that the defendant intended to abandon his suitcase and thereby forfeited any legitimate expectation of privacy in it. Mere disclaimer of ownership *alone,* however, may not provide sufficient indication of intent to abandon.

> Perea's statement that the duffel bag did not belong to him was a truthful statement of fact that cannot alone provide a basis for inferring an intent on his part to abandon the bag. While he may have also intended to disassociate himself from the incriminating contents of the bag, Professor LaFave has cautioned that "a mere disclaimer of ownership in an effort to avoid making an incriminating statement in response to police questioning should not alone be deemed to constitute abandonment." . . . The question is whether the owner has "voluntarily discarded, left behind, or otherwise relinquished his interest in the property in question so that he could no longer retain a reasonable expectation of privacy with regard to it at the time of the search." Thus, if a person lawfully arrested disclaims any interest in the container and declines to take it with him, his readiness to depart the scene and leave an object such as a suitcase or briefcase in the control of no one may fairly be characterized as abandonment. *United States v. Perea,* 848 F.Supp. 1101, 1103 (E.D.N.Y. 1994).

In other cases involving warrantless searches and seizures of objects, the object is often picked up by a law enforcement officer immediately after it is dropped, thrown away, or otherwise discarded by a person. In these cases, courts cannot rely on the length of time the object has been left unattended to determine whether the object has been abandoned. Courts must look to other circumstances such as the conduct of the defendant and the manner of disposal of the object. In *Smith v. Ohio,* 494 U.S. 541, 110 S.Ct. 1288, 108 L.Ed.2d 464 (1990), officers in an unmarked police vehicle observed the defendant carrying a brown paper grocery bag. One of the officers asked the defendant to "come here a minute" and identified himself as a police officer. The defendant threw the bag he was carrying onto the hood of his car and turned to face the approaching officer. The officer rebuffed the defendant's attempt to protect the bag, opened it, and discovered drug paraphernalia. The U.S. Supreme Court said: "[A] citizen who attempts to protect his private property from inspection, after throwing it on a car to respond to a police officer's inquiry, clearly has not abandoned that property." 494 U.S. at 543–44, 110 S.Ct. at 1290, 108 L.Ed.2d at 468. In *People v. Anderson,* 298 N.Y.S.2d 698, 246 N.E.2d 508 (N.Y. 1969), a police officer approached the defendant without probable cause to make an arrest, and the defendant dropped a tin box to the ground. The officer immediately picked up the box, opened it, and found heroin. The court held that the evidence was insufficient to constitute an abandonment:

> There is no proof that the defendant threw it away or attempted to dispose of it in any manner which might have manifested the requisite intention to abandon. Moreover, the police officer's testimony reveals that he picked up the box so soon after it had been dropped that it is impossible to determine whether or not the defendant, if given the opportunity, would have picked up the box himself. Absent any such proof, the seizure of the tin box under the circumstances of this case cannot be sustained. *People v. Anderson,* 298 N.Y.S.2d 698, 699, 246 N.E.2d 508, 509 (N.Y. 1969).

When, however, the manner of disposal indicates that a defendant intended to relinquish possession or control of property because of consciousness of guilt or fear of potential apprehension, the courts usually find abandonment. In *United States v. Morgan*, 936 F.2d 1561 (10th Cir. 1991), the court found that the defendant voluntarily abandoned a gym bag based on the following facts and circumstances:

- When he saw police, the defendant threw the bag off a porch.

- He made no attempt to retrieve the bag or to request officers or anyone else to retrieve it for him.

- He made no attempt to protect the bag or its contents from inspection.

- He made no manifestations, verbal or otherwise, to indicate that he retained a reasonable privacy interest in the bag.

The court noted that "[w]hile an abandonment must be voluntary, '[t]he existence of police pursuit or investigation at the time of abandonment does not of itself render the abandonment involuntary.'" 936 F.2d at 1570.

In *United States v. Morris*, 738 F.Supp. 20 (D.D.C. 1990), the court held that, once the defendant stuffed a plastic bag containing vials into the crevice between bus seats, he surrendered any reasonable expectation of privacy he may have had in the contents of the bag prior to that time. The court pointed out that the defendant's intent to relinquish possession and control was most clearly evidenced by the defendant's decision not to return to the row of seats in which he had left his bag.

> The critical fact in this case is that the defendant made a decision to place his property in a location that was out of control and open to the public. At the time he placed the bag between the seats and then left the area, nothing precluded another passenger from occupying that seat or the one next to it. Indeed, nothing would have prevented such a passenger from placing his/her hand between the seats and discovering the bag. 738 F.Supp. at 23.

Some courts find an intent to abandon property when the defendant fails to object or take any other affirmative action but merely allows evidence to be seized in the ordinary course of events. In *United States v. Cox*, 428 F.2d 683 (7th Cir. 1970), the defendant was in jail after being arrested for bank robbery. He was given a haircut pursuant to routine jail procedures, and the hair clippings were turned over to the FBI, at their request, and used as evidence. In response to the defendant's claim of an illegal search and seizure, the court said:

> At no time has defendant objected to the legality of the prison procedures under which he received his haircut. He has never claimed that the haircut was illegally or improperly given. The thrust of his contention is rather that a warrant should have been obtained before the shorn locks were appropriated by the state officer for analysis. Cox, however, never indicated any desire or intention to retain possession of the hair after it had been scissored from his head. Clippings such as those preserved in the instant case are ordinarily abandoned after being cut. Cox in fact left his hair and has never claimed otherwise. The deputy sheriff was not obliged to inform him that, if abandoned, his hair would be taken and analyzed. Having voluntarily abandoned his property, in this case his hair, Cox may not object to its appropriation by the government. 428 F.2d at 687–88.

MOTOR VEHICLES. Motor vehicles are unique for purposes of the discussion of abandonment in that they are treated both as premises and as objects. In *United States v. Hastamorir*, 881 F.2d 1551 (11th Cir. 1989), the court held that the defendant's repeated disclaimers of knowledge of, or interest in, a vehicle or its contents ended any reasonable expectation of privacy in the vehicle and was an abandonment of the vehicle for Fourth Amendment purposes. In *Thom v. State,* 450 S.W.2d 550 (Ark. 1970), the defendant, who was tampering with a cigarette machine, left his car in the street and fled on foot to avoid apprehension by an officer. The court said:

> Sometimes an automobile takes on the characteristics of a man's castle. Other times an automobile takes on the characteristic of an overcoat—that is, it is movable and can be discarded by the possessor at will. If appellant in his endeavors to avoid the clutches of the law had discarded his overcoat to make his flight more speedy, no one would think that an officer was unreasonably invading his privacy or security in picking up the overcoat and searching it thoroughly. In that situation most people would agree that the fleeing suspect had abandoned his coat as a matter of expediency as well as any rights relative to its search and seizure. What difference can there be when a fleeing burglar abandons his automobile to escape the clutches of the law? We can see no distinction and consequently hold that when property is abandoned officers in making a search thereof do not violate any rights or security of a citizen guaranteed under the Fourth Amendment. 450 S.W.2d at 552.

In *United States v. Tate,* 821 F.2d 1328 (8th Cir. 1987), the court held that the defendant, who fled on foot from a stolen truck after shooting two troopers who had legally stopped the truck, abandoned the truck and its contents and any expectation of privacy he might have had in either.

Note that if an officer has probable cause to search a motor vehicle, he or she may also be able to justify a search of the vehicle under the *Carroll* doctrine (see Chapter 11).

Lawfulness of Police Behavior

"An abandonment that occurs in response to proper police activity has not been coerced in violation of the Fourth Amendment." *United States v. Miller,* 974 F.2d 953, 958 (8th Cir. 1992). The following are examples of cases in which a person discarded or disclaimed ownership of an object in response to the lawful activities of the police, and courts considered the object abandoned and therefore seizable without a warrant or other justification:

- An officer asked the defendant, a bus passenger, whether she owned a tote bag on a rack above her seat and she denied ownership. *United States v. Lewis,* 921 F.2d 1294 (D.C.Cir. 1990).

- As Drug Enforcement Administration (DEA) agents were approaching the defendant's car to lawfully arrest him, the defendant opened the passenger door and threw down a packet later determined to contain cocaine. *United States v. Koessel,* 706 F.2d 271 (8th Cir. 1983).

- Officers in a public place asked the defendant questions about suitcases in the trunk of a car, and the defendant abandoned them by denying ownership of them. *United States v. Karman,* 849 F.2d 928 (5th Cir. 1988).

- Officers, attempting to execute a valid search warrant, temporarily detained the defendant at the scene of the search, and the defendant discarded a package containing incriminating evidence. *State v. Romeo,* 203 A.2d 23 (N.J. 1964).

In a case involving only *attempted* unlawful police activity, a law enforcement officer, without probable cause or reasonable articulable suspicion, pursued the defendant on mere suspicion of involvement in a drug transaction. As the officer approached the defendant, the defendant tossed away a small rock. A moment later, the officer tackled the defendant. The rock he threw away was later determined to be crack cocaine. The court held that, although the seizure of the defendant was illegal, the defendant tossed away the crack cocaine *before* he was seized. Therefore, the abandonment of the cocaine did not occur as a result of unlawful police *activity,* and the cocaine was admissible in court.

> [A]ssuming that [Officer] Pertoso's pursuit in the present case constituted a "show of authority" enjoining Hodari to halt, since Hodari did not comply with that injunction he was not seized until he was tackled. The cocaine abandoned while he was running was in this case not the fruit of a seizure, and his motion to exclude evidence of it was properly denied. *California v. Hodari D.,* 499 U.S. 621, 629, 111 S.Ct. 1547, 1552, 113 L.Ed.2d 690, 699 (1991).

"When an individual abandons an object in response to an officer's violation of his constitutional rights, the violation taints the abandonment making it involuntary." *United States v. Mendez,* 827 F.Supp. 1280, 1284 (S.D. Tex. 1993). A stop of two black occupants of a car parked with its engine running in a black neighborhood merely because the officer did not recognize the men was held illegal in *United States v. Beck,* 602 F.2d 726 (5th Cir. 1979). The court found that the discarding of drugs and paraphernalia by the men in connection with the stop was not a voluntary abandonment:

> While it is true that a criminal defendant's voluntary abandonment of evidence can remove the taint of an illegal stop or arrest . . . it is equally true that for this to occur the abandonment must be truly voluntary and not merely the product of police misconduct. . . . In this case, it seems clear that the contraband was abandoned because of the illegal stop of the Chevrolet. After the stop was made, and while [Officer] Spears was pulling his patrol car in front of the Chevrolet, he observed the marijuana cigarette thrown out Beck's window. The bag containing marijuana and the syringe were presumably discarded at the same time. These acts of abandonment do not reflect the mere coincidental decision of Beck and his passenger to discard their narcotics; it would be sheer fiction to presume they were caused by anything other than the illegal stop. Had Spears observed these items inside the Chevrolet during an unlawful stop they would be suppressed . . . ; the fact that Beck and his passenger threw them out the window onto the ground after the commencement of an illegal stop and just prior to an unlawful arrest does not change this result. 602 F.2d at 729–30.

Reasonable Expectation of Privacy in the Property

As shown in the discussion of the open fields doctrine, since the U.S. Supreme Court decision in *Katz v. United States,* the courts increasingly have analyzed the legality of warrantless searches and seizures in terms of their intrusion upon the defendant's reasonable expectation of privacy. This trend has extended also to cases involving vacated or discarded property. The Minnesota Supreme Court explained:

> In the law of property, the question . . . is whether the owner has voluntarily, intentionally, and unconditionally relinquished his interest in the property so that another, having acquired possession, may successfully assert his superior interest. In the law of search and seizure, however, the question is whether the defendant

has, in discarding the property, relinquished his reasonable expectation of privacy so that its seizure and search is reasonable within the limits of the Fourth Amendment. In essence, what is abandoned is not necessarily the defendant's property, but his reasonable expectation of privacy therein. *City of St. Paul v. Vaughn,* 237 N.W.2d 365, 370–71 (Minn. 1975).

In a case involving supposedly vacated premises, law enforcement officers were investigating a possible arson in a building gutted by fire. The fire occurred on April 14, 1968, and the officers entered the building, made observations, and took photographs on April 24, 1968. Evidence showed that the house had been boarded up on April 14. Thereafter the owner went to the house every day, and both she and the defendant kept some of their personal effects in the house. The defendant claimed that the observations and photographs of the officers were a product of an illegal search and seizure. The court said:

> The uncontradicted evidence before the court was that the building was not abandoned. On April 24, 1968, it still contained personal effects and had been boarded up to keep the public out.
>
> The test to be used in determining whether a place is a constitutionally protected area within the meaning of the Fourth Amendment is . . . "whether the person has exhibited a reasonable expectation of privacy, and, if so, whether that expectation has been violated by unreasonable governmental intrusion." In the instant matter the owner of the dwelling house clearly demonstrated her expectation of privacy as to the interior of the house and its contents by boarding up the doorways, which were damaged by fire. That expectation was violated by the intrusion of the police on April 24, 1968. *Swan v. Superior Court, County of Los Angeles,* 87 Cal.Rptr. 280, 282 (Cal. 1970).

Courts differ on the extent of a person's reasonable expectation of privacy in discarded objects. The controversy has centered around the search and seizure of trash or garbage by law enforcement officers. In a leading case in this area, law enforcement officers, acting without a warrant, found marijuana in a trash can in the open backyard area of the defendant's residence. The court held that the marijuana in the trash can was not abandoned for the following reasons:

> As we have seen, the trash can was within a few feet of the back door of defendants' home and required trespass for its inspection. It was an adjunct to the domestic economy. . . . Placing the marijuana in the trash can, so situated and used, was not an abandonment unless as to persons authorized to remove the receptacle's contents, such as trashmen. . . . The marijuana itself was not visible without "rummaging" in the receptacle. So far as appears defendants alone resided at the house. In the light of the combined facts and circumstances it appears that defendants exhibited an expectation of privacy, and we believe that expectation was reasonable under the circumstances of the case. We can readily ascribe many reasons why residents would not want their castaway clothing, letters, medicine bottles or other telltale refuse and trash to be examined by neighbors or others, at least not until the trash has lost its identity and meaning by becoming part of a large conglomeration of trash elsewhere. Half truths leading to rumor and gossip may readily flow from an attempt to "read" the contents of another's trash. *People v. Edwards,* 80 Cal.Rptr. 633, 638, 458 P.2d 713, 718 (Cal. 1969).

Other courts have generally agreed with the holding in the *Edwards* case and have found a violation of a defendant's reasonable expectation of privacy where the trash searched or seized was located within the curtilage of the defendant's house. *Ball v. State*, 205 N.W.2d 353 (Wis. 1973). In *United States v. Certain Real Property*, 719 F.Supp. 1396 (E.D.Mich. 1989), a police officer, disguised as a trash collector, walked up the defendant's driveway and invaded the curtilage to retrieve trash bags placed by the doorway for collection. In holding the seizure illegal, the court said that "the government decided to do directly what it already could do indirectly, and that trip up the side driveway makes all the difference for fourth amendment purposes." 719 F.Supp. at 1407. In a footnote the court said that the police could have had the regular garbage collector deliver the garbage bags to them after they had been removed from the curtilage of the home.

Where garbage is left *outside* the curtilage of the home, however, the U.S. Supreme Court held that the Fourth Amendment does not prohibit the warrantless search and seizure of the garbage. In *California v. Greenwood*, 486 U.S. 35, 108 S.Ct. 1625, 100 L.Ed.2d 30 (1988), police suspected the defendant of narcotics trafficking, but did not have probable cause to search the defendant's house. Police obtained from the regular trash collector garbage bags left at the curb in front of the defendant's house. On the basis of items found in the bags, police obtained a search warrant for the home and discovered controlled substances.

The defendants claimed an expectation of privacy with respect to their trash, but the Court held that even if they had an expectation of privacy, it was not one that society was prepared to accept as reasonable.

> [R]espondents exposed their garbage to the public sufficiently to defeat their claim to Fourth Amendment protection. It is common knowledge that plastic garbage bags left on or at the side of a public street are readily accessible to animals, children, scavengers, snoops, and other members of the public. . . . Moreover, respondents placed their refuse at the curb for the express purpose of conveying it to a third party, the trash collector, who might himself have sorted through respondent's trash or permitted others, such as the police, to do so. Accordingly, having deposited their garbage "in an area particularly suited for public inspection and, in a manner of speaking, public consumption, for the express purpose of having strangers take it," . . . respondents could have had no reasonable expectation of privacy in the inculpatory items that they discarded. . . . [T]he police cannot reasonably be expected to avert their eyes from evidence of criminal activity that could have been observed by any member of the public. 486 U.S. at 40–41, 108 S.Ct. at 1628–29, 100 L.Ed.2d at 36–37.

In *United States v. Dunkel*, 900 F.2d 105 (7th Cir. 1990), the court found that the defendant, a dentist, had no reasonable expectation of privacy in a dumpster located off the parking lot of a building that he owned and that housed several other businesses. All used the same dumpster, and the parking lot and dumpster were accessible to patients, employees, and the general public. No warrant was needed to search for and seize financial records discarded in the dumpster. In *United States v. Walker*, 624 F.Supp. 99 (D.Md. 1985), law enforcement officers found a paper shopping bag out in the open alongside a road in a sparsely populated rural setting. No attempt had been made to protect the bag from damage from the elements, from removal by a passerby, or from disturbance by an animal. The court held that, despite the defendant's claim that he did not intend to abandon the bag, by leaving the bag in the manner he did, the defendant was no longer retaining a reasonable expectation of privacy.

7. Property is abandoned, for purposes of the Fourth Amendment, if its owner has voluntarily discarded, left behind, or otherwise relinquished his or her interest in the property so as to no longer retain a reasonable expectation of privacy with regard to it. Such property may be searched and seized without a warrant or other justification and without the Fourth Amendment being violated.

8. Leaving property unattended for a long period of time is a strong indication of intent to abandon property.

9. Disclaimer of interest in property accompanied by departing the scene, making no attempt to retrieve or protect the property, and leaving the property in the care of no one are strong indications of intent to abandon property.

10. Discarding property as a direct result of the unlawful activity of a law enforcement officer is not voluntary abandonment but a forced response to the unlawful police behavior.

11. A person who establishes a reasonable expectation of privacy in property has not abandoned that property, and the property may not be searched or seized without a warrant or other legal justification.

12. When a person leaves garbage outside the curtilage of a home, the person no longer has a reasonable expectation of privacy in the garbage and the Fourth Amendment does not prohibit the warrantless search and seizure of the garbage.

Summary

A law enforcement officer may search for items of evidence lying in the open fields without probable cause, search warrant, or other legal justification without violating a person's Fourth Amendment rights and may seize items if he or she has probable cause to believe the items are "seizable" under the law of the officer's jurisdiction. An officer may also legally make observations from a vantage point in the open fields into constitutionally protected areas, to detect criminal activity or evidence.

The open fields are the area lying outside the curtilage of a person's home or business. Whether a piece of land or building falls within the curtilage can be determined by consideration of the following factors: the proximity of the area claimed to be curtilage to the home, the inclusion of the area within an enclosure surrounding the home, the nature of the uses to which the area is put, and the steps taken by the resident to protect the area from observation by passersby.

Since the 1967 U.S. Supreme Court decision in *Katz v. United States,* which held that "the Fourth Amendment protects people, not places," courts have increasingly analyzed the legality of warrantless searches in terms of the defendants' reasonable expectation of privacy, in addition to the concepts of curtilage and open fields. Law enforcement officers, therefore, must be careful to avoid warrantless intrusions not only into the curtilage of a person's house but also into any area that the person reasonably seeks to preserve as private.

A law enforcement officer, without probable cause, warrant, or other legal justification, may retrieve items of evidence that have been abandoned by their owners without violating Fourth Amendment rights. Property has been abandoned when its owner has voluntarily discarded, left behind, or otherwise relinquished his or her interest in the property so as to no longer retain a reasonable expectation of privacy with regard to it. Among the factors that the courts rely on in determining whether a given object has been abandoned by its owner are the following:

- *Indications of intent to abandon property.* Indications of intent to abandon *premises* can be divided into positive acts and omissions. Positive indications of intent to abandon include removing personal belongings, paying final rent and other bills, turning in keys, quitting local employment, and taking leave of friends. Omissions indicating intent to abandon include failing to pay rent for a long time, long absence from the premises, failure to communicate with anyone regarding the premises, and failure to attend to or care for the premises. Intent to abandon an *object* is indicated by leaving the object unattended for an unreasonable period of time, discarding the object out of consciousness of guilt or fear of apprehension, disclaiming interest in the object and leaving it unprotected in the care of no one, and allowing the object to be taken away in the ordinary course of events, without objection. Intent to abandon *vehicles* is determined by the same considerations as those for premises and objects.

- *Lawfulness of police behavior.* Objects discarded as a direct result of the unlawful activity of a law enforcement officer will not be considered voluntarily abandoned.
- *Reasonable expectation of privacy in the property.* Even though property has been vacated or thrown away, under certain circumstances, a person may reasonably retain an expectation of privacy with respect to the property. Such property is not considered abandoned, and a search and seizure of it, without a warrant or probable cause, will be illegal.

Determining whether property is abandoned is similar to determining whether it is in the open fields, in that both require a consideration not only of a person's property rights but also of the person's rights of privacy. Such determinations will always be difficult for the courts as well as for law enforcement officers. In the absence of an emergency, officers should obtain a search warrant whenever possible.

Key Holdings from Major Cases

Hester v. United States (1924). "[T]he special protection accorded by the Fourth Amendment to the people in their 'persons, houses, papers and effects' is not extended to the open fields." 265 U.S. 57, 59, 44 S.Ct. 445, 446, 68 L.Ed. 898, 900.

Oliver v. United States (1984). "[A]n individual may not legitimately demand privacy for activities conducted out of doors in fields, except in the area immediately surrounding the home." 466 U.S. 170, 178, 104 S.Ct. 1735, 1741, 80 L.Ed.2d 214, 224.

"[O]pen fields do not provide the setting for those intimate activities that the [Fourth] Amendment is intended to shelter from government interference or surveillance. There is no societal interest in protecting the privacy of those activities such as the cultivation of crops, that occur in open fields. Moreover, as a practical matter these lands usually are accessible to the public and the police in ways that a home, an office or commercial structure would not be. It is not generally true that fences or 'No Trespassing' signs effectively bar the public from viewing open fields in rural areas. And . . . the public and police lawfully may survey lands from the air. For these reasons, the asserted expectation of privacy in open fields is not an expectation that 'society recognizes as reasonable.'" 466 U.S. at 179, 104 S.Ct. at 1741, 80 L.Ed.2d at 224.

To determine whether property to be searched falls within the curtilage of a house, the law enforcement officer must consider "the factors that determine whether an individual reasonably may expect that an area immediately adjacent to the home will remain private." 466 U.S. at 180, 104 S.Ct. at 1742, 80 L.Ed.2d at 225.

"[T]he term 'open fields' may include any unoccupied or undeveloped area outside of the curtilage. An open field need be neither 'open' nor a 'field' as those terms are used in common speech. For example . . . a thickly wooded area nonetheless may be an open field as that term is used in construing the Fourth Amendment." 466 U.S. at 180 n.11, 104 S.Ct. at 1742 n.11, 80 L.Ed.2d at 225 n.11.

United States v. Dunn (1987). "[C]urtilage questions should be resolved with particular reference to four factors: the proximity of the area claimed to be curtilage to the home, whether the area is included within an enclosure surrounding the home, the nature of the uses to which the area is put, and the steps taken by the resident to protect the area from observation by people passing by." 480 U.S. 294, 301, 107 S.Ct. 1134, 1139, 94 L.Ed.2d 326, 334–35.

"[T]he primary focus [in determining curtilage] is whether the area in question harbors those intimate activities associated with domestic life and the privacies of the home." 480 U.S. at 301 n.4, 107 S.Ct. at 1139 n.4, 94 L.Ed.2d at 335 n.4 (1987).

California v. Ciraolo (1986). "That the area is within the curtilage does not itself bar all police observation. The Fourth Amendment protection of the home has never been extended to require law enforcement officers to shield their eyes when passing by a home on public thoroughfares. Nor does the mere fact that an individual has taken measures to restrict some views of his activities preclude an officer's observations from a public vantage point where he has a right to be and which renders the activities clearly visible." 476 U.S. 207, 213, 106 S.Ct. 1809, 1812, 90 L.Ed.2d 210, 216.

Dow Chemical Co. v. United States (1986). "[T]he open areas of an industrial plant complex with numerous plant structures spread over an area of 2,000 acres are not analogous to the 'curtilage' of a dwelling for purposes of aerial surveillance; such an industrial complex is more comparable to an open field and as such it is open to the view and observation of persons in aircraft lawfully in the public airspace immediately above or sufficiently near the area for the reach of cameras. . . . [T]he taking of aerial photographs of an industrial plant complex from navigable airspace is not a search prohibited by the Fourth Amendment." 476 U.S. 227, 239, 106 S.Ct. 1819, 1827, 90 L.Ed.2d 226, 238.

Florida v. Riley (1989). The defendant, who had left the sides and roof of his greenhouse partially open "could not reasonably have expected that his greenhouse was protected from public or official observation from a helicopter had it been flying within the navigable airspace for fixed-wing aircraft.

"Nor . . . does it make a difference for Fourth Amendment purposes that the helicopter was flying at 400 feet when the officer saw what was growing in the greenhouse through the partially open roof and sides of the structure. We would have a different case if flying at that altitude had been contrary to law or regulation. But helicopters are not bound by the lower limits of the navigable airspace allowed to other aircraft. Any member of the public could legally have been flying over Riley's property in a helicopter at the altitude of 400 feet and could have observed Riley's greenhouse." 488 U.S. 445, 449–53, 109 S.Ct. 693, 696–97, 102 L.Ed.2d 835, 842.

Abel v. United States (1960). "There can be nothing unlawful in the Government's appropriation of . . . abandoned property." 362 U.S. 217, 241, 80 S.Ct. 683, 698, 4 L.Ed.2d 668, 687.

Smith v. Ohio (1990). "[A] citizen who attempts to protect his private property from inspection, after throwing it on a car to respond to a police officer's inquiry, clearly has not abandoned that property." 494 U.S. 541, 543–44, 110 S.Ct. 1288, 1290, 108 L.Ed.2d 464, 468.

California v. Greenwood (1988). "[H]aving deposited their garbage 'in an area particularly suited for public inspection and, in a manner of speaking, public consumption, for the express purpose of having strangers take it,' . . . respondents could have had no reasonable expectation of privacy in the inculpatory items that they discarded. . . . [T]he police cannot reasonably be expected to avert their eyes from evidence of criminal activity that could have been observed by any member of the public." 486 U.S. 35, 40–41, 108 S.Ct. 1625, 1629, 100 L.Ed.2d 30, 36–37.

Review and Discussion Questions

1. Does the term *open fields* include any place that is public, including forests, lakes, city streets, and stadiums?

2. Which of the following, if any, would be considered a house for purposes of the Fourth Amendment?

   a. Tent

   b. Lean-to

   c. Motor home

   d. Sailboat

   e. Cave

3. The dissent in *California v. Hodari D.* said that "a police officer may now fire his weapon at an innocent citizen and not implicate the Fourth Amendment—as long as he misses his target." If a person throws away an item of criminal evidence after being illegally shot at by a police officer, is that item abandoned?

4. Would a person's Fourth Amendment rights be violated by law enforcement officers who, after illegally arresting the person, entered the person's fenced and posted rural property to observe a marijuana field surrounded by a forest?

5. Compare the plain view doctrine, the open fields doctrine, and the abandonment doctrine with respect to the reasonable expectation of privacy.

6. If a person abandons property inside the curtilage of someone else's property, may a law enforcement officer seize the abandoned property?

7. Is observing activities inside a house in the country by looking into a window with binoculars from a field or forest any different from observing activities in a tenth-story apartment from a window in an adjacent apartment building?

8. Does the value of an object have any bearing on the question of whether a person abandoned it? Can a person who runs away from his or her automobile to avoid apprehension by the police be said to give up all reasonable expectations of privacy in the vehicle? What if the person locks the vehicle before fleeing?

9. For each place listed in question 2, what indications of intent to abandon would give a law enforcement officer authority to search for and seize items left at that place?

10. If a person undergoes emergency surgery after being shot by police while driving a stolen automobile, which of the following, if any, has the person abandoned?

    a. Clothing worn at the time of the shooting

    b. Wallets and other items in the pockets of the clothing

    c. Bullets surgically removed

    d. The automobile

1. On April 28, 1995, at approximately 9:00 P.M., officer Jose Arroyo and his partner were on duty in plain clothes in an unmarked police van as part of the Taxi and Livery Task Force. Arroyo followed a yellow medallion cab for three blocks until it pulled over to the side of the road and discharged two passengers, one of whom was defendant. The defendant and the other man walked quickly away from the cab after exiting the vehicle. As the officers walked toward the cab to see if the driver was alright, the defendant and his companion stopped walking and looked in the officers' direction, whereupon the defendant dropped the backpack he had been carrying to the ground. Arroyo turned his attention to the defendant, who stood 12 to 15 feet away, and, pointing to the backpack, asked, "Is that your bag?" At the time, Arroyo was wearing his shield around his neck. The defendant responded, "No." Arroyo thereupon picked up the bag and, noticing that it was "dead-center heavy," placed his hand under the bag, squeezed it, and felt an L-shaped hard, metal object inside the bag. Arroyo then placed his hand inside the bag and felt a pistol and again asked the defendant, this time in Spanish, "This isn't your bag?" The defendant replied "Yes, it's my bag." Defendant was then placed under arrest.

   As the defendant was being handcuffed, Arroyo explained to defendant that he was being arrested for carrying the gun, at which point the defendant declared that the weapon belonged to a friend. A frisk of the defendant revealed a clip containing five bullets, which corresponded to the weapon found in the backpack. At the precinct, following *Miranda* warnings in Spanish, which the defendant stated he understood, the defendant told police that a friend had left him the weapon.

   Although crediting the testimony of Officer Arroyo, the hearing court nonetheless granted the motion to suppress the physical evidence and the defendant's statements on the basis that illegal police conduct precipitated the abandonment. Was the hearing court correct? *People v. Morales,* 663 N.Y.S.2d 200 (A.D.1 Dept. 1977).

2. On the morning of December 6, 1988, a state trooper and five other police officers went to 68 Calendar Street in the Dorchester section of Boston to execute an arrest warrant on the defendant. The warrant had been issued following the defendant's default on an assault with intent to murder charge in the Dorchester District Court. The police had information that the defendant was at the 68 Calendar Street address, a three-story single-family home occupied by the defendant's family.

   In response to a knock by the officers, the defendant's mother opened the front door of the house, and she was advised that the police were there to execute an arrest warrant for the defendant. The defendant's mother indicated that her son was upstairs. A police officer encountered the defendant as he was coming down the stairs from the second floor and placed him under arrest on the default warrant.

   Before the arrest occurred, a police officer, who had positioned himself behind the house to intercept the defendant if he tried to flee, saw a window opened on the second floor and a briefcase thrown to the yard below. The briefcase, which was thrown by the defendant, landed about six to ten feet from the house in the back yard between the house and a wrought iron fence that separated the yard from the adjacent sidewalk.

   The officer who observed the foregoing entered the back yard to retrieve the briefcase. The officer noticed that the right side latch of the briefcase was unlocked, leaving that side slightly ajar. He proceeded to pry open the right side of the briefcase and to look inside, where he saw a plastic glassine bag containing a white powdery substance which he believed (correctly, as it turned out) to be cocaine. The officer proceeded to explore fully the contents of the briefcase, which included other bags of white powder (cocaine totalling over 200 grams), an empty container of a cutting agent, plastic sandwich bags, $1,750 in cash, a jewelry box with the defendant's name on it, and a receipt for a gold watch.

   The defendant was again placed under arrest, this time for a violation of the controlled substances laws. At the police station, the defendant was advised of his *Miranda* rights and questioned. He admitted to purchasing the cocaine, and he told the police that, when they arrived at the house, he became "nervous" and threw the briefcase out of the second-floor window. Should the defendant's motion to suppress the contents of the briefcase and his statements be granted? *Commonwealth v. Straw,* 665 N.E.2d 80 (Mass. 1996).

3. The testimony and evidence at the hearing on defendant's motion showed that, on February 16, 1996, acting on an anonymous tip, Detectives Bennett and Stephens went to the defendant's property on Territorial Highway, halfway between Lorane and Curtin in rural Douglas County. The highway winds through a remote and heavily wooded area, and the defendant's residence is about a quarter of a mile from the highway, up a steep, narrow, single vehicle driveway. The defendant's mail and newspaper boxes were at the entrance to the driveway. At the right side of the driveway, a sign reading "No Hunting

or Trespassing Under Penalty of Law" was posted on a tree facing the highway. On the left side of the driveway entrance, another sign reading "Posted—No Hunting" was attached to a post. The sign on the left was sprayed with red paint, and a cable was attached to the post and circled around it. Directly across the driveway was a second post and, further to the right, a large tree to which the cable could be attached. The cable was not pulled across the driveway. The large tree and post on the right side had been knocked over in a storm a week or two before the officers' visit.

About 20 feet up the driveway, hanging at an angle, was a black and orange "KEEP OUT" sign posted on a sawed-off tree. The sign faced the driveway. Halfway up the driveway was a red and white sign reading "Guard Dog on Duty" with a picture of a dog. About 100 feet beyond was a large red "STOP" sign on the left-hand side of the driveway. Bennett testified that at the stop sign there was a "partially graveled roadway that goes to the right, looked like somebody was cutting wood off of." Bennett testified that he saw the "No Hunting or Trespassing Under Penalty of Law" sign at the entrance to the driveway, the "Guard Dog on Duty," sign and the "Stop" sign. Stephens testified that he saw the "No Hunting or Trespassing Under Penalty of Law" sign and the "Guard Dog" sign.

The officers proceeded up the driveway, noticing items that they recognized as associated with marijuana growing. In the second-story window of the defendant's residence, they saw a marijuana plant. After the defendant refused to permit the officers to search his residence, they applied for a warrant and searched the property. Holding that the defendant had excluded the public from his property, the trial court granted the defendant's motion to suppress. Was the trial court correct? *State v. Poulos*, 942 P.2d 901 (Or.App. 1997).

4. The Florida Highway Patrol obtained information that a stolen 1983 International truck was located in a gated lot at 5500 Pembroke Road in Hollywood, Florida. Once at that location, the troopers were able to look through the fence and identify the stolen truck. The troopers then made a warrantless entry onto the property to seize the stolen vehicle. While on the property, the troopers discovered other stolen property, which was not observable from outside the fence. After obtaining this information, the troopers applied for a warrant and returned to seize this additional contraband.

The property in question was a fenced private lot. Appellant held a leasehold interest in the property; the owner of the premises described the property as consisting of three adjacent "twenty-five (25) foot lots." The gate to the fence was closed but not locked. According to the testimony of one of the troopers, "the gate had a chain hanging from it and a lock hanging, but it was not

locked." There were vehicles and various vehicle parts located within the fence. A very small warehouse-type structure was situated in the middle of the lot all the way back against the rear fence. One of the troopers testified that the area in which the lot was located was mainly "residential." In any event, no one lived on the premises, and the appellant engaged in no open commercial activity there. Should the appellant's motion to suppress vehicles and vehicle parts seized from the lot be granted? *O'Neal v. State*, 689 So.2d 1135 (Fla.App. 4 Dist. 1997).

5. The evidence presented at the suppression hearing showed the following. Four drug agents of the Marietta-Cobb-Smyrna Narcotics Unit ("MCS") proceeded without a warrant to O'Bryant's home to speak with O'Bryant because they had received an anonymous tip of possible drug dealing. Two MCS agents testified they walked around to the side of the residence because they believed there was a living area in the basement. The state never proved there was a living area in that location and that this activity was not a pretext to further explore O'Bryant's property. Again, there was no response at this door. The agents noticed a black Toyota truck parked in the driveway on the side of the house. Agent Hathaway testified the same truck had been there during an earlier unsuccessful attempt to contact O'Bryant. Agent Cebula testified he had never before seen this truck. Although Agent Cebula testified no vehicles had been present when he visited O'Bryant's home on July 8, 1993, and in the fall of 1993, Agent Hathaway testified that Cebula had looked into the same Toyota truck on their fall 1993 visit and on that occasion discovered "marijuana roaches" in the ashtray.

Agent Cebula claimed he went over to the truck to determine whether the engine was still warm or if the keys were in the ignition. He admitted there was nothing the agents would have done differently if the engine were warm or the keys present, thus conceding he had no valid reason for walking over to the truck. While looking inside the closed and tinted windows, he claimed he was able to discern what appeared to be a plastic bag of marijuana, partially hidden under the driver's seat.

Agent Hathaway then left the residence and procured a search warrant for the house and the truck. The search warrant was based on their observation of marijuana on the floorboard, anonymous tips of purported drug activity involving O'Bryant, and the officers' observation of marijuana in the truck's ashtray in the fall of 1993. The warrant apparently was founded in part on Cebula's prior discovery of marijuana in the ashtray, a discovery that Cebula seemed to repudiate. Although Hathaway testified Cebula discovered marijuana in the truck on two different occasions, Cebula denied even seeing a vehicle on the premises before April 1994.

During the search of the house, drug agents discovered approximately 20 pounds of marijuana in the master bedroom, anabolic steroids, and a pound of marijuana on the floorboard of the truck. O'Bryant was indicted for possession with intent to distribute marijuana. Should O'Bryant's motion to suppress the marijuana be granted? *State v. O'Bryant,* 467 S.E.2d 342 (Ga.App. 1996).

6. On November 14, 1994, an investigator for the Douglas County District Attorney's office saw appellant's vehicle parked by the roadside. The investigator, Lt. Cosper, turned around to follow appellant, but appellant's vehicle was gone. Cosper saw another officer, Lt. Streetman, traveling in the same direction as appellant's car and radioed him to get the tag number. Streetman was in charge of inmate labor details at the sheriff's office; his pickup truck had no blue light or siren but did have a sheriff's star on each door and lettering showing it to be a "Sheriff's Corrections" vehicle. Appellant was driving too fast for Streetman to get the tag number, but Streetman caught up with appellant's car when it stopped at an intersection behind other cars. Streetman got the tag number, and appellant sped away and disappeared around a curve. When Streetman caught up with the car, it was parked by the side of the road.

Streetman did nothing to cause appellant to stop his vehicle. Appellant exited his vehicle but Streetman told him to get back in, and he did so. When Cosper arrived, appellant and his companion, Larry McCowan, got out of the car and ran into the woods. Streetman tackled McCowan. Another officer testified that appellant was captured without incident. Meanwhile, Cosper went to the abandoned vehicle and saw on the front seat a set of drug scales, which he seized. He also saw a bag on the passenger side on the floorboard, and in it he could clearly see what he thought to be drugs. The cocaine in the bag tested as weighing 110.8 grams with 84 percent purity. Should the appellant's motion to suppress the cocaine be granted? *Walker v. State,* 493 S.E.2d 193 (Ga.App. 1997).

PART FOUR

Admissions and Confessions and Pretrial Identification

CHAPTER THIRTEEN

Admissions and Confessions

OBJECTIVES

1. Know the history of the development of the test for the admissibility of a defendant's admission or confession.
   a. Voluntariness
   b. *Escobedo v. Illinois*
   c. *Miranda v. Arizona*

2. Be able to determine whether the *Miranda* requirements are applicable to a particular fact situation—that is, whether the suspect was subject to custodial interrogation.

3. Know under what circumstances further attempts at interrogation may be made after a suspect has exercised his or her right to remain silent, has requested the assistance of an attorney, or has waived the *Miranda* rights and submitted to interrogation.

4. Be able to determine whether the *Miranda* requirements have been satisfied in a case in which they apply—that is, whether the warnings were adequate, whether the rights were clearly waived, whether the suspect was competent to waive the rights, and whether the suspect's reasonable expectation of privacy was violated.

5. Understand the applicability of *Miranda* to misdemeanors and other miscellaneous situations.

6. Understand the effect of *Miranda* in court.

OUTLINE

1. Historical background—admissibility of admissions and confessions
   a. Voluntariness
   b. *Escobedo* and *Miranda*
2. Facts and holdings of *Miranda*
3. Issues of *Miranda*
4. Custody—definition and determination
   a. Focus of investigation
   b. Place of interrogation
      (1) Police stations
      (2) Prisons and jails
      (3) Homes
      (4) Places of business
      (5) Stores, restaurants, and other public places
      (6) Hospitals
      (7) Crime scenes
   c. Investigative and traffic stops
   d. Time of interrogation
   e. Presence of other persons
   f. Arrest or restraint
   g. Police coercion or domination
   h. Psychological restraints
   i. Interview initiated by suspect
5. Interrogation
   a. Volunteered statements
   b. Clarifying questions
   c. Routine questions
   d. Spontaneous questions
   e. Questions related to public safety
   f. Confrontation of suspect with evidence
   g. Confrontation of suspect with accomplice
   h. Statements or actions of officers
   i. Interrogation by private citizens
   j. Multiple attempts at interrogation
      (1) Attempts after right to silence is invoked
      (2) Attempts after right to counsel is invoked
      (3) Attempts after rights are waived
      (4) Attempts after an unwarned admission
      (5) Attempts after defendant is formally charged
6. Warnings
   a. Manner of giving warning
   b. Does the suspect require warnings?
      (1) Suspect knows his or her rights
      (2) Suspect is not indigent
      (3) Suspect has an attorney present
   c. Passage of time
7. Waiver
   a. Obtaining a waiver
   b. Words and actions indicating a waiver
   c. Voluntariness of the waiver
   d. Requisite level of comprehension
      (1) Suspect's need for additional useful information
      (2) Suspect's competency
8. Other *Miranda* issues
   a. Nontestimonial evidence
   b. Fourth Amendment violations
   c. Nature or severity of offense
   d. Undercover agents
9. Effect of *Miranda* in court

Since the U.S. Supreme Court decision in *Miranda v. Arizona*, 384 U.S. 436, 86 S.Ct. 1602, 16 L.Ed.2d 694 (1966), the name *Miranda* has become familiar to criminal justice personnel throughout the United States. The *Miranda* decision radically changed the course of law enforcement in the area of admissions, confessions, and interrogations. This chapter focuses on the *Miranda* decision and the multitude of other court decisions interpreting *Miranda*. Other aspects of the law governing admissions and confessions are also discussed.

Definitions of the terms *statement, admission,* and *confession,* as used in this chapter, will assist the reader in understanding the chapter. **Statement** is a broad term meaning simply any oral or written declaration or assertion. **Admission** means a statement or acknowledgment of facts by a person tending to incriminate that person, but not sufficient of itself to establish guilt of a crime. An admission, alone or in connection with other facts, tends to show the existence of one or more, but not all, elements of a crime. **Confession** means a statement or acknowledgment of facts by a person establishing that person's guilt of all elements of a crime. ■

Historical Background

To fully appreciate the effect and significance of the *Miranda* decision, one must understand the developments in the law leading up to that decision. This section discusses the important concept of **voluntariness** of admissions and confessions and the landmark case of *Escobedo v. Illinois*.

Voluntariness

Before 1964, the only test for the admissibility of a defendant's admission or confession was its "voluntariness." An involuntary statement was ruled inadmissible because it violated the due process clause of the Fifth and Fourteenth Amendments to the Constitution. Involuntary statements violate due process for the following reasons: First, an involuntary statement is considered to be inherently untrustworthy or unreliable, and convictions based on unreliable evidence violate due process. Second, coercive police practices are a violation of "fundamental fairness," an essential element of due process. Therefore, a confession coerced by the police violates due process, even if that confession is otherwise reliable. Third, free choice is an essential aspect of due process, and an involuntary confession cannot be the product of a person's free and rational choice. Finally, our system of justice is an accusatorial, not an inquisitorial, system. As stated by the U.S. Supreme Court:

> Our decisions under [the Fourteenth Amendment] have made clear that convictions following the admission into evidence of confessions which are involuntary, i.e., the product of coercion, either physical or psychological, cannot stand. This is so not because such confessions are unlikely to be true but because the methods used to extract them offend an underlying principle in the enforcement of our criminal law: that ours is an accusatorial and not an inquisitorial system—a system in which the State must establish guilt by evidence independently and freely secured and may not by coercion prove its charge against an accused out of his own mouth. . . . To be sure, confessions cruelly extorted may be and have been, to an unascertained extent, found to be untrustworthy. But the constitutional principle of excluding confessions that are involuntary does not rest

on this consideration. Indeed, in many of the cases in which the command of the Due Process Clause has compelled us to reverse state convictions involving the use of confessions obtained by impermissible methods, independent corroborating evidence left little doubt of the truth of what the defendant had confessed. *Rogers v. Richmond,* 365 U.S. 534, 540–41, 81 S.Ct. 735, 739–40, 5 L.Ed.2d 760, 766–67 (1961).

The voluntariness requirement was established in *Brown v. Mississippi,* 297 U.S. 278, 56 S.Ct. 461, 80 L.Ed. 682 (1936), in which the U.S. Supreme Court held that a confession coerced from a defendant by means of police brutality violated due process of law. Later cases established that various other forms of police coercive conduct, including the more subtle psychological pressures, might render a resulting confession involuntary and thus violative of due process. The test for voluntariness of a statement was stated in *Townsend v. Sain,* 372 U.S. 293, 307–08, 83 S.Ct. 745, 754, 9 L.Ed.2d 770, 782–83 (1963).

If an individual's "will was overborne" or if his confession was not "the product of a rational intellect and a free will," his confession is inadmissible because coerced. These standards are applicable whether a confession is the product of physical intimidation or psychological pressure. . . . Any questioning by police officers which in fact produces a confession which is not the product of a free intellect renders that confession inadmissible.

The following kinds of police conduct have been found to violate due process:

- Threats of violence. *Beecher v. Alabama,* 389 U.S. 35, 88 S.Ct. 189, 19 L.Ed.2d 35 (1967).

- Confinement of the suspect in a small space until the suspect confessed. *United States v. Koch,* 552 F.2d 1216 (7th Cir. 1977).

- Continued interrogation of an injured and depressed suspect in a hospital intensive care unit. *Mincey v. Arizona,* 437 U.S. 385, 98 S.Ct. 2408, 57 L.Ed.2d 290 (1978).

- Deprivation of food or sleep. *Greenwald v. Wisconsin,* 390 U.S. 519, 88 S.Ct. 1152, 20 L.Ed.2d 77 (1968).

- Extended periods of incommunicado interrogation. *Ashcraft v. Tennessee,* 322 U.S. 143, 64 S.Ct. 921, 88 L.Ed. 1192 (1944); *Davis v. North Carolina,* 384 U.S. 737, 86 S.Ct. 1761, 16 L.Ed.2d 895 (1966).

- Trickery or deception. *Spano v. New York,* 360 U.S. 315, 79 S.Ct. 1202, 3 L.Ed.2d 1265 (1959). However, some courts have adopted the view that "[c]onfessions generally are not vitiated when they are obtained by deception or trickery, as long as the means employed are not calculated to produce an untrue statement." *Matter of D.A.S.,* 391 A.2d 255, 258 (D.C.App. 1978).

- Obtaining of a statement during a period of unnecessary delay between arrest and presentment. *McNabb v. United States,* 318 U.S. 332, 63 S.Ct. 608, 87 L.Ed. 819 (1943); *Mallory v. United States,* 354 U.S. 449, 77 S.Ct. 1356, 1 L.Ed.2d 1479 (1957). The *McNabb* and *Mallory* cases apply only to federal courts and hold that any admission or confession obtained during an unreasonable delay between arrest and first appearance before a magistrate will be inadmissible in court. This rule was developed pursuant to the Court's supervisory power over the lower federal courts and is not applicable to the states as a constitutional rule would have been. The Court, clearly concerned about incommunicado interrogation and coerced confessions, designed the rule to implement the guarantees of

Rule 5 of the *Federal Rules of Criminal Procedure*. Rule 5 requires prompt arraignment, notification of rights, and provision for terms of bail. The Court never attempted to specify a minimum time after which delay in presenting a suspect for arraignment would invalidate confessions. Congress, however, enacted 18 U.S.C.A. § 3501(c), which "permits exclusion of a confession, regardless of voluntariness, where the confession is made after six hours following arrest but prior to arraignment and where the delay between arrest and arraignment is unreasonable in light of the means of transportation and the distance traveled to the nearest available magistrate." *United States v. Wilbon*, 911 F.Supp. 1420, 1432 (D.N.M. 1995). Several states have adopted similar provisions.

In contrast, courts have found the following practices, standing alone and without additional evidence of a suspect's will being overborne, insufficiently coercive to constitute a violation of due process:

- Promises of leniency. "[A] confession is not involuntary merely because the suspect was promised leniency if he cooperated with law enforcement officials." *United States v. Guarno*, 819 F.2d 28, 31 (2d Cir. 1987).

- Encouragement to cooperate.

  > Encouraging a suspect to tell the truth and suggesting that his cohorts might leave him "holding the bag" does not, as a matter of law, overcome a confessor's will. . . . Neither is a statement that the accused's cooperation will be made known to the court a sufficient inducement so as to render a subsequent incriminating statement involuntary. . . . A truthful and noncoercive statement of the possible penalties which an accused faces may be given to the accused without overbearing one's free will. Such an account may increase the chance that one detained will make a statement. However, as long as the statement results from an informed and intelligent appraisal of the risks involved rather than a coercive atmosphere, the statement may be considered to have been voluntarily made. . . . [T]elling the appellant in a noncoercive manner of the realistically expected penalties and encouraging her to tell the truth is no more than affording her the chance to make an informed decision with respect to her cooperation with the government. *United States v. Ballard*, 586 F.2d 1060, 1063 (5th Cir. 1978).

- Misrepresentations. *Evans v. Dowd*, 932 F.2d 739 (8th Cir. 1991), found a confession voluntary even though the officer misstated the purpose of the investigation and falsely stated that he had eyewitnesses.

- Promises of psychological treatment. *United States v. McClinton*, 982 F.2d 278, 283 (8th Cir. 1992), found the defendant's confession voluntary even though police "told him that he was not a bad person and that he would receive help for his drug and alcohol problems if he talked to them."

Courts also examine the personal characteristics of defendants in determining the voluntariness of an admission or confession. Some of the characteristics considered important are age; mental capacity; education level; physical or mental impairment from illness, injury, or intoxication; and experience in dealing with the police. The U.S. Supreme Court said that these personal characteristics are "relevant only in establishing a setting in which actual coercion might have been exerted to overcome the will of the suspect." *Procunier v. Atchley*, 400 U.S. 446, 453–54, 91 S.Ct. 485, 489, 27 L.Ed.2d 524, 531 (1971). The Court elaborated in *Colorado v. Connelly*, stating that while mental condition is surely relevant to an individual's susceptibility to police coercion, mere examination of the confessant's state of mind can never conclude the due process inquiry. . . . [C]oercive police activity is a necessary predicate to the finding that a confession is not "voluntary" within the meaning of the Due Process Clause of the Fourteenth Amendment. 479 U.S. 157, 165–67, 107 S.Ct. 515, 521–22, 93 L.Ed.2d 473, 483–84 (1986).

Therefore, absent coercive conduct by the police, every confession is considered to be voluntary. "Absent police conduct causally related to the confession, there is simply no basis for concluding that any state actor has deprived a criminal defendant of due process of law." 479 U.S. at 164, 107 S.Ct. at 520, 93 L.Ed.2d at 482.

Determination of the voluntariness of an admission or confession can be summarized as follows:

- If no police coercion occurred, any statement will be considered voluntary, regardless of the suspect's mental or physical condition.

- If police coercion occurred, the voluntariness of the statement will be evaluated on the basis of the totality of the circumstances surrounding the giving of the statement. Except for the use of physical violence by the police, no single fact or circumstance will be solely determinative.

Escobedo and *Miranda*

In 1964, a major change in the law took place. In the case of *Escobedo v. Illinois,* 378 U.S. 478, 84 S.Ct. 1758, 12 L.Ed.2d 977 (1964), the U.S. Supreme Court held that

where . . . the investigation is no longer a general inquiry into an unsolved crime but has begun to focus on a particular suspect, the suspect has been taken into police custody, the police carry out a process of interrogations that lends itself to eliciting incriminating statements, the suspect has requested and been denied an opportunity to consult with his lawyer, and the police have not effectively warned him of his absolute constitutional right to remain silent, the accused has been denied "the Assistance of Counsel" in violation of the Sixth Amendment to the Constitution as "made obligatory upon the States by the Fourteenth Amendment," . . . and . . . no statement elicited by the police during the interrogation may be used against him at a criminal trial. 378 U.S. at 491, 84 S.Ct. at 1765, 12 L.Ed.2d at 986.

The *Escobedo* case was significant not only because it shifted the area of inquiry from due process to the Sixth Amendment but also because it did not follow a totality-of-the-circumstances approach. Instead, the Court took a single circumstance and made it the single determinative factor in all cases in which it occurred. The Court said that "when the process shifts from investigatory to accusatory—when its focus is on the accused and its purpose is to elicit a confession . . . the accused must be permitted to consult with his lawyer." 378 U.S. at 492, 84 S.Ct. at 1766, 12 L.Ed.2d at 987. This has come to be known as the Escobedo *focus of investigation test.*

Miranda v. Arizona, decided two years later in 1966, again rejected a totality-of-the-circumstances approach, extended the *Escobedo* decision, and shifted the area of inquiry to the Fifth Amendment. In short, the *Miranda* case held that "the prosecution may not use statements, whether exculpatory or inculpatory, stemming from custodial interrogation of the defendant unless it demonstrates the use of procedural safeguards effective to secure the privilege against self-incrimination." 384 U.S. at

444, 86 S.Ct. at 1612, 16 L.Ed.2d at 706. Such statements may not be used to prove the case against the defendant even if the statements were otherwise voluntary. If the statements were not voluntary, they will be inadmissible even though the *Miranda* requirements were satisfied. Satisfaction of *Miranda* requirements is a relevant consideration in the determination of the voluntariness of a confession, but, as the following quotations indicate, is not conclusive.

> We do not suggest that compliance with *Miranda* conclusively establishes the voluntariness of a subsequent confession. But cases in which a defendant can make a colorable argument that a self-incriminating statement was "compelled" despite the fact that the law enforcement authorities adhered to the dictates of *Miranda* are rare. *Berkemer v. McCarty,* 468 U.S. 420, 433 n.20, 104 S.Ct. 3138, 3147 n.20, 82 L.Ed.2d 317, 330 n.20 (1984).

Furthermore, "[a]s the *Miranda* Court itself recognized, the failure to provide *Miranda* warnings in and of itself does not render a confession involuntary. . . ." *New York v. Quarles,* 467 U.S. 649, 655 n.5, 104 S.Ct. 2626, 2631 n.5, 81 L.Ed.2d 550, 556 n.5 (1984).

KEY POINTS

1. Coercive police activity is necessary for an admission or confession to be found involuntary. The totality of the circumstances surrounding the giving of the statement, including the defendant's mental or physical condition, must be evaluated to determine if the coercion overcame the defendant's will.

2. Satisfaction of *Miranda* requirements is a relevant consideration in determining the voluntariness of an admission or confession, but it is not conclusive.

3. Only voluntary admissions or confessions that are obtained in compliance with *Miranda* requirements will be admissible in court.

Facts and Holdings of *Miranda*

The U.S. Supreme Court's opinion in *Miranda v. Arizona* encompasses three other cases besides *Miranda,* all dealing with the admissibility of statements obtained from a person who is subjected to custodial police interrogation. A brief description of the facts of each case is presented to delineate the scope of the opinion.

In *Miranda v. Arizona* the defendant was arrested at his home for rape and taken to a police station, where he was identified by the complaining witness. The defendant was then interrogated and within two hours signed a written confession. At no time was the defendant informed of his right to consult with an attorney, his right to have an attorney present during the interrogation, or his right not to be compelled to incriminate himself.

In *Vignera v. New York* the defendant was apprehended in connection with a robbery and was taken to detective squad headquarters. The defendant was interrogated; he confessed and was then locked up. About eight hours later, the defendant was interrogated again and gave a written statement. At no time was the defendant informed of any of his rights.

In *Westover v. United States* the defendant was arrested by municipal police as a robbery suspect. The municipal police, and later the FBI, interrogated the defendant at the municipal police department. After two hours of questioning, the defendant signed two confessions. The Court noted that the FBI interrogation was conducted following the interrogation by municipal police in the same police station—in the same compelling surroundings.

In *California v. Stewart* the defendant was arrested at his home, where police found proceeds from a robbery. The defendant was then taken to a police station and placed in a cell where, over a period of five days, he was interrogated nine times. The Court noted that the defendant was isolated with his interrogators at all times except when he was being confronted by an accusing witness.

In each of these cases, the defendant was questioned by police officers, detectives, or a prosecuting attorney in unfamiliar surroundings, cut off from the outside world. In none of the cases was the defendant given a full and effective warning of his rights at the outset of the interrogation process. In all of the cases, the questioning elicited oral statements. In three of the cases, signed statements were also given, and those statements were admitted into evidence at trial. Thus, all the cases shared the features of incommunicado interrogation of a person in a police-dominated atmosphere, resulting in self-incriminating statements without full warnings of constitutional rights.

In the *Miranda* opinion, the Court reviewed the facts in each case and then discussed specific police interrogation techniques as prescribed in police manuals. In condemning those techniques, the Court said:

> It is obvious that such an interrogation environment is created for no purpose other than to subjugate the individual to the will of his examiner. This atmosphere carries its own badge of intimidation. To be sure, this is not physical intimidation, but it is equally destructive of human dignity. The current practice of incommunicado interrogation is at odds with one of our Nation's most cherished principles—that the individual may not be compelled to incriminate himself. Unless adequate protective devices are employed to dispel the compulsion inherent in custodial surroundings, no statement obtained from the defendant can truly be the product of his free choice. 384 U.S. at 457–58, 86 S.Ct. at 1619, 16 L.Ed.2d at 714.

The Court then established procedural safeguards to protect the privilege against self-incrimination. Those safeguards are the *Miranda* warnings so familiar to law enforcement personnel.

> [W]hen an individual is taken into custody or otherwise deprived of his freedom by the authorities in any significant way and is subjected to questioning, the privilege against self-incrimination is jeopardized. Procedural safeguards must be employed to protect the privilege and unless other fully effective means are adopted to notify the person of his right of silence and to assure that the exercise of the right will be scrupulously honored, the following measures are required. He must be warned prior to any question that he has the right to remain silent, that anything he says can be used against him in a court of law, that he has the right to the presence of an attorney, and that if he cannot afford an attorney one will be appointed for him prior to any questioning if he so desires. Opportunity to exercise these rights must be afforded to him throughout the interrogation. After such warnings have been given, and such opportunity afforded him, the individual may knowingly and intelligently waive these rights and agree to answer questions or make a statement. But unless and until such warnings and waiver are demonstrated by the prosecution at trial no evidence obtained as a result of interrogation can be used against him. 384 U.S. at 478–79, 86 S.Ct. at 1630, 16 L.Ed.2d at 726.

Issues of *Miranda*

The *Miranda* decision has raised many questions, and the issues can generally be divided into two categories:

- The first category is whether *Miranda* requirements apply to the particular case. The issues here are whether the defendant was in custody, whether the defendant's statements were the result of interrogation, whether the interrogator was a law enforcement officer or agent, and whether the seriousness of the offense has any bearing.

- The second category is whether *Miranda* requirements have been met in a case in which they apply. The issues here are whether the warnings were adequate, whether rights were clearly waived, whether the suspect was competent to waive the rights, and whether more than one interrogation is allowed under *Miranda*.

In short, the major issues of *Miranda* hinge on the meaning of four terms: **custody, interrogation, warning,** and **waiver.** The remainder of this chapter is devoted to a discussion of the meanings of these terms as well as a discussion of additional miscellaneous issues.

Custody

The warnings required by the *Miranda* case must be given before police question a person who is in custody or deprived of his or her freedom of action in any significant way.

> Although the circumstances of each case must certainly influence a determination of whether a suspect is "in custody" for purposes of receiving *Miranda* protection, the ultimate inquiry is simply whether there is a "formal arrest or restraint on freedom of movement" of the degree associated with a formal arrest. *California v. Beheler,* 463 U.S. 1121, 1125, 103 S.Ct. 3517, 3520, 77 L.Ed.2d 1275, 1279 (1983).

In other words, has there been a seizure tantamount to arrest? (See Chapter 4.) In answering this question, courts consider the totality of the circumstances under which the questioning occurred from the viewpoint of a reasonable person. The circumstances to be considered include:

> The time, the place and purpose of the encounter; the persons present during the interrogation; the words spoken by the officer to the defendant; the officer's tone of voice and general demeanor; the length and mood of the interrogation; whether any limitation of movement or other form of restraint was placed on the defendant during the interrogation; the officer's response to any questions asked by the defendant; whether directions were given to the defendant during the interrogation; and the defendant's verbal or nonverbal response to such directions. *People v. Horn,* 790 P.2d 816, 818 (Colo. 1990).

As stated by the U.S. Supreme Court, "the only relevant inquiry is how a reasonable man in the suspect's position would have understood his situation." *Berkemer v. Mc-*

Carty, 468 U.S. 420, 442, 104 S.Ct. 3138, 3151, 82 L.Ed.2d 317, 336 (1984). "The reasonable person through whom we view the situation must be neutral to the environment and to the purposes of the investigation—that is, neither guilty of criminal conduct and thus overly apprehensive nor insensitive to the seriousness of the circumstances." *United States v. Bengivenga,* 845 F.2d 593, 596 (5th Cir. 1988). The following discussion examines various factors considered by the courts in determining whether a person is in custody for *Miranda* purposes.

Focus of Investigation

The *Miranda* decision is generally understood to have abandoned the focus of investigation test of the *Escobedo* case to determine when an interrogated suspect is entitled to warnings. The U.S. Supreme Court specifically held that even though a suspect is clearly the focus of a criminal investigation, the suspect need not be given *Miranda* warnings if he or she is not otherwise in custody or deprived of freedom of action in any significant way. *Beckwith v. United States,* 425 U.S. 341, 96 S.Ct. 1612, 48 L.Ed.2d 1 (1976).

> Our cases make clear, in no uncertain terms, that any inquiry into whether the interrogating officers have focused their suspicions upon the individual being questioned (assuming those suspicions remain undisclosed) is not relevant for purposes of *Miranda. Stansbury v. California,* 511 U.S. 318, 326, 114 S.Ct. 1526, 1530, 128 L.Ed.2d 293, 301 (1994).

The focus concept may still have some vitality as one of the circumstances to be considered by a court in determining the custody issue, but only if an officer's views or beliefs were somehow manifested to the person under interrogation and would have affected how a reasonable person in that position would perceive his or her freedom to leave.

> An officer's knowledge or beliefs may bear upon the custody issue if they are conveyed, by word or deed, to the individual being questioned. . . . Those beliefs are relevant only to the extent they would affect how a reasonable person in the position of the individual being questioned would gauge the breadth of his or her "'freedom of action.'" . . . Even a clear statement from an officer that the person under interrogation is a prime suspect is not, in itself, dispositive of the custody issue, for some suspects are free to come and go until the police decide to make an arrest. The weight and pertinence of any communications regarding the officer's degree of suspicion will depend upon the facts and circumstances of the particular case. *Stansbury v. California,* 511 U.S. 318, 325, 114 S.Ct. 1526, 1530, 128 L.Ed.2d 293, 300 (1994).

Place of Interrogation

Court decisions interpreting *Miranda* hold that the place of interrogation is an important, but not conclusive, factor in determining custody. The following discussion analyzes cases that have relied heavily on the place of interrogation in determining the question of custody.

POLICE STATIONS. In all four of the cases decided by the *Miranda* opinion, the suspect was questioned in a police station after arrest. There is little question that custody exists in this type of situation. Other courts have held that even if a person is not under arrest but is present at a police station for questioning at the command of the police, the person is in custody for purposes of *Miranda*. *United States v. Pierce*, 397 F.2d 128 (4th Cir. 1968).

In *Oregon v. Mathiason*, 429 U.S. 492, 97 S.Ct. 711, 50 L.Ed.2d 714 (1977), however, the U.S. Supreme Court held that a suspect questioned in a police station is not necessarily in custody. In that case, the defendant, a parolee, was a suspect in a burglary. A state police officer asked him to come to the state police offices "to discuss something." When the defendant arrived, the officer took him into a closed office and told him that he was not under arrest. The officer then informed the defendant that he was a suspect in the burglary and falsely stated that the defendant's fingerprints had been found at the scene. Within five minutes, the defendant confessed to the burglary. He left the office one-half hour later.

The Court held that the *Miranda* warnings were not required because the defendant was not in custody.

> [T]here is no indication that the questioning took place in a context where respondent's freedom to depart was restricted in any way. He came voluntarily to the police station, where he was immediately informed that he was not under arrest. At the close of a ½-hour interview respondent did in fact leave the police station without hindrance. It is clear from these facts that Mathiason was not in custody "or otherwise deprived of his freedom of action in any significant way." . . . Any interview of one suspected of a crime by a police officer will have coercive aspects to it, simply by virtue of the fact that the police officer is part of a law enforcement system which may ultimately cause the suspect to be charged with a crime. But police officers are not required to administer *Miranda* warnings to everyone whom they question. Nor is the requirement of warnings imposed simply because the questioning takes place in the station house, or because the questioned person is one whom the police suspect. *Miranda* warnings are required only where there has been such a restriction on a person's freedom as to render him "in custody." It was that sort of coercive environment to which *Miranda* by its terms was made applicable, and to which it is limited. 429 U.S. at 495, 97 S.Ct. at 714, 50 L.Ed.2d at 719.

PRISONS AND JAILS. In *Mathis v. United States*, 391 U.S. 1, 88 S.Ct. 1503, 20 L.Ed.2d 381 (1968), a person who was incarcerated in a penitentiary for one offense was held to be in custody for purposes of an interrogation conducted by IRS (Internal Revenue Service) agents with respect to another offense. However, in *United States v. Conley*, 779 F.2d 970, 972–73 (4th Cir. 1985), the court said:

> We decline to read *Mathis* as compelling the use of *Miranda* warnings prior to all prisoner interrogations and hold that a prison inmate is not automatically always in "custody" within the meaning of *Miranda*. . . . A different approach to the custody determination is warranted in the paradigmatic custodial prison setting where, by definition, the entire population is under restraint of free movement. The Ninth Circuit has taken the position that "restriction" is a relative concept and that, in this context, it "necessarily implies a change in the surroundings of the prisoner which results in an added imposition on his freedom of movement." . . . We agree that this approach best reconciles *Mathis* and *Miranda* in the unique context of prisons and the problems peculiar to their administration.

Therefore, in *United States v. Cooper,* 800 F.2d 412 (4th Cir. 1986), the court found that questioning of a prisoner that took place in a disciplinary boardroom occurred in an inherently less restrictive area than the defendant's cell and that the questioning was therefore noncustodial.

HOMES. Ordinarily, interrogation of a person in that person's home is noncustodial because the person is in familiar surroundings and there is no "police-dominated atmosphere." For example, in *United States v. Gregory,* 891 F.2d 732 (9th Cir. 1989), the court concluded that the defendant was not in custody under the following circumstances:

> [H]e consented to be interviewed in his house, he was interviewed in the presence of his wife, the interview lasted only a brief time, and no coercion or force was used. Although the agents initially drew their guns, they returned them to their holsters prior to the interview. They stated that they wanted to question Gregory about some robberies committed in Phoenix and they made no suggestion that Gregory would not be free to leave. The entire interview lasted only a few minutes. 891 F.2d at 735.

However, in *Orozco v. Texas,* 394 U.S. 324, 89 S.Ct. 1095, 22 L.Ed.2d 311 (1969), a suspect was questioned at 4:00 A.M. in his bedroom by four officers, one of whom later testified that the suspect was under arrest. The Court held, that even though the questioning was brief and the suspect was in familiar surroundings, the interrogation was custodial. The key reasons for the decision were the time of the interrogation, the number of officers present, and the somewhat unclear evidence of formal arrest.

In *Sprosty v. Buchler,* 79 F.3d 635 (7th Cir. 1996), the court held that the defendant was in custody even though he was in his home, in the presence of his mother and at least one family friend, and not handcuffed or otherwise physically restrained. The court found that the degree to which the police dominated the scene was more important than the familiarity of the surroundings:

- When the police arrived at the defendant's mobile home, they surrounded his car, blocked the driveway from his car to the street, and escorted him inside.

- Four officers searched for the photographs while another officer, who was armed and in uniform, remained with the defendant to guard him.

- During the nearly three-hour period that the officers searched the home, they repeatedly asked the defendant to tell them where the incriminating photographs were located.

PLACES OF BUSINESS. Interrogation of a person at his or her place of business is usually held to be noncustodial. Like the home, the place of business represents a familiar surrounding. *United States v. Venerable,* 807 F.2d 745 (8th Cir. 1986). However, in *United States v. Steele,* 648 F.Supp. 1375 (N.D.Ind. 1986), a postal employee who was approached at her work station, asked to accompany two postal inspectors to a small room in the post office, and questioned for an hour and forty-five minutes was found to be in custody. The court said:

> The defendant was not subjected to severe restraint on her physical freedom. She was not handcuffed nor locked in any type of detention facility. In addition, she was not faced with a large number of police officers. She was, however, placed in a closely confined area and confronted by two government agents. Because this was an environment in which the defendant had no control, the physical

restraint used, and the show of authority made by the inspectors remain significant. 648 F.Supp. at 1379.

The court also noted that the postal inspectors represented not only law enforcement authority but the authority of the defendant's employer as well. The court found that "a reasonable person would not feel free to rebuff the inspectors out of fear of jeopardizing his or her job as well as encouraging criminal suspicion. Because the interrogators had the power to initiate criminal charges and to terminate the defendant's job, this situation involved coercion greater than the more common situation involving a suspect approached on the street by a police officer." 648 F.Supp. at 1378.

STORES, RESTAURANTS, AND OTHER PUBLIC PLACES. Public places such as stores, restaurants, bars, streets, and sidewalks are considered less familiar to a suspect than a home or office. Nevertheless, courts usually find that an interrogation conducted in these places is noncustodial, because the suspect is in a place of personal choice and is not isolated from the outside world. In addition, there is usually not a police-dominated atmosphere in a public place. In *United States v. Masse,* 816 F.2d 805 (1st Cir. 1987), brief, noncoercive questioning of the defendant on the public sidewalks by two nonuniformed Drug Enforcement Administration (DEA) agents was held to be noncustodial.

HOSPITALS. Questioning of a suspect who is confined in a hospital as a patient but not under arrest is usually held to be a noncustodial interrogation. *United States v. Martin,* 781 F.2d 671 (9th Cir. 1985). Factors supporting such a holding include a lack of a compelling atmosphere, the routine nature of the questioning, and a lack of any deprivation of the defendant's freedom by the police. In *State v. Lescard,* 517 A.2d 1158 (N.H. 1986), however, the court found that the defendant was clearly in custody, where he had been handcuffed at the scene of an accident and was attended by a police officer while at the hospital.

CRIME SCENES. In *Miranda,* the Court said that its decision was

> not intended to hamper the traditional function of police officers in investigating crime. . . . General on-the-scene questioning as to facts surrounding a crime or other general questioning of citizens in the fact-finding process is not affected by our holding. It is an act of responsible citizenship for individuals to give whatever information they may have to aid in law enforcement. In such situations the compelling atmosphere inherent in the process of in-custody interrogation is not necessarily present. 384 U.S. at 477–78, 86 S.Ct. at 1629–30, 16 L.Ed.2d at 725–26.

In *United States v. Wolak,* 923 F.2d 1193 (6th Cir. 1991), two police officers responded to a "disturbance" call at a store. They had no details on what was going on, if anything, before they arrived, and they did not know what to expect. One officer asked the defendant what happened, and the defendant replied that he had pulled a gun because he feared that another person was going to assault him. The court held that even though the officers were not letting anyone leave the store until they found out what was going on, this was not the type of "custody" envisioned by *Miranda.* The court said that, carried to its logical conclusion, applying *Miranda* in this type of situation "would require officers to announce *Miranda* warnings to everyone present immediately upon arriving at a possible crime scene before they knew what happened or before they could ask any questions." 923 F.2d at 1196.

Investigative and Traffic Stops

The ordinary *Terry*-type investigative stop and the ordinary traffic stop are noncustodial and do not require the administration of *Miranda* warnings. The U.S. Supreme Court's discussion of the issue in *Berkemer v. McCarty* is illuminating:

Two features of an ordinary traffic stop mitigate the danger that a person questioned will be induced "to speak where he would not otherwise do so freely" [citing *Miranda*]. First, detention of a motorist pursuant to a traffic stop is presumptively temporary and brief. The vast majority of roadside detentions last only a few minutes. A motorist's expectations, when he sees a policeman's light flashing behind him, are that he will be obliged to spend a short period of time answering questions and waiting while the officer checks his license and registration, that he may then be given a citation, but that in the end he most likely will be allowed to continue on his way. In this respect, questioning incident to an ordinary traffic stop is quite different from stationhouse interrogation, which frequently is prolonged, and in which the detainee often is aware that questioning will continue until he provides his interrogators the answers they seek. . . .

Second, circumstances associated with the typical traffic stop are not such that the motorist feels completely at the mercy of the police. To be sure, the aura of authority surrounding an armed, uniformed officer and the knowledge that the officer has some discretion in deciding whether to issue a citation, in combination, exert some pressure on the detainee to respond to questions. But other aspects of the situation substantially offset these forces. Perhaps most importantly, the typical traffic stop is public, at least to some degree. Passersby, on foot or in other cars, witness the interaction of officer and motorist. This exposure to public view both reduces the ability of an unscrupulous policeman to use illegitimate means to elicit self-incriminating statements and diminishes the motorist's fear that, if he does not cooperate, he will be subjected to abuse. The fact that the detained motorist typically is confronted by only one or at most two policemen further mutes his sense of vulnerability. In short, the atmosphere surrounding an ordinary traffic stop is substantially less "police dominated" than that surrounding the kinds of interrogation at issue in *Miranda* itself . . . and in the subsequent cases in which we have applied *Miranda*.

In both of these respects, the usual traffic stop is more analogous to a so-called "*Terry* stop," . . . than to a formal arrest. Under the Fourth Amendment . . . a policeman who lacks probable cause but whose "observations lead him reasonably to suspect" that a particular person has committed, is committing, or is about to commit a crime, may detain that person briefly in order to "investigate the circumstances that provoke suspicion." . . . "[T]he stop and inquiry must be 'reasonably related in scope to the justification for their initiation.'" . . . Typically, this means that the officer may ask the detainee a moderate number of questions to determine his identity and to try to obtain information confirming or dispelling the officer's suspicions. But the detainee is not obliged to respond. And, unless the detainee's answers provide the officer with probable cause to arrest him, he must then be released. The comparatively nonthreatening character of detentions of this sort explains the absence of any suggestion in our opinions that *Terry* stops are subject to the dictates of *Miranda*. The similarly noncoercive aspect of ordinary traffic stops prompts us to hold that persons temporarily detained pursuant to such stops are not "in custody" for the purposes of *Miranda*.

Berkemer v. McCarty, 468 U.S. 420, 437–40, 104 S.Ct. 3138, 3149–40, 82 L.Ed.2d 317, 333–35 (1983).

In *United States v. Murray,* 89 F.3d 459, 462 (7th Cir. 1996), the court held that where other aspects of a traffic stop were noncustodial, "the fact that Murray was questioned while seated in the back of the squad car did not put him 'in custody' for purposes of *Miranda* warnings."

Time of Interrogation

An interrogation conducted during business hours is less likely to be considered custodial than is an interrogation conducted in the late evening or early morning. The time of the interrogation (4:00 A.M.) was a significant reason for holding the interrogation at the suspect's home to be custodial in the *Orozco* case (see earlier discussion under "Homes").

Presence of Other Persons

The *Miranda* decision expressly indicated a concern for the suspect who is "cut off from the outside world." 384 U.S. at 445, 86 S.Ct. at 1612, 16 L.Ed.2d at 707. Courts have interpreted this to mean that the presence of family, friends, or neutral persons during the interrogation of a suspect may render the interrogation noncustodial. *People v. Butterfield,* 65 Cal.Rptr. 765 (Cal.App. 1968). Correspondingly, deliberately removing a suspect from the presence of family and friends is indicative of custody.

> A frequently recurring example of police domination concerns the removal of the suspect from the presence of family, friends, or colleagues who might lend moral support during the questioning and deter a suspect from making inculpatory statements, an established interrogation practice noted by the *Miranda* court. . . . Officers diminish the public character of, and assert their dominion over, an interrogation site by removing a suspect from the presence of third persons that could lend moral support. *United States v. Griffin,* 922 F.2d 1343, 1352 (8th Cir. 1990).

United States v. Carter, 884 F.2d 368 (8th Cir. 1989), found custody where the defendant was questioned at his place of employment but was removed from his work station, isolated from others that might have lent moral support, and not told that he was free to leave. Some courts speak of a "balance of power" and find custody to exist where the sheer number of police indicates a police-dominated atmosphere. *Orozco v. Texas,* 394 U.S. 324, 89 S.Ct. 1095, 22 L.Ed.2d 311 (1969).

Arrest or Restraint

A suspect who is told that he or she is under arrest is definitely in custody for *Miranda* purposes. *Duckett v. State,* 240 A.2d 332 (Md.Spec.App. 1968). Conversely, a suspect who is told that he or she is not under arrest and is free to leave at any time is usually not considered to be in custody for *Miranda* purposes. *United States v. Guarno,* 819 F.2d 28 (2d Cir. 1987). Nevertheless, a suspect who was questioned by an FBI agent while sitting handcuffed in the back of a police car was found to be in custody, even though he was told he was not under arrest. *United States v. Henley,* 984 F.2d 1040 (9th Cir. 1993).

"Physical restraint . . . is ordinarily associated with a custodial interrogation." *United States v. Levy,* 955 F.2d 1098, 1104 (7th Cir. 1992). By the same token, an absence of physical restraint has led courts to conclude that the defendant was not in custody. In *United States v. Hocking,* 860 F.2d 769 (7th Cir. 1988), questioning in the defendant's home was held to be noncustodial where no restraints were placed on the defendant's movements and he was free to leave the house or ask the officers to leave. "A person detained during the execution of a search warrant is normally not in custody for *Miranda* purposes." *United States v. Saadeh,* 61 F.3d 510, 520 (7th Cir. 1995). In the *Saadeh* case, the defendant was not handcuffed or physically restrained in any way and was not detained for an unreasonably long period of time.

If the physical restraint of a person is not accomplished by law enforcement officers, the restraint does not constitute custody for *Miranda* purposes. In *Wilson v. Coon,* 808 F.2d 688 (8th Cir. 1987), a brief restraint of the defendant by a medical technician for medical purposes was held not to constitute custody.

Police Coercion or Domination

Police use of force or other types or coercion and the creation of a police-dominated atmosphere are usually indicative of custody. If an officer holds a gun on a suspect, the officer clearly creates a custodial situation. "[A] 'reasonable person' in [the defendant's] position—crouched on the ground and held at gunpoint by a citizen and then by a police officer—would have understood the situation to constitute the requisite restraint on freedom of movement." *Fleming v. Collins,* 917 F.2d 850, 853 (5th Cir. 1990). However, if the suspect is also armed, a court is unlikely to find that the suspect was in custody. *Yates v. United States,* 384 F.2d 586 (5th Cir. 1967).

In *United States v. Longbehn,* 850 F.2d 450 (8th Cir. 1988), the court found custody requiring *Miranda* warnings where the defendant was detained at his place of employment beyond usual work hours; was compelled to accompany officers in a police vehicle to police headquarters and then to his residence; was forced to open his home and submit to the execution of its search by five officers, during which he was continuously chaperoned and overtly interrogated by three separate officers. The entire process took between two and one-half and four hours.

In *People v. Horn,* 790 P.2d 816 (Colo. 1990), the court found questioning of the defendant custodial, even though the defendant came to the police station voluntarily. The interview was conducted in a small, windowless room in the basement of the police station with only one officer and the defendant present. More important, a transcript of the interview strongly revealed police coercion and domination:

> The transcript reveals that the defendant initially denied involvement in any sexual assaults. It further indicates that [officer] Galyardt accused the defendant of lying on at least five occasions and twice left the defendant alone in the interview room to "reconsider" his prior responses. During the course of the interview, the defendant was urged to take a polygraph exam and encouraged to confess for the "therapeutic" effect it would have on the victim, who was now in the juvenile justice system. Although the defendant was repeatedly told that he was free to leave and that he would not be arrested that day, he was also confronted with the evidence against him and informed that charges would be filed against him regardless of his interview responses. 790 P.2d at 818–19.

In *United States v. Jones,* 630 F.2d 613, 616 (8th Cir. 1980), the court found the lack of police coercion or domination indicative of the absence of custody.

No strong arm tactics were used. The defendant had not previously been subjected to a police escort nor given commands by the interrogating agents intended to dictate the course of conduct followed by the defendant.

A probationer, although subject to a number of restrictive conditions governing various aspects of life, is not in custody for purposes of *Miranda* simply by reason of the probationer status. A probation interview, unlike a custodial arrest, is arranged by appointment at a mutually convenient time and is conducted in familiar, nonintimidating surroundings. It does not become custodial for *Miranda* purposes because the probation officer could compel attendance and truthful answers at the interview. *Minnesota v. Murphy,* 465 U.S. 420, 104 S.Ct. 1136, 79 L.Ed.2d 409 (1984).

Psychological Restraints

Even when a person is not physically restrained, psychological restraints may be so powerful as to create an atmosphere of coercion constituting custody for *Miranda* purposes. In *United States v. Beraun-Panez,* 812 F.2d 578 (9th Cir. 1987), the court said:

> Although not physically bound, Beraun-Panez was subjected to psychological restraints just as binding. Accusing Beraun-Panez repeatedly of lying, confronting him with false or misleading witness statements, employing good guy/bad guy tactics, taking advantage of Beraun-Panez's insecurities about his alien status, keeping him separated from his co-worker in a remote rural location, insisting on the "truth" until he told them what they sought, the officers established a setting from which a reasonable person would believe that he or she was not free to leave. 812 F.2d at 580.

Interview Initiated by Suspect

If a suspect summons the police or initiates the interview, or both, a court is likely to hold that subsequent police interrogation is noncustodial. In *United States v. Jonas,* 786 F.2d 1019 (11th Cir. 1986), the defendant learned indirectly that an FBI agent wanted to contact him. He called the agent, agreed to talk with the FBI, and appeared voluntarily at FBI offices. The interview was held to be noncustodial. And in *United States v. Dockery,* 736 F.2d 1232 (8th Cir. 1984), the court found no custody where the defendant initiated a second interview with officers and was advised that she did not have to answer any questions and was free to go.

KEY POINTS

4. The determination of whether a suspect is in custody for purposes of receiving *Miranda* protection depends on whether there is a formal arrest or restraint on freedom of movement of the degree associated with a formal arrest.

5. A suspect questioned in a police station is not necessarily in custody if his or her freedom to depart is not restricted in any way.

6. Interrogation of a person at his or her home or place of business, or in a public place, is usually held to be noncustodial.

7. *Miranda* warnings are not required before general on-the-scene questioning as to facts surrounding a crime or other general questioning of citizens in the fact-finding process.

8. *Miranda* warnings are not required in connection with the ordinary *Terry*-type investigative stop and the ordinary traffic stop, because these stops are usually noncustodial.

9. Police interrogation of a person after the person has summoned the police or otherwise initiated the conversation is usually found to be noncustodial.

Interrogation

The *Miranda* requirements apply only if a person in custody is subjected to interrogation. In *Rhode Island v. Innis,* 446 U.S. 291, 100 S.Ct. 1682, 64 L.Ed.2d 297 (1980), the U.S. Supreme Court recognized that the term *interrogation* in the *Miranda* opinion involved something more than express questioning.

> The concern of the Court in *Miranda* was that the "interrogation environment" created by the interplay of interrogation and custody would "subjugate the individual to the will of his examiner" and thereby undermine the privilege against compulsory self-incrimination. . . . The police practices that evoked this concern included several that did not involve express questioning. For example, one of the practices discussed in *Miranda* was the use of line-ups in which a coached witness would pick the defendant as the perpetrator. This was designed to establish that the defendant was in fact guilty as a predicate for further interrogation. . . . A variation on this theme discussed in *Miranda* was the so-called "reverse line-up" in which a defendant would be identified by coached witnesses as the perpetrator of a fictitious crime, with the object of inducing him to confess to the actual crime of which he was suspected in order to escape the false prosecution. . . . The Court in *Miranda* also included in its survey of interrogation practices the use of psychological ploys, such as to "posi[t]" "the guilt of the subject," to "minimize the moral seriousness of the offense," and "to cast blame on the victim or on society." . . . It is clear that these techniques of persuasion, no less than express questioning, were thought, in a custodial setting, to amount to interrogation. 446 U.S. at 299, 100 S.Ct. at 1688–89, 64 L.Ed.2d at 306–07.

The *Innis* Court went on to define interrogation for purposes of *Miranda*.

> [T]he Miranda safeguards come into play whenever a person in custody is subjected to either express questioning or its functional equivalent. That is to say, the term "interrogation" under Miranda refers not only to express questioning, but also to any words or actions on the part of police (other than those normally attendant to arrest and custody) that the police should know are reasonably likely to elicit an incriminating response from the suspect. 446 U.S. at 300–01, 100 S.Ct. at 1689, 64 L.Ed.2d at 307–08.

The Supreme Court further refined the definition by stating that an incriminating response is any response—whether inculpatory or exculpatory—that the prosecution may seek to introduce at trial. As stated by the Ninth Circuit Court of Appeals, "It can be in the form of a denial, an admission, an alibi, or any other inculpatory or exculpatory conduct." *Shedelbower v. Estelle,* 885 F.2d 570, 573 (9th Cir. 1989). Although this definition of interrogation is broad, many situations in which a person converses with, or gives information to, a law enforcement officer are not considered to be interrogation for *Miranda* purposes and do not require *Miranda* warnings.

Volunteered Statements

The most obvious situation not constituting interrogation is a volunteered statement—a statement made of a person's own volition and not in response to questioning by a law enforcement officer. In the *Miranda* opinion, the Supreme Court stated that "[v]olunteered statements of any kind are not barred by the Fifth Amendment and their admissibility is not affected by our holding today." 384 U.S. at 478, 86 S.Ct. at 1630, 16 L.Ed.2d at 726.

Volunteered statements sometimes occur when a person, intentionally or unintentionally, makes an incriminating statement in the presence of a law enforcement officer. *United States v. Wright,* 991 F.2d 1180 (4th Cir. 1993), found no interrogation where the defendant, standing in the doorway to his bedroom while it was being legally searched and without any provocation by police, admitted that he had purchased a rifle. Volunteered statements occur more frequently, however, when a person is in custody, either before, during, or after interrogation. *Deck v. United States,* 395 F.2d 89 (9th Cir. 1968). Volunteered statements may occur during interrogation when the suspect makes an incriminating statement that is not in response to an officer's question. For example, in *Parson v. United States,* 387 F.2d 944 (10th Cir. 1968), an officer asked the defendant where the key to his car was, so the car could be moved off the street and put in storage. The defendant replied that the car had been stolen. The court held that the statement that the car was stolen was not responsive to the inquiry about the key and was completely voluntary.

Law enforcement officers need not interrupt a volunteered statement to warn a suspect of *Miranda* rights. The *Miranda* decision specifically states that "[t]here is no requirement that police stop a person who enters a police station and states that he wishes to confess to a crime, or a person who calls the police to offer a confession or any other statement he desires to make." 384 U.S. at 478, 86 S.Ct. at 1630, 16 L.Ed.2d at 726.

Clarifying Questions

Because many volunteered statements are ambiguous, an officer hearing a statement may try to clarify what is being said. Courts have held that a statement is volunteered even if some questions are asked by police. The questions must not, however, be directed to expand on what the person originally intended to say but merely to clear up or explain the original statement. *People v. Sunday,* 79 Cal.Rptr. 752 (Cal.App. 1969).

In *People v. Savage,* 242 N.E.2d 446 (Ill.App. 1968), a man walked into a police station and said, "I done it; I done it; arrest me; arrest me." The officer asked him what he had done, and the man said he killed his wife. Then the officer asked him how, and the man replied, "With an axe, that's all I had." The court held that the officer's clarifying questions were not interrogation and that no *Miranda* warnings were required.

Routine Questions

In the determination of custody, routine questioning is usually indicative of a lack of custody. Courts have also held that routine questioning is not interrogation under *Miranda,* even if the suspect is in custody. Routine booking questions regarding a suspect's name, address, height, weight, eye color, date of birth, and current age to secure biographical data necessary to complete booking or pretrial services fall outside the protections of *Miranda. Pennsylvania v. Muniz,* 496 U.S. 582, 110 S.Ct. 2638, 110 L.Ed.2d 528 (1990). Likewise, in *United States v. Booth,* 669 F.2d 1231 (9th Cir. 1981), the court found no interrogation where a police officer investigating a robbery asked a person resembling the description of one of the perpetrators to state his name, age, and residence.

Routine questioning in connection with enforcement of implied consent laws is also not interrogation. For example, in *South Dakota v. Neville,* 459 U.S. 553, 565 n.15, 103 S.Ct. 916, 923 n.15, 74 L.Ed.2d 748, 759 n.15 (1983), the U.S. Supreme Court stated that "[i]n the context of an arrest for driving while intoxicated, a police inquiry of whether the suspect will take a blood-alcohol test is not an interrogation within the meaning of *Miranda.*" Nor is police questioning of a suspect to determine whether a suspect understands instructions as to how physical sobriety tests or breathalyzer tests are to be performed. *Pennsylvania v. Muniz,* 496 U.S. 582, 110 S.Ct. 2638, 110 L.Ed.2d 528 (1990).

When a police officer has reason to know that a suspect's answer may incriminate him or her, however, even routine questioning may amount to interrogation. Thus, although there is usually nothing objectionable about asking a detainee his place of birth, the same question assumes a completely different character when an Immigration and Naturalization Service (INS) agent asks it of a person he suspects is an illegal alien. *United States v. Gonzalez-Sandoval,* 894 F.2d 1043 (9th Cir. 1990), held that such a question was interrogation. Likewise, *United States v. Disla,* 805 F.2d 1340 (9th Cir. 1986), held that questioning a defendant as to his residence subjected him to interrogation, where the officer knew that a large quantity of cocaine and cash had been found at the defendant's apartment and that the residents of the apartment had not been identified. The officer suspected the defendant of cocaine possession and "should have known that the question regarding Disla's residence was reasonably likely to elicit an incriminating response." 805 F.2d at 1347.

Spontaneous Questions

When law enforcement officers ask questions spontaneously, impulsively, or in response to an emergency, the questions are usually held not to be interrogation. In *People v. Morse,* 76 Cal.Rptr. 391, 452 P.2d 607 (Cal. 1969), a jailer and a guard were called to a cell area where they found a prisoner near death from strangling. While tending to the injured prisoner, they asked the defendant, who was also a prisoner, about the incident and received incriminating replies. The court held that this questioning was couched in a context of "stupefied wonderment," not one of incisive inquiry, and that the questioning was not interrogation for purposes of *Miranda.*

In *Turner v. Sullivan,* 661 F.Supp. 535 (E.D.N.Y. 1987), a law enforcement officer asked, "What happened to you?" when the arrested defendant complained that his leg was hurting, and the defendant gave an incriminating response. The court held that there was no interrogation.

> [T]he officer's question was a natural response to petitioner's remark that his leg hurt. The statement at issue was part of a colloquy, initiated by petitioner, about his physical condition. The officer's inquiry was not an effort to elicit information, but rather evidenced the appropriate concern about petitioner's injuries. The officer could not have foreseen that the response might help the prosecution by placing defendant at the scene of the crime. Accordingly, because there was no interrogation and thus no *Miranda* violation, the statement was properly admitted. 661 F.Supp. at 538.

Questions Related to Public Safety

Closely related to spontaneous questions are questions asked by a law enforcement officer out of a concern for public safety. In *New York v. Quarles,* 467 U.S. 649, 104

S.Ct. 2626, 81 L.Ed.2d 550 (1984), two police officers were approached by a woman who told them that she had just been raped and that her assailant had entered a nearby supermarket and was carrying a gun. One of the officers entered the store and observed the defendant, who matched the description given by the woman. The officer pursued the defendant with a drawn gun and ordered him to stop and put his hands over his head. The officer frisked the defendant and discovered that he was wearing an empty shoulder holster. After handcuffing the defendant, the officer asked him where the gun was, and the defendant nodded toward some empty cartons and responded that "the gun is over there."

Although the defendant was in police custody when he made his statements and the facts fell within the coverage of *Miranda,* the U.S. Supreme Court held that there was a "public safety" exception to the requirement that *Miranda* warnings be given before a suspect's answers may be admitted into evidence. The Court said:

> The police in this case, in the very act of apprehending a suspect, were confronted with the immediate necessity of ascertaining the whereabouts of a gun which they had every reason to believe the suspect had just removed from his empty holster and discarded in the supermarket. So long as the gun was concealed somewhere in the supermarket, with its actual whereabouts unknown, it obviously posed more than one danger to the public safety: an accomplice might make use of it, a customer or employee might later come upon it. 467 U.S. at 657, 104 S.Ct. at 2632, 81 L.Ed.2d at 557–58.

The Court concluded that the need for answers to questions in a situation posing a threat to the public safety outweighed the need for the prophylactic rule protecting the Fifth Amendment's privilege against self-incrimination. Furthermore, the Court held that the availability of the public safety exception does not depend on the motivation of the individual officers involved. The Court recognized that in a spontaneous, emergency situation like the one in the *Quarles* case, most police officers act out of several different, instinctive motives: a concern for their own safety and that of others, and, perhaps, the desire to obtain incriminating evidence from the suspect. A rigid adherence to the *Miranda* rules is not required when police officers ask questions reasonably prompted by a concern for the public safety.

Finally, the Court acknowledged that the public safety exception lessens the clarity of the *Miranda* rule but expressed confidence that the police would instinctively respond appropriately in situations threatening the public safety.

> [W]e recognize here the importance of a workable rule "to guide police officers, who have only limited time and expertise to reflect on and balance the social and individual interests involved in the specific circumstances they confront." But we believe that the [public safety] exception lessens the necessity of that on-the-scene balancing process. The exception will not be difficult for police officers to apply because in each case it will be circumscribed by the exigency which justifies it. We think police officers can and will distinguish almost instinctively between questions necessary to secure their own safety or the safety of the public and questions designed solely to elicit testimonial evidence from a suspect. 467 U.S. at 658–59, 104 S.Ct. at 2633, 81 L.Ed.2d at 559.

Note that the ruling in the *Quarles* case is an exception to the *Miranda* rule, and as an exception, it must be construed narrowly.

As the *Quarles* Court indicated, the "public safety" exception applies only where there is "an objectively reasonable need to protect the police or the public from any immediate danger associated with [a] weapon." . . . Absent such circumstances posing an objective danger to the public or police, the need for the exception is not apparent, and the suspicion that the questioner is on a fishing expedition outweighs the belief that public safety motivated the questioning that all understand is otherwise improper. *United States v. Mobley,* 40 F.3d 688, 693 (4th Cir. 1994).

In the *Mobley* case, the court found no immediate danger requiring questioning regarding the presence of weapons where

- the defendant answered the door to his apartment naked;
- by the time he was arrested, the FBI had already made a protective sweep of the premises and found that he was the only one present; and
- the questioning took place as the defendant was being led away from his apartment.

Confrontation of Suspect with Evidence

In general, it is proper for a law enforcement officer to confront a suspect with evidence or other facts in a case being investigated. Often, after such a confrontation, a suspect may make incriminating statements. Are these incriminating statements voluntary, or are they the product of a form of "silent interrogation"?

Courts have decided the issue both ways depending on the circumstances of individual cases. When there is no verbal interrogation and the suspect is merely confronted with evidence, courts have held that incriminating statements made after the confrontation were not the product of interrogation. *People v. Doss,* 256 N.E.2d 753 (Ill. 1970). When, however, along with such a confrontation, an officer subtly attempts to get the suspect to talk, courts have found interrogation and have suppressed statements obtained without prior warnings. *State v. LaFernier,* 155 N.W.2d 93 (Wis. 1967). The crucial question under *Rhode Island v. Innis* (discussed earlier) is whether the officer's words or actions are reasonably likely to elicit an incriminating response. *Toliver v. Gathright,* 501 F.Supp. 148 (E.D.Va. 1980).

Confrontation of Suspect with Accomplice

In general, whether confronting a suspect with an accomplice to the crime is the functional equivalent of interrogation depends on what is or said in connection with the confrontation. As the Third Circuit Court of Appeals stated:

> Confronting a suspect with his alleged partner and informing him that his alleged partner has confessed is very likely to spark an incriminating response from a suspect if that suspect is in fact guilty. Accordingly we conclude that if the police, or [the alleged partner] at the police's instruction, had already confronted Nelson [the defendant] with the confession, then this case falls squarely under *Innis*'s prohibition of ploys reasonably likely to elicit an incriminating response. On the other hand, if Nelson had not been informed of the confession by the words or conduct of [the partner] or the police, then suppression of the remark was not required; we cannot say that merely placing a suspect in the same room with his partner in crime, without *any* additional stimulus, is reasonably likely to evoke an incriminating response. *Nelson v. Fulcomer,* 911 F.2d 928, 934 (3d Cir. 1990).

In *Shedelbower v. Estelle*, 885 F.2d 570 (9th Cir. 1989), however, the court found that it was not the functional equivalent of interrogation for an officer to correctly inform the defendant that a codefendant was in custody and to falsely add that the victim had identified his picture as one of the perpetrators. The court said that these were not the type of comments that would encourage the defendant to make some spontaneous incriminating remark.

Statements or Actions of Officers

A law enforcement officer may receive an incriminating response to his or her mere comment or statement or an action that is not a question. If the officer's words or actions were not such that "the police should know are reasonably likely to elicit an incriminating response from the suspect," they are not interrogation. In *Rhode Island v. Innis*, 446 U.S. 291, 100 S.Ct. 1682, 64 L.Ed.2d 297 (1980), a conversation between police officers in the presence of the defendant expressing concern that area children with disabilities might find a missing shotgun was held not to be interrogation.

> There is nothing in the record to suggest that the officers were aware that the respondent was peculiarly susceptible to an appeal to his conscience concerning the safety of handicapped children. Nor is there anything in the record to suggest that the police knew that the respondent was unusually disoriented or upset at the time of his arrest.
>
> The case thus boils down to whether, in the context of a brief conversation, the officers should have known that the respondent would suddenly be moved to make a self-incriminating response. Given the fact that the entire conversation appears to have consisted of no more than a few off hand remarks, we cannot say that the officers should have known that it was reasonably likely that Innis would so respond. This is not a case where the police carried on a lengthy harangue in the presence of the suspect. Nor does the record support the respondent's contention that, under the circumstances, the officers' comments were particularly "evocative." It is our view, therefore, that the respondent was not subjected by the police to words or actions that the police should have known were reasonably likely to elicit an incriminating response from him. 446 U.S. 291, 302–03, 100 S.Ct. 1682, 1690–91, 64 L.Ed.2d 297, 309.

In general, a law enforcement officer's informational response to a suspect's inquiry about the reasons for an arrest or investigation does not constitute interrogation. For example, it was held not to be interrogation for an officer, in response to a suspect's question about the reason for her arrest, to reply, "You can't be growing dope on your property like that." *United States v. Taylor*, 985 F.2d 3 (1st Cir. 1993).

If, however, the officer's statement is deliberately directed toward eliciting incriminating information, courts will consider the statement as tantamount to interrogation. In *United States v. Montana*, 958 F.2d 516, 518 (2d Cir. 1992), the court held that the officer's "unsolicited statement informing the defendants that any cooperation would be brought to the attention of the Assistant United States Attorney constituted 'interrogation.'" (See also *Brewer v. Williams*, 430 U.S. 387, 97 S.Ct. 1232, 51 L.Ed.2d 424 [1977], discussed later in this chapter under the heading "Attempts After Defendant Is Formally Charged.")

In *United States v. Samuels*, 938 F.2d 210 (D.C.Cir. 1991), the removal by an officer of a photograph of the defendant's son from the defendant's bag was held not to be the functional equivalent of interrogation. The court found that the officer could not have known that his action was reasonably likely to elicit an incriminating response.

Interrogation by Private Citizens

The *Miranda* warning requirements apply only to custodial interrogations conducted by *law enforcement officers*. Therefore, incriminating statements made by a person in response to custodial interrogation by a private citizen will be admissible in court despite a lack of prior warnings. In *United States v. Pace*, 833 F.2d 1307 (9th Cir. 1987), the defendant's cell mate, acting on his own initiative and without prior arrangement with the government, elicited incriminating statements from the defendant. The court held that, since the cell mate was not the government's agent, the government did not participate in any custodial interrogation in obtaining the confession, and no *Miranda* warnings were required. Similarly, a statement made to a nurse during routine performance of medical duties in a hospital emergency room was held not to be the product of interrogation. *United States v. Romero*, 897 F.2d 47 (2d Cir. 1990).

Multiple Attempts at Interrogation

In the *Miranda* opinion, the Court said:

> Once warnings have been given, the subsequent procedure is clear. If the individual indicates in any manner, at any time prior to or during questioning, that he wishes to remain silent, the interrogation must cease. At this point he has shown that he intends to exercise his Fifth Amendment privilege; any statement taken after the person invokes his privilege cannot be other than the product of compulsion, subtle or otherwise. Without the right to cut off questioning, the setting of in-custody interrogation operates on the individual to overcome free choice in producing a statement after the privilege has been once invoked. If the individual states that he wants an attorney, the interrogation must cease until an attorney is present. At that time the individual must have an opportunity to confer with the attorney and to have him present during any subsequent questioning. If the individual cannot obtain an attorney and he indicates that he wants one before speaking to police, they must respect his decision to remain silent. 384 U.S. at 473–74, 86 S.Ct. at 1627–28, 16 L.Ed.2d at 723.

The quoted language commands that, once a suspect indicates either a desire to remain silent or a desire for an attorney, all questioning must stop, at least until the suspect confers with an attorney. Nevertheless, under certain circumstances, some courts have admitted statements obtained after multiple attempts to question suspects.

ATTEMPTS AFTER RIGHT TO SILENCE IS INVOKED. The U.S. Supreme Court has, under limited conditions, allowed a second interrogation of a suspect who exercised the *Miranda* right of silence after being given warnings.

The* Mosley *Rule. In *Michigan v. Mosley*, 423 U.S. 96, 96 S.Ct. 321, 46 L.Ed.2d 313 (1975), the defendant was arrested early in the afternoon in connection with certain robberies and was given the *Miranda* warnings by a police detective. After indicating that he understood the warnings, the defendant declined to discuss the robberies, and the detective ceased the interrogation. Shortly after 6:00 P.M. the same day, after giving another set of *Miranda* warnings, a different police detective questioned the defendant about a murder that was unrelated to the robberies. The defendant made an incriminating statement that was used against him at his trial. He was convicted of the murder.

The Court held that admitting the defendant's statement into evidence did not violate *Miranda* principles. Even though the *Miranda* opinion states that the interrogation must cease when the person in custody indicates a desire to remain silent, the Court in the *Mosley* case held that "neither this passage nor any other passage in the *Miranda* opinion can sensibly be read to create a per se proscription of indefinite duration upon any further questioning by any police officer on any subject, once the person in custody has indicated a desire to remain silent." 423 U.S. at 102–03, 96 S.Ct. at 326, 46 L.Ed.2d at 320–21. The Court then gave several reasons that it allowed the second interrogation in the *Mosley* case:

- The defendant's right to cut off questioning had been "scrupulously honored" by the first detective.
- The first detective ceased the interrogation when the defendant refused to answer and did not try to wear down his resistance by repeated efforts to make him change his mind.
- The second interrogation was directed toward a different crime with a different time and place of occurrence.
- And, the second interrogation began after a significant time lapse and after the defendant had been given a fresh set of warnings.

In *United States v. Olof,* 527 F.2d 752 (9th Cir. 1975), the court held that a second interrogation by federal agents, conducted three hours after the defendant had refused to make a statement after being given the *Miranda* warnings, violated the defendant's rights. Although the agents gave the defendant fresh warnings, they pressured him to cooperate and they questioned him about the same crime for which the first warnings were given. In *Jackson v. Dugger,* 837 F.2d 1469 (11th Cir. 1988), however, the court held that the defendant's invocation of the right to silence was scrupulously honored where the police discontinued questioning after each invocation of the right, more than six hours elapsed between the initial invocation of the right and the confession, fresh warnings were given before the confession, and there was no allegation of overbearing police conduct.

These cases suggest the following guidelines for conducting a second custodial interrogation of a person who has exercised the *Miranda* right to remain silent.

- Scrupulously honor the person's right to terminate questioning at the initial interrogation.
- Allow a significant amount of time to intervene between the first and second interrogation attempts.
- Give the person complete *Miranda* warnings again.
- Do not employ any pressure to cooperate or other illegal tactics.

Invocation of the Right to Silence. In *United States v. Mikell,* 102 F.3d 470 (11th Cir. 1996), the court ruled that a suspect must articulate his desire to end questioning with sufficient clarity so that a reasonable police officer would understand that statement to be an assertion of the right to remain silent. Relying on *Davis v. United States* (see page 460), the court added that if the statement is ambiguous or equivocal, the police have no duty to clarify the suspect's intent, and they may proceed with the interrogation. No particular word or combination of words is required to invoke the Fifth Amendment right to remain silent. For example, a suspect who acknowledged that he understood his *Miranda* rights by nodding and then remained silent in response to all pedigree questions was held to have sufficiently asserted his right to remain silent. *United States v. Montana,* 958 F.2d 516 (2d Cir. 1992). However, the *Mikell* case held that a suspect's refusal to answer certain questions, but not others, is not tantamount to the invocation, either equivocal or unequivocal, of the constitutional right to remain silent and that questioning may continue until the suspect articulates in some manner that he wishes the questioning to cease.

ATTEMPTS AFTER RIGHT TO COUNSEL IS INVOKED. As the quotation at the beginning of this section indicates, *Miranda* created a rigid rule that an accused's request for an attorney is per se an invocation of Fifth Amendment rights, requiring that all interrogation cease. This rigid rule is based on an attorney's unique ability to protect the Fifth Amendment rights of a client undergoing custodial interrogation. Once an accused person indicates that he or she is not competent to deal with the authorities without legal advice, courts will closely examine any later choice to make a decision without counsel's presence. Therefore, although an accused may waive *Miranda* rights and submit to interrogation, the U.S. Supreme Court has recognized that additional safeguards are necessary after an accused has exercised the right to counsel.

The Edwards *Rule.* The Supreme Court established these safeguards in the case of *Edwards v. Arizona*, 451 U.S. 477, 101 S.Ct. 1880, 68 L.Ed.2d 378 (1981). In that case, the defendant voluntarily submitted to questioning but later stated that he wanted an attorney before the discussions continued. The following day, detectives accosted the defendant in the county jail, and when the defendant refused to speak with the detectives, he was told that he "had" to talk. The Court held that subsequent incriminating statements made without his attorney present violated the rights secured to the defendant by the Fifth and Fourteenth Amendments. The Court stated:

> [W]hen an accused has invoked his right to have counsel present during custodial interrogation, a valid waiver of that right cannot be established by showing only that he responded to further police-initiated custodial interrogation even if he has been advised of his rights. We further hold that an accused, such as [the defendant], having expressed his desire to deal with the police only through counsel, is not subject to further interrogation by the authorities until counsel has been made available to him, unless the accused himself initiates further communication, exchanges, or conversations with the police. 451 U.S. at 484–85, 101 S.Ct. at 1884–85, 68 L.Ed.2d at 386.

The requirement that counsel be "made available" refers to more than an opportunity to consult with an attorney outside the interrogation room. In *Minnick v. Mississippi*, 498 U.S. 146, 153, 111 S.Ct. 486, 491, 112 L.Ed.2d 489, 498 (1990), the U.S. Supreme Court held that

> a fair reading of *Edwards* and subsequent cases demonstrates that we have interpreted the rule to bar police-initiated interrogation unless the accused has counsel with him at the time of questioning. . . . [W]hen counsel is requested, interrogation must cease, and officials may not reinitiate interrogation without counsel *present,* whether or not the accused has consulted with his attorney. [Emphasis supplied.]

The *Minnick* rule has no time limitation and is effective as long as the suspect remains in custody. Therefore, once a defendant invokes the right to counsel, the police are forever barred from initiating further custodial interrogation of the defendant unless defense counsel is present at the interview. Moreover, the *Minnick* rule bars further police-initiated interrogation about unrelated charges unless counsel is present. *Arizona v. Roberson*, 486 U.S. 675, 108 S.Ct. 2093, 100 L.Ed.2d 704 (1988). In summary, unless counsel is present, or unless the accused initiates further conversations, a waiver of *Miranda* rights after invocation of the right to counsel is presumed involuntary. Incriminating statements obtained after such an involuntary waiver, regardless of their merit, will be suppressed.

Relying on the Sixth Amendment, the Supreme Court also prohibited further interrogation without counsel present after assertions of the right to counsel *made at or after the initiation of adversary judicial proceedings.* The Court held that "if police initiate interrogation after a defendant's assertion, at an arraignment or similar proceeding, of his right to counsel, any waiver of the defendant's right to counsel for that police-initiated interrogation is invalid." *Michigan v. Jackson,* 475 U.S. 625, 636, 106 S.Ct. 1404, 1411, 89 L.Ed.2d 631, 642 (1986). The Sixth Amendment right to counsel, however, unlike the *Miranda* Fifth Amendment right to counsel, is *offense-specific.* Invocation of the Sixth Amendment right bars police-initiated interrogation regarding *only* the offense at issue; it does not bar later police-initiated interrogation on an unrelated charge.

> The purpose of the Sixth Amendment counsel guarantee—and hence the purpose of invoking it—is to "protec[t] the unaided layman at critical confrontations" with his "expert adversary," the government, *after* "the adverse positions of government and defendant have solidified" with respect to a particular alleged crime. . . . The purpose of the *Miranda-Edwards* guarantee, on the other hand— and hence the purpose of invoking it—is to protect a quite different interest: the suspect's "desire to deal with the police only through counsel," . . . This is in one respect narrower than the interest protected by the Sixth Amendment guarantee (because it relates only to custodial interrogation) and in another respect broader (because it relates to interrogation regarding any suspected crime and attaches whether or not the "adversarial relationship" produced by a pending prosecution has yet arisen). To invoke the Sixth Amendment interest is, as a matter of *fact, not* to invoke the *Miranda-Edwards* interest. *McNeil v. Wisconsin,* 501 U.S. 171, 178–79, 111 S.Ct. 2204, 2208–09, 115 L.Ed.2d 158, 168 (1991).

Interrogation or Its Functional Equivalent. If police action after the suspect has invoked his or her right to counsel is not "interrogation" or the "functional equivalent" of interrogation, then neither the *Edwards* rule nor the *Jackson* rule apply, and the suspect's statements will be admissible. In *Arizona v. Mauro,* 481 U.S. 520, 107 S.Ct. 1931, 95 L.Ed.2d 458 (1987), the defendant, who was in custody on suspicion of murdering his son, indicated that he did not wish to be questioned further without a lawyer present, and the questioning then ceased. The defendant's wife, who was being questioned in another room, asked whether she could speak to her husband. They were allowed to speak, but an officer was present in the room, and the conversation was tape-recorded with the couple's knowledge. The recording was used against the defendant at his trial.

The U.S. Supreme Court held that the actions of the police were not the functional equivalent of police interrogation. No evidence indicated that the officers sent the wife in to see her husband for the purpose of eliciting incriminating statements. Nor was the officer's presence in the room improper, because there were legitimate reasons for his presence, including the wife's safety and various security considerations. Furthermore, it is improbable that the defendant would have felt he was being coerced to incriminate himself simply because he was told his wife would be allowed to speak to him. Even though the police knew there was a possibility that the defendant would incriminate himself, "[o]fficers do not interrogate a suspect simply by hoping that he will incriminate himself." 481 U.S. at 529, 107 S.Ct. at 1936, 95 L.Ed.2d at 468. The

Court held that the officers acted reasonably and that the defendant's tape-recorded statements could be used against him at trial. "Police departments need not adopt inflexible rules barring suspects from speaking with their spouses, nor must they ignore legitimate security concerns by allowing spouses to meet in private." 481 U.S. at 530, 107 S.Ct. at 1937, 95 L.Ed.2d at 468.

The following actions by police have been held to be interrogation, or the functional equivalent of interrogation, in violation of the *Edwards* rule prohibiting further interrogation after the defendant's invocation of the right to counsel.

- Reinterrogation about a separate offense. "[T]he presumption raised by a suspect's request for counsel—that he considers himself unable to deal with the pressures of custodial interrogation without legal assistance—does not disappear simply because the police have approached the suspect, still in custody, still without counsel, about a separate investigation." *Arizona v. Roberson,* 486 U.S. 675, 683, 108 S.Ct. 2093, 2099, 100 L.Ed.2d 704, 715 (1988).

- Resubmitting a waiver of rights form (which the defendant previously refused to sign) accompanied by an announcement that a victim of a shooting had died and that the charge was now murder. (The waiver of rights form is discussed later in this chapter.) *State v. Iovino,* 524 A.2d 556 (R.I. 1987).

- Offering to explain the operation of the criminal justice system to the defendant. (The court noted that despite their seeming innocence, such explanations are often designed to inform a defendant that cooperation may be beneficial.) *United States v. Johnson,* 812 F.2d 1329 (11th Cir. 1986).

- Exhibiting an incriminating document to the defendant ten minutes after he had invoked his *Miranda* right to counsel. *United States v. Walker,* 624 F.Supp. 103 (D.Md. 1985).

- Calling the defendant by the nickname of the person believed to have committed the particular offense. *State v. Dellorfano,* 517 A.2d 1163 (N.H. 1986).

- Confronting the defendant with an arrest warrant and photographs of his fingerprints taken at the crime scene. *Clark v. Marshall,* 600 F.Supp. 1520 (E.D.Ohio 1985).

- Questioning about the ownership of an automobile parked at the crime scene. *United States v. Monzon,* 869 F.2d 338 (7th Cir. 1989).

Other examples of what does and does not constitute interrogation appear on pages 449 through 455.

Invocation of the Right to Counsel. In *Patterson v. Illinois,* 487 U.S. 285, 108 S.Ct. 2389, 101 L.Ed.2d 261 (1988), the U.S. Supreme Court held that, under the *Edwards* rule, police-initiated interrogation will be barred only after the right to counsel is *invoked.* In that case, the defendant's Sixth Amendment right to counsel came into existence with his indictment, but, unlike the defendant in *Michigan v. Jackson,* he did not ask for counsel after receiving the *Miranda* warnings. The Court said that the interrogation of the defendant after indictment was indistinguishable from the interrogation of a person before indictment whose right to counsel is in existence and available to be exercised during questioning. The Court said:

> Preserving the integrity of an accused's choice to communicate with police only through counsel is the essence of *Edwards* and its progeny—not barring an accused from making an *initial* selection as to whether he will face the State's

officers during questioning with the aid of counsel, or go it alone. If an accused "knowingly and intelligently" pursues the latter course, we see no reason why the uncounseled statements he then makes must be excluded at his trial. 487 U.S. at 291, 108 S.Ct. at 2394, 101 L.Ed.2d at 271–72.

In *Smith v. Illinois,* 469 U.S. 91, 105 S.Ct. 490, 83 L.Ed.2d 488 (1984), the Court held that, after an accused has invoked the right to counsel, courts will not allow an accused's responses to further interrogation to be used to cast retrospective doubt on the clarity of the initial request itself. The Court said, "'No authority, and no logic, permits the interrogator to proceed . . . on his own terms and as if the defendant had requested nothing, in the hope that the defendant might be induced to say something casting retrospective doubt on his initial statement that he wished to speak through an attorney or not at all.'" 469 U.S. at 99, 105 S.Ct. at 494, 83 L.Ed.2d at 496.

Under *Edwards,* after a knowing and voluntary waiver of the *Miranda* rights, law enforcement officers may continue questioning until and unless the suspect clearly requests an attorney. Ambiguous or equivocal references to an attorney are insufficient to invoke a suspect's right to counsel.

> Although a suspect need not "speak with the discrimination of an Oxford don," . . . he must articulate his desire to have counsel present sufficiently clearly that a reasonable police officer in the circumstances would understand the statement to be a request for an attorney. If the statement fails to meet the requisite level of clarity, *Edwards* does not require that the officers stop questioning the suspect. *Davis v. United States,* 512 U.S. 452, 459, 114 S.Ct. 2350, 2355, 129 L.Ed.2d 362, 371 (1994).

Of course, when a suspect makes an ambiguous or equivocal statement, it will often be good police practice for the interviewing officers to clarify whether he or she actually wants an attorney.

> Clarifying questions help protect the rights of the suspect by ensuring that he gets an attorney if he wants one, and will minimize the chance of a confession being suppressed due to subsequent judicial second-guessing as to the meaning of the suspect's statement regarding counsel. But we decline to adopt a rule requiring officers to ask clarifying questions. If the suspect's statement is not an unambiguous or unequivocal request for counsel, the officers have no obligation to stop questioning him. 512 U.S. at 461–62, 114 S.Ct. at 2356, 129 L.Ed.2d at 373.

In the *Davis* case, the court held that the suspect's remark "Maybe I should talk to a lawyer" was not a clear request for a lawyer, and officers therefore were not required to stop questioning him.

Initiation of Further Communications. In *Oregon v. Bradshaw,* 462 U.S. 1039, 103 S.Ct. 2830, 77 L.Ed.2d 405 (1983), the U.S. Supreme Court attempted to explain what would constitute the initiation of further communication with the police:

> [T]here are undoubtedly situations where a bare inquiry by either a defendant or by a police officer should not be held to "initiate" any conversation or dialogue. There are some inquiries, such as a request for a drink of water or a request to use a telephone that are so routine that they cannot be fairly said to represent a desire on the part of an accused to open up a more generalized discussion relating directly or indirectly to the investigation. Such inquiries or statements, by either an accused or a police officer, relating to routine incidents of the custodial relationship, will not generally "initiate" a conversation in the sense in which

that word was used in Edwards. 462 U.S. at 1045, 103 S.Ct. at 2835, 77 L.Ed.2d at 412.

In *Bradshaw,* the Court found that the defendant's question to a police officer, after the defendant had asked for an attorney, as to what was going to happen to him now "evinced a willingness and a desire for a generalized discussion about the investigation; it was not merely a necessary inquiry arising out of the incidents of the custodial relationship." 462 U.S. at 412, 103 S.Ct. at 2835, 77 L.Ed.2d at 412.

Waiver of Rights. The *Edwards* case also established a second prerequisite to police interrogation of an accused who has invoked the right to have counsel present during custodial interrogation. Once it is established that the accused "initiated" further conversation or dialogue with the police, the next inquiry is

> whether a valid waiver of the right to counsel and the right to silence had occurred, that is, whether the purported waiver was knowing and intelligent and found to be so under the totality of the circumstances, including the necessary fact that the accused, not the police, reopened the dialogue with the authorities. 451 U.S. at 486 n.9, 101 S.Ct. at 1885 n.9, 68 L.Ed.2d at 387 n.9.

In the *Bradshaw* case, the Court found a knowing waiver where the police made no threats, promises, or inducements to talk; the defendant was properly advised of his rights and understood them; and within a short time the defendant changed his mind and decided to talk without any impropriety on the part of the police. In *Wyrick v. Fields,* 459 U.S. 42, 44, 103 S.Ct. 394, 396, 74 L.Ed.2d 214, 218 (1982), the U.S. Supreme Court held that by waiving his right to counsel at a polygraph examination, the accused also validly waived his right to have counsel present at posttest questioning, "unless the circumstances changed so seriously that his answers no longer were voluntary, or unless he no longer was making a 'knowing and intelligent relinquishment or abandonment' of his rights." (See the discussion of waiver later in this chapter.)

To summarize, before a suspect in custody can be subjected to further uncounseled interrogation after requesting an attorney, there must first be a showing that the suspect initiated communication with the authorities. Once this is established, it is still necessary to establish as a separate matter the existence of a knowing and intelligent waiver of the right to counsel and the right to silence. Once a valid waiver is made, interrogation may continue until the circumstances change so seriously that the answers are no longer voluntary or until the accused revokes the waiver.

ATTEMPTS AFTER RIGHTS ARE WAIVED. Often, a suspect may waive *Miranda* rights and submit to interrogation, and after an interval of time, police may wish to interrogate the suspect again. The general rule is that

> the *Miranda* rights "need not be repeated so long as the circumstances attending any interruption or adjournment of the process [are] such that the suspect has not been deprived of the opportunity to make an informed and intelligent assessment of his interest involved in the interrogation, including his right to cut off questioning." *Bivins v. State,* 642 N.E.2d 928, 939 (Ind. 1994).

The Supreme Court of Pennsylvania listed five significant factors in determining whether an accused must be reinformed of his or her *Miranda* rights:

> (1) the time lapse between the last *Miranda* warnings and the accused's statement; (2) interruptions in the continuity of the interrogation; (3) whether there

was a change of location between the place where the last *Miranda* warnings were given and the place where the accused's statement was made; (4) whether the same officer who gave the warnings also conducted the interrogation resulting in the accused's statement; and (5) whether the statement elicited during the complained of interrogation differed significantly from other statements which had been preceded by *Miranda* warnings. *Commonwealth v. Wideman,* 334 A.2d 594, 598 (Pa. 1975).

Where *Miranda* warnings are not repeated during an ongoing interrogation, the ultimate question is whether the defendant, with full knowledge of his or her legal rights, knowingly and intentionally relinquished those rights.

ATTEMPTS AFTER AN UNWARNED ADMISSION. In *Oregon v. Elstad,* 470 U.S. 298, 105 S.Ct. 1285, 84 L.Ed.2d 222 (1985), a law enforcement officer investigating a burglary obtained an admission from the defendant in a custodial setting without first giving him the *Miranda* warnings. Shortly thereafter, at the station house, the defendant received complete *Miranda* warnings, waived his rights, and gave a written confession.

The U.S. Supreme Court held that, although the initial unwarned admission was inadmissible in court, the written confession was admissible. The Court reasoned that, despite the *Miranda* violation before the officer obtained the first admission, there was no *constitutional* violation, since no coercion or other illegal means were used to break the defendant's will. (In other words, a *Miranda* violation is not a constitutional violation unless it is accompanied by other circumstances indicating that the defendant's statement was compelled.) Because the first admission was obtained without a constitutional violation, the "fruit of the poisonous tree" doctrine did not apply to the written confession obtained shortly thereafter. (That doctrine applies only to constitutional violations; see Chapter 3.)

The Court then evaluated the written statement as follows:

> We must conclude that, absent deliberately coercive or improper tactics in obtaining the initial statement, the mere fact that a suspect has made an unwarned admission does not warrant a presumption of compulsion. A subsequent administration of *Miranda* warnings to a suspect who has given a voluntary but unwarned statement ordinarily should suffice to remove the conditions that precluded admission of the earlier statement. In such circumstances, the finder of fact may reasonably conclude that the suspect made a rational and intelligent choice whether to waive or invoke his rights. 470 U.S. at 314, 105 S.Ct. at 1296, 84 L.Ed.2d at 235.

For the law enforcement officer, the lesson from the *Elstad* case is that, after an admission is obtained as a result of interrogating a suspect, the officer should carefully comply with all *Miranda* procedures in all subsequent interrogations, before obtaining further statements, no matter how much time has elapsed between interrogations. This will ensure that, even if an earlier statement is ruled inadmissible because of a *Miranda* violation, later statements will have a better chance of being admitted. Furthermore, even if an officer believes that a statement has been obtained in violation of *Miranda,* the officer need not warn that the statement cannot be used against the suspect. "Police officers are ill equipped to pinch-hit for counsel, construing the murky and difficult questions of when 'custody' begins or whether a given unwarned statement will ultimately be held inadmissible." 470 U.S. at 316, 105 S.Ct. at 1297, 84 L.Ed.2d at 237.

ATTEMPTS AFTER DEFENDANT IS FORMALLY CHARGED. In *Massiah v. United States,* 377 U.S. 201, 84 S.Ct. 1199, 12 L.Ed.2d 246 (1964), after the defendant was indicted, federal agents obtained incriminating statements from the defendant in the absence of his counsel. While the defendant was free on bail, his codefendant, in cooperation with the federal agents, engaged the defendant in conversation in the presence of a hidden radio transmitter. The Court held that the statements were inadmissible because the defendant was denied the basic protection of his Sixth Amendment right to assistance of counsel.

The *Massiah* decision has become less significant in recent years because the *Miranda* decision has resulted in courts shifting their emphasis from the Sixth Amendment to the Fifth Amendment. Nevertheless, as stated by the Fifth Circuit Court of Appeals:

> [I]t [*Massiah*] retains its vitality and stands as a supplement to *Miranda: Massiah* teaches that although the government may properly continue to gather evidence against a defendant after he has been indicted, it may not nullify the protection *Miranda* affords a defendant by using trickery to extract incriminating statements from him that otherwise could not be obtained without first giving the required warnings. Today *Massiah* simply means that after indictment and counsel has been retained the Fifth Amendment prevents law enforcement authorities from deliberately eliciting incriminating statements from a defendant by the surreptitious methods used in that case. *United States v. Hayles,* 471 F.2d 788, 791 (5th Cir. 1973).

The U.S. Supreme Court affirmed the continuing validity of the *Massiah* case in *Brewer v. Williams,* 430 U.S. 387, 97 S.Ct. 1232, 51 L.Ed.2d 424 (1977). In that case, the defendant had been arrested, arraigned, and jailed in Davenport, Iowa, for abducting a ten-year-old girl in Des Moines, Iowa, and was being transported by police to Des Moines to talk to his lawyer there. Both the defendant's Des Moines lawyer and the lawyer at his Davenport arraignment advised the defendant not to make any statements until after he had consulted with his Des Moines lawyer. The police officers who were to accompany the defendant on the trip agreed not to question him during the trip. Nevertheless, one of the police officers, who knew that the defendant was a former mental patient and was deeply religious, suggested that the defendant reveal the location of the girl's body because her parents were entitled to a Christian burial for the girl, who was taken away from them on Christmas Eve. The defendant eventually made several incriminating statements during the trip and finally directed the police to the girl's body.

The Court, citing *Massiah,* held that a person against whom adversary proceedings have commenced has a right to legal representation when the government interrogates him or her. Because the officer's "Christian burial" speech was tantamount to interrogation and the defendant had been formally charged, the defendant was entitled to the assistance of counsel at the time he made the incriminating statements. The Court found that the defendant did not waive his right to counsel and therefore held any evidence relating to or resulting from his statements inadmissible.

In *United States v. Henry,* 447 U.S. 264, 100 S.Ct. 2183, 65 L.Ed.2d 115 (1980), the Supreme Court held inadmissible statements made by an indicted and imprisoned defendant to a paid, undisclosed government informant who was in the same cell block. Although the informant did not question the defendant, the informant "stimulated" conversations with the defendant and developed a relationship of trust and confidence with the defendant. As a result, the defendant made incriminating statements without the assistance of counsel. This indirect and surreptitious type of interrogation was an impermissible interference with the defendant's right to the assistance of counsel in violation of *Massiah*. The Court emphasized the potential susceptibility of an incarcerated person to subtle influences of government undercover agents.

Furthermore, even when a confrontation between an accused and a police agent is initiated by the accused, the government may not deliberately attempt to elicit information without counsel being present. In *Maine v. Moulton*, 474 U.S. 159, 106 S.Ct. 477, 88 L.Ed.2d 481 (1985), the Supreme Court said that the guarantee of the Sixth Amendment includes the government's affirmative obligation not to act in a manner that circumvents the protections accorded the accused who invokes his or her right to rely on counsel as a "medium" between the accused and the government. The Court continued:

> [T]he Sixth Amendment is not violated whenever—by luck or happenstance—the State obtains incriminating statements from the accused after the right to counsel has attached. . . . However, knowing exploitation by the State of an opportunity to confront the accused without counsel being present is as much a breach of the State's obligation not to circumvent the right to assistance of counsel as is the intentional creation of such an opportunity. Accordingly, the Sixth Amendment is violated when the State obtains incriminating statements by knowingly circumventing the accused's right to have counsel present in a confrontation between the accused and a state agent. 474 U.S. at 176, 106 S.Ct. at 487, 88 L.Ed.2d at 496.

The *Henry* and *Moulton* cases illustrate that courts will carefully examine any attempts to circumvent the right of any formally charged person to have counsel present at a confrontation between the person and police agents. But, as the first sentence of the preceding quotation indicates, the defendant's Sixth Amendment rights are not violated when an informant, either through prior arrangement or voluntarily, reports the defendant's incriminating statements to the police. "[T]he defendant must demonstrate that the police and their informant took some action, beyond merely listening, that was designed deliberately to elicit incriminating remarks." *Kuhlmann v. Wilson*, 477 U.S. 436, 459, 106 S.Ct. 2616, 2630, 91 L.Ed.2d 364, 384–85 (1986).

This prohibition against attempts to elicit information in the absence of counsel is not intended to hamper police investigation of crimes other than the crime for which adversary proceedings have already commenced. The police need to investigate crimes for which formal charges have already been filed as well as new or additional crimes. Either type of investigation may require surveillance of persons already indicted. Moreover, police who are investigating a person suspected of committing one crime and formally charged with having committed another crime may seek to discover evidence useful at a trial of either crime. In seeking evidence relating to pending charges, however, police investigators are limited by the Sixth Amendment rights of the accused. Therefore, incriminating statements relating to pending charges will be inadmissible at the trial of those charges, even though police were also investigating other crimes if, in obtaining the evidence, the government violated the Sixth Amendment by knowingly circumventing the accused's right to the assistance of counsel. On the other hand, evidence relating to charges to which the Sixth Amendment right to counsel had not attached at the time the evidence was obtained will not be inadmissible merely because other charges were pending at the time. *Maine v. Moulton*, 474 U.S. 159, 106 S.Ct. 477, 88 L.Ed.2d 481 (1985).

10. Interrogation, for purposes of *Miranda*, refers not only to express questioning but also to any words or actions on the part of police (other than those normally attendant to arrest and custody) that the police should know are reasonably likely to elicit an incriminating response from the suspect. An incriminating response is any response—whether inculpatory or exculpatory—that the prosecution may seek to introduce at trial.

11. Law enforcement officers need not interrupt a volunteered statement to warn a suspect of *Miranda* rights.

12. Routine booking questions regarding a suspect's name, address, height, weight, eye color, date of birth, and current age to secure biographical data necessary to complete booking or pretrial services are not considered interrogation for purposes of *Miranda*.

13. Questions asked by law enforcement officers in situations posing a threat to public safety need not be preceded by *Miranda* warnings.

14. *Miranda* warning requirements apply only to custodial interrogations conducted by law enforcement officers and not to questioning by private citizens.

15. If, after receiving *Miranda* warnings, a person indicates a desire to remain silent, the interrogation must cease. If the person requests an attorney, the interrogation must cease until an attorney is present.

16. Generally, a second custodial interrogation of a person who has exercised the *Miranda* right of silence is permissible after a lapse of a significant time period, if the person's right to terminate questioning at the first interrogation was scrupulously honored, fresh *Miranda* warnings are given, and no pressure to cooperate or other illegal tactics are used.

17. Whether the right to counsel is invoked during custodial interrogation or at an arraignment or similar proceeding, at or after which the defendant's Sixth Amendment right to counsel has attached, police may not further interrogate the defendant without counsel present unless the defendant initiates further communication with the police. If the defendant initiates further communication, interrogation may proceed if the defendant makes a voluntary, knowing, and intelligent waiver of the right to counsel and the right to silence.

18. If an initial statement was obtained in violation of *Miranda*, but without coercion or other illegal means to break the defendant's will, a subsequent statement obtained after warnings and a valid waiver of *Miranda* rights is admissible.

19. After a person has been indicted and has retained counsel, the Fifth Amendment prevents law enforcement authorities from deliberately eliciting incriminating statements from the person by surreptitious methods.

Warnings

The warnings that must be given to a suspect by a law enforcement officer before conducting a custodial interrogation are stated in the *Miranda* decision.

> He must be warned prior to any questioning that he has the right to remain silent, that anything he says can be used against him in a court of law, that he has the right to the presence of an attorney, and that if he cannot afford an attorney one will be appointed for him prior to any questioning if he so desires. 384 U.S. at 479, 86 S.Ct. at 1630, 16 L.Ed.2d at 726.

The *Miranda* warnings need not be given in the exact form described in the *Miranda* decision, so long as the warnings reasonably convey to a suspect his or her rights as required by *Miranda*. *California v. Prysock*, 453 U.S. 355, 101 S.Ct. 2806, 69 L.Ed.2d 696 (1981). For example, the standard *Miranda* warnings used by the Federal Bureau of Investigation provide as follows:

> Before we ask you any questions, you must understand your rights.
> You have the right to remain silent.

Anything you say can be used against you in court.

You have the right to talk to a lawyer for advice before we ask you any questions and to have a lawyer with you during questioning.

If you cannot afford a lawyer, one will be appointed for you before any questioning if you wish.

If you decide to answer questions now without a lawyer present, you will still have the right to stop answering at any time. You also have the right to stop answering at any time until you talk to a lawyer. *Duckworth v. Eagan,* 492 U.S. 195, 202 n.4, 109 S.Ct. 2875, 2879 n.4, 106 L.Ed.2d 166, 176 n.4 (1989).

Most law enforcement agencies distribute *Miranda* warning cards to their officers to be used when informing persons subjected to custodial interrogation of their rights.

Manner of Giving Warnings

Miranda warnings must be stated clearly and in an unhurried manner, so that the person warned understands his or her rights and feels free to claim them without fear. The warnings should not be given in a careless, indifferent, and superficial manner. When warnings are given to an immature, illiterate, or mentally impaired person, the warnings must be given in language that the person can comprehend and on which the person can knowingly act. If necessary, the officer should explain and interpret the warnings. The test is whether the words used by the officer, in view of the age, intelligence, and demeanor of the individual being interrogated, convey a clear understanding of all *Miranda* rights. *Anderson v. State,* 253 A.2d 387 (Md.Spec.App. 1969).

Does the Suspect Require Warnings?

Although some suspects arguably may not need to be informed of their *Miranda* rights, the safest procedure for police is to administer the warnings in situations where they are required.

SUSPECT KNOWS HIS OR HER RIGHTS. The *Miranda* opinion made it clear that law enforcement officers are not to assume that any suspect knows his or her rights:

> The Fifth Amendment privilege is so fundamental to our system of constitutional rule and the expedient of giving an adequate warning as to the availability of the privilege so simple, we will not pause to inquire in individual cases whether the defendant was aware of his rights without a warning being given. Assessments of the knowledge the defendant possessed, based on information as to his age, education, intelligence, or prior contact with authorities, can never be more than speculation; a warning is a clearcut fact. More important, whatever the background of the person interrogated, a warning at the time of the interrogation is indispensable to overcome its pressures and to insure that the individual knows he is free to exercise the privilege at that point in time. 384 U.S. at 468–69, 86 S.Ct. at 1625, 16 L.Ed.2d at 720.

SUSPECT IS NOT INDIGENT. If a suspect is known to be financially able to afford a lawyer, officers need not give the warning that a lawyer will be appointed in case of indigency. However, a law enforcement officer may not always be able to determine a person's financial status correctly, and "the expedient of giving a warning is too simple and the rights involved too important to engage in ex post facto inquiries into financial ability when there is any doubt at all on that score." 384 U.S. at 473, 86 S.Ct. at 1627, 16 L.Ed.2d at 723. Therefore, officers should give the complete set of *Miranda* warnings before conducting any custodial interrogation.

SUSPECT HAS AN ATTORNEY PRESENT. The *Miranda* opinion implies that the warnings are not required to be given to persons who have an attorney present with them:

> The presence of counsel . . . would be the adequate protective device necessary to make the process of police interrogation conform to the dictates of the privilege. His presence would insure that statements made in the government-established atmosphere are not the product of compulsion. 384 U.S. at 466, 86 S.Ct. at 1623, 16 L.Ed.2d at 719.

Passage of Time

The mere passage of time does not compromise a *Miranda* warning. Courts have consistently upheld the integrity of *Miranda* warnings even in cases in which several hours have elapsed between the reading of the warning and the interrogation. In *United States v. Frankson,* 83 F.3d 79 (4th Cir. 1996), the defendant contended that *Miranda* requires the police to readvise suspects of their rights when the interrogation does not immediately follow the *Miranda* warning or the interrogation is delayed. The court held that the defendant's "initial *Miranda* warning was in no way compromised by the passage of two and one-half hours between the issuance of his warning and the point at which he began to confess his crimes and cooperate with the police." 83 F.3d at 83.

KEY POINTS

20. Before custodial interrogation of a person, he or she must be warned (1) of the right to remain silent; (2) that anything said can be used against the person in a court of law; (3) of the right to the presence of an attorney; and (4) that if he or she cannot afford an attorney, one will be appointed prior to any questioning.

21. *Miranda* warnings need not be given in the exact form described in the *Miranda* decision, so long as the warnings reasonably convey to a suspect his or her rights as required by *Miranda*.

22. Law enforcement officers should give complete *Miranda* warnings before conducting custodial interrogations, even if they believe that the suspect knows his or her rights or that the suspect is not indigent.

Waiver

The *Miranda* case stated that, after warnings of *Miranda* rights have been given to a person subjected to custodial interrogation and opportunity to exercise the rights afforded the person, "the individual may knowingly and intelligently waive these rights and agree to answer questions or make a statement. But unless and until such warnings and waiver are demonstrated by the prosecution at trial no evidence obtained as a result of interrogation can be used against him." 384 U.S. at 478–79, 86 S.Ct. at 1630, 16 L.Ed.2d at 726. A *waiver* is a voluntary and intentional relinquishment of a known right. The *Miranda* decision held that the defendant may waive the rights conveyed in the *Miranda* warnings "provided the waiver is made voluntarily, knowingly and intelligently." 384 U.S. at 475, 86 S.Ct. at 1628, 16 L.Ed.2d at 724. The inquiry whether the defendant has made a full and effective waiver has two distinct dimensions. As stated by the U.S. Supreme Court:

> First the relinquishment of the right must have been voluntary in the sense that it was the product of a free and deliberate choice rather than intimidation, coercion or deception. Second, the waiver must have been made with a full awareness both of the nature of the right being abandoned and the consequences of the decision to abandon it. Only if "the totality of the circumstances surrounding the interrogation" reveal both an uncoerced choice and the requisite level of comprehension may a court properly conclude that the Miranda rights have been waived. *Moran v. Burbine,* 475 U.S. 412, 421, 106 S.Ct. 1135, 1141, 89 L.Ed.2d 410, 421 (1986).

To satisfy this totality-of-the-circumstances test, law enforcement officers must know what constitutes a waiver and must follow recommended procedures in obtaining the waiver. They also must be aware of the legal concerns involved in the two-dimensional inquiry regarding the validity of a waiver: (1) voluntariness and (2) requisite level of comprehension.

Obtaining a Waiver

After the *Miranda* warnings have been administered, the law enforcement officer should first ask the suspect whether he or she understands the rights that have been explained. The officer should then ask the suspect whether he or she wishes to talk without first consulting a lawyer or having a lawyer present during questioning. If the officer receives an affirmative answer to both questions, the officer should carefully note the exact language in which the answer was given, preserving it for possible future use in court. The officer may then proceed with the interrogation.

If possible, the officer should always try to obtain a written waiver of rights from the suspect before questioning. A written waiver is almost always held to be sufficient if the suspect is literate and there is no evidence of police coercion. *Menendez v. United States,* 393 F.2d 312 (5th Cir. 1968). Exhibit 13.1 is a suggested form for obtaining a written waiver of *Miranda* rights.

Law enforcement officers may not always be able to obtain express written or oral waivers. The U.S. Supreme Court held that "an explicit statement of waiver is not invariably necessary to support a finding that the defendant waived the right to remain silent or the right to counsel guaranteed by the *Miranda* case." *North Carolina v. Butler,* 441 U.S. 369, 375–76, 99 S.Ct. 1755, 1759, 60 L.Ed.2d 286, 293–94 (1979).

> An express written or oral statement of waiver of the right to remain silent or of the right to counsel is usually strong proof of the validity of that waiver, but is not inevitably either necessary or sufficient to establish waiver. The question is not one of form, but rather whether the defendant in fact knowingly and voluntarily waived the rights delineated in the *Miranda* case. As was unequivocally said in *Miranda,* mere silence is not enough. That does not mean that the defendant's silence, coupled with an understanding of his rights and a course of conduct indicating waiver, may never support a conclusion that a defendant has waived his rights. The courts must presume that a defendant did not waive his rights; the prosecution's burden is great; but in at least some cases waiver can be

Case File _____ Police Dept. _____

Date _____ Time _____ Place _____

STATEMENT OF RIGHTS

THE FOLLOWING SEVEN STATEMENTS MUST BE FULLY UNDER-STOOD BY YOU BEFORE WE CAN CONTINUE. IF YOU DO NOT UNDERSTAND A STATEMENT, ASK THAT IT BE EXPLAINED:

1. You have the right to remain silent.
2. Anything you say can and will be used against you in a court of law.
3. You have the right to talk to a lawyer and have the lawyer present with you while you are being questioned.
4. If you cannot afford to hire a lawyer, one will be appointed to represent you before any questioning, if you wish.
5. You can decide at any time to exercise these rights and not answer any questions or make any statements.
6. Do you understand each of these rights I have explained to you?
7. Having these rights in mind, do you wish to talk to us now without a lawyer present?

ACKNOWLEDGEMENT AND WAIVER OF RIGHTS

THE ABOVE STATEMENT OF MY RIGHTS HAS BEEN READ AND EX-PLAINED TO ME AND I FULLY UNDERSTAND WHAT MY RIGHTS ARE. KNOWING THIS I AM WILLING TO ANSWER QUESTIONS OR TO MAKE A STATEMENT WITHOUT A LAWYER PRESENT.

Witness _____ Signed _____
    (Advising Officer or Witness)   (Individual Advised of Rights)

Witness _____ Education _____
    (Officer or Witness)   (Name of school and last grade completed)

STATEMENT

Page No. _____ of _____ Page Statement

I have read the above statement, have signed each page of the statement, and acknowledge receipt of a true copy of the statement.

                  I give this statement without threat, coercion or promise of any kind.

Witness _____

Witness _____ Signed _____

EXHIBIT 13.1A   Suggested Form for Waiver of *Miranda* Rights, Page 1

Page No. _____ of _____ Page Statement   Date _____

Page No. _____ of _____ Page Statement

I have read the above statement, have signed each page of the statement, and acknowledge receipt of a true copy of the statement.

I give this statement without threat, coercion or promise of any kind.

Witness _____

Witness _____ Signed _____

EXHIBIT 13.1B   Suggested Form for Waiver of *Miranda* Rights, Page 2

clearly inferred from the actions and words of the person interrogated. 441 U.S. at 373, 99 S.Ct. at 1757, 60 L.Ed.2d at 292.

The Court went on to say that the question of waiver must be determined "on the 'particular facts and circumstances surrounding that case, including the background, experience, and conduct of the accused.'" 441 U.S. at 374–75, 99 S.Ct. at 1758, 60 L.Ed.2d at 293. Suspects may express themselves through an infinite variety of words and actions, which courts may or may not determine to be valid waivers of *Miranda* rights. Some suspects may be indecisive and may never clearly claim or waive their rights. Nevertheless, waiver of *Miranda* rights must be proved by the prosecution by a preponderance of the evidence. *Colorado v. Connelly,* 479 U.S. 157, 107 S.Ct. 515, 93 L.Ed.2d 473 (1986). Moreover, the absence of any evidence of waiver will result in a finding of no waiver and the exclusion of any statement obtained. *Tague v. Louisiana,* 444 U.S. 469, 100 S.Ct. 652, 62 L.Ed.2d 622 (1980). Therefore, when no written waiver or unambiguous oral waiver can be obtained, law enforcement officers should write down all circumstances surrounding the attempt to obtain the waiver so that the prosecution will have evidence to prove that the waiver was voluntary, knowing, and intelligent.

Some courts require officers to cease all questioning if a suspect's exercise of the right to counsel is ambiguous. These courts allow further questioning only after the suspect's intention is clarified and the right to counsel is unequivocally waived. *United States v. Nordling,* 804 F.2d 1466 (9th Cir. 1986). Questions may be asked only to clarify the defendant's wishes with respect to the request for counsel. *United States v. Fouche,* 833 F.2d 1284 (9th Cir. 1987).

Words and Actions Indicating a Waiver

When a defendant has been fully informed of his or her *Miranda* rights, any comprehensible oral statement of understanding and willingness to speak is usually acceptable as a waiver of rights. Examples of valid waivers are cases in which a suspect said, "I might as well tell you about it," *United States v. Boykin,* 398 F.2d 483, 484 (3d Cir. 1968); "I'll tell you," *State v. Kremens,* 245 A.2d 313, 315 (N.J. 1968); or, "I know all that," *State v. Brown,* 202 So.2d 274, 279 (La. 1967). Courts have also approved nonverbal waivers such as nods, shrugs, or other body language. *United States v. Chapa-Garza,* 62 F.3d 118 (5th Cir. 1995). After receiving a waiver in any of these forms, the law enforcement officer may begin questioning.

Often a suspect will indicate an understanding of *Miranda* rights and then simply begin to make a statement without any other verbal or nonverbal indication of waiver. Most courts have held that, once the suspect has been informed of *Miranda* rights and indicates an understanding of those rights, choosing to speak without a lawyer present is sufficient evidence of a knowing and voluntary waiver of the rights. *United States v. Puig,* 810 F.2d 1085 (11th Cir. 1987). However, this rule is probably valid only if the statement of the suspect follows closely after the suspect indicates an understanding of the warnings. *Billings v. People,* 466 P.2d 474 (Colo. 1970). In *Watkins v. Callahan,* 724 F.2d 1038 (1st Cir. 1984), the court found a valid waiver where the defendant indicated he was ready to make a statement after calling his family instead of calling an attorney. A suspect who indicates a desire to talk to a lawyer at some time in the future but agrees to answer questions without a lawyer has waived the right to counsel. *Thompson v. State,* 235 So.2d 354 (Fla.App. 1970).

A request to see someone other than a lawyer is not considered to be an assertion of rights under *Miranda,* although a denial of such a request may have some bearing on the voluntariness of the statements. For example, in *Fare v. Michael C.,* 442 U.S.

707, 99 S.Ct. 2560, 61 L.Ed.2d 197 (1979), the U.S. Supreme Court held that a juvenile waived his *Miranda* rights even though he had been denied a request to speak to his probation officer. The Court found that the request, made by an experienced older juvenile with an extensive prior record, did not per se constitute a request to remain silent, nor was it tantamount to a request for an attorney. However, some states require a parent, guardian, or other interested adult to be notified before a juvenile may be found to have waived *Miranda* rights. A request for counsel made by a suspect to a friend or relative is not the same as a request to the police. Therefore, even if the police are aware of such a request, the request does not operate as an exercise of *Miranda* rights. *People v. Smith,* 246 N.E.2d 689 (Ill.App. 1969).

Once a suspect has been given *Miranda* warnings, the suspect's refusal to give a written statement outside the presence of his or her attorney does not render ineffective the suspect's clear waiver of rights for the purpose of giving an oral statement. In *Connecticut v. Barrett,* 479 U.S. 523, 107 S.Ct. 828, 93 L.Ed.2d 920 (1987), the suspect, who was in custody on a sexual assault charge, was given the *Miranda* warnings and indicated to the police that he would not make a written statement outside the presence of his attorney. He then clearly expressed his willingness to speak with the police without an attorney and made an oral statement admitting his involvement in the sexual assault. The Court held that the defendant's exercise of his right to counsel was limited by its terms to the making of written statements and did not prohibit further police questioning leading to the oral confession. Although the settled approach to questions of waiver requires giving a broad rather than a narrow interpretation to a defendant's request for counsel, the Court said:

> Interpretation is only required where the defendant's words, understood as ordinary people would understand them, are ambiguous. Here, however, Barrett made clear his intentions, and they were honored by police. To conclude that respondent invoked his right to counsel for all purposes requires not a broad interpretation of an ambiguous statement, but a disregard of the ordinary meaning of respondent's statement. 479 U.S. at 529–30, 107 S.Ct. at 832, 93 L.Ed.2d at 928.

Other examples of valid selective waivers are a defendant's assertion that "it would depend on the questions and he would answer some questions if he thought it appropriate. . . ." *United States v. Eaton,* 890 F.2d 511, 513 (1st Cir. 1989), and the defendant's statement, "Well, ask your questions and I will answer those I see fit." *Bruni v. Lewis,* 847 F.2d 561, 564 (9th Cir. 1988). When a suspect indicates, after giving a valid written or oral waiver, a desire not to have any notes taken, this may suggest that the suspect erroneously believes that oral statements cannot be used as evidence in court. The law enforcement officer should explain that oral statements can be used against the suspect in court. Otherwise, a court might invalidate the waiver. *Frazier v. United States,* 419 F.2d 1161 (D.C.Cir. 1969).

Voluntariness of the Waiver

In *Colorado v. Connelly,* 479 U.S. 157, 107 S.Ct. 515, 93 L.Ed.2d 473 (1986), the U.S. Supreme Court held that the voluntariness inquiry in the *Miranda* waiver context was the same as that in the Fifth Amendment confession context. The Court said:

> The sole concern of the Fifth Amendment, on which *Miranda* was based, is governmental coercion. . . . The voluntariness of a waiver of this privilege has always depended on the absence of police overreaching, not on "free choice" in any broader sense of the word. 479 U.S. at 170, 107 S.Ct. at 523, 93 L.Ed.2d at 486.

Therefore, absent evidence that a suspect's will was overborne and his or her capacity for self-determination critically impaired because of coercive police conduct, the suspect's waiver of *Miranda* rights will be considered voluntary. The *Connelly* case holds that, even if a suspect is compelled to waive *Miranda* rights for some psychological or other reason, if the compulsion did not flow from the police, the waiver will not be held involuntary.

Psychological tactics, such as playing on the defendant's sympathies or explaining that honesty is the best policy, have been variously interpreted by courts in determining the voluntariness of a defendant's waiver. Some courts apply a totality-of-the-circumstances test to determine whether the defendant's will was overborne or his or her capacity for self-determination was critically impaired. In *United States v. Pelton,* 835 F.2d 1067 (4th Cir. 1987), the court said:

> Agents may properly initiate discussions on cooperation, and may indicate that they will make this cooperation known. . . . General encouragement to cooperate is far different from specific promises of leniency. 835 F.2d at 1073.

With respect to the use of psychological tactics, the Third Circuit Court of Appeals said:

> These ploys may play a part in the suspect's decision to confess, but so long as that decision is a product of the suspect's own balancing of competing considerations the confession is voluntary. The question . . . is whether . . . statements were so manipulative or coercive that they deprived [the defendant] of his ability to make an unconstrained, autonomous decision to confess. *Miller v. Fenton,* 796 F.2d 598, 605 (3d Cir. 1986).

Requisite Level of Comprehension

The requirement that a waiver must be made with full awareness of both the right being abandoned and the consequences of the decision to abandon that right is satisfied by careful administration of the *Miranda* warnings to a suspect. As stated by the U.S. Supreme Court:

> The Constitution does not require that a criminal suspect know and understand every possible consequence of a waiver of the Fifth Amendment privilege. . . . The Fifth Amendment's guarantee is both simpler and more fundamental: A defendant may not be compelled to be a witness against himself in any respect. The *Miranda* warnings protect this privilege by insuring that a suspect knows that he may choose not to talk to law enforcement officers, to talk only with counsel present, or to discontinue talking at any time. The *Miranda* warnings ensure that a waiver of these rights is knowing and intelligent by requiring that the suspect be fully advised of this constitutional privilege, including the critical advice that whatever he chooses to say may be used as evidence against him. *Colorado v. Spring,* 479 U.S. 564, 574, 107 S.Ct. 851, 857–58, 93 L.Ed.2d 954, 966 (1987).

Patterson v. Illinois, 487 U.S. 285, 108 S.Ct. 2389, 101 L.Ed.2d 261 (1988), held that the *Miranda* warnings are also sufficient to inform a defendant of the right to have counsel present during *postindictment* questioning and the consequences of a decision to waive the Sixth Amendment right during such questioning.

> [W]hatever warnings suffice for *Miranda*'s purposes will also be sufficient in the context of postindictment questioning. The State's decision to take an additional step and commence formal adversarial proceedings against the accused does not

substantially increase the value of counsel to the accused at questioning, or expand the limited purpose that an attorney serves when the accused is questioned by authorities. With respect to this inquiry, we do not discern a substantial difference between the usefulness of a lawyer to a suspect during custodial interrogation, and his value to an accused at postindictment questioning. 487 U.S. at 298–99, 108 S.Ct. at 2398, 101 L.Ed.2d at 276.

SUSPECT'S NEED FOR ADDITIONAL USEFUL INFORMATION. Suspects often claim that their waivers of *Miranda* rights were involuntary because police or prosecutors failed to give them enough information on which to base the decision to waive or not waive the rights. In *Moran v. Burbine*, 475 U.S. 412, 106 S.Ct. 1135, 89 L.Ed.2d 410 (1986), the U.S. Supreme Court held that the police are not required to inform an uncharged suspect of an attorney's attempts to reach him or her, or to otherwise keep the suspect abreast of the status of his or her legal representation, before giving *Miranda* warnings and obtaining a waiver of *Miranda* rights. In the *Burbine* case, an attorney who was contacted by the suspect's sister (without the suspect's knowledge) attempted to telephone the suspect, who was in custody at the police station. The police assured the attorney that the suspect would not be questioned any further that day. Later that evening, however, police informed the suspect of his *Miranda* rights, the suspect executed a series of valid written waivers, and the suspect eventually confessed to a murder. At no point during the course of interrogation, which occurred before arraignment, did the suspect request an attorney.

The Court held that the police's failure to inform the suspect of the attorney's phone call did not deprive the suspect of information essential to his ability to knowingly waive his Fifth Amendment rights. The Court said:

> Events occurring outside the presence of the suspect and entirely unknown to him surely can have no bearing on the capacity to comprehend and knowingly relinquish a constitutional right. . . . Once it is determined that a suspect's decision not to rely on his rights was uncoerced, that he at all times knew he could stand mute and request a lawyer, and that he was aware of the state's intention to use his statements to secure a conviction, the analysis is complete and the waiver is valid as a matter of law. 475 U.S. at 422–23, 106 S.Ct. at 1141–42, 89 L.Ed.2d at 421–22.

Furthermore, whether the police conduct in the case was intentional or inadvertent, the Court held that the police's state of mind was irrelevant to the question of the intelligence and voluntariness of the suspect's election to abandon his rights. Finally, there was no violation of the suspect's Sixth Amendment right to counsel. The Court reasoned that if that right had attached, the police would have been prohibited from interfering with the attorney's efforts to assist the suspect. But because the interrogation took place *before* the initiation of adversary judicial proceedings, the right to counsel did not attach, and the suspect could not have his confession suppressed for a violation of a right he did not have.

The Court frowned upon the police's deception of the attorney, but it found that this conduct was not so offensive as to deprive the defendant of the fundamental fairness guaranteed by the due process clause of the Fourteenth Amendment. The Court specifically warned, however, that a more flagrant violation by the police might rise to the level of a due process violation. Therefore, the *Burbine* case should not be interpreted as generally approving dishonest or shady dealings by the police with defense attorneys in interrogation situations occurring before the initiation of formal charges. In fact, some states have explicitly rejected the ruling in *Moran v. Burbine* based on state constitutional law. The California Supreme Court held as follows:

[W]hether or not a suspect in custody has previously waived his rights to silence and counsel, the police may not deny him the opportunity, before questioning begins or resumes, to meet with his retained or appointed counsel who has taken diligent steps to come to his aid.

If the lawyer comes to the station before interrogation begins or while it is still in progress, the suspect must promptly be told, and if he then wishes to see his counsel, he must be allowed to do so. Moreover, the police may not engage in conduct, intentional or grossly negligent, which is calculated to mislead, delay, or dissuade counsel in his efforts to reach his client. Such conduct constitutes a denial of a California suspect's *Miranda* rights to counsel, and it invalidates any subsequent statements. *People v. Houston,* 230 Cal.Rptr. 141, 149, 724 P.2d 1166, 1174–75 (Cal. 1986).

In *Colorado v. Spring,* 479 U.S. 564, 107 S.Ct. 851, 93 L.Ed.2d 954 (1987), the defendant contended that the failure of police to inform him of the potential subjects of interrogation constituted police trickery and deception as condemned in *Miranda,* and rendered his waiver of *Miranda* rights invalid. The U.S. Supreme Court declined to hold that "mere silence by law enforcement officials as to the subject matter of an interrogation is 'trickery' sufficient to invalidate a suspect's waiver of *Miranda* rights. . . ." 479 U.S. at 576, 107 S.Ct. at 858, 93 L.Ed.2d at 967. Citing *Moran v. Burbine,* the Court said that a valid waiver does not require that police supply a suspect with all useful information to help the suspect calibrate his or her self-interest in deciding whether to speak or to stand by his or her rights. The Court concluded as follows:

> This Court's holding in *Miranda* specifically required that the police inform a criminal suspect that he has the right to remain silent and that anything he says may be used against him. There is no qualification of this broad and explicit warning. The warning, as formulated in *Miranda,* conveys to a suspect the nature of his constitutional privilege and the consequences of abandoning it. Accordingly, we hold that a suspect's awareness of all the possible subjects of questioning in advance of interrogation is not relevant to determining whether the suspect voluntarily, knowingly, and intelligently waived his Fifth Amendment privilege. 479 U.S. at 577, 107 S.Ct. at 859, 93 L.Ed.2d at 968.

In *United States v. Tapp,* 812 F.2d 177 (5th Cir. 1987), the court held that the interrogating officer's failure to inform the defendant that he was the target of the investigation did not render the defendant's waiver of *Miranda* rights involuntary.

SUSPECT'S COMPETENCY. The inquiry as to whether the suspect has the requisite level of comprehension to validly waive *Miranda* rights is also directed at the competency of the suspect. In determining competency to waive *Miranda* rights, courts will examine the totality of the circumstances surrounding the waiver, with no single factor controlling. Among the factors to be considered are the defendant's

- education—*Stawicki v. Israel,* 778 F.2d 380 (7th Cir. 1985);
- intelligence—*Henry v. Dees,* 658 F.2d 406 (5th Cir. 1981);
- literacy—*United States v. Binder,* 769 F.2d 595 (9th Cir. 1985);
- familiarity with the criminal justice system—*United States v. Scarpa,* 897 F.2d 63 (2d Cir. 1990);
- physical and mental condition—*United States v. Lewis,* 833 F.2d 1380 (9th Cir. 1987);

- ingestion of drugs or alcohol—*United States v. D'Antoni,* 856 F.2d 975 (7th Cir. 1988);

- language barriers—*United States v. Boon San Chong,* 829 F.2d 1572 (11th Cir. 1987);

- age—*Woods v. Clusen,* 794 F.2d 293 (7th Cir. 1986).

In a case involving a juvenile, the U.S. Supreme Court stated:

> This totality of circumstances approach is adequate to determine whether there has been a waiver even where interrogation of juveniles is involved. . . . The totality approach permits—indeed, it mandates—inquiry into all the circumstances surrounding the interrogation. This includes evaluation of the juvenile's age, experience, education, background, and intelligence, and into whether he had the capacity to understand the warnings given him, the nature of his Fifth Amendment rights, and the consequences of waiving those rights. *Fare v. Michael C.,* 442 U.S. 707, 725, 99 S.Ct. 2560, 2572, 61 L.Ed.2d 197, 212 (1979).

Additional circumstances to be considered in determining a waiver of a juvenile's rights are as follows: (1) knowledge of the accused as to the substance of the charge, if any has been filed; (2) whether the accused is held incommunicado or allowed to consult with relatives, friends, or an attorney; (3) whether the accused was interrogated before or after formal charges had been filed; (4) method used in interrogation; (5) length of interrogations; and (6) whether the accused refused to voluntarily give statements on prior occasions. *West v. United States,* 399 F.2d 467 (5th Cir. 1968).

In general, the officer should carefully observe the suspect and take notes on all indications of the suspect's competence or incompetence to waive *Miranda* rights. In *State v. Addington,* 518 A.2d 449 (Me. 1986), the court found that the suspect's refusal to talk to officers and refusal to undergo certain tests supported the conclusion that his waiver of *Miranda* rights was voluntary, knowing, and intelligent. Unless an officer is positive that the suspect is incapable of understanding and waiving *Miranda* rights, the officer should not refrain from trying to obtain a lawful confession. It is the duty of the courts, not of the law enforcement officer, to determine finally whether there was a voluntary, knowing, and intelligent waiver and a voluntary and trustworthy confession.

KEY POINTS

23. After warnings of *Miranda* rights have been given to a person subjected to custodial interrogation and opportunity to exercise the rights afforded the person, the person may voluntarily, knowingly, and intelligently waive the rights and agree to answer questions or make a statement. But unless and until such warnings and waiver are demonstrated by the prosecution at trial, no evidence obtained as a result of interrogation can be used against the person.

24. To constitute a full and effective waiver of *Miranda* rights, (1) the relinquishment of the right must have been voluntary in the sense that it was the product of a free and deliberate choice rather than police intimidation, coercion, or deception; and (2) the waiver must have been made with a full awareness both of the nature of the right being abandoned and the consequences of the decision to abandon it. This second requirement is satisfied by careful administration of the *Miranda* warnings to a competent suspect.

25. A request to see someone other than a lawyer is not considered to be an assertion of rights under *Miranda,* although a denial of such a request may have some bearing on the voluntariness of the statements.

26. The police are not required to inform an uncharged suspect of an attorney's attempts to reach him or her, or to otherwise keep the suspect abreast of the status of his or her legal representation or of other information useful to the person's defense, before giving *Miranda* warnings and obtaining a waiver of *Miranda* rights.

Other *Miranda* Issues

This section discusses issues collateral to the four core issues of *Miranda:* custody, interrogation, warning, and waiver. Included here are the application of *Miranda* to nontestimonial evidence; Fourth Amendment considerations; application of *Miranda* to minor offenses and civil proceedings; and implications of the use of undercover agents.

Nontestimonial Evidence

The self-incrimination clause of the Fifth Amendment provides that no "person . . . shall be compelled in any criminal case to be a witness against himself." U.S. Const., Amend. 5. Although the text of the amendment does not set out the ways in which a person might be a "witness against himself," the U.S. Supreme Court has long held that the privilege does not protect a suspect from being compelled by the state to produce "real or physical evidence." Rather the privilege "protects an accused only from being compelled to testify against himself, or otherwise provide the State with evidence of a testimonial or communicative nature. . . ." *Schmerber v. California,* 384 U.S. 757, 761, 86 S.Ct. 1826, 1830, 16 L.Ed.2d 908, 914 (1966). "[I]n order to be testimonial, an accused's communication must itself, explicitly or implicitly, relate a factual assertion or disclose information. Only then is a person compelled to be a 'witness' against himself." *Doe v. United States,* 487 U.S. 201, 210, 108 S.Ct. 2341, 2347, 101 L.Ed.2d 184, 197 (1988). In *Pennsylvania v. Muniz,* 496 U.S. 582, 597, 110 S.Ct. 2638, 2648, 110 L.Ed.2d 528, 549 (1990), the Court elaborated further:

> Whenever a suspect is asked for a response requiring him to communicate an express or implied assertion of fact or belief, the suspect confronts the 'trilemma' of truth, falsity, or silence and hence the response (whether based on truth or falsity) contains a testimonial component.

In the *Muniz* case, the defendant was arrested for driving under the influence and was asked a series of questions without being given the *Miranda* warnings. In responding, his confusion and failure to speak clearly indicated a state of drunkenness. The Court held that the defendant's responses were not rendered inadmissible by *Miranda* merely because the slurred nature of his speech was incriminating.

> Under *Schmerber* and its progeny . . . any slurring of speech and other evidence of lack of muscular coordination revealed by Muniz's responses to [the officer's] direct questions constitute nontestimonial components of those responses. Requiring a suspect to reveal the physical manner in which he articulates words, like requiring him to reveal the physical properties of the sound produced by his voice [see *United States v. Dionisio,* 410 U.S. 1, 93 S.Ct. 764, 35 L.Ed.2d 67 (1973)] does not, without more, compel him to provide a "testimonial" response for purposes of the privilege. 496 U.S. at 592, 110 S.Ct. at 2645, 110 L.Ed.2d at 546.

In *California v. Byers,* 402 U.S. 424, 431–32, 91 S.Ct. 1535, 1539–40, 29 L.Ed.2d 9, 19 (1971), the U.S. Supreme Court held that a state statutory requirement that a driver involved in an accident stop at the scene and give his or her name and address was not testimonial in the Fifth Amendment sense:

> The act of stopping is no more testimonial—indeed less so in some respects— than requiring a person in custody to stand or walk in a police lineup, to speak

prescribed words, or to give samples of handwriting, fingerprints, or blood. *United States v. Wade,* 388 U.S. 218, 221–223, 87 S.Ct. 1926, 1929–1930,18 L.Ed.2d 1149 (1967); *Schmerber v. California,* 384 U.S. 757, 764 and n.8, 86 S.Ct. 1826, 1832, 16 L.Ed.2d 908 (1966). . . . Disclosure of name and address is an essentially neutral act.

Fourth Amendment Violations

For purposes of this chapter, when a law enforcement officer attempts to obtain a statement from a person, not only must the voluntariness and *Miranda* requirements be satisfied, but the officer must not violate the person's reasonable expectation of privacy. Thus, even though a law enforcement officer has satisfied all the *Miranda* requirements in obtaining a statement from a person, the statement may still be inadmissible in court if it was obtained in violation of the person's Fourth Amendment rights.

The leading case on this subject is *Katz v. United States,* 389 U.S. 347, 88 S.Ct. 507, 19 L.Ed.2d 576 (1967), in which the defendant, who was in a telephone booth, was eavesdropped on by federal agents, who had attached an electronic listening and recording device to the outside of the booth. The Court held that despite the lack of an intrusion into a constitutionally protected area, the defendant's statements were inadmissible in court because they were taken in violation of his reasonable expectation of privacy. The Court said that

> once it is recognized that the Fourth Amendment protects people—and not simply "areas"—against unreasonable searches and seizures, it becomes clear that the reach of that Amendment cannot turn upon the presence or absence of a physical intrusion into any given enclosure. 389 U.S. at 353, 88 S.Ct. at 512, 19 L.Ed.2d at 583.

In *Halpin v. Superior Court,* 101 Cal.Rptr. 375, 495 P.2d 1295 (Cal. 1972), the incarcerated defendant's wife visited him at the jail during regular visiting hours. A detective allowed the defendant and his wife to use his office to converse, and the detective left the office. The conversation was secretly taped and was used in court against the defendant. The court ruled the tapes inadmissible, stating that law enforcement officers may not deliberately create an expectation of privacy so that a prisoner and his or her visitor will be lulled into believing their conversations will be confidential.

In *United States v. Fisch,* 474 F.2d 1071 (9th Cir. 1973), law enforcement officers were investigating a narcotics smuggling operation. The officers obtained a motel room adjacent to that of the suspects, and, by listening at the door, the officers heard a discussion of criminal acts. The officers used no electronic devices and committed no trespass. The court ruled that the statements were admissible, holding that the defendants had no justifiable expectation of privacy in their conversations. The court emphasized that a person's interest in privacy must be balanced against the public's interest in the investigation and prosecution of crime:

> Upon balance, appraising the public and private interests here involved, we are satisfied that the expectations of the defendants as to their privacy, even were such expectations to be considered reasonable despite their audible disclosures, must be subordinated to the public interest in law enforcement. In sum, there has been no justifiable reliance, the expectation of privacy not being "one that society is prepared to recognize as 'reasonable.'" 474 F.2d at 1078–79.

Nature or Severity of Offense

The U.S. Supreme Court held that "a person subjected to custodial interrogation is entitled to the benefit of the procedural safeguards enunciated in *Miranda*, regardless of the nature or severity of the offense of which he is suspected or for which he was arrested." *Berkemer v. McCarty*, 468 U.S. 420, 434, 104 S.Ct. 3138, 3147, 82 L.Ed.2d 317, 331 (1984). The Court explained:

> The occasions on which the police arrest and then interrogate someone suspected only of a misdemeanor traffic offense are rare. The police are already well accustomed to giving Miranda warnings to persons taken into custody. Adherence to the principle that *all* suspects must be given such warnings will not significantly hamper the efforts of the police to investigate crimes. 468 U.S. at 434, 104 S.Ct. at 3147, 82 L.Ed.2d at 331.

Miranda has been held inapplicable to civil proceedings such as customs procedures, civil commitments, extradition proceedings, and license revocation proceedings.

Undercover Agents

Miranda was concerned with the inherently compelling pressures generated by a police-dominated atmosphere "which work to undermine the individual's will to resist and to compel him to speak where he would not otherwise do so freely." 384 U.S. at 467, 86 S.Ct. at 1624, 16 L.Ed.2d at 719. Coercion is determined from the perspective of the suspect. Conversations between suspects and undercover agents do not implicate the concerns underlying *Miranda*, because a suspect speaking to those whom he assumes are not officers would not feel compelled to speak by the fear of reprisal for remaining silent or in the hope of more lenient treatment should he or she confess.

In *Hoffa v. United States*, 385 U.S. 293, 87 S.Ct. 408, 17 L.Ed.2d 374 (1966), the U.S. Supreme Court held that placing an undercover agent near a suspect to gather incriminating information was permissible under the Fifth Amendment. In *Hoffa*, while the defendant was on trial, he met often with a person named Partin, who, unbeknownst to Hoffa, was cooperating with law enforcement officials. Partin reported to officials that Hoffa had divulged his attempts to bribe jury members. The Court approved using Hoffa's statements at his subsequent trial for jury tampering, on the rationale that no claim had been or could have been made that his incriminating statements were the product of any sort of coercion, legal or factual. In addition, the Court found that the fact that Partin had fooled Hoffa into thinking that Partin was a sympathetic colleague did not affect the voluntariness of the statements.

In *Illinois v. Perkins*, 495 U.S. 292, 110 S.Ct. 2394, 110 L.Ed.2d 243 (1990), police placed undercover agent Parisi in a jail cellblock with the defendant, who was incarcerated on charges unrelated to the murder that Parisi was investigating. When Parisi asked him whether he had ever killed anyone, the defendant made statements implicating himself in the murder. The Court said that

> [t]he only difference between this case and *Hoffa* is that the suspect here was incarcerated, but detention, whether or not for the crime in question, does not warrant a presumption that the use of an undercover agent to speak with an incarcerated suspect makes any confession thus obtained involuntary. 495 U.S. at 298, 110 S.Ct. at 2398, 110 L.Ed.2d at 252.

It is the premise of *Miranda* that the danger of coercion results from the interaction of custody and official interrogation. The Court rejected the argument that *Miranda* warnings are required whenever a suspect is in custody in a technical sense and converses with someone who happens to be a government agent. *Miranda* forbids coercion, not mere strategic deception by taking advantage of a suspect's misplaced trust in one he or she supposes to be a fellow prisoner.

> *Miranda* was not meant to protect suspects from boasting about their criminal activities in front of persons whom they believe to be their cellmates. . . . Respondent had no reason to feel that undercover agent Parisi had any legal authority to force him to answer questions or that Parisi could affect respondent's future treatment. Respondent viewed the cellmate-agent as an equal and showed no hint of being intimidated by the atmosphere of the jail. In recounting the details of the Stephenson murder, respondent was motivated solely by the desire to impress his fellow inmates. He spoke at his own peril. 495 U.S. at 298, 110 S.Ct. at 2398, 110 L.Ed.2d at 252.

KEY POINTS

27. The privilege against self-incrimination does not protect a suspect from being compelled by the state to produce real or physical evidence but only protects an accused from being compelled to testify against him- or herself, or otherwise provide the state with evidence of a testimonial or communicative nature. To be testimonial, an accused's communication must itself, explicitly or implicitly, relate a factual assertion or disclose information.

28. When a law enforcement officer attempts to obtain a statement from a person, not only must the voluntariness and *Miranda* requirements be satisfied, but the officer must not violate the person's reasonable expectation of privacy.

29. *Miranda* requirements apply regardless of the nature or severity of the offense being investigated.

30. *Miranda* is inapplicable to civil proceedings such as customs procedures, civil commitments, extradition proceedings, and license revocation proceedings.

31. Undercover agents need not administer *Miranda* warnings to suspects before obtaining statements, unless the suspect is coerced in some way.

Effect of *Miranda* in Court

Statements taken in violation of *Miranda* requirements will be inadmissible in court as substantive evidence in the prosecution's case in chief to prove the defendant's guilt of crime. In recent years, however, courts have allowed the use of statements taken in violation of *Miranda* for purposes other than the proof of a defendant's guilt. In *Harris v. New York*, 401 U.S. 222, 91 S.Ct. 643, 28 L.Ed.2d 1 (1971), and *Oregon v. Hass,* 420 U.S. 714, 95 S.Ct. 1215, 43 L.Ed.2d 570 (1975), the Court admitted testimony of previous inconsistent statements taken from a defendant in violation of his *Miranda* rights solely for the purpose of impeaching the defendant's testimony at trial. Stressing that the trustworthiness of the defendant's earlier conflicting statements must satisfy legal standards, the Court in *Harris* said:

> The shield provided by *Miranda* cannot be perverted into a license to use perjury by way of a defense, free from the risk of confrontation with prior inconsistent utterances. We hold, therefore, that petitioner's credibility was appropriately impeached by use of his earlier conflicting statements. 401 U.S. at 226, 91 S.Ct. at 646, 28 L.Ed.2d at 5.

Similarly, a statement taken in violation of the rule of *Edwards v. Arizona* and *Michigan v. Jackson* (see pages 457–461)—that once a criminal defendant invokes the Fifth Amendment right to counsel at a custodial interrogation or the Sixth Amendment right to counsel at a postarraignment interrogation, a subsequent waiver of that right, even if voluntary, knowing, and intelligent under traditional standards, is presumed invalid if secured pursuant to police-initiated conversation—may be used to impeach a defendant's false or inconsistent testimony at trial, even though the same statement may not be used as substantive evidence. *Michigan v. Harvey*, 494 U.S. 344, 110 S.Ct. 1176, 108 L.Ed.2d 293 (1990).

Law enforcement officers should not interpret the *Harris, Hass,* and *Harvey* cases as providing an opportunity to evade the requirements of the *Miranda, Edwards,* and *Jackson* cases. An admission or confession obtained in compliance with the latter cases is much more valuable to the prosecution than is an illegally obtained voluntary statement to be used only for impeachment. In addition, *involuntary* statements obtained from a defendant cannot be used for any purpose in a criminal trial. The U.S. Supreme Court stated that "*any* criminal trial use against a defendant of his *involuntary* statement is a denial of due process of law, 'even though there is ample evidence aside from the confession to support the conviction.'" *Mincey v. Arizona*, 437 U.S. 385, 398, 98 S.Ct. 2408, 2416, 57 L.Ed.2d 290, 303 (1978). The only exception to this rule allows admission of an involuntary statement if the admission is found to be harmless error. *Arizona v. Fulminante*, 499 U.S. 279, 111 S.Ct. 1246, 113 L.Ed.2d 302 (1991).

In *United States v. Hale*, 422 U.S. 171, 95 S.Ct. 2133, 45 L.Ed.2d 99 (1975), and *Doyle v. Ohio*, 426 U.S. 610, 96 S.Ct. 2240, 49 L.Ed.2d 91 (1976), the U.S. Supreme Court held that a defendant's silence after receiving the *Miranda* warnings could not be used against the defendant at trial for the purpose of impeaching his or her trial testimony. The Court quoted the *Hale* case in the *Doyle* case as follows:

> "'[W]hen a person under arrest is informed as *Miranda* requires, that he may remain silent, that anything he says may be used against him, and that he may have an attorney if he wishes, it seems to me that it does not comport with due process to permit the prosecution during the trial to call attention to his silence at the time of arrest and to insist that because he did not speak about the facts of the case at that time, as he was told he need not do, an unfavorable inference might be drawn as to the truth of his trial testimony. . . .'" 426 U.S. at 619, 96 S.Ct. at 2245, 49 L.Ed.2d at 98.

The *Doyle* rule does not apply, however, to a defendant's silence before *Miranda* warnings are given.

> [T]he Constitution does not prohibit the use for impeachment purposes of a defendant's silence prior to arrest . . . or after arrest if no *Miranda* warnings are given. . . . Such silence is probative and does not rest on any implied assurance by law enforcement authorities that it will carry no penalty. *Brecht v. Abrahamson*, 507 U.S. 619, 628, 113 S.Ct. 1710, 1716, 123 L.Ed.2d 353, 366 (1993).

KEY POINTS

32. Statements taken in violation of *Miranda, Edwards,* and *Jackson* requirements are inadmissible in court as substantive evidence in the prosecution's case in chief to prove the defendant's guilt of crime, but they may be used for the purpose of impeaching the defendant's testimony at trial.

33. Involuntary statements obtained from a defendant cannot be used for any purpose in a criminal trial.

34. A defendant's silence *after* receiving the *Miranda* warnings may not be used against the defendant at trial for the purpose of impeaching his or her trial testimony.

Summary

An admission or confession obtained by a law enforcement officer is inadmissible in court unless (1) it is voluntary and (2) the requirements of the U.S. Supreme Court case of *Miranda v. Arizona* are satisfied. Courts find a statement involuntary if the statement is a product of police coercion, whether by force or by subtler forms of coercion, and if, in the totality of the circumstances, the statement is not the result of a person's free and rational choice. In making the determination of voluntariness, courts will consider the personal characteristics of the defendant, such as age, mental capacity, physical or mental impairment, and experience with the police, in establishing the setting in which coercion might operate to overcome the will of the defendant.

The *Miranda* case held that a statement obtained by police during a custodial interrogation of a defendant is inadmissible unless the police used certain procedural safeguards to secure the defendant's privilege against self-incrimination. Those procedural safeguards are the giving of warnings of rights and the obtaining of a valid waiver of those rights before an interrogation is begun. The major issues of *Miranda* can thus be broken down into four categories: custody, interrogation, warnings, and waiver.

A person is in custody if there is a formal arrest or restraint on freedom of movement of the degree associated with a formal arrest. Custody is determined by examining, from a reasonable person's point of view, the totality of facts and circumstances surrounding an encounter between a person and law enforcement authorities, including the place; the time; the presence of family, friends, or other persons; physical restraint; and coercion or domination by the police.

Interrogation refers not only to express questioning but also to any words or actions on the part of police that the police should know are reasonably likely to elicit an incriminating response. Nevertheless, clarifying questions, spontaneous questions, and routine questions are not considered to be interrogation for *Miranda* purposes. In addition, volunteered statements are not the product of interrogation and are not subject to the *Miranda* requirements. Multiple attempts at interrogation are permitted after a defendant's invocation of the right to silence, but the defendant's right to cut off questioning must be scrupulously honored, fresh warnings must be given, and no coercion or other pressures may be employed. If the defendant has exercised the right to counsel, further interrogation without counsel may be conducted only upon the initiation of the defendant and the waiver of *Miranda* rights. After a defendant has been formally charged and has retained counsel, law enforcement authorities are prohibited from using any methods, however surreptitious or indirect, to elicit incriminating evidence from the defendant in the absence of counsel.

Before persons in custody may be subjected to interrogation, they must be given the familiar *Miranda* warnings:

- You have the right to remain silent.

- Anything you say can and will be used against you in a court of law.

- You have the right to consult with a lawyer and to have the lawyer present with you while you are being questioned.

- If you cannot afford to hire a lawyer, a lawyer will be appointed to represent you before any questioning, if you wish.

These warnings must be recited clearly and unhurriedly and must be carefully explained to immature, illiterate, or mentally impaired persons.

If a person waives the *Miranda* rights to remain silent and to have an attorney, that person may be questioned. To be effective, a waiver of *Miranda* rights must be voluntary and made with a full awareness of both the nature of the right being abandoned and the consequences of the decision to abandon that right. Waiver will not be inferred from mere silence but may be expressed by a great variety of words and gestures. If possible, an officer should obtain a written waiver of rights, because this provides the best evidence of a voluntary and intentional relinquishment of a known right.

Even though the voluntariness and *Miranda* requirements have been met, a statement may still be inadmissible if the officer violates a person's reasonable expectation of privacy in obtaining the statement. *Miranda* requirements apply regardless of the nature or severity of the offense being investigated. *Miranda* is inapplicable, however, to civil proceedings such as customs procedures, civil commitments, extradition proceedings, and license revocation proceedings.

Key Holdings from Major Cases

Brown v. Mississippi (1936). "[T]he trial . . . is a mere pretense where the state authorities have contrived a conviction resting solely upon confessions obtained by violence. The due process clause requires 'that state action, whether through one agency or another, shall be consistent with the fundamental principles of liberty and justice which lie at the base of all our civil and political institutions.' . . . It would be difficult to conceive of methods more revolting to the sense of justice than those taken to procure the confessions of these petitioners [beatings and whippings], and the use of the confessions thus obtained as the basis for conviction and sentence was a clear denial of due process." 297 U.S. 278, 286, 56 S.Ct. 461, 465, 80 L.Ed. 682, 687.

Townsend v. Sain (1963). "If an individual's 'will was overborne' or if his confession was not 'the product of a rational intellect and a free will,' his confession is inadmissible because coerced. These standards are applicable whether a confession is the product of physical intimidation or psychological pressure. . . . Any questioning by police officers which in fact produces a confession which is not the product of a free intellect renders that confession inadmissible." 372 U.S. 293, 307–08, 83 S.Ct. 745, 754, 9 L.Ed.2d 770, 782–83.

Colorado v. Connelly (1986). "[W]hile mental condition is surely relevant to an individual's susceptibility to police coercion, mere examination of the confessant's state of mind can never conclude the due process inquiry. . . . [C]oercive police activity is a necessary predicate to the finding that a confession is not 'voluntary' within the meaning of the Due Process Clause of the Fourteenth Amendment." 479 U.S. 157, 165–67, 107 S.Ct. 515, 521–22, 93 L.Ed.2d 473, 483–84.

Waiver of *Miranda* rights must be proved by the prosecution by a preponderance of the evidence. 479 U.S. 157, 107 S.Ct. 515, 93 L.Ed.2d 473.

"The sole concern of the Fifth Amendment, on which *Miranda* was based, is governmental coercion. . . . The voluntariness of a waiver of this privilege has always depended on the absence of police overreaching, not on 'free choice' in any broader sense of the word." 479 U.S. at 170, 107 S.Ct. at 523, 93 L.Ed.2d at 486.

Escobedo v. Illinois (1964). "[W]here . . . the investigation is no longer a general inquiry into an unsolved crime but has begun to focus on a particular suspect, the suspect has been taken into police custody, the police carry out a process of interrogations that lends itself to eliciting incriminating statements, the suspect has requested and been denied an opportunity to consult with his lawyer, and the police have not effectively warned him of his absolute constitutional right to remain silent, the accused has been denied 'the Assistance of Counsel' in violation of the Sixth Amendment to the Constitution as 'made obligatory upon the States by the Fourteenth Amendment,' . . . and . . . no statement elicited by the police during the interrogation may be used against him at a criminal trial." 378 U.S. 478, 491, 84 S.Ct. 1758, 1765, 12 L.Ed.2d 977, 986.

Miranda v. Arizona (1966) "[T]he prosecution may not use statements, whether exculpatory or inculpatory, stemming from custodial interrogation of the defendant unless it demonstrates the use of procedural safeguards effective to secure the privilege against self-incrimination. By custodial interrogation, we mean questioning initiated by law enforcement officers after a person has been taken into custody or otherwise deprived of his freedom of action in any significant way. As for the procedural safeguards to be employed, unless other fully effective means are devised to inform accused persons of their right of silence and to assure a continuous opportunity to exercise it, the following measures are required. Prior to any questioning, the person must be warned that he has a right to remain silent, that any statement he does make may be used as evidence against him, and that he has a right to the presence of an attorney, either retained or appointed. The defendant may waive effectuation of these rights provided the waiver is made voluntarily, knowingly, and intelligently. If, however, he indicates in any manner and at any stage of the process that he wishes to consult with an attorney before speaking there can be no questioning. Likewise, if the individual is alone and indicates in any manner that he does not wish to be interrogated, the police may not question him. The mere fact that he may have answered some questions or volunteered some statements on his own does not deprive him of the right to refrain from answering any further inquiries until he has consulted with an attorney and thereafter consents to be questioned." 384 U.S. 436, 444–45, 86 S.Ct. 1602, 1612, 16 L.Ed.2d 694, 706–07.

"The presence of counsel . . . would be the adequate protective device necessary to make the process of police interrogation conform to the dictates of the privilege. His presence would insure that statements made in the government-established atmosphere are not the product of compulsion." 384 U.S. at 466, 86 S.Ct. at 1623, 16 L.Ed.2d at 719.

"The Fifth Amendment privilege is so fundamental to our system of constitutional rule and the expedient of giving an adequate warning as to the availability of the privilege so simple, we will not pause to inquire in individual cases whether the defendant was aware of his rights without a warning being given. Assessments of the knowledge the defendant possessed, based on information as to his age, education, intelligence, or prior contact with authorities, can never be more than speculation; a warning is a clearcut fact. More important, whatever the background of the person interrogated, a warning at the time of the interrogation is indispensable to overcome its pressures and to insure that the individual knows he is free to exercise the privilege at that point in time." 384 U.S. at 468–69, 86 S.Ct. at 1625, 16 L.Ed.2d at 720.

"[T]he expedient of giving a warning is too simple and the rights involved too important to engage in ex post facto inquiries into financial ability when there is any doubt at all on that score." 384 U.S. at 473, 86 S.Ct. at 1627, 16 L.Ed.2d at 723.

"Once warnings have been given, the subsequent procedure is clear. If the individual indicates in any manner, at any time prior to or during questioning, that he wishes to remain silent, the interrogation must cease. At this point he has shown that he intends to exercise his Fifth Amendment privilege; any statement taken after the person invokes his privilege cannot be other than the product of compulsion, subtle or otherwise. Without the right to cut off questioning, the setting of in-custody interrogation operates on the individual to overcome free choice in producing a statement after the privilege has been once invoked. If the individual states that he wants an attorney, the interrogation must cease until an attorney is present. At that time the individual must have an opportunity to confer with the attorney and to have him present during any subsequent questioning. If the individual cannot obtain an attorney and he indicates that he wants one before speaking to police, they must respect his decision to remain silent." 384 U.S. at 473–74, 86 S.Ct. at 1627–28, 16 L.Ed.2d at 723.

"There is no requirement that police stop a person who enters a police station and states that he wishes to confess to a crime, or a person who calls the police to offer a confession or any other statement he desires to make. Volunteered statements of any kind are not barred by the Fifth Amendment and their admissibility is not affected by our holding today." 384 U.S. at 478, 86 S.Ct. at 1630, 16 L.Ed.2d at 726.

"[W]hen an individual is taken into custody or otherwise deprived of his freedom by the authorities in any significant way and is subjected to questioning, the privilege against self-incrimination is jeopardized. Procedural safeguards must be employed to protect the privilege and unless other fully effective means are adopted to notify the person of his right of silence and to assure that the exercise of the right will be scrupulously honored, the following measures are required. He must be warned prior to any question that he has the right to remain silent, that anything he says can be used against him in a court of law, that he has the right to the presence of an attorney, and that if he cannot afford an attorney one will be appointed for him prior to any questioning if he so desires. Opportunity to exercise these rights must be afforded to him throughout the interrogation. After such warnings have been given, and such opportunity afforded him, the individual may knowingly and intelligently waive these rights and agree to answer questions or make a statement. But unless and until such warnings and waiver are demonstrated by the prosecution at trial no evidence obtained as a result of interrogation can be used against him." 384 U.S. at 478–79, 86 S.Ct. at 1630, 16 L.Ed.2d at 726.

California v. Beheler (1983). "Although the circumstances of each case must certainly influence a determination of whether a suspect is 'in custody' for purposes of receiving *Miranda* protection, the ultimate inquiry is simply whether there is a 'formal arrest or restraint on freedom of movement' of the degree associated with a formal arrest." 463 U.S. 1121, 1125, 103 S.Ct. 3517, 3520, 77 L.Ed.2d 1275, 1279.

Stansbury v. California (1994). "[A]ny inquiry into whether the interrogating officers have focused their suspicions upon the individual being questioned (assuming those suspicions remain undisclosed) is not relevant for purposes of *Miranda.*" 511 U.S. 318, 326, 114 S.Ct. 1526, 1530, 128 L.Ed.2d 293, 301.

Oregon v. Mathiason (1977). "Any interview of one suspected of a crime by a police officer will have coercive aspects to it, simply by virtue of the fact that the police officer is part of a law enforcement system which may ultimately cause the suspect to be charged with a crime. But police officers are not required to administer *Miranda* warnings to everyone whom they question. Nor is the requirement of warnings imposed simply because the questioning takes place in the station house, or because the questioned person is one whom the police suspect. *Miranda* warnings are required only where there has been such a restriction on a person's freedom as to render him 'in custody.' It was that sort of coercive environment to which *Miranda* by its terms was made applicable, and to which it is limited." 429 U.S. 492, 495, 97 S.Ct. 711, 714, 50 L.Ed.2d 714, 719.

Berkemer v. McCarty (1984). "Under the Fourth Amendment . . . a policeman who lacks probable cause but whose 'observations lead him reasonably to suspect' that a particular person has committed, is committing, or is about to commit a crime, may detain that person briefly in order to 'investigate the circumstances that provoke suspicion.' . . . '[T]he stop and inquiry must be "reasonably related in scope to the justification for their initiation."' . . . Typically, this means that the officer may ask the detainee a moderate number of questions to determine his identity and to try to obtain information confirming or dispelling the officer's suspicions. But the detainee is not obliged to respond. And, unless the detainee's answers provide the officer with probable cause to arrest him, he must then be released. The comparatively nonthreatening character of detentions of this sort explains the absence of any suggestion in our opinions that *Terry* stops are subject to the dictates of *Miranda.* The similarly noncoercive aspect of ordinary traffic stops prompts us to hold that persons temporarily detained pursuant to such stops are not 'in custody' for the purposes of *Miranda.*" 468 U.S. 420, 439–40, 104 S.Ct. 3138, 3150, 82 L.Ed.2d 317, 334–35.

Rhode Island v. Innis (1980). "[T]he *Miranda* safeguards come into play whenever a person in custody is subjected to either express questioning or its functional equivalent. That is to say, the term 'interrogation' under *Miranda* refers not only to express questioning, but also to any words or actions on the part of police (other than those normally attendant to arrest and custody) that the police should know are reasonably likely to elicit an incriminating response from the suspect." 446 U.S. 291, 300–01, 100 S.Ct. 1682, 1689, 64 L.Ed.2d 297, 307–08.

South Dakota v. Neville (1983). "In the context of an arrest for driving while intoxicated, a police inquiry of whether the suspect will take a blood-alcohol test is not an interrogation within the meaning of *Miranda*." 459 U.S. 553, 565 n.15, 103 S.Ct. 916, 923 n.15, 74 L.Ed.2d 748, 759 n.15.

New York v. Quarles (1984). "[T]here is a 'public safety' exception to the requirement that *Miranda* warnings be given before a suspect's answers may be admitted into evidence, and . . . the availability of that exception does not depend upon the motivation of the individual officers involved." 467 U.S. 649, 655–56, 104 S.Ct. 2626, 2631, 81 L.Ed.2d 550, 557.

"[T]he need for answers to questions in a situation posing a threat to the public safety outweighs the need for the prophylactic rule protecting the Fifth Amendment's privilege against self-incrimination. We decline to place officers . . . in the untenable position of having to consider, often in a matter of seconds, whether it best serves society for them to ask the necessary questions without the *Miranda* warnings and render whatever probative evidence they uncover inadmissible, or for them to give the warnings in order to preserve the admissibility of evidence they might uncover but possibly damage or destroy their ability to obtain that evidence and neutralize the volatile situation confronting them." 467 U.S. at 657–58, 104 S.Ct. at 2632, 81 L.Ed.2d at 558.

Michigan v. Mosley (1975). Even though the *Miranda* opinion states that the interrogation must cease when the person in custody indicates a desire to remain silent, "neither this passage nor any other passage in the *Miranda* opinion can sensibly be read to create a per se proscription of indefinite duration upon any further questioning by any police officer on any subject, once the person in custody has indicated a desire to remain silent." 423 U.S. 96, 102–03, 96 S.Ct. 321, 326, 46 L.Ed.2d 313, 320–21.

Edwards v. Arizona (1981). "[W]hen an accused has invoked his right to have counsel present during custodial interrogation, a valid waiver of that right cannot be established by showing only that he responded to further police-initiated custodial interrogation even if he has been advised of his rights. We further hold that an accused . . . having expressed his desire to deal with the police only through counsel, is not subject to further interrogation by the authorities until counsel has been made available to him, unless the accused himself initiates further communication, exchanges, or conversations with the police." 451 U.S. 477, 484–85, 101 S.Ct. 1880, 1884–85, 68 L.Ed.2d 378, 386.

Minnick v. Mississippi (1990). "[W]hen counsel is requested, interrogation must cease, and officials may not reinitiate interrogation without counsel present, whether or not the accused has consulted with his attorney." 498 U.S. 146, 153, 111 S.Ct. 486, 491, 112 L.Ed.2d 489, 498.

Michigan v. Jackson (1986). "[I]f police initiate interrogation after a defendant's assertion, at an arraignment or simi-

lar proceeding, of his right to counsel, any waiver of the defendant's right to counsel for that police-initiated interrogation is invalid." 475 U.S. 625, 636, 106 S.Ct. 1404, 1411, 89 L.Ed.2d 631, 642.

McNeil v. Wisconsin (1991). "The purpose of the Sixth Amendment counsel guarantee—and hence the purpose of invoking it—is to 'protec[t] the unaided layman at critical confrontations' with his 'expert adversary,' the government, *after* 'the adverse positions of government and defendant have solidified' with respect to a particular alleged crime. . . . The purpose of the *Miranda-Edwards* guarantee, on the other hand—and hence the purpose of invoking it—is to protect a quite different interest: the suspect's 'desire to deal with the police only through counsel,' . . . This is in one respect narrower than the interest protected by the Sixth Amendment guarantee (because it relates only to custodial interrogation) and in another respect broader (because it relates to interrogation regarding any suspected crime and attaches whether or not the 'adversarial relationship' produced by a pending prosecution has yet arisen). To invoke the Sixth Amendment interest is, as a matter of *fact, not* to invoke the *Miranda-Edwards* interest." 501 U.S. 171, 178–79, 111 S.Ct. 2204, 2208–09, 115 L.Ed.2d 158, 168.

Arizona v. Mauro (1987). "Officers do not interrogate a suspect simply by hoping that he will incriminate himself." 481 U.S. 520, 529, 107 S.Ct. 1931, 1936, 95 L.Ed.2d 458, 468.

"Police departments need not adopt inflexible rules barring suspects from speaking with their spouses, nor must they ignore legitimate security concerns by allowing spouses to meet in private." 481 U.S. at 530, 107 S.Ct. at 1937, 95 L.Ed.2d at 468.

Arizona v. Roberson (1988). "[T]he presumption raised by a suspect's request for counsel—that he considers himself unable to deal with the pressures of custodial interrogation without legal assistance—does not disappear simply because the police have approached the suspect, still in custody, still without counsel, about a separate investigation." 486 U.S. 675, 683, 108 S.Ct. 2093, 2099, 100 L.Ed.2d 704, 715.

Patterson v. Illinois (1988). "Preserving the integrity of an accused's choice to communicate with police only through counsel is the essence of *Edwards* and its progeny—not barring an accused from making an *initial* selection as to whether he will face the State's officers during questioning with the aid of counsel, or go it alone. If an accused 'knowingly and intelligently' pursues the latter course, we see no reason why the uncounseled statements he then makes must be excluded at his trial." 487 U.S. 285, 291, 108 S.Ct. 2389, 2394, 101 L.Ed.2d 261, 271–72.

"[W]hatever warnings suffice for *Miranda*'s purposes will also be sufficient in the context of postindictment questioning. The State's decision to take an additional step and commence formal adversarial proceedings against the accused does not substantially increase the value of counsel to the accused at questioning, or expand the limited purpose that an attorney serves when the accused is questioned by authorities. With respect to this inquiry, we do not discern a substantial difference between the usefulness of a lawyer to a suspect during custodial interrogation, and his value to an accused at postindictment questioning." 487 U.S. at 298–99, 108 S.Ct. at 2398, 101 L.Ed.2d at 276.

Smith v. Illinois (1984). "'No authority, and no logic, permits the interrogator to proceed . . . on his own terms and as if the defendant had requested nothing, in the hope that the defendant might be induced to say something casting retrospective doubt on his initial statement that he wished to speak through an attorney or not at all.'" 469 U.S. 91, 99, 105 S.Ct. 490, 494, 83 L.Ed.2d 488, 496.

Davis v. United States (1994). "Although a suspect need not 'speak with the discrimination of an Oxford don,' . . . he must articulate his desire to have counsel present sufficiently clearly that a reasonable police officer in the circumstances would understand the statement to be a request for an attorney. If the statement fails to meet the requisite level of clarity, *Edwards* does not require that the officers stop questioning the suspect." 512 U.S. 452, 459, 114 S.Ct. 2350, 2355, 129 L.Ed.2d 362, 371.

Oregon v. Bradshaw (1983). "[T]here are undoubtedly situations where a bare inquiry by either a defendant or by a police officer should not be held to 'initiate' any conversation or dialogue. There are some inquiries, such as a request for a drink of water or a request to use a telephone that are so routine that they cannot be fairly said to represent a desire on the part of an accused to open up a more generalized discussion relating directly or indirectly to the investigation. Such inquiries or statements, by either an accused or a police officer, relating to routine incidents of the custodial relationship, will not generally 'initiate' a conversation in the sense in which that word was used in *Edwards*." 462 U.S. 1039, 1045, 103 S.Ct. 2830, 2835, 77 L.Ed.2d 405, 412.

Oregon v. Elstad (1985). "[A]bsent deliberately coercive or improper tactics in obtaining the initial statement, the mere fact that a suspect has made an unwarned admission does not warrant a presumption of compulsion. A subsequent administration of *Miranda* warnings to a suspect who has given a voluntary but unwarned statement ordinarily should suffice to remove the conditions that precluded admission of the earlier statement. In such circumstances, the finder of fact may reasonably conclude that the suspect made a rational and intelligent choice whether to waive or invoke his rights." 470 U.S. 298, 314, 105 S.Ct. 1285, 1296, 84 L.Ed.2d 222, 235.

Massiah v. United States (1964). "[T]he petitioner was denied the basic protections of [the Sixth Amendment guarantee to assistance of counsel] when there was used against him at his trial evidence of his own incriminating words, which federal agents had deliberately elicited from him after

he had been indicted and in the absence of his counsel. . . . '[I]f such a rule is to have any efficacy it must apply to indirect and surreptitious interrogations as well as those conducted in the jailhouse. . . . Massiah was more seriously imposed upon . . . because he did not even know that he was under interrogation by a government agent.'" 377 U.S. 201, 206, 84 S.Ct. 1199, 1203, 12 L.Ed.2d 246, 250.

Brewer v. Williams (1977). "Whatever else it may mean, the right to counsel granted by the Sixth and Fourteenth Amendments means at least that a person is entitled to the help of a lawyer at or after the time that judicial proceedings have been initiated against him—'whether by way of formal charge, preliminary hearing, indictment, information, or arraignment.'" 430 U.S. 387, 398, 97 S.Ct. 1232, 1239, 51 L.Ed.2d 424, 436.

"[T]he clear rule of *Massiah* is that once adversary proceedings have commenced against an individual, he has a right to legal representation when the government interrogates him." 430 U.S. at 401, 97 S.Ct. at 1240, 51 L.Ed.2d at 438.

Maine v. Moulton (1985). "[T]he Sixth Amendment is not violated whenever—by luck or happenstance—the State obtains incriminating statements from the accused after the right to counsel has attached. . . . However, knowing exploitation by the State of an opportunity to confront the accused without counsel being present is as much a breach of the State's obligation not to circumvent the right to assistance of counsel as is the intentional creation of such an opportunity. Accordingly, the Sixth Amendment is violated when the State obtains incriminating statements by knowingly circumventing the accused's right to have counsel present in a confrontation between the accused and a state agent." 474 U.S. 159, 176, 106 S.Ct. 477, 487, 88 L.Ed.2d 481, 496.

Kuhlmann v. Wilson (1986). The defendant's Sixth Amendment rights are not violated when an informant, either through prior arrangement or voluntarily, reports the defendant's incriminating statements to the police. "[T]he defendant must demonstrate that the police and their informant took some action, beyond merely listening, that was designed deliberately to elicit incriminating remarks." 477 U.S. 436, 459, 106 S.Ct. 2616, 2630, 91 L.Ed.2d 364, 384–85.

Duckworth v. Eagan (1989). "Reviewing courts . . . need not examine *Miranda* warnings as if construing a will or defining the terms of an easement. The inquiry is simply whether the warnings reasonably 'conve[y] to [a suspect] his rights as required by *Miranda*.'" 492 U.S. 195, 203, 109 S.Ct. 2875, 2880, 106 L.Ed.2d 166, 177.

Moran v. Burbine (1986). The inquiry whether the defendant has made a full and effective waiver of *Miranda* rights has two distinct dimensions. "First, the relinquishment of the right must have been voluntary in the sense that it was the product of a free and deliberate choice rather than intimidation, coercion or deception. Second, the waiver must have been made with a full awareness both of the nature of the right being abandoned and the consequences of the decision to abandon it. Only if 'the totality of the circumstances surrounding the interrogation' reveal both an uncoerced choice and the requisite level of comprehension may a court properly conclude that the Miranda rights have been waived." 475 U.S. 412, 421, 106 S.Ct. 1135, 1141, 89 L.Ed.2d 410, 421.

"Events occurring outside the presence of the suspect and entirely unknown to him surely can have no bearing on the capacity to comprehend and knowingly relinquish a constitutional right. . . . Once it is determined that a suspect's decision not to rely on his rights was uncoerced, that he at all times knew he could stand mute and request a lawyer, and that he was aware of the State's intention to use his statements to secure a conviction, the analysis is complete and the waiver is valid as a matter of law." 475 U.S. at 422–23, 106 S.Ct. at 1141, 89 L.Ed.2d at 421–22.

Connecticut v. Barrett (1987). "It is undisputed that Barrett desired the presence of counsel before making a written statement. Had the police obtained such a statement without meeting the waiver standards of *Edwards,* it would clearly be inadmissible. Barrett's limited requests for counsel, however, were accompanied by affirmative announcements of his willingness to speak with the authorities. The fact that officials took the opportunity provided by Barrett to obtain an oral confession is quite consistent with the Fifth Amendment. *Miranda* gives the defendant a right to choose between speech and silence, and Barrett chose to speak." 479 U.S. 523, 529, 107 S.Ct. 828, 832, 93 L.Ed.2d 920, 928.

Colorado v. Spring (1987). "The Constitution does not require that a criminal suspect know and understand every possible consequence of a waiver of the Fifth Amendment privilege. . . . The Fifth Amendment's guarantee is both simpler and more fundamental: A defendant may not be compelled to be a witness against himself in any respect. The *Miranda* warnings protect this privilege by insuring that a suspect knows that he may choose not to talk to law enforcement officers, to talk only with counsel present, or to discontinue talking at any time. The *Miranda* warnings ensure that a waiver of these rights is knowing and intelligent by requiring that the suspect be fully advised of this constitutional privilege, including the critical advice that whatever he chooses to say may be used as evidence against him." 479 U.S. 564, 574, 107 S.Ct. 851, 857–58, 93 L.Ed.2d 954, 966.

"This Court's holding in *Miranda* specifically required that the police inform a criminal suspect that he has the right to remain silent and that anything he says may be used against him. There is no qualification of this broad and explicit warning. The warning, as formulated in *Miranda,* conveys to a suspect the nature of his constitutional privilege and the consequences of abandoning it. Accordingly, we hold that a suspect's awareness of all the possible subjects of questioning in advance of interrogation is not relevant to determining whether the suspect voluntarily, knowingly, and intelligently waived his Fifth Amendment privilege." 479 U.S. at 577, 107 S.Ct. at 859, 93 L.Ed.2d at 968.

Fare v. Michael C. (1979). "This totality of circumstances approach is adequate to determine whether there has been a waiver even where interrogation of juveniles is involved. . . . The totality approach permits—indeed, it mandates—inquiry into all the circumstances surrounding the interrogation. This includes evaluation of the juvenile's age, experience, education, background, and intelligence, and into whether he had the capacity to understand the warnings given him, the nature of his Fifth Amendment rights, and the consequences of waiving those rights." 442 U.S. 707, 725, 99 S.Ct. 2560, 2572, 61 L.Ed.2d 197, 212.

Schmerber v. California (1966). The privilege against self-incrimination "protects an accused only from being compelled to testify against himself, or otherwise provide the State with evidence of a testimonial or communicative nature. . . ." 384 U.S. 757, 761, 86 S.Ct. 1826, 1830, 16 L.Ed.2d 908, 914.

Doe v. United States (1988). "[I]n order to be testimonial, an accused's communication must itself, explicitly or implicitly, relate a factual assertion or disclose information. Only then is a person compelled to be a 'witness' against himself." 487 U.S. 201, 210, 108 S.Ct. 2341, 2347, 101 L.Ed.2d 184, 197.

Pennsylvania v. Muniz (1990). "Requiring a suspect to reveal the physical manner in which he articulates words, like requiring him to reveal the physical properties of the sound produced by his voice . . . does not, without more, compel him to provide a 'testimonial' response for purposes of the privilege." 496 U.S. 582, 592, 110 S.Ct. 2638, 2645, 110 L.Ed.2d 528, 546.

Illinois v. Perkins (1990). "[A]n undercover law enforcement officer posing as a fellow inmate need not give *Miranda* warnings to an incarcerated suspect before asking questions that may elicit an incriminating response." 496 U.S. 292, 300, 110 S.Ct. 2394, 2399, 110 L.Ed.2d 243, 253.

Harris v. New York (1971). "The shield provided by *Miranda* cannot be perverted into a license to use perjury by way of a defense, free from the risk of confrontation with prior inconsistent utterances. We hold, therefore, that petitioner's credibility was appropriately impeached by use of his earlier conflicting statements." 401 U.S. 222, 226, 91 S.Ct. 643, 646, 28 L.Ed.2d 1, 5.

Doyle v. Ohio (1976). "'[W]hen a person under arrest is informed as *Miranda* requires, that he may remain silent, that anything he says may be used against him, and that he may have an attorney if he wishes, it seems to me that it does not comport with due process to permit the prosecution during the trial to call attention to his silence at the time of arrest and to insist that because he did not speak about the facts of the case at that time, as he was told he need not do, an unfavorable inference might be drawn as to the truth of his trial testimony. . . .'" 426 U.S. 610, 619, 96 S.Ct. 2240, 2245, 49 L.Ed.2d 91, 98.

Brecht v. Abrahamson (1993). "[T]he Constitution does not prohibit the use for impeachment purposes of a defendant's silence prior to arrest . . . or after arrest if no *Miranda* warnings are given. . . . Such silence is probative and does not rest on any implied assurance by law enforcement authorities that it will carry no penalty." 507 U.S. 619, 628, 113 S.Ct. 1710, 1716, 123 L.Ed.2d 353, 366.

Review and Discussion Questions

1. Would any of the following actions cause a statement of a suspect to be involuntary?

   a. Making an appeal to the suspect's moral or religious beliefs

   b. Confronting the suspect with the deceased or seriously injured victim of the crime in question

   c. Starting an argument with, challenging, or baiting the suspect

2. Does a person need a lawyer to help decide whether to waive *Miranda* rights? Is the compelling atmosphere of a custodial setting just as likely to influence a person's decision to waive rights as it is to influence the decision to confess?

3. Is a person's giving of consent to search an inculpatory or exculpatory statement? Should a person in custody be given *Miranda* warnings before being asked for a consent to search?

4. Assume that a person has been formally arrested for one crime, and police want to question that person about another, unrelated crime. Are *Miranda* warnings required to be given before the questioning? If the answer is no, what additional circumstances might cause *Miranda* warnings to be required?

5. It is reasonable to assume that a person under investigation for a crime might think that complete silence in the face of an accusation might not look good to a judge or a jury. Should the *Miranda* warnings include a statement that a person's silence may not be used against the person in any way?

6. Should suspects be told the nature and seriousness of the offense for which they are being interrogated? What if a person believes that he or she is being investigated for an accident caused by driving while intoxicated but does not know that a person in the other vehicle has died?

7. What would be the advantages and disadvantages of requiring law enforcement officers to tape-record the entire process of administration of *Miranda* warnings and the suspect's invocation or waiver of rights?

8. Is it proper for a law enforcement officer to inform a suspect who has just invoked the *Miranda* right to counsel that the case against the suspect is strong and that immediate cooperation with the authorities would be beneficial in the long run? If the suspect says, "What do you mean?" would this be considered an initiation of further communication by the suspect and a waiver of the right to counsel?

9. Considering the confusion and pressures associated with being arrested and transported to a police station, should arrested persons be advised, in addition to the *Miranda* warnings, of where they are being taken, what is going to happen to them, how long they will be held, and with whom they may communicate?

10. Would the *Massiah* rule be violated if conversations of an indicted and imprisoned person were obtained by means of a listening device installed in that person's cell?

REAL-LIFE FACT SITUATIONS

1. On October 13, 1994, Albany County Deputy Sheriff William Riley was dispatched to the intersection of County Route 353 and Littner Road in the Town of Rensselaerville, Albany County, to investigate a report that a vehicle operated by defendant had been abandoned in a ditch. Upon arriving at his destination, Riley was advised by an unidentified individual that the defendant was walking on nearby Lake Road harassing people. Upon locating the defendant, Riley informed him that he had a warrant for his arrest and then began to question defendant as to how he arrived in Rensselaerville and whether he had been drinking, in response

to which the defendant made incriminating admissions. Should the defendant's statements be admitted in evidence? *People v. Duncan*, 660 N.Y.S.2d 81 (A.D.3 Dept. 1997).

2. On the evening of July 25, 1996, Stillwater police officers Allen and Felsch received a call that cars were drag racing. When the officers arrived at the scene, there had been an accident. Officer Allen was told by a witness that the witness's car had been struck from behind by Aron Edrozo. He also stated that Edrozo had tried to run over the witness and four other persons while they were standing on the sidewalk.

While the officers were interviewing other witnesses, Edrozo's vehicle drove by. They pursued and then stopped the vehicle. Edrozo was not driving. He and another person in the vehicle, Benjamin Easton, were first placed in Officer Felsch's car, then moved to Officer Allen's car. Unbeknownst to Edrozo and Easton, Officer Felsch activated a tape recorder in Officer Allen's car. Edrozo made incriminating statements to Easton while seated in the vehicle. Neither Edrozo nor Easton was given a *Miranda* warning.

Edrozo's car was impounded and on July 29, 1996, he and his mother went to the Stillwater Police Department and then the impound lot to retrieve some things from the vehicle. Investigator Davin Miller accompanied Edrozo to the lot. Edrozo made voluntary and incriminating statements to Miller. The statements were not taped, and Edrozo had previously refused to talk without the presence of counsel. Miller refused to speak with Edrozo at the impound lot. No *Miranda* warning was given. Should Edrozo's motion to suppress the statements made in the back of the police car and the statements made to Miller be granted? *State v. Edrozo*, 567 N.W.2d 59 (Minn.App 1997).

3. On August 28, 1995, at approximately 12:45 A.M., Officer William C. Muse of the State College Police Department was in full uniform and operating a marked patrol vehicle when he observed two unoccupied vehicles in the parking area of Orchard Park located in State College, Pennsylvania. According to the State College Borough Ordinance, no one was permitted in the park after sunset. This rule was posted at the various entrances to the park. Believing that the occupants of the vehicle were in the park in violation of the ordinance, Officer Muse exited his patrol car and entered the park on foot. As he proceeded through an area of trees, he observed five males sitting in an open grassy area approximately twenty feet from his location. The officer then illuminated the five males with his flashlight and instructed them to approach. After the males approached him, Officer Muse requested that they each take a seat on the ground. The males all complied with the officer's request. At some point during this event, Officer Muse radioed for assistance.

Officer Michael McDannel responded to Officer Muse's request for assistance. The two officers then requested and examined the males' identification. Officer Muse also checked the area for signs of illegal activity. Particularly, the officer searched for evidence of drugs or alcohol consumption. After finding no evidence of illegal activity, Officer Muse returned the identification cards to the males, instructed them that he was not going to cite them for violating the borough's ordinance and indicated that they were free to leave the area. As Officer Muse was handing Prosek his identification card, he recognized him as a newly initiated brother into the fraternity where Officer Muse was the chapter adviser. Moreover, while Prosek was being questioned by Officer McDannel, Officer Muse heard Prosek announce that he was academically suspended from the Pennsylvania State University. After handing Prosek his identification card, Officer Muse asked Prosek if he could speak to him. Prosek agreed, and the two conversed for approximately two minutes about Prosek's grades, suspension, and possible readmission into the university. Officer Muse then asked Prosek what he was doing in the park and whether he was smoking marijuana. Prosek responded that he was smoking marijuana. The officer asked Prosek if he had a pipe. Prosek stated that he did and then handed the pipe to Officer Muse. Officer Muse inspected the bowl of the pipe and found evidence of marijuana. Based upon Prosek's admission and the seized pipe, the officer announced that he was going to search all of the males. Officer Muse then lifted Charles Lechian's shirt and observed a clear plastic baggie containing marijuana in his waistband. No *Miranda* warnings were given to Prosek or to any of the other males by either Officer Muse or Officer McDannel. Should Prosek's motion to suppress his statements and the pipe be granted? *Commonwealth v. Prosek*, 700 A.2d 1305 (Pa.Super. 1997).

4. The defendant/appellant was arrested for trafficking in cocaine and conspiracy to traffic in cocaine by the undercover officer who had worked on setting up a drug transaction with him. Although appellant had spoken in English with the officer prior to discovering that he was a police officer, he refused to speak to him further after the arrest and spoke only in Creole. According to the arresting officer, it was clear that appellant did not want to talk with him. Thereafter, appellant was booked into the jail. Officer Poliard was summoned to the jail to try to get a statement from appellant. He went into appellant's jail cell in an undercover capacity, wearing a T-shirt, shorts, and sneakers. He was told to sit in the cell and see if appellant wanted to talk. Since Poliard could speak both Creole and English, he spoke to appellant in both languages. Poliard initiated the contact by asking appellant

what he was in for, to which appellant responded "cocaine." Appellant asked Poliard the same, and Poliard said he had a bad tag on his car, cocaine on his person, and his probation would be violated which would result in a five year prison sentence. Appellant said that the police told him that he would have to do ten years. Poliard asked why, and appellant said he set up a deal for two kilos of cocaine with a police officer but denied ever touching or delivering the cocaine. Appellant continued to give Poliard details of the crime.

The appellant moved to suppress the statements made to Officer Poliard, contending that the method used in acquiring the incriminating statements violated appellant's right to due process. However, relying on *Illinois v. Perkins,* 496 U.S. 292, 110 S.Ct. 2394, 110 L.Ed.2d 243 (1990), the trial court denied the motion, finding that the words spoken between appellant and the officer were a conversation and not an interrogation. Was the appellant or the trial court correct? *Voltaire v. State,* 697 So.2d 1002 (Fla.App. 4 Dist. 1997).

5. The victim testified that she awoke one night to find Anderson, whom she knew from her neighborhood, pulling her up by the throat. Anderson took her upstairs to a bedroom, removed the bottom portion of her clothing, and sodomized her. He then forced the victim to perform oral sex on him, after which he had vaginal intercourse with her and attempted, but failed, to penetrate her anally. The victim testified that she did not consent to any of these acts.

In his first enumeration of error, Anderson argues that the trial court improperly admitted into evidence an in-custody statement he gave to Officer Chuck Gammill. Prior to trial, the trial court held a *Jackson-Denno* hearing regarding Anderson's in-custody statement. Officer Gammill testified that when he first met with Anderson at the Clarke County Jail, he read Anderson his *Miranda* rights. According to Gammill, Anderson stated that he wanted to speak with an attorney. As described by Gammill: "I told him that that was fine. That the only reason I was there was to get his side of the story. If there was something that I needed to know that he may want to go ahead and tell me." The trial court asked Gammill why he did not stop the interview when Anderson asked for counsel. Gammill explained: "Well, at that point I told [Anderson] that I was there to get his side of the story. I wanted to know his perspective on the events that had occurred. And if there was anything else that I needed to be looking into from anything that he told me that I would continue the investigation from there. At that point I said but it's your right not to talk to me. If you don't want to, you don't have to. I then started down the steps in order to go get the deputies to put him back into the cell, and he said wait. I do want to talk to you. He summoned me back up the steps, and at that point I

[again read him his *Miranda* rights and] took a statement from him." Should Anderson's in-custody statement have been excluded from evidence? *Anderson v. State,* 492 S.E.2d 252 (Ga.App. 1997).

6. The trial court found that when the police responded to a crime scene in Forest Park on December 5, 1995, they discovered Jack Barnhill lying wounded in a van (he had been struck in the head with a stick) and Ritter sitting on the van's step. Ritter was arrested at the scene and, after being read his *Miranda* rights, told the police he understood his rights and did not want to say anything. As he was driven to the police station, Ritter inquired after the victim but the officer transporting him, knowing of Ritter's invocation of his rights, did not respond or speak to Ritter. Ritter also inquired after the victim while he was being booked, at which time he was asked only routine booking questions. The trial court found that Detective Cox, the officer in charge of the investigation, was informed of Ritter's invocation of his right to remain silent and also about Ritter's repeated inquiries into the victim's well-being.

The next day, December 6, Detective Cox had Ritter moved from his jail cell to an "interview room." Ritter had not requested to speak with the police; the questioning was initiated and orchestrated by the police. The evidence supports the trial court's finding that Detective Cox knew Jack Barnhill had died as a result of the wounds he had received and that Cox had obtained a warrant for the arrest of Ritter on charges of murder and armed robbery before the December 6 interview. Detective Cox testified at the hearing that he informed Ritter prior to the interview that Ritter was charged with aggravated assault, but did not tell him of the murder or armed robbery charges. Cox began an almost hour-long interrogation by volunteering that Barnhill was "awake now and conscious and all that good stuff. I talked to him yesterday after I got him up." In response to Ritter's inquiry whether Barnhill was "okay," Cox responded "yeah, I think he's going to be okay. He's going to have a bad headache now for a while." Cox testified at the hearing that he was afraid that if he told Ritter the truth, i.e., that the victim had died, Ritter would not talk to the police or would invoke his right to remain silent. Cox further testified that he read Ritter his *Miranda* rights again; asked Ritter if he wanted to talk; and after Ritter responded, "I do not know," immediately started questioning Ritter. The evidence supports the trial court's finding that Ritter stated at the beginning of the interrogation that he thought he needed an attorney, that Ritter repeated that statement later in the questioning, and that Ritter asked once at the end of the interrogation if he needed an attorney. Should Ritter's December 6 statements be excluded from evidence? *State v. Ritter,* 485 S.E.2d 492 (Ga. 1997).

CHAPTER FOURTEEN

Pretrial Identification Procedures

OBJECTIVES

1. Know the meanings of the terms *showup, lineup,* and *confrontation.*

2. Understand the reasons that the presence of counsel is required at a pretrial confrontation with witnesses conducted after the initiation of adversary judicial proceedings.

3. Know the proper procedures for conducting a lineup.

4. Know when a law enforcement officer may use a one-person showup and the ways in which the inherent suggestiveness of the showup may be reduced.

5. Know the factors that indicate accuracy or reliability of an identification even though the identification procedure was unnecessarily suggestive.

6. Know the proper procedures for conducting a photographic identification procedure.

OUTLINE

P retrial confrontation of a suspected criminal with witnesses to, or victims of, a crime has long been an accepted law enforcement technique to identify perpetrators of crime and also to clear from suspicion those who are innocent. In 1967, the U.S. Supreme Court decided three major cases governing this area of the law: *United States v. Wade,* 388 U.S. 218, 87 S.Ct. 1926, 18 L.Ed.2d 1149; *Gilbert v. California,* 388 U.S. 263, 87 S.Ct. 1951, 18 L.Ed.2d 1178; and *Stovall v. Denno,* 388 U.S. 293, 87 S.Ct. 1967, 18 L.Ed.2d 1199. These decisions provide the groundwork for most of the law applicable to pretrial identification procedures today.

The discussion of the *Wade, Gilbert,* and *Stovall* cases uses the terms *showup, lineup,* and *confrontation* throughout. A **showup** is the presentation of a single suspect to a victim or witness of a crime for the purpose of identifying the perpetrator of the crime. A **lineup** is the presentation at one time of several persons, including a suspect, to a victim or witness of a crime for the purpose of identifying the perpetrator of the crime. A lineup gives the victim or witness several choices. A **confrontation** includes both showups and lineups and is *any* presentation of a suspect to a victim or witness of a crime for the purpose of identifying the perpetrator of the crime. These terms are also sometimes used in connection with photographic or voice identifications. Thus, for example, a photographic showup would be a presentation of a single photograph of a suspect to a victim or witness of a crime. ■

Requirement of Counsel— The *Wade-Gilbert* Rule

In the *Wade* and *Gilbert* decisions, the Supreme Court decided that

> a post-indictment pretrial lineup at which the accused is exhibited to identifying witnesses is a critical stage of the criminal prosecution; that police conduct of such a lineup without notice to and in the absence of his counsel denies the accused his Sixth Amendment right to counsel and calls in question the admissibility at trial of the in-court identifications of the accused by witnesses who attended the lineup. *Gilbert v. California,* 388 U.S. 263, 272, 87 S.Ct. 1951, 1956, 18 L.Ed.2d 1178, 1186.

Furthermore, if the suspect is unable to afford a lawyer, he or she is entitled to have one appointed by the court. This ruling is an extension of the right of all accused persons to have the assistance of counsel for their defense at all critical stages of their criminal prosecution as guaranteed by the Sixth Amendment to the Constitution. (See pages 21–23.)

Basis of the Court's Decision

The Supreme Court's reasoning in the *Wade* and *Gilbert* cases was based on (1) the inherent unreliability of eyewitness identifications and (2) the possibility of improper suggestions being made to witnesses during the confrontation procedure. The Court said:

> [T]he confrontation compelled by the State between the accused and the victim or witnesses to a crime to elicit identification evidence is peculiarly riddled with innumerable dangers and variable factors which might seriously, even crucially, derogate from a fair trial. The vagaries of eyewitness identification are well-

known; the annals of criminal law are rife with instances of mistaken identification. . . . The identification of strangers is proverbially untrustworthy. . . . A major factor contributing to the high incidence of miscarriage of justice from mistaken identification has been the degree of suggestion inherent in the manner in which the prosecution presents the suspect to witnesses for pretrial identification. A commentator has observed that "[t]he influence of improper suggestion upon identifying witnesses probably accounts for more miscarriages of justice than any other single factor—perhaps it is responsible for more such errors than all other factors combined." . . . Suggestion can be created intentionally or unintentionally in many subtle ways. And the dangers for the suspect are particularly grave when the witness's opportunity for observation was insubstantial, and thus his susceptibility to suggestion the greatest.

Moreover, "(i)t is a matter of common experience that, once a witness has picked out the accused at the line-up, he is not likely to go back on his word later on, so that in practice the issue of identity may (in the absence of other relevant evidence) for all practical purposes be determined there and then, before the trial." 388 U.S. at 228–29, 87 S.Ct. at 1933, 18 L.Ed.2d at 1158–59.

The Court was concerned that, as with secret interrogations, there would be serious difficulty determining what happened at a lineup or other identification confrontation conducted in secret.

[T]he defense can seldom reconstruct the manner and mode of lineup identification for judge or jury at trial. Those participating in a lineup with the accused may often be police officers; in any event, the participants' names are rarely recorded or divulged at trial. The impediments to an objective observation are increased when the victim is the witness. Lineups are prevalent in rape and robbery prosecutions and present a particular hazard that a victim's understandable outrage may excite vengeful or spiteful motives. In any event, neither witnesses nor lineup participants are apt to be alert for conditions prejudicial to the suspect. And if they were, it would likely be of scant benefit to the suspect since neither witnesses nor lineup participants are likely to be schooled in the detection of suggestive influences. Improper influences may go undetected by a suspect, guilty or not, who experiences the emotional tension which we might expect in one being confronted with potential accusers. Even when he does observe abuse, if he has a criminal record he may be reluctant to take the stand and open up the admission of prior convictions. Moreover any protestations by the suspect of the fairness of the lineup made at trial are likely to be in vain; the jury's choice is between the accused's unsupported version and that of the police officers present. In short, the accused's inability effectively to reconstruct at trial any unfairness that occurred at the lineup may deprive him of his only opportunity meaningfully to attack the credibility of the witness' courtroom identification. 388 U.S. at 230–32, 87 S.Ct. at 1934–35, 18 L.Ed.2d at 1159–60.

The Court believed that the presence of counsel at the pretrial confrontation with witnesses would prevent misconduct by those conducting the confrontation. In addition, counsel would have firsthand knowledge of events at the confrontation and could, therefore, conduct an intelligent cross-examination of witnesses at a later suppression hearing or trial and point out any improprieties that might have occurred. The Court said:

Since it appears that there is grave potential for prejudice, intentional or not, in the pretrial lineup, which may not be capable of reconstruction at trial, and since presence of counsel itself can often avert prejudice and assure a meaningful confrontation at trial, there can be little doubt that for Wade the post-indictment lineup was a critical stage of the prosecution at which he was "as much entitled to such aid [of counsel] . . . as at the trial itself." . . . Thus both Wade and his counsel should have been notified of the impending lineup, and counsel's presence should have been a requisite to conduct of the lineup, absent an "intelligent waiver." 388 U.S. at 236–37, 87 S.Ct. at 1937, 18 L.Ed.2d at 1162–63.

The Court's ruling recognized the realities of modern criminal prosecution and the defendant's need for assistance at critical stages of the prosecution, formal or informal, in court or out, where the absence of counsel might adversely affect the right to a fair trial.

When the Bill of Rights was adopted, there were no organized police forces as we know them today. The accused confronted the prosecutor and the witnesses against him, and the evidence was marshalled, largely at the trial itself. In contrast, today's law enforcement machinery involves critical confrontations of the accused by the prosecution at pretrial proceedings where the results might well settle the accused's fate and reduce the trial itself to a mere formality. In recognition of these realities of modern criminal prosecution, our cases have construed the Sixth Amendment guarantee to apply to "critical" stages of the proceedings. The guarantee reads: "In all criminal prosecutions, the accused shall enjoy the right * * * to have the Assistance of Counsel for his defence." The plain wording of this guarantee thus encompasses counsel's assistance whenever necessary to assure a meaningful "defence." 388 U.S. at 224–25, 87 S.Ct. at 1931, 18 L.Ed.2d at 1156.

Waiver of Right to Counsel

Suspects may waive their right to the presence of counsel at a pretrial confrontation.

A waiver is ordinarily an intentional relinquishment or abandonment of a known right or privilege. The determination of whether there has been an intelligent waiver of right to counsel must depend, in each case, upon the particular facts and circumstances surrounding that case, including the background, experience, and conduct of the accused. *Johnson v. Zerbst,* 304 U.S. 458, 464, 58 S.Ct. 1019, 1023, 82 L.Ed. 1461, 1466 (1938).

Before suspects can intelligently and understandingly waive their right to presence of counsel, they should be clearly advised of their rights. The form appearing as Exhibit 14.1 is suggested for this purpose. In *United States v. Sublet,* 644 F.2d 737 (8th Cir. 1981), the court found an intelligent waiver of the right to counsel, even though the defendant refused to sign the waiver form. In that case, the defendant consented to being placed in the lineup after its purpose was explained. Furthermore, "[t]he fact that another suspect requested an attorney and the lineup was delayed until counsel arrived is strong evidence that Sublet was not denied his right to counsel." 644 F.2d at 741–42.

Substitute Counsel

If a suspect requests the advice and presence of his or her own lawyer and that lawyer is not immediately available, a substitute lawyer may sometimes be called for the purpose of the confrontation. *Zamora v. Guam,* 394 F.2d 815 (9th Cir. 1968). As stated in *United States v. Wade:*

Although the right to counsel usually means a right to the suspect's own counsel, provision for substitute counsel may be justified on the ground that the substitute counsel's presence may eliminate the hazards which render the lineup a critical stage for the presence of the suspect's own counsel. 388 U.S. at 237 n.9, 87 S.Ct. at 1938 n.9, 18 L.Ed.2d at 1163–64 n.9.

KEY POINTS

1. A postindictment pretrial lineup at which the accused is exhibited to identifying witnesses is a critical stage of the criminal prosecution. Police conduct of such a lineup without notice to and in the absence of his counsel denies the accused his Sixth Amendment right to counsel and calls in question the admissibility at trial of the in-court identifications of the accused by witnesses who attended the lineup.

Guidelines for Lineup Identifications

As a general rule, the decision to conduct a lineup is made at the discretion of the police or prosecution. Although the police, the prosecution, or the court may grant a suspect's request for a lineup, there is no requirement that such a request be granted. *United States v. Harvey,* 756 F.2d 636 (8th Cir. 1985). The following are guidelines for the law enforcement officer in conducting a lineup identification procedure.

Before the Lineup

- No lineup identification procedure should be conducted by a law enforcement officer without the officer discussing with the prosecuting attorney the legal advisability of the lineup.

- A lineup should be conducted as soon after the arrest of a suspect as is practicable. Promptly conducted lineups enable the release of innocent arrestees, guarantee the freshness of witnesses' memories, and ensure that crucial identification evidence is obtained before the suspect is released on bail or for other reasons. When possible, lineup arrangements (such as contacting witnesses and locating innocent participants) should be completed before the arrest of the suspect.

- A person in custody may be compelled to participate in a lineup without Fourth or Fifth Amendment rights being violated. Most courts hold that once a person is in custody, his or her liberty is not further infringed by that person's being presented in a lineup for witnesses to view. *People v. Hodge,* 526 P.2d 309 (Colo. 1974). Furthermore, "compelling the accused merely to exhibit his person for observation by a prosecution witness prior to trial involves no compulsion of the accused to give evidence having testimonial significance. It is compulsion of the accused to exhibit his physical characteristics, not compulsion to disclose any knowledge he might have." *United States v. Wade,* 388 U.S. 218, 222, 87 S.Ct. 1926, 1930, 18 L.Ed.2d 1149, 1154–55 (1967).

    Compelling persons who are not in custody to appear in a lineup involves a much greater intrusion on liberty and is usually done only by order of a court or grand jury, or by authority of statute in some states. Some courts have upheld the ordering of a person not in custody to appear in a lineup in serious cases in which the public interest in law enforcement outweighed the privacy interests of the person. *Wise v. Murphy*, 275 A.2d 205 (D.C.App. 1971). Other courts have held that a person not in custody cannot be ordered to participate in a lineup unless there is probable cause to arrest. *Alphonso C. v. Morgenthau*, 50 A.D.2d 97, 376 N.Y.S.2d 126 (N.Y .1975).

- If the suspect has the right to counsel at the lineup, the suspect should be informed of that right. If the suspect chooses to waive the right to counsel, a careful record should be made of the suspect's waiver and agreement to voluntarily participate in the lineup. (See Exhibit 14.1.)

- If the suspect chooses to have an attorney present at the lineup proceedings, the lineup should be delayed a reasonable time to allow the attorney to appear. The attorney must be allowed to be present from the beginning of the lineup, or "the moment [the suspect] and the other lineup members were within the sight of witnesses." *United States v. LaPierre*, 998 F.2d 1460, 1464 (9th Cir. 1993). The attorney should be allowed to consult with the suspect before the lineup and be given every opportunity to observe all the proceedings, take notes, and tape-record the identification process in whole or in part. If the attorney has any suggestions that might improve the fairness of the proceedings, the officer in charge may follow them if they are reasonable and practicable. However, the attorney should not be allowed to control the proceedings in any way.

  Note that the suspect's attorney must be made aware that an identification is taking place. The attorney's mere presence will not satisfy the *Wade-Gilbert* rule. In a case in which the suspect and his attorney were unaware that witnesses had identified the suspect during his arraignment, the suspect's right to counsel was held to be violated. *Mason v. United States*, 414 F.2d 1176 (D.C.Cir. 1969). Counsel's purpose is to ensure that the identification is conducted fairly and to reconstruct the procedures at trial. Counsel can do neither if he or she is unaware that an identification is taking place.

- Even when the suspect's counsel is not required at a lineup (see the following section entitled "Exceptions to the *Wade-Gilbert* Rule"), the officer conducting the lineup should consider allowing counsel to be present to minimize subsequent challenges to the fairness of the lineup. *State v. Taylor*, 210 N.W.2d 873 (Wis. 1973).

- The names of all persons participating in the lineup, the names of the officers conducting the lineup, and the name of the suspect's attorney, if any, should be recorded and preserved.

- The witness or victim viewing the lineup should be advised of the purpose for which the lineup is being conducted, but the officer should not suggest that the suspect is one of those in the lineup or even that the suspect is in police custody. Moreover, all witnesses who are to view the lineup should be prevented from seeing the suspect in custody, particularly in handcuffs, or in any other circumstances that would indicate the identity of the suspect in question.

- If possible, witnesses should not be allowed to view photographs of the suspect before the lineup. If a witness has viewed photographs before the lineup, the officer conducting the lineup should inform the suspect's counsel and the court of any identification of the suspect's photograph, any failure to identify the suspect's photograph, and any identification of a photograph of someone other than the suspect.

Pretrial Identification Warning and Waiver

Name: _____ Address: _____

Age: _____ Place: _____

Date:_____ Time: _____

Warning

Before appearing at any confrontation with any witnesses being conducted by (Name of Police Department) in relation to (Description of Offense), you are entitled to be informed of your legal rights.

The results of the confrontation can and will be used against you in court.

You have the right to the presence and advice of an attorney of your choice at any such confrontation.

If you cannot afford an attorney and you want one, an attorney will be appointed for you at no expense, before any confrontation is held.

Waiver

I have been advised of my right to the advice of an attorney and to have an attorney present at any confrontation with witnesses, and that if I cannot afford an attorney, one will be appointed for me before any such confrontation occurs. I understand these rights.

I do not want an attorney and I understand and know what I am doing.

No promises have been made to me and no pressures of any kind have been used against me.

_____
Signature of Suspect

Certification

I, (Name of Officer), hereby certify that I read the above warning to (Name of Suspect) on (Date), that this person indicated an understanding of the rights, and that this person signed the WAIVER form in my presence.

_____
Signature of Officer

_____
Witness

EXHIBIT 14.1 Pretrial Identification Warning and Waiver

- Before viewing the lineup, each witness should be required to give to the officer in charge of the lineup a written description of the perpetrator of the crime. A copy should be made available to the suspect's counsel.

During the Lineup

- Insofar as possible, all persons in the lineup should be of the same general weight, height, age, and race; should have the same general physical characteristics; and should be dressed similarly. A suspect, and other participants in the lineup, may be required to wear particular kinds of clothing at the lineup. *United States v. King*, 433 F.2d 937 (9th Cir. 1970). In addition, a suspect may be required to shave, trim his or her hair, or even grow a beard before participating in a lineup. *United States v. O'Neal*, 349 F.Supp. 572 (N.D.Ohio 1972). If a suspect fails to cooperate with identification procedures or attempts to change his or her appearance, the officer conducting the lineup should keep a careful record of this behavior.

- The suspect should be allowed to choose his or her initial position in the lineup and to change that position after each viewing. This promotes fairness and eliminates any claim that the positioning of the suspect in the lineup was unduly suggestive.

- Nonsuspects participating in the lineup should be instructed not to act in any way that singles out the suspect.

- If any body movement or gesture is necessary, it should be made one time only by each person in the lineup and repeated only at the express request of the observing witness or victim. Again, the officer conducting the lineup should keep a careful record of any person's failure to cooperate.

- Lineup participants may be compelled to speak for purposes of voice identification. As stated by the U.S. Supreme Court in the *Wade* case, "[C]ompelling Wade to speak within hearing distance of the witnesses, even to utter words purportedly uttered by the robber, was not compulsion to utter statements of a 'testimonial' nature; he was required to use his voice as an identifying physical characteristic, not to speak his guilt." 388 U.S. at 222–23, 87 S.Ct. at 1930, 18 L.Ed.2d at 1155. Each person in the lineup should be asked to speak the same words.

- A color photograph or videotape (or both) of the lineup should be made, and copies should be provided to the suspect's counsel as soon as possible after the lineup.

- If more than one witness is called to view a lineup, the persons who have already viewed the lineup should not be allowed to converse with the persons who have not yet viewed the lineup. It is good practice to keep witnesses who have viewed the lineup in a room separate from witnesses who have not yet viewed the lineup. Furthermore, only one witness at a time should be present in the room where the lineup is being conducted.

- The officer conducting the lineup should not engage in unnecessary conversation with witnesses. Most important, the officer should not indicate by word, gesture, or otherwise his or her opinion as to the guilt of the suspect.

- The officer conducting the lineup should not allow unnecessary persons in the lineup room. A suggested group of people to include is the witness, the officer conducting the lineup, the prosecuting attorney, the suspect's attorney, and an investigator.

- Upon entering the room in which the lineup is being conducted, each witness should be handed a form for use in the identification. The form should be signed by the witness and the law enforcement officer conducting the lineup. A suggested form appears as Exhibit 14.2.

Lineup Identification Form for Witnesses

Your Name: _____ Date of Birth: _____

Address: _____

Telephone Number: _____ Case Number: _____

Place Viewed: _____ Officer: _____

Agency: _____

TO THE WITNESS: You have been asked to look at a lineup. This is either a presentation in person of several individuals or a presentation of several photographs. You may or may not be able to identify a person in the lineup. Please look at all the persons before making any choice. If you do not identify a person in the lineup, please indicate below. If you do identify a person, please indicate the number of the person on this form.

You must look at this display and make an independent identification *without assistance*. Do not ask any questions about the people being shown. You may, however, ask the officer to have persons in the lineup say certain words, do certain things, or wear certain clothing, if you think it will aid you. Do not ask anyone for help or discuss this with anyone except the officer. There is no "right" answer, so do not ask whether you have made the "right" choice.

Please mark your choice with an "X":

I do not identify anyone

I identify   1   2   3   4   5   6   7   8

COMMENTS: _____

_____

_____

_____

Thank you for your cooperation.

_____ Date and Time _____
Viewer's Signature

_____ Date and Time _____
Officer's Signature/Badge Number

EXHIBIT 14.2   Lineup Identification Form for Witnesses

- A copy of the witness identification form should be given to the suspect's attorney at the time each witness completes his or her viewing of the lineup.

- Use of a one-way mirror in a lineup, so that the suspect is unable to know what occurs on the other side of the mirror, has been held to be a prima facie violation of constitutional due process. This means that a lineup identification in which a one-way mirror is so used will be illegal, unless the officer conducting the lineup can show that particularly compelling or exigent circumstances made the use of the mirror necessary. *State v. Northup,* 303 A.2d 1, 5 (Me. 1973). When the suspect's counsel is present, however, one-way mirrors may be permitted because counsel can observe the conduct of the lineup and preserve the suspect's rights. A one-way mirror may also be used to protect witnesses who fear retaliation. *Commonwealth v. Lopes,* 287 N.E.2d 118 (Mass. 1972).

After the Lineup

- The officer conducting the lineup should take complete notes of everything that takes place at the lineup and should prepare an official report of all the proceedings, to be filed in the law enforcement agency's permanent records. The report should include the time, location, identity of persons present, statements made, and photographs or videotapes of the lineup. A copy should be sent to the prosecuting attorney and made available to the suspect's attorney. The lineup identification form (see Exhibit 14.2) for each witness viewing the lineup should be included as part of the officer's report.

- A defendant has no right to have his or her counsel present at a postlineup police interview with an identifying witness. *Hallmark v. Cartwright,* 742 F.2d 584 (10th Cir. 1984).

- Any officer who observed a lineup must disclose to the court that reviews the lineup any evidence that might affect the accuracy of the identification, whether the evidence was observed before, during, or after the lineup. Failure to do so may be a violation of the suspect's due process rights.

- Multiple lineups involving the same suspect and witness are inherently suggestive and strongly discouraged. In *Foster v. California,* 394 U.S. 440, 89 S.Ct. 1127, 22 L.Ed.2d 402 (1969), the eyewitness was unable to make a positive identification at the first lineup where Foster was placed with men considerably shorter than he. Even after the eyewitness met one-on-one with Foster, the identification was tentative with the eyewitness still indicating he was not sure Foster was the one. At a second lineup, the eyewitness was finally convinced Foster committed the crime and positively identified him. Foster was the only person who was used in both lineups. The U.S. Supreme Court reversed the conviction:

  > The suggestive elements in this identification procedure made it all but inevitable that David would identify petitioner whether or not he was in fact "the man." In effect, the police repeatedly said to the witness, "This is the man." . . . This procedure so undermined the reliability of the eyewitness identification as to violate due process. 394 U.S. at 443, 89 S.Ct. at 1129, 22 L.Ed.2d at 407.

Exceptions to the *Wade-Gilbert* Rule

The *Wade* and *Gilbert* decisions have caused much controversy, generating many conflicting opinions in subsequent court decisions. Some lower courts have limited *Wade* and *Gilbert* to their particular facts. Others have created exceptions to the broad holdings implicit in the decisions. Several of those exceptions are discussed here.

Identifications Conducted Before the Initiation of Adversary Judicial Proceedings

Most identification procedures take place before the defendant is indicted. The following discussion explains at what point in the judicial process the right to counsel attaches and what standards govern identification procedures conducted before the right to counsel attaches.

KIRBY v. ILLINOIS. At what stage of a criminal proceeding does a suspect have a right to counsel at an identification procedure? The U.S. Supreme Court decided this issue in *Kirby v. Illinois*, 406 U.S. 682, 92 S.Ct. 1877, 32 L.Ed.2d 411 (1972). In the *Kirby* case, the Court held that the right to counsel attaches to lineups and showups held

> at or after the initiation of adversary judicial criminal proceedings—whether by way of formal charge, preliminary hearing, indictment, information or arraignment. . . .
> The initiation of judicial criminal proceedings is far from a mere formalism. It is the starting point of our whole system of adversary criminal justice. For it is only then that the government has committed itself to prosecute, and only then that the adverse positions of government and defendant have solidified. It is then that a defendant finds himself faced with the prosecutorial forces of organized society, and immersed in the intricacies of substantive and procedural criminal law. It is this point, therefore, that marks the commencement of the "criminal prosecutions" to which alone the explicit guarantees of the Sixth Amendment are applicable. 406 U.S. at 689–90, 92 S.Ct. at 1882, 32 L.Ed.2d at 417–18.

Therefore, a law enforcement officer need not warn a suspect of the right to counsel at a confrontation, if criminal proceedings have not been initiated.

Courts differ in their interpretations of when criminal proceedings are initiated. The Supreme Court of Pennsylvania, for example, affords an accused a right to counsel at all lineups held after arrest. *Commonwealth v. Richman*, 320 A.2d 351 (Pa. 1974). In *People v. Blake*, 361 N.Y.S.2d 881, 320 N.E.2d 625 (N.Y. 1974), the court concluded that a complaint for an arrest warrant triggers the right to counsel since it is an "accusatory instrument." Other courts have held that the filing of a complaint and issuance of an arrest warrant do not trigger the right to counsel. *United States v. Smith*, 778 F.2d 925 (2d Cir. 1985). And in *Ellis v. Grammer*, 664 F.Supp. 1292 (D.Neb. 1987), the court held that a defendant who has been formally charged for one offense does not have a right to counsel at a lineup conducted for a different offense of which the defendant is suspected. An officer conducting a confrontation with witnesses must determine at what point in the criminal justice process the right to counsel at pretrial identification procedures attaches under the law applicable to the officer's jurisdiction.

Even though a suspect has no right to counsel at a confrontation with witnesses held before the initiation of adversary judicial criminal proceedings, the suspect retains the right to have the identification procedure conducted in a fair and impartial manner. In the *Kirby* case, the Court said:

> What has been said is not to suggest that there may not be occasions during the course of a criminal investigation when the police do abuse identification procedures. Such abuses are not beyond the reach of the Constitution. As the Court pointed out in *Wade* itself, it is always necessary to "scrutinize *any* pretrial confrontation. . . ." 388 U.S. at 227, 87 S.Ct. at 1932. The Due Process Clause of the Fifth and Fourteenth Amendments forbids a lineup that is unnecessarily suggestive and conducive to irreparable mistaken identification. *Stovall v. Denno,* 388 U.S. 293, 87 S.Ct. 1967, 18 L.Ed.2d 1199; *Foster v. California,* 394 U.S. 440, 89 S.Ct. 1127, 22 L.Ed.2d 402. When a person has not been formally charged with a criminal offense, *Stovall* strikes the appropriate constitutional balance between the right of a suspect to be protected from prejudicial procedures and the interest of society in the prompt and purposeful investigation of an unsolved crime. 406 U.S. at 690–91, 92 S.Ct. at 1883, 32 L.Ed.2d at 418–19.

STOVALL v. DENNO. The case of *Stovall v. Denno,* 388 U.S. 293, 87 S.Ct. 1967, 18 L.Ed.2d 1199 (1967), mentioned in the previous quote from the *Kirby* case, held that the due process clause of the Fifth and Fourteenth Amendments to the Constitution forbids any pretrial identification procedure that is unnecessarily suggestive and conducive to irreparable mistaken identification. Furthermore, "a claimed violation of due process of law in the conduct of a confrontation depends on the totality of the circumstances surrounding it. . . ." 388 U.S. at 302, 87 S.Ct. at 1972, 18 L.Ed.2d at 1206. For the law enforcement officer, this simply means that *all* lineups and showups must be conducted in a fair and impartial manner. The word *all* is emphasized because the *Stovall* test applies whether or not a suspect is represented by an attorney at the identification procedure.

The *Stovall* case is particularly important with respect to confrontations occurring *before* the initiation of adversary judicial criminal proceedings against a suspect. Courts will carefully scrutinize identification procedures for fairness and impartiality in these instances, because suspects are without the benefit of an attorney to protect their rights. Therefore, when a law enforcement officer conducts a *lineup* to identify a suspect, before the suspect has been formally charged, the officer should carefully follow the recommended procedures in the section of this chapter entitled "Guidelines for Lineup Identifications."

When a *showup* rather than a lineup is used, the officer must exercise great care to ensure that identification procedures are not unnecessarily suggestive and conducive to irreparable mistaken identification. Unarranged spontaneous showups are not considered impermissibly suggestive. For example, in *United States v. Boykins,* 966 F.2d 1240 (8th Cir. 1992), an unaccompanied witness, while walking toward the courtroom on the day of trial, recognized the defendant as one of the armed intruders into her home. She told the prosecuting attorney, who accompanied her down the hall to confirm the identification. She later identified the defendant in court. The court allowed the in-court identification, finding that the witness recognized the defendant without any suggestion from the government. "While a lineup is certainly the preferred method of identification, a witness who spontaneously recognized a defendant should be allowed to testify to that fact." 966 F.2d at 1243.

Showups resulting from a crime victim or witness cruising the area of the crime in a police car also present few problems of suggestiveness. Cruising the area is an accepted investigative technique when police have no suspect of a crime that has just occurred. Witness memories are still fresh, and perpetrators are still likely to be in the area and not have had opportunity to change their clothes or appearance. Of course, police should not coach witnesses by suggesting that persons observed look suspicious or have bad reputations.

A more common type of showup is the **on-the-scene showup,** in which a suspect is arrested or apprehended at or near the scene of a crime and is immediately brought before victims or witnesses by a law enforcement officer for identification purposes. Clearly, so long as adversary judicial criminal proceedings have not been initiated, the suspect has no right to counsel at this type of confrontation. But does an on-the-scene showup satisfy the *Stovall* requirements regarding suggestiveness?

Although courts differ on this question, the prevailing view is that practical considerations may justify a prompt on-the-scene showup under the *Stovall* test. In *Russell v. United States,* 408 F.2d 1280 (D.C. Cir. 1969), the court said that the delay required to assemble a lineup "may not only cause the detention of an innocent suspect; it may also diminish the reliability of any identification obtained." 480 F.2d at 1284. The court also suggested that only "fresh" on-the-scene identifications that occur within minutes of the witnessed crime would satisfy the *Stovall* standard. In *Johnson v. Dugger,* 817 F.2d 726 (11th Cir. 1987), the court said:

> Although show-ups are widely condemned . . . immediate confrontations allow identification before the suspect has altered his appearance and while the witness' memory is fresh, and permit the quick release of innocent persons. . . . Therefore, show-ups are not unnecessarily suggestive unless the police aggravate the suggestiveness of the confrontation. 817 F.2d at 729.

In *Bates v. United States,* 405 F.2d 1104 (D.C. Cir. 1968), the court said:

> There is no prohibition against a viewing of a suspect alone in what is called a "one-man showup" when this occurs near the time of the alleged criminal act; such a course does not tend to bring about misidentification but rather in some circumstances to insure accuracy. The rationale underlying this is in some respects not unlike that which the law relies on to make an exception to the hearsay rule, allowing spontaneous utterances a standing which they would not be given if uttered at a later point in time. An early identification is not error. Of course, proof of infirmities and subjective factors, such as hysteria of a witness, can be explored on cross-examination and in argument. Prudent police work would confine these on-the-spot identifications to situations in which possible doubts as to identification needed to be resolved promptly; absent such need the conventional lineup viewing is the appropriate procedure. 405 F.2d at 1106.

The following fact situation from *United States v. Watson,* 76 F.3d 4, 6 (1st Cir. 1996), illustrates the type of on-the-scene showup identification procedure that courts do not find unnecessarily suggestive.

> As Alexander Milette was bicycling home to the Cathedral Project, a Porsche drove past him and stopped in front of his house. Trevor Watson got out of the car, carrying a loaded pistol of the type favored by the Boston police, a Glock 9mm semi-automatic. After accusing Milette of liking "hitting on" women, Watson aimed the gun at Milette's stomach. Someone said "Don't shoot him."
>
> Instead, Watson pistol-whipped Milette's head, causing the gun to fire into a building and then to jam. Milette, bleeding, ran while Watson unjammed the gun and fired again, hitting the building Milette ran behind. Milette sought sanctuary at a friend's house and was helped with his bleeding head.

Watson had jumped back into the Porsche, only to have it stall out in a deep puddle. A nearby off-duty Boston Police officer, Officer Christopher Shoulla, heard the shots, drove to the project, and put out a call on his police radio. Officer Shoulla saw Watson and asked him to stop. Watson instead fled, clutching his right pocket, and, ironically, ran right past Milette and past another youth. Two other Boston officers arrived and gave chase. Watson threw the gun, as he ran, into a small garden. Officer Shoulla stopped Watson at gunpoint. When the officers patted down Watson and determined he had no gun, they retraced Watson's steps and found it within forty seconds.

One officer saw Milette, still holding a bloody towel to his head, and had the others bring Watson over. Watson was brought over by patrol car and Milette was asked by the police, "What's the story?" Milette looked, and identified Watson as his assailant. He later testified he was 100% sure of that identification. Watson was also identified by the other youth past whom he had run.

Law enforcement officers should use on-the-scene showups only when a suspect can be shown to a witness minutes after the crime has occurred. Furthermore, officers should not add in any way to the already inherent suggestiveness of the on-the-scene identification. For example, the officer should not say or do anything to lead the witness to believe that the suspect is believed to be the perpetrator or that the suspect has been formally arrested, has confessed, or has been found in possession of incriminating items. If there is a significant delay between the commission of the crime and the confrontation, officers should take the suspect to the station and conduct a lineup in accordance with suggested procedures in the section of this chapter entitled "Guidelines for Lineup Identifications."

NEIL v. BIGGERS. Despite the advice in the preceding paragraph, law enforcement officers have often conducted showups several days, weeks, or even months after a crime has occurred. Before 1972, most courts, applying the standards of *Stovall v. Denno,* held that delayed one-on-one confrontations were impermissibly suggestive and violative of due process. Evidence obtained from identifications made under these circumstances was held inadmissible in court.

In 1972, however, the U.S. Supreme Court decided the case of *Neil v. Biggers,* 409 U.S. 188, 93 S.Ct. 375, 34 L.Ed.2d 401, in which the Court noted that "[i]t is the likelihood of misidentification that violates a defendant's right to due process. . . . Suggestive confrontations are disapproved because they increase the likelihood of misidentification, and unnecessarily suggestive ones are condemned for the further reason that the increased chance of misidentification is gratuitous." 409 U.S. at 198, 93 S.Ct. at 381–82, 34 L.Ed.2d at 410–11. Thus, the Court focused on whether the identification was accurate or reliable despite the suggestiveness of the identification procedure. *Neil v. Biggers* involved a defendant who had been convicted of rape on evidence consisting, in part, of the victim's visual and voice identification of the defendant at a station house showup seven months after the crime. At the time of the crime, the victim was in her assailant's presence for nearly a half hour, and the victim directly observed her assailant indoors and under a full moon outdoors. The victim testified at trial that she had no doubt that the defendant was her assailant. Immediately after the crime, she gave the police a thorough description of the assailant that matched the description of the defendant. The victim had also made no identification of others presented at previous showups or lineups or through photographs.

Despite its concern about the seven-month delay between the crime and the confrontation, the Court held that the central question was "whether under 'the totality of the circumstances' the identification was reliable even though the confrontation procedure was suggestive." 409 U.S. at 199, 93 S.Ct. at 382, 34 L.Ed.2d at 411. The Court listed the following five factors to be considered in evaluating the likelihood of misidentification:

1. Witness's opportunity to view the criminal at the time of the crime
2. Witness's degree of attention
3. Accuracy of the witness's prior description of the criminal
4. Level of certainty demonstrated by the witness at the confrontation
5. Length of time between the crime and the confrontation

Applying these considerations to the facts of the case, the Court found no substantial likelihood of misidentification and held the evidence of the identification to be admissible in court.

MANSON v. BRATHWAITE. In *Manson v. Brathwaite,* 432 U.S. 98, 97 S.Ct. 2243, 53 L.Ed.2d 140 (1977), the U.S. Supreme Court reiterated the five reliability factors of *Biggers* and emphasized that they should be balanced against the corrupting effect of the suggestive identification itself. The *Brathwaite* case involved an undercover drug officer's viewing of a single photograph of a drug crime suspect that had been left in his office by a fellow officer. Two days had elapsed between the crime and the viewing of the photograph. After finding that the single photographic display was unnecessarily suggestive, the Court considered the five factors affecting the reliability of an identification set out in *Neil v. Biggers.* The Court found that the undercover officer was no casual observer but a trained police officer, that the officer had sufficient opportunity to view the suspect for two or three minutes in natural light, that the officer accurately described the suspect in detail within minutes of the crime, that the officer positively identified the photograph in court as that of the drug seller, and that the officer made the photographic identification only two days after the crime.

The Court's analysis of the five factors indicated that the undercover drug officer was able to make an accurate identification of the defendant. The Court did not end its discussion at this stage as it did in the *Biggers* case, however. Instead, it took the additional step of analyzing the corrupting effect of the suggestive identification and then weighing that against the factors indicating reliability. The Court said:

> Although identifications arising from single-photograph displays may be viewed in general with suspicion, . . . we find in the instant case little pressure on the witness to acquiesce in the suggestion that such a display entails. D'Onofrio had left the photograph at Glover's office and was not present when Glover first viewed it two days after the event. There thus was little urgency and Glover could view the photograph at his leisure. And since Glover examined the photograph alone, there was no coercive pressure to make an identification arising from the presence of another. The identification was made in circumstances allowing care and reflection. 432 U.S. at 116, 97 S.Ct. at 2254, 53 L.Ed.2d at 155.

Under the totality of the circumstances, the Court held that the identification was reliable and that evidence of the identification was admissible in court.

The following quotation from the *Brathwaite* case sets out the basic test for determining the admissibility of evidence of identifications that take place before the initiation of adversary judicial criminal proceedings:

> We therefore conclude that reliability is the linchpin in determining the admissibility of identification testimony for both pre- and post-*Stovall* confrontations. The factors to be considered are set out in *Biggers.* 409 U.S. at 199–200, 93

S.Ct. at 382. These include the opportunity of the witness to view the criminal at the time of the crime, the witness' degree of attention, the accuracy of his prior description of the criminal, the level of certainty demonstrated at the confrontation, and the time between the crime and the confrontation. Against these factors is to be weighed the corrupting effect of the suggestive identification itself. 432 U.S. at 114, 97 S.Ct. at 2253, 53 L.Ed.2d at 154.

The lesson of the *Biggers* and *Brathwaite* cases is that, even though an officer conducts an unnecessarily suggestive identification procedure, the evidence is not necessarily lost because it may still be admitted in court if the identification was otherwise reliable. However, these cases should not be interpreted as evidencing a lack of concern about conducting fair and impartial identification procedures. As the Court stated in the *Brathwaite* case:

> [I]t would have been better had D'Onofrio presented Glover with a photographic array including "so far as practicable . . . a reasonable number of persons similar to any person then suspected whose likeness is included in the array." . . . The use of that procedure would have enhanced the force of the identification at trial and would have avoided the risk that the evidence would be excluded as unreliable. 432 U.S. at 117, 97 S.Ct. at 2254, 53 L.Ed.2d at 155.

In *United States v. Thody*, 978 F.2d 625 (10th Cir. 1992), the court applied the *Biggers-Brathwaite* factors to find an identification of a bank robber reliable despite an impermissibly suggestive lineup.

> Each witness had an adequate opportunity to observe Thody closely during the two robberies. All three witnesses testified at the suppression hearing that at least once they were within a few feet of Thody, and that they were able to observe McIntosh and him for several minutes. Woods and Harshfield were within arm's reach of Thody while complying with his instructions. The light was good, and there is no question that the attention of these three employees was riveted on Thody and his companion. Dillard testified that she had been trained to remember the descriptions of robbers. When the second robbery took place Harshfield immediately recognized Thody from the July 12 robbery, exclaiming to Woods, "It's him!" The descriptions of the robbers given by Harshfield, Woods, and Dillard after the robberies also corroborated one another to the degree that descriptions of subtleties in nose size, presence or lack of facial hair, and hair color corresponded significantly.
>
> The witnesses were unequivocal in their testimony, both at trial and at the suppression hearing. Despite attempts by defense counsel to unearth inconsistencies, no significant inconsistencies materialized. Also, only one week separated the confrontation from the robbery. 978 F.2d at 629.

In contrast, *United States v. De Jesus-Rios*, 990 F.2d 672 (1st Cir. 1993), found that a boat captain's identification of a woman who had contracted for cargo transport was *not* otherwise reliable after an impermissibly suggestive one-person showup. The court had no problem with the first, second, and fifth *Biggers-Brathwaite* factors but was troubled by application of the third and fourth factors:

> Agent Marti testified that, on the date the cocaine was discovered, February 8, 1991, Rivera [the boat captain] described the suspect as "white" and approximately five feet, two inches tall. Rivera's testimony at the suppression hearing and Agent Dania's trial testimony revealed that during his February 11, 1991, interview with Agent Dania, Rivera again described her as "white." It was not until after the February 16, 1991, showup that Rivera described the suspect as

having "light brown" skin. Moreover, Rivera also failed to provide an accurate description of her height (five feet, six inches) at either of his pre-showup descriptions.

The record also contains uncontroverted evidence that, despite having been asked at the February 16, 1991, showup to signal the agents when he positively identified Eva Rios, Rivera waited until after she approached the agents and began speaking with them (as scheduled) to signal. We hardly think that this constitutes a high degree of certainty on Rivera's part, particularly in light of the showup procedure at issue here. Prior to that showup, Rivera was informed that the agents were meeting the suspect in front of the customs building at a specific time. While a few other women also may have walked by the customs building that morning, only Eva Rios stopped to speak with the agents.

Law enforcement officers have control over the conduct of the identification procedures, but they have little or no control over the five factors determining the reliability of the identification. Therefore, officers should conduct all identification procedures fairly and impartially. To avoid the risk that identification evidence will be excluded as unreliable, officers should follow the guidelines for lineup identifications set out earlier in this chapter. When photographs are used, officers should follow the guidelines for photographic identifications appearing later in this chapter.

Emergency Identifications

In an emergency, courts are more likely to condone one-person showups and violations of the *Wade* right-to-counsel rule, because an immediate identification by a witness may be the only identification possible. For identification purposes, an **emergency** can be defined as a witness in danger of death or blindness or a suspect in danger of death. The leading case on emergency identifications is *Stovall v. Denno*, 388 U.S. 293, 87 S.Ct. 1967, 18 L.Ed.2d 1199 (1967). In that case, the defendant was arrested for stabbing a doctor to death and seriously wounding his wife, who was hospitalized for major surgery. Without affording the defendant time to retain counsel, police arranged with the wife's surgeon to bring the defendant to her hospital room. The wife identified the defendant as her assailant. The court held that "a claimed violation of due process of law in the conduct of a confrontation depends on the totality of the circumstances surrounding it, and the record in the present case reveals that the showing of the defendant to the wife in an immediate hospital confrontation was imperative."

> Here was the only person in the world who could possibly exonerate Stovall. Her words, and only her words, "He is not the man" could have resulted in freedom for Stovall. The hospital was not far distant from the courthouse and jail. No one knew how long Mrs. Behrendt might live. Faced with the responsibility of identifying the attacker, with the need for immediate action and with the knowledge that Mrs. Behrendt could not visit the jail, the police followed the only feasible procedure and took Stovall to the hospital room. Under these circumstances, the usual police station line-up, which Stovall now argues he should have had, was out of the question. 388 U.S. at 302, 87 S.Ct. at 1972–73, 18 L.Ed.2d at 1206.

In *Trask v. Robbins*, 421 F.2d 773 (1st Cir. 1970), the defendant, who was being held in jail on a charge of robbing a store, was presented to a hospitalized victim of a separate assault and robbery offense that was under investigation. It was uncertain whether the defendant had retained a lawyer on the store robbery charge, and no lawyer was contacted for the identification proceeding in the separate assault and robbery crime. The defendant was transported to the hospital by a deputy sheriff. The victim spontaneously and positively identified the defendant as his assailant. The defendant claimed that he should have been represented by a lawyer at this pretrial confrontation with the victim.

Applying the *Stovall* totality-of-the-circumstances test, the court found that the circumstances surrounding the identification were not unnecessarily suggestive and conducive to irreparable mistaken identification: (1) no preliminary statements were made to the victim, (2) the victim's words of identification were spontaneous and positive, (3) the defendant said nothing in the presence of the victim, (4) the case was merely in the investigatory stage, and (5) the critically injured victim (thought to be dying) was about to be moved to a distant hospital. Under these emergency conditions, the fact that a lawyer was not present did not void the identification.

Note that identification procedures involving critically injured persons should only be conducted with the approval of medical authorities. The importance of obtaining an identification is secondary in importance to the treatment and care of an injured person.

Preparatory Steps

The *Wade* decision made clear that there is no right to counsel at preparatory steps in the gathering of the prosecution's evidence, such as "systematized or scientific analyzing of the accused's fingerprints, blood sample, clothing, hair, and the like."

> We think there are differences which preclude such stages being characterized as critical stages at which the accused has the right to the presence of his counsel. Knowledge of the techniques of science and technology is sufficiently available, and the variables in techniques few enough, that the accused has the opportunity for a meaningful confrontation of the Government's case at trial through the ordinary processes of cross-examination of the Government's expert witnesses and the presentation of the evidence of his own experts. The denial of a right to have his counsel present at such analyses does not therefore violate the Sixth Amendment; they are not critical stages since there is minimal risk that his counsel's absence at such stages might derogate from his right to a fair trial. 388 U.S. at 227–28, 87 S.Ct. at 1932–33, 18 L.Ed.2d at 1158.

KEY POINTS

2. The suspect's right to counsel at a pretrial confrontation with witnesses attaches at or after the initiation of adversary judicial criminal proceedings—whether by way of formal charge, preliminary hearing, indictment, information, or arraignment.

3. Due process requires that the totality of the circumstances surrounding an identification must not be so overly suggestive as to cause a substantial likelihood of irreparable misidentification. All lineups and showups must be conducted in a fair and impartial manner.

4. The central question surrounding an identification is whether under the totality of the circumstances the identification was reliable even though the confrontation procedure was suggestive. Factors to be considered in evaluating the reliability of an identification are (1) the witness's opportunity to view the criminal at the time of the crime, (2) the witness's degree of attention, (3) the accuracy of the witness's prior description of the criminal, (4) the level of certainty demonstrated by the witness at the confrontation, (5) the length of time between the crime and the confrontation, and (6) the corrupting effect of the suggestive identification.

Photographic Identifications

A common and accepted method of police investigation is the showing of mug shots or photographs to witnesses to aid in identifying or eliminating criminal suspects. In *Simmons v. United States,* 390 U.S. 377, 88 S.Ct. 967, 19 L.Ed.2d 1247 (1968), the U.S. Supreme Court approved this procedure, subject to the same standards of fairness set out in *Stovall v. Denno.* Furthermore, the Court held that there is no right to counsel at any photographic identification procedure, whether that procedure is held before or after the initiation of adversary judicial criminal proceedings. *United States v. Ash,* 413 U.S. 300, 93 S.Ct. 2568, 37 L.Ed.2d 619 (1973). The basic rationale of *Ash* is that "[s]ince the accused himself is not present at the time of the photographic display, . . . no possibility arises that the accused might be misled by his lack of familiarity with the law. . . ." 413 U.S. at 317, 93 S.Ct. at 2577, 37 L.Ed.2d at 631. In addition, the Court stated that the accused has sufficient opportunity at trial to contest the identification without being present at the time the photographs are shown. Therefore, unless at the pretrial stage there was involved the physical presence of the accused at a trial-like confrontation at which the accused requires the guiding hand of counsel, the Sixth Amendment does not guarantee the assistance of counsel.

Applying similar reasoning, the court in *United States v. Amrine,* 724 F.2d 84 (8th Cir. 1983), held that the defendant was not entitled to counsel at the showing of a videotaped lineup in which the defendant was one of the participants. The court said that the videotape was not to be considered an actual lineup but, rather, was more aptly categorized as a photographic display. And in *United States v. Dupree,* 553 F.2d 1189 (8th Cir. 1977), the court held that there was no right to counsel at the playing of a tape-recorded voice array.

Each case must be decided on the totality of the circumstances surrounding it, and the identification evidence will be excluded in court "only if the photographic identification procedure was so impermissibly suggestive as to give rise to a very substantial likelihood of irreparable misidentification" 390 U.S. at 384, 88 S.Ct. at 971, 19 L.Ed.2d at 1253, and if the identification fails to satisfy the basic reliability test set out in the previous discussion of *Manson v. Brathwaite.*

The following guidelines, based on the *Simmons* case, are suggested for photographic identifications:

- More than one photograph should be shown to a witness. In the *Simmons* case, six photographs were shown to several witnesses, and the Supreme Court suggested that even more than six would be preferable. "In the absence of exigent circumstances, presentation of a single photograph to the victim of a crime amounts to an unnecessarily suggestive photographic identification procedure." *United States v. Jones,* 652 F.Supp. 1561, 1570 (S.D.N.Y. 1986).

- The people appearing in the photographs should be of the same general age, height, weight, hair color, and skin color.

- No group of photographs should be arranged in such a way that the photograph of a single person recurs or is in any way emphasized. Furthermore, the officer conducting the photographic identification should do nothing to indicate which picture is that of the suspect. *Cikora v. Wainwright,* 661 F.Supp. 813 (S.D.Fla. 1987).

- If there are two or more suspects, no two should appear together in a group photo.

- Witnesses should be handled in a manner similar to that suggested in the guidelines for lineup identifications presented earlier in this chapter.

- If there are several witnesses, only some of them should be shown the photographs to obtain an initial identification. Then the suspect should be displayed to the remaining witnesses in a more reliable lineup. By following this procedure, the officer helps ensure that the perceptions of the witnesses at the lineup are not influenced by a viewing of the photographs.

- After the photographs have been shown to the witnesses, they should be numbered and preserved as evidence. The officer conducting the photographic identification should take careful notes of all remarks made by witnesses while viewing photos and of all positive identifications and all failures to identify the suspect. Proper record keeping is essential. The ability to exactly reconstruct a photographic identification procedure may help to counter defense claims of undue suggestiveness and to support the validity of a later in-court identification. Some courts hold that a photo array that is not preserved is presumed to be unduly suggestive.

    > By failing to show the defendant or the court the photos, the state virtually assures that the defendant will be unable to argue the suggestiveness of the photographs. Unless the witness or officer admits to the suggestiveness of the array, there will be no means available to contest the identification procedures. *Smith v. Campbell,* 781 F.Supp. 521, 527–28 (M.D.Tenn. 1991).

- It is good practice to have an identifying witness initial and date the back of the photograph selected. Care should be taken, however, to avoid allowing later witnesses to see an earlier witness's initials on the back of a photograph.

- After a witness selects a photograph from a photographic display, that witness should not be shown the same photograph in later displays. Such a procedure would tend to fix the image of the photograph in the witness's mind and blur the image actually perceived at the crime. *United States v. Eatherton,* 519 F.2d 603 (1st Cir. 1975).

- Photographs of suspects in the act of committing the crime (such as bank robbery surveillance photographs) do not present any problems of suggestiveness and mistaken identification. Courts have held that presenting such photographs to witnesses shows the actual perpetrator of the crime in the act rather than suggesting a number of possible perpetrators. The photographs refresh the witness's memory of the actual crime and thereby strengthen the reliability of the witness's in-court identification. *United States v. Browne,* 829 F.2d 760 (9th Cir. 1987).

- If possible, a mug shot of a suspect should not be displayed in a photographic array alongside ordinary photographs of other persons. Mug shots may prejudice the suspect by implying that he or she has a criminal record. Nevertheless, use of mug shots is often unavoidable. Therefore, it is suggested that only frontal views be used and that the photographs be presented in a manner that disguises their identity as mug shots. Of course, if police have no suspect, the display of a mug book to a witness or victim for identification purposes presents no problems of suggestivity. A reasonable number of photographs should be shown and careful records kept of all pictures shown and any pictures identified.

- A photograph in a photographic display may be altered (to show what the person would look like with a beard or a hat, for example) so long as all other photographs in the display are altered in the same way. *United States v. Dunbar,* 767 F.2d 72 (3d Cir. 1985).

- "Once law enforcement officers obtain from a witness a photographic identification of a suspect which is both untainted and positive, they may show other pictures of that properly and positively identified suspect to the witness without implicating the concerns of *Simmons* and its progeny." *United States v. Jones,* 652 F.Supp. 1561 (S.D.N.Y. 1986).

- Photographic identification should not be used once a suspect's identity is known and the suspect is in police custody. A lineup is preferable in these circumstances because lineups are normally more accurate than photographic identifications. *Simmons v. United States,* 390 U.S. at 386 n.6, 88 S.Ct. at 972 n.6, 19 L.Ed.2d at 1254 n.6 (1968).

These guidelines are only suggested; different circumstances may require different identification procedures. The law requires that the totality of the circumstances surrounding an identification must not be so overly suggestive as to cause a substantial likelihood of irreparable misidentification. As discussed earlier, courts will look beyond the mere fact of a suggestive photographic identification procedure in determining whether there was a substantial likelihood of irreparable misidentification. Courts will analyze each case with respect to the five factors determining the reliability of the identification as set out in *Neil v. Biggers.* Courts will then weigh those factors against the corrupting effect of the suggestive identification, as was done in *Manson v. Brathwaite.* Law enforcement officers should follow the guidelines for photographic identifications set out in this section to minimize the suggestiveness of identification procedures and to help ensure that identification evidence will not be excluded as unreliable.

KEY POINTS

5. A suspect has no right to counsel at any photographic identification procedure, whether that procedure is held before or after the initiation of adversary judicial criminal proceedings.

Effect of an Improper Identification Procedure

To enforce the standards set out by the U.S. Supreme Court with respect to pretrial identifications, certain rules have been established for the admission of identification evidence in court. If a pretrial identification is made in violation of defendant's right to counsel, or if the identification is unreliable and thereby violates a defendant's right to due process of law, the court must exclude at trial

- any evidence of the pretrial identification presented as a part of the prosecutor's direct case and
- any identification of the perpetrator of the crime made by a witness in court.

If, however, the prosecution can establish by clear and convincing evidence that a witness has a source independent from the illegal confrontation for identifying the perpetrator of the crime, the court may allow in-court identification testimony. *Frisco v. Blackburn,* 782 F.2d 1353 (5th Cir. 1986). A court will find that an in-court identification has an **independent source** when the court is convinced that the identifying witness, by drawing on personal memory of the crime and observations of the defendant during the crime, has such a clear and definite image of the defendant that the witness can make an identification unaffected by the illegal confrontation. Some factors considered by judges in determining an independent source were set out in the *Wade* case.

> Application of [the independent source test] requires consideration of various factors; for example, the prior opportunity to observe the alleged criminal act, the existence of any discrepancy between any pre-lineup description and the defendant's actual description, any identification prior to the lineup of another person, the identification by picture of the defendant prior to lineup, failure to identify the defendant on a prior occasion, and the lapse of time between the alleged act and the lineup identification. It is also relevant to consider those facts which, despite the absence of counsel, are disclosed concerning the conduct of the lineup. 388 U.S. at 241, 87 S.Ct. at 1940, 18 L.Ed.2d at 1165.

In *McKinon v. Wainwright*, 705 F.2d 419 (11th Cir. 1983), the court found an independent source for the identification of the accused at trial where the witness had known the accused long before the crime was committed and had spent several days with the accused on the day of the crime. Law enforcement officers should gather information on these factors from witnesses and record the information in their reports. Officers should obtain as much detail as possible because strong evidence of an independent source for identification of a criminal can salvage an improperly conducted identification procedure. Of course, if the defendant does not meet the threshold requirement of showing that the in-court identification was tainted by impermissible suggestiveness, then "independent reliability [of the in-court identification] is not a constitutionally required condition of admissibility . . . and the reliability of the identification is simply a question for the jury." *Jarrett v. Headley*, 802 F.2d 34, 42 (2d Cir. 1986).

The same independent-source factors are used by courts to determine the admissibility of in-court identifications that violate the defendant's Fourth Amendment rights. For example, in *United States v. Slater*, 692 F.2d 107 (10th Cir. 1982), the photograph used for an out-of-court identification had been obtained through an illegal arrest. The court held that the in-court identification of the defendant was admissible, however, because

> the witnesses . . . had each actually seen the crime committed at close hand, there was little discrepancy between the pretrial descriptions and the defendant's actual description, there was no identification of another person or failure to identify the defendant, and the person who committed the crime made no attempt to conceal his face. 692 F.2d at 108.

Summary

A criminal suspect has a right to counsel at all lineups and showups conducted *at or after* the initiation of adversary judicial criminal proceedings against the suspect. The emergency showup is the only possible exception to this rule. In every other case, the suspect should be warned of the right to counsel in accordance with the form appearing as Exhibit 14.1.

If a lineup or showup is conducted *before* adversary judicial criminal proceedings are initiated against a suspect,

the suspect is *not* entitled to the presence or advice of counsel. Nevertheless, *all* pretrial identification procedures, whether lineups or showups, must be conducted in accordance with due process, which forbids any pretrial identification procedure that is unnecessarily suggestive and conducive to irreparable mistaken identification. As further interpreted by the U.S. Supreme Court, due process simply requires that all pretrial identifications be reliable in the totality of the circumstances, or evidence of the identification will be inadmissible in court. Factors to be considered in determining reliability are the witness's opportunity to view the criminal at the time of the crime, the witness's degree of attention, the accuracy of the witness's prior description of the criminal, the level of certainty demonstrated by the witness at the confrontation, and the length of time between the crime and the confrontation. These factors are to be weighed against the corrupting effect of any suggestive identification. Officers conducting lineups are advised to follow the guidelines for lineup identifications presented in this chapter.

A criminal suspect is not entitled to the presence or advice of counsel at *photographic* identification procedures no matter when those procedures are held. Nevertheless, such procedures must be conducted as fairly and impartially as possible, and identifications will be evaluated by the reliability test described in the preceding paragraph. Officers are advised to follow the guidelines for photographic identifications provided in this chapter.

Key Holdings from Major Cases

Gilbert v. California (1967). "[A] post-indictment pretrial lineup at which the accused is exhibited to identifying witnesses is a critical stage of the criminal prosecution; . . . police conduct of such a lineup without notice to and in the absence of his counsel denies the accused his Sixth Amendment right to counsel and calls in question the admissibility at trial of the in-court identifications of the accused by witnesses who attended the lineup." 388 U.S. 263, 272, 87 S.Ct. 1951, 1956, 18 L.Ed.2d 1178, 1186.

United States v. Wade (1967). "Since it appears that there is grave potential for prejudice, intentional or not, in the pretrial lineup, which may not be capable of reconstruction at trial, and since presence of counsel itself can often avert prejudice and assure a meaningful confrontation at trial, there can be little doubt that for Wade the post-indictment lineup was a critical stage of the prosecution at which he was 'as much entitled to such aid [of counsel] . . . as at the trial itself.' . . . Thus both Wade and his counsel should have been notified of the impending lineup, and counsel's presence should have been a requisite to conduct of the lineup, absent an 'intelligent waiver.'" 388 U.S. 218, 236–37, 87 S.Ct. 1926, 1937, 18 L.Ed.2d 1149, 1162–63.

Kirby v. Illinois (1972). "The initiation of judicial criminal proceedings is far from a mere formalism. It is the starting point of our whole system of adversary criminal justice. For it is only then that the Government has committed itself to prosecute, and only then that the adverse positions of Government and defendant have solidified. It is then that a defendant finds himself faced with the prosecutorial forces of organized society, and immersed in the intricacies of substantive and procedural criminal law. It is this point, therefore, that marks the commencement of the 'criminal prosecutions' to which alone the explicit guarantees of the Sixth Amendment are applicable.

"In this case we are asked to import into a routine police investigation an absolute constitutional guarantee historically and rationally applicable only after the onset of formal prosecutorial proceedings. We decline to do so. Less than a year after *Wade* and *Gilbert* were decided, the Court explained

the rule of those decisions as follows: 'The rationale of those cases was that an accused is entitled to counsel at any "critical stage of the prosecution," and that a postindictment lineup is such a "critical stage."' We decline to depart from that rationale today by imposing a *per se* exclusionary rule upon testimony concerning an identification that took place long before the commencement of any prosecution whatever." 406 U.S. 682, 689–90, 92 S.Ct. 1877, 1882–83, 32 L.Ed.2d 411, 417–18.

Stovall v. Denno (1967). The Constitution forbids any identification procedure that is "so unnecessarily suggestive and conducive to irreparable mistaken identification that he was denied due process of law. This is a recognized ground of attack upon a conviction independent of any right to counsel claim. . . . The practice of showing suspects singly to persons for the purpose of identification, and not as part of a lineup, has been widely condemned. However, a claimed violation of due process of law in the conduct of a confrontation depends on the totality of the circumstances surrounding it. . . ." 388 U.S. 293, 302, 87 S.Ct. 1967, 1972, 18 L.Ed.2d 1199, 1206.

Manson v. Brathwaite (1977). "[R]eliability is the linchpin in determining the admissibility of identification testimony for both pre- and post-*Stovall* confrontations. The factors to be considered are set out in *Biggers.* 409 U.S., at 199–200, 93 S.Ct., at 382. These include the opportunity of the witness to view the criminal at the time of the crime, the witness' degree of attention, the accuracy of his prior description of the criminal, the level of certainty demonstrated at the confrontation, and the time between the crime and the confrontation. Against these factors is to be weighed the corrupting effect of the suggestive identification itself." 432 U.S. 98, 114, 97 S.Ct. 2243, 2253, 53 L.Ed.2d 140, 154.

Simmons v. United States (1968). Evidence obtained from a photographic identification procedure will be excluded "only if the photographic identification procedure was so impermissibly suggestive as to give rise to a very substantial likelihood of irreparable misidentification." 390 U.S. 377, 384, 88 S.Ct. 967, 971, 19 L.Ed.2d 1247, 1253.

Review and Discussion Questions

1. What circumstances might justify the use of a one-way mirror during a lineup procedure? What if a witness or victim refuses to view a lineup unless a one-way mirror is used?

2. Why should a person not have a right to demand an immediate lineup to clear him- or herself and avoid the many inconveniences associated with being arrested?

3. State three ways in which a law enforcement officer conducting a lineup can decrease the suggestibility of the lineup. State three ways in which a law enforcement officer can decrease the suggestibility of a one-person showup.

4. Assume that a suspect is about to be placed in a lineup and is told by a law enforcement officer that she has a right to counsel at the lineup. If the suspect asks, "Why do I need a lawyer?" what should the officer tell her?

5. Why should photographic identification procedures not be used when a physical lineup is contemplated? What arguments would a defense attorney make at a suppression hearing under each of the following circumstances?

   a. The witness identified the defendant's photograph at a pretrial photographic display but failed to identify the defendant at a later physical lineup.

   b. The witness failed to identify the defendant's photograph at a pretrial photographic display but identified the defendant at a later physical lineup.

   c. The witness identified the defendant's photograph at a pretrial photographic display and also identified the defendant at a later physical lineup.

6. Is it possible to conduct a fair lineup when the suspect is unusually tall or short or has very distinctive features or deformities?

7. Would an emergency one-person showup be justified if the suspect and not the victim were seriously injured? In what ways could the suggestibility of the showup be decreased?

8. Would certain suggestive pretrial identification procedures be excusable in a small rural police department as opposed to a large urban police department? What procedures might be excusable and why?

9. Discuss the following quotation from Justice William J. Brennan's dissenting opinion in *United States v. Ash,* 413 U.S. 300, 344, 93 S.Ct 2568, 2591, 37 L.Ed.2d 619, 646–47 (1973), in which the U.S. Supreme Court held that there is no right to counsel at any photographic identification procedure: "There is something ironic about the Court's conclusion today that a pretrial lineup identification is a 'critical stage' of the prosecution because counsel's presence can help to compensate for the accused's deficiencies as an observer, but that a pretrial photographic identification is not a 'critical stage' of the prosecution because the accused is not able to observe at all."

10. Would there be any need for counsel at a lineup if the entire lineup procedure were recorded on both audiotape and videotape?

REAL-LIFE FACT SITUATIONS

1. Defendant Joseph Arthur Emanuele was convicted of robbing two Integra Banks, the "Millvale Bank" and the "Waterworks Bank". Martha Hottel, a teller, observed the man who robbed the Millvale Bank standing at a writing table before he came to her window and demanded money. Five weeks later, when shown a six-photo array, she selected a photograph of defendant but stated that she "wasn't 100 percent sure" of her choice. When shown a second array several weeks later, Hottel selected the photograph of someone other than defendant. The bank's security cameras malfunctioned without photographing the robber, and latent fingerprints

from the writing table and bank door did not match those of defendant.

The man who robbed the Waterworks Bank demanded money from Lorraine Woessner, a teller. Woessner observed the man for several minutes at close range in the well-lit bank lobby. Shown a six-photo array that included a photograph of defendant shortly after the crime, Woessner was unable to identify the robber. The one fingerprint taken from the Waterworks Bank did not match that of defendant, but the Waterworks Bank security cameras did photograph the robber.

The two tellers were subpoenaed by the government to testify, and after checking in at the U.S. Attorney's

Office, they were directed to sit outside the courtroom. There, the tellers saw defendant led from the courtroom in manacles by U.S. Marshals. Though later Woessner could not remember for certain who had spoken first, outside the courtroom the two tellers talked to each other about defendant, telling each other "it has to be him."

Having learned of the encounter, defendant's attorney moved to suppress the tellers' anticipated in-court identification testimony as violative of defendant's right to due process, or in the alternative, for a court-ordered lineup. The government conceded that it had been "careless," but argued that because the confrontation was inadvertent no constitutional violation had occurred. Was the defendant's right to due process violated? *United States v. Emanuele*, 51 F.3d 1123 (3d Cir. 1995).

2. At the suppression hearing on identification, the undercover officer who made the drug purchase testified at length about the factors that assisted him in identifying the defendant (Jones), including that he was unusually large; that he was in close proximity to Jones for several minutes, in good light, while making the purchase; and that he had been trained to observe the physical characteristics of individuals in order to make such identifications. It is, however, also worthy of note that the officer apparently missed Jones's weight by over one hundred pounds. He estimated Jones's weight at 210 to 220 pounds, but the testimony indicates that Jones weighed over 300 pounds at the time of the offense.

The undercover officer also testified that he saw a photograph of Jones, supplied to him by a local officer six days after the transaction. The local officer had told the undercover officer that his description of the suspect matched that of Franklin Jones. The undercover officer testified that he had looked at the picture only to verify this. The undercover officer unequivocally testified that the defendant was the person from whom he made the purchase and that his identification was made solely from his observations of the defendant at the time of the offense. Should the undercover officer's in-court testimony be allowed? *Jones v. State*, 944 S.W.2d 50 (Tex.App.—Texarkana 1997).

3. At about 3 A.M. on April 17, 1995, Jay Dereke Shea and an accomplice, Jonathan Jackson, broke into a truck and removed several pieces of stereo equipment. The victim of the crime, Michael McKay, watched the theft from his bedroom window 15 feet away and called the police on his cellular telephone. McKay watched the suspects leave the scene and heard the sound of a loud car exhaust system. An officer arrived within minutes and was in the process of obtaining a description from McKay when a car drove by with a loud exhaust system. McKay identified the sound of the car and the officer pulled the car over. Two white males and several pieces of stereo equipment were found inside.

McKay was taken to where the suspects stood handcuffed on the side of the road and identified them. Jackson admitted to police that he and Shea had taken the items from McKay's truck and further told officers that additional items were in Shea's car. McKay identified two stolen compact disc containers while standing outside the car. Shea contends that the "showup" identification was unduly suggestive and violated his right to due process. Was Shea's right to due process violated? *State v. Shea*, 930 P.2d 1232 (Wash.App. Div. 2 1997).

4. Amelia Martin, a sixteen-year old, and her mother, Sheila Jones, testified at the hearing. Ms. Martin stated that, while sitting on her front porch, she observed the defendant walk around the block a few times. She then saw the defendant shoot the victim, an elderly man who lived next door. The shooting occurred on May 20, 1995, at approximately 7:30.

On August 21, 1995 the police brought a photographic lineup to Ms. Martin. The detective told her that they had a suspect, but needed to identify him to be sure. The detective spread the photographs across the table. Ms. Martin picked out the photo of the defendant, stating that it was the man she saw.

Ms. Sheila Jones testified that she was inside at the time of the actual shooting. The children sitting on the front porch ran in, saying that a man had a gun and shot "Candy." Ms. Jones went outside and saw a man coming down the stairs. Ms. Jones stated that she did not have "long at all" to view the defendant. She got a look at his face because he turned and looked at her as he was going down the stairs.

On August 21, 1995 when the police brought the photographic lineup to Amelia Martin, her mother, Ms. Jones, was sitting next to her. After Amelia Martin identified the defendant, Ms. Jones also selected the defendant's photograph. Ms. Jones testified that she had also recognized another of the pictures and thought that maybe the other photograph was of the man who shot the victim but then identified the photo as being the picture of someone else who broke into the car in front of the door a few weeks before. After looking again, she selected the defendant's picture.

Ms. Jones related that the defendant wore jeans shorts and a T-shirt top. He was wearing an earring. Her daughter had testified that the man wore blue jean pants and a white T-shirt. Ms. Jones estimated that the man was around five-eight or five-nine. Both witnesses stated that the defendant was slender. The mother, Ms. Jones, also testified that she was the one who called the police. She gave a description of the defendant to the police over the phone. Ms. Jones stated that she was also interviewed on another occasion and gave the police a description.

The defendant argues that the photographic lineup was suggestive because Ms. Jones was present while Amelia Martin made her identification. Furthermore, Ms. Jones found that two photographs looked familiar, but did not select the defendant's photo until after her daughter had. The state argues that, even if the procedure was suggestive, the identification is still reliable and should be admitted. Is the defendant or the State correct? *State v. Sterling*, 684 So.2d 74 (La.App. 4 Cir. 1996).

5. In the early morning hours of September 15, 1995, the defendant and the victim Anthony Sanders were observed entering the stairwell of an apartment building located at 456 DeKalb Avenue. A few moments later gun shots were heard and the defendant was then seen running from the apartment building. Tara Leech, the victim's girlfriend, Cooley Sanders, the victim's brother, William Dickerson and Anthony Johnson, were witnesses to these events.

On September 16, 1995, Tara Leech identified the defendant from a photo array, which was subsequently lost by Detective Howard. The defendant was apprehended approximately two months later and on November 10, 1995, Leech, Dickerson and Sanders picked the defendant out of a lineup. The defendant's attorney was present at the precinct while the lineup was conducted. However, the attorney was not permitted to be in the viewing room with the witnesses because those witnesses were afraid of retaliation, specifically, that the attorney would relate to the defendant who had identified him. Following this lineup, the defendant was placed under arrest.

On November 12, 1995, Rita Sanders, the victim's mother and Anthony Johnson, another witness, viewed a second photo array and identified the defendant. The defendant now moves to suppress all of the identification evidence on various Sixth Amendment grounds. Should the identification evidence be suppressed? *People v. Adams*, 660 N.Y.S.2d 950 (Sup. 1997).

6. On the 6th day of July, 1979, John Griffin (the alleged victim) and Billy Wayne Davis, employees of the Sonic Drive-In, were closing the restaurant around 12:30 A.M. when two men allegedly appeared and demanded their money. One of the men was armed with a rifle and was wearing dark clothing. The other person was wearing light clothing. During the course of the robbery, two Lanett policemen drove up, and the two men fled on foot behind the restaurant into a wooded area. The officers chased the fugitives, but they did not apprehend them.

Adjacent to the Sonic Drive-In was a vacant parking lot and a building called the Snow Cap Drive-In. The parking lot was customarily filled with unattended parked cars. During the course of the chase, the officers observed an unattended car in the Snow Cap Drive-In parking lot, and they went over, looked into the car, and removed an Alabama driver's license from the vehicle.

Officer Hutchison then showed the driver's license to the employees of the Sonic Drive-In, and they identified the picture on the license as the one who robbed them. Later that day, Billy Wayne Davis was taken to the police station and was shown a mug shot of Lewis Floyd, Jr., whom he identified as one of the robbers. During the afternoon of July 6, Lewis Floyd, Jr. was picked up and arrested by the Lanett Police and was taken into custody. At the police station, Floyd informed the investigators that he desired a lawyer to be present at the station. However, a lawyer was not furnished, and he was promptly placed in a lineup and was identified by John Griffin who had previously been shown Floyd's drivers license.

During lengthy testimony and argument on a pretrial motion to suppress evidence as to the identification of defendant, he contended "that the whole identification process is tainted." He particularized the grounds for his contention by urging (1) that the testimony by Griffin and Davis as to the identity of defendant as one of the robbers was tainted by the fact that they had been shown the driver's license picture of defendant that the officers had taken from the unattended automobile and (2) that the in-court identification of defendant by John Griffin was additionally tainted by a lineup procedure subsequent to his seeing the photograph of defendant on the mentioned driver's license, at which lineup defendant was not afforded a lawyer, as requested by him. Should the identification evidence be suppressed? *Floyd v. State*, 387 So.2d 291 (Ala.Crim.App. 1980).

Glossary

Definitions for this glossary are taken from Ferdico's *Criminal Law and Justice Dictionary,* also published by Wadsworth Publishing Company.

ABANDONED PROPERTY. Property whose owner has voluntarily discarded, left behind, or otherwise relinquished his or her interest in the property in question so that the owner could no longer retain a reasonable expectation of privacy with regard to it. Law enforcement officers may lawfully seize abandoned property without a warrant or probable cause because the Fourth Amendment is inapplicable.

ACQUITTAL. A judgment of a court, based either on the verdict of a jury or of a judicial officer in a nonjury trial, that the defendant is not guilty of the offense for which he or she has been tried. An acquittal on all charges is a final court disposition terminating criminal jurisdiction over the defendant.

ADMINISTRATIVE SEARCH. A routine inspection of a home or business by governmental authorities responsible for determining compliance with various statutes and regulations. An administrative search seeks to enforce fire, health, safety, and housing codes, licensing provisions, and the like. It differs from a criminal search in that a criminal search is directed toward gathering evidence in order to convict a person of a crime. An administrative search ordinarily does not result in a criminal prosecution.

ADMISSION. A statement or acknowledgment of a fact by a person tending to incriminate the person but not sufficient of itself to establish guilt of a crime. An admission, alone or in connection with other facts, tends to show the existence of one or more, but not all, of the elements of a crime. *See* CONFESSION.

AFFIDAVIT. A written statement sworn to or affirmed before an officer authorized to administer an oath or affirmation. An affidavit may be distinguished from a deposition in some contexts in that an affidavit requires no notice to the adverse party or opportunity for cross-examination. In the criminal law, affidavits are used by law enforcement officers and others to provide information to a magistrate to establish probable cause for the issuance of an arrest warrant or a search warrant.

ANTICIPATORY SEARCH WARRANT. A warrant to search a particular place for a particular seizable item that has not yet arrived at the place where the search is to be executed.

APPEAL. An application to or proceeding in an appellate court for review or rehearing of a judgment, decision, or order of a lower court or other tribunal in order to correct alleged errors or injustices in the trial below. A successful appeal results in the reversal or modification of the lower court judgment, decision, or order. An appeal may be either on the record of the proceedings below or de novo. In an appeal on the record only, matters of law may be reviewed. In an appeal de novo, matters of fact as well as law may be reviewed.

APPELLATE JURISDICTION. Lawful authority or power of a court to review a decision made by a lower court or to hear an appeal from a judgment of a lower court.

ARRAIGNMENT. The hearing before a court having jurisdiction in a criminal case, in which the identity of the defendant is established, the defendant is informed of the charge and of his or her rights, and the defendant is required to enter a plea. The defendant's entering of a plea is the crucial distinguishing element of the arraignment. Besides the pleas of guilty or not guilty, courts of many states and the federal courts permit pleas of nolo contendere and some accept pleas of not guilty by reason of insanity or former jeopardy.

ARREST. The taking of a person into the custody of the law for the purpose of charging the person with a criminal offense or a delinquent act or status offense. The basic elements necessary to constitute a formal arrest are:

1. a purpose or intention of a law enforcement officer to effect an arrest;
2. a law enforcement officer acting under real or pretended authority;
3. an actual or constructive seizure or detention of the person to be arrested by an officer having the present power to control the person; and
4. an understanding by the person to be arrested that it is the intention of the arresting officer then and there to arrest and detain him or her.

In order to make a lawful formal arrest without a warrant, a law enforcement officer must either have probable cause to believe that the person to be arrested is committing or has committed a felony or the person to be arrested must be committing a misdemeanor in the officer's presence.

Even though an officer does not intend to make a formal arrest, a court may find that the officer's actions are tantamount to an arrest if they are indistinguishable from an arrest in important respects. If an officer seizes (*see* SEIZURE, definition 1) or detains a person significantly, beyond a mere stop or other minor investigatory detention, the seizure or detention may nevertheless be considered an arrest for purposes of the Fourth Amendment, even if the officer does not comply with all the requirements of a formal arrest. As such, the seizure or detention will be ruled illegal unless it is supported by probable cause.

ARREST WARRANT. A written order issued by a magistrate or other proper judicial officer, upon probable cause, directing a law enforcement officer to arrest a particular person. An arrest warrant is issued on the basis of a sworn complaint charging that the accused person has committed a crime. The arrest warrant must identify the person to be arrested by name and/or other unique characteristics and must describe the crime.

ATTENUATION OF TAINT. *See* FRUIT OF THE POISONOUS TREE DOCTRINE.

AUTOMOBILE EXCEPTION. *See* CARROLL DOCTRINE.

BAIL. To obtain the release from custody of an arrested or imprisoned person by pledging money or other property as a guarantee of the person's appearance in court at a specified date and time. The purposes of bail are to prevent the imprisonment of an accused prior to trial and to ensure his or her appearance at trial. The court may or may not require that the pledge of money or property be secured. Pledges may be secured in several ways. The most common way is by employment of a bail bondsman, to whom a nonrefundable fee is paid. In other cases the court can require a deposit of money before the person is released. The requirement can be for the full amount pledged, or for a percentage of the amount pledged.

BEEPER. A radio transmitter, usually battery operated, which emits periodic signals that can be picked up by a radio receiver.

BENCH TRIAL. Same as NONJURY TRIAL.

BOOKING. A police administrative procedure officially recording an arrest in a police register. Booking involves, at the minimum, recording the name of the person arrested, the officer making the arrest, and the time of, place of, circumstances of, and reason for the arrest. The meaning of booking, however, is sometimes expanded to include other procedures that take place in the station house after an arrest. Booking may include a search of the arrested person, including in some cases a search of body cavities, fingerprinting, photographing, a lineup, or other identification procedures. Booking is usually completed before the arrested person is taken for his or her initial appearance before the magistrate.

BURDEN OF PROOF. The duty to establish a particular issue or proposition by the quantity of evidence required by law. The prosecution has the burden of proof to establish every element of the crime charged beyond a reasonable doubt.

CARROLL DOCTRINE. The search and seizure doctrine, originating in the case of *Carroll v. U.S.*, 267 U.S. 132, 45 S.Ct. 280, 69 L.Ed. 543 (1925), that a warrantless search of a motor vehicle under exigent circumstances by a law enforcement officer who has probable cause to believe that the vehicle contains items subject to seizure is not unreasonable under the Fourth Amendment. The doctrine is sometimes referred to as the automobile exception to the search warrant requirement. "As a general rule, [the U.S. Supreme Court has] required the judgment of a magistrate on the probable cause issue and the issuance of a warrant before a search is made. Only in exigent circumstances will the judgment of the police as to probable cause serve as a sufficient authorization for a search." *Chambers v. Maroney*, 399 U.S. 42, 51, 90 S.Ct. 1975, 1981, 26 L.Ed.2d 419, 428 (1970). Usually, exigent circumstances are established by demonstrating specific facts showing either that the vehicle may be moved to an unknown location out of the jurisdiction, making a search under authority of a warrant impossible, or that items subject to seizure may be removed from the vehicle and concealed or destroyed. The U.S. Supreme Court has held, however, that this is not necessary and that the exigent circumstances requirement is automatically satisfied in the case of a readily mobile motor vehicle. "If a car is readily mobile and probable cause exists to believe it contains contraband, the Fourth Amendment . . . permits police to search the vehicle without more." *Pennsylvania v. Labron*, 518 U.S. 938, 940, 116 S.Ct. 2485, 2487, 135 L.Ed.2d 1031, 1036 (1996).

CHALLENGE FOR CAUSE. A formal objection to a prospective juror directed toward the qualifications of that juror. The party exercising a challenge for cause has an unlimited number of such challenges. Each challenge for cause, however, must be supported by a satisfactory reason or the judge will not dismiss the challenged juror. A general challenge for cause is an objection that the prospective juror is unqualified to serve in any case because of conviction of crime, unsoundness of mind, etc. A special or particular challenge for cause is an objection that the juror is unqualified to serve in the case to be tried because the juror has formed an opinion in the case, has a bias toward one of the parties, etc.

CIVIL RIGHTS. Generally, the constitutionally guaranteed rights of a person by virtue of the person's status as a member of civil society, except those rights involving participation in the establishment, support, or management of the government. Examples of civil rights are those rights to personal liberty established by the bill of rights and by the Thirteenth and Fourteenth Amendments to the Constitution and other congressional acts.

CLOSING ARGUMENT. The part of a trial after all the evidence has been presented and the jury has been instructed in which each party recapitulates the facts and evidence it has presented and attempts to convince the judge or jury of the correctness of its position.

COLLATERAL ESTOPPEL DOCTRINE. When an issue of ultimate fact has once been determined by a valid and final judgment, that issue cannot again be litigated between the same parties in any future lawsuit.

COMMON LAW. The system of law, originated and developed in England, based on court decisions and on custom and usage, rather than on written laws created by legislative enactment. "The common law does not consist of absolute, fixed, and inflexible rules, but rather of broad and comprehensive principles based on justice, reason, and common sense. It is of judicial origin and promulgation. Its principles have been determined by the social needs of the community and have changed with changes in such needs. These principles are susceptible of adaptation to new conditions, interests, relations and usages as the progress of society may require." *Miller v. Monsen,* 37 N.W.2d 543, 547 (Minn. 1949).

COMPLAINT. A sworn written statement presented to a magistrate or other proper judicial officer alleging that a specified person has committed a specified crime and requesting prosecution. The complaint must state the essential facts constituting the crime charged, including the time and place of its commission and the name or description of the defendant. If the defendant has been arrested without an arrest warrant, the complaint may serve as the charging document upon which the preliminary examination is held. If the defendant has not been arrested, the complaint serves as the basis for determining whether there is probable cause to justify the issuance of a warrant for the arrest. Most jurisdictions call the charging document filed in a misdemeanor case or at the first step of a felony case a complaint, and the document filed to initiate trial proceedings at the second step of a felony case an information. In some jurisdictions, the document filed to bind over a defendant until a grand jury decides whether or not to issue an indictment is also called a complaint.

COMPULSORY PROCESS. Coercive means used by courts to procure the attendance in court of persons wanted as witnesses or otherwise. Examples of compulsory process are subpoenas and arrest warrants. The Sixth Amendment to the U.S. Constitution guarantees a defendant the right to have compulsory process to obtain witnesses in his or her favor. The right makes the subpoena power of the court available to a defendant only with respect to competent, material witnesses subject to the court's process, whose expected testimony will be admissible.

CONFESSION. A statement whereby a person admits facts revealing his or her guilt as to all elements of a particular crime. *See* ADMISSION.

CONFRONTATION. 1. The right of confrontation is the right of an accused person to come face to face with an adverse witness in the court, so the accused person has the opportunity to object to the testimony of the witness and to cross-examine the witness. The Sixth Amendment to the U.S. Constitution guarantees the right of confrontation to defendants in federal criminal prosecutions. The due process clause of the Fourteenth Amendment makes this Sixth Amendment guarantee applicable to the states. **2.** Any presentation of a suspect to a victim or witness of a crime for the purpose of identifying the perpetrator of the crime. The term confrontation includes both lineups and showups.

CONSENT SEARCH. A search of a person's body, premises, or belongings conducted by a law enforcement officer with the person's permission. A consent search is lawful only if the totality of circumstances surrounding the search indicate that the consent was voluntary. A person may limit the scope of a consent search by words or actions and may revoke the consent to search at any time. A person may not consent to the search of a third person's premises or property unless the third person has specifically given the person authority to do so or the person possesses "common authority over or other sufficient relationship to the premises or effects sought to be inspected." Common authority rests "on mutual use of the property by persons generally having joint access or control for most purposes, so that it is reasonable to recognize that any of the co-inhabitants has the right to permit the inspection in his own right and that the others have assumed the risk that one of their number might permit the common area to be searched." *U.S. v. Matlock,* 415 U.S. 164, 171 n.7, 94 S.Ct. 988, 993 n.7, 39 L.Ed.2d 242, 250 n.7 (1974).

CONTRABAND. Goods the possession of which is prohibited.

CORROBORATE. To support or enhance the believability of a fact or assertion by presenting additional information that confirms or strengthens the truthfulness of the fact or assertion. A law enforcement officer applying for a search warrant or arrest warrant based on information from an informant may increase the likelihood of the warrant issuing by presenting in the affidavit information that corroborates the information provided by the informant.

COURT OF GENERAL JURISDICTION. Speaking only of criminal courts, a court that has trial jurisdiction over all criminal offenses, including all felonies, and that may or may not hear appeals. A court of general jurisdiction has original jurisdiction over all felonies and frequently has appellate jurisdiction over the decisions of a court of limited jurisdiction. The decisions of a court of general jurisdiction may be reviewed by an appellate court. Courts of general jurisdiction are commonly named superior court, district court, and circuit court. The factual determination of a court of general jurisdiction is final. Appeals are on the record and on matters of law rather than on matters of fact.

COURT OF LIMITED JURISDICTION. Speaking only of criminal courts, a court whose trial jurisdiction either includes no felonies or is limited to less than all felonies, and which may or may not hear appeals. A court of limited jurisdiction is limited to a particular class or classes of cases, and cannot try every felony. A court of limited jurisdiction often has jurisdiction over misdemeanor or traffic cases, over the initial setting of bail and preliminary hearings in felony cases, and occasionally over felony trials where the penalty prescribed for the offense is below a statutorily specified limit. In these cases, the courts of general jurisdiction maintain concurrent jurisdiction over those felonies that the courts of limited jurisdiction are also empowered to try. In some jurisdictions a court of general jurisdiction may hear appeals from a court of limited jurisdiction, and in some cases may review decisions of a court of limited jurisdiction de novo. In other jurisdictions, appeals from a court of limited jurisdiction are made directly to an appellate court, bypassing the court of general jurisdiction. With respect to civil actions, a court of limited jurisdiction may be limited to a certain type of case, or to cases where the amount in controversy is below a statutorily specified limit. Courts of limited jurisdiction are commonly named city court, county court, district court, domestic relations court, family court, justice court, magistrate court, municipal court, police court, probate court, small claims court, and traffic court.

CROSS-EXAMINATION. The questioning of a witness by the party opposed to the party producing the witness. Cross-examination comes after direct examination of the witness by the party producing the witness. The purpose of cross-examination is to discredit the witness's information and impeach the witness's credibility as a means of testing the accuracy of his or her testimony. The scope of cross-examination is usually limited to matters covered during direct examination.

CURTILAGE. The ground and buildings immediately surrounding a dwelling and used for domestic purposes in connection with the dwelling. Under the Fourth Amendment to the U.S. Constitution, "[t]he right of the people to be secure in their persons, houses, papers, and effects, against unreasonable searches and seizures, shall not be violated. . . ." Courts have extended the meaning of houses under the Fourth Amendment to include the curtilage. To determine whether property falls within the curtilage of a house, one must consider "the factors that determine whether an individual reasonably may expect that an area immediately adjacent to the home will remain private." *Oliver v. United States,* 466 U.S. 170, 180, 104 S.Ct. 1735, 1742, 80 L.Ed.2d 214, 225 (1984). The U.S. Supreme Court described those factors in another case: "[W]e believe that curtilage questions should be resolved with particular reference to four factors: the proximity of the area claimed to be curtilage to the home, whether the area is included within an enclosure surrounding the home, the nature of the uses to which the area is put, and the steps taken by the resident to protect the area from observation by people passing by." *United States v. Dunn,* 480 U.S. 294, 301, 107 S.Ct. 1134, 1139, 94 L.Ed.2d 326, 334–35 (1987). The Court emphasized that "the primary focus is whether the area in question harbors those intimate activities associated with domestic life and the privacies of the home." 480 U.S. at 301 n.4, 107 S.Ct. at 1139 n.4, 94 L.Ed.2d at 335 n.4.

CUSTODIAL ARREST. An arrest in which the person arrested is taken into custody and not merely given a ticket, citation, or notice to appear. Whether or not an arrest is custodial is a determining factor in justifying a search incident to arrest. The U.S. Supreme Court held that "in the case of lawful custodial arrest, a full search of the person is not only an exception to the warrant requirement of the Fourth Amendment, but is also a 'reasonable' search under that Amendment." *United States v. Robinson,* 414 U.S. 218, 235, 94 S.Ct. 467, 477, 38 L.Ed.2d 427, 441 (1973).

CUSTODY. 1. Legal or physical control of a person or thing; legal, supervisory or physical responsibility for a person or thing. The term custody has several degrees of meaning, depending on the context in which it is used, and may mean actual imprisonment or the mere power, legal or physical, to imprison or take into physical possession. It ranges from the clearest legal and physical control and responsibility, as when a legally arrested person is in the custody of a police officer, to physical control without legal justification, as when a jail holds prisoners in its custody who are legally under the jurisdiction of a state prison system. Custody also applies to physical objects, such as evidence taken into custody by law enforcement investigators. **2.** A person is in custody for purposes of *Miranda v. Arizona* when the person is deprived of freedom of action in any significant way. The U.S. Supreme Court said: "Although the circumstances of each case must certainly influence a determination of whether a suspect is 'in custody' for purposes of receiving *Miranda* protection, the ultimate inquiry is simply whether there is a 'formal arrest or restraint on freedom of movement' of the degree associated with a formal arrest." *California v. Beheler,* 463 U.S. 1121, 1125, 103 S.Ct. 3517, 3520, 77 L.Ed.2d 1275, 1279 (1983).

DEPOSITION. Out-of-court testimony of a witness, taken under oath prior to trial and reduced to writing. A deposition is taken either orally or upon written interrogatories with notice to the adverse party so that the adverse party may attend and cross-examine. If it appears that a prospective witness may be unable to attend or be prevented from attending a trial or hearing, that the witness's testimony is material, and that it is necessary to take the witness's deposition to prevent a failure of justice, the court may, upon motion and notice to the parties, order that the witness's testimony be taken by deposition. At the trial or hearing, the deposition, or any part of it, may be used if the court finds that:

- the witness is dead;
- the witness is out of the jurisdiction, unless the court finds that the absence of the witness was procured by the party offering the deposition;
- the witness is unable to attend or testify because of sickness or infirmity; or
- the party offering the deposition has been unable to procure the attendance of the witness by subpoena.

A deposition may also be used by any party for the purpose of contradicting or impeaching the testimony of the deponent as a witness.

DERIVATIVE EVIDENCE. *See* FRUIT OF THE POISONOUS TREE DOCTRINE.

DIRECT EXAMINATION. The first interrogation or examination of a witness in a trial by the party on whose behalf the witness is called. The direct examination consists of specific questions asked by the attorney for the party calling the witness, and the witness is expected to give testimony favorable to the party calling the witness.

DISCOVERY. A procedure by which a party obtains a legal right to compel the opposing party to allow him or her to obtain, inspect, copy, or photograph items within the possession or control of the opposing party. Among the items subject to discovery are tangible objects, tape recordings, books, and papers, including written or recorded statements made by the defendants or witnesses, and the results or reports of physical examinations and scientific tests, experiments, and comparisons. Information usually not subject to discovery includes investigators' notes, lawyers' work product, and anything that would violate the defendant's constitutional privilege against compelled self-incrimination.

The general purpose of discovery is "to promote the orderly ascertainment of the truth" during trial. Ordinarily, to obtain the right to discovery, a party must make a motion before the court and must show that the specific items sought may be material to the preparation of its case and that its request is reasonable. A recent development is automatic informal discovery for certain types of evidence, without the necessity for motions and court orders. The state of the law governing discovery is constantly changing, but the trend appears to be in favor of broadening the right of discovery for both the defense and the prosecution. The federal government and the states have varying statutes and rules relating to the nature and scope of the information required to be disclosed in the discovery process.

DOUBLE JEOPARDY. A legal doctrine that "protects against a second prosecution for the same offense after acquittal, against a second prosecution for the same offense after conviction, and against multiple punishments for the same offense." *Justices of Boston Municipal Court v. Lydon,* 466 U.S. 294, 306–07, 104 S.Ct. 1805, 1812, 80 L.Ed.2d 311, 323 (1984). The Fifth Amendment to the U.S. Constitution prohibits placing a person in double jeopardy ("nor shall any person be subject for the same offense to be twice put in jeopardy of life or limb"). "Same offense," under two different tests, means either an offense requiring the same evidence to sustain a conviction or an offense arising from the same criminal act or transaction. The stage of the prosecution at which a person is considered to be in danger of conviction differs in different jurisdictions. Generally, however, an accused is in legal jeopardy in a trial at the moment the jury is sworn or, in nonjury trials, when the first witness is sworn. The constitutional protection against double jeopardy is extended to state prosecutions through the due process clause of the Fourteenth Amendment as a result of the U.S. Supreme Court decision in *Benton v. Maryland,* 395 U.S. 784, 89 S.Ct. 2056, 23 L.Ed.2d 707 (1989). Nevertheless, the double jeopardy clause does not bar a state prosecution of a defendant who was acquitted on a federal charge arising out of the same criminal act.

DUAL SOVEREIGNTY DOCTRINE. The doctrine under which, "[w]hen a defendant in a single act violates the 'peace and dignity' of two sovereigns by breaking the laws of each, he has committed two distinct 'offences.'" *Heath v. Alabama,* 474 U.S. 82, 88, 106 S.Ct. 433, 437, 88 L.Ed.2d 387 (1985). The dual sovereignty doctrine is limited, by its own terms, to cases where the two entities that seek successively to prosecute a defendant for the same course of conduct can be termed separate sovereigns. This determination turns on whether the two entities draw their authority to punish the offender from distinct sources of power, not on

whether they are pursuing separate interests. Double jeopardy does not arise when a single act exposes a defendant to prosecution by two separate sovereigns such as the federal government and a state government or the governments of two different states.

DUE PROCESS OF LAW. Another name for governmental fair play, i.e., laws and procedures that conform to the rules and principles established in our system of justice for the enforcement and protection of individual rights. Some of the essential elements of due process of law, with respect to criminal justice, are: a law creating and clearly defining the offense and punishment; an impartial tribunal having jurisdictional authority over the case; accusation in proper form; notice and opportunity to appear, to be heard, and to defend against charges; trial according to established procedure; and discharge from all restraints or obligations unless convicted. The Fifth Amendment to the U.S. Constitution provides that "nor [shall any person] be deprived of life, liberty, or property, without due process of law." This provision applies only to actions of the federal government. The due process requirement was made applicable to the states by the Fourteenth Amendment, Section 1, which states "nor shall any State deprive any person of life, liberty, or property, without due process of law." The meaning of due process of law is not fixed but changes with changing jurisprudential attitudes of fair play. In his concurring opinion in the 1951 case of *Joint Anti-Fascist Refugee Committee v. McGrath,* Justice Frankfurter said:

> The requirement of "due process" is not a fair weather or timid assurance. It must be respected in periods of calm and in times of trouble; it protects aliens as well as citizens. But "due process," unlike some legal rules, is not a technical conception with a fixed content unrelated to time, place and circumstances. Expressing as it does in its ultimate analysis respect enforced by law for that feeling of just treatment which has been evolved through centuries of Anglo-American constitutional history and civilization, "due process" cannot be imprisoned within the treacherous limits of any formula. Representing a profound attitude of fairness between man and man, and more particularly between the individual and government, "due process" is compounded of history, reason, the past course of decisions, and stout confidence in the strength of the democratic faith which we profess. Due process is not a mechanical instrument. It is not a yardstick. It is a process. It is a delicate process of adjustment inescapably involving the exercise of judgment by those whom the Constitution entrusted with the unfolding of the process. 341 U.S. 123, 162–63, 71 S.Ct. 624, 643–44, 95 L.Ed. 817, 849.

In *Green v. State,* 247 A.2d 117, 121 (Me. 1968), the court said:

> Due process . . . does not restrict the State to any particular mode of procedure. It protects against the exercise of arbitrary governmental power and guarantees equal and impartial dispensation of law according to the settled course of judicial proceedings or in accordance with fundamental principles of distributive justice.

DUPLICITOUS INDICTMENT OR INFORMATION. An indictment or information that unites two or more separate and distinct offenses in the same count. By obscuring the exact charge, duplicitous indictments or informations may violate the defendant's constitutional right to notice of charges and may impair the defendant's ability to plead double jeopardy in a subsequent prosecution.

EMERGENCY. A serious situation developing suddenly and unexpectedly and demanding immediate action; a pressing necessity; an exigency; exigent circumstances.

EQUAL PROTECTION OF THE LAWS. The Fourteenth Amendment to the U.S. Constitution provides, in part, that no state shall "deny to any person within its jurisdiction the equal protection of the laws." This constitutional guarantee prohibits states from denying any person or class of persons the same protection of the law enjoyed by other persons or other classes of persons in similar circumstances. No state may adopt laws, regulations, or policies that establish categories of people receiving unequal treatment on the basis of race, religion, or national origin. Thus, racial segregation in public schools and other public places, laws that prohibit the sale of use of property to certain minority groups, and laws that prohibit interracial marriage have been struck down. Furthermore, the U.S. Supreme Court held that purely private acts of discrimination can be in violation of the equal protection clause if they are customarily enforced throughout the state, whether or not there is a specific law or other explicit manifestation of action by the state.

No specific equal protection clause applies to the federal government, but the federal government is prohibited from denying a person equal protection of federal laws by judicial interpretations of the due process clause of the Fifth Amendment.

EVIDENCE. Anything offered to a court or jury through the medium of witnesses, documents, exhibits, or other objects, to demonstrate or ascertain the truth of facts in issue in a case; the means by which facts are proved or disproved in court.

EXCLUSIONARY RULE. A rule, developed by the U.S. Supreme Court, stating that evidence obtained in violation of a person's constitutional rights by law enforcement officers or agents will be inadmissible in a criminal prosecution against the person whose rights were violated. "The exclusionary rule prohibits introduction into evidence of tangible materials seized during an unlawful search, *Weeks v. United States,* 232 U.S. 383, 34 S.Ct. 341, 58 L.Ed. 652 (1914), and of testimony concerning knowledge acquired during an unlawful search, *Silverman v. United States,* 365 U.S. 505, 81 S.Ct. 679, 5 L.Ed.2d 734 (1961). Beyond that, the exclusionary rule also prohibits the introduction of derivative evidence, both tangible and testimonial, that is the product of the primary evidence, or that is otherwise acquired as an indirect result of the unlawful search, up to the point at which the connection with the unlawful search becomes 'so attenuated as to dissipate the taint,' *Nardone v. United States,* 308 U.S. 338, 341, 60 S.Ct. 266, 268, 84 L.Ed. 307 (1939)." *Murray v. United States,* 478 U.S. 533, 536–37, 108 S.Ct. 2529, 2532–33, 101 L.Ed.2d 472, 480 (1988). The purpose of the exclusionary rule is to deter law enforcement officers and other government officials from violating the constitutional rights of suspects by removing the incentive for obtaining illegally seized evidence. The rule does not apply to evidence obtained by persons other than government officials.

EXIGENT CIRCUMSTANCES. Generally, an emergency, a pressing necessity, or a set of circumstances requiring immediate attention or swift action. In the criminal procedure context, exigent circumstances means "an emergency situation requiring swift action to prevent imminent danger to life or serious damage to property, or to forestall the imminent escape of a suspect or destruction of evidence. There is no ready litmus test for determining whether such circumstances exist, and in each case the claim of an extraordinary situation must be measured by the facts known to the officers." *People v. Ramey,* 127 Cal.Rptr. 629, 637, 545 P.2d 1333, 1341 (Cal. 1976).

EX POST FACTO. *Latin.* "After the fact." An ex post facto law is "one which makes that criminal which was not so at the time the action was performed, or which increases the punishment, or, in short, in relation to the offense or its consequences, alters the situation of a party to his disadvantage." *Lindsey v. Washington,* 301 U.S. 397, 57 S.Ct. 797, 81 L.Ed. 1182 (1937). Ex post facto laws are prohibited by Article I, Sections 9 and 10, of the U.S. Constitution and similar provisions of state constitutions.

EXTRADITION. The surrender of an accused or convicted person by one state (asylum state), to which the person has fled, to the state with jurisdiction to try or punish the person (demanding state), upon demand of the latter state, so that the person may be dealt with according to its laws. The demand occurs in the form of an extradition warrant issued by the governor of the demanding state. The delivery of the person to the demanding state will occur under the executive or judicial authorization of the asylum state. The U.S. Constitution, Article IV, Section 2, requires the officials of a state to arrest and return an accused fugitive to another state for trial upon demand of the governor of the latter state. Most states have adopted the Uniform Criminal Extradition Act, which provides uniform extradition procedures among the states.

FELONY. In general, a crime of a more serious nature than those designated as misdemeanors. Felonies are distinguished from misdemeanors by place of punishment and possible duration of punishment as defined by statute. The statutory definition of felony may differ between states and between the federal government and various states. Typically a felony is a crime with a possible punishment of death or imprisonment in a state or federal prison facility for a period of one year or more.

FRESH PURSUIT. Immediate pursuit of a fleeing criminal with intent to apprehend him or her. Fresh pursuit generally refers to the situation in which a law enforcement officer attempts to make a valid arrest of a criminal within the officer's jurisdiction, and the criminal flees outside the jurisdiction to avoid arrest, with the officer immediately pursuing. An arrest made in fresh pursuit will be legal if the pursuit was started promptly and maintained continuously. Many states have adopted the Uniform Act on Fresh Pursuit to govern fresh pursuits that take an arresting officer into a neighboring state.

FRISK. A modified search consisting of a careful exploration of the outer surfaces of a person's clothing all over his or her body in an attempt to find weapons. The 1968 U.S. Supreme Court case of *Terry v. Ohio* set out the limits on law enforcement officers' authority to frisk persons. "[T]here must be a narrowly drawn authority to permit a reasonable search for weapons for the protection of the police officer, where he has reason to believe that he is dealing with an armed and dangerous individual, regardless of whether he has probable cause to arrest the individual for a crime." 392 U.S. 1, 27, 88 S.Ct. 1868, 1883, 20 L.Ed.2d 889, 909. In a later case, the Court extended the permissible scope of a frisk to include the passenger compartment of an automobile. "[T]he search of the passenger compartment of an automobile, limited to those areas in which a weapon may be placed or hidden, is permissible if the police officer possesses a reasonable belief based on 'specific and articulable facts which, taken together with the rational inferences from those facts, reasonably warrant' the officers in believing that the suspect is dangerous and the suspect may gain immediate control of weapons." *Michigan v. Long,* 463 U.S. 1032, 1049, 103 S.Ct. 3469, 3480, 77 L.Ed.2d 1201, 1220 (1983).

FRUIT OF THE POISONOUS TREE DOCTRINE. The doctrine that evidence will be inadmissible in court if it was indirectly obtained by exploitation of some prior unconstitutional police activity (such as an illegal arrest or search or a coerced confession). The evidence indirectly obtained is sometimes called derivative evidence. The doctrine derives its name from the idea that once a tree is poisoned (illegal police activity), then the fruit of the tree (derivative evidence obtained by exploiting the illegal activity) is likewise poisoned or tainted and should not be used. If, however, evidence is obtained by means sufficiently distinguishable to be purged of the taint of the primary illegality, the primary illegality has not been exploited and the evidence will be admissible. Courts refer to this as attenuation or dissipation of the taint and require the prosecution to prove at least an intervening act by the defendant or a third party that breaks the causal chain linking the illegality and evidence in such a way that the evidence is not in fact obtained by exploitation of that illegality. *Example*: Assume that the police arrest a man illegally merely because he is walking in an area where a bank robbery has occurred. Then they take him to the bank and the teller identifies him as the robber. The derivative evidence of the teller's identification of the man at the bank would be "fruit of the poisonous tree" and would be inadmissible in court because the identification was obtained by exploitation of the prior illegal arrest. Assume further that the arrested person was arraigned and released on his own recognizance, but returned several days later to make a full confession of the robbery. The confession would be admissible because the connection between the arrest and the confession "had become so attenuated as to dissipate the taint." *Wong Sun v. U.S.* 371 U.S. 471, 491, 83 S.Ct. 407, 419, 9 L.Ed.2d 441, 457 (1963).

GOOD-FAITH EXCEPTION. An exception to the exclusionary rule for illegal searches conducted in good faith.

Under this exception, whenever a law enforcement officer acting with objective good faith has obtained a search warrant from a detached and neutral judge or magistrate and acted within its scope, evidence seized pursuant to the warrant will not be excluded, even though the warrant is later determined to be invalid. In determining what is good faith on the part of an officer, the Court said that "our good-faith inquiry is confined to the objectively ascertainable question whether a reasonably well-trained officer would have known that the search was illegal despite the magistrate's authorization. In making this determination, all of the circumstances, including whether the warrant application has previously been rejected by a different magistrate, may be considered." *United States v. Leon,* 468 U.S. 897, 922–23 n.23, 104 S.Ct. 3405, 3421 n.23, 82 L.Ed.2d 677, 698 n.23 (1984). The good-faith exception has been extended to protect police who acted in good-faith reliance upon a statute (subsequently found invalid) that authorized warrantless administrative searches. *Illinois v. Krull,* 480 U.S. 340, 107 S.Ct. 1160, 94 L.Ed.2d 364 (1987).

GRAND JURY. A jury, usually of 16 to 23 persons, selected according to law and sworn, whose duty is to receive criminal complaints, hear the evidence put forth by the prosecution, and find indictments when they are satisfied that there is probable cause that an accused person has committed a crime and should be brought to trial. Grand juries may also investigate criminal activity generally and investigate the conduct of public agencies and officials. In many states all felony charges must be considered by a grand jury before filing in the trial court. Ordinarily a prosecutor presents to the grand jury for its consideration a list of charges and evidence related to a specific criminal event. The grand jury may then, after deliberation, decide to indict or not to indict. The grand jury may call witnesses and may even compel witnesses to appear or produce documents by having them served with subpoenas. Grand jury proceedings are kept secret for the following reasons:

- to prevent an escape from the jurisdiction of someone who is not yet in custody but whose indictment may be contemplated;
- to provide the utmost freedom for the grand jury in its deliberations and to protect jury members from outside influences;
- to prevent tampering with witnesses who may testify before the grand jury and later appear at the trial of those indicted;
- to encourage the free and unrestrained disclosure of information by persons who have information on the commission of crimes; and
- to protect innocent persons who are exonerated of charges from disclosure of the fact that they were under grand jury investigation.

A trial jury is distinguished from a grand jury in that a trial jury hears a case in order to render a verdict of guilty or not guilty. A grand jury only decides whether there is sufficient evidence to cause a person to be brought to trial for a crime.

HABEAS CORPUS. The name of a writ issued by a court and directed to a person detaining or confining another (usually the superintendent of a confinement facility) commanding him or her to bring the body of the person detained before a judicial officer and to show cause whether the detention is legal. Article I, Section 9, Clause 2, of the U.S. Constitution provides that "[t]he privilege of the Writ of Habeas Corpus shall not be suspended, unless when in Cases of Rebellion or Invasion the public Safety may require it." The right of a person to the writ depends on the legality of the detention and not on the person's guilt or innocence. The major grounds for issuance of the writ are lack of jurisdiction of the court in which the prisoner was convicted and violation of the petitioner's constitutional rights. Habeas corpus is an extraordinary remedy to be used only in cases of special urgency and not when relief can be obtained by other adequate remedies, such as a motion for a new trial or an appeal. The writ of habeas corpus is also called the great writ.

HEARSAY EVIDENCE. Evidence of a statement made other than by a witness testifying at a trial or hearing offered to prove the truth of the matter asserted. The statement may be oral or written or may be nonverbal conduct intended as a substitute for words.

HEARSAY RULE. The hearsay rule, simply stated, is that hearsay evidence is inadmissible. The basis of the hearsay rule is that the credibility of the person making a statement is the most important factor in determining the truth of the statement. If a statement is made out of court, there is no opportunity to cross-examine the person making the statement or to observe the person's demeanor. Without these methods of determining the truth of the statement, the statement may not be admitted into evidence. Many exceptions to the hearsay rule allow the admission of hearsay evidence for various reasons of trustworthiness of the evidence and practical necessity.

HOT PURSUIT. The immediate pursuit by a law enforcement officer of a person into a house or other constitutionally protected area in response to an emergency. Examples of emergencies that will justify a hot pursuit are escape of a fleeing felon or other dangerous person, avoidance of arrest by a person suspected of a crime, and prevention of the destruction or concealment of evidence. Once inside the house or other constitutionally protected area, officers may search the premises if necessary to alleviate the emergency and any items of evidence observed lying open to view may be legally seized under the plain view doctrine. *Warden v. Hayden*, 387 U.S. 294, 87 S.Ct. 1642, 18 L.Ed.2d 782 (1967).

IMMUNITY. Freedom or exemption from prosecution granted to a witness to compel answers to questions or the production of evidence, which the witness might otherwise refuse to do on the grounds of the Fifth Amendment privilege against self-incrimination. Two types of immunity that may be granted are transactional immunity and use immunity. Under transactional immunity a witness may be compelled to testify despite the privilege against self-incrimination, but the witness is protected from any prosecution for crimes to which his or her compelled testimony relates. Under use immunity a witness may be compelled to testify despite the privilege against self-incrimination, but the witness is protected from the use of the compelled testimony and any evidence derived from it. Use immunity would still permit prosecution for related offenses based upon evidence derived from independent sources. A witness's failure to answer questions or produce evidence within the subject of the investigation as ordered by the court constitutes contempt of court.

IMPOUND. To take a vehicle, document, or other object into the custody of the law or of a court or law enforcement agency for safekeeping or examination. The U.S. Supreme Court approved the impounding of motor vehicles under certain circumstances in *South Dakota v. Opperman.*

> In the interests of public safety and as part of what the Court has called "community caretaking functions," automobiles are frequently taken into police custody. Vehicle accidents present one such occasion. To permit the uninterrupted flow of traffic and in some circumstances to preserve evidence, disabled or damaged vehicles will often be removed from the highways or streets at the behest of police engaged solely in caretaking and traffic-control activities. Police will also frequently remove and impound automobiles which violate parking ordinances and which thereby jeopardize both the public safety and the efficient movement of vehicular traffic. The authority of police to seize and remove from the streets vehicles impeding traffic or threatening public safety and convenience is beyond challenge. 428 U.S. 364, 368–69, 96 S.Ct. 3092, 3097, 49 L.Ed.2d 1000, 1005 (1976).

INDEPENDENT SOURCE. An exception to the fruit of the poisonous tree doctrine that allows the admission of tainted evidence if that evidence was also obtained through a source wholly independent of the primary constitutional violation. The independent source exception is compatible with the underlying rationale of the exclusionary rule: the deterrence of police misconduct. As stated by the U.S. Supreme Court, "The independent source doctrine teaches us that the interest of society in deterring unlawful police conduct and the public interest in having juries receive all probative evidence of a crime are properly balanced by putting the police in the same, not a *worse*, position than they would have been in if no police error or misconduct had occurred." *Nix v. Williams*, 467 U.S. 431, 443, 104 S.Ct. 2501, 2509, 81 L.Ed.2d 377, 387 (1984).

INDICTMENT. A formal written accusation submitted by a grand jury to a court, alleging that a specified person has committed a specific offense. An indictment, like an information, is usually used to initiate a felony prosecution. In some jurisdictions, all felony accusations must be by indictment, but in others felony trials will ordinarily be initiated by the filing of an information by a prosecutor. Ordinarily, the prosecutor presents allegations and evidence (often called a bill of indictment) to the grand jury, which endorses on it "a true bill" if it decides that there is sufficient evidence to sustain the accusation and that a trial should be had. The indictment delivered to the court states the facts about the alleged crime as found by the grand jury and cites the penal code sections believed to have been violated. If the grand jury ignores the bill of indictment, it endorses "no true bill," "not a true bill," or "not found" on it. When a grand jury takes notice of an offense on its own initiative and delivers an indictment, it is sometimes called a grand jury original or a presentment.

INEVITABLE DISCOVERY. A variation of the independent source doctrine allowing the admission of tainted evidence if it would inevitably have been discovered in the normal course of events. Under this exception, the prosecution must establish by a preponderance of the evidence that, even though the evidence was actually discovered as the result of a constitutional violation, the evidence would ultimately or inevitably have been discovered by lawful means, for example, as the result of the predictable and routine behavior of a law enforcement agency, some other agency, or a private person.

> [I]f the government can prove that the evidence would have been obtained inevitably and, therefore, would have been admitted regardless of any overreaching by the police, there is no rational basis to keep that evidence from the jury in order to ensure the fairness of the trial proceedings. In that situation, the State has gained no advantage at trial and the defendant has suffered no prejudice. Indeed, suppression of the evidence would operate to undermine the adversary system by putting the State in a *worse* position than it would have occupied without any police misconduct. *Nix v. Williams,* 467 U.S. 431, 447, 104 S.Ct. 2501, 2511, 81 L.Ed.2d 377, 389–90 (1984).

INFORMANT. A person who gives information to the police regarding criminal activity.

INFORMATION. A formal, written accusation submitted to a court by a prosecutor, without the approval or intervention of a grand jury, alleging that a specified person has committed a specific offense. An information is similar in nature and content to an indictment and serves as an alternative to the indictment in some jurisdictions to initiate usually felony prosecutions. Some jurisdictions initiate felony prosecutions only through indictment and others allow use of the information only after the defendant has waived an indictment.

INITIAL APPEARANCE. The first appearance of an accused person in the first court having jurisdiction over his or her case. Various procedural steps may be taken during the initial appearance. In minor misdemeanor cases the initial appearance may be the only one, and judgment and penalty, if any, will be determined at that time. When the charge is more serious, the accused at initial appearance may be informed of the charges, a plea may be entered and bail set, or the accused may merely be informed of his or her rights and of the general nature of the proceedings and it may be determined whether he or she has counsel. In any given jurisdiction, the initial appearance may be characterized by the major step taken in that court at that point. Thus, it may be called a preliminary arraignment, preliminary hearing, magistrate's preliminary hearing, or presentment. The timing of an initial appearance is largely determined by whether the defendant is in custody, and by the laws concerning the maximum period a person can be held in custody without court appearance. In most states an arrested person has a right to be brought forthwith before a court or magistrate for an initial appearance.

INSTRUCTION. A direction or explanation given by a trial judge to a jury informing them of the law applicable to the case before them. Attorneys for both sides normally furnish the judge with suggested instructions.

INTERROGATION. The questioning of a person suspected of a crime with the intent of eliciting incriminating admissions from the person. The U.S. Supreme Court explained the meaning of interrogation for purposes of the *Miranda v. Arizona* decision as follows: "[T]he *Miranda* safeguards come into play whenever a person in custody is subjected to either express questioning or its functional equivalent. That is to say, the term 'interrogation' under Miranda refers not only to express questioning, but also to any words or actions on the part of police (other than those normally attendant to arrest and custody) that the police should know are reasonably likely to elicit an incriminating response from the suspect." *Rhode Island v. Innis,* 446 U.S. 291, 300–01, 100 S.Ct. 1682, 1689, 64 L.Ed.2d 297, 307–08 (1980). The Court further refined the definition by stating that an incriminating response is any response, whether inculpatory or exculpatory, that the prosecution may seek to introduce at trial. Volunteered statements, questions directed at clarifying a suspect's statement, brief, routine questions, spontaneous questions, and questions necessary to protect the safety of the police and public are not considered interrogation for purposes of *Miranda.*

INVENTORY SEARCH. The routine practice of police departments of securing and recording the contents of a lawfully impounded vehicle. In *South Dakota v. Opperman,* 428 U.S. 364, 96 S.Ct. 3092, 49 L.Ed.2d 1000 (1976), the U.S. Supreme Court approved this limited type of search for the purposes of protecting the vehicle owner's property while it remains in custody and protecting the police from potential danger and from claims or disputes over lost or stolen property. This inventory procedure is not considered to be a search for purposes of the Fourth Amendment because its object is not to find incriminating evidence as part of a criminal investigation. Rather, it is considered to be a routine administrative-custodial procedure, and it may not be used as a pretext to conduct an exploratory search for incriminating evidence in order to circumvent the warrant requirement. If, however, incriminating evidence is found under circumstances satisfying the plain view doctrine, that evidence may be seized and is admissible in court. The validity of an inventory search depends on whether the officers conducting the inventory followed standard inventory procedures of their law enforcement agency.

ITEMS SUBJECT TO SEIZURE. Items for which a search warrant may be issued. Federal Rule of Criminal Procedure 41 (b) specifies that "[a] warrant may be issued under this rule to search for and seize any (1) property that constitutes evidence of the commission of a criminal offense; or (2) contraband, the fruits of crime, or things otherwise criminally possessed; or (3) property designed or intended for use or which is or has been used as the means of committing a criminal offense. . . ." Most states have similar rules.

JOINDER. Generally, the uniting or combining of two or more persons, parties, charges, causes of action, etc. to be considered together. In criminal proceedings, joinder means the naming of two or more defendants and/or the listing of two or more charges in a single charging document.

JUDGMENT. 1. The statement of a court's decision of conviction or acquittal of a person charged with a crime. The date of a judgment of conviction is an important item in calculations of elapsed time in those jurisdictions where a sentence must be pronounced within a time limit. The count begins the day the judgment is pronounced. Judgment is sometimes used to mean any court decision, such as a judgment of conviction, an acquittal, a court order, or a sentence. **2.** Generally, the determination or decision of a court upon a matter within its jurisdiction; the final conclusion of a court as to matters of fact and law. Sometimes judgment is used only in the sense of a final or authoritative decision.

JUDICIAL REVIEW. "Judicial review is the exercise by courts of their responsibility to determine whether acts of the other two branches are illegal and void because those acts violate the constitution. The doctrine authorizes courts to determine whether a law is constitutional, not whether it is necessary or useful. In other words, judicial review is the power to say what the constitution means and not whether such a law reflects a wise policy. Adherence to the doctrine of judicial review is essential to achieving balance in our government. . . . Judicial review, coupled with the specified constitutional provisions which keep the judicial branch separate and independent of the other branches of government and with those articles of the constitution that protect the impartiality of the judiciary from public and political pressure, enables the courts to ensure that the constitutional rights of each citizen will not be encroached upon by either the legislative or the executive branch of the government." *State v. LaFrance,* 471 A.2d 340, 343–44 (N.H. 1983).

JURISDICTION. 1. The territory, subject matter, or person over which lawful authority may be exercised by a court or other justice agency, as determined by statute or constitution. *Example:* Criminal cases are not within the jurisdiction of the probate court. **2.** The lawful authority or power of a court or an administrative agency to act upon or deal with a matter. *Example:* Police agencies do not have jurisdiction over most private disputes. **3.** The jurisdiction of a court, more specifically, is the lawful authority or power to hear or act upon a case or question and to pass and enforce judgment on it. A particular court can have more than one kind of jurisdiction. *Example:* An appellate court has appellate jurisdiction over felony cases and original jurisdiction for the issuance of certain writs, but no jurisdiction to conduct trials.

JURY. A body of persons, selected and sworn according to law, to inquire into certain matters of fact and to render a verdict or true answer based on evidence presented before them.

JURY NULLIFICATION. The power of a jury to acquit regardless of the strength of the evidence against a defendant. Nullification usually occurs when the defendant is particularly sympathetic, or when the defendant is prosecuted for violating an unpopular law.

JURY PANEL. The group of persons summoned to appear in court as potential jurors for a particular trial, or the persons selected from the group of potential jurors to sit in the jury box, from which second group those acceptable to the prosecution and the defense are finally chosen as the jury. The group of persons who are asked to sit in the jury box are usually selected by the court clerk by lot. As individuals are dismissed from the box for various reasons, replacements are chosen, also by lot.

LINEUP. A confrontation (definition 2) involving the presentation at one time of several persons, including a person suspected of committing a crime, to a victim or witness of the crime for the purpose of identifying the perpetrator of the crime. The presentation is usually conducted by a law enforcement official or a prosecuting attorney. In *United States v. Wade,* 388 U.S. 218, 87 S.Ct. 1926, 18 L.Ed.2d 1149 (1967), the U.S. Supreme Court held that a pretrial confrontation is a critical stage in the legal proceedings against a suspect and that the suspect has a right to the presence of a lawyer at the lineup. Furthermore, if the suspect cannot afford a lawyer, he or she is entitled to have one appointed by the court. In *Kirby v. Illinois,* 406 U.S. 682, 689, 92 S.Ct. 1877, 1882, 32 L.Ed.2d 411, 417 (1972), the Court held that the right to counsel attaches only to lineups held "at or after the initiation of adversary judicial criminal proceedings, whether by way of formal charge, preliminary hearing, indictment, information or arraignment." Nevertheless, even though a suspect may not have a right to counsel at a confrontation, the due process clause of the Fifth and Fourteenth Amendments to the Constitution forbids any pretrial identification procedure that is unnecessarily suggestive and conducive to irreparable mistaken identification. *Stovall v. Denno,* 388 U.S. 293, 87 S.Ct. 1967, 18 L.Ed.2d 1199 (1967). If an officer conducts an unnecessarily suggestive identification procedure, the identification evidence will be inadmissible in court unless the identification is otherwise reliable under the totality of the circumstances.

> [R]eliability is the linchpin in determining the admissibility of identification testimony for both pre- and post-Stovall confrontations. The factors to be considered are set out in Biggers. 409 U.S., at 199–200, 93 S.Ct., at 382. These include the opportunity of the witness to view the criminal at the time of the crime, the witness' degree of attention, the accuracy of his prior description of the criminal, the level of certainty demonstrated at the confrontation, and the time between the crime and the confrontation. Against these factors is to be weighed the corrupting effect of the suggestive identification itself. *Manson v. Brathwaite,* 432 U.S. 98, 114, 97 S.Ct. 2243, 2253, 53 L.Ed.2d 140, 154 (1977).

MAGISTRATE. A judicial officer of a court of limited jurisdiction or with limited or delegated authority. Among the duties of a magistrate are the issuance of arrest warrants, search warrants, and summonses, the setting of bail, the ordering of release on bail, and the conduct of arraignments and preliminary examinations of persons charged with serious crimes. A magistrate may also have limited authority to try minor cases or to dispose of cases on a guilty plea. The authority of a magistrate in a particular jurisdiction depends on the statutes, rules, and customs of that jurisdiction.

MISDEMEANOR. In general, a crime of less serious nature than those designated as felonies. In jurisdictions that recognize the felony-misdemeanor distinction, a misdemeanor is any crime that is not a felony. Misdemeanors are usually punished by fine or by incarceration in a local confinement facility rather than a state prison or penitentiary. The maximum period of confinement that may be imposed for a misdemeanor is defined by statute and is usually less than one year. Court procedures for handling misdemeanors are usually different from those for felonies.

MOTION. An oral or written request made to a court at any time before, during, or after court proceedings, asking the court to make a specified finding, decision, or order. In criminal proceedings a motion can be made by the prosecution, the defense, or the court itself.

MULTIPLICITOUS INDICTMENT OR INFORMATION. An indictment or information that charges the commission of a single offense in several counts. The evil of a multiplicitous indictment or information is that it may lead to multiple sentences for the same offense, or it may have some psychological effect upon a jury by suggesting that the defendant has committed more than one crime.

NOLO CONTENDERE. *Latin.* "I do not wish to contest." A defendant's plea to a criminal charge in which the defendant states that he or she does not contest the charge, but neither admits guilt nor claims innocence. A plea of nolo contendere subjects the defendant to the same legal consequences as a guilty plea. Both pleas can be followed by a judgment of conviction without a trial or verdict, and by a sentencing disposition. The major difference between the two pleas is that a plea of nolo contendere cannot constitute evidence in a civil action that relevant facts have been admitted; a guilty plea can. A court may not accept a plea of nolo contendere unless the court is satisfied, after inquiry, that the defendant committed the crime charged and that the plea is made voluntarily with an understanding of the nature of the charge.

NONJURY TRIAL. A trial in which there is no jury and in which a judicial officer determines all issues of fact and law.

OPEN FIELDS. The portions of a person's premises lying outside the curtilage of his or her home or business. The open fields doctrine states that "the special protection accorded by the Fourth Amendment to the people in their 'persons houses, papers, and effects,' is not extended to the open fields. *Hester v. U.S.* 265 U.S. 57, 59, 44 S.Ct. 445, 446, 68 L.Ed. 898, 900 (1924). This doctrine simply means that a law enforcement officer may search for and seize items of evidence lying in the open fields without probable cause or other legal justification without violating a person's Fourth Amendment rights.

OPENING STATEMENT. The part of a trial before the presentation of evidence in which the attorney for each party gives an outline of what that party intends to prove by the evidence it will present. The primary purpose of the opening statement is to acquaint the judge and jury in a general way with the nature of the case.

ORIGINAL JURISDICTION. Jurisdiction of a court or administrative agency to hear or act upon a case from its beginning and to pass judgment on the law and the facts.

PEREMPTORY CHALLENGE. A formal objection to a prospective juror for which no reason need be given. The judge will automatically dismiss a juror to whom a peremptory challenge is made. The number of peremptory challenges available to each party is limited by statute or court rule.

PLAIN FEEL DOCTRINE. Same as PLAIN TOUCH DOCTRINE

PLAIN TOUCH DOCTRINE. The doctrine stating that if police are lawfully in a position from which they *feel* an object, if its incriminating character is *immediately apparent,* and if the officers have a lawful right of access to the object, they may seize it without a warrant. If, however, the police lack probable cause to believe that the object felt is subject to seizure without conducting some further search of the object, its seizure is not justified.

PLAIN VIEW DOCTRINE. The doctrine stating that "if police are lawfully in a position from which they view an object, if its incriminating character is apparent, and if the officers have a lawful right of access to the object, they may seize it without a warrant." *Minnesota v. Dickerson,* 508 U.S. 366, 375, 113 S.Ct. 2130, 2136–37, 124 L.Ed.2d 334, 345 (1993). The plain view doctrine has four requirements, all of which must be satisfied before seizure of an item of evidence can be legally justified.

1. The officer, as the result of a prior valid intrusion, must be in a position in which he or she has legal right to be, such as effecting an arrest, executing a search warrant, or responding to an emergency.
2. The officer must not unreasonably intrude on any person's reasonable expectation of privacy.
3. The incriminating character of the object to be seized must be immediately apparent to the officer.
4. The discovery of the item of evidence by the officer need not be inadvertent.

PLEA. A defendant's formal answer in court to the charge contained in a complaint, information, or indictment, that he or she is guilty or not guilty of the offense charged, or does not contest the charge. The pleas in a criminal case are guilty, nolo contendere, not guilty, and not guilty by reason of insanity.

PLEA BARGAINING. The exchange of prosecutorial or judicial concessions, or both, in return for a guilty plea. Common concessions include a lesser charge, the dismissal of other pending charges, a recommendation by the prosecutor for a reduced sentence, or a combination of these. The guilty plea arrived at through the process of plea bargaining is sometimes called a negotiated plea.

Plea bargaining has been approved by the U.S. Supreme Court and is governed by rules of court in federal and in many state courts. The U.S. Supreme Court stated:

The disposition of criminal charges by agreement between the prosecutor and the accused, sometimes loosely called "plea bargaining," is an essential component of the administration of justice. Properly administered, it is to be encouraged. If the criminal charge were subjected to a full-scale trial, the States and the Federal Government would need to multiply by many times the number of judges and court facilities.

Disposition of charges after plea discussions is not only an essential part of the process but a highly desirable part for many reasons. It leads to prompt and largely final disposition of most criminal cases; it avoids much of the corrosive impact of enforced idleness during pretrial confinement for those who are denied release pending trial; it protects the public from those accused persons who are prone to continue criminal conduct even while on pretrial release; and, by shortening the time between charge and disposition, it enhances whatever may be the rehabilitative prospects of the guilty when they are ultimately imprisoned. *Santobello v. N.Y.,* 404 U.S. 257, 260–61, 92 S.Ct. 495, 498, 30 L.Ed.2d 427, 432 (1971).

PRELIMINARY HEARING. The proceeding before a judicial officer in which three matters must be decided: whether a crime was committed; whether the crime occurred within the territorial jurisdiction of the court; and whether there is probable cause to believe that the defendant committed the crime.

A chief purpose of the preliminary hearing is to protect the accused from an inadequately based prosecution in felony cases by making a judicial test of the existence of probable cause early in the proceedings. In felony cases in states where a felony trial can be initiated by the filing of an information by the prosecutor, the preliminary hearing (usually in a lower court) is a key step at which it is determined whether proceedings will continue. If the court does find probable cause, bail may be set or reset, and the defendant will be bound over or held to answer the charge in the trial court.

In felony cases in states where the grand jury indictment is used to initiate proceedings in the trial court, defendants often waive the preliminary hearing, because the grand jury will make the probable cause determination. But some defendants request a preliminary hearing because it affords opportunity to acquire information about the basis of the prosecution's case or to move for dismissal of the case.

Whether the defendant has the right to a preliminary hearing in a misdemeanor case depends upon the jurisdiction.

PROBABLE CAUSE. Probable cause exists when the facts and circumstances within a person's knowledge and of which he or she has reasonably trustworthy information are sufficient in themselves to justify a person of reasonable caution and prudence in believing that something is true. It means something less than certainty, but more than mere suspicion, speculation, or possibility. The U.S. Supreme Court defined probable cause to search as "a fair probability that contraband or evidence of a crime will be found in a particular place." *Illinois v. Gates,* 462 U.S. 213, 238, 103 S.Ct. 2317, 2332, 76 L.Ed.2d 527, 548 (1983).

Probable cause is required to justify the issuance of an arrest warrant or search warrant, all arrests made without a warrant, and most searches made without a warrant. The quality and amount of information needed to establish probable cause to arrest or search are the same in either case. The kind of information needed to justify an arrest, however, is different from that to justify a search. Probable cause to arrest arises from facts tending to show that a specific crime has been or is being committed and that a particular person committed or is committing it. Probable cause to search arises from facts tending to show that the items searched for are items subject to seizure and that they will be located in a particular place at a particular time.

Information to establish probable cause may come to a person through any of his or her five senses or through a third person or informant. When the information comes through an informant, the information must satisfy the "totality of the circumstances" test set out in the U.S. Supreme Court case of *Illinois v. Gates.* Even though the *Gates* case dealt with a search warrant, the "totality of the circumstances" test must be satisfied to establish probable cause for a warrantless search and for arrests made both with and without a warrant.

Probable cause to believe that a particular person committed a particular crime is also required to initiate prosecution. In felony cases the existence of probable cause will be established in court in a hearing usually called a preliminary hearing, or by a grand jury, before felony trial proceedings begin. Whether the defendant has the right to a preliminary hearing in a misdemeanor case depends upon the jurisdiction.

PROBATION. The conditional freedom without imprisonment granted by a judicial officer to an alleged or adjudicated adult or juvenile offender, as long as the person meets certain conditions of behavior. Probation differs from parole, in that it is conditional freedom ordered by a court, whereas parole is conditional freedom granted by a paroling authority after commitment to a period of confinement. Probation is usually a continuation of freedom previously granted by the court during court proceedings. It may be granted after conviction, but also may be granted before adjudication, as when the defendant concedes guilt, prosecution is suspended, and the subject placed on probation.

Probation is usually granted to young offenders and first offenders who have committed minor crimes. Typical conditions of adult probation, as set forth by the court that granted the probation, frequently include maintaining regular employment, abstaining from drugs and alcohol, not associating with known offenders or other specified persons, regularly reporting to a probation officer or other designated person, and/or remaining within a designated geographic area. Not committing another offense is always a condition of probation. A grant of probation after conviction often includes another kind of sentencing disposition as a condition: confinement in jail, payment of restitution in the form of money or public service, a fine, etc. Conditions of probation unique to a person may also be imposed, such as payment of personal debts. Some courts commit offenders to prison with a period of probationary status, instead of parole, to follow. This is often called shock probation.

The limits of probationary periods are usually set by statute and can be longer than the maximum sentence of confinement, or series of sentences to confinement, provided by law for a given offense. Some jurisdictions limit probationary periods for felonies to the maximum possible period of imprisonment for the offense.

Violation of any of the conditions of probation may lead to probation revocation and the execution of a suspended sentence or the imposition and execution of a sentence if one has not already been imposed.

Juvenile probation is often designated as informal or formal, depending upon the authority granting it and the nature of the conditions. Juveniles may be placed on informal probation by a probation officer in lieu of the filing of a juvenile petition.

REASONABLE DOUBT. An accused person is presumed innocent until proven guilty beyond a reasonable doubt. Beyond a reasonable doubt requires little interpretation, although many courts have attempted to formulate somewhat involved definitions that add little to the plain meaning of the term. Some examples of these definitions are "fully satisfied," "entirely convinced," "reasonably certain," and "satisfied to a moral certainty." Suffice it to say that proof beyond a reasonable doubt requires that the fact be established to a reasonable, but not absolute or mathematical, certainty. A possibility or probability is not sufficient.

In the U.S. Supreme Court decision holding that due process required the use of the reasonable doubt standard in criminal prosecutions, Justice John M. Harlan concurred, writing: "I view the requirement of proof beyond a reasonable doubt in a criminal case as bottomed on a fundamental value determination of our society that it is far worse to convict an innocent man than to let a guilty man go free." *In re Winship,* 397 U.S. 358, 372, 90 S.Ct. 1068, 1077, 25 L.Ed.2d 368, 380 (1970). In the *Winship* decision, the Court also decided that the Fourteenth Amendment required proof beyond a reasonable doubt in state juvenile delinquency proceedings during the adjudicatory stage, when the juvenile was charged with an act that would constitute a crime if committed by an adult. Furthermore, the *Winship* decision held that due process requires "proof beyond a reasonable doubt of every fact necessary to constitute the crime with which [the defendant] is charged." 397 U.S. at 364, 90 S.Ct. at 1073, 25 L.Ed.2d at 375. This means that the prosecution must establish every element of the offense beyond a reasonable doubt.

REDACTION. In evaluating the constitutional sufficiency of a search warrant, the practice of invalidating clauses in the warrant that are constitutionally insufficient for lack of probable cause or particularity while preserving clauses that satisfy the Fourth Amendment.

SEARCH. Under the Fourth Amendment prohibition against unreasonable searches and seizures, a search can be defined as an examination or inspection of a location, vehicle, or person by a law enforcement officer or other authorized person for the purpose of locating objects relating to or believed to relate to criminal activities or wanted persons. Mere observation of objects lying open to view by a law enforcement officer who is in a position in which he or she has a legal right to be does not constitute a search. In recent years courts have increasingly analyzed search and seizure issues in terms of violation of the right of privacy and have expanded the definition of search to include any official intrusion into matters and activities as to which a person has exhibited a reasonable expectation of privacy. "A 'search' occurs when an expectation of privacy that society is prepared to consider reasonable is infringed." *U.S. v. Jacobsen,* 466 U.S. 109, 113, 104 S.Ct. 1652, 1656, 80 L.Ed.2d 85, 94 (1984).

The general rule is that any search conducted without a search warrant is unreasonable. Courts have fashioned several well-defined exceptions to this rule, however. A warrant is not required, therefore, for a search incident to arrest; a consent search; an observation of evidence falling under the plain view doctrine; an emergency search of a motor vehicle under the *Carroll* doctrine; searches conducted in the open fields; observations and seizures of abandoned property; and frisks conducted as a part of an investigative stop (see STOP AND FRISK).

SEARCH INCIDENT TO ARREST. A recognized exception to the search warrant requirement, allowing a law enforcement officer who legally arrests a person to conduct a warrantless search of that person contemporaneous with the arrest. The basic legal requirements of a search incident to arrest are stated in the 1969 U.S. Supreme Court case of *Chimel v. California:*

> When an arrest is made, it is reasonable for the arresting officer to search the person arrested in order to remove any weapons that the latter might seek to use in order to resist arrest or effect his escape. Otherwise, the officer's safety might well be endangered, and the arrest itself frustrated. In addition, it is entirely reasonable for the arresting officer to search for and seize any evidence on the arrestee's person in order to prevent its concealment or destruction. And the area into which an arrestee might reach in order to grab a weapon or evidentiary items must, of course, be governed by a like rule. A gun on a table or in a drawer in front of one who is arrested can be as dangerous to the arresting officer as one concealed in the clothing of the person arrested. There is ample justification, therefore, for a search of the arrestee's person and the area "within his immediate control" construing that phrase to mean the area from within which he might gain possession of a weapon or destructible evidence. 395 U.S. 752, 762–63, 89 S.Ct. 2034, 2040, 23 L.Ed.2d 685, 694.

SEARCH WARRANT. An order in writing, issued by a magistrate or other proper judicial officer in the name of the people of a state or of the nation, directed to a law enforcement officer and commanding him or her to search a specified person or premises for specified property and to bring it before the judicial authority named in the warrant. Generally, the types of property for which a search warrant may be issued, as set out in statutes or rules of court, are weapons, contraband, fruits of crime, instrumentalities of crime, and other evidence of crime (*see* ITEMS SUBJECT TO SEIZURE). The Fourth Amendment to the U.S. Constitution states that "no warrants shall issue, but upon probable cause, supported by Oath or affirmation, and particularly describing the place to be searched and the persons or things to be seized." The judicial officer, before issuing the warrant, must determine whether there is probable cause to search based on information supplied in an affidavit by a law enforcement officer or other person.

SEIZABLE ITEMS. Same as ITEMS SUBJECT TO SEIZURE.

SEIZURE. 1. Under the Fourth Amendment prohibition against unreasonable searches and seizures, a seizure of the person can be defined as follows: "[A] person has been 'seized' within the meaning of the Fourth Amendment only if, in view of all of the circumstances surrounding the incident, a reasonable person would have believed that he was not free to leave. Examples of circumstances that might indicate a seizure even where the person did not attempt to leave, would be the threatening presence of several officers, the display of a weapon by an officer, some physical touching of the person of the citizen, or the use of language or tone of voice indicating that compliance with the officer's request might be compelled. . . . In the absence of some such evidence, otherwise inoffensive contact between a member of the public and the police cannot, as a matter of law, amount to a seizure of that person." *U.S. v. Mendenhall*, 446 U.S. 544, 554–55, 100 S.Ct. 1870, 1877, 64 L.Ed.2d 497, 509 (1980).

The least intrusive type of seizure of the person governed by the Fourth Amendment is the so-called *Terry*-type investigative stop (*see* STOP AND FRISK). At a still higher level of intensity are police contacts with members of the public involving a detention or temporary seizure of a person that is more intrusive on a person's freedom of action than a brief investigatory stop, but that does not satisfy the four elements of a formal arrest. An example would be an officer's handcuffing a suspect and transporting him or her to the station for questioning without formally arresting the person. In this type of situation, a court may find that the officer's actions are tantamount to an arrest if they are indistinguishable from an arrest in important respects. The seizure or detention will be ruled illegal unless it is supported by probable cause. This type of seizure is sometimes referred to as a seizure tantamount to arrest.

The highest level of seizure of the person governed by the Fourth Amendment is the formal arrest.

2. Under the Fourth Amendment's prohibition against unreasonable searches and seizures, a seizure of property "occurs when there is some meaningful interference with an individual's possessory interests in that property." *U.S. v. Jacobsen*, 466 U.S. 109, 113, 104 S.Ct. 1652, 1656, 80 L.Ed.2d 85, 94 (1984). Usually a seizure involves the taking into custody by a law enforcement officer of an item of property relating to or believed to relate to criminal activity. Ordinarily property is seized after a search conducted pursuant to a search warrant or pursuant to one of the recognized exceptions to the warrant requirement. In certain situations, however, such as seizures of items under the plain view doctrine, seizures of items found in the open fields, and seizures of abandoned property, the seizure may be made without any preceding search. Because a search and seizure are often combined in one transaction, they are often referred to together by the term "search and seizure," and the legal principles applicable to searches and seizures are referred to as the law of search and seizure.

SENTENCE. The penalty imposed by a court upon a person convicted of a crime. The types of sentences are death, commitment to confinement, probation or a suspended sentence, and a fine. The determination of the sentence is perhaps the most sensitive and difficult decision the judge has to make because of the effect it will have on the defendant's life. For this reason, most states have laws directing and guiding the judge in this determination. A typical provision requires the judge to impose sentence without unreasonable delay. This protects the defendant from a prolonged period of uncertainty about the future. In addition, before imposing sentence, the judge is usually required to address the defendant personally and ask if the defendant desires to be heard before the imposition of sentence. The defendant may be heard personally or by counsel or both. The purpose of this provision is to enable the defendant to present any information that may be of assistance to the court in determining punishment.

Another typical statutory provision that is designed to assist the court in fixing sentence allows the court, in its discretion, to direct the state probation and parole board to make a presentence investigation and presentence report to the court before the imposition of sentence. This report will contain any prior criminal record of the defendant and such other information on personal characteristics, financial condition, and the circumstances affecting the defendant's behavior as may be helpful to the court in reaching its decision.

The court has a number of alternatives open to it with respect to sentencing, depending largely on individual state criminal statutes. Some criminal statutes have mandatory sentences, some have fixed maximum sentences, some have fixed minimum sentences, and others leave the matter of sentencing to the judge. Therefore, depending upon the offense for which the defendant has been convicted, the court may have a very broad discretion in fixing sentence, or no discretion whatsoever. In a few states, the jury has the power to fix the sentence as well as to determine guilt or innocence.

SHOWUP. A confrontation (definition 2) involving the presentation of a single suspect to a victim or witness of a crime for the purpose of identifying the perpetrator of the crime.

STANDING. The legal right of a person to judicially challenge the conduct of another person or the government. In general, standing depends on whether the person seeking relief has a legally sufficient personal interest at stake to obtain judicial resolution of merits of the dispute. The "gist of the question of standing" is whether the party seeking relief has "alleged such a personal stake in the outcome of the controversy as to assure that concrete adverseness which sharpens the presentation of issues upon which the court so largely depends for illumination of difficult constitutional questions." *Baker v. Carr,* 369 U.S. 186, 204, 82 S.Ct. 691, 703, 7 L.Ed.2d 663, 678 (1962).

To invoke the exclusionary rule to challenge the admissibility of evidence, a defendant must have standing. A defendant has standing when his or her own constitutional rights have been violated.

"Fourth Amendment rights are personal rights which, like some other constitutional rights, may not be vicariously asserted." . . . A person who is aggrieved by an illegal search and seizure only through the introduction of damaging evidence secured by a search of a third person's premises or property has not had any of his Fourth Amendment rights infringed. . . . And since the exclusionary rule is an attempt to effectuate the guarantees of the Fourth Amendment, . . . it is proper to permit only defendants whose Fourth Amendment rights have been violated to benefit from the rule's protections. *Rakas v. Illinois,* 439 U.S. 128, 133–34, 99 S.Ct. 421, 425, 58 L.Ed.2d 387, 394–95 (1978).

In determining whether a defendant's Fourth Amendment rights have been violated, courts will analyze whether the defendant had a reasonable expectation of privacy in the area searched or the item seized.

STOP AND FRISK. A shorthand term for the law enforcement practice involving the temporary investigative seizure of a person and the pat-down search of the person's outer clothing for weapons. A stop and frisk is a much less severe and less extensive restraint on a person than that of an arrest and search. A stop and frisk may be initiated on a lesser justification than probable cause for the purposes of crime prevention and investigation and for the protection of the law enforcement officer carrying out the investigation. In order to protect society's interest in effective crime prevention or detection, a law enforcement officer may stop or temporarily detain a person for the purpose of investigating possibly criminal behavior, even though there is no probable cause to make an arrest. The officer making the stop, however, must have an articulable suspicion—specific and articulable facts that, taken together with rational inferences from those facts, reasonably warrant that intrusion. Also, the extent of the officer's interference with the person must be reasonable under the circumstances.

In order to protect the officer and others from possible violence by persons being investigated for crime, a law enforcement officer may frisk or pat-down the outer clothing of a person for weapons. The officer conducting the frisk must have reason to believe that he or she is dealing with an armed and dangerous person and must be able to justify the stop by pointing to specific facts and specific reasonable inferences that the officer is entitled to draw from the facts in light of his or her experience. Also, the frisk must be limited to what is minimally necessary for self-protection and the protection of others and therefore must be limited initially to a pat-down of the outer clothing for weapons. If a weapon-like object is felt, the officer may seize it. If a weaponlike object is not felt, the officer must discontinue the search immediately.

The basic principles of the law of stop and frisk are discussed in the U.S. Supreme Court case of *Terry v. Ohio*, 392 U.S. 1, 88 S.Ct. 1868, 20 L.Ed.2d 889 (1968). Note that these basic principles have been applied to other limited detention and search situations involving objects such as motor vehicles and packages in the mail.

SUBPOENA. A written order issued by a judicial officer requiring a specified person to appear in a designated court at a specified time in order to testify in a case under the jurisdiction of that court, or to bring a document, piece of evidence or other thing for use or inspection by the court. A subpoena to serve as a witness is called a subpoena ad testificandum. A subpoena to bring a document, piece of evidence, or other thing into court is called a subpoena duces tecum. Subpoenas can be served in various ways. They may be served in person by a law enforcement officer, or by another person authorized to do so. In some jurisdictions some types of subpoenas may be served by mail or by telephone. Failure to obey a subpoena is contempt of court.

SUMMONS. A written order issued by a judicial officer requiring a person accused of a criminal offense to appear in a designated court at a specified time to answer the charge or charges. Rules of court and statutes usually provide that if a defendant fails to appear in response to a summons, an arrest warrant will be issued for his or her arrest. The summons is usually used when the offense charged in a complaint is a violation of a municipal ordinance or some other misdemeanor or petty offense. If the offender is a citizen with "roots firmly established in the soil of the community," and thus can be easily found for service of a warrant if the summons is ignored, the summons procedure is a much easier and better way of inducing a defendant to appear in court than is arresting the defendant and taking him or her into custody.

TESTIMONIAL COMMUNICATION. The Fifth Amendment protects a person against being incriminated by his or her own compelled testimonial communications. This protection is applicable to the states through the Fourteenth Amendment. *Malloy v. Hogan*, 378 U.S. 1, 84 S.Ct. 1489, 12 L.Ed.2d 653 (1964). To be testimonial, a "communication must itself, explicitly or implicitly, relate a factual assertion or disclose information" that is "the expression of the contents of an individual's mind." *Doe v. United States*, 487 U.S. 201, 210 n.9, 108 S.Ct. 2341, 2347 n.9, 101 L.Ed.2d 184, 197 n.9 (1988). Therefore, the privilege against self-incrimination is not violated by compelling a person to appear in a lineup, to produce voice exemplars, to furnish handwriting samples, to be fingerprinted, to shave a beard or mustache, or to take a blood-alcohol or breathalyzer test.

TRIAL DE NOVO. A new trial or retrial in which the whole case is gone into again as if no trial whatever had been held before. In a trial de novo, matters of fact as well as law may be considered, witnesses may be heard, and new evidence may be presented, regardless of what happened at the first trial.

VENUE. The geographical area from which the jury is drawn and in which a court with jurisdiction may hear and determine a case. Venue is usually the county or district in which the crime is alleged to have been committed. The Sixth Amendment to the U.S. Constitution grants an accused "the right to a speedy and public trial, by an impartial jury of the State and district wherein the crime shall have been committed, which district shall have been previously ascertained by law. . . ."

VERDICT. The decision made by a jury in a jury trial, or by a judicial officer in a nonjury trial, that a defendant is either guilty or not guilty of the offense for which he or she has been tried. In entering a judgment, a judicial officer has the power to reject a jury verdict of guilty, but must accept a jury verdict of not guilty. Thus a jury verdict of not guilty results in a judgment of acquittal, but a verdict of guilty does not necessarily result in a judgment of conviction.

VOIR DIRE. *French.* "To speak the truth." **1.** An examination conducted by the court or by the attorneys of a prospective juror or witness to determine if he or she is competent or qualified for service. **2.** During a trial, a hearing conducted by the court out of the presence of the jury on some issue upon which the court must make an initial determination as a matter of law.

WAIVER. "[T]he intentional relinquishment or abandonment of a known right or privilege." *Johnson v. Zerbst*, 304 U.S. 458, 464, 58 S.Ct. 1019, 1023, 82 L.Ed. 1461, 1466 (1938).

WARRANT. A written order or writ issued by a judicial officer or other authorized person commanding a law enforcement officer to perform some act incident to the administration of justice.

WITNESS. 1. A person who directly sees or perceives an event or thing or who has expert knowledge relevant to a case. **2.** A person who testifies to what he or she has seen or perceived or what he or she knows. **3.** A person who signs his or her name to a document to attest to its authenticity. Such a person is sometimes called an attesting witness.

WRIT OF ASSISTANCE. A form of general warrant issued by the British Colonial courts against the American colonists in the mid-eighteenth century to enforce the Trade Acts. Writs of assistance authorized royal customs officers to search houses and ships at will in order to discover and seize smuggled goods or goods on which the required duties had not been paid. The reaction of the colonists against the writs of assistance was strong and was one of the major causes of the American Revolution.

WRIT OF CERTIORARI. A discretionary writ issued from an appellate court for the purpose of obtaining from a lower court the record of its proceedings in a particular case. In the U.S. Supreme Court, and in some states, this writ is the mechanism for discretionary review. A request for review is made by petitioning for a writ of certiorari, and granting of review is indicated by issuance of the writ.

Table of Cases

Joe, Commonwealth v., 247
Joe R., In re, 326
Johns, United States v., 378, 382–383, 397
Johns, United States v., 159–160
Johnson, Ohio v., 16
Johnson, People v., 372–373
Johnson, State v., 327, 332
Johnson, United States v., 301, 302–303, 459
Johnson v. Dugger, 503
Johnson v. Louisiana, 64
Johnson v. United States, 157, 209–210
Johnson v. Zerbst, 22, 494
Johnston, United States v., 360
Jonas, United States v., 448
Jones, People v., 313
Jones, State v., 352–353
Jones (1980), United States v., 447–448
Jones (1985), United States v., 109
Jones (1986), United States v., 509, 511
Jones (1988), United States v., 326–327
Jones v. Commonwealth, 130
Jones v. State, 515
Jones v. United States, 157, 181, 210–211
Joseph, United States v., 181
Judge, United States v., 387
Justices of Boston Municipal Court v. Lydon, 16

K

Kaluna, State v., 303
Kampbell, United States v., 323
Kaplan, United States v., 323, 330
Kapperman, United States v., 332
Karman, United States v., 421
Karo, United States v., 168, 394, 398
Katz v. United States, 88, 89–90, 92, 98, 199, 200, 344, 358, 410, 412, 413, 414, 422, 425, 478
Kellam, State v., 341
Kelley, United States v., 337
Kelly, United States v., 338
Kentucky (*see also* opposing party v.)
Kentucky v. Stincer, 21
Ker v. California, 78, 95–96, 137, 220–221
Khoury, United States v., 388–389
Kidd v. O'Neil, 128
King, State v., 264
King, United States v., 498
Kirby v. Illinois, 22, 328, 501–502, 513
Klein, United States v., 169
Knotts, United States v., 393–394, 398

Koch, United States v., 435
Kock, State v., 380
Koelling, United States v., 171
Koessel, United States v., 421
Kotteakos v. United States, 70
Kremens, State v., 471
Krull, Illinois v., 87, 98
Kuebel, Schilb v., 24
Kuhlmann v. Wilson, 464, 486
Kurtzman, Lemon v., 12–13
Kyles v. Whitley, 55

L

Labron, Pennsylvania v., 379, 397
Ladd, United States v., 212
LaDuca, State v., 405
Lafayette, Illinois v., 141–142, 149, 386, 397
LaFernier, State v., 453
Lahti, Commonwealth v., 83
Laing, United States v., 275–276
Laird, State v., 372
Lambert, State v., 185, 231
Lambert, United States v., 77
Lane, State v., 400
LaPierre, United States v., 496
Larson, United States v., 339
Lasanta, United States v., 305
Laury, United States v., 162
Lavicky v. Burnett, 381
Lawrence, People v., 230
Leach, State v., 336
Lee, United States v., 419
Lee, Winton v., 143–144, 167–168
Lemon, United States v., 66
Lemon v. Kurtzman, 12–13
Leon, United States v., 85–87, 97
Lescard, State v., 444
Levesque, United States v., 379
Levy, United States v., 447
Lewis, Bruni v., 472
Lewis, Cardwell v., 380, 392, 398
Lewis, State v., 334, 383
Lewis, United States v., 421, 475
Lewis v. United States, 58
Lima, United States v., 221–222
Limatoc, United States v., 355
Lindsey, Alexander v., 123
Litwin, People v., 340
Llanos, People v., 214
Lockhart v. Fretwell, 23
Lo-Ji Sales, Inc. v. New York, 159, 171
Long, Michigan v., 273–274, 291, 354, 370
Long, United States v., 342
Longbehn, United States v., 447
Longwell, People v., 304
Lopes, Commonwealth v., 500

Lopez v. United States, 197–198
Lorenzana v. Superior Court of Los Angeles County, 413–414
Louisiana (*see* opposing party v.)
Lucas, Giacalone v., 305
Lucas, United States v., 307
Lydon, Justices of Boston Municipal Court v., 16
Lyles, United States v., 385

M

MacDougall, Boag v., 34
Mackenzie, Robbins v., 331
Mackey, United States v., 225–226
Macklin, United States v., 201
Macon, Maryland v., 90–91
Madison, Marbury v., 6
Maez, United States v., 326
Magluta, United States v., 132
Maine (*see also* opposing party v.)
Maine v. Moulton, 464, 486
Maine v. Thornton, 410
Malley v. Briggs, 146, 161
Mallory v. United States, 435
Malloy v. Hogan, 17, 76–77, 97
Manfredi, United States v., 122
Manley v. Commonwealth, 166
Manning, United States v., 418
Manson v. Brathwaite, 505–506, 509, 513
Manuel, United States v., 327
Mapp v. Ohio, 76, 78, 80, 96–97
Marbury v. Madison, 6
Marcus v. Search Warrant, 169
Maroney, Chambers v., 377–378, 396–397
Marron v. United States, 168, 210
Marshall, Clark v., 459
Marshall v. Barlow's, Inc., 189
Marshall v. United States, 361–362
Martin, United States v., 444
Martinez, United States v., 277
Martinez-Fuerte, United States v., 278
Martino, United States v., 203
Marx, United States v., 188
Maryland (*see also* opposing party v.)
Maryland v. Buie, 308, 315
Maryland v. Craig, 20
Maryland v. Garrison, 167, 186–187
Maryland v. Macon, 90–91
Maryland v. Wilson, 266, 290
Mason v. United States, 496
Massachusetts v. Sheppard, 86
Masse, United States v., 444
Massiah v. United States, 22, 463, 464, 486
Mathews v. Eldridge, 27
Mathiason, Oregon v., 442
Mathis v. United States, 442

Index